W9-BUB-516

Advance praise for *Head First Servlets & JSP™*

"This Head First Servlets & JSP book is as good as the Head First EJB book, which made me laugh AND gave me 97% on the exam!"

— Jef Cumps, J2EE consultant, Cronos

"For our Servlet/JSP classes, we bought more than ten books, without finding any one really satisfying our teaching needs... Until we found the pedagogical gem you now hold in your hands! Head First books simply make us better teachers."

— Philippe Maquet: Senior Instructor at Loop Factory, Brussels.

Praise for *Head First EJB™* and the *Head First* approach

"Java technology is everywhere—in mobile phones, cars, cameras, printers, games, PDAs, ATMs, smart cards, gas pumps, sports stadiums, medical devices, Web cams, servers, you name it. If you develop software and haven't learned Java, it's definitely time to dive in—***Head First.***"

— Scott McNealy, Sun Microsystems Chairman, President and CEO

[Note from marketing: this is the best you could get from Scott? See if you can get him to add something like, "If we'd had Head First books two years ago, we might still have that bubble..."]

"Astoundingly enjoyable book on this complex, involved body of knowledge.
As a Professor at Purdue University, specializing in advanced software development using Java-based technologies, I am always on the lookout for motivational background materials that provide comprehensive subject matter examination while at the same time does not put students to sleep. "Head First EJB" overwhelmingly fits the bill ! Books like this are extremely rare.
I have added this book as one of the required texts for future offerings of my advanced undergraduate "Enterprise Application Development" course. Kudos to the authors; Keep up the great work !"

— Dan Gill, Professor, Purdue University, Department of Computer Technology

"Beyond the engaging style that drags you forward from know-nothing into exalted Java warrior status, Head First Java covers a huge amount of practical matters that other texts leave as the dreaded "exercise for the reader..." It's clever, wry, hip and practical—there aren't a lot of textbooks that can make that claim and live up to it while also teaching you about object serialization and network launch protocols. "

— Dr. Dan Russell, Director of User Sciences and Experience Research
IBM Almaden Research Center (and teaches Artificial Intelligence at Stanford University)

What a fantastic way to learn!!! I CAN NOT PUT THIS BOOK DOWN!!! My 3 year old woke up at 1:40 a.m. this morning, and I put him back to bed with book in hand and a flashlight so I could continue to read for about another hour.

— Ross Goldberg

"Kathy and Bert's 'Head First Java' transforms the printed page into the closest thing to a GUI you've ever seen. In a wry, hip manner, the authors make learning Java an engaging 'what're they gonna do next?' experience."

— Warren Keuffel, Software Development Magazine

Praise for the *Head First* approach

"It's fast, irreverent, fun, and engaging. Be careful—you might actually learn something!"

— Ken Arnold, former Senior Engineer at Sun Microsystems
Co-author (with James Gosling, creator of Java), "The Java Programming Language"

"I passed the exam SCBCD with 94%. Really this "HF EJB" Rocks! I completed reading this book in 10 days..."

— Basavaraj Devershetty

"...the only way to decide the worth of a tutorial is to decide how well it teaches. Head First Java excels at teaching. OK, I thought it was silly... then I realized that I was thoroughly learning the topics as I went through the book."

"The style of Head First Java made learning, well, easier."

— slashdot (honestpuck's review)

"I could not have imagined a person smiling while studying an IT book! Using Head First EJB materials, I got a great score (91%) and set a world record as the youngest SCBCD, 14 years."

— Afsah Shafquat (world's youngest SCBCD)

"This stuff is so fricking good it makes me wanna WEEP! I'm stunned."

— Floyd Jones, Senior Technical Writer/Poolboy, BEA

"If you want to *learn* Java, look no further: welcome to the first GUI-based technical book! This perfectly-executed, ground-breaking format delivers benefits other Java texts simply can't... Prepare yourself for a truly remarkable ride through Java land."

— Neil R. Bauman, Captain & CEO, Geek Cruises (www.GeekCruises.com)

"If anyone in the world is familiar with the concept of 'Head First,' it would be me. This book is so good, I'd marry it on TV!"

— Rick Rockwell, Comedian
The original FOX Television "Who Wants to Marry a Millionaire" groom

"Head First Java is like Monty Python meets the gang of four... the text is broken up so well by puzzles and stories, quizzes and examples, that you cover ground like no computer book before."

— Douglas Rowe, Columbia Java Users Group

" 'Head First Java'... gives new meaning to their marketing phrase `There's an O Reilly for that.` I picked this up because several others I respect had described it in terms like 'revolutionary' and a described a radically different approach to the textbook. They were (are) right... In typical O'Reilly fashion, they've taken a scientific and well considered approach. The result is funny, irreverent, topical, interactive, and brilliant...Reading this book is like sitting in the speakers lounge at a view conference, learning from – and laughing with – peers... If you want to UNDERSTAND Java, go buy this book."

— Andrew Pollack, www.thenorth.com

"Remember when you were in kindergarten? No? Well, how about when you were first learning your ABC's? Can't think back that far? Well, no matter. Read Head First Java and you will once again experience fun in learning...For people who like to learn new programming languages, and do not come from a computer science or programming background, this book is a gem... This is one book that makes learning a complex computer language fun. I hope that there are more authors who are willing to break out of the same old mold of 'traditional' writing styles. Learning computer languages should be fun, not onerous."

— Judith Taylor, Southeast Ohio Macromedia User Group

"A few days ago I received my copy of Head First Java by Kathy Sierra and Bert Bates. I'm only part way through the book, but what's amazed me is that even in my sleep-deprived state that first evening, I found myself thinking, 'OK, just one more page, then I'll go to bed.' "

— Joe Litton

"FINALLY - a Java book written the way I would'a wrote it if I were me.
Seriously though - this book absolutely blows away every other software book I've ever read...
A good book is very difficult to write... you have to take a lot of time to make things unfold in a natural, "reader oriented" sequence. It's a lot of work. Most authors clearly aren't up to the challenge. Congratulations to the Head First EJB team for a first class job!

P.S. When is Head First J2EE architect coming out! And Head First Web Component Developer! And how can I make my VCR record a football game while I'm at work?"

— Wally Flint

"If you're relatively new to programming and you are interested in Java, here's your book...Covering everything from objects to creating graphical user interfaces (GUI), exception (error) handling to networking (sockets) and multithreading, even packaging up your pile of classes into one installation file, this book is quite complete...If you like the style...I'm certain you'll love the book and, like me, hope that the Head First series will expand to many other subjects!"

— LinuxQuestions.org

"When I read "Head First Java" by the same author I thought, it is just impossible to write another book (that too on EJB) in that lucid way. But now they have left us amazed by this even more lovable book. The Head First Books are now acting like something necessary (MUST) on every topic. I wish I were a child, so that I could learn every thing the HF way."

— Anshu Mishra

I worked in EJB about 4 years ago and found it to be a counter intuitive mess. After reading the 2.1 and 2.0 specs I found it's just a steaming t*** that got bigger. Your book answered most of the zillions of questions banging around in my peanut sized brain and allowed me to pass the test with a 92% score...
Handily beating that 14 year old dude by 1 point. :-) Thanks alot,

— Jim Steiner

"I was ADDICTED to the book's short stories, annotated code, mock interviews, and brain exercises."

— Michael Yuan, author, Enterprise J2ME

Other Java books from O'Reilly

Ant: The Definitive Guide™
Better, Faster, Lighter Java™
Enterprise JavaBeans™
Head First EJB™
Head First Java™
Hibernate: A Developer's Notebook
Java™ 1.5 Tiger: A Developer's Notebook
Java™ Cookbook
Java™ in a Nutshell
Java™ Network Programming
Java™ Servlet & JSP Cookbook
Java™ Swing
JavaServer Faces™
JavaServer Pages™
Programming Jakarta Struts
Tomcat: the Definitive Guide

Be watching for more books in the Head First series!

Head First Servlets & JSP™

Wouldn't it be dreamy if there were a Servlets book that was more stimulating than deleting spam from your inbox? It's probably just a fantasy...

Bryan Basham
Kathy Sierra
Bert Bates

Beijing • Cambridge • Köln • Paris • Sebastopol • Taipei • Tokyo

Head First Servlets & JSP™

by Bryan Basham, Kathy Sierra, and Bert Bates

Copyright © 2004 O'Reilly Media, Inc. All rights reserved.

Printed in the United States of America.

Published by O'Reilly Media, Inc., 1005 Gravenstein Highway North, Sebastopol, CA 95472.

O'Reilly Media books may be purchased for educational, business, or sales promotional use. Online editions are also available for most titles (safari.oreilly.com). For more information, contact our corporate/institutional sales department: (800) 998-9938 or corporate@oreilly.com.

Editor: Mike Loukides

Cover Designer: Edie Freedman

Interior Decorators: Kathy Sierra and Bert Bates

Anthropomorphizer: Kathy Sierra

Servlet Wrangler: Bryan Basham

Assistant to the Front Controller: Bert Bates

Printing History:

August 2004: First Edition.

The O'Reilly logo is a registered trademark of O'Reilly Media, Inc. Java and all Java-based trademarks and logos are trademarks or registered trademarks of Sun Microsystems, Inc., in the United States and other countries. O'Reilly Media, Inc. is independent of Sun Microsystems.

Many of the designations used by manufacturers and sellers to distinguish their products are claimed as trademarks.

Where those designations appear in this book, and O'Reilly Media, Inc. was aware of a trademark claim, the designations have been printed in caps or initial caps.

While every precaution has been taken in the preparation of this book, the publisher and the authors assume no responsibility for errors or omissions, or for damages resulting from the use of the information contained herein.

In other words, if you use anything in *Head First Servlets & JSP™* to, say, run a nuclear power plant or air traffic control system, you're on your own.

The authors hope you remember them, should you create a huge, successful dot com as a result of reading this book. We'll take stock options, beer, or dark chocolate.

ISBN: 0-596-00540-7

[M] [8/05]

This book is dedicated to whoever decided that the EL implicit object for a *context* param should be named *init*Param...

Perpetrators of the Head First series (and this book)

Bert is a long-time software developer and architect, but a decade-long stint in artificial intelligence drove his interest in learning theory and technology-based training. He spent the first decade of his software career traveling the world to help broadcasting clients like Radio New Zealand, the Weather Channel, and the Arts and Entertainment Network (A&E). He's currently a member of the development team for several of Sun's Java Certification exams, including the new SCWCD.

Bert is a long-time, hopelessly addicted *go* player, and has been working on a *go* program for way too long. Java may finally be a language expressive enough for him to finish the project. He's a fair guitar player and is now trying his hand at banjo. His latest adventure is the purchase of an Icelandic horse which should give his training skills a new challenge...

Kathy has been interested in learning theory and the brain since her days as a game designer (she wrote games for Virgin, MGM, and Amblin') and an AI developer. She developed much of the Head First format while teaching New Media Interactivity for UCLA Extension's Entertainment Studies program. More recently, she's been a master trainer for Sun Microsystems, teaching Sun's Java instructors how to teach the latest Java technologies, and developing several of Sun's certification exams, including the SCWCD. Together with Bert Bates, she has been actively using the Head First concepts to teach throusands of developers. She founded one of the largest Java community websites in the world, javaranch.com, which won a 2003 and 2004 Software Development magazine Productivity Award. She likes running, skiing, horses, skateboarding, and weird science.

Bryan has over twenty years of software development experience including time at NASA developing advanced automation software using AI techniques. He also worked for a consulting firm developing custom OO business apps. Currently, Bryan is a Course Developer for Sun, concentrating on Java and OO design principles. He's worked on a large range of Sun's Java courses including those on JDBC, J2EE, Servlets and JSP, and OO Software Development. He was also the lead designer of both the original and new version of the SCWCD exam.

Bryan is a practicing Zen Buddhist, Ultimate Frisbee player, audiophile, and telemark skier.

Write to us at:
terrapin@wickedlysmart.com
kathy@wickedlysmart.com
bryan@wickedlysmart.com

Table of Contents (summary)

Table of Contents

Intro

Your brain on Servlets. Here *you* are trying to *learn* something, while here your *brain* is doing you a favor by making sure the learning doesn't *stick*. Your brain's thinking, "Better leave room for more important things, like which wild animals to avoid and whether naked snowboarding is a bad idea." So how *do* you trick your brain into thinking that your life depends on knowing Servlets?

1 Why use servlets & JSPs?

Web applications are hot. How many GUI apps do you know that are used by millions of users world-wide? As a web app developer, you can free yourself from the grip of deployment problems all standalone apps have, and deliver your app to anyone with a browser. But you need servlets and JSPs. Because plain old static HTML pages are so, well, 1999. Learn to move from web *site* to web *app*.

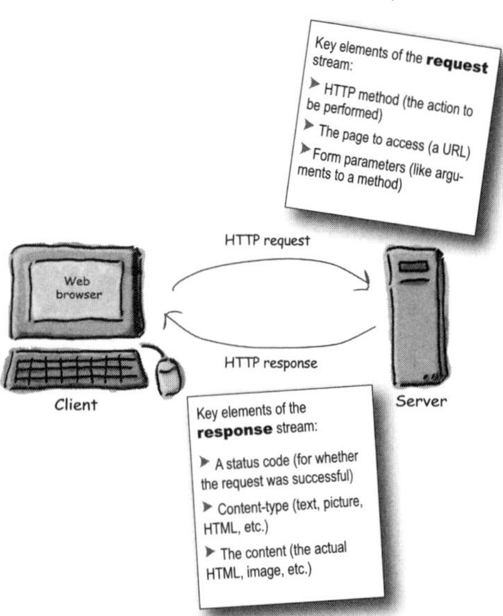
Key elements of the **request** stream:
➤ HTTP method (the action to be performed)
➤ The page to access (a URL)
➤ Form parameters (like arguments to a method)
HTTP request
Web browser
HTTP response
Client
Server
Key elements of the **response** stream:
➤ A status code (for whether the request was successful)
➤ Content-type (text, picture, HTML, etc.)
➤ The content (the actual HTML, image, etc.)

2 Web app architecture

Servlets need help. When a request comes in, somebody has to instantiate the servlet or at least allocate a thread to handle the request. Somebody has to call the servlet's doPost() or doGet() method. Somebody has to get the request and the response to the servlet. Somebody has to manage the life, death, and resources of the servlet. In this chapter, we'll look at the Container, and we'll take a first look at the MVC pattern.

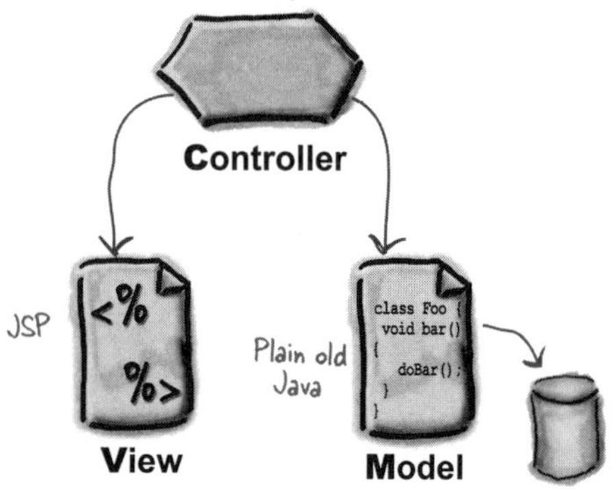
Servlet
Controller
JSP
<%
%>
View
Plain old Java
class Foo {
void bar()
{
doBar();
}
}
Model

3 Mini MVC tutorial

Create and deploy an MVC web app. It's time to get your hands dirty writing an HTML form, a servlet controller, a model (plain old Java class), an XML deployment descriptor, and a JSP view. Time to build it, deploy it, and test it. But first, you need to set up your *development* environment. Next, you need to set up your *deployment* environment following the servlet and JSP specs and Tomcat requirements.True, this *is* a small app...but there's almost NO app that's too small to use MVC.

Tomcat-specific

tomcat
webapps
Beer-v1

This directory name also represents the "context root" which Tomcat uses when resolving URLs. We'll explore this concept in great detail in the deployment chapter.

Part of the servlets spec

WEB-INF
form.html
result.jsp
classes
lib
web.xml

This web.xml file MUST be in WEB-INF

Your app

com
example
web
model
BeerSelect.class
BeerExpert.class

This package structure is exactly what we used in the development environment. Unless you're deploying your classes in a JAR (we'll talk about that later in the book), then you MUST put the package directory structure immediately under WEB-INF/classes.

4 Being a servlet

Servlets live to service clients. A servlet's job is to take a client's ***request*** and send back a ***response***. The request might be simple: *"get me the Welcome page."* Or it might be complex: *"Complete my shopping cart check-out."* The **request** carries crucial data, and your servlet code has to know how to *find* it and how to *use* it. And your servlet code has to know how to *send* a **response**. Or *not*...

Idempotency is nothing to be ashamed of...

NOT Idempotent

POST

Servlet uses the POST data to update the database.

DB

Servlet

Client

Servlet sends back a response with a generated HTML page.

Being a web app

No servlet stands alone. In today's modern web app, many components work together to accomplish a goal. You have models, controllers, and views. You have parameters and attributes. You have helper classes. But how do you tie the pieces together? How do you let components *share* information? How do you *hide* information? *How do you make information thread-safe?* Your job might depend on the answers.

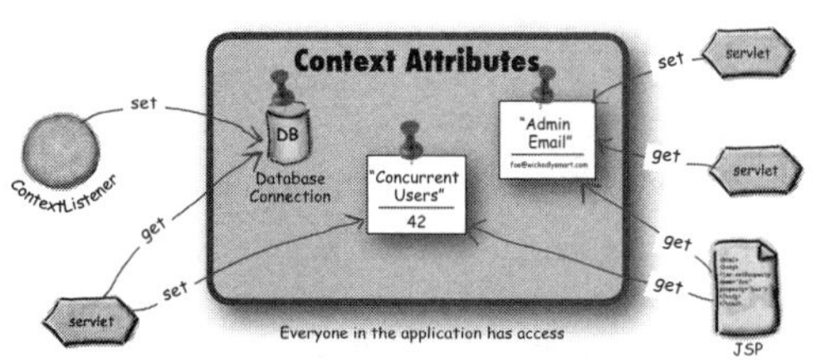

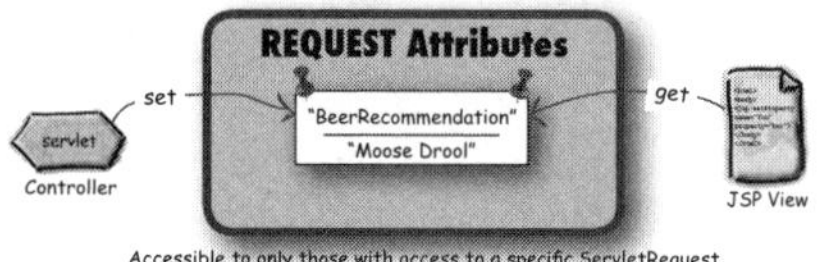

6 Conversational state

Web servers have no short-term memory. As soon as they send you a response, they forget who you are. The next time you make a request, they don't recognize you. They don't remember what you've requested in the past, and they don't remember what they've sent you in response. Nothing. But sometimes you need to keep conversational state with the client *across multiple requests.* A shopping cart wouldn't work if the client had to make all his choices and then checkout *in a single request.*

Cookies
Here's your cookie with the session ID inside...
"Set-Cookie" is just another header sent in the response.
HTTP/1.1 200 OK
Set-Cookie: JSESSIONID=0AAB6C8DE415
HTTP Response
OK, here's the cookie with my request
"Cookie" is another header sent in the request.
POST /select/selectBeerTaste2.do HTTP/1.1
Cookie: JSESSIONID=0AAB6C8DE415
HTTP Request

7 Being a JSP

A JSP becomes a servlet. A servlet that *you* don't create. The Container looks at your JSP, translates it into Java source code, and compiles it into a full-fledged Java servlet class. But you've got to know what happens when the code you write in the JSP is turned into Java code. You *can* write Java code in your JSP, but should you? And if not Java code, what *do* you write? How does it *translate* into Java code? We'll look at six different kinds of JSP elements—each with its own purpose and, yes, *unique syntax*. You'll learn how, why, and what to write in your JSP. And you'll learn what *not* to write.

writes
is translated to
MyJSP.jsp
compiles to
MyJSP_jsp.java
loaded and initialized
Servlet object
MyJSP_jsp.class
MyJSP_jsp Servlet

Script-free pages

Lose the scripting. Do your web page designers really have to know Java? Do they expect server-side Java programmers to be, say, graphic designers? And even if it's just *you* on the team, do you really want a pile of bits and pieces of Java code in your JSPs? Can you say, "maintenance nightmare"? Writing scriptless pages is not just *possible*, it's become much *easier* and more flexible with the new JSP 2.0 spec, thanks to the new Expression Language (EL). Patterned after JavaScript and XPATH, web designers feel right at home with EL, and you'll like it too (once you get used to it). But there are some traps... EL *looks* like Java, but isn't. Sometimes EL behaves differently than if you used the same syntax in Java, so pay attention!

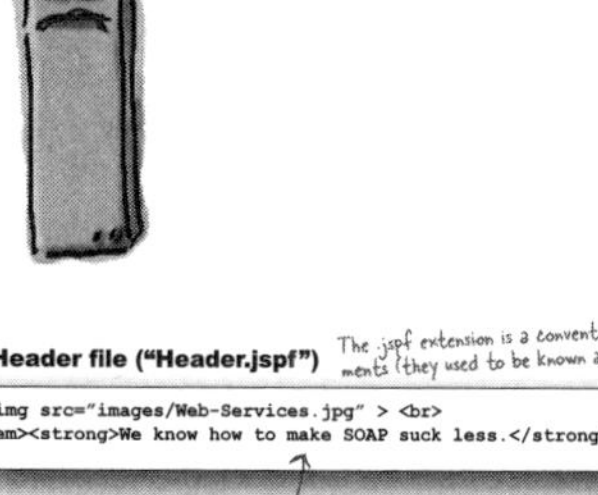
Don't expect ME to strip out your redundant opening and closing tags.

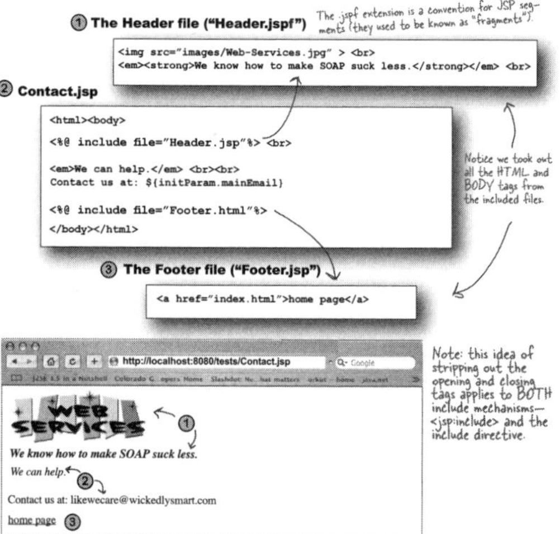
① The Header file ("Header.jspf")
The .jspf extension is a convention for JSP segments (they used to be known as "fragments").
<img src="images/Web-Services.jpg" >
<em><strong>We know how to make SOAP suck less.</strong></em>
② Contact.jsp
<html><body>
<%@ include file="Header.jsp"%>
<em>We can help.</em>

Contact us at: ${initParam.mainEmail}
<%@ include file="Footer.html"%>
</body></html>
Notice we took out all the HTML and BODY tags from the included files.
③ The Footer file ("Footer.jsp")
<a href="index.html">home page</a>
http://localhost:8080/tests/Contact.jsp
WEB SERVICES
We know how to make SOAP suck less.
We can help.
Contact us at: likewecare@wickedlysmart.com
home page
Note: this idea of stripping out the opening and closing tags applies to BOTH include mechanisms—<jsp:include> and the include directive.

9 Custom tags are powerful

Sometimes you need more than EL or standard actions. What if you want to loop through the data in an array, and display one item per row in an HTML table? You *know* you could write that in two seconds using a for loop in a scriptlet. But you're trying to get away from scripting. No problem. When EL and standard actions aren't enough, you can use *custom tags*. They're as easy to use in a JSP as standard actions. Even better, someone's already written a pile of the ones you're most likely to need, and bundled them into the JSP Standard Tag Library (JSTL). In *this* chapter we'll learn to *use* custom tags, and in the next chapter we'll learn to create our own.

<table>
The ArrayList request attribute
<c:forEach var="listElement" items="${movies}" >
<c:forEach var="movie" items="${listElement}" >
<tr>
<td>${movie}</td>
</tr>
</c:forEach>
</c:forEach>
</table>
inner loop
outer loop
One of the String arrays that was assigned to the outer loop's "var" attribute.
From the first String array
From the second String array
Matrix Revolutions
Kill Bill
Boondock Saints
Amelie
Return of the King
Mean Girls

10 When even JSTL isn't enough...

Sometimes JSTL and standard actions aren't enough. When you need something custom, and you don't want to go back to scripting, you can write your *own* tag handlers. That way, your page designers can use your *tag* in their pages, while all the *hard* work is done behind the scenes in your tag handler *class*. But there are three different ways to build your own tag handlers, so there's a lot to learn. Of the three, two were introduced with JSP 2.0 to make your life easier (Simple Tags and Tag Files).

But why? why didn't you tell him you could do it?

I didn't know about custom tags... I thought I was stuck with only JSTL, and nothing in JSTL could do what the manager wanted. Oh if only I'd known I could build my own... but it's too late for me. Learn this and... save yourself...

11 Deploying your web app

Finally, your web app is ready for prime time. Your pages are polished, your code is tested and tuned, and your deadline was two weeks ago. But where does everything go? So many directories, so many rules. What do *you* name your directories? What does the *client* think they're named? What does the client actually request, and how does the Container know where to look?

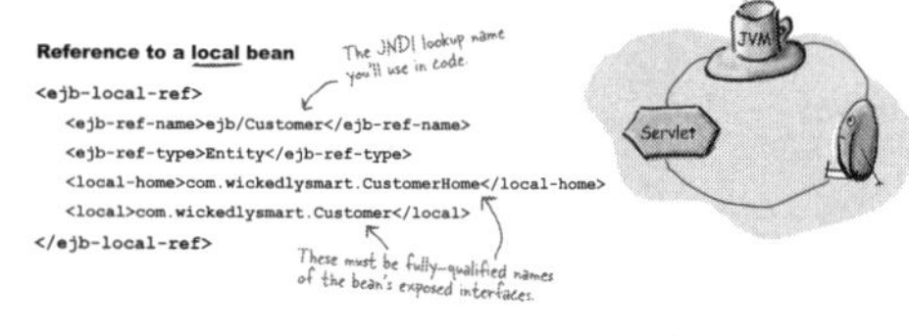

Reference to a remote bean

```
<ejb-ref>
   <ejb-ref-name>ejb/LocalCustomer</ejb-ref-name>
   <ejb-ref-type>Entity</ejb-ref-type>
   <home>com.wickedlysmart.CustomerHome</home>
   <remote>com.wickedlysmart.Customer</remote>
</ejb-ref>
```

12 Keep it secret, keep it safe

Your web app is in *danger*. Trouble lurks in every corner of the network. You don't want the Bad Guys listening in to your online store transactions, picking off credit card numbers. You don't want the Bad Guys convincing your server that they're actually the Special Customers Who Get Big Discounts. And you don't want *anyone* (good OR bad) looking at sensitive employee data. Does Jim in marketing really need to know that Lisa in engineering makes three times as much as he does?

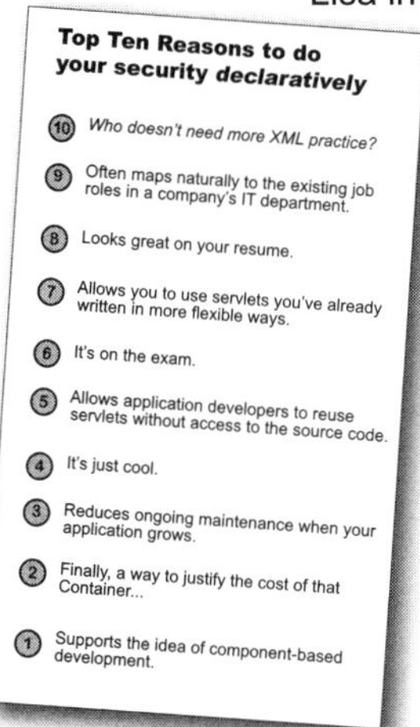

Top Ten Reasons to do your security *declaratively*

10. *Who doesn't need more XML practice?*
9. Often maps naturally to the existing job roles in a company's IT department.
8. Looks great on your resume.
7. Allows you to use servlets you've already written in more flexible ways.
6. It's on the exam.
5. Allows application developers to reuse servlets without access to the source code.
4. It's just cool.
3. Reduces ongoing maintenance when your application grows.
2. Finally, a way to justify the cost of that Container...
1. Supports the idea of component-based development.

13 The power of filters

Filters let you intercept the request. And if you can intercept the *request*, you can also control the *response*. And best of all, **the servlet remains clueless**. It never knows that someone stepped in between the client request and the Container's invocation of the servlet's service() method. What does that mean to you? More vacations. Because the time you would have spent rewriting just *one* of your servlets can be spent instead writing and configuring a filter that has the ability to affect *all* of your servlets. Want to add user request tracking to *every* servlet in your app? No problem. Manipulate the output from ever *servlet* in your app? No problem. And you don't even have to *touch* the servlet.

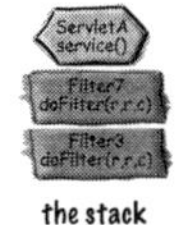
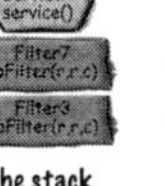

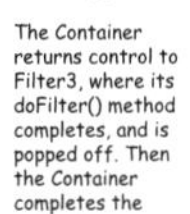

the stack ❶ Upon getting the request, the Container calls Filter3's doFilter() method, which runs until it encounters its chain.doFilter() call.

the stack ❷ The Container pushes Filter7's doFilter() method on the top of the stack - where it executes until it reaches its chain. doFilter ()call.

the stack ❸ The Container pushes ServletA's service() method on the top of the stack where it executes to completion, and is then popped off the stack.

the stack ❹ The Container returns control to Filter7, where its doFilter() method completes and is then popped off.

the stack ❺ The Container returns control to Filter3, where its doFilter() method completes, and is popped off. Then the Container completes the response.

14 Enterprise design patterns

Someone has done this already. If you're just starting to develop web applications in Java, you're lucky. You get to exploit the collective wisdom of the tens of thousands of developers who've been down that road and got the t-shirt. Using both J2EE-specific and *other* design patterns, you can can simplify your code *and* your life. And the most significant design pattern for web apps, MVC, even has a wildly popular framework, Struts, that'll help you craft a flexible, maintainable servlet Front Controller. You owe it to yourself to take advantage of everyone *else's* work so that you can spend more time on the more important things in life...

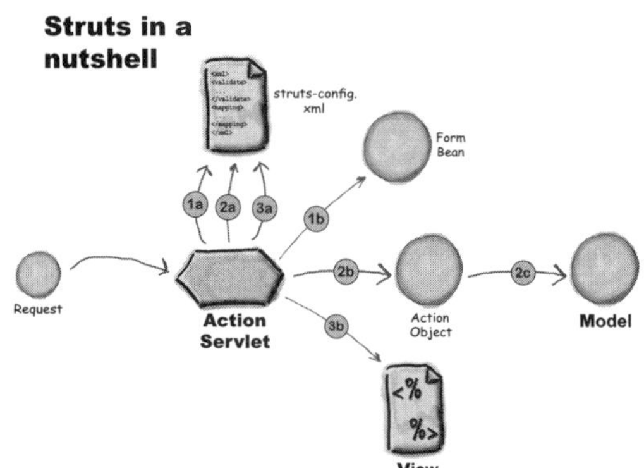

A

The final Coffee Cram Mock Exam. This is it. 69 questions. The tone, topics, and difficulty level are virtually identical to the *real* exam. *We know.*

how to use this book

Intro

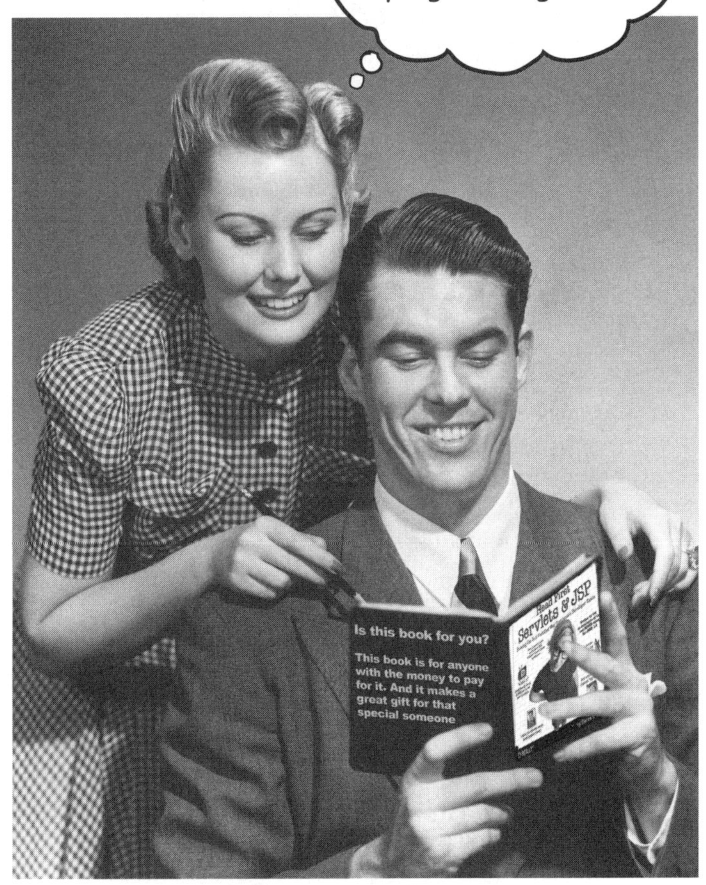

In this section, we answer the burning question:
"So, why DID they put that in a programming book?"

Who is this book for?

If you can answer "yes" to ***all*** of these:

1. **Do you know Java? (You don't need to be a guru.)**

2. Do you want to **learn, understand, and *remember*** servlets and JSPs, with a goal of developing web components for web applications? (And, possibly, passing the **SCWCD** for J2EE 1.4).

3. **Do you prefer stimulating dinner party conversation to dry, dull, academic lectures?**

this book is for you.

Who should probably back away from this book?

If you can answer "yes" to any ***one*** of these:

1. **Are you completely new to Java?**
(You don't need to be advanced, but you should definitely have some experience. If not, go get a copy of Head First Java, right now, today, and then come back and get *this* book.)

2. Are you a kick-butt Java developer looking for **a *reference* book?**

3. Are you **a J2EE veteran** looking for ultra-advanced server techniques, server-specific how-to's, enterprise architecture, and complex, robust real-world code?

4. Are you **afraid to try something different**? Would you rather have a root canal than mix stripes with plaid? Do you believe that a technical book can't be serious if Java components are anthropomorphized?

this book is ***not*** for you.

[note from marketing: this book is for anyone who can afford it.]

We know what you're thinking.

"How can *this* be a serious programming book?"

"What's with all the graphics?"

"Can I actually *learn* it this way?"

"Do I smell pizza?"

And we know what your *brain* is thinking.

your brain thinks THIS is important.

Your brain craves novelty. It's always searching, scanning, *waiting* for something unusual. It was built that way, and it helps you stay alive.

Today, you're less likely to be a tiger snack. But your brain's still looking. You just never know.

So what does your brain do with all the routine, ordinary, normal things you encounter? Everything it *can* to stop them from interfering with the brain's *real* job—recording things that *matter*. It doesn't bother saving the boring things; they never make it past the "this is obviously not important" filter.

How does your brain *know* what's important? Suppose you're out for a day hike and a tiger jumps in front of you, what happens inside your head and body?

Neurons fire. Emotions crank up. *Chemicals surge.*

And that's how your brain knows...

This must be important! Don't forget it!

But imagine you're at home, or in a library. It's a safe, warm, tiger-free zone. You're studying. Getting ready for an exam. Or trying to learn some tough technical topic your boss thinks will take a week, ten days at the most.

Great. Only
637 more dull, dry,
boring pages.

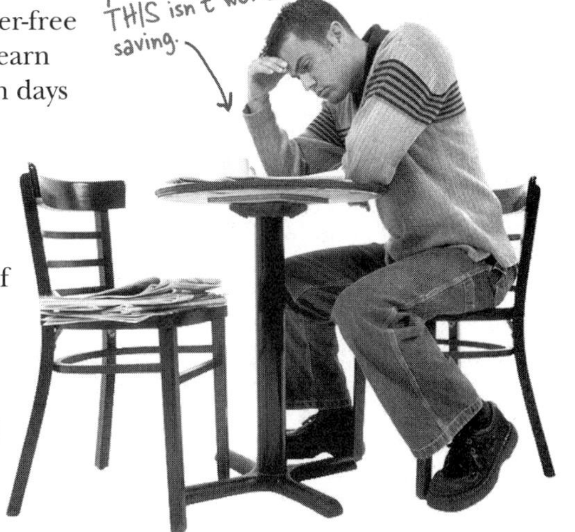
your brain thinks THIS isn't worth saving.

Just one problem. Your brain's trying to do you a big favor. It's trying to make sure that this *obviously* non-important content doesn't clutter up scarce resources. Resources that are better spent storing the really *big* things. Like tigers. Like the danger of fire. Like how you should never again snowboard in shorts.

And there's no simple way to tell your brain, "Hey brain, thank you very much, but no matter how dull this book is, and how little I'm registering on the emotional Richter scale right now, I really *do* want you to keep this stuff around."

We think of a "Head First" reader as a learner.

So what does it take to *learn* something? First, you have to *get* it, then make sure you don't *forget* it. It's not about pushing facts into your head. Based on the latest research in cognitive science, neurobiology, and educational psychology, *learning* takes a lot more than text on a page. We know what turns your brain on.

Some of the Head First learning principles:

Make it visual. Images are far more memorable than words alone, and make learning much more effective (up to 89% improvement in recall and transfer studies). It also makes things more understandable. **Put the words within or near the graphics** they relate to, rather than on the bottom or on another page, and learners will be up to *twice* as likely to solve problems related to the content.

It really sucks to be an abstract method. You don't have a body.

Use a conversational and personalized style. In recent studies, students performed up to 40% better on post-learning tests if the content spoke directly to the reader, using a first-person, conversational style rather than taking a formal tone. Tell stories instead of lecturing. Use casual language. Don't take yourself too seriously. Which would *you* pay more attention to: a stimulating dinner party companion, or a lecture?

```
abstract void roam();
```

No method body! End it with a semicolon.

Does it make sense to say Tub IS-A Bathroom? Bathroom IS-A Tub? Or is it a HAS-A relationship?

Get the learner to think more deeply. In other words, unless you actively flex your neurons, nothing much happens in your head. A reader has to be motivated, engaged, curious, and inspired to solve problems, draw conclusions, and generate new knowledge. And for that, you need challenges, exercises, and thought-provoking questions, and activities that involve both sides of the brain, and multiple senses.

Get—and keep—the reader's attention. We've all had the "I really want to learn this but I can't stay awake past page one" experience. Your brain pays attention to things that are out of the ordinary, interesting, strange, eye-catching, unexpected. Learning a new, tough, technical topic doesn't have to be boring. Your brain will learn much more quickly if it's not.

Touch their emotions. We now know that your ability to remember something is largely dependent on its emotional content. You remember what you care about. You remember when you feel something. No, we're not talking heart-wrenching stories about a boy and his dog. We're talking emotions like surprise, curiosity, fun, "what the...?", and the feeling of "I Rule!" that comes when you solve a puzzle, learn something everybody else thinks is hard, or realize you know something that "I'm more technical than thou" Bob from engineering *doesn't*.

Metacognition: thinking about thinking

If you really want to learn, and you want to learn more quickly and more deeply, pay attention to how you pay attention. Think about how you think. Learn how you learn.

Most of us did not take courses on metacognition or learning theory when we were growing up. We were *expected* to learn, but rarely *taught* to learn.

But we assume that if you're holding this book, you want to learn servlets. And you probably don't want to spend a lot of time. And since you're going to take the exam, you need to *remember* what you read. And for that, you've got to understand it. To get the most from this book, or *any* book or learning experience, take responsibility for your brain. Your brain on *this* content.

I wonder how I can trick my brain into remembering this stuff...

The trick is to get your brain to see the new material you're learning as Really Important. Crucial to your well-being. As important as a tiger. Otherwise, you're in for a constant battle, with your brain doing its best to keep the new content from sticking.

So just how *DO* you get your brain to treat servlets like it's a hungry tiger?

There's the slow, tedious way, or the faster, more effective way. The slow way is about sheer repetition. You obviously know that you *are* able to learn and remember even the dullest of topics, if you keep pounding on the same thing. With enough repetition, your brain says, "This doesn't *feel* important to him, but he keeps looking at the same thing *over* and *over* and *over*, so I suppose it must be."

The faster way is to do ***anything that increases brain activity,*** especially different *types* of brain activity. The things on the previous page are a big part of the solution, and they're all things that have been proven to help your brain work in your favor. For example, studies show that putting words *within* the pictures they describe (as opposed to somewhere else in the page, like a caption or in the body text) causes your brain to try to makes sense of how the words and picture relate, and this causes more neurons to fire. More neurons firing = more chances for your brain to *get* that this is something worth paying attention to, and possibly recording.

A conversational style helps because people tend to pay more attention when they perceive that they're in a conversation, since they're expected to follow along and hold up their end. The amazing thing is, your brain doesn't necessarily *care* that the "conversation" is between you and a book! On the other hand, if the writing style is formal and dry, your brain perceives it the same way you experience being lectured to while sitting in a roomful of passive attendees. No need to stay awake.

But pictures and conversational style are just the beginning.

Here's what WE did:

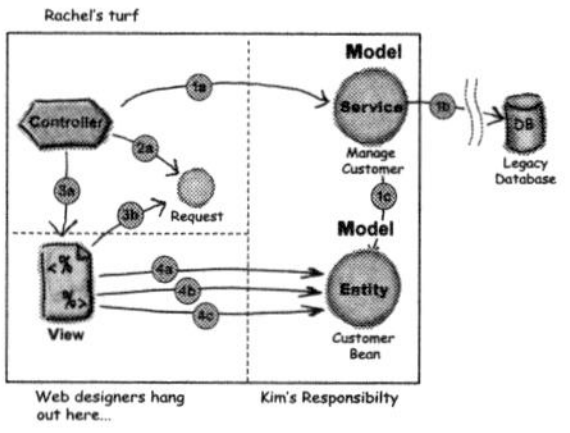

We used ***pictures***, because your brain is tuned for visuals, not text. As far as your brain's concerned, a picture really *is* worth 1024 words. And when text and pictures work together, we embedded the text *in* the pictures because your brain works more effectively when the text is *within* the thing the text refers to, as opposed to in a caption or buried in the text somewhere.

We used ***repetition***, saying the same thing in different ways and with different media types, and *multiple senses*, to increase the chance that the content gets coded into more than one area of your brain.

We used concepts and pictures in ***unexpected*** ways because your brain is tuned for novelty, and we used pictures and ideas with at least *some* ***emotional*** *content*, because your brain is tuned to pay attention to the biochemistry of emotions. That which causes you to *feel* something is more likely to be remembered, even if that feeling is nothing more than a little ***humor***, ***surprise***, or ***interest.***

We used a personalized, ***conversational style***, because your brain is tuned to pay more attention when it believes you're in a conversation than if it thinks you're passively listening to a presentation. Your brain does this even when you're *reading*.

We included more than 40 ***activities***, because your brain is tuned to learn and remember more when you ***do*** things than when you *read* about things. And we made the exercises challenging-yet-do-able, because that's what most *people* prefer.

We used ***multiple learning styles***, because *you* might prefer step-by-step procedures, while someone else wants to understand the big picture first, while someone else just wants to see a code example. But regardless of your own learning preference, *everyone* benefits from seeing the same content represented in multiple ways.

We include content for ***both sides of your brain***, because the more of your brain you engage, the more likely you are to learn and remember, and the longer you can stay focused. Since working one side of the brain often means giving the other side a chance to rest, you can be more productive at learning for a longer period of time.

And we included ***stories*** and exercises that present ***more than one point of view,*** because your brain is tuned to learn more deeply when it's forced to make evaluations and judgements.

We included ***challenges***, with exercises, and by asking ***questions*** that don't always have a straight answer, because your brain is tuned to learn and remember when it has to *work* at something. Think about it—you can't get your *body* in shape just by *watching* people at the gym. But we did our best to make sure that when you're working hard, it's on the *right* things. That ***you're not spending one extra dendrite*** processing a hard-to-understand example, or parsing difficult, jargon-laden, or overly terse text.

We used ***people***. In stories, examples, pictures, etc., because, well, because *you're* a person. And your brain pays more attention to *people* than it does to *things*.

We used an ***80/20*** approach. We assume that if you're going for a PhD in JSP, this won't be your only book. So we don't talk about *everything*. Just the stuff you'll actually *need*.

Here's what YOU can do to bend your brain into submission

So, we did our part. The rest is up to you. These tips are a starting point; listen to your brain and figure out what works for you and what doesn't. Try new things.

cut this out and stick it on your refridgerator.

1. **Slow down. The more you understand, the less you have to memorize.**

   Don't just *read*. Stop and think. When the book asks you a question, don't just skip to the answer. Imagine that someone really *is* asking the question. The more deeply you force your brain to think, the better chance you have of learning and remembering.

2. **Do the exercises. Write your own notes.**

   We put them in, but if we did them for you, that would be like having someone else do your workouts for you. And don't just *look* at the exercises. **Use a pencil.** There's plenty of evidence that physical activity *while* learning can increase the learning.

3. **Read the "There are No Dumb Questions"**

   That means all of them. They're not optional side-bars—*they're part of the core content!* Don't skip them.

4. **Don't do all your reading in one place.**

   Stand-up, stretch, move around, change chairs, change rooms. It'll help your brain *feel* something, and keeps your learning from being too connected to a particular place. Remember, you won't be taking the exam in your bedroom.

5. **Make this the last thing you read before bed. Or at least the last *challenging* thing.**

   Part of the learning (especially the transfer to long-term memory) happens *after* you put the book down. Your brain needs time on its own, to do more processing. If you put in something new during that processing-time, some of what you just learned will be lost.

6. **Drink water. Lots of it.**

   Your brain works best in a nice bath of fluid. Dehydration (which can happen before you ever feel thirsty) decreases cognitive function. Beer, or something stronger, is called for when you pass the exam.

7. **Talk about it. Out loud.**

   Speaking activates a different part of the brain. If you're trying to understand something, or increase your chance of remembering it later, say it out loud. Better still, try to explain it out loud to someone else. You'll learn more quickly, and you might uncover ideas you hadn't known were there when you were reading about it.

8. **Listen to your brain.**

   Pay attention to whether your brain is getting overloaded. If you find yourself starting to skim the surface or forget what you just read, it's time for a break. Once you go past a certain point, you won't learn faster by trying to shove more in, and you might even hurt the process.

9. **Feel something!**

   Your brain needs to know that this *matters*. Get involved with the stories. Make up your own captions for the photos. Groaning over a bad joke is *still* better than feeling nothing at all.

10. **Take the final Coffee Cram Mock Exam only AFTER you finish the book.**

    If you take it too soon, you won't get a clear picture of how ready you are for the exam. Wait until you think you're close to ready, then take the exam, giving yourself exactly 135 minutes—the length of the real SCWCD.

What you need for this book:

Besides your brain and a pencil, **you need Java, Tomcat 5 and a computer.**

You do *not* need any other development tool, such as an Integrated Development Environment (IDE). We strongly recommend that you *not* use anything but a basic editor until you complete this book. A servlet/JSP-aware IDE can protect you from some of the details that really matter (and that you'll be tested on), so you're much better off developing the bean code completely by hand. Once you really understand what's happening, you can move to a tool that automates some of the servlet/JSP creation and deployment steps. If you already know how to use Ant, then after chapter 3, you can switch to using it to help you deploy, but we don't recommend using Ant until after you've completely memorized the web app deployment structure.

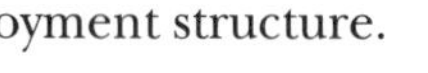

GETTING TOMCAT

- If you don't already have a 1.3 or greater **J2SE SDK**, you need it. (1.4 preferred.)
- If you don't already have Tomcat 5, go get it from:
  http://jakarta.apache.org/site/binindex.cgi
  Scroll down to the page to the Tomcat 5.0.xxx listing.
  Select the appropriate download (usually by machine type).
- Save the installation file in a temporary directory.
- Install Tomcat.
  For Windows, that means double-clicking the install .exe file and following the installer wizard instructions.
  For the others, unpack the install file into the place on your hard drive where you want Tomcat to be.
- To make it easier to follow the book instructions, name the Tomcat home directory "tomcat" (or set up a "tomcat" alias to the real Tomcat home).
- Set environment variables for **JAVA_HOME** and **TOMCAT_HOME**, in whatever way you normally set them for your system.
- You should have a copy of the specs, although you do not need them in order to pass the exam. At the time of this writing, the specs are at:
  Servlet 2.4 (JSR #154) **http://jcp.org/en/jsr/detail?id=154**
  JSP 2.0 (JSR #152) **http://jcp.org/en/jsr/detail?id=152**
  JSTL 1.1 (JSR #52) **http://jcp.org/en/jsr/detail?id=52**

  Go to the JSR page and click on the Download Page for the final release.
- Test Tomcat by launching the tomcat/bin/startup script (which is startup.sh) for Linux/Unix/OSX). Point your browser to:
  http://localhost:8080/ and you'll see the Tomcat welcome page.

Java 2 *Standard* Edition 1.4

Tomcat 5

The exam covers the following specs:

- Servlets 2.4
- JSP 2.0
- JSTL 1.1

Last-minute things you need to know:

This is a learning experience, not a reference book. We deliberately stripped out everything that might get in the way of *learning* whatever it is we're working on at that point in the book. And the first time through, you need to begin at the beginning, because the book makes assumptions about what you've already seen and learned.

We use simple UML-*like* diagrams.

Although there's a good chance you already know UML, it's not covered on the exam, and it's not a prerequisite for the book. So you won't have to worry about learning servlets, JSP, JSTL *and* UML at the same time.

We use a simpler, modified faux-UML

Director
getMovies getOscars() getKevinBaconDegrees()

We don't cover every single picky detail from the spec.

The exam *is* pretty detailed, though, and so are we. But if there's a detail in the spec that's not covered in the exam, we don't talk about it unless it's important to most component developers. What you need to know to begin developing web components (servlets and JSPs), and what you need to pass the exam, overlap about 85%. We cover a few things not on the exam, but we point them out so you don't have to try to memorize them. We created the *real* exam, so we know where you should focus your energy! If there's a chance that this one picky detail might be on one question on the exam, but the effort to learn it isn't really worth it, we might skip it, or cover it only very lightly, or only in a mock exam question.

The activities are NOT optional.

The exercises and activities are not add-ons; they're part of the core content of the book. Some of them are there to help with memory, some for understanding, some to help you apply what you've learned. *Don't skip anything.*

The redundancy is intentional and important.

One thing that's distinctly different in a Head First book is that *we want you to really really really get it.* And we want you to finish the book *remembering* what you've learned. Most information or reference books don't necessarily have retention and recall as a goal, but in this book you'll see some of the same concepts come up more than once.

The code examples are as lean as possible

Our readers tell us that it's frustrating to wade through 200 lines of code looking for the two lines they need to understand. Most examples in this book are shown within the smallest possible context, so that the part you're trying to learn is clear and simple. Don't expect the code to be robust, or even complete. That's *your* assignment for after you finish the book. The book examples are written specifically for *learning*, and aren't always fully-functional. We sometimes make code examples available at wickedlysmart.com.

About the SCWCD (for J2EE 1.4) exam

Do I first have to pass the SCJP?

Yes. The Web Component Developer exam, the Business Component Developer exam, The Mobile Application Developer exam, the Web Services Developer exam, and the Developer exam all require you to be a Sun Certified Java Programmer.

How many questions?

You'll get 69 questions when you take the exam. Not everyone gets the same 69 questions; there are many different versions of the exam. But everyone gets the same degree of difficulty, and the same balance of topics. On the real exam, expect to see at least one question from each exam objective, and there are a few objectives where you'll get *more* than one question.

How much time do I get to complete the exam?

You get two hours and 15 minutes (135 minutes). Most people don't find this to be a problem, because these questions don't lend themselves to long, complicated, puzzles. Most questions are very short multiple-choice, and you either know the answer or you don't.

What are the questions like?

They are almost exactly like our mock exam questions, with one big difference—the *real* exam tells you how many answers are correct, where we do not. You will see a handful of drag-and-drop questions, however, that we can't do here. But drag-and-drop questions are just the interactive way of matching one thing to another.

How many do I have to answer correctly?

You must get 43 questions correct (62%) to pass the exam. When you finish answering all of the questions, hold your mouse cursor over the done button until you have the courage to click it. Because in, like, six nanoseconds, you'll know whether you passed (of course you *will*).

Why don't the mock exams in the book tell you how many options to choose for the correct answer?

We want our exams to be just a little more difficult than the real exam, to give you the most realistic picture of whether you're ready to take the exam. People tend to get higher scores on book mock exams because they retake the same test more than once, and we don't want you to get a false picture of your readiness to take the exam. Readers have reported that the score they get on the real exam is very close to the score they get on the mock final exam in this book.

What do I get after I take the exam?

Before you leave the testing center, be sure to get your exam report. It shows a summary of your score in each major area, and whether you passed or failed. *Keep this!* It's your initial proof that you've been certified. A few weeks after the test, you'll get a little package from Sun Educational Services that includes your *real* printed certificate, a congratulations letter from Sun, and a lovely lapel pin that says Sun Certified Web Component Developer in a font so incredibly small that you could pretty much claim to be certified in anything you like, and nobody could read it to tell the difference. It does not include the alcohol you'll be wanting after you pass the exam.

How much does it cost, and how do I register?

The exam costs U.S. $150. Which is why you need this book... to make sure you pass the first time. You register through Sun Educational Services, by giving them your credit card number. In exchange, you'll get a *voucher* number, which you'll use to schedule an appointment at a Prometric Testing Center nearest you.

To get the details online and buy an exam voucher, start at: http://suned.sun.com. If you're in the U.S., go to http://suned.sun.com/US/certification. If you're not in the U.S., you can select a country from the main page.

What's the exam software like?

It's dead simple to use—you get a question, and you answer it. If you don't want to answer it, you can skip it and come back to it later. If you do answer it, but aren't sure, and you want to come back to it if you have more time, you can "mark" a question. Once you're done, you'll see a screen that shows all of the questions you haven't answered, or have marked, so that you can go back to them.

At the very beginning of the exam you'll get a short tutorial on how to use the software, where you get a little practice test (not on Servlets). The time you spend in the tutorial does not count as time spent on the SCWCD exam. The clock doesn't start until you've finished the exam software tutorial and you're ready to begin.

Where can I find a study group, and how long will it take to prepare?

The best online discussion group for this exam just happens to be the one that the authors moderate! (Gosh, what are the odds?) Stop by javaranch.com and go to the Big Moose Saloon (that's where all the discussion forums are). You can't miss it. There will always be *someone* there to answer your questions, including *us*. Javaranch is the friendliest Java community on the internet, so you're welcome no matter what level you're at with Java. If you still need to take the SCJP, we'll help you with that one too.

How long it takes you to get ready for the exam depends a lot on how much servlets and JSP experience you've had. If you're *new* to servlets and JSP, you might need anywhere from six to twelve weeks, depending on how much time you can devote to it each day. Those with a lot of recent servlets and JSP experience can often be ready in as little as three weeks.

Beta testers

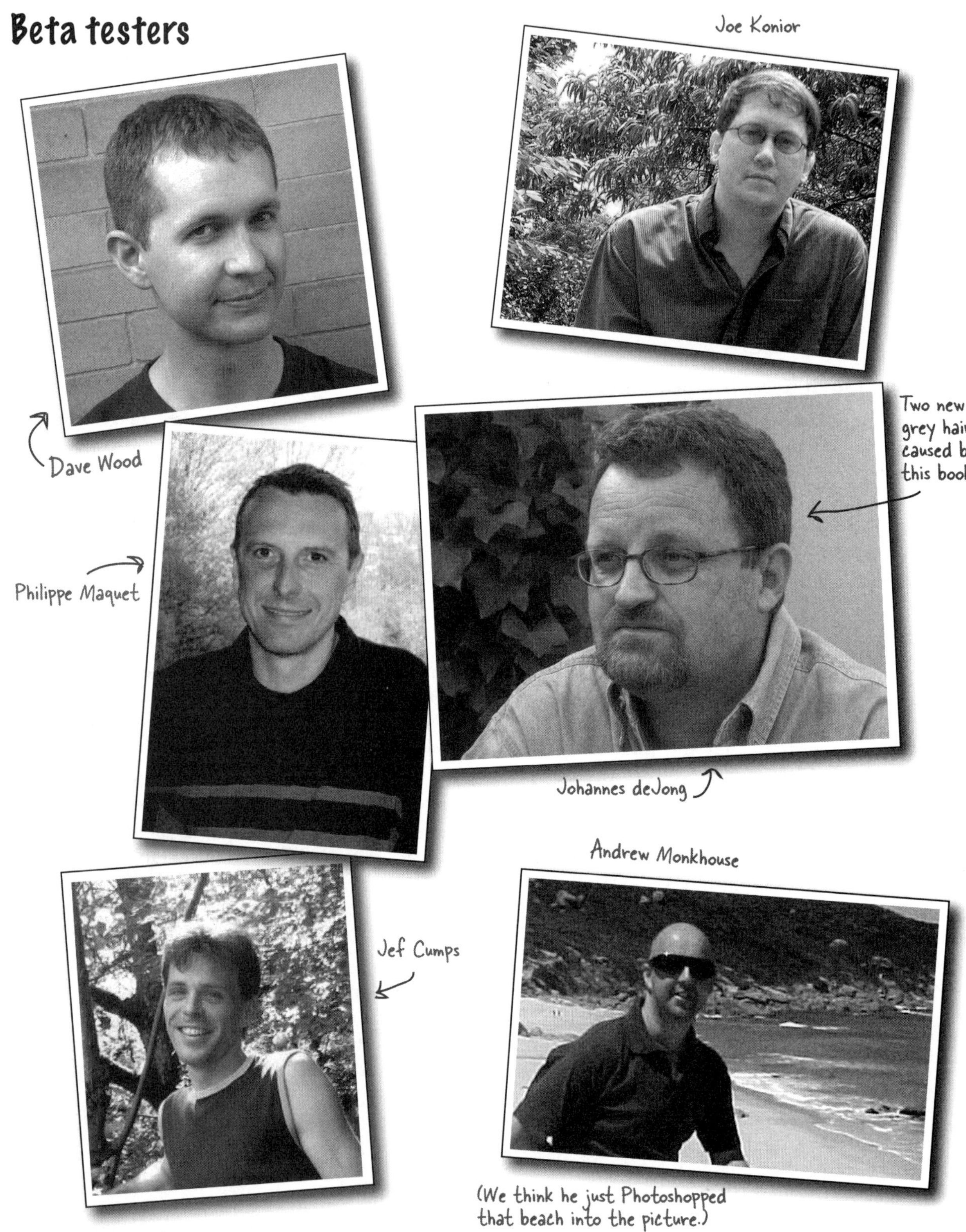

Other people to ~~blame~~ credit:

At O'Reilly:

Our biggest thanks to **Mike Loukides** at O'Reilly, for starting it all, and helping to shape the Head First concept into a series. We love having an editor who is a Real Java Guy. And a big thanks to the driving force behind Head First, **Tim O'Reilly**. Lucky for us, he's always thinking about the future, and enjoys being a disruptive influence. Thanks to the clever Head First "series mom" **Kyle Hart** for figuring out how Head First fits into the rest of the computer book world.

Jason Menard

Our intrepid reviewers:

OK, so the book took a little longer than we'd planned. But without Javaranch review manager **Johannes deJong**, it would have been *scarily* late. You are our hero, Johannes. And our special thanks to **Joe Konior,** whose feedback on each chapter was pretty much the same *size* as the chapter. We deeply appreciate the relentless effort and expertise (and cheerfulness) of **Philippe Macquet**. All three of the authors love him so much we want to marry him...but that would be weird. And we're very grateful to **Andrew Monkhouse** for both technical feedback *and* help with the subtle English-to-Australian translations. **Jef Cumps**, your MP3 rendition of the "setHeader" song was terrific (except for maybe being a bit *emo*), and your technical comments were *really* helpful.

Dave Wood hammered us on *everything*, and was fond of pointing to early pages and saying, "*That's* not very Head Firsty." And now Dave's working on his *own* Head First book that *we'll* be reviewing. Two words Dave: *payback time.*

We also got some excellent feedback from Javaranch moderators **Jason Menard**, **Dirk "fish face" Schreckmann**, **Rob Ross**, **Ernest Friedman-Hill**, and **Thomas Paul**. And as always, thanks especially to the javaranch.com Trail Boss, **Paul Wheaton**.

Dirk Schreckmann

Mock Exam Questions

Don't hate us for the hard questions. Hate **Dave Wood** (yes, same guy) and **Bruce Perry** instead; they wrote a a lot the questions, some of which are even tougher than in the *real* exam. Dave is co-author of O'Reilly's *Java Swing*, and has been a Java Guy since he went to work for Sun Microsystems in 1997. He left Sun to make his millions in the dot-com boom, and is currently a thousandaire. Bruce Perry is an independent Java consultant with Parker River Net Solutions: www.parkerriver.com. He also recently published the O'Reilly book *Java Servlet & JSP Cookbook.*

Even more people*

From Bryan Basham

I could start by thanking my Mom, but that's been done before...My knowledge of Java web development is founded in a few medium-scale applications that I have written, but that foundation was honed and refined by years of debate on a Java instructor email alias internal to Sun. In particular, I would like to thank Steve Stelting, Victor Peters, Lisa Morris, Jean Tordella, Michael Judd, Evan Troyka, and Keith Ratliff. There were many people that carved my knowledge, but these six have been the knives that have cut me the deepest.

As with all book projects, the last three months were pretty difficult. I want to thank my fiance, Kathy Collina, for being patient with me. I want to thank Karma and Kiwi (our cats) for the late night sessions of lap-sitting and keyboard trouncing.

Lastly, and most importantly, I must thank Kathy and Bert for even suggesting that we take on this project. Kathy Sierra is truly unique in the world. Her knowledge of metacognition and instructional design is matched only by her creative juice that pours out of her Head First books. I have worked in education for five years now and I have learned nearly everything I know from Kathy... Oh, don't worry about my Mom; she will get a big dedication in my next Head First book. I love you, Mom!

From Kathy and Bert

That was so mushy Bryan, *geez.* (Not that Kathy doesn't appreciate the sucking up.) We agree about your fiance, though. But it's not like she *missed* you, out playing Ultimate all summer long while *we* were working like dogs at our Powerbooks. But you really made this a rewarding experience Bryan, and you're the best[1] co-author we've ever had! It's almost frightening how calm and happy you are *all the time.*

We all appreciate the hard-working Sun exam certification team, especially Java cert manager Evelyn Cartagena, and we thank all the folks who helped develop the JSR's for the Servlet and JSP specs.

*The large number of acknowledgements is because we're testing the theory that everyone mentioned in a book acknowledgement will buy at least one copy, probably more, what with relatives and everything. If you'd like to be in the acknowledgement of our *next* book, and you have a large family, write to us.

[1]Point of clarification: Bryan is the *only* co-author we've ever had, but that in no way diminishes the intent.

1 intro and overview

Why use Servlets & JSPs?

Web applications are hot. Sure, GUI applications might use exotic Swing widgets, but how many GUI apps do you know that are used by millions of users world-wide? As a web app developer, you can free yourself from the grip of deployment problems all standalone apps have, and deliver your app to anyone with a browser. But to build a truly powerful web app, you need Java. You need servlets. You need JSPs. Because plain old static HTML pages are so, well, 1999. Today's users expect sites that are dynamic, interactive, and custom-tailored. Within these pages you'll learn to move from web *site* to web *app*.

Servlets & JSP overview

1.1 For each of the HTTP Methods (such as GET, POST, HEAD, and so on):

* Describe benefits of the HTTP Method

* Describe functionality of the HTTP Method

* List triggers that might cause a Client (usually a Web browser) to use the method

Also part of Objective 1.1, but not covered in this chapter:

* Identify the HttpServlet method that corresponds to the HTTP Method

Coverage Notes:

The objectives in this section are covered completely in another chapter, so think of this chapter as a first-look foundation for what comes later. In other words, don't worry about finishing this chapter knowing (and remembering) anything specific from these objectives; just use it for background. If you already know these topics, you can just skim this chapter and jump to chapter 2. You won't have any mock exam questions on these topics until you get to the more specific chapter where those topics are covered.

Everybody wants a web site

You have a killer idea for a web site. To destroy the competition, you need a flexible, scalable architecture. You need servlets and JSPs.

Before we start building, let's take a look at the World Wide Web from about 40k feet. What we care most about in this chapter are how web ***clients*** and web ***servers*** talk to one another.

These next several pages are probably all review for you, especially if you're already a web application developer, but it'll give us a chance to expose some of the terminology we use throughout the book.

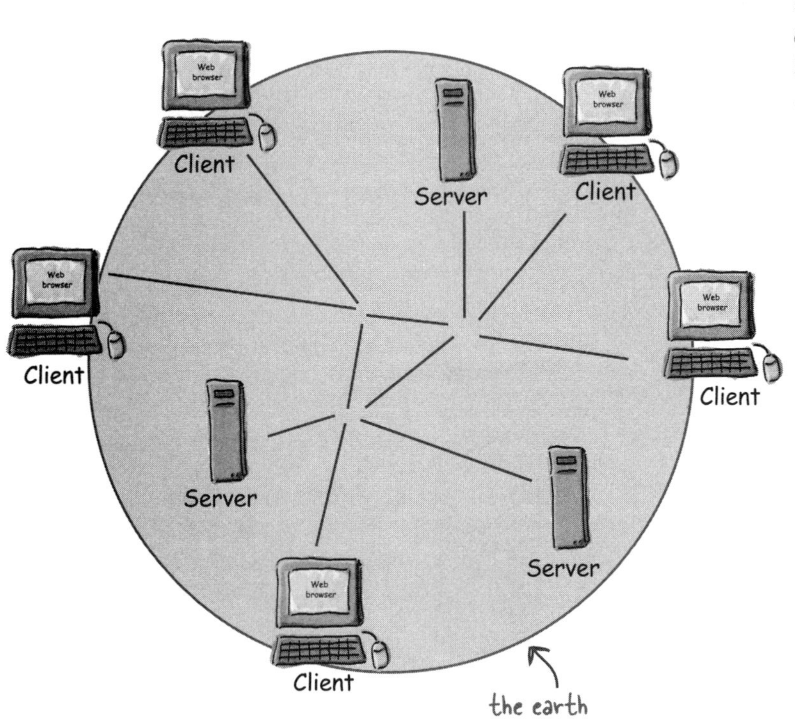

The web consists of gazillions of clients (using browsers like Mozilla or Safari) and servers (using web server apps like Apache) connected through wires and wireless networks. Our goal is to build a web application that clients around the globe can access. And to become obscenely rich.

What does your web server do?

A web server takes a client request and gives something back to the client.

A web *browser* lets a user request a *resource.* The web *server* gets the request, finds the resource, and returns something to the user. Sometimes that resource is an *HTML page.* Sometimes it's a *picture.* Or a *sound* file. Or even a *PDF* document. Doesn't matter—the client asks for the thing (resource) and the server sends it back.

Unless the thing isn't there. Or at least it's not where the server is expecting it to be. You're of course quite familiar with the "404 Not Found" error—the response you get when the server can't find what it thinks you asked for.

When we say "server", we mean *either* the physical machine (hardware) or the web server application (software). Throughout the book, if the difference between server hardware and software matters, we'll explicitly say which one (hardware or software) we're talking about.

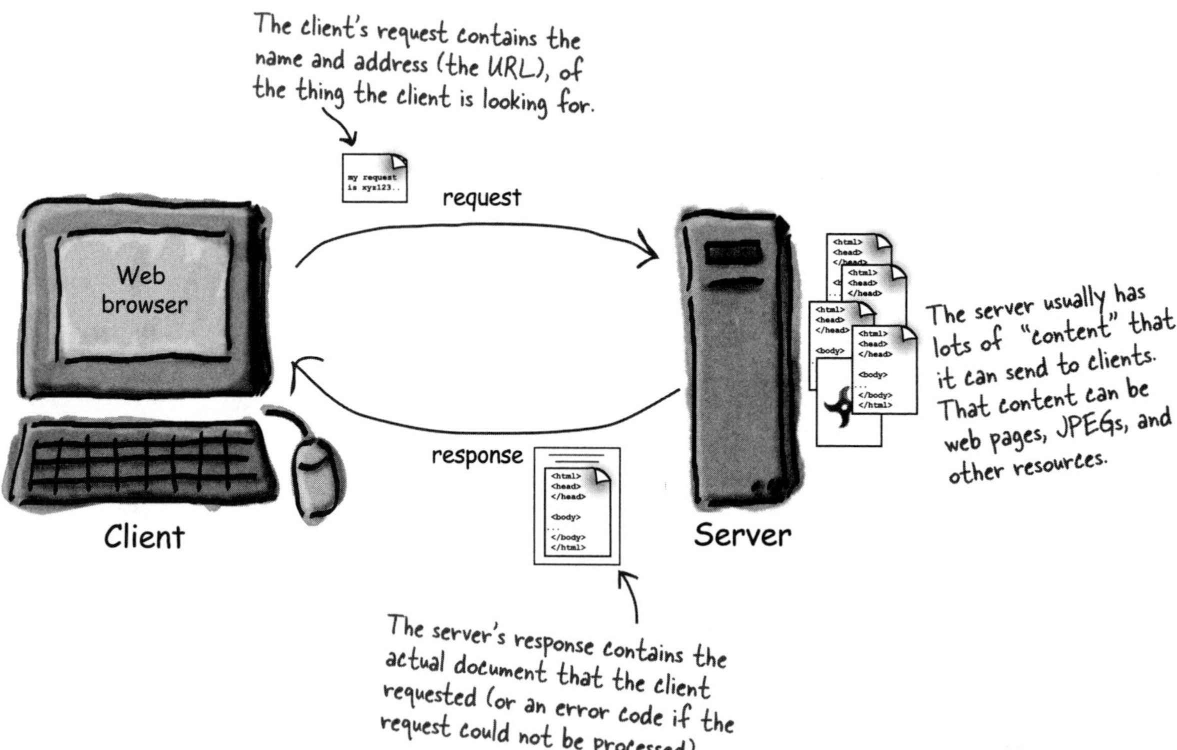
The client's request contains the name and address (the URL), of the thing the client is looking for.
my request is xyz123..
request
Web browser
Client
response
Server
The server usually has lots of "content" that it can send to clients. That content can be web pages, JPEGs, and other resources.
The server's response contains the actual document that the client requested (or an error code if the request could not be processed).

What does a web client do?

A web client lets the user request something on the server, and shows the user the result of the request.

When we talk about *clients*, though, we usually mean both (or either) the *human* user and the browser *application.*

The *browser* is the piece of software (like Netscape or Mozilla) that knows how to communicate with the server. The browser's other big job is interpreting the HTML code and *rendering* the web page for the user.

So from now on, when we use the term *client*, we usually won't care whether we're talking about the human user *or* the browser app. In other words, the *client* is the *browser app doing what the user asked it to do.*

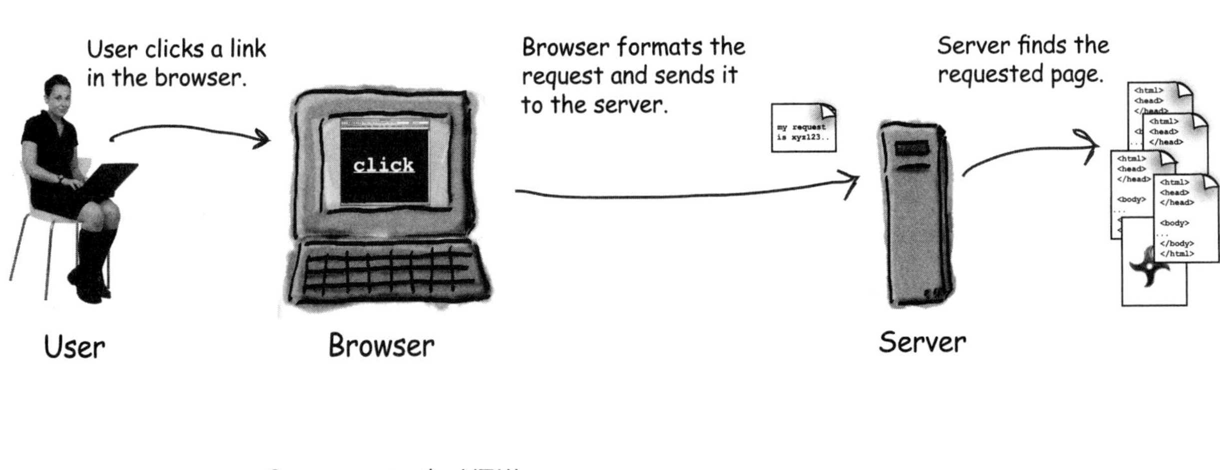
User clicks a link in the browser.
click
Browser formats the request and sends it to the server.
my request is xyz123..
Server finds the requested page.
User
Browser
Server

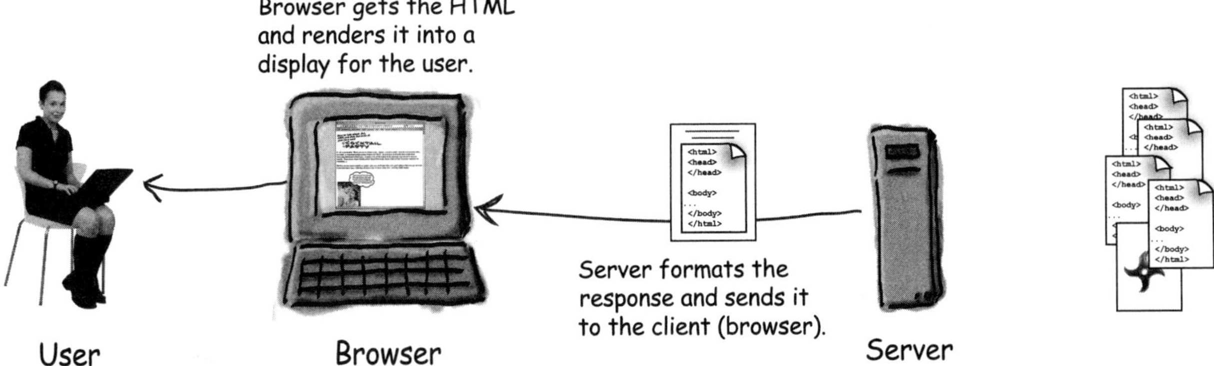
Browser gets the HTML and renders it into a display for the user.
Server formats the response and sends it to the client (browser).
User
Browser
Server

Clients and servers know HTML and HTTP

HTML

When a server answers a request, the server usually sends some type of content to the browser so that the browser can display it. Servers often send the browser a set of instructions written in HTML, the HyperText Markup Language. The HTML tells the browser how to present the content to the user.

All web browsers know what to do with HTML, although sometimes an *older* browser might not understand parts of a page that was written using *newer* versions of HTML.

But how do the clients and servers talk to each other?
A wise question. In order to communicate, they must share a common language. On the web, clients and servers must speak HTTP, and browsers must know HTML.

HTML tells the browser how to display the content to the user.

HTTP

Most of the conversations held on the web between clients and servers are held using the HTTP protocol, which allows for simple request and response conversations. The client sends an HTTP request, and the server answers with an HTTP response. Bottom line: ***if you're a web server, you speak HTTP.***

When a web server sends an HTML page to the client, it sends it using HTTP. (You'll see the details on how all this works in the next few pages.)

(FYI: HTTP stands for HyperText Transfer Protocol.)

HTTP is the protocol clients and servers use on the web to communicate.

The server uses HTTP to send HTML to the client.

Two-minute HTML guide

When you develop a web page, you use HTML to describe what the page should look like and how it should behave.

HTML has dozens of ***tags*** and hundreds of tag ***attributes***. The goal of HTML is to take a text document and add tags that tell the browser how to format the text. Below are the tags we use in the next several chapters. If you need a more complete understanding of HTML, we recommend the book *HTML & XHTML The Definitive Guide.*

Tag	Description
`<!-- -->`	where you put your *comments*
`<a>`	*anchor* - usually for putting in a hyperlink
`<align>`	*align* the contents left, right, centered, or justified
`<body>`	define the boundaries of the document's *body*
` `	a *line break*
`<center>`	*center* the contents
`<form>`	define a *form* (which usually provides input fields)
`<h1>`	the first level *heading*
`<head>`	define the boundaries of the document's *header*
`<html>`	define the boundaries of the HTML *document*
`<input type>`	defines an *input widget* to a form
`<p>`	a new *paragraph*
`<title>`	the HTML document's *title*

(Technically, the <center> and <align> tags have been deprecated in HTML 4.0, but we're using them in some of our examples because it's simpler to read than the alternative, and you're not here to learn HTML anyway.)

What you write...
(the HTML)

Imagine you're creating a login page. The simple HTML might look something like this:

```
    <html>
    <!-- Some sample HTML -->        <-- An HTML comment
    <head>
A     <title>A Login Page</title>
    </head>
    <body>
B   <h1 align="center">Skyler's Login Page</h1>

    <p align="right">
C     <img src="SKYLER2.jpg" width="130" height="150"/>
    </p>

    <form action="date2">     <-- The servlet to send the request to.
D          Name: <input type="text" name="param1"/><br/>
      Password: <input type="text" name="param2"/><br/><br/><br/>

      <center>
        <input type="SUBMIT"/>
E     </center>
    </form>

    </body>
    </html>
```

The <img> tag is nested inside a paragraph <align> tag in order to place the image roughly where we want it. (Remember, <align> is deprecated, but we're using it because it's simple to read.)

We'll talk more about forms later, but briefly, the browser can collect the user's input and return it to the server.

The <br> tags cause line breaks.

The "submit" button in the form.

Relax ***You need only the most basic HTML knowledge.***

HTML pops up all over the exam. But you're not being *tested* on your HTML knowledge. You'll see HTML in the context of a large chunk of questions, though, so you need at least some idea of what's happening when you see simple HTML.

What the browser creates...

The browser reads through the HTML code, creates the web page, and renders it to the user's display.

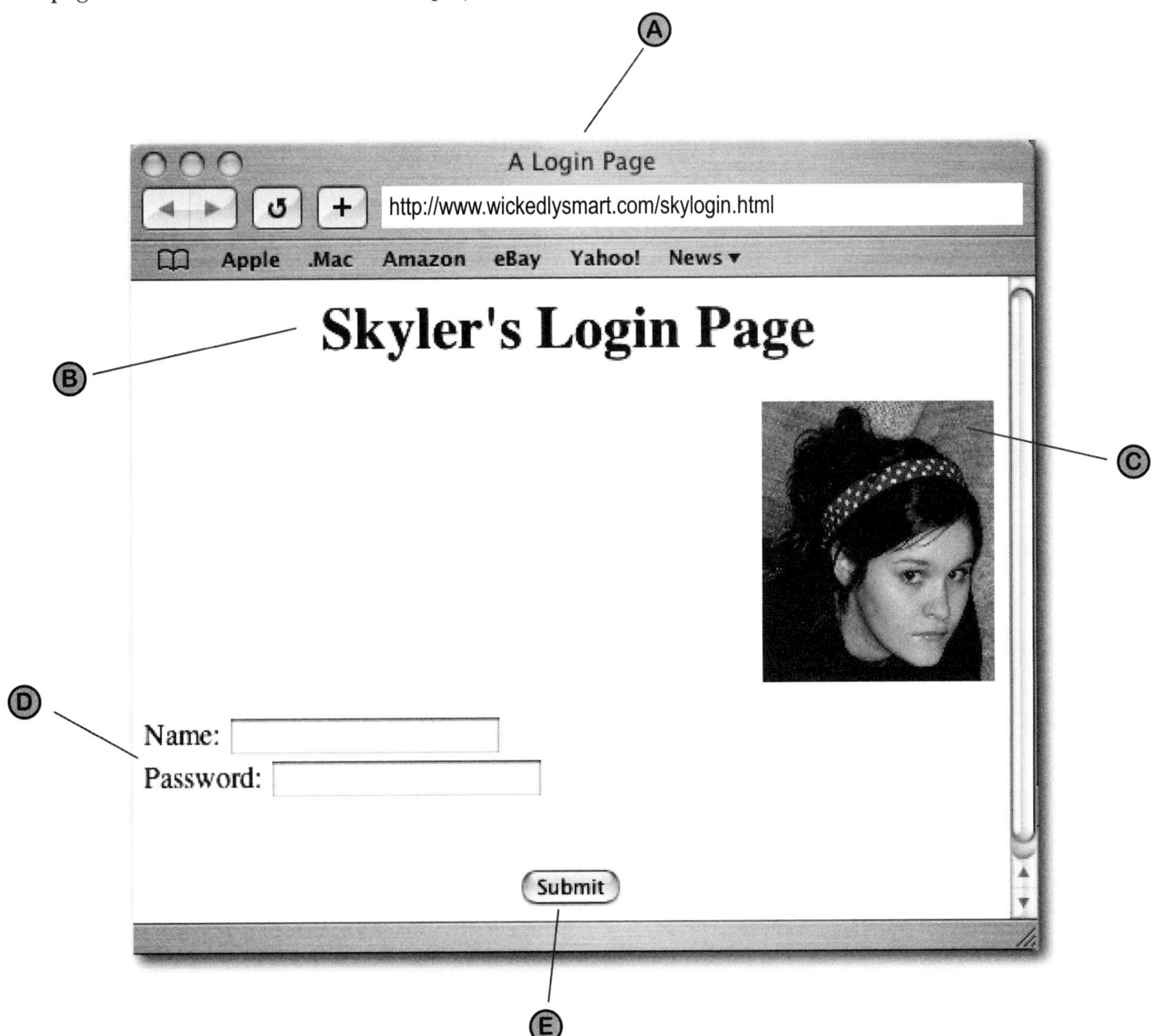

What is the HTTP protocol?

HTTP runs on top of TCP/IP. If you're not familiar with those networking protocols, here's the crash course: TCP is responsible for making sure that a file sent from one network node to another ends up as a complete file at the destination, even though the file is split into chunks when it's sent. IP is the underlying protocol that moves/routes the chunks (packets) from one host to another on their way to the destination. HTTP, then, is another network protocol that has Web-specific features, but it depends on TCP/IP to get the complete request and response from one place to another. The structure of an HTTP conversation is a simple **Request/Response** sequence; a browser *requests,* and a server *responds.*

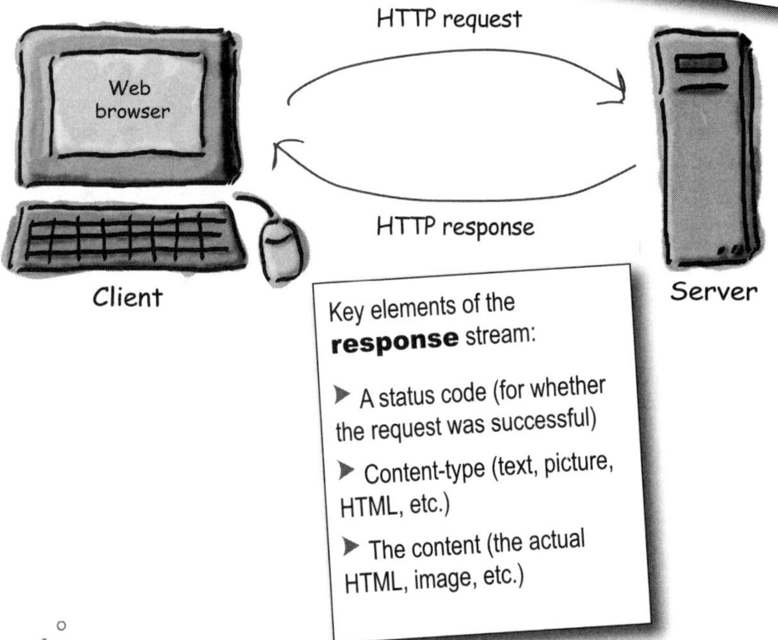

Key elements of the **request** stream:
HTTP method (the action to be performed)
The page to access (a URL)
Form parameters (like arguments to a method)
HTTP request
Web browser
HTTP response
Client
Server
Key elements of the **response** stream:
A status code (for whether the request was successful)
Content-type (text, picture, HTML, etc.)
The content (the actual HTML, image, etc.)

Relax ***You don't have to memorize the HTTP spec.***

The HTTP protocol is an IETF standard, RFC 2616. If you care. (Fortunately, the exam doesn't expect you to.) Apache is an example of a Web server that processes HTTP requests. Mozilla is an example of a Web browser that provides the user with the means to make HTTP requests and to view the documents returned by the server.

HTML is part of the HTTP response

An HTTP response can *contain* HTML. HTTP adds header information to the top of whatever content is in the response (in other words, the *thing* coming back from the server). An HTML browser uses that header info to help process the HTML page. Think of the HTML content as data pasted inside an HTTP response.

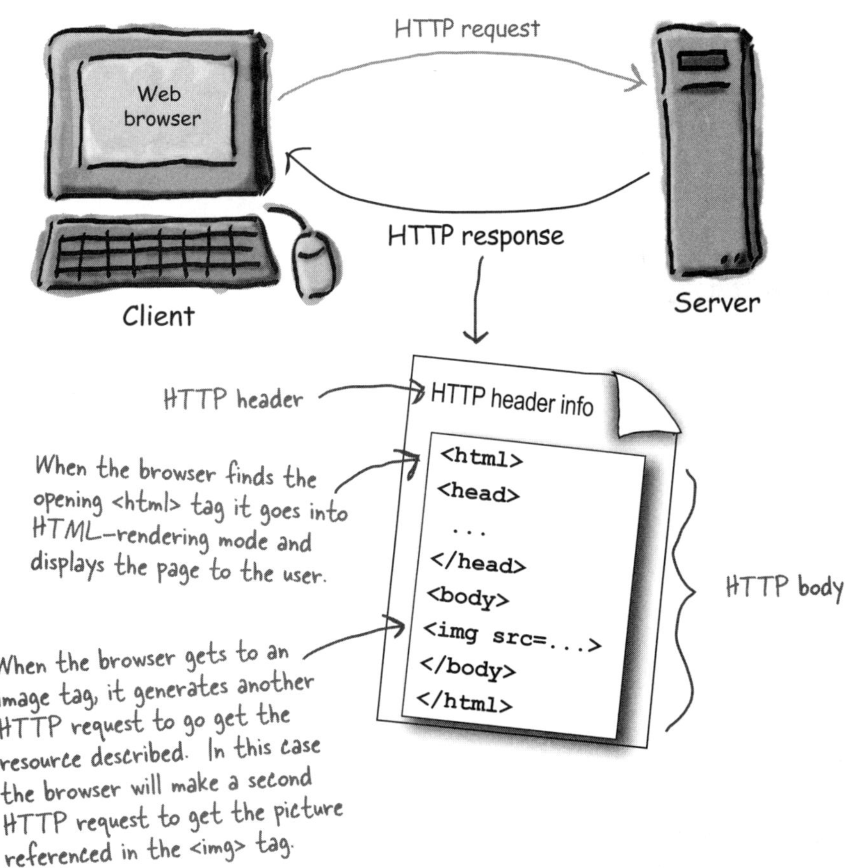

If that's the response, what's in the request?

The first thing you'll find is an HTTP *method* name. These aren't *Java* methods, but the idea is similar. The method name tells the server the kind of request that's being made, and how the rest of the message will be formatted. The HTTP protocol has several methods, but the ones you'll use most often are *GET* and *POST*.

GET

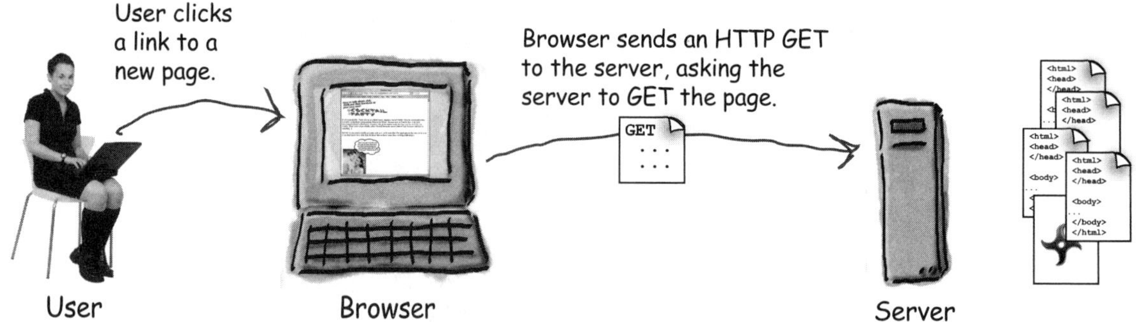

User clicks a link to a new page.
Browser sends an HTTP GET to the server, asking the server to GET the page.
GET
User
Browser
Server

POST

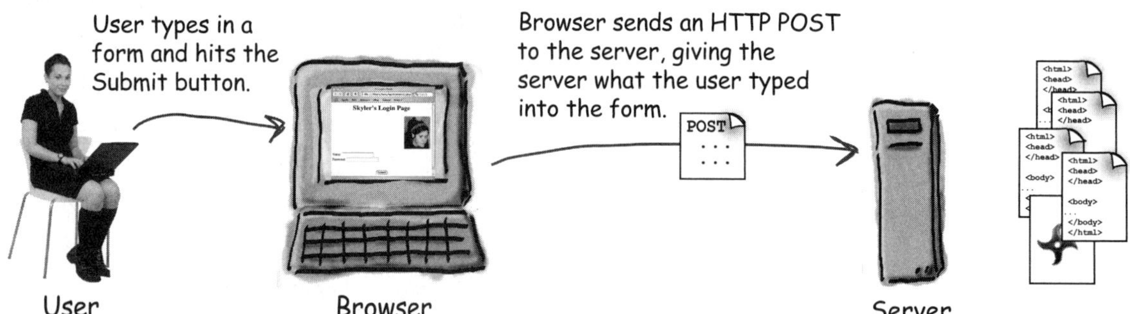

User types in a form and hits the Submit button.
Browser sends an HTTP POST to the server, giving the server what the user typed into the form.
POST
User
Browser
Server

GET is a simple request, POST can send user data

GET is the simplest HTTP method, and its main job in life is to ask the server to *get* a resource and send it back. That resource might be an HTML page, a JPEG, a PDF, etc. Doesn't matter. The point of GET is to *get* something back from the server.

POST is a more powerful request. It's like a GET plus plus. With POST, you can *request* something and at the same time *send* form data to the server (later in this chapter we'll see what the server might do with that data).

Wait a minute... I could swear I've seen GET requests that *did* send some parameter data to the server.

there are no Dumb Questions

Q: So what about the other HTTP methods besides GET and POST?

A: Those are the two big ones that everybody uses. But there are a few rarely used methods (and Servlets can handle them) including HEAD, TRACE, PUT, DELETE, OPTIONS, and CONNECT.

You really don't need to know much about these others for the exam, although you might see them appear in a question. The Life and Death of a Servlet chapter covers the rest of the HTTP method details you'll need.

It's true... you *can* send a little data with HTTP GET

But you might not want to. Reasons you might use POST instead of GET include:

1. The total amount of characters in a GET is really limited (depending on the server). If the user types, say, a long passage into a "search" input box, the GET might not work.

2. The data you send with the GET is appended to the URL up in the browser bar, so whatever you send is exposed. Better not put a password or some other sensitive data as part of a GET!

3. Because of number two above, the user can't bookmark a form submission if you use POST instead of GET. Depending on your app, you may or may not want users to be able to bookmark the resulting request from a form submission.

The "?" separates the path and the parameters (the extra data). The amount of data you can send along with the GET is limited, and it's exposed up here in the browser bar for everyone to see. Together, the entire String is the URL that is sent with the request.

The original URL before the extra parameters.

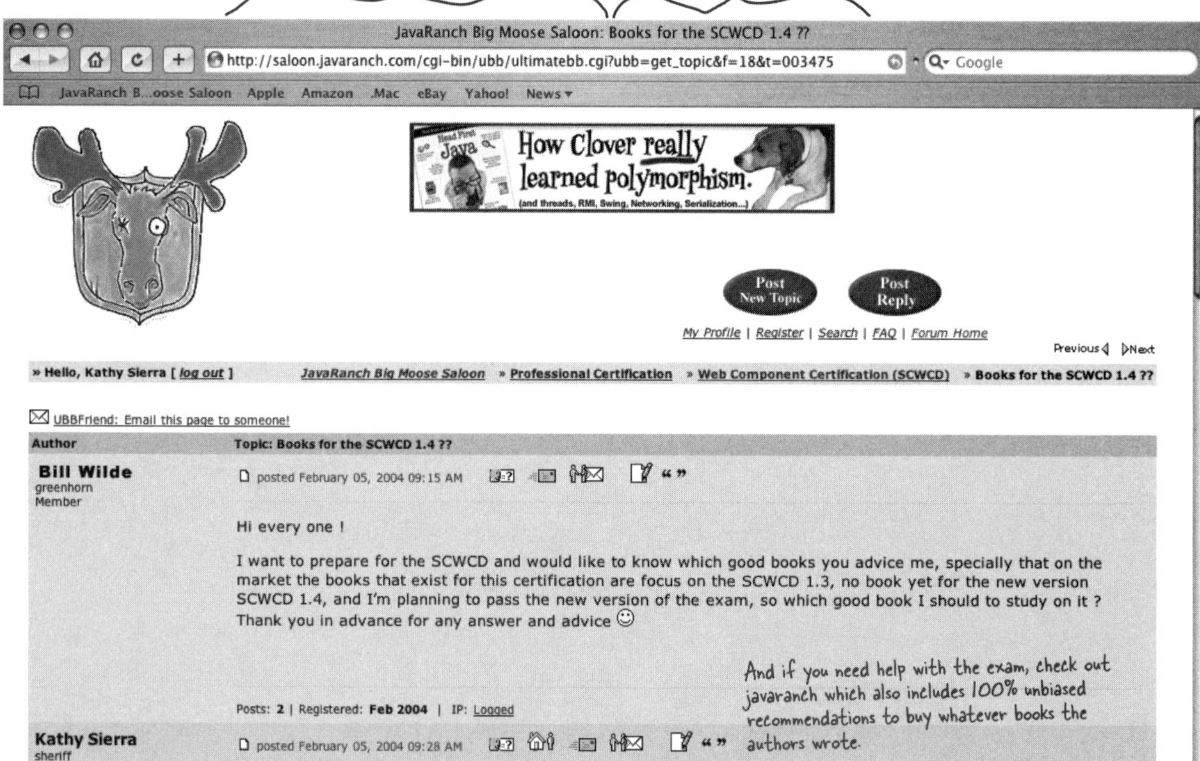

Anatomy of an HTTP GET request

The path to the resource, and any parameters added to the URL are all included on the "request line".

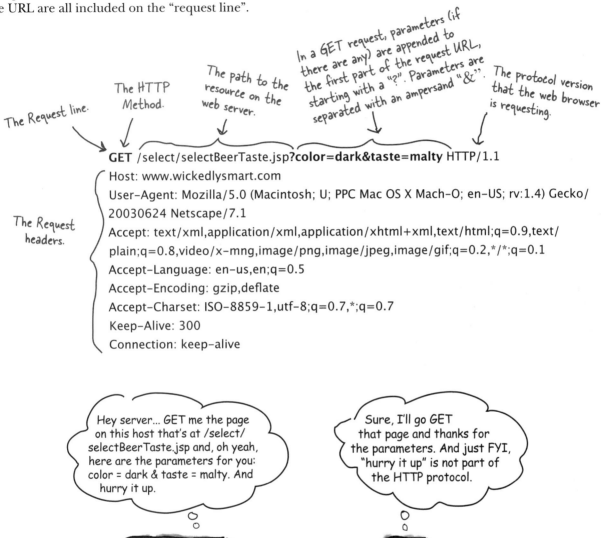

The Request line.

The HTTP Method.

The path to the resource on the web server.

In a GET request, parameters (if there are any) are appended to the first part of the request URL, starting with a "?". Parameters are separated with an ampersand "&".

The protocol version that the web browser is requesting.

The Request headers.

```
GET /select/selectBeerTaste.jsp?color=dark&taste=malty HTTP/1.1
Host: www.wickedlysmart.com
User-Agent: Mozilla/5.0 (Macintosh; U; PPC Mac OS X Mach-O; en-US; rv:1.4) Gecko/
20030624 Netscape/7.1
Accept: text/xml,application/xml,application/xhtml+xml,text/html;q=0.9,text/
plain;q=0.8,video/x-mng,image/png,image/jpeg,image/gif;q=0.2,*/*;q=0.1
Accept-Language: en-us,en;q=0.5
Accept-Encoding: gzip,deflate
Accept-Charset: ISO-8859-1,utf-8;q=0.7,*;q=0.7
Keep-Alive: 300
Connection: keep-alive
```

Hey server... GET me the page on this host that's at /select/selectBeerTaste.jsp and, oh yeah, here are the parameters for you: color = dark & taste = malty. And hurry it up.
Sure, I'll go GET that page and thanks for the parameters. And just FYI, "hurry it up" is not part of the HTTP protocol.
Web browser
HTTP request
GET
Client
Server

Anatomy of an HTTP POST request

HTTP POST requests are designed to be used by the browser to make complex requests on the server. For instance, if a user has just completed a long form, the application might want all of the form's data to be added to a database. The data to be sent back to the server is known as the "message body" or "payload" and can be quite large.

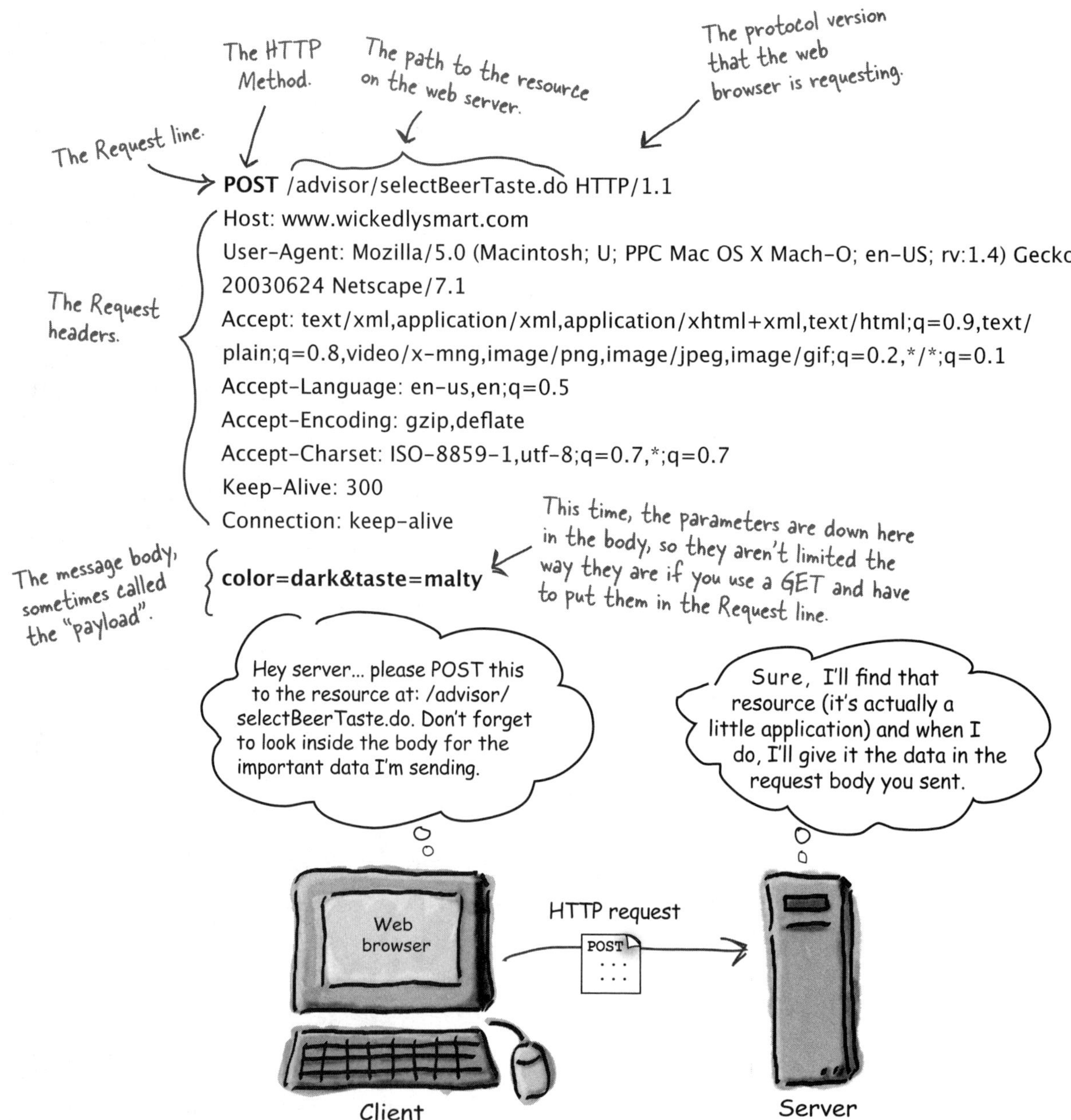
The HTTP Method.
The path to the resource on the web server.
The protocol version that the web browser is requesting.
The Request line.
POST /advisor/selectBeerTaste.do HTTP/1.1
Host: www.wickedlysmart.com
User-Agent: Mozilla/5.0 (Macintosh; U; PPC Mac OS X Mach-O; en-US; rv:1.4) Gecko/20030624 Netscape/7.1
Accept: text/xml,application/xml,application/xhtml+xml,text/html;q=0.9,text/plain;q=0.8,video/x-mng,image/png,image/jpeg,image/gif;q=0.2,*/*;q=0.1
Accept-Language: en-us,en;q=0.5
Accept-Encoding: gzip,deflate
Accept-Charset: ISO-8859-1,utf-8;q=0.7,*;q=0.7
Keep-Alive: 300
Connection: keep-alive
The Request headers.
This time, the parameters are down here in the body, so they aren't limited the way they are if you use a GET and have to put them in the Request line.
The message body, sometimes called the "payload".
color=dark&taste=malty
Hey server... please POST this to the resource at: /advisor/selectBeerTaste.do. Don't forget to look inside the body for the important data I'm sending.
Sure, I'll find that resource (it's actually a little application) and when I do, I'll give it the data in the request body you sent.
Web browser
HTTP request
POST
Client
Server

Anatomy of an HTTP response, and what the heck is a "MIME type"?

Now that we've seen the requests from the browser to the server, let's look at what the server sends back in response. An HTTP response has both a header and a body. The header info tells the browser about the protocol being used, whether the request was successful, and what kind of content is included in the body. The body contains the contents (for example, HTML) for the browser to display.

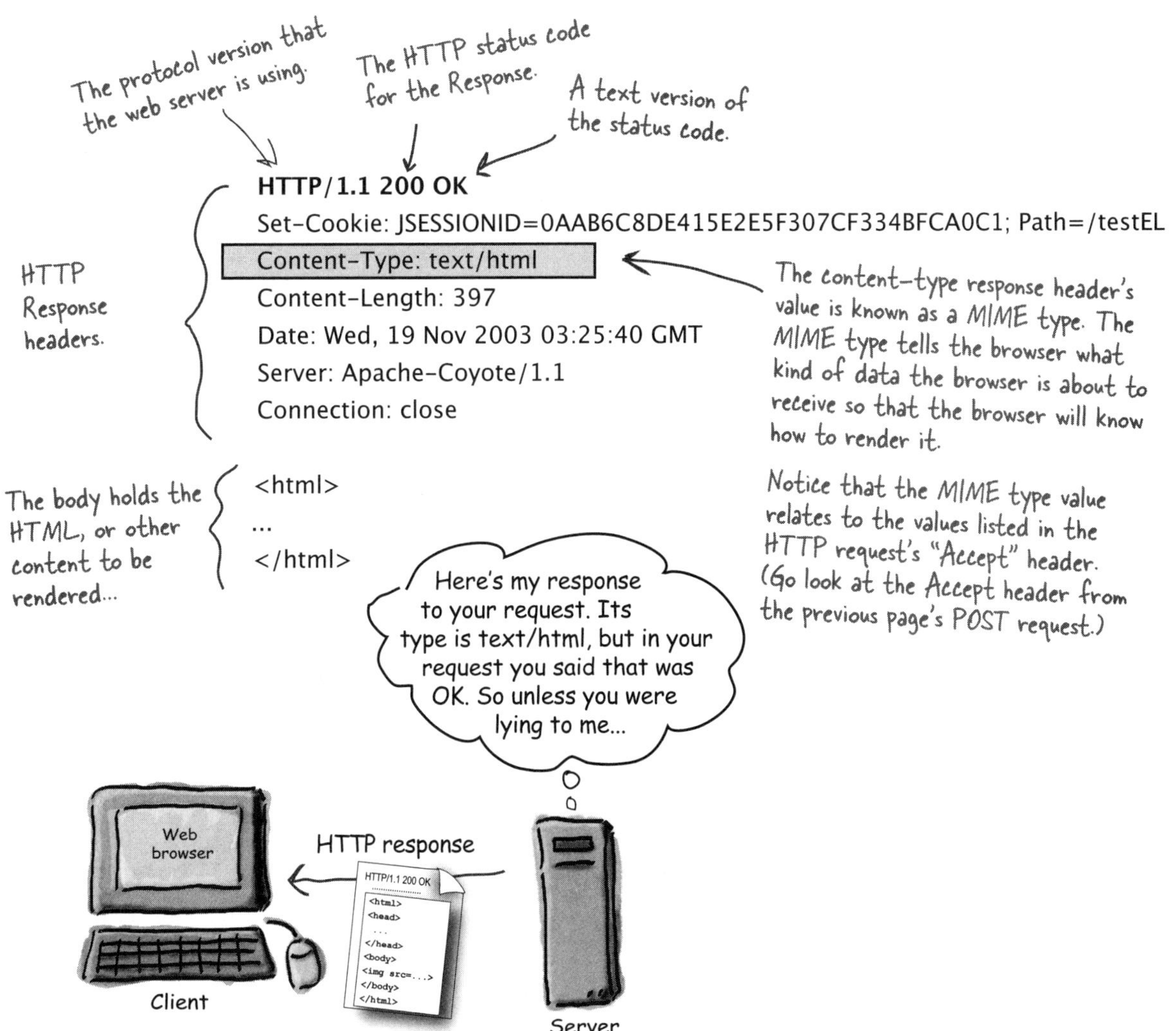

The protocol version that the web server is using.
The HTTP status code for the Response.
A text version of the status code.
HTTP/1.1 200 OK
Set-Cookie: JSESSIONID=0AAB6C8DE415E2E5F307CF334BFCA0C1; Path=/testEL
Content-Type: text/html
Content-Length: 397
Date: Wed, 19 Nov 2003 03:25:40 GMT
Server: Apache-Coyote/1.1
Connection: close
HTTP Response headers.
The content-type response header's value is known as a MIME type. The MIME type tells the browser what kind of data the browser is about to receive so that the browser will know how to render it.
<html>
...
</html>
The body holds the HTML, or other content to be rendered...
Notice that the MIME type value relates to the values listed in the HTTP request's "Accept" header. (Go look at the Accept header from the previous page's POST request.)
Here's my response to your request. Its type is text/html, but in your request you said that was OK. So unless you were lying to me...
Web browser
HTTP response
HTTP/1.1 200 OK
Client
Server

All the pieces. On one page.

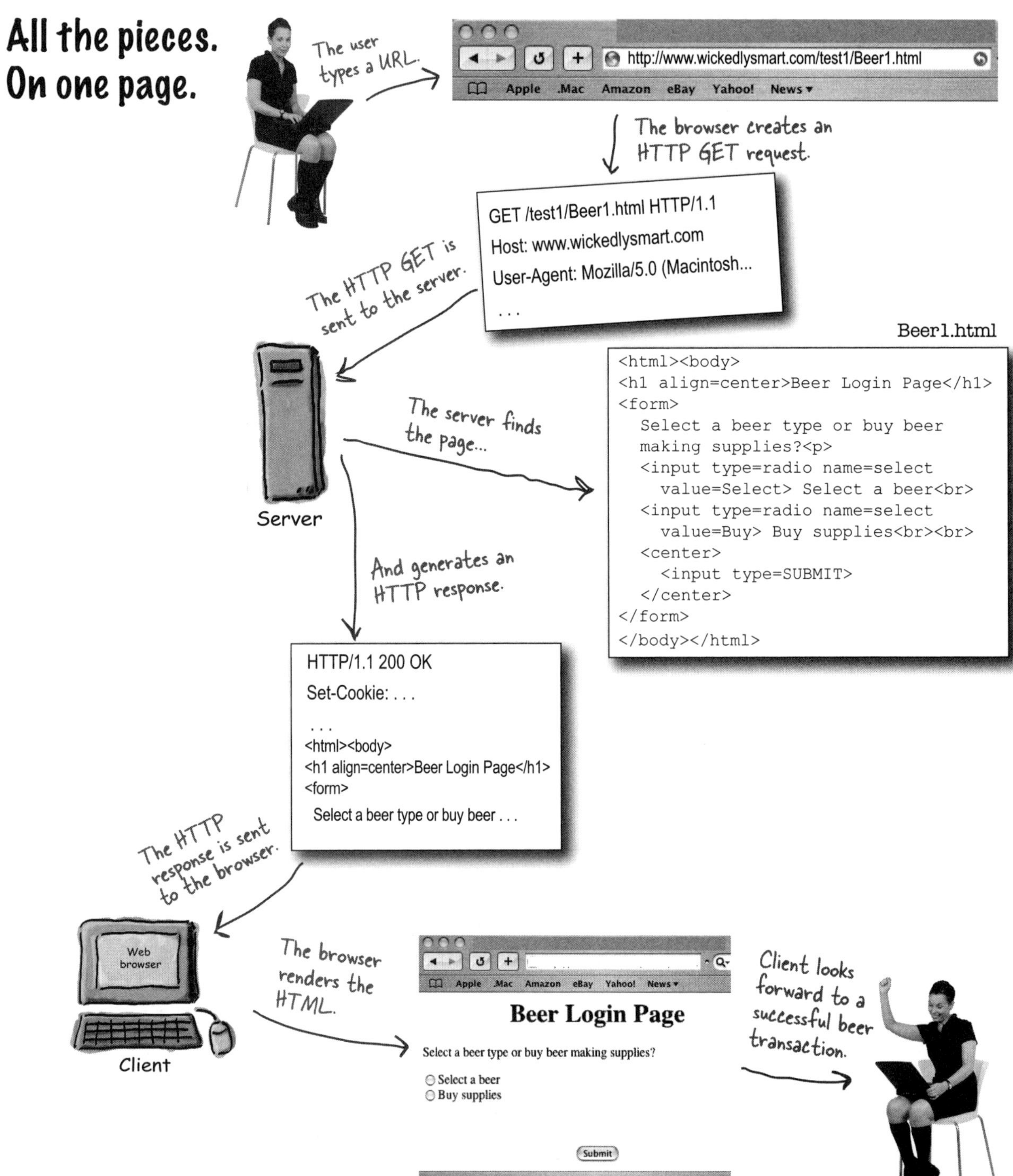

GET or POST?

For each description, circle either POST or GET depending on which HTTP method you'd choose for implementing that functionality. If you think it could be either, circle both. But be prepared to defend your answers...

POST GET *A user is returning a login name and password.*

POST GET *A user is requesting a new page via a hyperlink.*

POST GET *A chat room user is sending a written response.*

POST GET *A user hits the 'next' button to see the next page.*

POST GET *A user hits the 'log out' button on a secure banking site.*

POST GET *A user hits the 'back' button on the browser.*

POST GET *A user sends a name and address form to the server.*

POST GET *A user makes a radio button selection.*

URL. Whatever you do, don't pronounce it "Earl".

When you get to the U's in the acronym dictionary there's a traffic jam... URI, URL, URN, where does it end? For now, we're going to focus on the URLs, or **U**niform **R**esource **L**ocators, that you know and love. Every resource on the web has its own unique address, in the URL format.

Protocol: Tells the server which communications protocol (in this case HTTP) will be used.

Port: This part of the URL is optional. A single server supports many ports. A server application is identified by a port. If you don't specify a port in your URL, then port 80 is the default, and as luck would have it, that's the default port for web servers.

Resource: The name of the content being requested. This could be an HTML page, a servlet, an image, PDF, music, video, or anything else the server feels like serving. If this optional part of the URL is left out, most web servers will look for index.html by default.

```
http://www.wickedlysmart.com:80/beeradvice/select/beer1.html
```

Server: The unique name of the physical server you're looking for. This name maps to a unique IP address. IP addresses are numeric and take the form "xxx.yyy.zzz.aaa". You can specify an IP address here instead of a server name, but a server name is a lot easier to remember.

Path: The path to the location, on the server, of the resource being requested. Because most of the early servers on the web ran Unix, Unix syntax is still used to describe the directory hierarchies on the web server.

Not shown:

Optional Query String: Remember, if this was a GET request, the extra info (parameters) would be appended to the end of this URL, starting with a question mark "?", and with each parameter (name/value pair) separated by an ampersand "&".

A TCP port is just a number

A 16-bit number that identifies a specific software program on the server hardware.

Your internet web (HTTP) server software runs on port 80. That's a standard. If you've got a Telnet server, it's running on port 23. FTP? 21. POP3 mail server? 110. SMTP? 25. The Time server sits at 37. Think of ports as unique identifiers. A port represents a logical connection to a particular piece of software running on the server *hardware*. That's it. You can't spin your hardware box around and find a TCP port. For one thing, you have 65536 of them on a server (0 to 65535). For another, they do *not* represent a place to plug in physical devices. They're just numbers representing a server application.

Without port numbers, the server would have no way of knowing which application a client wanted to connect to. And since each application might have its own unique protocol, think of the trouble you'd have without these identifiers. What if your web browser, for example, landed at the POP3 mail server instead of the HTTP server? The mail server won't know how to parse an HTTP request! And even if it did, the POP3 server doesn't know anything about serving back an HTML page.

If you're writing services (server programs) to run on a company network, you should check with the sys-admins to find out which ports are already taken. Your sys-admins might tell you, for example, that you can't use any port number below, say, 3000.

Well-known TCP port numbers for common server applications

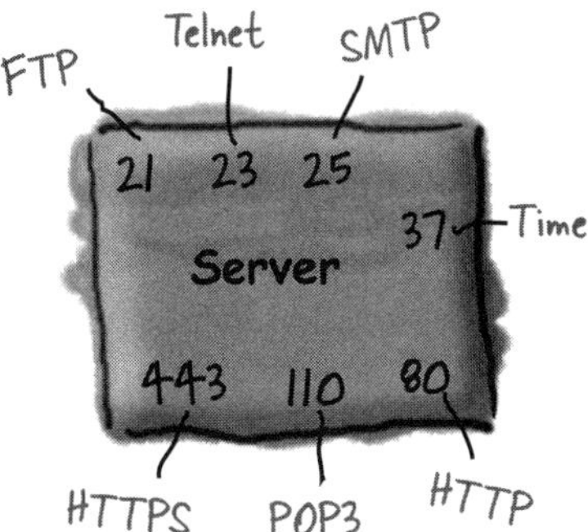

Using one server app per port, a server can have up to 65536 different server apps running (although it's possible to run more than one app on the same port if the apps use different protocols).

The TCP port numbers from 0 to 1023 are reserved for well-known services (including the Big One we care about—port 80). Don't use these ports for your own custom server programs!

Directory structure for a simple Apache web site

We'll talk more about Apache and Tomcat later, but for now let's assume that our simple web site is using Apache (the extremely popular, open source web server you're probably already using). What would the directory structure look like for a web site called www.wickedlysmart.com, hosting two applications, one giving skiing advice, and the other beer-related advice? Imagine that the Apache application is running on port 80.

The .html pages are each marked with a letter (A, B, C, D) for the exercise on the opposite page.

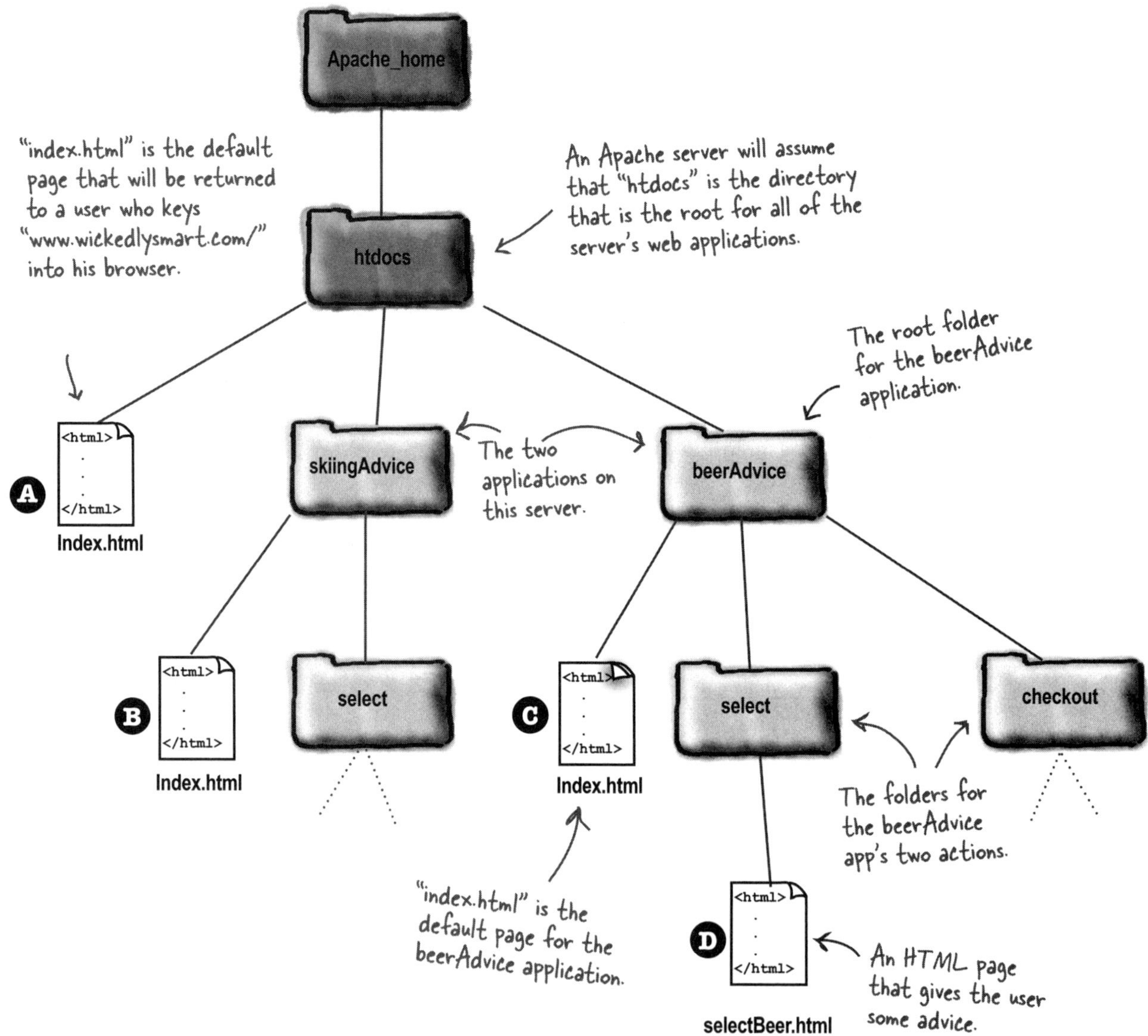

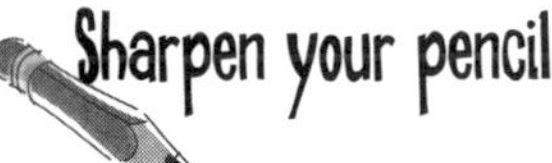

Mapping URLs to content

Look at the directory structure on the opposite page, then write in a URL that would get you to each of the four .html pages marked with the A, B, C, and D. We did the first one (A) for you, because that's the kind of people we are. For the exercise, assume Apache is running on port 80. (The answers are at the bottom of the next page.)

will cause the server to return to you the index.html page at location 

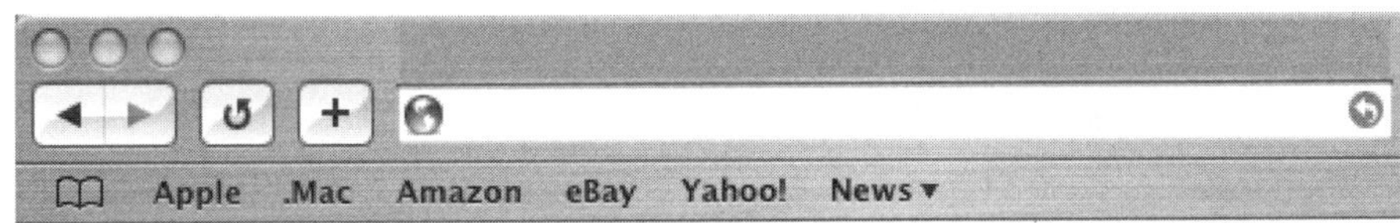

will cause the server to return to you the index.html page at location 

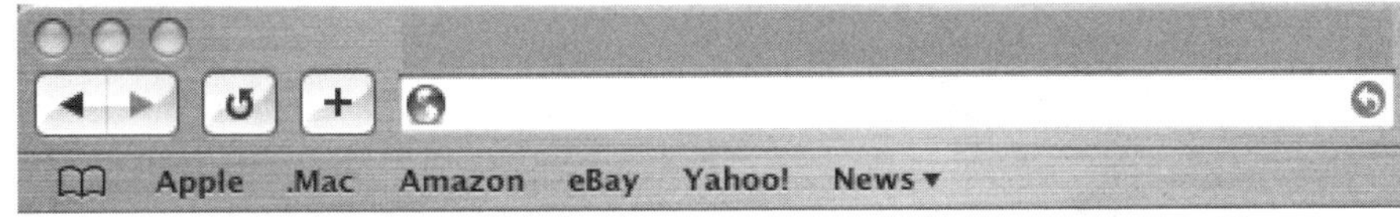

will cause the server to return to you the index.html page at location 

will cause the server to return to you the selectBeer.html page at location 

Web servers love serving static web pages

This is what I do. Ask me for a page, I find it, and I hand it back. With a few headers. But that's it. Do NOT ask me to, like, *do* anything to the page.

A <u>static</u> page just sits there in a directory. The server finds it and hands it back to the client as-is. Every client sees the same thing.

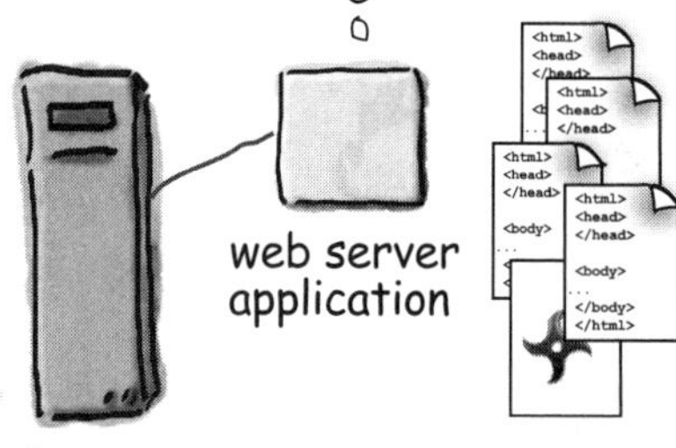

These pages go straight to the client just exactly as they were put on the server.

But what if I want, say, the current time to show up on my page? What if I want a page that has something *dynamic*? Can't I have something like a *variable* inside my HTML?

What if we want to stick something variable inside the HTML page?

```
<html>
<body>
The current time is [insertTimeOnServer].
</body>
</html>
```

Answers from previous page:
B- www.wickedlysmart.com/skiingAdvice/
C- www.wickedlysmart.com/beerAdvice/
D- www.wickedlysmart.com/beerAdvice/select/selectBeer.html

But sometimes you need more than just the web server

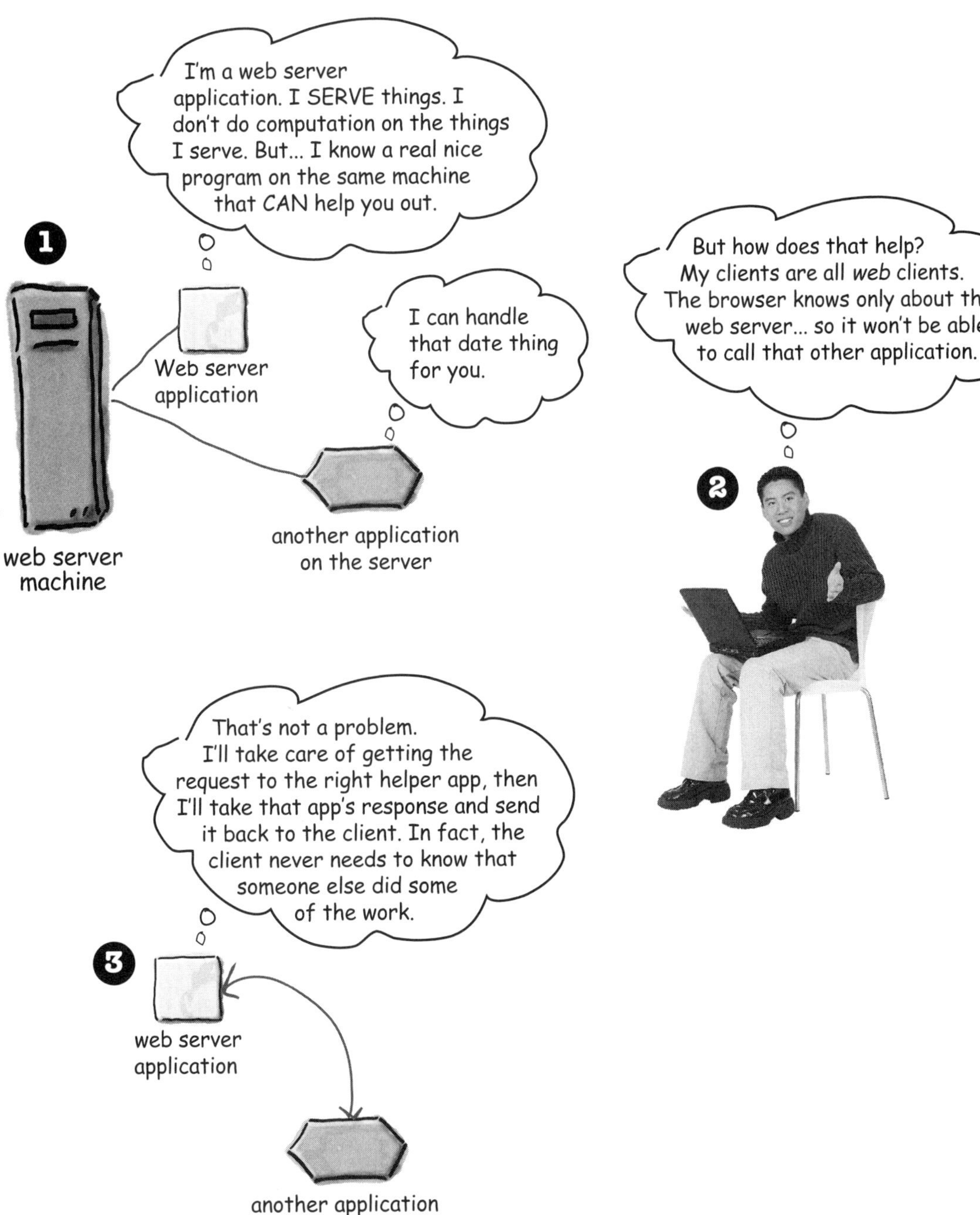

1
I'm a web server application. I SERVE things. I don't do computation on the things I serve. But... I know a real nice program on the same machine that CAN help you out.
Web server application
I can handle that date thing for you.
web server machine
another application on the server
2
But how does that help? My clients are all *web* clients. The browser knows only about the web server... so it won't be able to call that other application.
3
That's not a problem. I'll take care of getting the request to the right helper app, then I'll take that app's response and send it back to the client. In fact, the client never needs to know that someone else did some of the work.
web server application
another application on the server

Two things the web server alone won't do

If you need just-in-time pages (dynamically-created pages that don't exist before the request) and the ability to write/save data on the server (which means writing to a file or database), you can't rely on the web server alone.

1 Dynamic content

The web server application serves only static pages, but a separate "helper" application that the web server can communicate with can build non-static, just-in-time pages. A dynamic page could be anything from a catalog to a weblog or even just a page that randomly chooses pictures to display.

Just-in-time pages don't exist before the request comes in. It's like making an HTML page out of thin air.

The request comes in, the helper app "writes" the HTML, and the web server gets it back to the client.

When instead of this:

```
<html>
<body>
The current time is
always 4:20 PM
on the server
</body>
</html>
```

You want this:

```
<html>
<body>
The current time is
[insertTimeOnServer]
on the server
</body>
</html>
```

2 Saving data on the server

When the user submits data in a form, the web server sees the form data and thinks, "So? Like I care?". To process that form data, either to save it to a file or database or even just to use it to generate the response page, you need another app. When the web server sees a request for a helper app, the web server assumes that parameters are meant for that app. So the web server hands over the parameters, and gives the app a way to generate a response to the client.

The non-Java term for a web server helper app is "CGI" program

Most CGI programs are written as Perl scripts, but many other languages can work including C, Python, and PHP. (CGI stands for Common Gateway Interface, and we don't care why it's called that.)

Using CGI, here's how it might work for a dynamic web page that has the current server date.

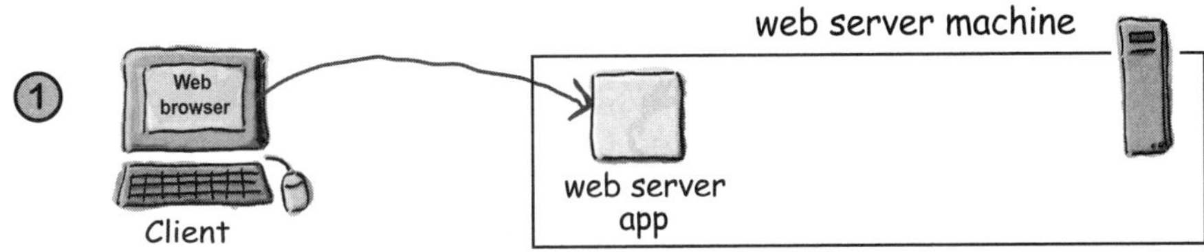

User clicks a link that has a URL to a CGI program instead of a static page.

Web server application "sees" that the request is for a helper program, so the web server launches and runs the program. The web server app sends along any parameters from a GET or POST.

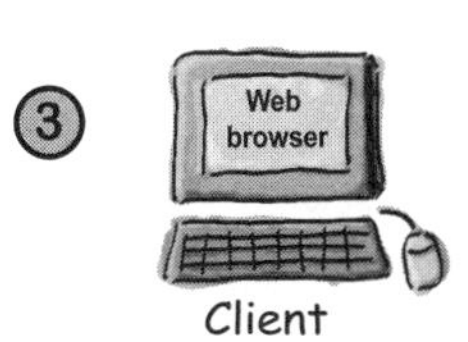

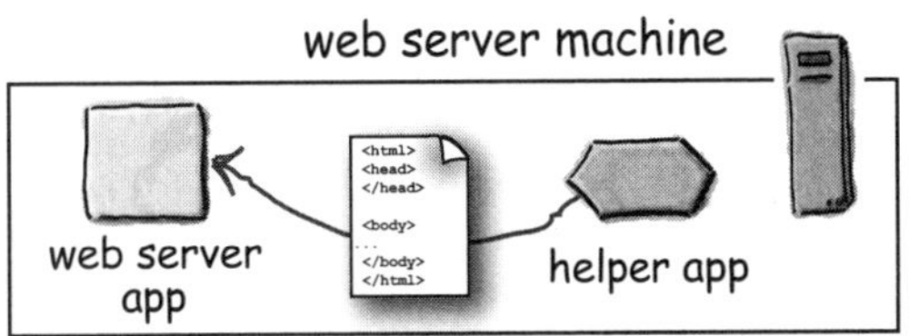

The helper app constructs the brand new page (that has the current date inserted) and sends the HTML back to the server.

As far as the web server is concerned, the HTML from the helper app is a static page.

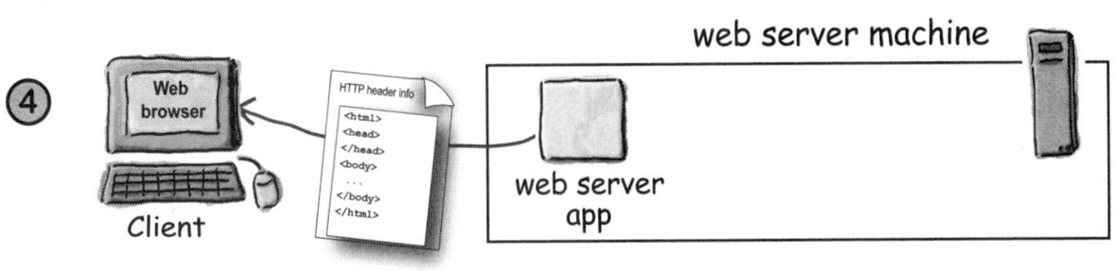

The helper application is shut down, and the client gets back an HTML page that has the current date as part of its now-static content.

Servlets and CGI both play the role of a helper app in the web server

Listen in as our two black-belts discuss the pros and cons of CGI and Servlets.

CGI

Servlets

CGI: CGI is better than Servlets. We write CGI scripts in Perl at our shop, because everybody knows Perl.

Servlets: I doubt *everybody* knows Perl. I like Perl, but we're all Java programmers in our shop so we prefer Java.

CGI: I guess that's fine if you use Java, since you know it. But it's certainly not worth it for us to switch to Java. There's no advantage.

Servlets: With much respect, master, there are many advantages to using Java over Perl for the things you want to do with CGI.

CGI: You challenge me? On what grounds?

Servlets: Performance, for one thing. With Perl, the server has to launch a heavy-weight process for each and every request for that resource!

CGI: This is no different from Java... what do you call the JVM? Is not every instance of the JVM a heavy-weight process?

Servlets: Ah, yes, but you see Servlets stay loaded and client requests for a Servlet resource are handled as separate *threads* of a single running Servlet. There's no overhead of starting the JVM, loading the class, and all that...

CGI: I see you have forgotten much. Web servers now are able to keep a single Perl program running between client requests. So the additional overhead argument is worthless.

Servlets: I have not forgotten, master. But it is not all web servers that can do that. You are talking about a special case which does not apply to all Perl CGI programs. But Servlets will always be more efficient in that way. And let's not forget that a Servlet can be a J2EE client, while a Perl CGI program cannot.

CGI: What are you talking about? Any CORBA-compliant thing can be a J2EE client.

Servlets: I do not mean a client *to* a J2EE program, I mean a client that *is* J2EE. A Servlet running in a J2EE web container can participate in security and transactions right along with enterprise beans and there are—

CGI: Stop—I'm late for my Pilates class. But this is not over. We'll have to finish it later.

to be continued...

Sharpen your pencil

Request Response

Fill in the boxes with a description of what happens during that step in the process. This is a duplicate of page 18, so when you're finished, flip back to that page to compare your answers.

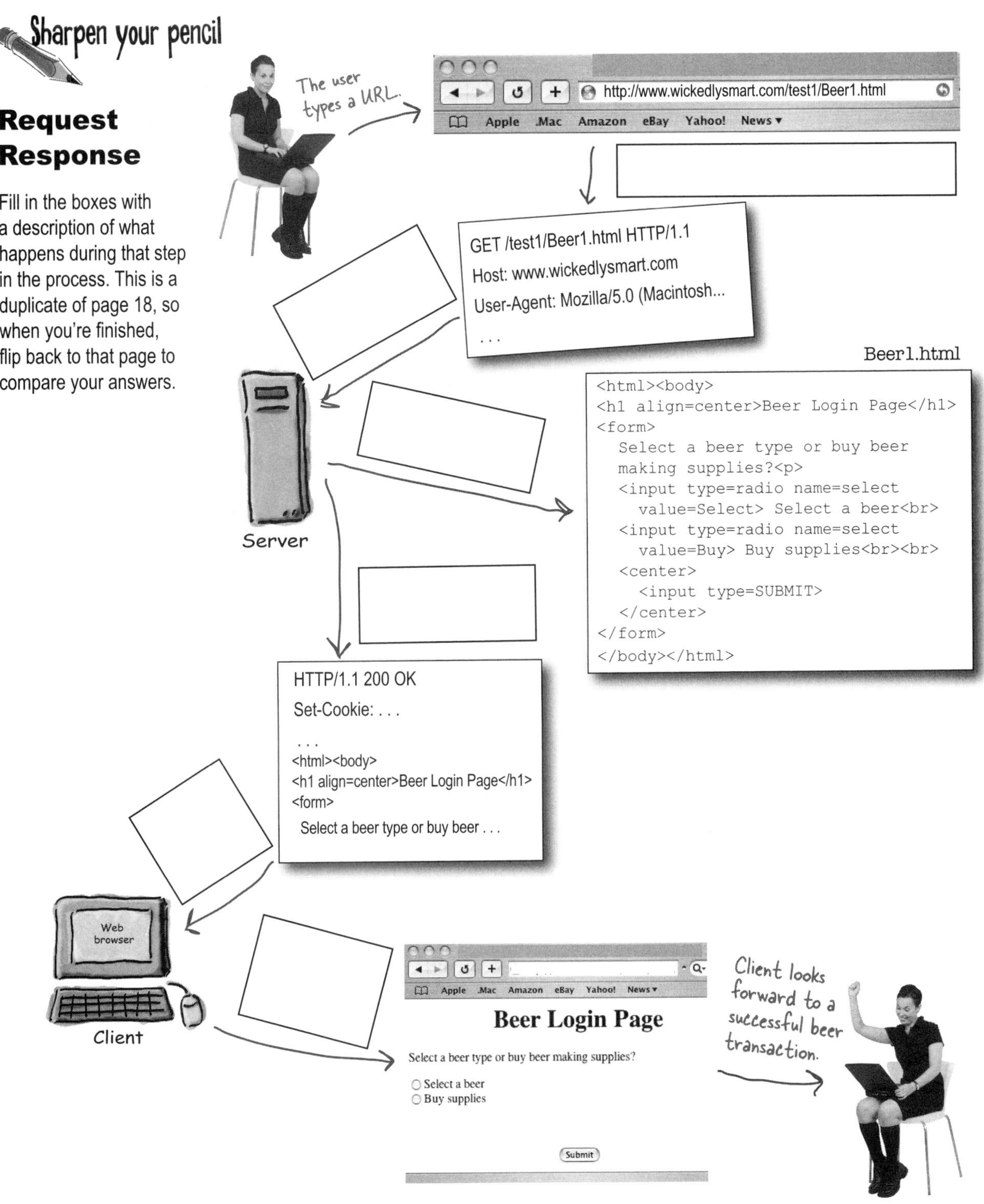

Servlets Demystified (write, deploy, run)

Just so those new to servlets can stop holding their breath, here's a quick guide to writing, deploying, and running a servlet. This might create more questions than it answers—***don't panic***, you don't have to *do* this right now. It's just a quick demonstration for those who can't wait. The next chapter includes a more thorough tutorial.

1. Build this directory tree (somewhere *not* under tomcat).

project1
src
classes
etc
```
Servlet {
  doGet(
  ...
}
```
Ch1Servlet.java
```
<webapp>
.
.
</webapp>
```
web.xml

2. Write a servlet named Ch1Servlet.java and put it in the *src* directory (to keep this example simple, we aren't putting the servlet in a package, but after this, all other servlet examples in the book will be in packages).

```
import javax.servlet.*;
import javax.servlet.http.*;
import java.io.*;

public class Ch1Servlet extends HttpServlet {

  public void doGet(HttpServletRequest request,
                    HttpServletResponse response)
                    throws IOException {

    PrintWriter out = response.getWriter();
    java.util.Date today = new java.util.Date();
    out.println("<html> " +
             "<body>" +
             "<h1 align=center>HF\'s Chapter1 Servlet</h1>"
             + "<br>" + today +  "</body>" + "</html>");
  }
}
```

Standard servlet declarations (there will be about 400 pages describing this stuff).

HTML imbedded in a Java program. Looks lovely, doesn't it?

3. Create a deployment descriptor (DD) named web.xml, put it in the *etc* directory

```
<web-app xmlns="http://java.sun.com/xml/ns/j2ee"
     xmlns:xsi="http://www.w3.org/2001/XMLSchema-instance"
    xsi:schemaLocation="http://java.sun.com/xml/ns/j2ee
    web-app_2_4.xsd"
    version="2.4">
   <servlet>
     <servlet-name>Chapter1 Servlet</servlet-name>
     <servlet-class>Ch1Servlet</servlet-class>
   </servlet>

   <servlet-mapping>
     <servlet-name>Chapter1 Servlet</servlet-name>
     <url-pattern>/Serv1</url-pattern>
   </servlet-mapping>
</web-app>
```

Highlights:

- One DD per web application.
- A DD can declare many servlets.
- A <servlet-name> ties the <servlet> element to the <servlet-mapping> element.
- A <servlet-class> is the Java class.
- A <url-pattern> is the name the client uses for the request.

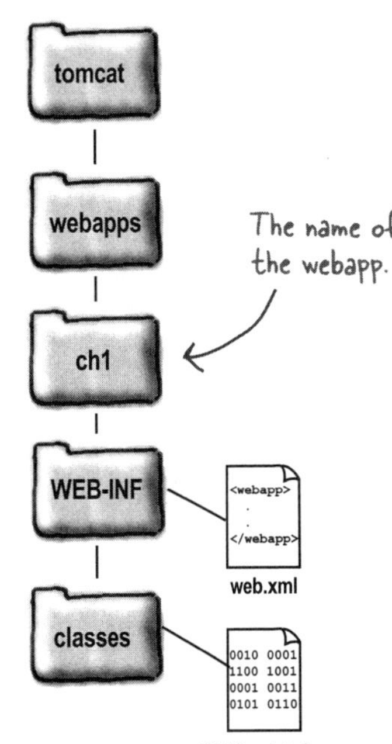

4. Build this directory tree under the existing *tomcat* directory...

5. From the *project1* directory, compile the servlet...

```
%javac -classpath /your path/tomcat/common/lib/
servlet-api.jar -d classes src/Ch1Servlet.java
```

(This is all one command.)

(the Ch1Servlet.class file will end up in *project1/classes*)

6. Copy the Ch1Servlet.class file to *WEB-INF/classes*, and copy the web.xml file to *WEB-INF*.

7. From the *tomcat* directory, start Tomcat...

```
%bin/startup.sh
```

8. Launch your browser and type in:

```
http://localhost:8080/ch1/Serv1
```

The webapp is named 'ch1' and the servlet is named 'Serv1'.

it should display:

9. For now, every time you update either a servlet class or the deployment descriptor, shutdown Tomcat:

```
%bin/shutdown.sh
```

No offense here, but there's something SERIOUSLY wrong with this servlets picture... trying to stuff HTML inside a println()?? That can't be right...

This is how you create a dynamic web page in a servlet. You have to print the whole thing to an output stream (it's really part of the HTTP response stream that you're printing to).

```
out.println("<html> " +
            "<body>" +
            "<h1>Skyler\'s Login Page</h1>" +
            "<br>" + today +
            "</body>" +
            "</html>");
```

Actually, trying to format HTML inside a servlet's out.println() pretty much sucks.

This is one of the worst parts (no, *the* worst part) of servlets. Stuffing properly formatted HTML tags into the println(), just so that you can insert variables and method calls, is just brutal. Don't even *think* about doing anything the least bit sophisticated.

there are no Dumb Questions

Q: It can't be *that* bad... why can't I just copy a whole page of HTML from my web page editor, like Dreamweaver, and paste it into the println(). It's not like I have to be able to *read* the code in there.

A: Obviously, you haven't tried this yet. It *sounds* good. Yes. I'll just make my page in a decent web page editor (or even a simple text file would be easier than in my Java code) and then a quick copy and paste into the println() and voila!

Except you get about 1,378 compiler errors.

Remember, you can't have a carriage return (a real one) inside a String literal. And while we're talking about Strings... what about all your HTML that has double-quote marks in it?

Oh if only there were a way to put Java inside an HTML page instead of putting HTML inside a Java class.

She doesn't know about JSP

```
<html>
<body>
<h1>Skyler's Login Page</h1>
<br>
<%= new java.util.Date() %>
</body>
</html>
```

Whoa! This looks like a little Java, right in the middle of HTML !?

skylerlogin.jsp

A JSP page looks just like an HTML page, except you can put Java and Java-related things inside the page. So it really is like inserting a variable into your HTML.

JSP is what happened when somebody introduced Java to HTML

Putting Java into HTML is a solution for two issues:

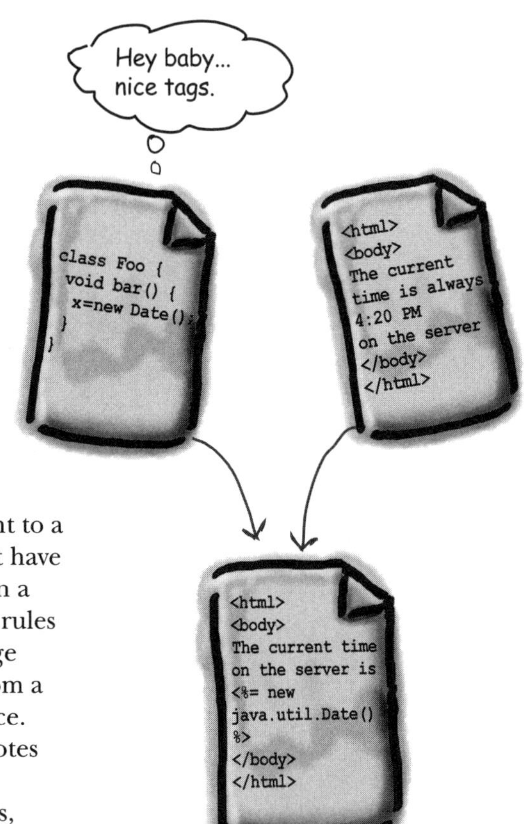

1 Not all HTML page designers know Java

App developers know Java. Web page designers know HTML. With JSP, Java developers can do Java and HTML developers can do web pages.

2 Formatting HTML into a String literal is REALLY ugly

Putting even marginally complex HTML into the argument to a println() is a compiler error waiting to happen. You might have to do a ton of work to get the HTML formatted properly in a way that still works in the client's browser, yet satisfies Java rules for what's allowed in a String literal. You can't have carriage returns, for example, yet most of the HTML you'll pull from a web page editor will have real carriage returns in the source. Quotes can be a problem too—a lot of HTML tags use quotes around attribute values, for example. And you know what happens when the compiler sees a double quote... it thinks, "This must be the end of the String literal." Sure, you can go back and replace each of your double quotes with escape codes... but it all gets insanely error prone.

Q: Wait... there's still something wrong here! Benefit number one says "Not all page designers know Java..." but the HTML page designer still has to write Java inside the JSP page!! JSP lets the Java programmer off the hook for writing HTML, but it doesn't really help the HTML designer. It might be *easier* to write HTML in a JSP rather than in a println(), but the HTML developer still has to know Java.

A: Looks that way, doesn't it? But with the new JSP spec, and by following best practices, the page designer should be putting very little (or *no*) real Java into a JSP. They do have to learn *something*... but it's more like putting in labels that *call* real Java methods rather than embedding the actual Java code into the page itself. They have to learn JSP syntax, but not the Java language.

BULLET POINTS

- HTTP stands for HyperText Transfer Protocol, and is the network protocol used on the Web. It runs on top of TCP/IP.
- HTTP uses a request/response model—the client makes an HTTP request, and the web server gives back and HTTP response that the browser then figures out how to handle (depending on the content type of the response).
- If the response from the server is an HTML page, the HTML is added to the HTTP response.
- An HTTP request includes the request URL (the resource the client is trying to access), the HTTP method (GET, POST, etc.), and (optionally) form parameter data (also called the "query string").
- An HTTP response includes a status code, the content-type (also known as MIME type), and the actual content of the response (HTML, image, etc.)
- A GET request appends form data to the end of the URL.
- A POST request includes form data in the body of the request.
- A MIME type tells the browser what kind of data the browser is about to receive so that the browser will know what to do with it (render the HTML, display the graphic, play the music, etc.)
- URL stands for Uniform Resource Locator. Every resource on the web has its own unique address in this format. It starts with a protocol, followed by the server name, an optional port number, and usually a specific path and resource name. It can also include an optional query string, if the URL is for a GET request.
- Web servers are good at serving static HTML pages, but if you need dynamically-generated data in the page (the current time, for example), you need some kind of helper app that can work with the server. The non-Java term for these helper apps (most often written in Perl) is CGI (which stands for Common Gateway Interface).
- Putting HTML inside a println() statement is ugly and error-prone, but JSPs solve that problem by letting you put Java into an HTML page rather than putting HTML into Java code.

2 high-level overview

Web App Architecture

Servlets need help. When a request comes in, somebody has to instantiate the servlet or at least make a new thread to handle the request. Somebody has to call the servlet's doPost() or doGet() method. And, oh yes, those methods have crucial arguments—the HTTP request and HTTP response objects. Somebody has to get the request and the response to the servlet. Somebody has to manage the life, death, and resources of the servlet. That somebody is the web Container. In this chapter, we'll look at how your web application runs in the Container, and we'll take a first look at the structure of a web app using the Model View Controller (MVC) design pattern.

High-level Web App Achitecture

1.1 For each of the HTTP Methods (such as GET, POST, HEAD, and so on), describe the purpose of the method and the technical characteristics of the HTTP Method protocol, list triggers that might cause a client (usually a Web browser) to use the Method, and identify the HttpServlet method that corresponds to the HTTP Method.

1.4 Describe the purpose and event sequence of the servlet life cycle: (1) servlet class loading, (2) servlet instantiation, (3) call the init method, (4) call the service method, and (5) call the destroy method.

2.1 Construct the file and directory structure of a Web Application that may contain (a) static content, (b) JSP pages, (c) servlet classes, (d) the deployment descriptor, (e) tag libraries, (f) JAR files, and (g) Java class files; and describe how to protect resource files from HTTP access.

2.2 Describe the purpose and semantics for each of the following deployment descriptor elements: servlet instance, servlet name, servlet class, servlet initialization parameters, and URL to named servlet mapping.

Coverage Notes:

All of the objectives in this section are covered completely in other chapters, so think of this chapter as a first-look foundation for what comes later. In other words, don't worry about finishing this chapter knowing (and remembering) anything specific from these objectives.
You won't have any mock exam questions on these topics until you get to the more specific chapter where those topics are covered.
Enjoy this nice, simple, background material while you can!
BUT... you do need to know this stuff before moving on. If you already have some servlet experience, you can probably just skim the pages, look at the pictures, do the exercises, and move on to chapter 3.

What *is* a Container?

Servlets don't have a main() method. They're under the control of another Java application called a *Container.*

Tomcat is an example of a Container. When your web server application (like Apache) gets a request for a *servlet* (as opposed to, say, a plain old static HTML page), the server hands the request not to the servlet itself, but to the Container in which the servlet is *deployed*. It's the Container that gives the servlet the HTTP request and response, and it's the Container that calls the servlet's methods (like doPost() or doGet()).

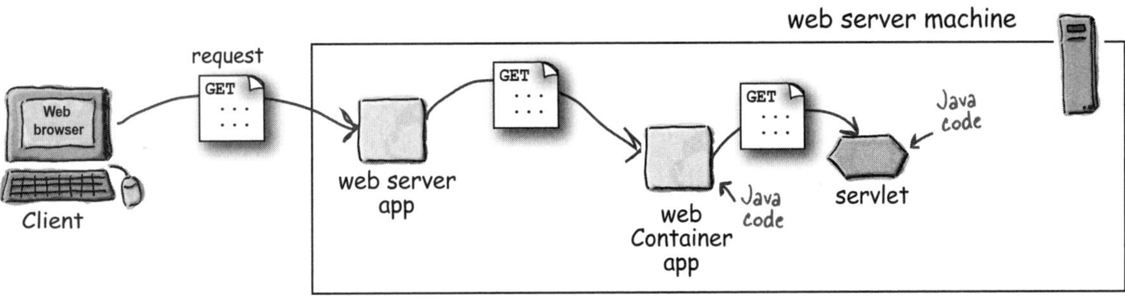

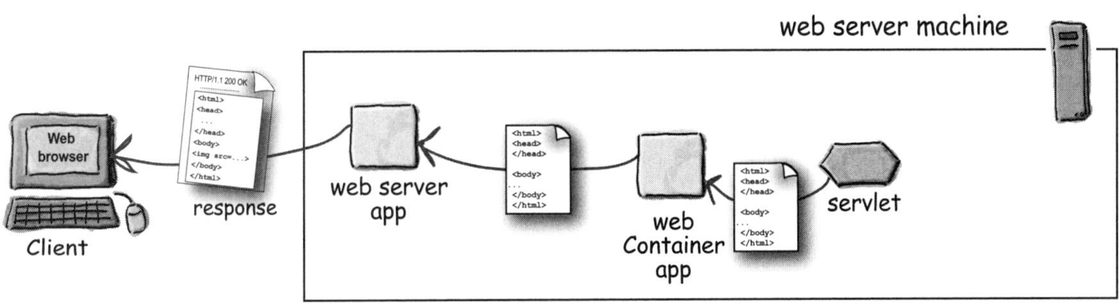

What if you had Java, but no servlets or Containers?

What if you had to write a Java program to handle dynamic requests that come to a web server application (like Apache) but without a Container like Tomcat? In other words, imagine there's no such thing as servlets, and all you have are the core J2SE libraries? (Of course, you can assume you have the capability of configuring the web server application so that it can invoke your Java application.) It's OK if you don't yet know much about what the Container does. Just imagine you need server-side support for a web application, and all you have is plain old Java.

A true warrior would not use a Container. He would write everything using only J2SE and his bare hands.

List some of the functions you would have to implement in a J2SE application if no Container existed:

* Create a socket connection with the server, and create a listener for the socket.

Possible answers: create a thread manager, implement security, how about filtering for things like logging, JSP support - yikes, memory management...

What does the Container give you?

We know that it's the Container that manages and runs the servlet, but *why*? Is it worth the extra overhead?

Communications support The container provides an easy way for your servlets to talk to your web server. You don't have to build a ServerSocket, listen on a port, create streams, etc. The Container knows the protocol between the web server and itself, so that your servlet doesn't have to worry about an API between, say, the Apache web server and your own web application code. All you have to worry about is your own business logic that goes in your Servlet (like accepting an order from your online store).

Lifecycle Management The Container controls the life and death of your servlets. It takes care of loading the classes, instantiating and initializing the servlets, invoking the servlet methods, and making servlet instances eligible for garbage collection. With the Container in control, *you* don't have to worry as much about resource management.

Multithreading Support The Container automatically creates a new Java thread for every servlet request it receives. When the servlet's done running the HTTP service method for that client's request, the thread completes (i.e. dies). This doesn't mean you're off the hook for thread safety—you can still run into synchronization issues. But having the server create and manage threads for multiple requests still saves you a lot of work.

Declarative Security With a Container, you get to use an XML deployment descriptor to configure (and modify) security without having to hard-code it into your servlet (or any other) class code. Think about that! You can manage and change your security without touching and recompiling your Java source files.

JSP Support You already know how cool JSPs are. Well, who do you think takes care of translating that JSP code into real Java? Of course. The *Container.*

Thanks to the Container, YOU get to concentrate more on your own business logic instead of worrying about writing code for threading, security, and networking.

You get to focus all your energy on making a fabulous online bubble wrap store, and leave the underlying services like security and JSP processing up to the container.

Now all I have to worry about is how to sell my scratch-n-sniff bubble wrap, instead of having to write all that code for the things the Container's gonna do for me...

How the Container handles a request

We'll save some of the juicier bits for later in the book, but here's a quick look:

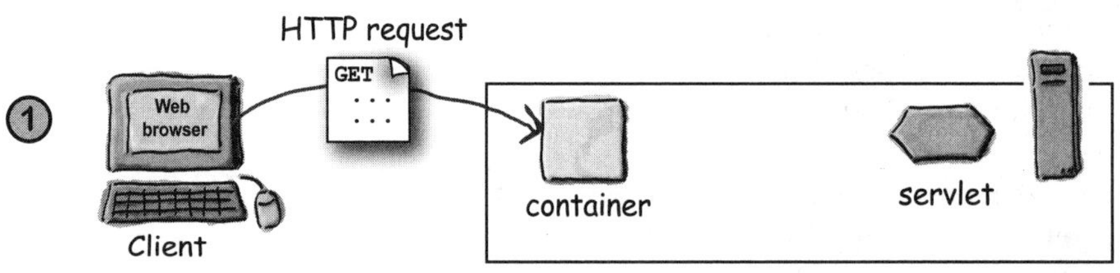

1. User clicks a link that has a URL to a servlet instead of a static page.

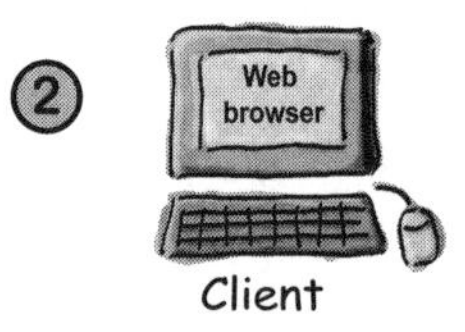

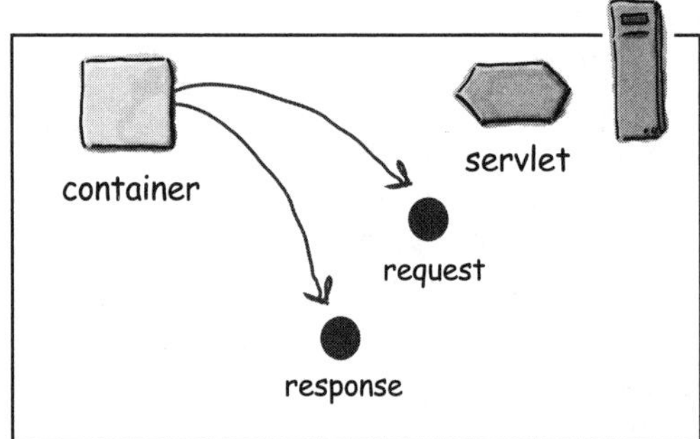

2. The container "sees" that the request is for a servlet, so the container creates two objects:

   1) HttpServletResponse

   2) HttpServletRequest

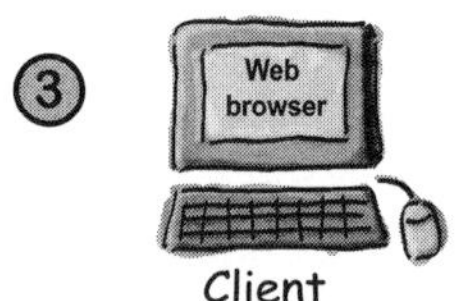

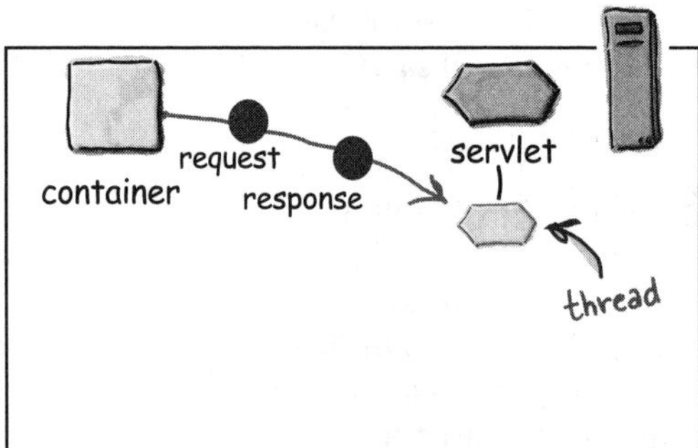

3. The container finds the correct servlet based on the URL in the request, creates or allocates a thread for that request, and passes the request and response objects to the servlet thread.

4

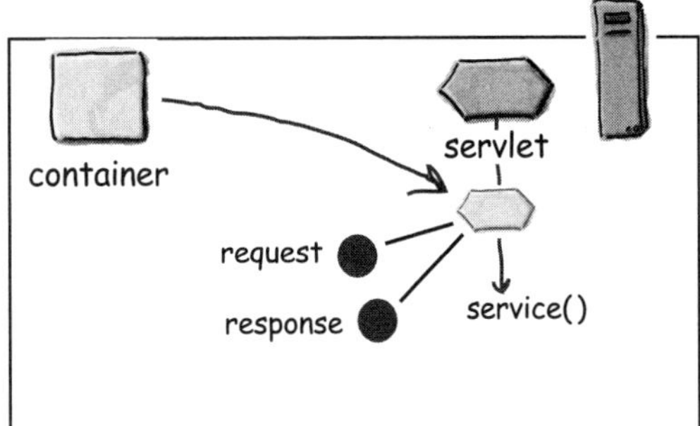

The container calls the servlet's service() method. Depending on the type of request, the service() method calls either the doGet() or doPost() method.

For this example, we'll assume the request was an HTTP GET.

5

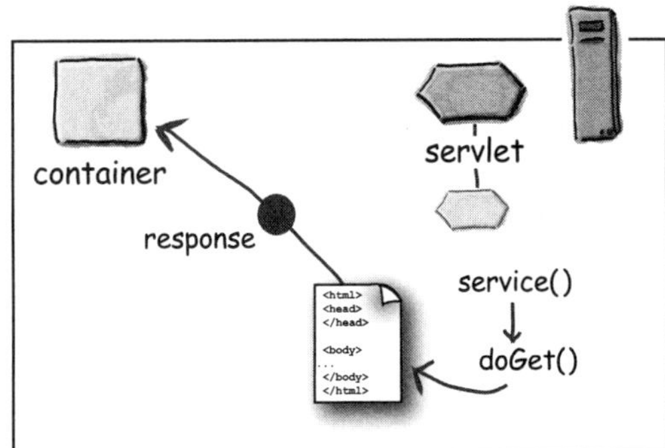

The doGet() method generates the dynamic page and stuffs the page into the response object. Remember, the container still has a reference to the response object!

6

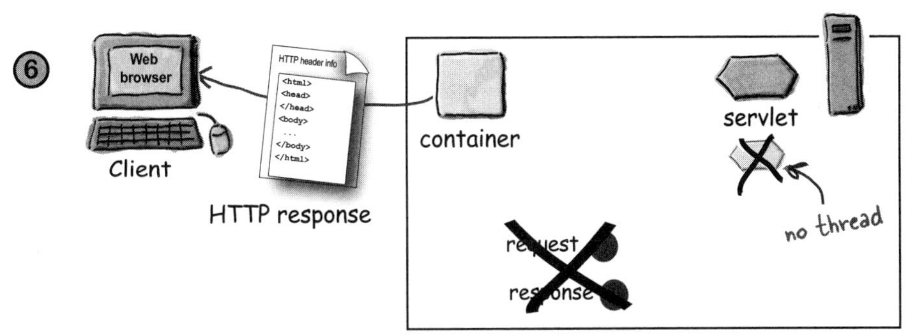

The thread completes, the container converts the response object into an HTTP response, sends it back to the client, then deletes the request and response objects.

How it looks in code (what makes a servlet a servlet)

In the real world, 99.9% of all servlets override either the doGet() or doPost() method.

Notice... no main() method. The servlet's lifecycle methods (like doGet()) are called by the Container.

99.9999% of all servlets are HttpServlets.

```
import javax.servlet.*;
import javax.servlet.http.*;
import java.io.*;

public class Ch2Servlet extends HttpServlet {

  public void doGet(HttpServletRequest request,
                    HttpServletResponse response)
                    throws IOException {

    PrintWriter out = response.getWriter();
    java.util.Date today = new java.util.Date();
    out.println("<html> " +
            "<body>" +
            "<h1 style="text-align:center>" +
            "HF\'s Chapter2 Servlet</h1>" +
            "<br>" + today +
            "</body>" +
            "</html>");
  }
}
```

This is where your servlet gets references to the request and response objects which the container creates.

You can get a PrintWriter from the response object your servlet gets from the Container. Use the PrintWriter to write HTML text to the response object. (You can get other output options, besides PrintWriter, for writing, say, a picture instead of HTML text.)

there are no Dumb Questions

Q: I remember seeing *doGet()* and *doPost()*, but on the previous page, you show a *service()* method? Where did the *service()* method come from?

A: Your servlet inherited it from HttpServlet, which inherited it from GenericServlet which inherited it from... ahhh, we'll do class hierarchies to death in the Being a Servlet chapter, so you just need a little more patience.

Q: You wimped out on explaining how the container *found* the correct servlet... like, how does a URL relate to a servlet? Does the user have to type in the exact path and class file name of the servlet?

A: No. Good question, though. But it points to a Really Big Topic (servlet mapping and URL patterns), so we'll take only a quick look on the next few pages, but go into much more detail later in the book (in the Deployment chapter).

You're wondering how the Container found the Servlet...

Somehow, the URL that comes in as part of the request from the client is *mapped* to a specific servlet on the server. This mapping of URLs to servlets might be handled in a number of different ways, and it's one of the most fundamental issues you'll face as a web app developer. The user request must map to a particular servlet, and it's up to you to understand and (usually) *configure* that mapping. What do you think?

FLEX YOUR MIND

How should the Container map servlets to URLs?

The user does *something* in the browser (clicks a link, hits the "Submit" button, enters a URL, etc.) and that *something* is supposed to send the request to a *specific* servlet (or other web app resource like a JSP) you built. How might that happen?

For each of the following approaches, think about the pros and cons.

1. *Hardcode the mapping into your HTML page. In other words, the client is using the exact path and file (class) name of the servlet.*

   PROS:

   CONS:

2. *Use your Container vendor's tool to do the mapping:*

   PROS:

   CONS:

3. *Use some sort of properties table to store the mappings:*

   PROS:

   CONS:

A servlet can have THREE names

A servlet has a *file path name*, obviously, like classes/registration/SignUpServlet.class (a path to an actual class file). The original developer of the servlet class chose the *class* name (and the package name that defines part of the directory structure), and the location on the server defines the full path name. But anyone who deploys the servlet can also give it a special *deployment name*. A deployment name is simply a *secret internal* name that doesn't have to be the same as the class or file name. It *can* be the same as the servlet *class* name (registration.SignUpServlet) or the relative path to the class *file* (classes/registration/SignUpServlet.class), but it can also be something completely different (like *EnrollServlet*).

Finally, the servlet has a *public URL name*—the name the *client* knows about. In other words, the name coded into the HTML so that when the user clicks a link that's supposed to go to that servlet, this public URL name is sent to the server in the HTTP request.

1

Client-known *URL* name

The client sees a URL for the servlet (in the HTML), but doesn't really know how that servlet name maps to real directories and files back on the server. The public URL name is a fake name, made up for clients.

2

Deployer-known *secret internal* name

The deployer can create a name that's known only to the deployer and others in the real operational environment. This name, too, is a fake name, made up just for the deployment of the servlet. It doesn't have to match the public URL used by the client, OR the real file and path name of the servlet class.

3

Actual *file* name

The developer's servlet *class* has a fully-qualified name that includes both the class name and the package name. The servlet class *file* has a real path and file name, depending on where the package directory structure lives on the server.

Well isn't that special how everyone gets to express their creativity and come up with their very own name for the same darn thing. But what's the point!? Really? Why don't we all just use the one, real, non-confusing file name?

Mapping servlet names improves your app's flexibility and security.

Think about it.

So you've hard-coded the real path and file name into all the JSPs and other HTML pages that use that servlet. Great. Now what happens when you need to reorganize your application, and possibly move things into different directory structures? ***Do** you really want to force everyone who uses that servlet to know (and forever follow) that same directory structure?*

By mapping the name instead of coding in the real file and path name, you have the flexibility to move things around without having the maintenance nightmare of tracking down and changing client code that refers to the old location of the servlet files.

And what about security? Do you really want the client to know exactly how things are structured on your server? Do you want them to, say, attempt to navigate directly to the servlet without going through the right pages or forms? Because if the end-user can see the *real* path, she can type it into her browser and try to access it directly.

Using the Deployment Descriptor to map URLs to servlets

When you deploy your servlet into your web Container, you'll create a fairly simple XML document called the Deployment Descriptor (DD) to tell the Container how to run your servlets and JSPs. Although you'll use the DD for more than just mapping names, you'll use two XML elements to map URLs to servlets—one to map the client-known *public URL* name to your own *internal* name, and the other to map your own *internal* name to a fully-qualified *class name.*

The two DD elements for URL mapping:

1. **<servlet>**
   maps internal name to fully-qualified class name

2. **<servlet-mapping>**
   maps internal name to public URL name

This web app has two servlets.

There is a LOT more that goes into this opening <web-app> tag, but we don't want to show it right now (there's an example at the end of this chapter).

The <servlet-name> element is used to tie a <servlet> element to a specific <servlet-mapping> element. The end-user NEVER sees this name; it's used only in other parts of the DD.

```
<web-app ...>

  <servlet>
    <servlet-name>Internal name 1</servlet-name>
    <servlet-class>foo.Servlet1</servlet-class>
  </servlet>

  <servlet>
    <servlet-name>Internal name 2</servlet-name>
    <servlet-class>foo.Servlet2</servlet-class>
  </servlet>
  ........................................................................

  <servlet-mapping>
    <servlet-name>Internal name 1</servlet-name>
    <url-pattern>/Public1</url-pattern>
  </servlet-mapping>

 <servlet-mapping>
    <servlet-name>Internal name 2</servlet-name>
    <url-pattern>/Public2</url-pattern>
 </servlet-mapping>

</web-app>
```

The <servlet> element tells the Container which class files belong to a particular web application.

You put in the fully-qualified name of the class (but you don't add the ".class" extension).

Think of the <servlet-mapping> element as what the Container uses at runtime when a request comes in, to ask, "which servlet should I invoke for this requested URL?".

This is what the client sees (and uses) to get to the servlet... but it's a made-up name that is NOT the name of the actual servlet class.

It's possible to use wildcards in the <url-pattern> element... more on that and paths later.

But wait! There's more you can do with the DD

Besides mapping URLs to actual servlets, you can use the DD to customize other aspects of your web application including security roles, error pages, tag libraries, initial configuration information, and if it's a full J2EE server, you can even declare that you'll be accessing specific enterprise javabeans.

Don't worry about the details yet. The crucial point for now is that the DD gives you a way to declaratively modify your application without changing source code!

Think about this... it means that even those who aren't Java programmers can customize your Java web application without having to drag you back from your tropical vacation.

The deployment descriptor (DD), provides a "declarative" mechanism for customizing your web applications without touching source code!

DD Benefits

- Minimizes touching source code that has already been tested.
- Lets you fine tune your app's capabilities, even if you don't *have* the source code.
- Lets you adapt your application to different resources (like databases), without having to recompile and test any code.
- Makes it easier for you to maintain dynamic security info like access control lists and security roles.
- Lets non-programmers modify and deploy your web applications while *you* can focus on the more interesting things. Like how appropriate your wardrobe isn't for a trip to Hawaii.

there are no Dumb Questions

Q: I'm confused. Looking at the DD, you still don't have anything that indicates the actual path name of the servlet! It just says the class name. This still doesn't answer the question of how the Container uses that class name to find a specific servlet class file. Is there yet ANOTHER mapping somewhere that says that such and such a class name maps to such and such a file in such and such a location?

A: You noticed. You're right that we put only the *class* name (fully-qualified to include the package name) into the <servlet-class> element. That's because the Container has a specific place it will look for all servlets for which you've specified a mapping in the DD.

In fact, the Container uses a sophisticated set of rules for finding a match between the URL that comes in from the client request and an actual Java class sitting somewhere on the server. But we'll get into that in a later chapter (on Deployment). Right now, the key point to remember is that you can do this mapping.

Story: Bob Builds a Matchmaking Site

Dating is tough today. Who has the time when there's always another disk to defrag? Bob, who wants a piece of the dot com action (what's left of it, anyway), believes that creating a geek-specific dating site is his ticket out of the Dilbertian job he has now.

The problem is, Bob's been a software manager for so long that he's, um, a little out of touch with contemporary software engineering practices. But he knows some buzzwords and some Java and he's read a little about servlets, so he makes a quick design and starts to code...

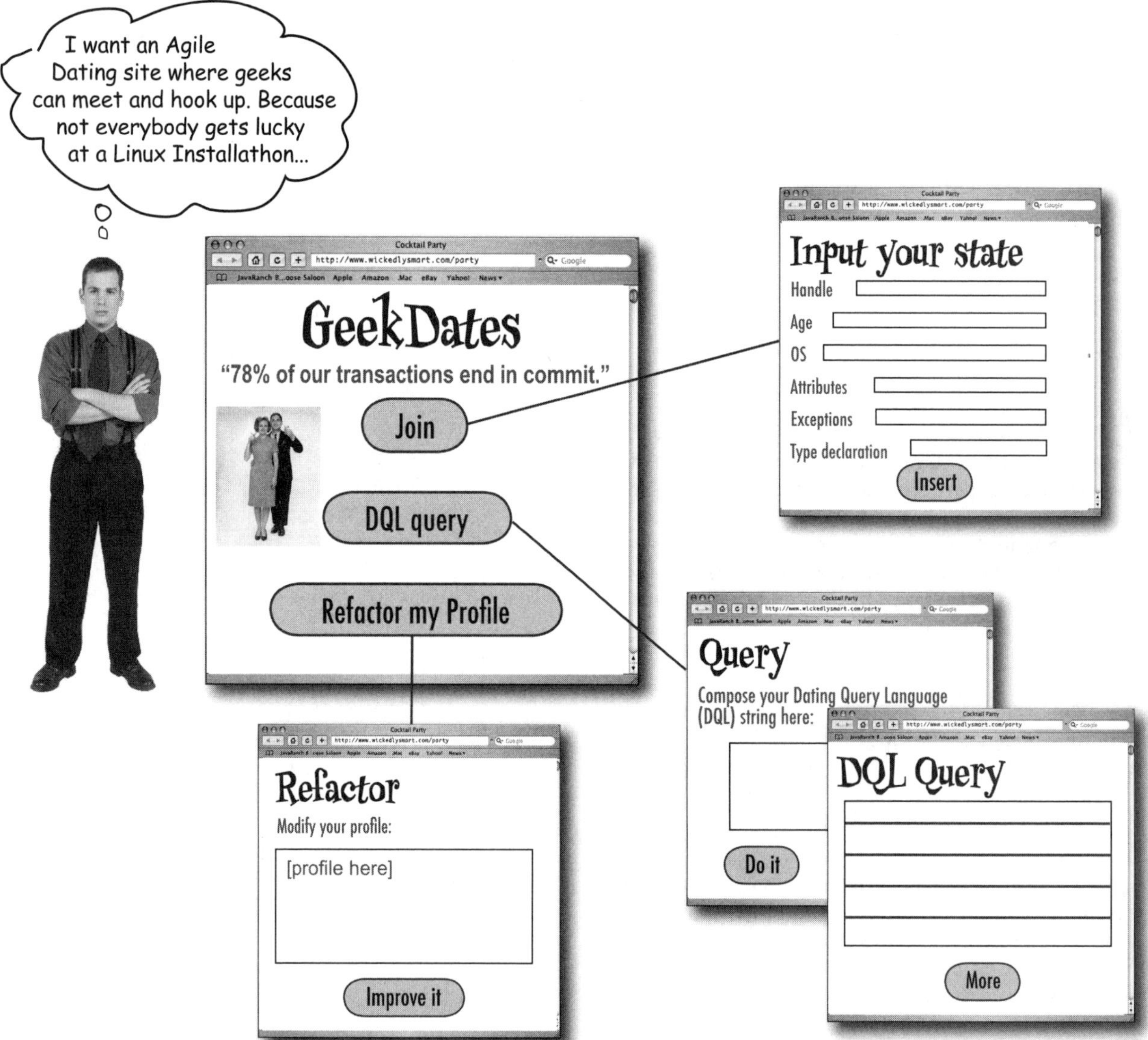

He starts to build a bunch of servlets... one for each page

He considered having just a single servlet, with a bunch of *if* tests, but decided that separate servlets would be more OO—each servlet should have one responsibility like the query page, the sign-up page, the search results page, etc.

Each servlet will have all the business logic it needs to modify or read the database, and prints the HTML to the response stream back to the client.

This is a great OO design. All my servlets have exactly one job.

```
// import statements

public class DatingServlet extends HttpServlet {

  public void doGet(HttpServletRequest request,
                    HttpServletResponse response)
                    throws IOException {

    // business logic goes here, depending
    // on what this servlet is supposed to do
    // (write to the database, do the query, etc.)

    PrintWriter out = response.getWriter();

    // compose the dynamic HTML page
    out.println( "something really ugly goes here");
  }
}
```

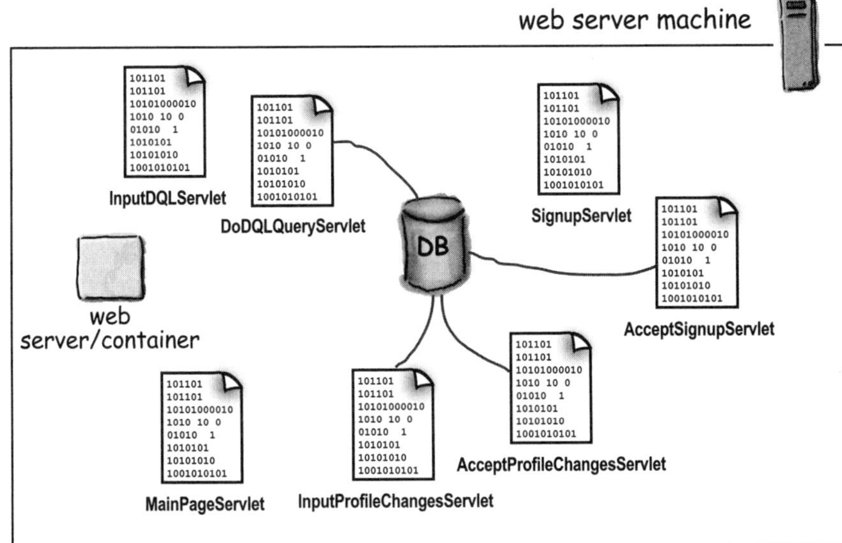

The servlet does whatever it needs to do to process the request (like insert or search the database) and returns the HTML page in the HTTP response.

All of the business logic AND the client HTML page response is inside the servlet code.

But then it gets ugly, so he adds JSPs

Those pesky println() statements for the output response get really ugly, really quickly. So he reads up on JSPs and decides to have each servlet do whatever business logic it needs to do (query the database, insert or update a new record, etc.) *then forward the request to a JSP* to do the HTML for the response. This also separates the *business logic* from the *presentation*... and since he's been reading up on design, he knows that *separation of concerns* is a Good Thing.

This JSP design is much cooler. Now the servlet code is cleaner... each servlet runs its own business logic and then invokes a specific JSP to handle the HTML for the response, separating business logic from presentation.

```
// import statements

public class DatingServlet extends HttpServlet {

  public void doGet(HttpServletRequest request,
                    HttpServletResponse response)
                    throws IOException {

     // business logic goes here, depending
     // on what this servlet is supposed to do
     // (write to the database, do the query, etc.)

     // forward the request to a specific JSP page
     // instead of trying to print the HTML
     // to the output stream
   }
}
```

InputSignupServlet — InputSignupJSP
AcceptSignupServlet — AcceptSignupJSP
InputProfileChangesServlet — InputProfileChangesJSP
AcceptProfileChangesServlet — AcceptProfileChangesJSP
MainPageServlet — MainPageJSP
InputDQLServlet — InputDQLJSP
DoDQlQueryServlet — DoDQLQueryJSP

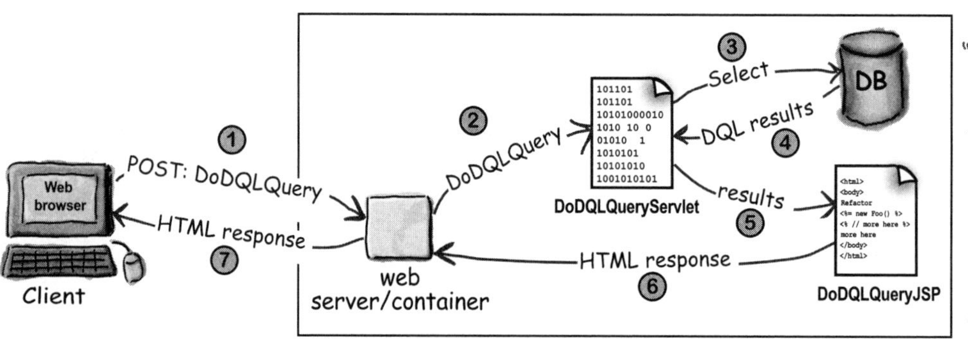

Client fills out the DQL query form and clicks the "Do it" button. This sends an HTTP POST request for the DoDQLQuery. The web server invokes the servlet, the servlet runs the query on the database, then the request is forwarded to the appropriate JSP. The JSP builds the response HTML and sends it back.

But then his friend says, "You ARE using MVC, right?"

Kim wants to know if the dating service can be accessed from a Swing GUI application. Bob says, "No, I hadn't thought of that." So Kim says, "Well, it's not a problem because I'm sure you used MVC, so we can just whip up a Swing GUI client that can access the business logic classes."

And Bob says, "Gulp."

And Kim says, "Don't tell me... you did ***not*** use MVC?"

And Bob says, "Well, I did separate out the presentation from the business logic..."

Kim says, "That's a start... but let me guess... your business logic is all inside *servlets*!?"

Bob realizes, suddenly, why he went into management.

But he's determined to do this right, so he asks Kim to give him a quick crash overview of MVC.

What if you want to make a Swing GUI app for the dating service, and it uses the same business logic?

With MVC the business logic is not only *separate* from the presentation... it doesn't even know that there *IS* a presentation.

The essence of MVC is that you separate the business logic from the presentation, but put something *between* them so that the business logic can stand on its own as a reusable Java class, and doesn't have to know anything about the view.

Bob was partly there, by separating out the business logic from the presentation, but his business logic still has an intimate *connection* to the view. In other words, *he mixed the business logic into a servlet,* and that means he can't reuse his business logic for some other kind of view (like a Swing GUI or even a wireless app). His business logic is stuck in a servlet when it should be in a standalone Java class he can reuse!

The Model-View-Controller (MVC) Design Pattern fixes this

If Bob had understood the MVC design pattern, he would have known that the business logic shouldn't be stuffed inside a servlet. He would have realized that with the business logic embedded in a servlet, he'd be screwed if he one day needed a different way to access the dating service. Like from a Swing GUI app. We'll talk a lot more about MVC (and other patterns) later in the book, but you need a quick understanding now because the tutorial app we build at the end of this chapter uses MVC.

If you're already familiar with it, then you know that MVC is not specific to servlets and JSPs—the clean separation of business logic and presentation is just as valid in any other kind of application. But with web apps, it's *really* important, because you should never assume that your business logic will be accessed *only* from the web! We're sure you've worked in this business long enough to know the only guarantee in software development: ***the spec always changes.***

Model*View*Controller (MVC) takes the business logic out of the servlet, and puts it in a "Model"– a reusable plain old Java class. The Model is a combination of the business data (like the state of a Shopping Cart) and the methods (rules) that operate on that data.

MVC in the Servlet & JSP world

Servlet

Controller

CONTROLLER

Takes user input from the request and figures out what it means to the model.

Tells the model to update itself, and makes the new model state available for the view (the JSP).

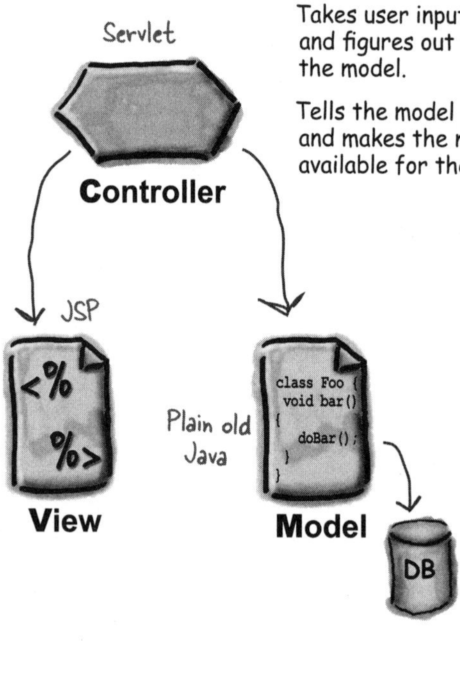

JSP

<%

%>

View

VIEW

Responsible for the presentation. It gets the state of the model from the Controller (although not directly; the Controller puts the model data in a place where the View can find it). It's also the part that gets the user input that goes back to the Controller.

Plain old Java

```
class Foo {
 void bar()
 {
   doBar();
 }
}
```

Model

DB

MODEL

Holds the real business logic and the state. In other words, it knows the rules for getting and updating the state.

A Shopping Cart's contents (and the rules for what to do with it) would be part of the Model in MVC.

It's the only part of the system that talks to the database (although it probably uses *another* object for the actual DB communication, but we'll save *that* pattern for later...)

Applying the MVC pattern to the matchmaking web app

So, Bob knows what he has to do. Separate out the business logic from the servlets, and create a regular Java class for each one... to represent the Model.

Then the original servlet will be the Controller, the new business logic class will be the Model, and the JSP will be the View.

For each page in the app, he now has a servlet Controller, a Java class Model, and a JSP View.

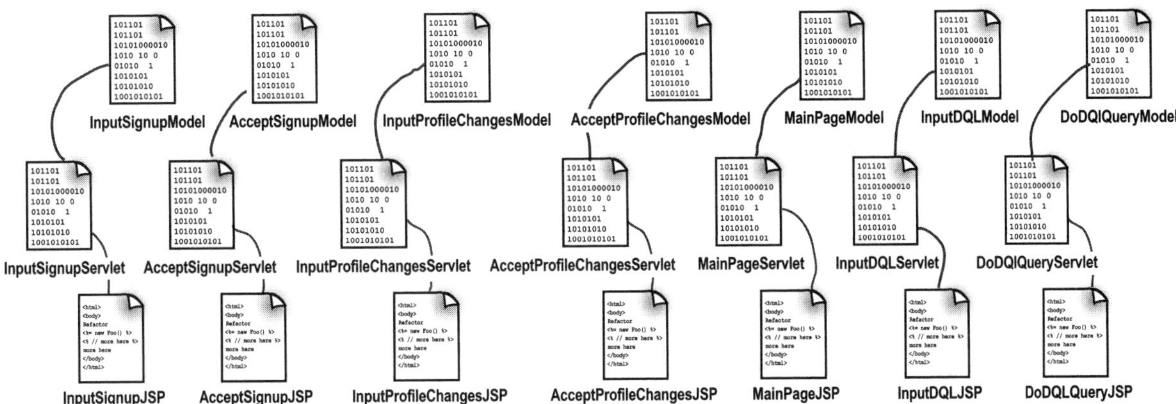

What do you think? Am I good or am I good? A perfect MVC design.

But then his friend Kim takes a look

Kim comes in and says that while it IS an MVC design, it's a dumb one. Sure, the business logic has been pulled out into a Model, and the servlets act as the Controllers working between the Models and Views so that the Models can be brain-dead about the Views. That's all good. But look at all those little servlets.

What do they even *do*? Now that the business logic is safely tucked away in the Model, the servlet Controller isn't doing much except some generic application stuff for this app, and, oh yeah, it does update the Model and then it kicks the View into gear.

But the worst part is that all that generic application logic is duplicated in every single frickin' servlet! If one thing needs to change, it has to change everywhere. A maintenance train wreck waiting to happen.

"Yeah, I felt a little weird about the duplicate code, " says Bob, "but what else can I do? Surely you don't mean for me to put everything in a single servlet again? How could *that* be good?"

What a completely lame design! Look at all the duplicate code in each servlet. You have to add the same overall application code, like security, in almost every servlet.

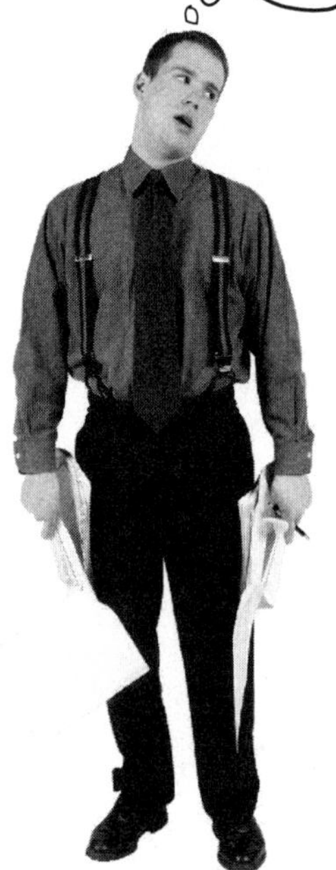

Come on... you don't SERIOUSLY expect me to put it all back in one non-OO servlet...

Is there an answer?

Should Bob go back to just one servlet Controller, to avoid duplicate code? Would that be bad OO, because the servlets really are doing different things? Does Keanu Reeves really know Kung Fu?

FLEX YOUR MIND

Leave this for you to ponder, we will.

What do you think? Do you know the answer? IS there an answer? Would you agree with Bob, and leave the servlets as they are, or would you put the code into just one servlet Controller? And if you do use just one Controller for everything, how will the Controller know which Model and View to call?

The answer to this question won't come until the very *end* of the book, so think about this for a few moments, then put it in a mental background thread...

Sharpen your pencil

1. Using MVC in a servlet & JSP world, each of these three components (JSP, Java class, Servlet) plays one of the three MVC roles. Circle the "M", the "V", or the "C" depending on which MVC part that component plays. Circle only one letter per component.

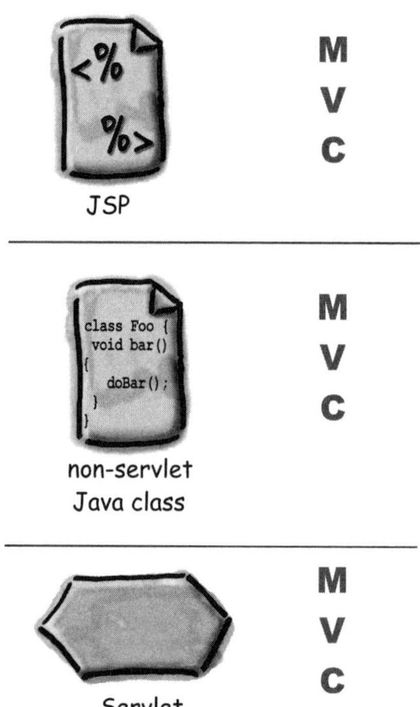

M V C

M V C

M V C

2. What do the letters MVC represent in the MVC design pattern?

M stands for ____________________

V stands for ____________________

C stands for ____________________

BULLET POINTS

- The Container gives your web app communications support, lifecycle management, multithreading support, declarative security, and support for JSPs, so that you can concentrate of your own business logic.
- The Container creates a request and response object that servlets (and other parts of the web app) can use to get information about the request and send information to the client.
- A typical servlet is a class that extends HttpServlet and overrides one or more service methods that correspond to HTTP methods invoked by the browser (doGet() doPost(), etc.).
- The deployer can map a servlet class to a URL that the client can use to request that servlet. The name may have nothing to do with the actual class *file* name.

Who's responsible?

Fill in the table below, indicating whether the web server, the web container, or a servlet is most responsible for the task listed. In a few cases more than one answer may be true for a given task. For extra credit, add a brief comment describing the process.

Task	Web server	Container	Servlet
Creates the request & response objects			
Calls the service() method			
Starts a new thread to handle requests			
Converts a response object to an HTTP response			
Knows HTTP			
Adds HTML to the response object			
Has a reference to the response objects			
Finds URLs in the DD			
Deletes the request and response objects			
Coordinates making dynamic content			
Manages lifecycles			
Has a name that matches the <servlet-class> element in the DD			

Code Magnets

A working servlet,and its DD are scrambled up on the fridge. Can you add the code snippets on the right to the incomplete listings on the left to make a working servlet and DD whose URL ends with **/Dice**? There might be some extra magnets on the right that you won't use at all!

Servlet

```
public class

extends HttpServlet {

public void doGet(

throws IOException {
```

```
    String d1 = Integer.toString((int)((Math.random()*6)+1));
    String d2 = Integer.toString((int)((Math.random()*6)+1));

    out.println("<html> <body>" +
       "<h1 align=center>HF\'s Chap 2 Dice Roller</h1>" +
       "<p>" + d1 + " and " + d2 + " were rolled" +
       "</body> </html>");
  }
}
```

DD

```
<web-app ... >
```

(Remember, this isn't the complete <web-app> opening tag--a complete example is at the end of this chapter. It doesn't affect this exercise.)

```
C2dice </servlet-name>

</web-app>
```

Code Magnets, continued...

```
import javax.servlet.*;
import javax.servlet.http.*;
import java.io.*;
```

```
</url-pattern>
```

```
public void service(
```

```
C2dice
```

```
Ch2Dice
```

```
<servlet-name>
```

```
ServletRequest request,
```

```
PrintWriter out = response.getWriter();
```

```
HttpServletResponse response)
```

```
<servlet-mapping>
```

```
C2dice
```

```
ServletResponse response,
```

```
<servlet-name>
```

```
</servlet-class>
```

```
/Dice
```

```
Ch2Dice
```

```
HttpServletRequest request,
```

```
<servlet>
```

```
PrintWriter out = request.getWriter();
```

```
/Dice
```

```
</servlet-name>
```

```
Ch2Dice
```

```
<url-pattern>
```

```
<servlet-class>
```

```
</servlet>
```

```
</servlet-mapping>
```

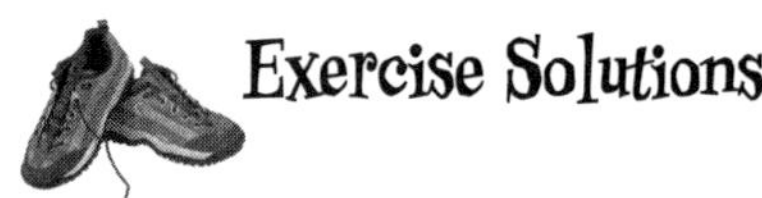

Exercise Solutions

Task	Web server	Container	Servlet
Creates the request & response objects		Just before starting the thread.	
Calls the service() method		Then service() method calls doGet() or doPost().	
Starts a new thread to handle requests		Starts a servlet thread.	
Converts a response object to an HTTP response		Generates the HTTP response stream from the data in response object.	
Knows HTTP	Uses it to talk to the client browser.		
Adds HTML to the response object			The dynamic content for the client.
Has a reference to the response objects		Container gives it the servlet.	Uses it to print a response.
Finds URLs in the DD		To find the correct servlet for the request.	
Deletes the request and response objects		Once the servlet is finished.	
Coordinates making dynamic content	Knows how to forward to the Container.	Knows who to call.	
Manages lifecycles		Calls service method (and others you'll see).	
Has a name that matches the <servlet-class> element in the DD			public class Whatever

Exercise Solutions, continued...

Servlet

```
import javax.servlet.*;
import javax.servlet.http.*;
import java.io.*;

public class Ch2Dice extends HttpServlet {

  public void doGet( HttpServletRequest request,
                     HttpServletResponse response)
                     throws IOException {

    PrintWriter out = response.getWriter();

    String d1 = Integer.toString((int)((Math.random()*6)+1));
    String d2 = Integer.toString((int)((Math.random()*6)+1));

    out.println("<html> <body>" +
       "<h1 align=center>HF\'s Chap 2 Dice Roller</h1>" +
       "<p>" + d1 + " and " + d2 + " were rolled" +
       "</body> </html>");
  }
}
```

DD

```
<web-app ...>
  <servlet>
    <servlet-name> C2dice </servlet-name>
    <servlet-class> Ch2Dice </servlet-class>
  </servlet>

  <servlet-mapping>
    <servlet-name> C2dice </servlet-name>
    <url-pattern> /Dice </url-pattern>
  </servlet-mapping>
</web-app>
```

A "working" Deployment Descriptor (DD)

Don't worry about what any of this really means (you'll see and be tested on this in *other* chapters). Here, we just wanted to show you a web.xml DD that actually *works*. The other examples in this chapter were missing a lot of the pieces that go into the opening <web-app> tag. (You can see why we don't usually include it in our examples.)

The way we usually show it in the book

```
<web-app   ...>

  <servlet>
    <servlet-name>Ch3 Beer</servlet-name>
    <servlet-class>com.example.web.BeerSelect</servlet-class>
  </servlet>

  <servlet-mapping>
    <servlet-name>Ch3 Beer</servlet-name>
    <url-pattern>/SelectBeer.do</url-pattern>
  </servlet-mapping>

</web-app>
```

This opening <web-app> tag isn't complete.

You do NOT have to memorize any of this opening tag, ever. Just copy it in when you're using a Container that's compliant with servlet spec 2.4 (like Tomcat 5).

The way it REALLY works

```
<web-app xmlns="http://java.sun.com/xml/ns/j2ee"
    xmlns:xsi="http://www.w3.org/2001/XMLSchema-instance"
    xsi:schemaLocation="http://java.sun.com/xml/ns/j2ee/web-app_2_4.xsd"
    version="2.4">

  <servlet>
    <servlet-name>Ch3 Beer</servlet-name>
    <servlet-class>com.example.web.BeerSelect</servlet-class>
  </servlet>

  <servlet-mapping>
    <servlet-name>Ch3 Beer</servlet-name>
    <url-pattern>/SelectBeer.do</url-pattern>
  </servlet-mapping>

</web-app>
```

How J2EE fits into all this

The Java 2 Enterprise Edition is kind of a super-spec—it incorporates other specifcations, including the Servlets 2.4 spec and the JSP 2.0 spec. That's for the web Container. But the J2EE 1.4 spec also includes the Enterprise JavaBean 2.1 specification, for the EJB Container. In other words, the web Container is for *web* components (Servlets and JSPs), and the EJB Container is for *business* components.

A fully-compliant J2EE application server must have *both* a web Container and an EJB Container (plus other things including a JNDI and JMS implementation). Tomcat is just a web Container! It is still compliant with the portions of the J2EE spec that address the web Container.

Tomcat is a web Container, not a full J2EE application server, because Tomcat does not have an EJB Container.

A J2EE application server includes both a web Container AND an EJB Container.

Tomcat is a web Container, but NOT a full J2EE application server.

A J2EE 1.4 server includes the Servlet spec 2.4, JSP spec 2.0, and EJB spec 2.1.

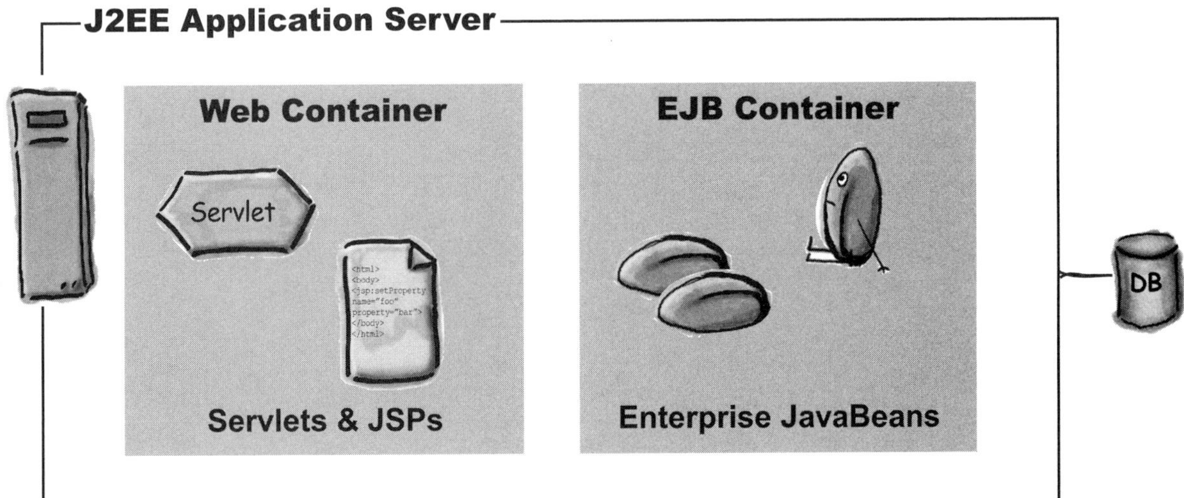

Q: So Tomcat is a standalone web Container... does that mean there are standalone EJB Containers?

A: In the old days, say, the year 2000, you could find complete J2EE application servers, standalone web Containers, and standalone EJB Containers. But today, virtually all *EJB* Containers are part of full J2EE servers, although there are still a few standlone *web* Containers, including Tomcat and Resin. Standalone web Containers are usually configured to work with an HTTP web server (like Apache), although the Tomcat Container *does* have the ability to act as a basic HTTP server. But for HTTP server capability, Tomcat is not nearly as robust as Apache, so the most common non-EJB web apps usually use Apache and Tomcat configured together—with Apache as the HTTP web *Server*, and Tomcat as the web *Container.*

Some of the most common J2EE servers are BEA's WebLogic, the open source JBoss AS, and IBM's WebSphere.

3 hands-on MVC

Mini MVC Tutorial

Create and deploy an MVC web app. It's time to get your hands dirty writing an HTML form, a servlet controller, a model (plain old Java class), an XML deployment descriptor, and a JSP view. Time to build it, deploy it, and test it. But first, you need to set up your *development* environment—a project directory structure that's separate from your actual deployed app. Next, you need to set up your *deployment* environment following the servlet and JSP specs and Tomcat requirements. Then you're ready to start writing, compiling, deploying, and running. True, this is a very small app we're building. But there's almost NO app that's too small to use MVC. Because today's small app is tomorrow's dot com success...

Web Application Deployment

2.1 Construct the file and directory structure of a web application that may contain (a) static content, (b) JSP pages, (c) servlet classes, (d) the deployment descriptor, (e) tag libraries, (f) JAR files, and (g) Java class files. Describe how to protect resource files from HTTP access.

2.2 Describe the purpose and semantics for each of the following deployment descriptor elements: error-page, init-param, mime-mapping, servlet, servlet-class, servlet-mapping, servlet-name, and welcome-file.

2.3 Construct the correct structure for each of the following deployment descriptor elements: error-page, init-param, mime-mapping, servlet, servlet-class, servlet-name, and welcome-file.

Coverage Notes:

All of the objectives in this section are covered completely in the Deployment chapter; this is just a first look. This chapter is the only complete start-to-finish tutorial in the book, so if you skip it, you might have trouble later testing some of the other examples in later chapters (where we don't go through every detail again).

As with the previous two chapters, you don't need to focus on memorizing the content in this chapter. Just get in there and do it.

Let's build a real (small) web application

We looked at the role of a container, we talked a bit about deployment descriptors, and we took a first look at the Model 2 MVC architecture. But you can't just sit here and *read* all day—now it's time to actually *do* something.

The four steps we'll follow:

1. Review the **user's *views*** (what the browser will display), and the high level ***architecture***.

2. Create the ***development* environment** that we will use for this project (which you can use for any other example in the book).

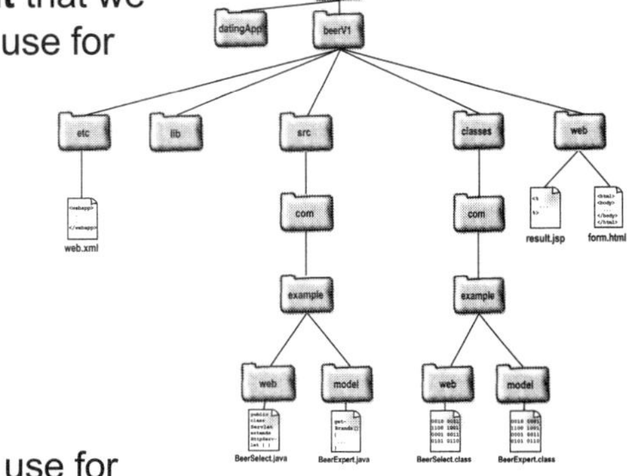

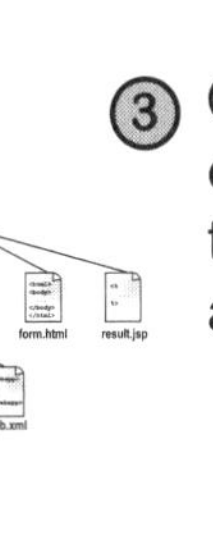

3. Create the ***deployment* environment** that we will use for this project (which you can use for any other example in the book).

4. Perform ***iterative* development and testing** on the various components of our web application. (OK, this is more of a strategy than a step.)

   Note: We recommend iterative development and testing, although we won't always show *all* the steps in this book.

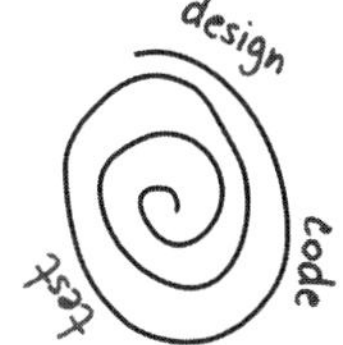

The User's View of the web application—a Beer Advisor

Our web application is a Beer Advisor. Users will be able to surf to our app, answer a question, and get back stunningly useful beer advice.

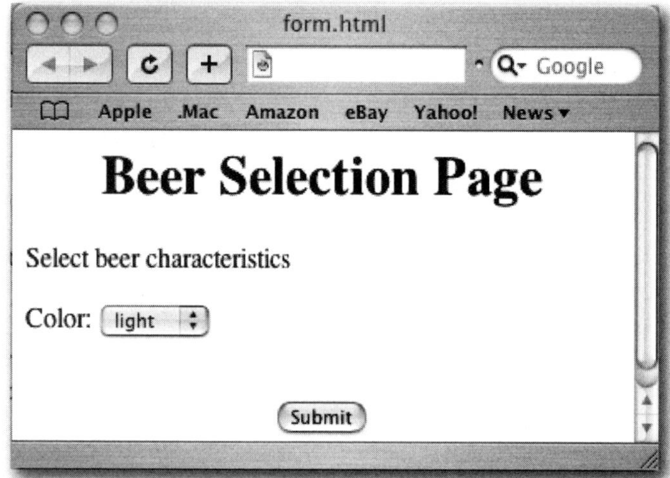

This page will be written in HTML, and will generate an HTTP Post request, sending the user's color selection as a parameter.

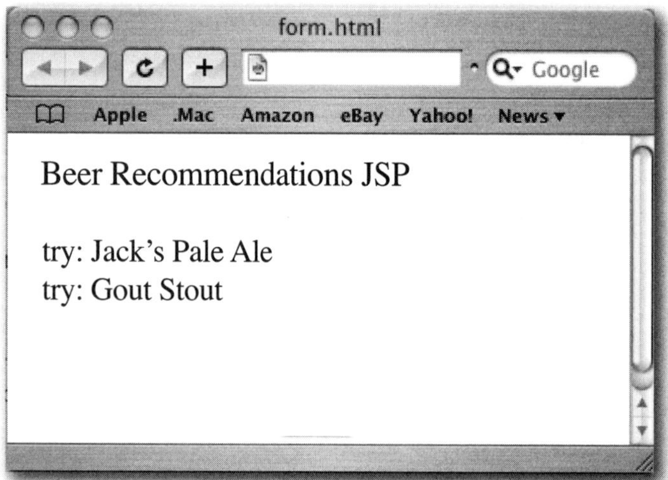

This page will be a JSP that gives the advice based on the user's choice.

Q: Why are we writing a web application that gives beer advice?

A: After an exhaustive marketing research effort, we concluded that 90% of our readers appreciate beer. The other 10% can simply substitute the word "coffee" for "beer".

Here's the architecture...

Even though this is a tiny application, we'll build it using a simple MVC architecture. That way, when it becomes THE hottest site on the web, we'll be ready to extend the application.

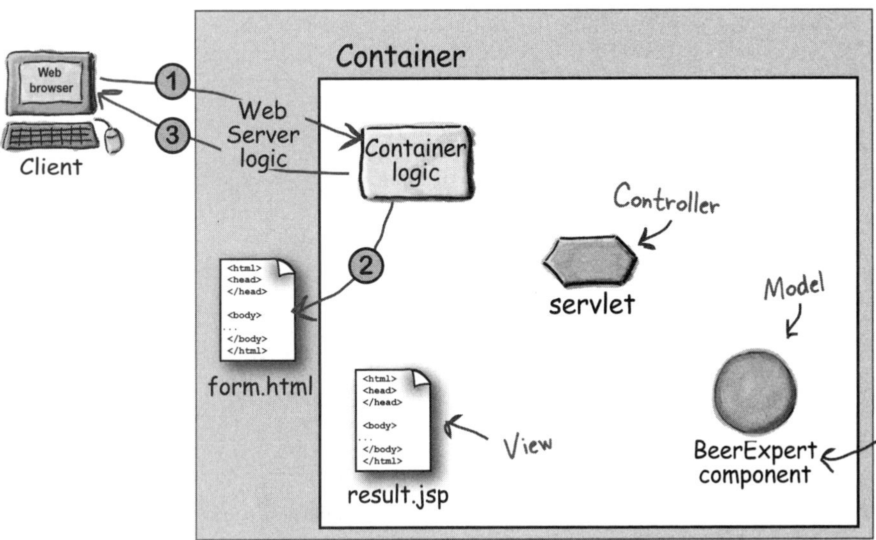

1 - The client makes a request for the *form.html* page.

2 - The Container retrieves the *form.html* page.

3 - The Container returns the page to the browser, where the user answers the questions on the form and...

Just a POJO (Plain Old Java Object).

Container

Web browser

Client

Container logic

servlet

BeerExpert component

result.jsp

request

4 - The browser sends the request data to the container.

5 - The Container finds the correct servlet based on the URL, and passes the request to the servlet.

6 - The servlet calls the BeerExpert for help.

7 - The expert class returns an answer, which the servlet adds to the request object.

8 - The servlet forwards the request to the JSP.

9 - The JSP gets the answer from the request object.

10 - The JSP generates a page for the Container.

11 - The container returns the page to the happy user.

From here on out when you don't see the web server, assume it's there.

Creating your development environment

There are lots of ways you could organize your development directory structure, but here's what we recommend for small- and medium-sized projects. When it's time to deploy the web app, we'll copy a portion of this into wherever our particular Container wants the pieces to go. (In this tutorial, we're using Tomcat 5.)

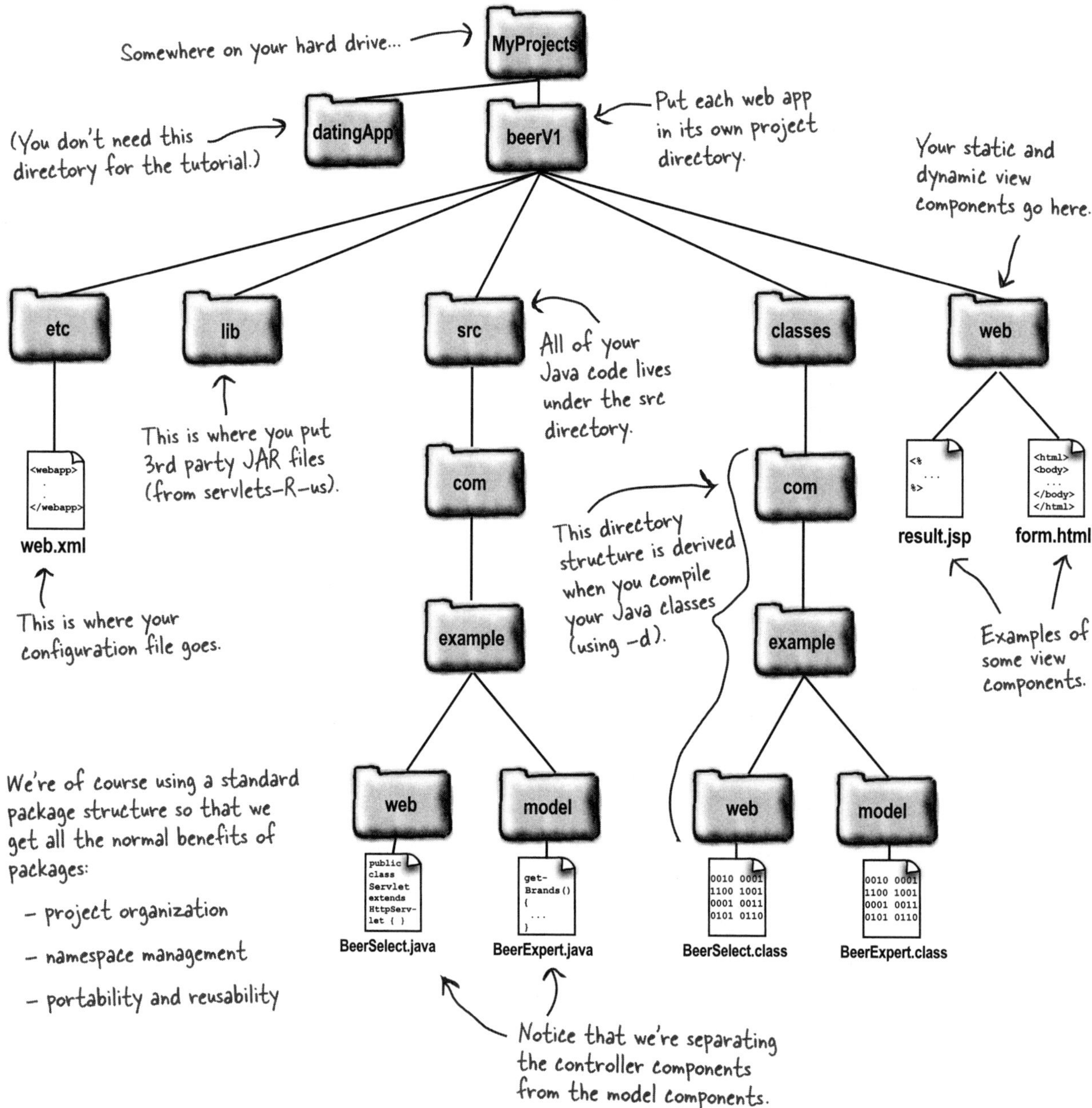

Somewhere on your hard drive...
MyProjects
(You don't need this directory for the tutorial.)
datingApp
beerV1
Put each web app in its own project directory.
Your static and dynamic view components go here.
etc
lib
src
classes
web
All of your Java code lives under the src directory.
<webapp>
</webapp>
web.xml
This is where you put 3rd party JAR files (from servlets-R-us).
This is where your configuration file goes.
com
example
This directory structure is derived when you compile your Java classes (using -d).
<%
%>
result.jsp
<html>
<body>
</body>
</html>
form.html
Examples of some view components.
We're of course using a standard package structure so that we get all the normal benefits of packages:
- project organization
- namespace management
- portability and reusability
web
model
public class Servlet extends HttpServlet { }
BeerSelect.java
get-Brands() { ... }
BeerExpert.java
0010 0001
1100 1001
0001 0011
0101 0110
BeerSelect.class
BeerExpert.class
Notice that we're separating the controller components from the model components.

Creating the deployment environment

Deploying a web app involves both Container-specific rules and requirements of the Servlets and JSP specifications. (If you're not deploying to Tomcat, you'll have to figure out exactly where your web app should be relative to *your* Container.) In our example, everything below the "Beer-v1" directory is the same *regardless* of your Container!

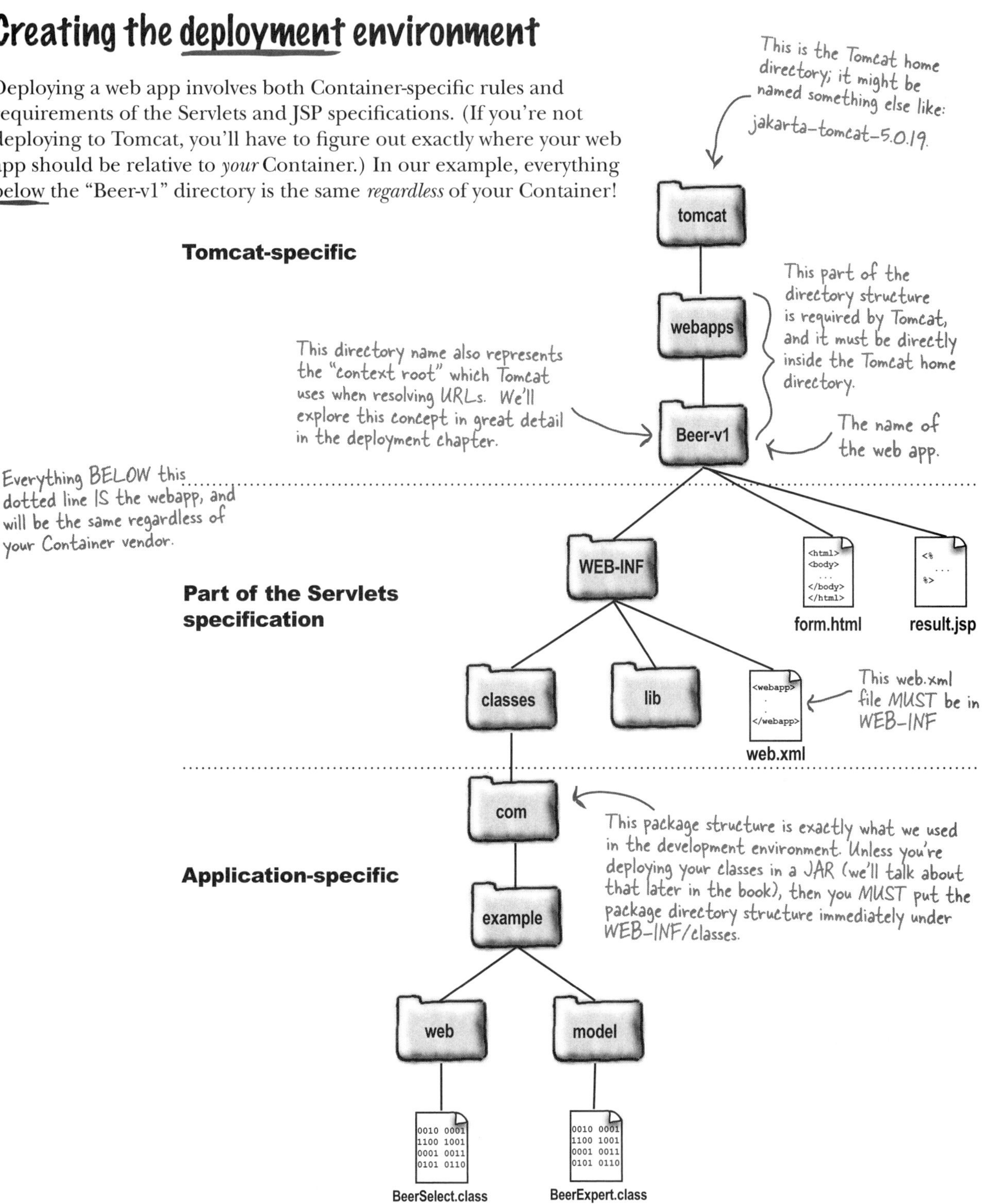

Our roadmap for building the app

When we started this chapter we outlined a four-step process for developing our web app. So far we've:

1 - reviewed the user *views* for our web app

2 - looked at the *architecture*

3 - setup the *development* and *deployment* environments for creating and deploying the app

Now it's time for step 4, *creating* the app.

We borrow from several popular development methodologies (a little from extreme programming, iterative development), and mangle them for our own evil purposes...

The five steps we'll follow (in step 4):

4a **Build and test the HTML** form that the user will first request.

4b **Build and test version 1 of the controller servlet** with the HTML form. This version is invoked via the HTML form and prints the parameter it receives.

4c **Build a test class** for the expert / model class, then build and test the expert / model class itself.

4d **Upgrade the servlet to version 2.** This version adds the capability of calling the model class to get beer advice.

4e ***Build the JSP, upgrade the servlet to version 3*** (which adds the capability of dispatching to the JSP), and test the whole app.

The HTML for the initial form page

The HTML is simple—it puts up the heading text, the drop-down list from which the user selects a beer color, and the submit button.

```
<html><body>
<h1 align="center">Beer Selection Page</h1>
<form method="POST"
  action="SelectBeer.do">
  Select beer characteristics<p>
  Color:
  <select name="color" size="1">
    <option>light
    <option>amber
    <option>brown
    <option>dark
  </select>
  <br><br>
  <center>
    <input type="SUBMIT">
  </center>
</form></body></html>
```

Why did we choose POST instead of GET ?

This is what the HTML thinks the servlet is called. There is NOTHING in your directory structure named "SelectBeer.do"! It's a logical name...

This is how we created the pull down menu, your options may vary.

(Did you figure out size="1" ?)

Q: Why is the form submitting to "SelectBeer.do" when there is NO servlet with that name? In the directory structures we looked at earlier, I didn't see anything that had the name "SelectBeer.do". And what's with the ".do" extension anyway?

A: SelectBeer.do is a logical name, not an actual file name. It's simply the name we want the client to use! In fact the client will NEVER have direct access to the servlet class file, so you won't, for example, create an HTML page with a link or action that includes a path to a servlet class file.

The trick is, we'll use the XML Deployment Descriptor (web.xml) to map from what the client requests ("SelectBeer.do") to an actual servlet class file the Container will use when a request comes in for "SelectBeer.do". For now, think of the ".do" extension as simply part of the logical name (and not a *real* file type). Later in the book, you'll learn about other ways in which you can use extensions (real or made-up/logical) in your servlet mappings.

Deploying and testing the opening page

To test it, you need to deploy it into the Container (Tomcat) directory structure, start Tomcat, and bring up the page in a browser.

tomcat

webapps

Beer-v1

<html>
<body>
...
</body>
</html>

form.html

① Create the HTML in your *development* environment

Create this HTML file, call it *form.html*, and save it in your development environment under the */beerV1/web/* directory.

② Copy the file into the *deployment* environment

Place a copy of the *form.html* file into *tomcat/webapps/Beer-v1/*. (Remember, your tomcat home directory might have a different name).

③ Start Tomcat

Throughout this book we're using Tomcat as both the web *Server* and the web *Container*. In the real world, you probably use a more robust Web Server (like Apache) configured with a Web Container (like Tomcat). But Tomcat makes a perfectly decent Web Server for everything we need to do in this book.

To start Tomcat, cd into the tomcat home directory and run *bin/startup.sh.*

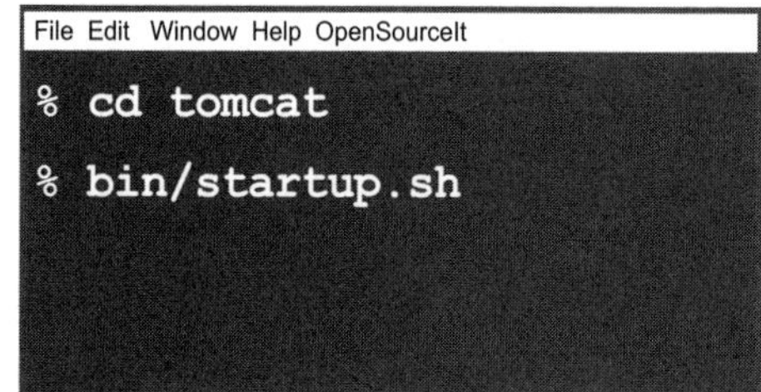

④ Test the page

Open the HTML page in your browser and type:

http://localhost:8080/Beer-v1/form.html

You should see something like the screen shot here.

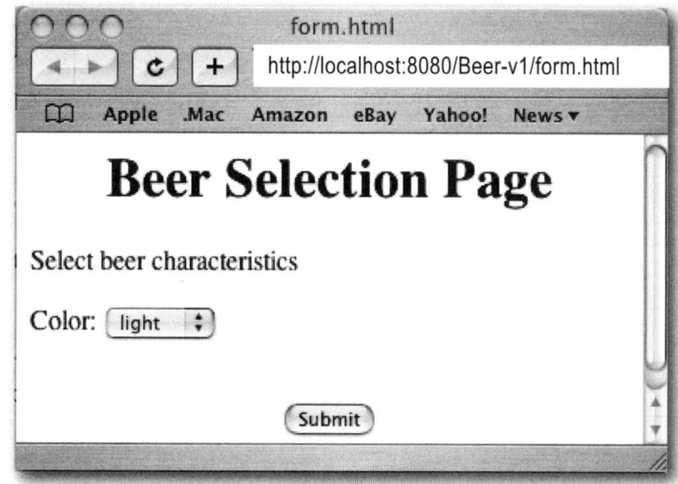

Note: the steps on this page won't work until you also do the steps on the NEXT page...

Creating the Deployment Descriptor (DD)

The main job of this DD is to define the mapping between the logical name the client uses for the request ("SelectBeer.do") and the actual servlet class file (com.example.web.BeerSelect).

① Create the DD in your *development* environment

Create this XML document, name it *web.xml*, and save it in your development environment under the */beerV1/etc/* directory.

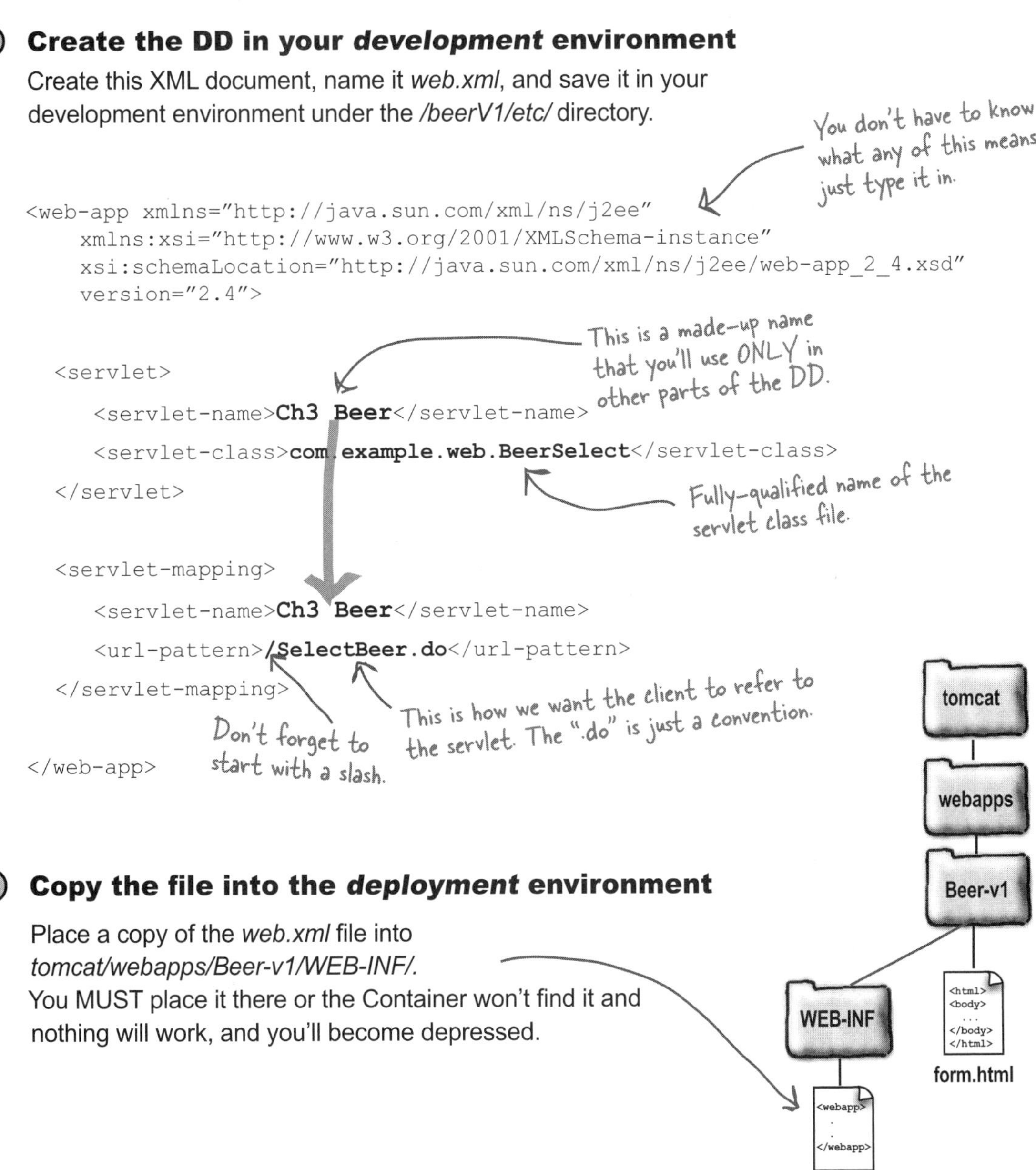
You don't have to know what any of this means, just type it in.
This is a made-up name that you'll use ONLY in other parts of the DD.
Fully-qualified name of the servlet class file.
Don't forget to start with a slash.
This is how we want the client to refer to the servlet. The ".do" is just a convention.
tomcat
webapps
Beer-v1
WEB-INF
form.html
web.xml

```
<web-app xmlns="http://java.sun.com/xml/ns/j2ee"
    xmlns:xsi="http://www.w3.org/2001/XMLSchema-instance"
    xsi:schemaLocation="http://java.sun.com/xml/ns/j2ee/web-app_2_4.xsd"
    version="2.4">

  <servlet>
    <servlet-name>Ch3 Beer</servlet-name>
    <servlet-class>com.example.web.BeerSelect</servlet-class>
  </servlet>

  <servlet-mapping>
    <servlet-name>Ch3 Beer</servlet-name>
    <url-pattern>/SelectBeer.do</url-pattern>
  </servlet-mapping>

</web-app>
```

② Copy the file into the *deployment* environment

Place a copy of the *web.xml* file into *tomcat/webapps/Beer-v1/WEB-INF/.* You MUST place it there or the Container won't find it and nothing will work, and you'll become depressed.

Mapping the logical name to a servlet class file

(1) Diane fills out the form and hits submit. The browser generates the request URL:

/Beer-v1/SelectBeer.do

The host server root. The web app context root. The logical resource name.

```
POST /Beer-v1/SelectBeer.do
HTTP/1.1
Host: www.wickedlysmart.com
User-Agent: Mozilla/5.0 (Macintosh; U;
PPC Mac OS X Mach-O; en-US; rv:1.4)
Gecko/20030624 Netscape/7.1
Accept: text/xml,application/
xml,application/xhtml+xml,text/
html;q=0.9,text/plain;q=0.8,video/x-
mng,image/png,image/jpeg,image/
gif;q=0.2,*/*;q=0.1
```

Client

Container

In the HTML, the "/Beer-v1/" isn't part of the path. In the HTML, it just says:

<form method="POST"

action="SelectBeer.do">

But the browser prepends "/Beer-v1/" on to the request, because that's where the client request is coming from. In other words, the "SelectBeer.do" in the HTML is relative to the URL of the page it's on. In this case, relative to the root of the web app, "/Beer-v1".

(2) The Container searches the DD and finds a <servlet-mapping> with a <url-pattern> that matches /SelectBeer.do, where the slash (/) represents the context root of the web app, and SelectBeer.do is the *logical* name of a resource.

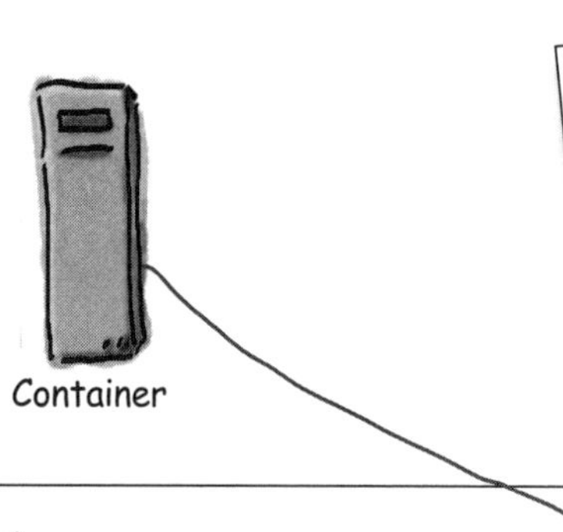

Container

```
<web-app>
  <servlet>
    <servlet-name>
      Ch3 Beer
    </servlet-name>
    <servlet-class>
      com.example.web.BeerSelect
    </servlet-class>
  </servlet>

  <servlet-mapping>
    <servlet-name>
      Ch3 Beer
    </servlet-name>
    <url-pattern>
      /SelectBeer.do
    </url-pattern>
  </servlet-mapping>
</web-app>
```

(3) The Container sees that the <servlet-name> for this <url-pattern> is "Ch3 Beer". But that isn't the name of an actual servlet class file. "Ch3 Beer" is the name of a *servlet*, not a servlet *class*!

To the Container, a servlet is something named in the DD under a <servlet> tag. The name of the servlet is simply the name used in the DD so that other parts of the DD can map to it.

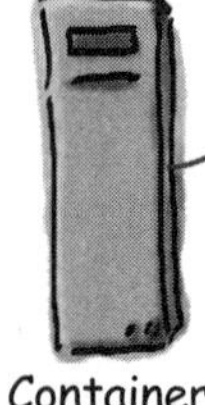

Container

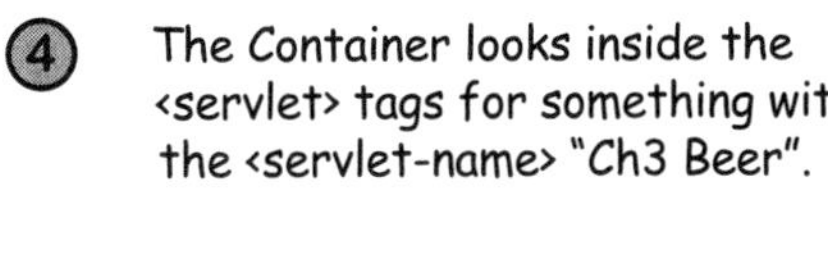

4. The Container looks inside the <servlet> tags for something with the <servlet-name> "Ch3 Beer".

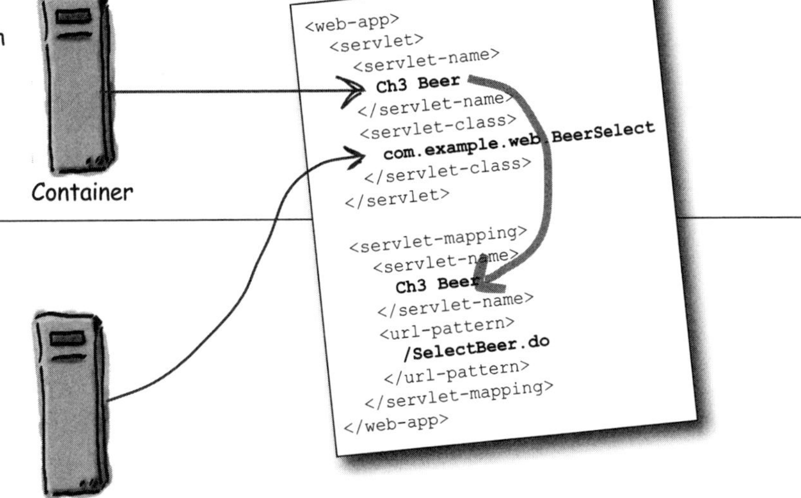

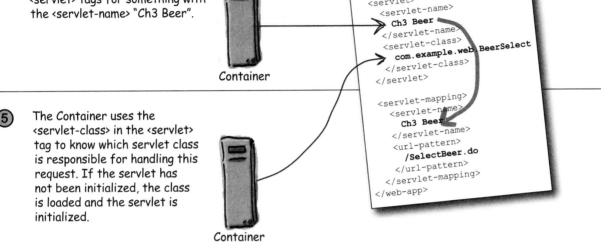

```
<web-app>
  <servlet>
    <servlet-name>
      Ch3 Beer
    </servlet-name>
    <servlet-class>
      com.example.web.BeerSelect
    </servlet-class>
  </servlet>

  <servlet-mapping>
    <servlet-name>
      Ch3 Beer
    </servlet-name>
    <url-pattern>
      /SelectBeer.do
    </url-pattern>
  </servlet-mapping>
</web-app>
```


5. The Container uses the <servlet-class> in the <servlet> tag to know which servlet class is responsible for handling this request. If the servlet has not been initialized, the class is loaded and the servlet is initialized.

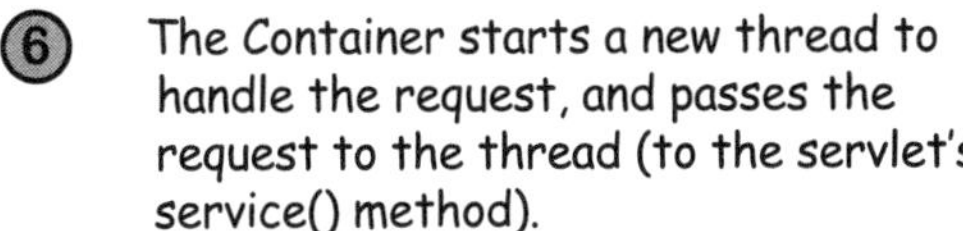

6. The Container starts a new thread to handle the request, and passes the request to the thread (to the servlet's service() method).

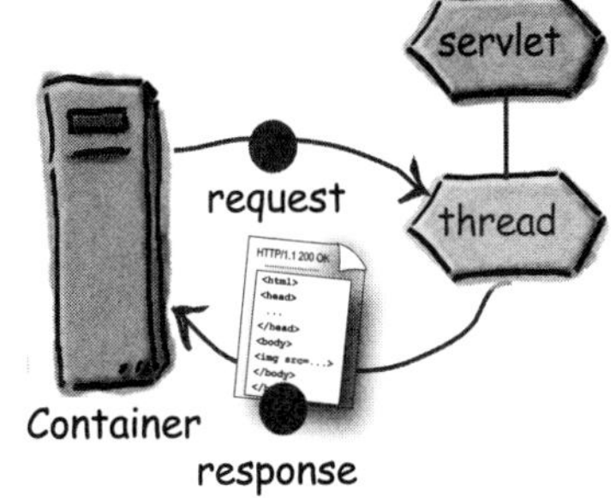

7. The Container sends the response (through the Web Server, of course) back to the client.

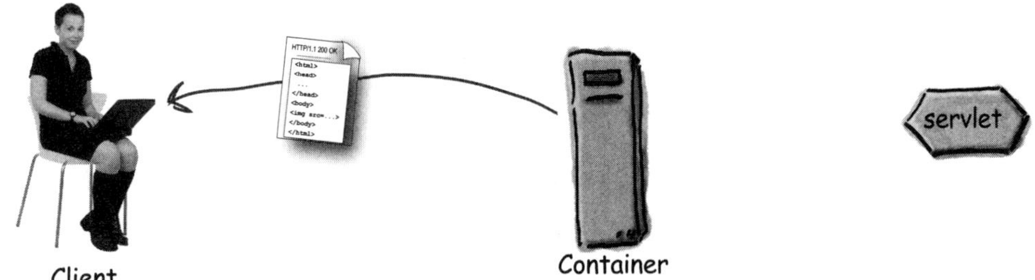

The first version of the controller servlet

Our plan is to build the servlet in stages, testing the various communication links as we go. In the end, remember, the servlet will accept a parameter from the request, invoke a method on the model, save information in a place the JSP can find, and forward the request to the JSP. But for this first version, our goal is just to make sure that the HTML page can properly invoke the servlet, and that the servlet is receiving the HTML parameter correctly.

Servlet code

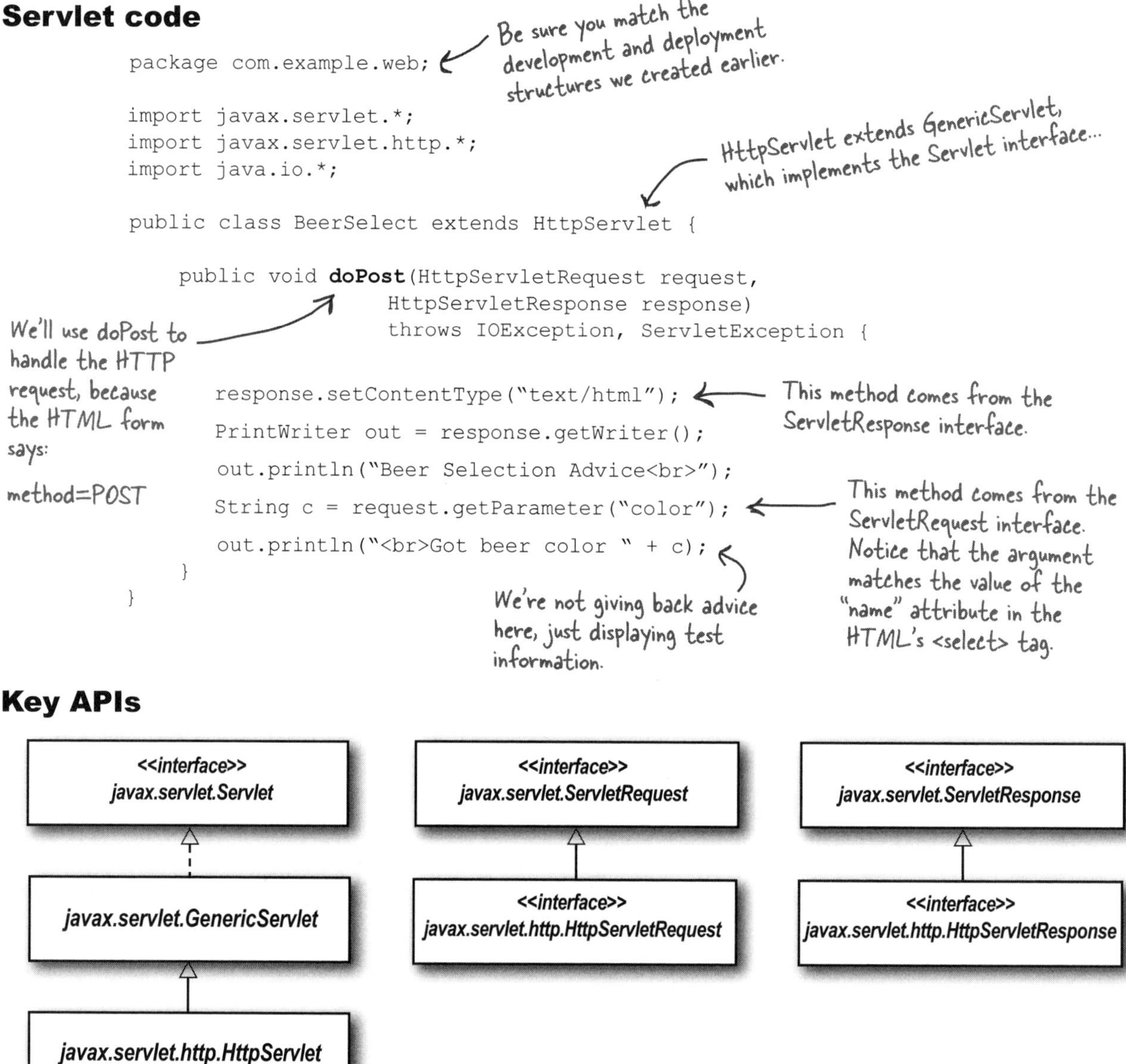

```
package com.example.web;

import javax.servlet.*;
import javax.servlet.http.*;
import java.io.*;

public class BeerSelect extends HttpServlet {

    public void doPost(HttpServletRequest request,
                       HttpServletResponse response)
                       throws IOException, ServletException {

        response.setContentType("text/html");
        PrintWriter out = response.getWriter();
        out.println("Beer Selection Advice<br>");
        String c = request.getParameter("color");
        out.println("<br>Got beer color " + c);
    }
}
```

Be sure you match the development and deployment structures we created earlier.
HttpServlet extends GenericServlet, which implements the Servlet interface...
We'll use doPost to handle the HTTP request, because the HTML form says:
method=POST
This method comes from the ServletResponse interface.
This method comes from the ServletRequest interface. Notice that the argument matches the value of the "name" attribute in the HTML's <select> tag.
We're not giving back advice here, just displaying test information.

Key APIs

Compiling, deploying, and testing the controller servlet

Ok, we've built, deployed, and tested our HTML, and we've built and deployed our DD (well, we put the web.xml into the deployment environment, but technically the DD won't be deployed until we restart Tomcat). Now it's time to compile the first version of the servlet, deploy it, and test it via the HTML form. Now we'll restart Tomcat to make sure that it "sees" the web.xml and servlet class.

Compiling the servlet

Compile the servlet with the -d flag to put the class in the *development* environment.

Adjust this to match your own directory path to your system! Everything after "tomcat/" will be the same.

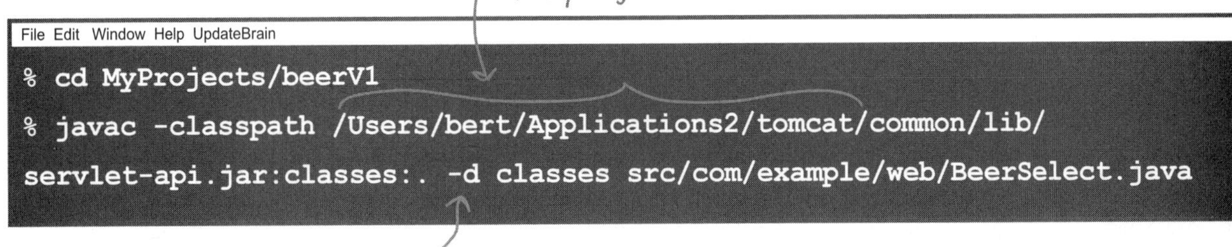

File Edit Window Help UpdateBrain
% cd MyProjects/beerV1
% javac -classpath /Users/bert/Applications2/tomcat/common/lib/
servlet-api.jar:classes:. -d classes src/com/example/web/BeerSelect.java

Use the -d option to tell the compiler to put the .class file into the classes directory within the correct package structure. Your .class file will end up in /beerV1/classes/com/example/web/.

Deploying the servlet

To deploy the servlet, make a copy of the .class file and move it to the /Beer-v1/WEB-INF/classes/com/example/web/ directory in the deployment structure.

Testing the servlet

1 - **Restart tomcat!**

2 - Launch your browser and go to: http://localhost:8080/Beer-v1/form.html

4 - Select a beer color and hit "Submit"

5 - If your servlet is working, you should see the servlet's response in your browser as something like:

Beer Selection Advice
Got beer color brown

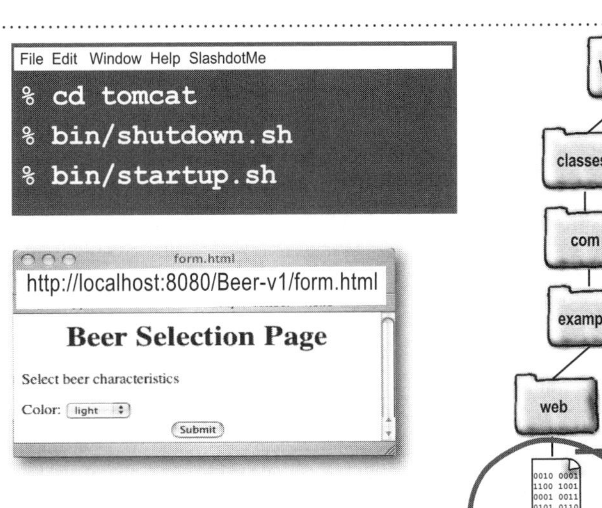

Building and testing the model class

In MVC, the model tends to be the "back-end" of the application. It's often the legacy system that's now being exposed to the web. In most cases it's just plain old Java code, with no knowledge of the fact that it might be called by servlets. The model shouldn't be tied down to being used by only a single web app, so it should be in its own utility packages.

The specs for the model

- Its package should be **com.example.model**
- Its directory structure should be /WEB-INF/classes/com/example/model
- It exposes one method, **getBrands()**, that takes a preferred beer color (as a String), and returns an ArrayList of recommended beer brands (also as Strings).

Build the test class for the model

Create the test class for the model (yes, *before* you build the model itself). You're on your own here; we don't have one in this tutorial. Remember, the model will still be in the development environment when you first test it—it's just like any other Java class, and you can test it without Tomcat.

Build and test the model

Models can be extremely complicated. They often involve connections to legacy databases, and calls to complex business logic. Here's our sophisticated, rule-based expert system for the beer advice:

```
package com.example.model;
import java.util.*;

public class BeerExpert {
  public List getBrands(String color) {
    List brands = new ArrayList();
    if (color.equals("amber")) {
       brands.add("Jack Amber");
       brands.add("Red Moose");
    }
    else {
       brands.add("Jail Pale Ale");
       brands.add("Gout Stout");
    }
    return(brands);
  }
}
```

Notice how we've captured complex, expert knowledge of the beer paradigm using advanced conditional expressions.

```
File Edit Window Help Skateboard
% cd beerV1
% javac -d classes src/com/example/model/BeerExpert.java
```

Enhancing the servlet to call the model, so that we can get REAL advice...

In this version *two* servlet we'll enhance the doPost() method to call the model for advice (version *three* will make the advice come from a JSP). The code changes are trivial, but the important part is understanding the redeployment of the enhanced web app. You can try to write the code, recompile, and deploy on your own, or you can turn the page and follow along...

Enhance the servlet, version two

Forget about servlets for a minute, let's just think Java. What are the steps we have to take to accomplish the following?

1 - Enhance the doPost() method to call the model.

2 - Compile the servlet.

3 - Deploy and test the updated web app.

```
public class BeerSelect extends HttpServlet {
```

Servlet version two code

Remember, the model is just plain old Java, so we call it like we'd call any other Java method—instantiate the model class and call its method!

```
package com.example.web;

import com.example.model.*;
import javax.servlet.*;
import javax.servlet.http.*;
import java.io.*;
import java.util.*;

public class BeerSelect extends HttpServlet {

    public void doPost(HttpServletRequest request,
                       HttpServletResponse response)
                       throws IOException, ServletException {

        response.setContentType("text/html");
        PrintWriter out = response.getWriter();
        out.println("Beer Selection Advice<br>");
        String c = request.getParameter("color");

        BeerExpert be = new BeerExpert();
        List result = be.getBrands(c);
        Iterator it = result.iterator();
        while(it.hasNext()) {
           out.print("<br>try: " + it.next());
        }

    }
}
```

Don't forget the import for the package that BeerExpert is in.

We're modifying the original servlet, not making a new class.

Instantiate the BeerExpert class and call getBrands().

Print out the advice (beer brand items in the ArrayList returned from the model). In the final (third) version, the advice will be printed from a JSP instead of the servlet.

Key steps for servlet version two

We have two main things to do: ***recompile the servlet*** and ***deploy the model class.***

Compiling the servlet

We'll use the same compiler command that we used when we built the first version of the servlet.

```
File Edit Window Help PlayGo
% cd beerV1
% javac -classpath /Users/bert/Applications2/tomcat/common/lib/
servlet-api.jar:classes:. -d classes src/com/example/web/BeerSelect.java
```

Deploying and testing the web app

Now, in addition to the servlet, we also have to deploy the model. The key steps are:

1 - Move a copy of the servlet .class file to:
../Beer-v1/WEB-INF/classes/com/example/web/
This ***replaces*** the version one servlet class file!

2 - Move a copy of the model's .class file to:
../Beer-v1/WEB-INF/classes/com/example/model/

3 - Shutdown and **restart tomcat**

```
File Edit Window Help SellHigh
% cd tomcat
% bin/shutdown.sh
% bin/startup.sh
```

4 - **Test the app** via form.html, the final browser output should be something like:

Beer Selection Advice
try: Jack Amber
try: Red Moose

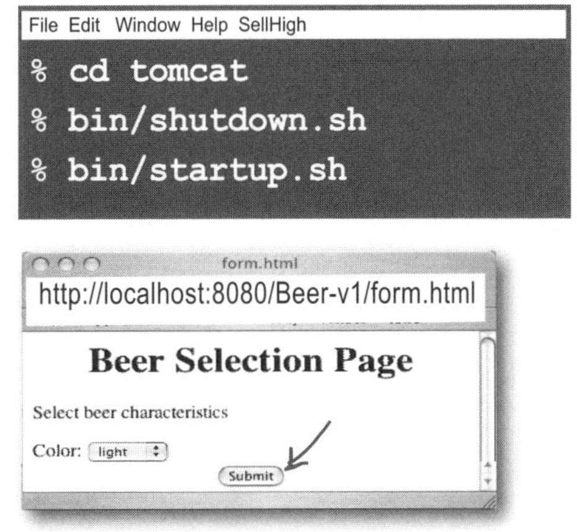

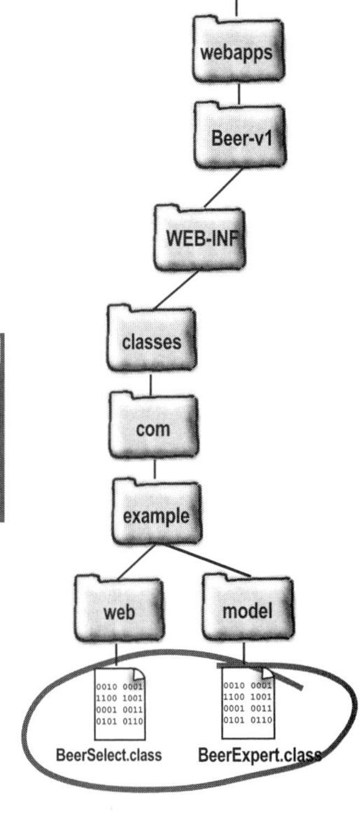

Review the partially completed, MVC beer advice web application

What's working so far...

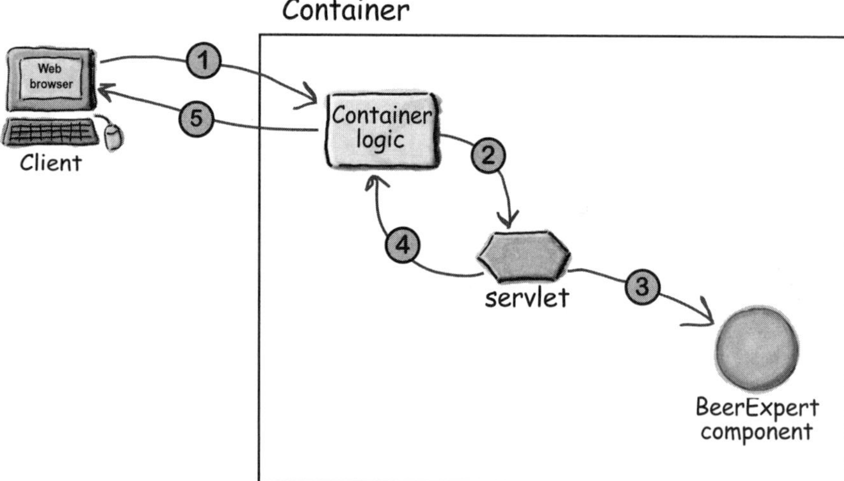

1 - The browser sends the request data to the Container.

2 - The Container finds the correct servlet based on the URL, and passes the request to the servlet.

3 - The servlet calls the BeerExpert for help.

4 - The servlet outputs the response (which prints the advice).

5 - The Container returns the page to the happy user.

What we WANT...

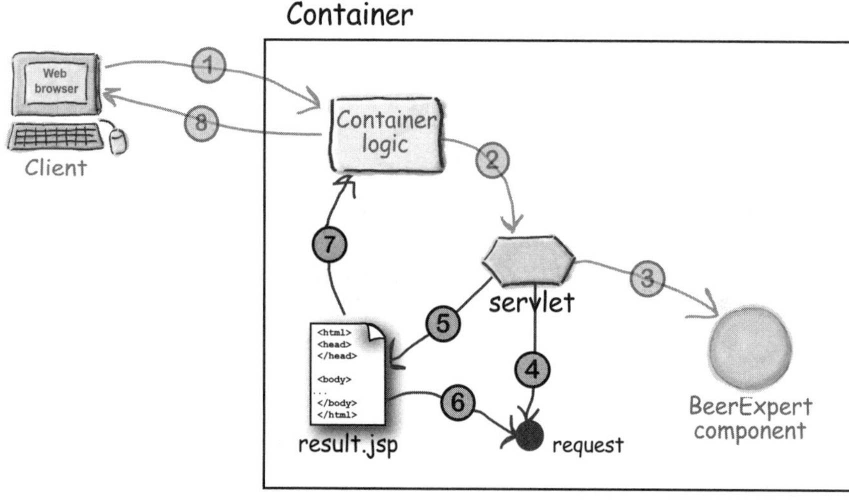

1 - The browser sends the request data to the Container.

2 - The Container finds the correct servlet based on the URL, and passes the request to the servlet.

3 - The servlet calls the BeerExpert for help.

4 - The expert class returns an answer, which the servlet adds to the request object.

5 - The servlet forwards the request to the JSP.

6 - The JSP gets the answer from the request object.

7 - The JSP generates a page for the Container.

8 - The Container returns the page to the happy user.

Create the JSP "view" that gives the advice

Don't get your hopes up. You're going to have to wait for a few chapters before we really start talking about JSPs. This JSP isn't actually a particularly good one, either (because of its scriptlet code, which we'll talk about later in the book). For now it should be pretty easy to read, and if you want to experiment a little, go for it. Although we *could* test this JSP now from the browser, we'll wait until after we modify the servlet (version three) to see if it works.

Here's the JSP...

```
<%@ page import="java.util.*" %>

<html>
<body>
<h1 align="center">Beer Recommendations JSP</h1>
<p>

<%
  List styles = (List)request.getAttribute("styles");
  Iterator it = styles.iterator();
  while(it.hasNext()) {
    out.print("<br>try: " + it.next());
  }
%>

</body>
</html>
```

This is a "page directive" (we're thinking it's pretty obvious what this one does).

Some standard HTML (which is known as "template text" in the JSP world).

Here we're getting an attribute from the request object. A little later in the book, we'll explain everything about attributes and how we managed to get the request object...

Some standard Java sitting inside <% %> tags (this is known as scriptlet code).

Deploying the JSP

We don't compile the JSP (the Container does that at first request). But we *do* have to:

1 - Name it "result.jsp".

2 - Save it in the *development* environment, in: */web/*.

3 - Move a copy of it to the *deployment* environment in */Beer-v1/*.

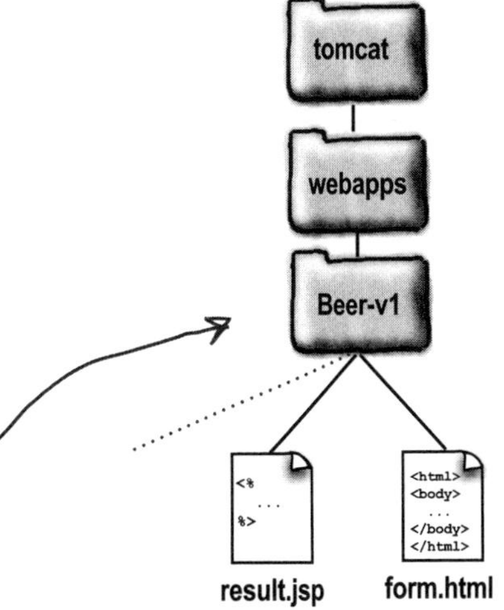

Enhancing the servlet to "call" the JSP (version three)

In this step we're going to modify the servlet to "call" the JSP to produce the output (view). The Container provides a mechanism called "request dispatching" that allows one Container-managed component to call another, and that's what we'll use—the servlet will get the info from the model, save it in the request object, then ***dispatch the request to the JSP.***

The important changes we must make to the servlet:

1 - Add the model component's answer to the request object, so that the JSP can access it. (Step 4)

2 - Ask the Container to forward the request to "result.jsp". (Step 5)

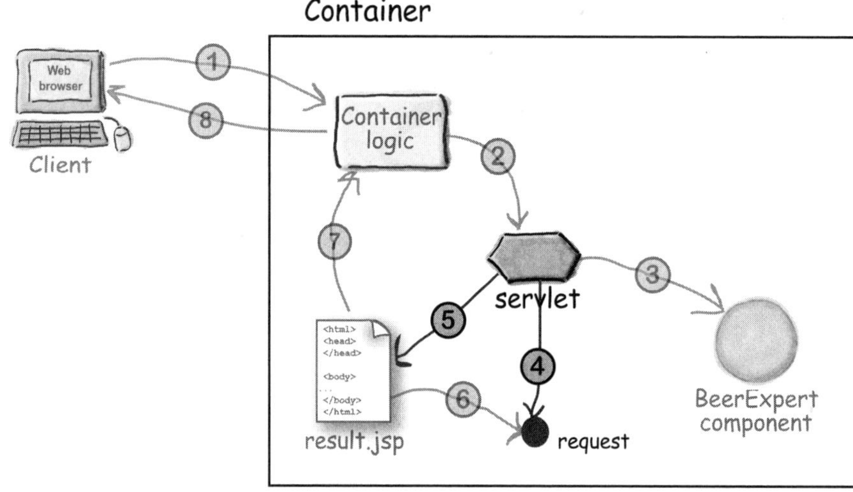

1 - The browser sends the request data to the container.

2 - The Container finds the correct servlet based on the URL, and passes the request to the servlet.

3 - The servlet calls the BeerExpert for help.

4 - The expert class returns an answer, which the servlet adds to the request object.

5 - The servlet dispatches to the JSP.

6 - The JSP gets the answer from the request object.

7 - The JSP generates a page for the Container.

8 - The Container returns the page to the happy user.

Code for servlet version three

Here's how we modified the servlet to add the model component's answer to the request object (so the JSP can retrieve it), and how we asked the Container to dispatch to the JSP.

```
package com.example.web;

import com.example.model.*;
import javax.servlet.*;
import javax.servlet.http.*;
import java.io.*;
import java.util.*;

public class BeerSelect extends HttpServlet {

    public void doPost(HttpServletRequest request,
                       HttpServletResponse response)
          throws IOException, ServletException {

       // response.setContentType("text/html");

       // remove the old test output
       // PrintWriter out = response.getWriter();
       // out.println("Beer Selection Advice<br>");

       String c = request.getParameter("color");

       // out.println("<br>Got beer color " + c);

       BeerExpert be = new BeerExpert();
       List result = be.getBrands(c);


       request.setAttribute("styles", result);


       RequestDispatcher view =
            request.getRequestDispatcher("result.jsp");

       view.forward(request, response);
    }
}
```

Now that the JSP is going to produce the output, we should remove the test output from the servlet. We commented it out so that you could still see it here.

Add an attribute to the request object for the JSP to use. Notice the JSP is looking for "styles".

Instantiate a request dispatcher for the JSP.

Use the request dispatcher to ask the Container to crank up the JSP, sending it the request and response.

Compile, deploy, and test the final app!

In this chapter we've built an entire (albeit tiny) MVC application using HTML, servlets and JSPs. You can add this to your resume.

Compiling the servlet

We'll use the same compiler command that we used earlier:

```
File Edit Window Help RunItsATrap
% cd beerV1
% javac -classpath /Users/bert/Applications2/tomcat/common/lib/
servlet-api.jar:classes:. -d classes src/com/example/web/BeerSelect.java
```

Deploying and testing the web app

Now it's time to redploy the servlet.

1 - Move a copy of the servlet's .class file to ../Beer-v1/WEB-INF/classes/com/example/web/ (again, this will ***replace*** the previous version two class file).

3 - Shutdown and restart tomcat

```
File Edit Window Help SaveYourself
% cd tomcat
% bin/shutdown.sh
% bin/startup.sh
```

4 - Test the app via form.html

form.html
http://localhost:8080/Beer-v1/form.html
Beer Selection Page
Select beer characteristics
Color: light
Submit

Here's what you should see!

form.html
Beer Recommendations JSP
try: Jack's Pale Ale
try: Gout Stout

OK so now he can do an MVC app, but he still has no clue how to use the JSP expression language, or JSTL, or write a custom tag, or use a filter, and I caught him playing a Weezer CD and it was AFTER the green album. He still has SO much to learn...

There is still so much to learn.

The party's over. You had three whole chapters to cruise along, write a little code, review the whole HTTP request/response thing.

But there's still 200 mock exam questions waiting for you in this book, and they start with the next chapter. Unless you're already familiar with servlet development and deployment, you really shouldn't turn the page until after you actually *do* the tutorial in this chapter.

Not that we're trying to pressure you or guilt-trip you or anything...

4 request AND response

Being a Servlet

He used a GET request to update the database. The punishment will be most severe... no "Yoga with Suzy" classes for 90 days.

Servlets live to service clients. A servlet's job is to take a client's ***request*** and send back a ***response***. The request might be simple: *"get me the Welcome page."* Or it might be complex: *"Complete my shopping cart check-out."* The request carries crucial data, and your servlet code has to know how to *find* it and how to *use* it. The response carries the info the browser needs to render a page (or download bytes), and your servlet code has to know how to *send* it. Or *not*... your servlet can decide to pass the request to something *else* (another page, servlet, or JSP) instead.

The Servlet Technology Model

1.1 For each of the HTTP Methods (such as GET, POST, HEAD, and so on), describe the purpose of the method and the technical characteristics of the HTTP Method protocol, list triggers that might cause a client (usually a Web browser) to use the Method, and identify the HttpServlet method that corresponds to the HTTP Method.

1.2 Using the HttpServletRequest interface, write code to retrieve HTML form parameters from the request, retrieve HTTP request header information, or retrieve cookies from the request.

1.3 Using the HttpServletResponse interface, write code to set an HTTP response header, set the content type of the response, acquire a text stream for the response, acquire a binary stream for the response, redirect an HTTP request to another URL, or add cookies to the response.*

1.4 Describe the purpose and event sequence of the servlet lifecycle: (1) servlet class loading, (2) servlet instantiation, (3) call the init() method, (4) call the service() method, and (5) call the destroy() method.

Coverage Notes:

All of the objectives in this section are covered completely in this chapter, with the exception of the cookies part of objective 1.3. A lot of the content in this chapter was touched on in chapter two, but in chapter two we said, "Don't worry about memorizing it."
In this chapter, you DO have to slow down, really study, and memorize the content. No other chapter will cover these objectives in detail, so this is it.
Do the exercises in the chapter, review the material, then take your first mock exam at the end of the chapter. If you don't get at least 80% correct, go back through the chapter to figure out what you missed, BEFORE you move on to chapter five.
Some of the mock exam questions that belong with these objectives have been moved into chapters 5 and 6, because the questions require additional knowledge of some of the topics we don't cover until those chapters. That means there are fewer mock exam questions in this chapter, and more in later chapters, to avoid testing you on topics you haven't covered.

Important note: while the first three chapters covered background information, from this page forward in the book, virtually everything you're going to see is directly related to or explicitly part of the exam.

* We won't say much about the objectives related to cookies until the Sessions chapter.

Servlets are controlled by the Container

In chapter two we looked at the Container's overall role in a servlet's life—it creates the request and response objects, creates or allocates a new thread for the servlet, and calls the servlet's service() method, passing the request and response references as arguments. Here's a quick review...

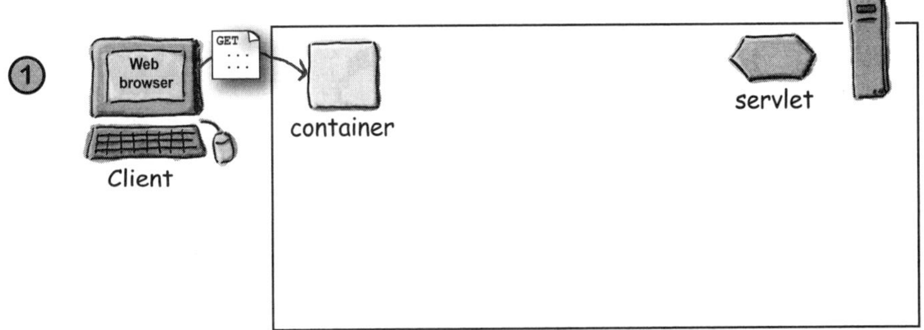

User clicks a link that has a URL to a servlet.

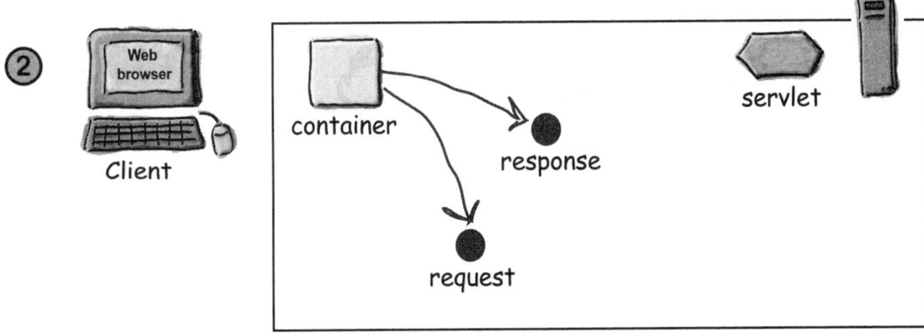

The Container "sees" that the request is for a servlet, so the container creates two objects:

1) HttpServletResponse

2) HttpServletRequest

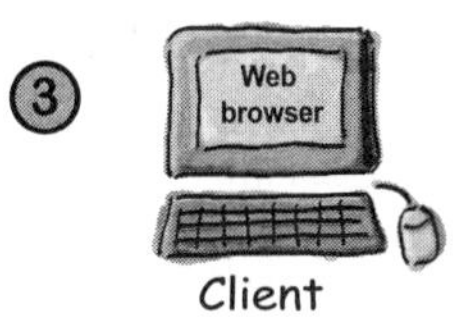

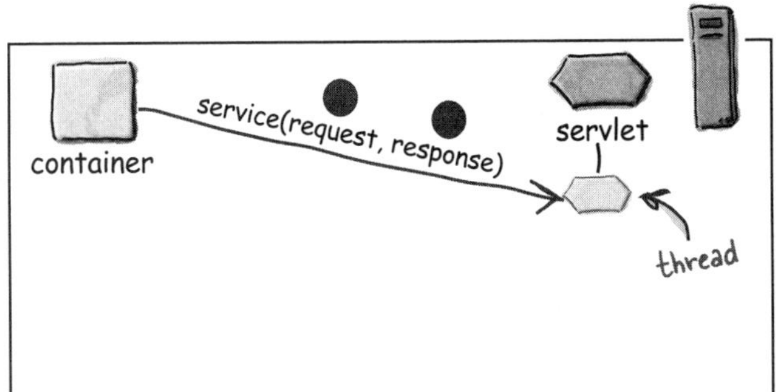

The Container finds the correct servlet based on the URL in the request, creates or allocates a thread for that request, and calls the servlet's service() method, passing the request and response objects as arguments.

The story continues...

4

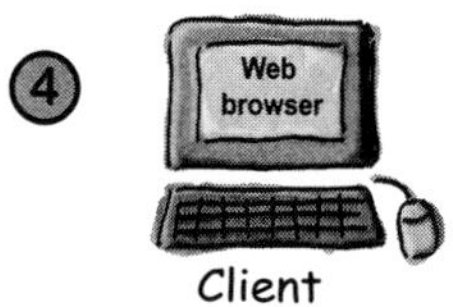

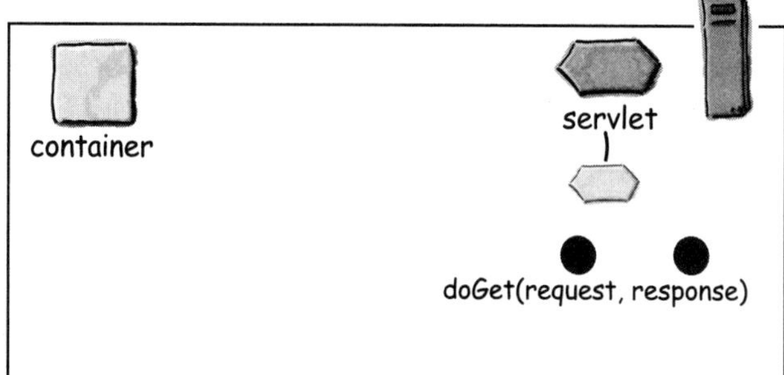

The service() method figures out which servlet method to call based on the HTTP Method (GET, POST, etc.) sent by the client.

The client sent an HTTP GET request, so the service() method calls the servlet's doGet() method, passing the request and response objects as arguments.

5

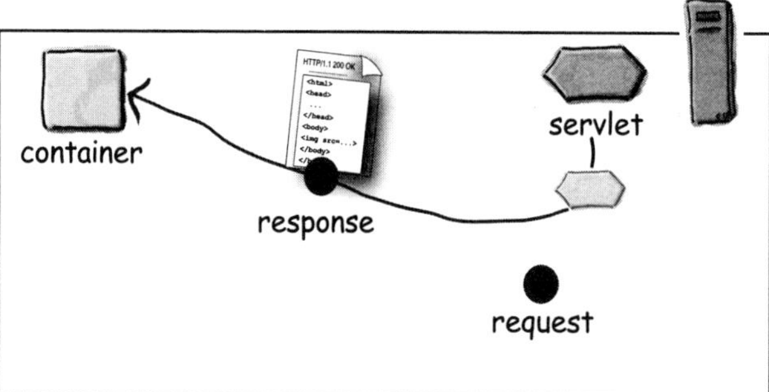

The servlet uses the response object to write out the response to the client. The response goes back through the Container.

6

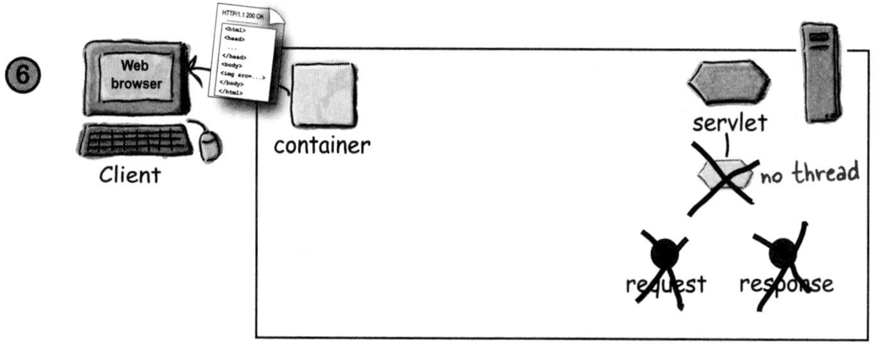

The service() method completes, so the thread either dies or returns to a Container-managed thread pool. The request and response object references fall out of scope, so these objects are toast (ready for garbage collection).

The client gets the response.

But there's more to a servlet's life

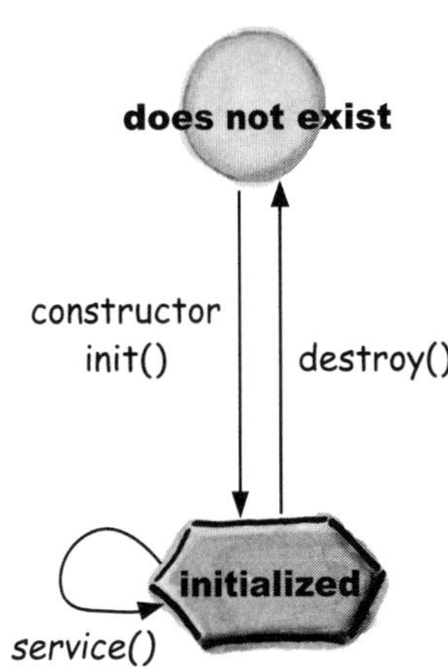

We stepped into the middle of the servlet's life, but that still leaves questions: when was the servlet class loaded? When did the servlet's constructor run? How long does the servlet object live? When should your servlet initialize resources? When should it clean up its resources?

The servlet lifecycle is simple; there's only one main state—***initialized***. If the servlet isn't initialized, then it's either *being initialized* (running its constructor or init()method), *being destroyed* (running its destroy() method), or it simply ***does not exist.***

Web Container | **Servlet Class** | **Servlet Object**

Container

Load class → AServlet.class

Instantiate servlet (constructor runs)

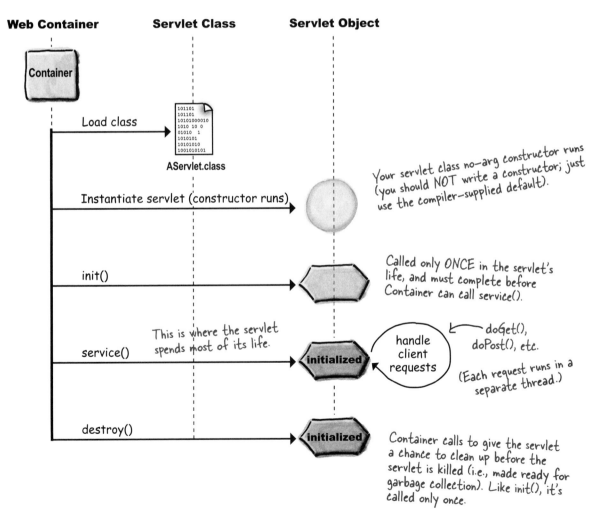

Your servlet class no-arg constructor runs (you should NOT write a constructor; just use the compiler-supplied default).

init()

Called only ONCE in the servlet's life, and must complete before Container can call service().

service() → initialized

This is where the servlet spends most of its life.

handle client requests

doGet(), doPost(), etc.

(Each request runs in a separate thread.)

destroy() → initialized

Container calls to give the servlet a chance to clean up before the servlet is killed (i.e., made ready for garbage collection). Like init(), it's called only once.

Your servlet <u>inherits</u> the lifecycle methods

NOTE: do <u>NOT</u> try to memorize all of these now! Just get a feel for how the API works...

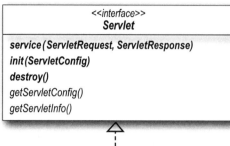

<<interface>>
Servlet

service(ServletRequest, ServletResponse)
init(ServletConfig)
destroy()
getServletConfig()
getServletInfo()

Servlet interface
(javax.servlet.Servlet)

The Servlet interface says that all servlets have these five methods (the three in bold are lifecycle methods).

GenericServlet

service(ServletRequest, ServletResponse)
init(ServletConfig)
init()
destroy()
getServletConfig()
getServletInfo()
getInitParameter(String)
getInitParameterNames()
getServletContext()
log(String)
log(String, Throwable)

GenericServlet class
(javax.servlet.GenericServlet)

GenericServlet is an abstract class that implements most of the basic servlet methods you'll need, including those from the Servlet interface. You will probably NEVER extend this class yourself. Most of your servlet's "servlet behavior" comes from this class.

HttpServlet

service(HttpServletRequest, HttpServletResponse)
service(ServletRequest, ServletResponse)
doGet(HttpServletRequest, HttpServletResponse)
doPost(HttpServletRequest, HttpServletResponse)
doHead(HttpServletRequest, HttpServletResponse)
doOptions(HttpServletRequest, HttpServletResponse)
doPut(HttpServletRequest, HttpServletResponse)
doTrace(HttpServletRequest, HttpServletResponse)
doDelete(HttpServletRequest, HttpServletResponse)
getLastModified(HttpServletRequest)

HttpServlet class
(javax.servlet.http.HttpServlet)

HttpServlet (also an abstract class) implements the service() method to reflect the HTTPness of the servlet—the service() method doesn't take just ANY old servlet request and response, but an HTTP-specific request and response.

MyServlet

doPost(HttpServletRequest, HttpServletResponse)
myBizMethod()

MyServlet class
(com.wickedlysmart.foo)

Most of your servletness is handled by superclass methods. All you do is override the HTTP methods you need.

The Three Big Lifecycle Moments

init()

When it's called

The Container calls init() on the servlet instance *after* the servlet instance is created but *before* the servlet can service any client requests.

What it's for

Gives you a chance to initialize your servlet before handling any client requests.

Do you override it?

Possibly.

If you have initialization code (like getting a database connection or registering yourself with other objects), then you'll override the init() method in your servlet class.

service()

When it's called

When the first client request comes in, the Container starts a new thread or allocates a thread from the pool, and causes the servlet's service() method to be invoked.

What it's for

This method looks at the request, determines the HTTP method (GET, POST, etc.) and invokes the matching doGet(), doPost(), etc. on the servlet.

Do you override it?

No. Very unlikely.

You should NOT override the service() method. Your job is to override the doGet() and/or doPost() methods and let the service() implementation from HTTPServlet worry about calling the right one.

doGet()

and/or

doPost()

When it's called

The service() method invokes doGet() or doPost() based on the HTTP method (GET, POST, etc.) from the request.

(We're including only doGet() and doPost() here, because those two are probably the only ones you'll ever use.)

What it's for

This is where *your* code begins! This is the method that's responsible for whatever the heck your web app is supposed to be DOING.

You can call other methods on other objects, of course, but it all starts from here.

Do you override it?

ALWAYS at least ONE of them! (doGet() or doPost())

Whichever one(s) you override tells the Container what you support. If you don't override doPost(), for example, then you're telling the Container that this servlet does not support HTTP POST requests.

I think I got this... so the Container calls my servlet's init() method, but if I don't override init(), the one from GenericServlet runs. Then when a request comes in, the Container starts or allocates a thread and calls the service() method, which I *don't* override, so the service() method from HttpServlet runs. The HttpServlet service() method then calls my overridden doGet() or doPost(). So each time my doGet() or doPost() runs, it's in a separate thread.

The service() method is always called in its own stack...

Servlet initialization

Thread A

The Container calls init() on the servlet instance *after* the servlet instance is created but *before* the servlet can service any client requests.

If you have initialization code (like getting a database connection or registering yourself with other objects), then you'll override the init() method in your servlet class. Otherwise, the init() method from GenericServlet runs.

Client request 1

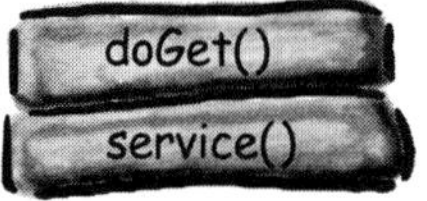

Thread B

When the first client request comes in, the Container starts (or finds) a thread and causes the servlet's service() method to be invoked.

You normally will NOT override the service() method, so the one from HttpServlet will run. The service() method figures out which HTTP method (GET, POST, etc.) is in the request, and invokes the matching doGet() or doPost() method. The doGet() and doPost() inside HttpServlet don't do anything, so you have to override one or both. This thread dies (or is put back in a Container-managed pool) when service() completes.

Client request 2

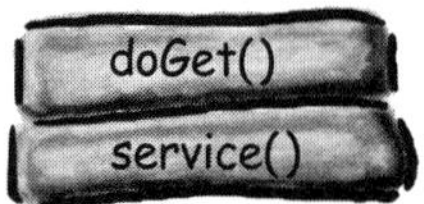

Thread C

When the second (and all other) client requests come in, the Container again creates or finds a another thread and causes the servlet's service() method to be invoked.

So, the service() -> doGet() method sequence happens each time there's a client request. At any given time, you'll have at least as many runnable threads as there are client requests, limited by the resources or policies/configuration of the Container. (You might, for example, have a Container that lets you specify the maximum number of simultaneous threads, and when the number of client requests exceeds that, some clients will just have to wait.)

Each request runs in a separate thread!

You might hear people say things like, "Each instance of the servlet..." but that's just *wrong*. There aren't multiple *instances* of any servlet class, except in one special case (called SingleThreadModel, which is inherently evil), but we're not talking about that special case yet.

The Container runs multiple *threads* to process multiple requests to a single servlet.

And every client request generates a new pair of request and response objects.

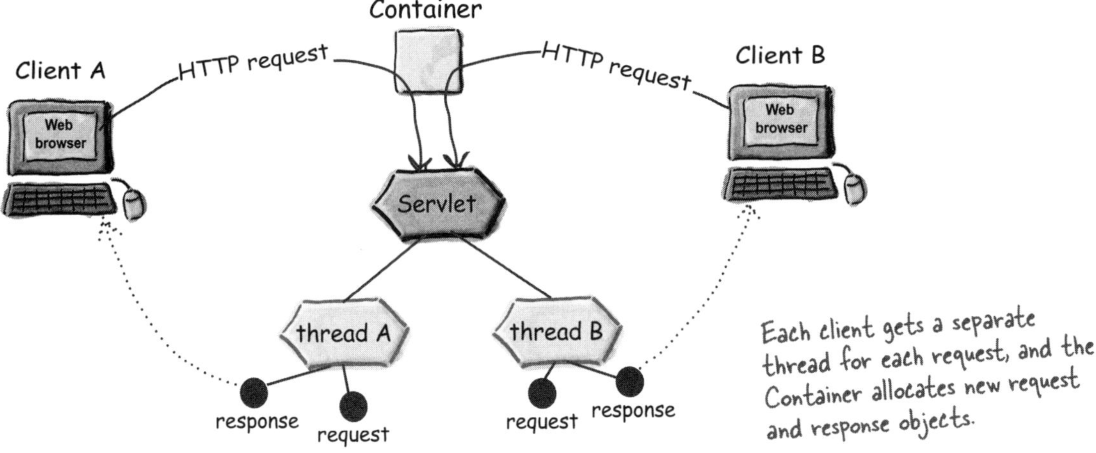

---

there are no Dumb Questions

Q: This is confusing... in the picture above you show two different clients, each with its own thread. What happens if the *same* client makes multiple requests? Is it one thread per *client* or one thread per *request*?

A: One thread per request. The Container doesn't care who makes the request—every incoming request means a new thread/stack.

Q: What if the Container uses clustering, and distributes the app on more than one JVM?

A: Imagine the picture above is for a single JVM, and each JVM has the same picture. So for a distributed web app, there would be one instance of a particular servlet per JVM, but each JVM would still have only a single instance of that servlet.

Q: I noticed that *HttpServlet* is in a different package from *GenericServlet*... how many servlet packages are there?

A: Everything related to servlets (but excluding JSP stuff) is in either *javax.servlet* or *javax.servlet.http*. And it's easy to tell the difference... things that have to do with HTTP is in the javax.servlet.http package, and the rest (generic servlet classes and interfaces) are in javax.servlet. We'll see JSP-related chapters later in the book.

In the beginning: loading and initializing

The servlet starts life when the Container finds the servlet class file. This virtually always happens when the Container starts up (for example, when you run Tomcat). When the Container starts, it looks for deployed web apps and then starts searching for servlet class files. (In the Deployment chapter, we'll go into more details of how, why, and where the Container looks for servlets.)

Finding the class is the first step.

Loading the class is the second step, and it happens either on *Container startup* or *first client use.* Your Container might give you a choice about class loading, or it might load the class whenever it wants. Regardless of whether your Container gets the servlet ready early or does it just-in-time when the first client needs it, a servlet's *service() method will not run until the servlet is fully initialized.*

Your servlet is always loaded and initialized BEFORE it can service its first client request.

init() always completes before the first call to service()

FLEX YOUR MIND

Why is there an init() method? In other words, why isn't the *constructor* enough for initializing a servlet?

What kind of code would you put in the init() method?

Hint: the init() method takes an object reference argument. What do you think the argument to the init() method might be, and how (or why) would you use it?

does not exist
constructor
init()
destroy()
initialized
service()

The init() runs only once in a servlet's life, so don't blow it! And don't try to do things too soon... the constructor is too early to do servlet-specific things.

Servlet Initialization: when an object becomes a servlet

The proudest moment of my life is when the Grand Master Container makes me a *servlet*, by making a ServletConfig for me, and calling my init(). Before that, I'm just an ordinary object. But as a servlet, I have special privileges (besides the secret handshake), like the ability to log events, get references to other resources, and store attributes for other servlets...

A servlet moves from *does not exist* to *initialized* (which really means *ready to service client requests*), beginning with a constructor. But the constructor makes only an *object*, not a *servlet*. To be a servlet, the object needs to be granted *servletness*.

When an object becomes a servlet, it gets all the unique privileges that come with being a servlet, like the ability to use its *ServletContext* reference to get information from the Container.

Why do we care about initialization details?

Because somewhere between the constructor and the init() method, the servlet is in a *Schroedinger's* servlet* state. You might have servlet initialization code, like getting web app configuration info, or looking up a reference to another part of the application, that will **fail** if you run it too *early* in the servlet's life. It's pretty simple though, if you remember to put nothing in the servlet's constructor!

There's nothing that can't wait until init().

* If your quantum mechanics is a little rusty—you might want to do a Google search on "Schroedinger's Cat". (Warning: pet lovers, just don't go there.) When we refer to a *Schroedinger state*, we mean something that is neither fully dead or fully alive, but in some really weird place in between.

What does 'being a servlet' buy you?

What happens when a servlet goes from this:

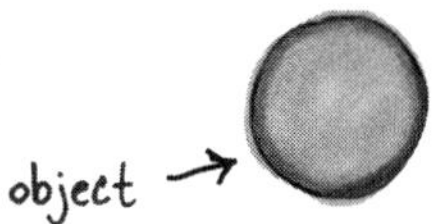

to this?

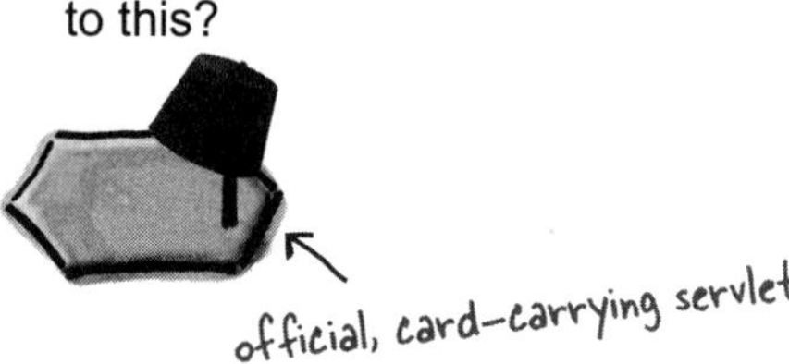

Don't confuse ServletConfig parameters with ServletContext parameters!

*We don't really talk about these until the **next** chapter, but so many people get them confused that we want to plant the seed early: **pay attention to the differences.***

*Start by looking at the names: Servlet**Config** has the word "config" in it for "configuration". It's about deploy-time values you've configured for the servlet (one per servlet). Things your servlet might want to access that you don't want to hard code, like maybe a database name.*

ServletConfig parameters won't change for as long as this servlet is deployed and running. To change them, you'll have to redeploy the servlet.

*Servlet**Context** should have been named AppContext (but they didn't listen to us), because there's only one per web app, NOT one per servlet. Anyway, we'll get into all this in the next chapter—this is just a heads-up.*

① A ServletConfig object

- One ServletConfig object per servlet.
- Use it to pass deploy-time information to the servlet (a database or enterprise bean lookup name, for example) that you don't want to hard-code into the servlet (servlet init parameters).
- Use it to access the ServletContext.
- Parameters are configured in the Deployment Descriptor.

② A ServletContext

- One ServletContext per web app. (They should have named it AppContext.)
- Use it to access web app *parameters* (also configured in the Deployment Descriptor).
- Use it as a kind of application bulletin-board, where you can put up messages (called attributes) that other parts of the application can access (way more on this in the next chapter).
- Use it to get server info, including the name and version of the Container, and the version of the API that's supported.

But a Servlet's REAL job is to handle requests. That's when a servlet's life has meaning.

In the next chapter we'll look at ServletConfig and ServletContext, but for now, we're digging into details of the request and response. Because the ServletConfig and ServletContext exist only to support your servlet's One True Job: to handle client requests! So before we look at how your context and config objects can help you do your job, we have to back up a little and look at the fundamentals of the request and response.

You already know that you're handed a request and response as arguments to the doGet() or doPost() method, but what *powers* do those request and response objects give you? What can you do with them and why do you care?

Sharpen your pencil

Label the missing pieces (the empty boxes) of this lifecycle timeline. (Check your answers with the timeline shown earlier in this chapter.)

Add your own annotations as well to help you remember the details.

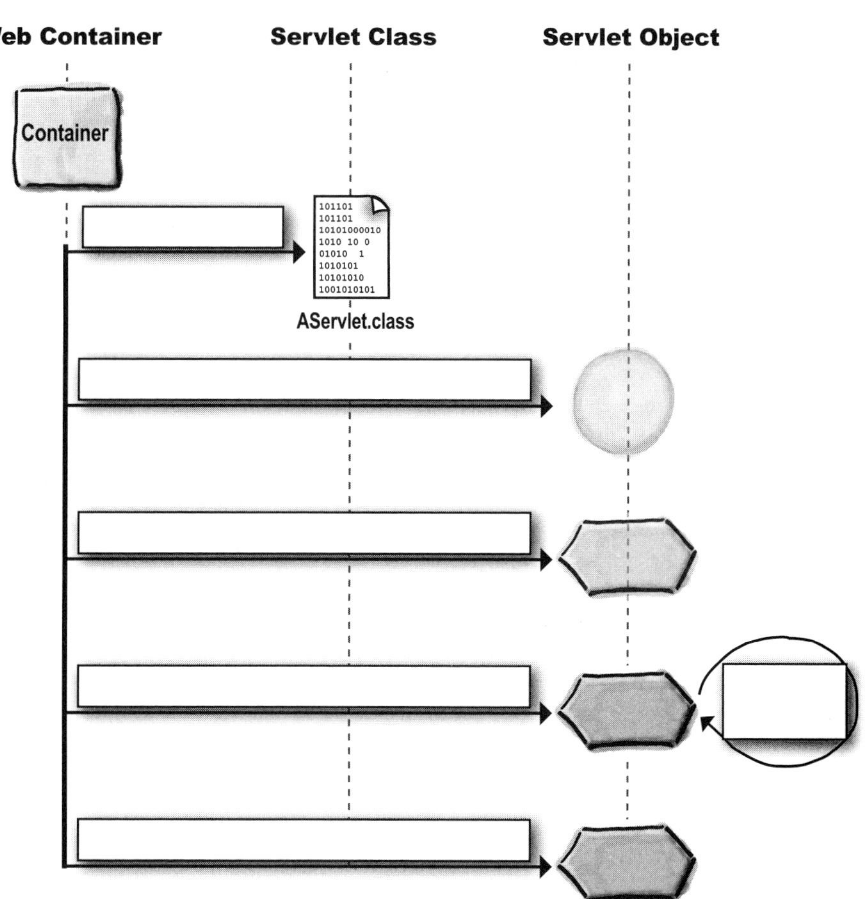

Request and Response: the key to everything, and the arguments to service()*

ServletRequest interface
(javax.servlet.ServletRequest)

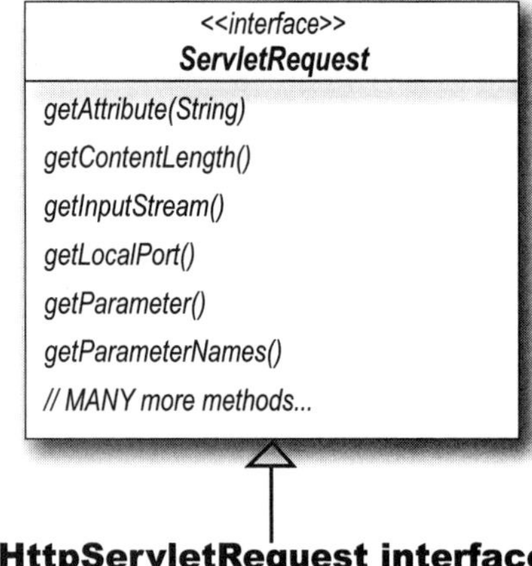

ServletResponse interface
(javax.servlet.ServletResponse)

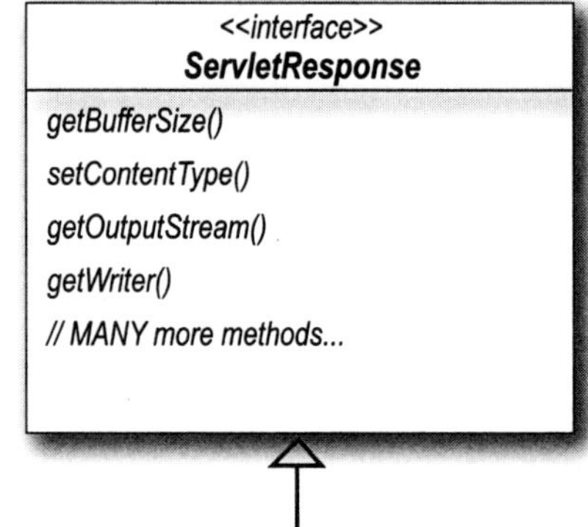

HttpServletRequest interface
(javax.servlet.http.HttpServletRequest)

<<interface>>
HttpServletRequest

getContextPath()
getCookies()
getHeader(String)
getQueryString()
getSession()
getMethod()
// MANY more methods...

The HttpServletRequest methods are about HTTP things like cookies, headers, and sessions.

HttpServletRequest interface adds the methods that relate to the HTTP protocol... what your servlet uses to communicate with the client/browser.

HttpServletResponse interface
(javax.servlet.http.HttpServletResponse)

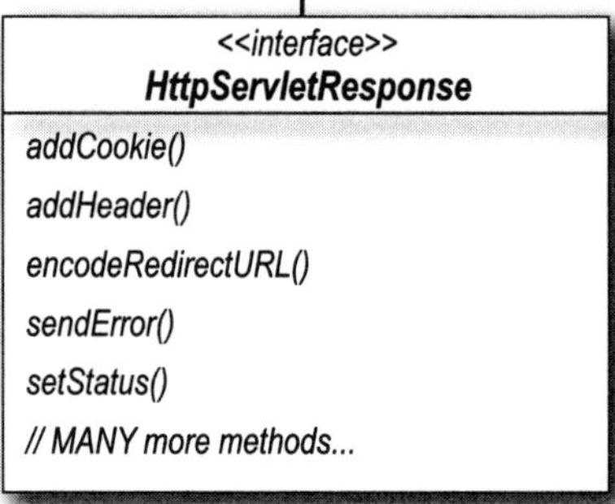

Same thing with the response... the HttpServletResponse adds methods you care about when you're using HTTP—things like errors, cookies, and headers.

*The request and response objects are also arguments to the *other* HttpServlet methods that *you* write— doGet(), doPost(), etc.

there are no Dumb Questions

Q: Who implements the interfaces for HttpServletRequest and HttpServletResponse? Are those classes in the API?

A: The Container, and No. The classes aren't in the API because they're left to the vendor to implement. The good news is, you don't have to worry about it. Just trust that when the service() method is called in your servlet, it'll be handed references to two perfectly good objects that *implement* HttpServletRequest and HttpServletResponse. You should never care about the actual implementation class name or type. All you care about is that you'll get something that has all the functionality from HttpServletRequest and HttpServletResponse.

In other words, all you need to know are *the methods you can call* on the objects the Container gives you as part of the request! The actual class in which they're implemented doesn't matter to you—you're referring to the request and response objects *only by the interface type.*

Q: Am I reading this UML correctly? Are those interfaces *extending* interfaces?

A: Yes. Remember, interfaces can have their own inheritance tree. When one interface *extends* another interface (which is all they *can* do—interfaces can't *implement* interfaces), it means that whoever implements an interface must implement *all* the methods defined in both the interface and its superinterfaces. This means, for example, that whoever implements HttpServletRequest must provide implementation methods for the methods declared in the HttpServletRequest interface and the methods in the ServletRequest interface.

Q: I'm still confused about why there's a GenericServlet and ServletRequest and ServletResponse. If nobody's doing anything except HTTP servlets... then what's the point?

A: We didn't say *nobody*. Somebody, somewhere, one could imagine, is using the servlet technology model without the HTTP protocol. Just nobody we've met personally or read about. Ever.

Still, the flexibility was designed into the servlet model for those who might want to use servlets with, say, SMTP or perhaps a proprietary custom protocol. The only support built-in to the API, though, is for HTTP, and that's what virtually everyone's using.

The exam doesn't expect you to know how to develop with non-HTTP servlets.

You're not expected to know anything about how you might use servlets with a protocol other than HTTP. You are, however, still supposed to know how the class hierarchy works. So you DO have to know that HttpServletRequest and HttpServletResponse extend from ServletRequest and ServletResponse, and that most of an HttpServlet's implementation actually comes from GenericServlet.

But that's it. The exam assumes you're an HttpServlet developer.

The HTTP request Method determines whether doGet() or doPost() runs

The client's request, remember, always includes a specific HTTP Method. If the HTTP Method is a GET, the service() method calls doGet(). If the HTTP request Method is a POST, the service() method calls doPost().

```
GET /select/selectBeerTaste.
do?color=dark&taste=malty
HTTP/1.1
Host: www.wickedlysmart.com
User-Agent: M
U; PPC Mac OS
rv:1.4) Gecko/
Accept: text/
xml,applicati
html;q=0.9,t
```

```
POST /select/selectBeer-
Taste2.do HTTP/1.1
Host: www.wickedlysmart.com
User-Agent: Mozilla/5.0 (Macintosh;
U; PPC Mac OS X Mach-O; en-US;
rv:1.4) Gecko/20030624 Netscape/7.1
Accept: text/xml,application/
xml,application/xhtml+xml,text/
html;q=0.9,text/plain;q=0.8,video/x-
mng,image/png,image/jpeg,image/
gif;q=0.2,*/*;q=0.1
```

HTTP requests

You keep showing doGet() and doPost() like they're the only ones... but I KNOW there are ***eight*** methods in HTTP 1.1.

You probably won't care about any HTTP Methods except GET and POST

Yes, there *are* other HTTP 1.1 Methods besides GET and POST. There's also HEAD, TRACE, OPTIONS, PUT, DELETE, and CONNECT.

All but one of the eight has a matching doXXX() method in the HttpServlet class, so besides doGet() and doPost(), you've got doOptions(), doHead(), doTrace(), doPut(), and doDelete(). There's no mechanism in the servlet API for handling doConnect(), so it's not part of HttpServlet.

But while the other HTTP Methods might matter to, say, a web serv*er* developer, a serv*let* developer rarely uses anything but GET and POST.

For most (or probably *all*) servlet development, you'll use either doGet() (for simple requests) or doPost() (to accept and process form data), and you won't have to think about the others.

So if they're not important to me... of COURSE that means they'll be on the exam.

Actually, one or more of the other HTTP Methods might make a (brief) appearance on the exam...

If you're preparing for the exam, you should be able to recognize all of them from a list, and have at least the briefest idea of what they're used for. But don't spend much time here!

In the real servlet world, you care about GET and POST.

In the exam world, you care just a tiny bit about the other HTTP Methods as well.

GET Asks to *get* the thing (resource / file) at the requested URL.

POST Asks the server to *accept* the body info attached to the request, and give it to the thing at the requested URL It's like a fat GET... a GET with extra info sent with the request.

HEAD Asks for only the *header* part of whatever a GET would return. So it's just like GET, but with no body in the response. Gives you info about the requested URL without actually getting back the real *thing.*

TRACE Asks for a loopback of the request message, so that the client can see what's being received on the other end, for testing or troubleshooting.

PUT Says to *put* the enclosed info (the body) at the requested URL.

DELETE Says to *delete* the thing (resource / file) at the requested URL.

OPTIONS Asks for a *list* of the HTTP methods to which the thing at the requested URL can respond.

CONNECT Says to *connect* for the purposes of tunneling.

Example of a response to an HTTP OPTIONS request:

```
HTTP/1.1 200 OK
Server: Apache-Coyote/1.1
Date: Thu, 20 Apr 2004 16:
20:00 GMT
Allow: OPTIONS, TRACE,
GET, HEAD, POST
Content-Length: 0
```

The difference between GET and POST

POST has a body. That's the key. Both GET and POST can send parameters, but with GET, the parameter data is limited to what you can stuff into the Request line.

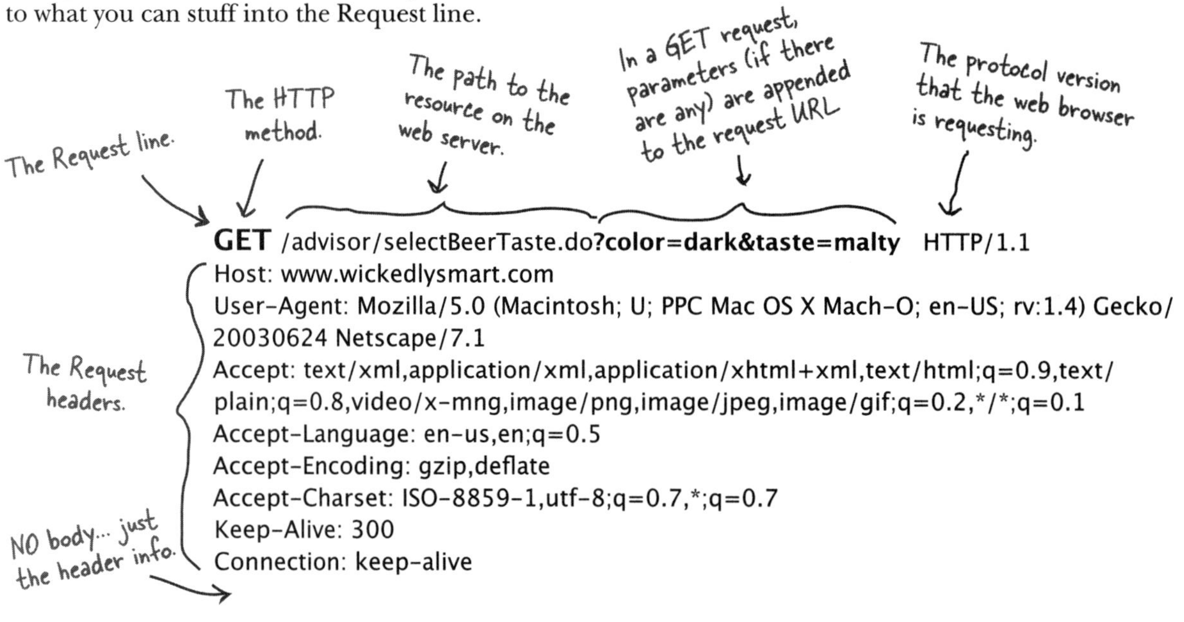

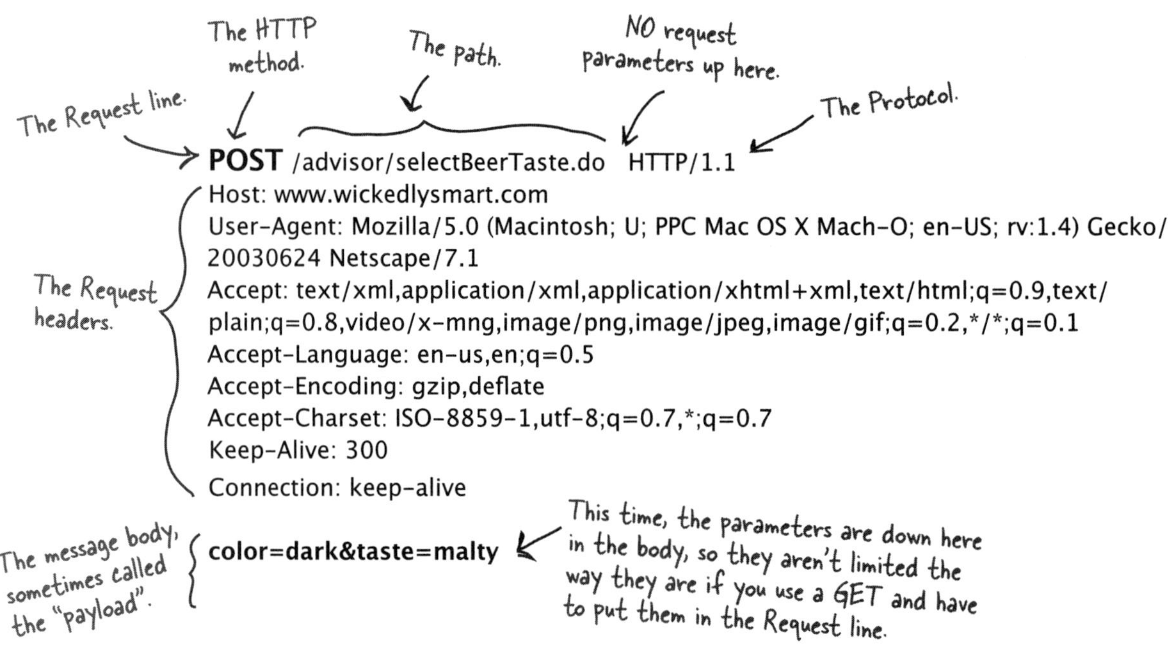

The HTTP method.
The path.
NO request parameters up here.
The Request line.
The Protocol.
POST /advisor/selectBeerTaste.do HTTP/1.1
Host: www.wickedlysmart.com
User-Agent: Mozilla/5.0 (Macintosh; U; PPC Mac OS X Mach-O; en-US; rv:1.4) Gecko/20030624 Netscape/7.1
Accept: text/xml,application/xml,application/xhtml+xml,text/html;q=0.9,text/plain;q=0.8,video/x-mng,image/png,image/jpeg,image/gif;q=0.2,*/*;q=0.1
Accept-Language: en-us,en;q=0.5
Accept-Encoding: gzip,deflate
Accept-Charset: ISO-8859-1,utf-8;q=0.7,*;q=0.7
Keep-Alive: 300
Connection: keep-alive
The Request headers.
color=dark&taste=malty
The message body, sometimes called the "payload".
This time, the parameters are down here in the body, so they aren't limited the way they are if you use a GET and have to put them in the Request line.

Sounds like the difference between GET and POST is the *size* of the parameter data you can send?

No, it's not just about the size

We talked about other issues with GET in chapter one, remember?

When you use GET, the parameter data shows up in the browser's input bar, right after actual URL (and separated with a "?"). Imagine a scenario in which you would not want the parameters to be visible.

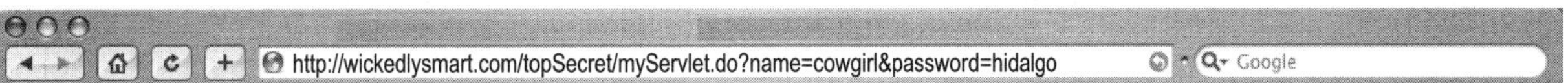

So, security might be another issue.

Still another issue is whether you need or want end-users to be able to bookmark the request page. GET requests can be bookmarked; POST requests cannot. That might be really important if you have, say, a page that lets users specify search criteria. The users might want to come back a week later and try the same search again now that there's new data on the server.

But *besides* size, security, and bookmarking, there's another crucial difference between GET and POST—the way they're *supposed* to be used. GET is meant to be used for *getting* things. Period. Simple retrieval. Sure, you might use the parameters to help figure out what to send back, but the point is—you're not making any changes on the server! POST is meant to be used for *sending data to be processed.* This could be as simple as query parameters used to figure out what to send back, just as with a GET, but when you think of POST, think: *update.* Think: use the data from the POST body to *change something on the server.*

And that brings up another issue... whether the request is *idempotent.* If it's *not,* you could get into the kind of trouble a little blue pill can't fix. If you're not familiar with the way the term "idempotent" is used in the web world, keep reading...

The story of the non-idempotent request

Diane has a need. She's trying desperately to purchase Head First Knitting from the Wickedly Smart online book shop which, unbeknownst to Diane, is still in beta. Diane's low on money—she has just enough in her debit account to cover *one* book. She considered buying directly from Amazon or the O'Reilly.com site, but decided she wanted an *autographed* copy, available only from the Wickedly Smart site. A choice she would later come to regret...

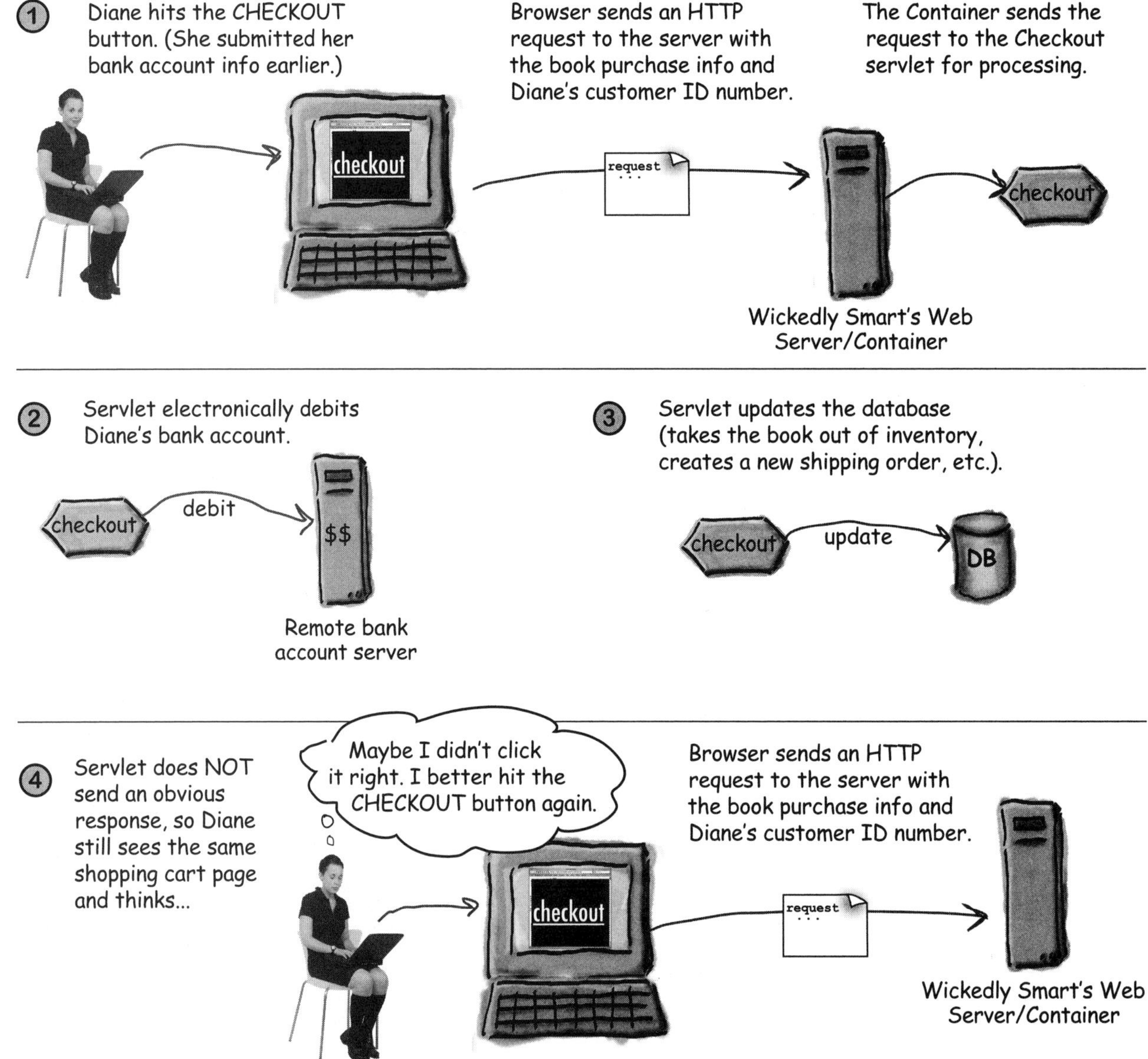

1
Diane hits the CHECKOUT button. (She submitted her bank account info earlier.)
checkout
Browser sends an HTTP request to the server with the book purchase info and Diane's customer ID number.
request
The Container sends the request to the Checkout servlet for processing.
checkout
Wickedly Smart's Web Server/Container
2
Servlet electronically debits Diane's bank account.
checkout
debit
$$
Remote bank account server
3
Servlet updates the database (takes the book out of inventory, creates a new shipping order, etc.).
checkout
update
DB
4
Servlet does NOT send an obvious response, so Diane still sees the same shopping cart page and thinks...
Maybe I didn't click it right. I better hit the CHECKOUT button again.
checkout
Browser sends an HTTP request to the server with the book purchase info and Diane's customer ID number.
request
Wickedly Smart's Web Server/Container

Our story continues...

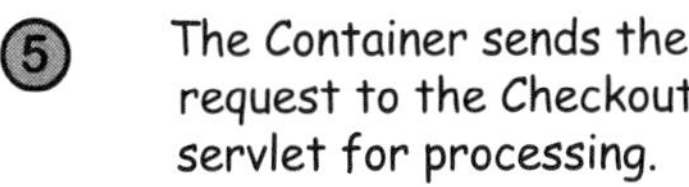

5 The Container sends the request to the Checkout servlet for processing.

Wickedly Smart's Web Server/Container

6 The servlet does not have a problem with Diane buying the same book she bought before.

I guess she really likes this knitting book a lot... she's buying it twice. Cool.

checkout

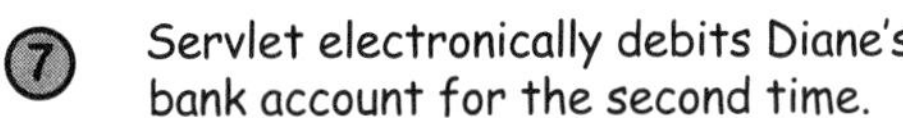

7 Servlet electronically debits Diane's bank account for the second time.

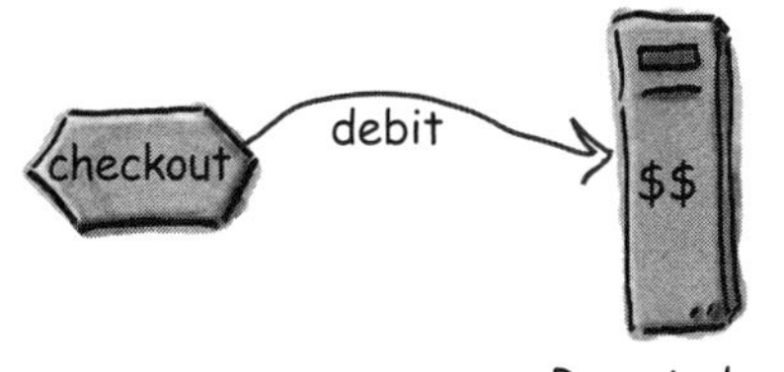

Remote bank account server

8 Diane's bank accepts the debit, but charges her a hefty overdraft fee.

We'll let her buy this book, but we'll charge her an extra $25.00 for being overdrawn. Bad, bad Diane!

Remote bank account server

---

9 Eventually Diane navigates to the Check Order Status page and sees that she has TWO orders for the knitting book...

This is not right... I meant to buy only ONE book. What stupid web app developer made THIS? It should have recognized a duplicate transaction...

10 Hello bank? This wickedly stupid web programmer made a mistake...

Which of the HTTP methods do you think are (or should be) idempotent? (Based on your previous understanding of the word and/or the Diane double-purchase story you just read.) Answers are at the bottom of this page.)

- ❑ GET
- ❑ POST
- ❑ PUT
- ❑ HEAD

(We left off CONNECT deliberately, since it's not part of HttpServlet.)

FLEX YOUR MIND

What went wrong with Diane's transaction?

(And it's not just ONE thing... there are probably several problems the developer must fix.)

What are some of the ways in which a developer could reduce the risk of this?

(Hint: they might not all be *programmatic* solutions.)

The HTTP 1.1 spec declares GET, HEAD, and PUT as idempotent, even though you CAN write a non-idempotent doGet() method yourself (but shouldn't). POST is considered idempotent by the HTTP 1.1 spec.

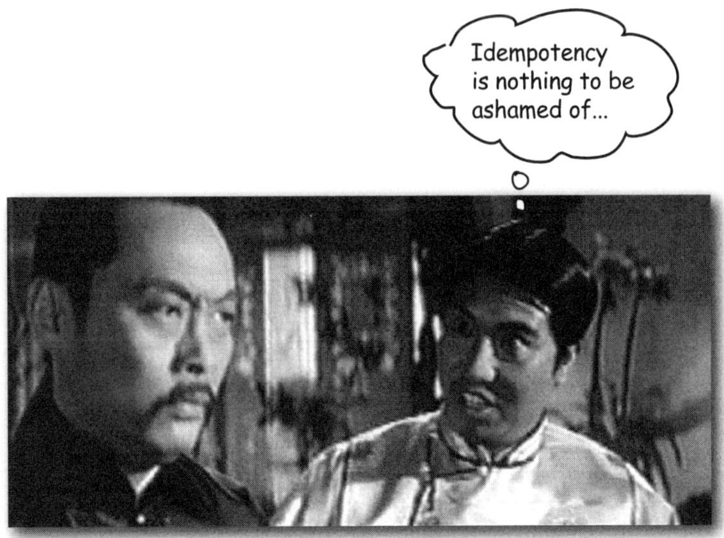

Being idempotent is GOOD. It means you can do the same thing over and over again, with no unwanted side effects!

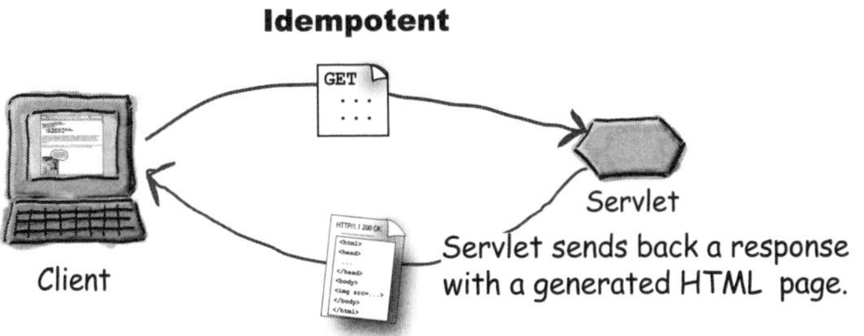

Idempotent
GET
Servlet
Servlet sends back a response
with a generated HTML page.
Client

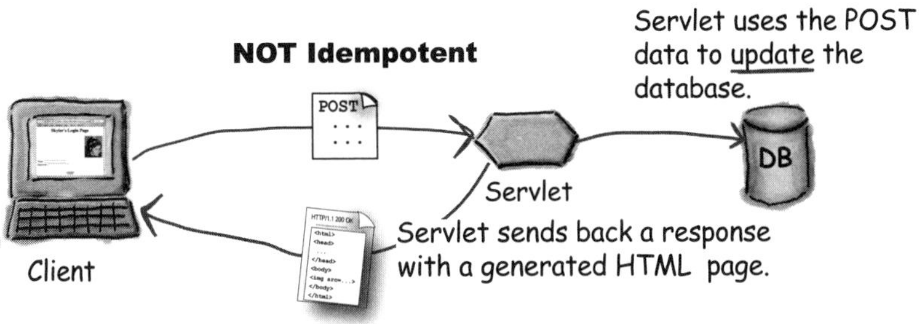

NOT Idempotent
Servlet uses the POST
data to update the
database.
POST
DB
Servlet
Servlet sends back a response
with a generated HTML page.
Client

POST is not idempotent

An HTTP GET is just for *getting* things, and it's not supposed to *change* anything on the server. So a GET is, by definition (and according to the HTTP spec) idempotent. It can be executed more than once without any bad side effects.

POST is *not* idempotent—the data submitted in the body of a POST might be destined for a transaction that can't be reversed. So you have to be careful with your doPost() functionality!

GET is idempotent. POST is not. It's up to *you* to make sure that your web app logic can handle scenarios like Diane's, where the POST comes in more than once.

What's to stop me from using the parameters in GET to update the server?

GET is always considered idempotent in HTTP 1.1...

...even if you see code on the exam that uses the GET parameters in a way that causes side-effects! In other words, ***GET is idempotent according to the HTTP spec.*** *But there's nothing to stop you from implementing a non-idempotent doGet() method in your servlet. The client's GET request is supposed to be idempotent, even if what YOU do with the data causes side-effects. Always keep in mind the difference between the HTTP GET method and your servlet's doGet() method.*

Note: there are several different uses of the word "idempotent"; we're using it in the HTTP/servlet way to mean that the same request can be made twice with no negative consequences on the server. We do *not* use "idempotent" to mean that the same request always returns the same response, and we do NOT mean that a request has NO side effects.

What determines whether the browser sends a GET or POST request?

GET

a simple hyperlink always means a GET.

```
<A HREF="http://www.wickedlysmart.com/index.html/">click here</A>
```

POST

if you explicitly SAY method="POST", then, surprisingly, it's a POST.

```
<form method="POST"  action="SelectBeer.do">
  Select beer characteristics<p>
  <select name="color" size="1">
    <option>light
    <option>amber
    <option>brown
    <option>dark
  </select>
  <center>
    <input type="SUBMIT">
  </center>
</form>
```

When the user clicks the "SUBMIT" button, the parameters are sent in the body of the POST request. In this example, there's just one parameter, named "color", and the value is the <option> beer color the user selected (light, amber, brown, or dark).

What happens if you do NOT say method="POST" in your <form>?

This time, there's no method="POST" here.

```
<form  action="SelectBeer.do">
  Select beer characteristics<p>
  <select name="color" size="1">
    <option>light
    <option>amber
    <option>brown
    <option>dark
  </select>
  <center>
    <input type="SUBMIT">
  </center>
</form>
```

NOW what happens to the parameters when the user clicks SUBMIT, if the form doesn't have a method= "POST"?

POST is NOT the default!

If you don't put **method="POST"** into your form, the default is an HTTP GET request. That means the browser sends the parameters in the request header, but that's the least of your problems. Because if the request comes in as a GET, that means you'll run into big trouble at runtime if you have only a doPost() and not a doGet() in your servlet!

If you do this:

No "method=POST" in the HTML form.

```
<form   action="SelectBeer.do">
```

And then this:

```
public class BeerSelect extends HttpServlet {

   public void doPost(HttpServletRequest request, HttpServletResponse response)
                                                throws IOException, ServletException {
     // code here
   }

}
```

No doGet() method in the servlet.

You'll get this:

FAILURE! If your HTML form uses GET instead of POST, then you MUST have doGet() in your servlet class. The default method for forms is GET.

Q: What if I want to support both GET and POST from a single servlet?

A: Developers who want to support both methods usually put logic in doGet(), then delegate to doGet() from the doPost() method if needed.

```
public void doPost(...)
                     throws ... {
   doGet(request, response);
}
```

Sending and using a single parameter

HTML form

```
<form method="POST"   action="SelectBeer.do">
  Select beer characteristics<p>
  <select name="color" size="1">
    <option>light
    <option>amber
    <option>brown
    <option>dark
  </select>
  <center>
    <input type="SUBMIT">
  </center>
</form>
```

The browser will send one of these four options in the request body, for the parameter named "color". For example, "color=amber".

HTTP POST request

```
POST /advisor/SelectBeer.do HTTP/1.1
Host: www.wickedlysmart.com
User-Agent: Mozilla/5.0 (Macintosh; U; PPC Mac OS X Mach-O; en-US; rv:1.4) Gecko/20030624
Netscape/7.1
Accept: text/xml,application/xml,application/xhtml+xml,text/html;q=0.9,text/
plain;q=0.8,video/x-mng,image/png,image/jpeg,image/gif;q=0.2,*/*;q=0.1
Accept-Language: en-us,en;q=0.5
Accept-Encoding: gzip,deflate
Accept-Charset: ISO-8859-1,utf-8;q=0.7,*;q=0.7
Keep-Alive: 300
Connection: keep-alive

color=dark
```

Remember, the browser generates this request, so you don't have to worry about creating it, but here's what it looks like coming over to the server...

Servlet class

```
public void doPost(HttpServletRequest request, HttpServletResponse response)
                                              throws IOException, ServletException {
   String colorParam = request.getParameter("color");
     // more enlightening code here...
}
```

(In this example, the String colorParam has a value of "dark".)

This matches the name in the form.

Sending and using TWO parameters

HTML form

```
<form method="POST"   action="SelectBeerTaste.do">
  Select beer characteristics<p>
  COLOR:
  <select name="color" size="1">
    <option>light
    <option>amber
    <option>brown
    <option>dark
  </select>
  BODY:
  <select name="body" size="1">
    <option>light
    <option>medium
    <option>heavy
  </select>
  <center>
    <input type="SUBMIT">
  </center>
</form>
```

The browser will send one of these four options in the request, associated with the name "color".

The browser will send one of these three options in the request, associated with the name "body".

HTTP POST request

POST /advisor/SelectBeerTaste.do HTTP/1.1
Host: www.wickedlysmart.com
User-Agent: Mozilla/5.0 (Macintosh; U; PPC Mac OS X Mach-O; en-US; rv:1.4) Gecko/20030624 Netscape/7.1
Accept: text/xml,application/xml,application/xhtml+xml,text/html;q=0.9,text/plain;q=0.8,video/x-mng,image/png,image/jpeg,image/gif;q=0.2,*/*;q=0.1
Accept-Language: en-us,en;q=0.5
Accept-Encoding: gzip,deflate
Accept-Charset: ISO-8859-1,utf-8;q=0.7,*;q=0.7
Keep-Alive: 300
Connection: keep-alive

color=dark&body=heavy

Now the POST request has both parameters, separated by an ampersand.

Servlet class

```
public void doPost(HttpServletRequest request, HttpServletResponse response)
                                             throws IOException, ServletException {
   String colorParam = request.getParameter("color");
   String bodyParam = request.getParameter("body");
      // more code here
}
```

Now the String variable colorParam has a value of "dark" and bodyParam has a value of "heavy".

You can have multiple values for a single parameter! That means you'll need getParameterValues() that returns an array, instead of getParameter() that returns a String.

Some form input types, like a set of checkboxes, can have more than one value. That means a single parameter ("sizes", for example) will have multiple values, depending on how many boxes the user checked off. A form where a user can select multiple beer sizes (to say that he's interested in ALL of those sizes) might look like this:

```
<form method=POST
  action="SelectBeer.do">
  Select beer characteristics<p>
  Can Sizes: <p>
  <input type=checkbox name=sizes value="12oz"> 12 oz.<br>
  <input type=checkbox name=sizes value="16oz"> 16 oz.<br>
  <input type=checkbox name=sizes value="22oz"> 22 oz.<br>
  <br><br>

  <center>
    <input type="SUBMIT">
  </center>
</form>
```

In your code, you'll use the getParameterValues() method that returns an array:

```
String one = request.getParameterValues("sizes")[0];

String [] sizes = request.getParameterValues("sizes");
```

If you want to see everything in the array, just for fun or testing, you can use:

```
String [] sizes = request.getParameterValues("sizes");
for(int x=0; x < sizes.length ; x++) {
   out.println("<br>sizes: " + sizes[x]);
}
```

(assume that "out" is a PrintWriter you got from the response)

Besides parameters, what else can I get from a Request object?

The ServletRequest and HttpServletRequest interfaces have a ton of methods you can call, but you don't need to memorize them all. On your own, you *really* should look at the full API for javax.servlet.ServletRequest and javax.servlet.http.HttpServletRequest, but here we'll look at only the methods you're most likely to use in your work (and which might also show up on the exam).

In the real world, you'll be lucky (or *un*lucky, depending on your perspective), to use more than 15% of the request API. ***Don't worry if you aren't clear about how or why you'd use each of these***; we'll see more details on some of them (especially cookies) later in the book.

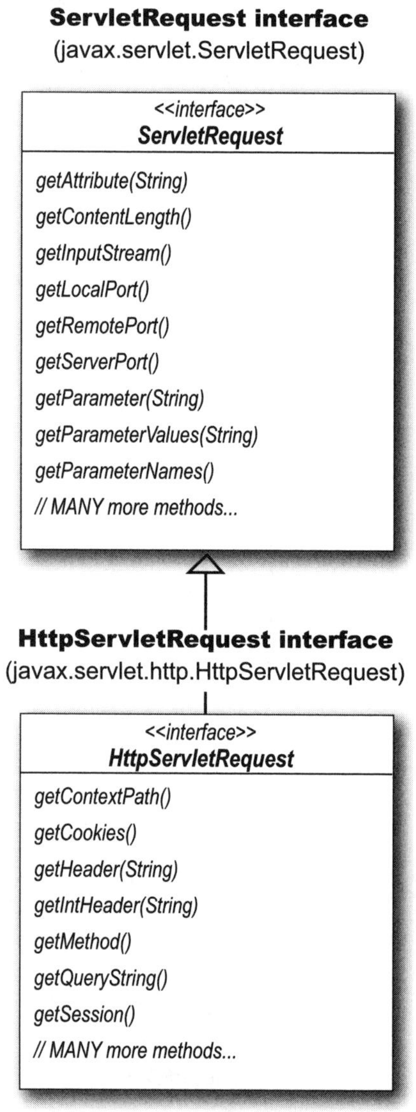

The client's *platform* and *browser* info

```
String client = request.getHeader("User-Agent");
```

The *cookies* associated with this request

```
Cookie[] cookies = request.getCookies();
```

The *session* associated with this client

```
HttpSession session = request.getSession();
```

The HTTP Method of the request

```
String theMethod = request.getMethod();
```

An *input stream* from the request

```
InputStream input = request.getInputStream();
```

ServletRequest interface
(javax.servlet.ServletRequest)

<<interface>>
ServletRequest

getAttribute(String)
getContentLength()
getInputStream()
getLocalPort()
getRemotePort()
getServerPort()
getParameter(String)
getParameterValues(String)
getParameterNames()
// MANY more methods...

HttpServletRequest interface
(javax.servlet.http.HttpServletRequest)

<<interface>>
HttpServletRequest

getContextPath()
getCookies()
getHeader(String)
getIntHeader(String)
getMethod()
getQueryString()
getSession()
// MANY more methods...

there are no Dumb Questions

Q: Why would I ever *want* to get an InputStream from the request?

A: With a GET request, there's nothing but the request header info. In other words, there's no body to care about. BUT... with an HTTP POST, there's body info. Most of the time, all you care about from the body is sucking out the parameter values (for example, "color=dark") using request.getParameter(), but those values might be large. If you want to get at the raw bytes of everything that comes in with the request, you can do it with the getInputStream() method. With the input stream you could, for example, strip out all the header info and process the raw bytes of the payload (the body) of the request, immediately writing it to a file on the server, perhaps.

Q: What's the difference between getHeader() and get*Int*Header()? Far as I can tell, headers are *always Strings!* Even the getIntHeader() method takes a String representing the name of the header, so what's the *int* about?

A: Headers have both a *name* (like "User-Agent" or "Host") and a *value* (like "Mozilla/5.0 (Macintosh; U; PPC Mac OS X Mach-O; en-US; rv:1.4) Gecko/20030624 Netscape/7.1" or "www.wickedlysmart.com"). The values that come back from headers are always in a String form, but for a few headers, the String represents a number. The "Content-Length" header returns the number of bytes that make up the message-body. The "Max-Forwards" HTTP header, for example, returns an integer indicating how many router hops the request is allowed to make. (You might want to use this header if you're trying to trace a request that you think is getting stuck in a loop somewhere.)

You could get the value of the "Max-Forwards" header by using getHeader():

```
String forwards = request.getHeader("Max-Forwards");
int forwardsNum = Integer.parseInt(forwards);
```

And that works fine. But if you *know* the value of the header is supposed to represent an int, you can use getIntHeader() as a ***convenience*** method to save the extra step of parsing the String to an int:

```
int forwardsNum = request.getIntHeader("Max-Forwards");
```

BANG!

getServerPort(), getLocalPort(), and getRemotePort() are confusing!

*The getServerPort() should be obvious... until you ask what getLocalPort() means. So let's do the easy one first: getRemotePort(). First you should ask, "remote to whom?" In this case, since it's the server asking, it's the CLIENT that's the remote thing. The client is remote to the server, so get**Remote**Port() means "get the **client's** port". In other words, the port number on the client from which the request was sent. Remember: if you're a servlet, **remote** means **client**.*

*The difference between get**Local**Port() and get**Server**Port() is more subtle—getServerPort() says, "to which port was the request originally SENT?" while getLocalPort() says, "on which port did the request END UP?" Yes, there's a difference, because although the requests are **sent** to a single port (where the **server** is listening), the server turns around and finds a **different** local port for each thread so that the app can handle multiple clients at the same time.*

Review: servlet lifecycle and API

BULLET POINTS

- The Container initializes a servlet by loading the class, invoking the servlet's no-arg constructor, and calling the servlet's init() method.
- The init() method (which the developer can override) is called only once in a servlet's life, and always before the servlet can service any client requests.
- The init() method gives the servlet access to the ServletConfig and ServletContext objects, which the servlet needs to get information about the servlet configuration and the web app.
- The Container ends a servlet's life by calling its destroy() method.
- Most of a servlet's life is spent running a service() method for a client request.
- Every request to a servlet runs in a separate thread! There is only one instance of any particular servlet class.
- Your servlet will almost always extend javax.servlet.http. HttpServlet, from which it inherits an implementation of the service() method that takes an HttpServletRequest and an HttpServletResponse.
- HttpServlet extends javax.servlet.GenericServlet—an abstract class that implements most of the basic servlet methods.
- GenericServlet implements the Servlet interface.
- Servlet classes (except those related to JSPs) are in one of two packages: javax.servlet or javax.servlet.http.
- You can override the init() method, and you must override at least one service method (doGet(), doPost(), etc.).

<<interface>>
javax.servlet.Servlet

service(ServletRequest, ServletResponse)
init(ServletConfig)
destroy()
getServletConfig()
getServletInfo()

javax.servlet.GenericServlet

service(ServletRequest, ServletResponse)
init(ServletConfig)
init()
destroy()
getServletConfig()
getServletInfo()
getInitParameter(String)
getInitParameterNames()
getServletContext()
log(String)
log(String, Throwable)

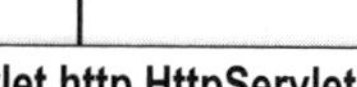

javax.servlet.http.HttpServlet

service(HttpServletRequest, HttpServletResponse)
service(ServletRequest, ServletResponse)
doGet(HttpServletRequest, HttpServletResponse)
doPost(HttpServletRequest, HttpServletResponse)
doHead(HttpServletRequest, HttpServletResponse)
doOptions(HttpServletRequest, HttpServletResponse)
doPut(HttpServletRequest, HttpServletResponse)
doTrace(HttpServletRequest, HttpServletResponse)
doDelete(HttpServletRequest, HttpServletResponse)
getLastModified(HttpServletRequest)

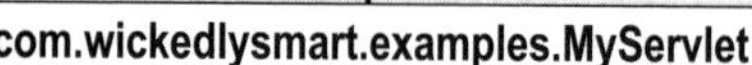

com.wickedlysmart.examples.MyServlet

doPost(HttpServletRequest, HttpServletResponse)
myBizMethod()

Review: HTTP and HttpServletRequest

BULLET POINTS

- The HttpServlet's doGet() and doPost() methods take an HttpServletRequest and an HttpServletResponse.
- The service() method determines whether doGet() or doPost() runs based on the HTTP Method (GET, POST, etc.) of the HTTP request.
- POST requests have a body; GET requests do not, although GET requests can have request parameters appended to the request URL (sometimes called "the query string").
- GET requests are inherently (according to the HTTP spec) idempotent. They should be able to run multiple times without causing any side effects on the server. GET requests shouldn't *change* anything on the server. But you *could* write a bad, non-idempotent doGet() method.
- POST is inherently not idempotent, so it's up to you to design and code your app in such a way that if the client sends a request twice by mistake, you can handle it.
- If an HTML form does not explicitly say "method=POST", the request is sent as a GET, not a POST. If you do not have a doGet() in your servlet, the request will fail.
- You can get parameters from the request with the getParameter("paramname") method. The return value is always a String.
- If you have multiple parameter values for a given parameter name, use the getParameterValues("paramname") method that returns a String array.
- You can get *other* things from the request object including headers, cookies, a session, the query string, and an input stream.

ServletRequest interface
(javax.servlet.ServletRequest)

<<*interface*>> ***ServletRequest***
getAttribute(String)
getContentLength()
getInputStream()
getLocalPort()
getRemotePort()
getServerPort()
getParameter(String)
getParameterValues(String)
getParameterNames()
// MANY more methods...

HttpServletRequest interface
(javax.servlet.http.HttpServletRequest)

<<*interface*>> ***HTTPServletRequest***
getContextPath()
getCookies()
getHeader(String)
getIntHeader(String)
getMethod()
getQueryString()
getSession()
// MANY more methods...

So that's the Request... now let's see the Response

The response is what goes back to the client. The thing the browser gets, parses, and renders for the user. Typically, you use the response object to get an output stream (usually a Writer) and you use that stream to write the HTML (or some other type of content) that goes back to the client. The response object has other methods besides just the I/O output, though, and we'll look at some of them in a bit more detail.

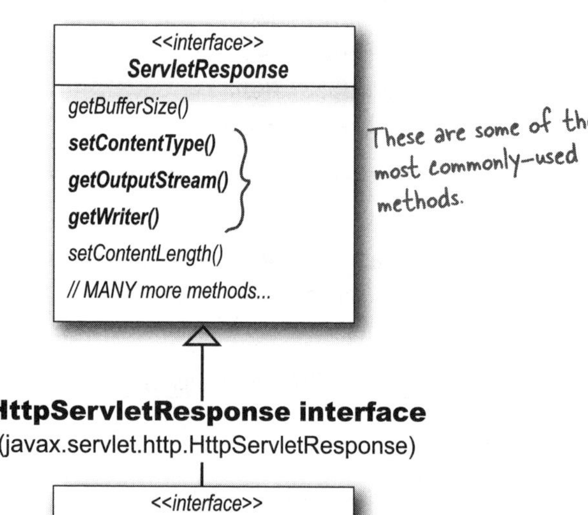

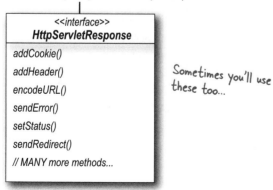

Most of the time, you use the Response just to send data back to the client.

You call two methods on the response: setContentType() and getWriter().

After that, you're simply doing I/O to write HTML (or something else) to the stream.

But you can also use the response to set other headers, send errors, and add cookies.

Wait a minute... I thought we weren't going to send HTML from a servlet because it's so ugly to format it for the output stream...

Using the response for I/O

OK, yes, we should be using JSPs rather than sending HTML back in the response output stream from a servlet. Formatting HTML to stick in an output stream's println() method *hurts.*

But that doesn't mean you'll never have to work with an output stream from your servlet.

Why?

1) Your hosting provider might not support JSPs. There are plenty of older servers and containers out there that support servlets but not JSPs, so you're stuck with it.

2) You don't have the option of using JSPs for some other reason, like, you have an incredibly stupid manager who won't let you use JSPs because in 1998 his brother-in-law told him that JSPs were bad.

3) Who said that *HTML* was the only thing you could send back in a response? You might send something *other* than HTML back to the client. Something for which an output stream makes perfect sense.

Turn the page for an example...

Imagine you want to send a JAR to the client...

Let's say you've created a download page where the client can get code from JAR files. Instead of sending back an HTML page, the response contains the bytes representing the JAR. You *read* the bytes of the JAR file, then *write* them to the response's output stream.

1. Diane is desperate to download the JAR of code for the book she's using to learn servlets and JSPs. She navigates to the book's website and clicks the "code jar" link, which refers to a servlet named "Code.do".

Browser sends an HTTP request to the server with the name of the requested servlet ("Code.do")

The Container sends the request to the CodeReturn servlet (mapped to the name "Code.do" in the DD) for processing.

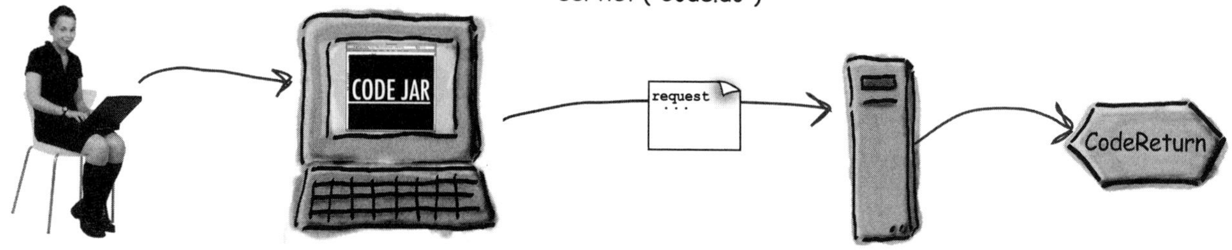

CODE JAR

request

CodeReturn

---

2. The JAR starts downloading onto the client's machine. Diane is pleased.

The CodeReturn servlet gets the bytes for the JAR, then gets an output stream from the response, and writes out the bytes representing the JAR.

down-loading...

The HTTP response now holds the bytes representing the JAR.

Code JAR

read

CodeReturn

write

response

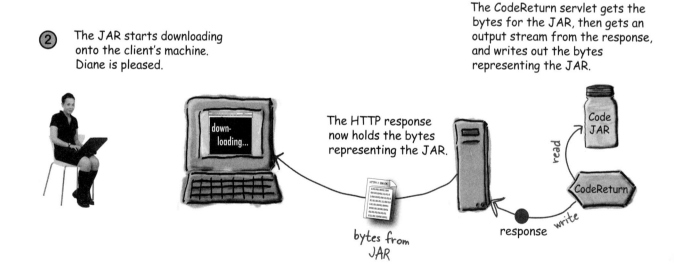

bytes from JAR

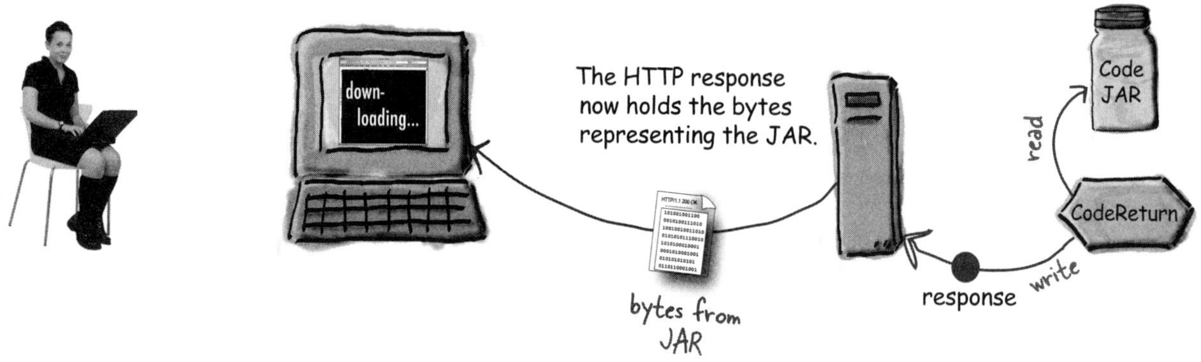

Servlet code to download the JAR

```
// a bunch of imports here

public class CodeReturn extends HttpServlet {

   public void doGet(HttpServletRequest request, HttpServletResponse response)
                                          throws IOException, ServletException {

      response.setContentType("application/jar");

      ServletContext ctx = getServletContext();
      InputStream is = ctx.getResourceAsStream("/bookCode.jar");

      int read = 0;
      byte[] bytes = new byte[1024];

      OutputStream os = response.getOutputStream();
      while ((read = is.read(bytes)) != -1) {
         os.write(bytes, 0, read);
      }
      os.flush();
      os.close();
   }
}
```

We want the browser to recognize that this is a JAR, not HTML, so we set the content type to "application/jar".

This just says, "give me an input stream for the resource named bookCode.jar".

Here's the key part, but it's just plain old I/O!! Nothing special, just read the JAR bytes, then write the bytes to the output stream that we get from the response object.

---

there are no Dumb Questions

Q: Where was the "bookCode.jar" JAR file located? In other words, where does the getResourceAsStream() method LOOK to find the file? How do you deal with the path?

A: The getResourceAsStream() requires you to start with a forward slash ("/"), which represents the root of your web app. Since the web app was named ***JarDownload***, then the directory structure looks like the directories in the picture. The ***JarDownload*** directory is inside ***webapps*** (as a peer directory to all the other web app directories), then inside ***JarDownload*** we put the ***WEB-INF*** directory, and the code JAR itself. So the file "bookCode.jar" is sitting at the root level of the ***JarDownload*** web app. (Don't worry, we'll go into deep penetrating details about the deployment directory structure when we get to the deployment chapter.)

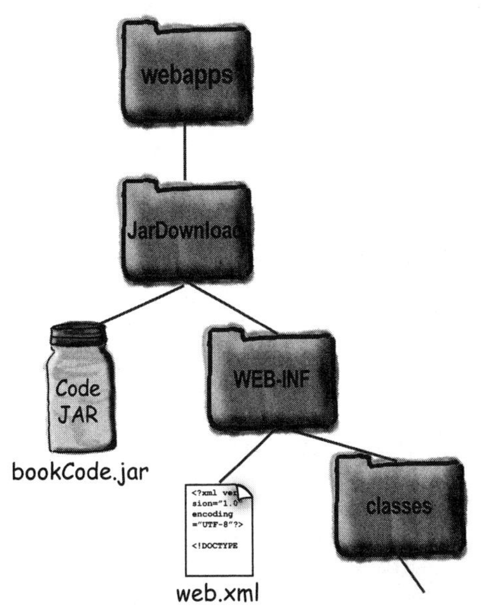

Whoa. What's the deal with content type?

You might be wondering about this line:

```
response.setContentType("application/jar");
```

Or at least you *should* be. You have to tell the browser what you're sending back, so the browser can ***do the right thing:*** launch a "helper" app like a PDF viewer or video player, render the HTML, save the bytes of the response as a downloaded file, etc. And since you're wondering, yes when we say *content type* we mean the same thing as MIME type. Content type is an HTTP header that *must* be included in the HTTP response.

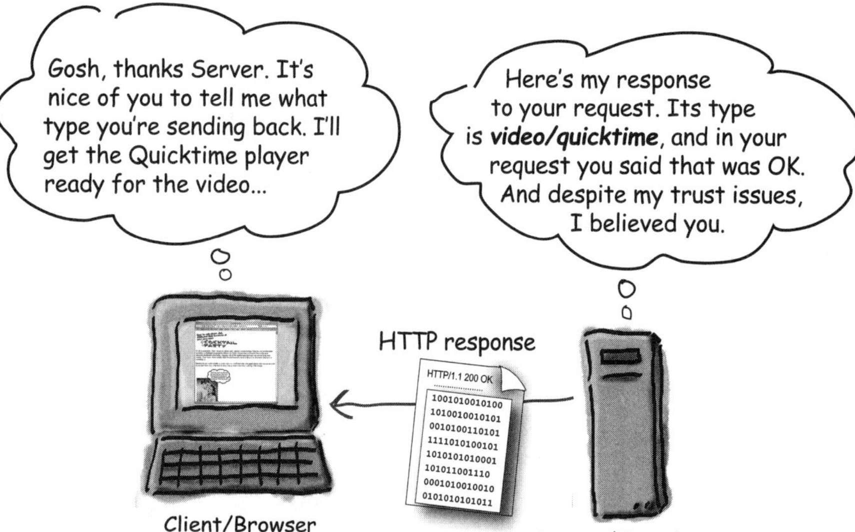

Gosh, thanks Server. It's nice of you to tell me what type you're sending back. I'll get the Quicktime player ready for the video...
Here's my response to your request. Its type is **video/quicktime**, and in your request you said that was OK. And despite my trust issues, I believed you.
HTTP response
HTTP/1.1 200 OK
Client/Browser
Server/Container

Common MIME types:

text/html
application/pdf
video/quicktime
application/java
image/jpeg
application/jar
application/octet-stream
application/x-zip

You don't need to memorize a bunch of content types.

Relax

You should know what setContentType() does, and how you use it, but you don't have to know even the most common content types except text/html. What you need to know about setContentType() is mostly common sense... for example, it won't do you any good to change the content type AFTER you write to the response output stream. Duh. But that does mean that you can't set a content type, write some stuff, and then change the content type and write something different. But think about it—how would the browser deal with that? It can handle only one type of THING at a time from the response.

To make sure everything works correctly, your best practice (and in some cases a requirement) is to always call setContentType() first, BEFORE you call the method that gives you your output stream (getWriter() or getOutputStream()). That'll guarantee you won't run into conflicts between the content type and the output stream.

there are no Dumb Questions

Q: Why do you have to set the content type? Can't servers figure it out from the extension of the file?

A: Most servers *can*, for static content. In Apache, for example, you can set up MIME types by mapping a specific file extension (.txt, .jar, etc.) to a specific content type, and Apache will use that to set the content type in the HTTP header. But we're talking about what happens inside a servlet where there IS no file! You're the one who is sending back the response; the Container has no idea what you're sending.

Q: But what about that last example where you read a specific JAR file? Can't the Container see that you're reading a JAR?

A: No. All we did from the servlet was read the bytes of a file (that just happened to be a JAR file), and turn around and write those bytes to the output stream. The Container has no idea what we were up to when we read those bytes. For all it knows we're reading from one type of thing and writing something completely different in the response.

Q: How can I find out what the common content types are?

A: Do a Google search. Seriously. New MIME types are being added all the time, but you can easily find lists on the Web. You can also look in your browser preferences for a list of those that have been configured for your browser, and you can check your Web server configuration files as well. Again, you don't have to worry about this for the exam, and it's not likely to cause you much stress in the real world either.

Q: Wait a second... why would you use a servlet to send back that JAR file when you can just have the web server send it back as a resource? In other words, why wouldn't you have the user click a link that goes to the JAR instead of to a servlet? Can't the server be configured to send back the JAR directly without even GOING through a servlet?

A: Yes. Good question. You COULD configure the web server so that the user clicks an HTML link that goes to, say, the JAR file sitting on the server (just like any other static resource including JPEGs and text files), and the server just sends it back in the response.

But... we're assuming that you might have other things that you want to do in that servlet BEFORE sending back the stream. You might, for example, need logic in the servlet that determines *which* JAR file to send. Or you might be sending back bytes that you're creating right there on-the-fly. Imagine a system where you take input parameters from the user, and then use them to dynamically generate a sound that you send back. Sound that didn't previously exist. In other words, sound that's not sitting on the server as a file somewhere. You just made it up, and now you're sending it back in the response.

So you're right, perhaps our example of just sending back a JAR sitting on the server is a little contrived, but come on... use your imagination here and embellish it with all sorts of things you might add to make it *worth* being a servlet. Maybe it's something as simple as putting code in your servlet that—along with sending back the JAR—writes some info to a database about this particular user. Or maybe you have to check to see if he's even allowed to download this JAR, based on something you first read from the database.

You've got two choices for output: characters or bytes

This is just plain old java.io, except the ServletResponse interface gives you only *two* streams to choose from: ServletOutputStream for bytes, or a PrintWriter for character data.

➤ PrintWriter

Example:

```
PrintWriter writer = response.getWriter();

writer.println("some text and HTML");
```

Use it for:

Printing text data to a character stream. Although you *can* still write character data to an OutputStream, this is the stream that's designed to handle character data.

➤ OutputStream

Example

```
ServletOutputStream out = response.getOutputStream();

out.write(aByteArray);
```

Use it for:

Writing *anything else!*

You MUST memorize these methods

*You have to know these for the exam. And it's tricky. Notice that to write to a Servlet**OutputStream** you **write()**, but to write to a **Print-Writer** you... **println()**! It's natural to assume that you write to a writer, but you don't. If you already use java.io, then you've been down this road. But if you haven't, just remember:*

println()** to a **PrintWriter
write()** to an **ServletOutputStream

Make sure you remember that the method names for getting the stream or the writer both drop the first word in the returned type:

ServletOutputStream
*response.get**OutputStream()***

PrintWriter
*response.get**Writer()***

You need to recognize WRONG method names like:

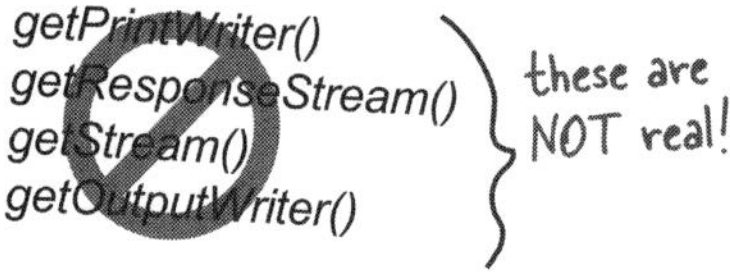

FYI: The PrintWriter actually "wraps" the ServletOutputStream. In other words, the PrintWriter has a reference to the ServletOutputStream and delegates calls to it. There's just ONE output stream back to the client, but the PrintWriter "decorates" the stream by adding higher-level character-friendly methods.

You can set response headers, you can add response headers

And you can wonder what the difference is. But think about it for a second, then do this exercise.

Match the method call with its behavior

Draw a line from the HttpResponse method to the method's behavior. We did the most obvious one for you.

```
response.setHeader("foo", "bar");

response.addHeader("foo", "bar");

response.setIntHeader("foo", 42);
```

Adds a new header and value to the response, or adds an additional value to an existing header.

A convenience method that replaces the value of an existing header with this integer value, or adds a new header and value to the response.

If a header with this name is already in the response, the value is replaced with this value. Otherwise, adds a new header and value to the response.

Pretty obvious when you see them all together.

But for the exam, you should have them memorized so that if next Tuesday the guy down the hall asks, "What's that response method that lets me add a value to an existing header?" you can, without the slightest pause, say "It's addHeader, and it takes two Strings for the name and value." Just like that.

Both setHeader() and addHeader() will add a header and value to the response if the header (the first argument to the method)is not already in the response. The difference between set and add shows up when the header *is* there. In that case:

***set*Header() overwrites the existing value**

***add*Header() adds an additional value**

When you call setContentType("text/html"), you're setting a header just as if you said:

setHeader("content-type", "text/html");

So what's the difference? No difference... *assuming you type the "content-type" header correctly*. The setHeader() method won't complain if you misspell the header names—it just thinks you're adding a new kind of header. But something else will fail later, because now you haven't properly set the content type of the response!

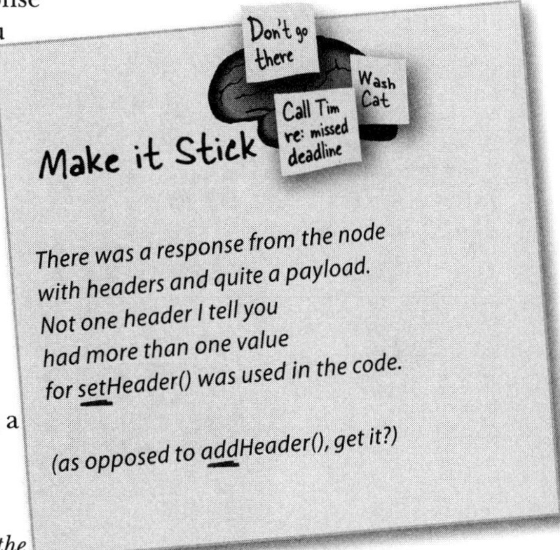

Don't go there
Wash Cat
Call Tim re: missed deadline
Make it Stick
There was a response from the node
with headers and quite a payload.
Not one header I tell you
had more than one value
for setHeader() was used in the code.
(as opposed to addHeader(), get it?)

(The first person to send us an mp3 file of them actually reciting this poem, with the right timing and everything, gets a special edition t-shirt.)

But sometimes you just don't want to deal with the response yourself...

You can choose to have something else handle the response for your request. You can either *redirect* the request to a completely different URL, or you can *dispatch the request* to some other component in your web app (typically a JSP).

Redirect

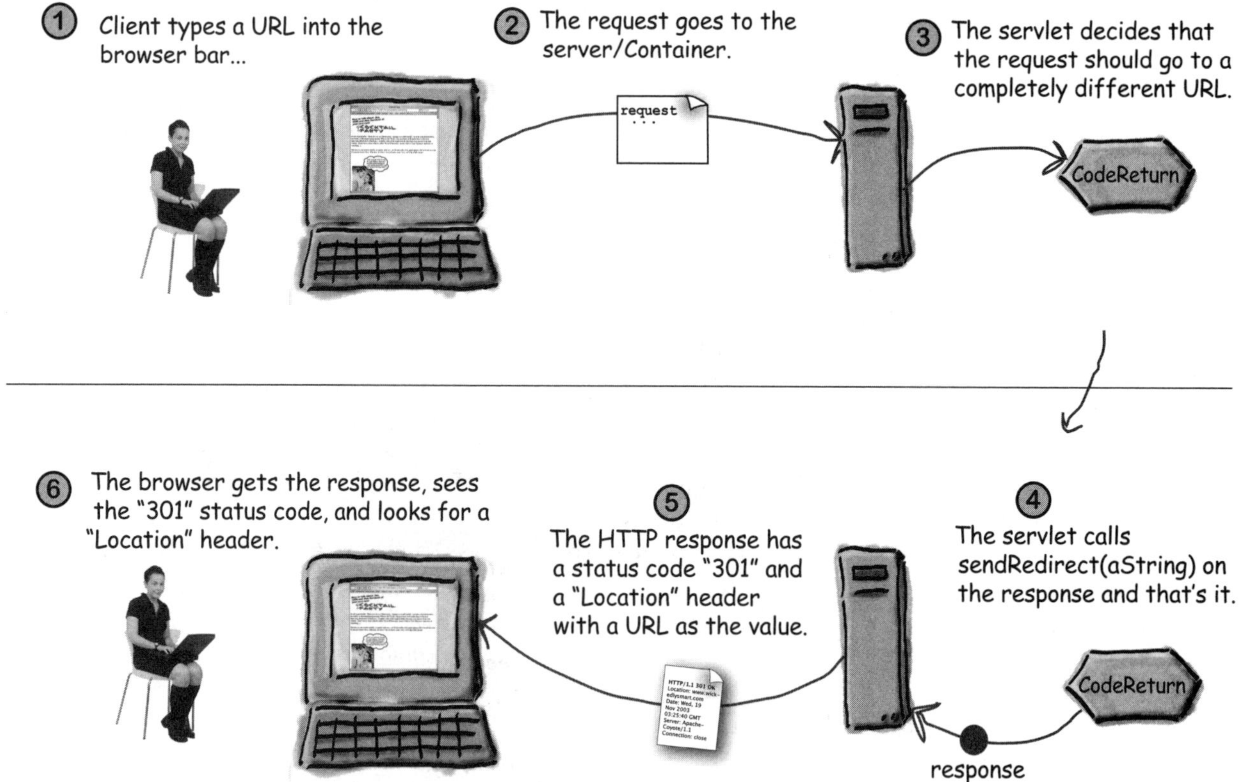

1 Client types a URL into the browser bar...
2 The request goes to the server/Container.
request
3 The servlet decides that the request should go to a completely different URL.
CodeReturn
6 The browser gets the response, sees the "301" status code, and looks for a "Location" header.
5 The HTTP response has a status code "301" and a "Location" header with a URL as the value.
4 The servlet calls sendRedirect(aString) on the response and that's it.
CodeReturn
response

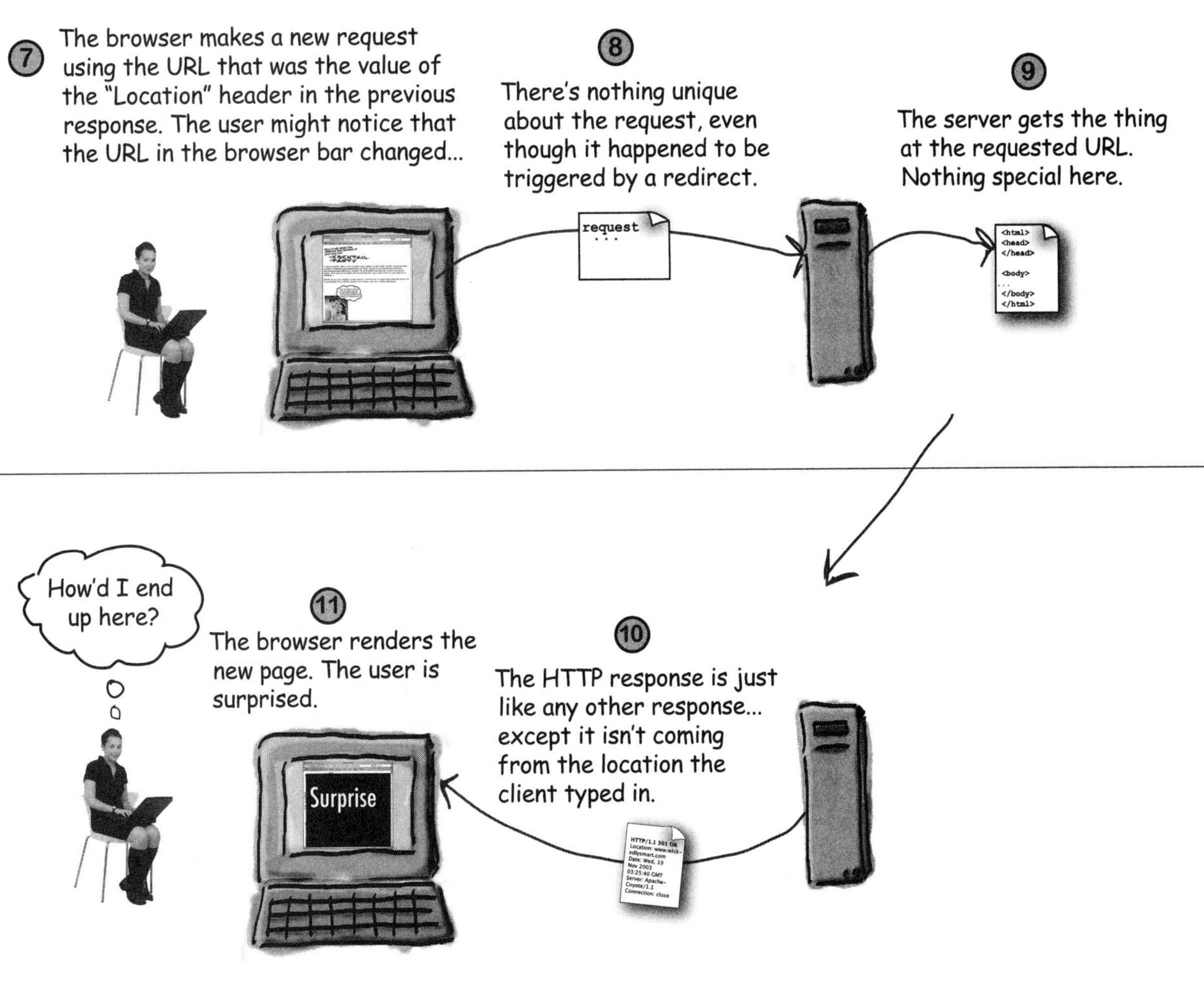

7 The browser makes a new request using the URL that was the value of the "Location" header in the previous response. The user might notice that the URL in the browser bar changed...
8 There's nothing unique about the request, even though it happened to be triggered by a redirect.
request
9 The server gets the thing at the requested URL. Nothing special here.
How'd I end up here?
11 The browser renders the new page. The user is surprised.
10 The HTTP response is just like any other response... except it isn't coming from the location the client typed in.
Surprise

Servlet redirect makes the browser do the work

A redirect lets the servlet off the hook completely. After deciding that it can't do the work, the servlet simply calls the *sendRedirect()* method:

```
if (worksForMe) {
  // handle the request
} else {
   response.sendRedirect("http://www.oreilly.com");
}
```

The URL you want the browser to use for the request. This is what the client will see.

Using relative URLs in sendRedirect()

You can use a *relative* URL as the argument to sendRedirect(), instead of specifying the whole "http://www..." thing. Relative URLs come in two flavors: with or without a starting forward slash ("/").

Imagine the client originally typed in:

```
http://www.wickedlysmart.com/myApp/cool/bar.do
```

When the request comes into the servlet named "bar.do", the servlet calls sendRedirect() with a relative URL that does NOT start with a forward slash:

```
sendRedirect("foo/stuff.html");
```

The Container builds the full URL (it needs this for the "Location" header it puts in the HTTP response) relative to the original request URL:

```
http://www.wickedlysmart.com/myApp/cool/foo/stuff.html
```

The Container knows the original request URL started from the myApp/cool path, so if you don't use a forward slash, that part of the path is prepended to the front of "foo/stuff.html".

But if the argument to sendRedirect() DOES start with a forward slash:

```
sendRedirect("/foo/stuff.html");
```

The forward slash at the beginning means "relative to the root of this web Container".

The Container builds the complete URL relative to the web Container itself, instead of relative to the original URL of the request. So the new URL will be:

```
http://www.wickedlysmart.com/foo/stuff.html
```

"foo" is a web app, separate from the "myApp" web app.

Watch it!

You can't do a sendRedirect() after writing to the response!

That's probably obvious, but it's the LAW so we're just making sure.

If you look up sendRedirect() in the API, you'll see that it throws an IllegalStateException if you try to invoke it after "the response has already been committed."

*By "committed", they mean that the response has been **sent**. That just means the data has been flushed to the stream. For practical purposes, it means **you can't write to the response and then call sendRedirect()!***

But some picky professor will tell you that technically, you could write to the stream without flushing, and then sendRedirect() wouldn't cause an exception. But it would be a completely stupid thing to do, so we won't talk about it. (Except that we just did... talk about it...)

In your servlet, for gosh sakes make a decision! Either handle the request or do a sendRedirect() to have someone ELSE handle the request.

(By the way, this idea that "once it's committed it's too late" also applies to setting headers, cookies, status codes, the content-type, and so on...)

sendRedirect() takes a String, NOT a URL object!

Well, it takes a String that IS a URL. The point is, sendRedirect() does NOT take an object of type URL. You pass it a String that's either a complete URL or a relative one. If the Container can't build a relative URL into a full one, it'll throw an IllegalStateException. The tricky part is to remember that THIS is wrong:

```
sendRedirect(new URL("http://www.oreilly.com"));
```

No! It looks so right, but it's SO wrong. sendRedirect() takes a String. Period.

A request dispatch does the work on the server side

And that's the big difference between a redirect and a request dispatch—*redirect* makes the *client* do the work while *request dispatch* makes something else on the *server* do the work. So remember: redirect = *client*, request dispatch = *server*. We'll say more about request dispatch in a later chapter, but these two pages should give you a quick look at the highlights.

Request Dispatch

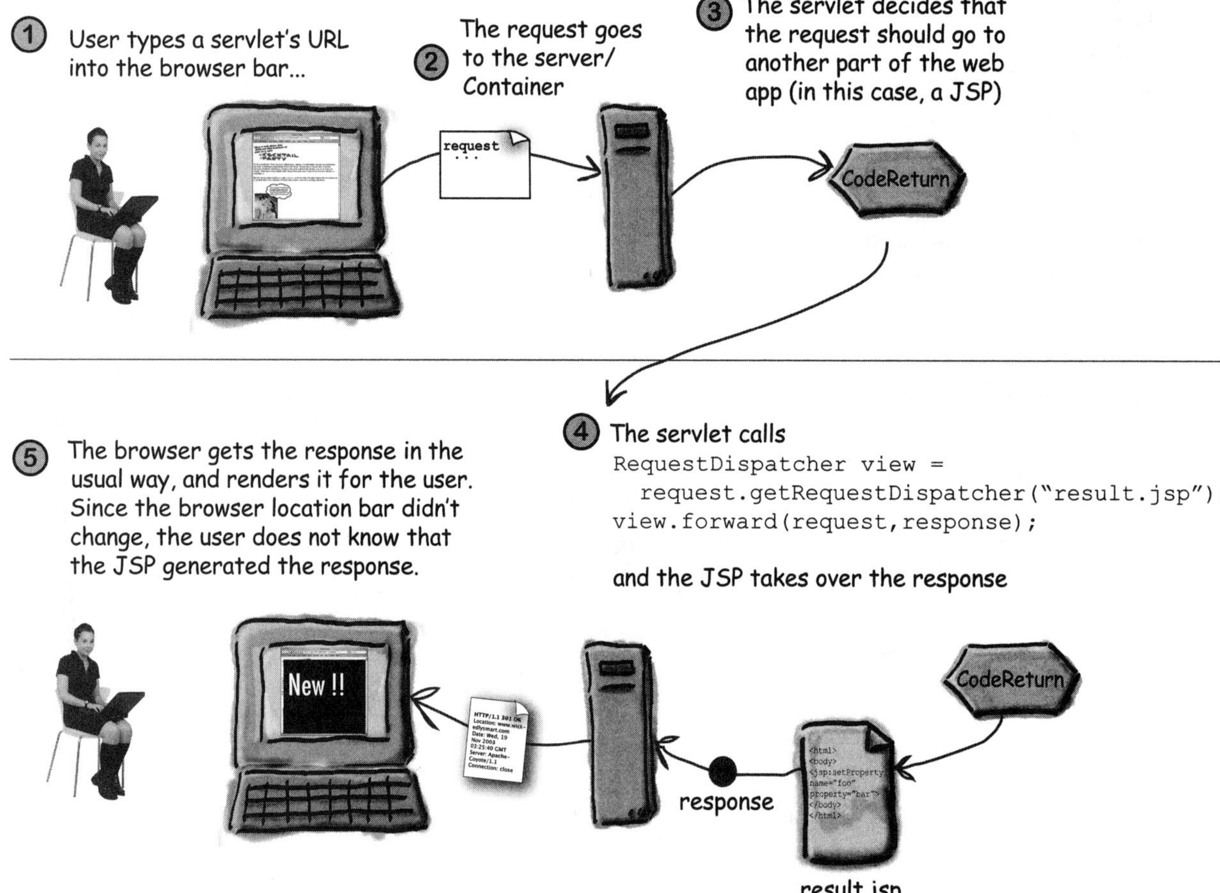

1 User types a servlet's URL into the browser bar...
2 The request goes to the server/ Container
3 The servlet decides that the request should go to another part of the web app (in this case, a JSP)
request
CodeReturn
4 The servlet calls
RequestDispatcher view =
request.getRequestDispatcher("result.jsp");
view.forward(request,response);
and the JSP takes over the response
5 The browser gets the response in the usual way, and renders it for the user. Since the browser location bar didn't change, the user does not know that the JSP generated the response.
New !!
response
CodeReturn
result.jsp

Redirect vs. Request Dispatch

I don't have time for this! Tell you what—why don't you call Barney. Maybe HE has time for this crap.

Redirect

Hey Kari, this is Dan... I want your help with a client. I'll forward you the details on how to get back to him, but I need you to take over now.

Yes I KNOW you have needs too... yes, I KNOW how important the View is in Model View Controller...no, I don't think I can find another JSP just like that... what? I didn't catch that? You're breaking up... sorry-- can't hear a thing... losing packets...

When a servlet does a **request dispatch**, it's like asking a co-worker to take over working with a client. The co-worker ends up responding to the client, but the client doesn't care as long as someone responds.

The user never knows someone else took over, because the URL in the browser bar doesn't change.

When a servlet does a **redirect**, it's like asking the client to call someone else instead. In this case, the client is the browser, not the user. The browser makes the new call on the user's behalf, after the originally-requested servlet says, "Sorry, call this guy instead..."

The user sees the new URL in the browser.

Review: HttpServletResponse

BULLET POINTS

- You use the Response to send data back to the client.
- The most common methods you'll call on the response object (HttpServletResponse) are setContentType() and getWriter().
- Be careful—many developers assume the method is get*Print*Writer(), but it's getWriter().
- The getWriter() method lets you do character I/O to write HTML (or something else) to the stream.
- You can also use the response to set headers, send errors, and add cookies.
- In the real world, you'll probably use a JSP to send most HTML responses, but you may still use a response stream to send binary data (like a JAR file, perhaps) to the client.
- The method you call on your response for getting a binary stream is getOutputStream().
- The setContentType() method tells the browser how to handle the data coming in with the response. Typical content types are "text/html", "application/pdf", and "image/jpeg".
- You don't have to memorize content types (also known as MIME types).
- You can set response headers using addHeader() or setHeader(). The difference depends on whether the header is already part of the response. If it is, *set*Header() will *replace* the value, but *add*Header will *add an additional value* to the existing response. If the header is not already part of the response, then setHeader() and addHeader() behave in exactly the same way.
- If you don't want to respond to a request, you can redirect the request to a different URL. The browser takes care of sending the new request to the URL you provide.
- To redirect a request, call sendRedirect(aStringURL) on the response.
- You cannot call sendRedirect() after the response is committed! In other words, if you've already written something to the stream, it's too late to do a redirect.
- A request *redirect* is different from a request *dispatch*. A request *dispatch* (covered more in another chapter) happens on the *server*, while a *redirect* happens on the *client*. A request dispatch hands the request to another component on the server, usually within the same web app. A request *redirect* simply tells the browser to go a different URL.

ServletResponse interface
(javax.servlet.ServletResponse)

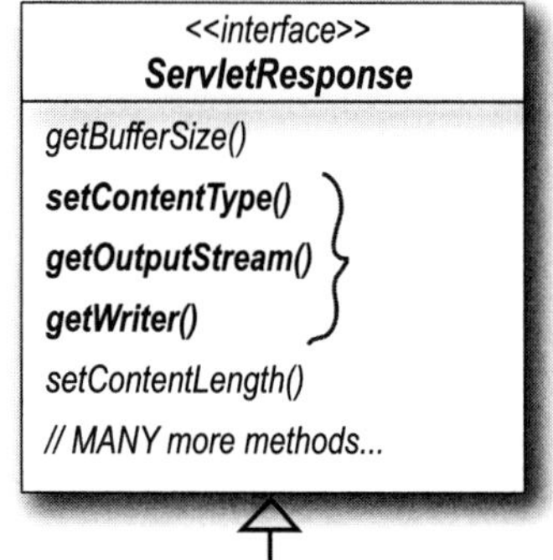

HttpServletResponse interface
(javax.servlet.http.HttpServletResponse)

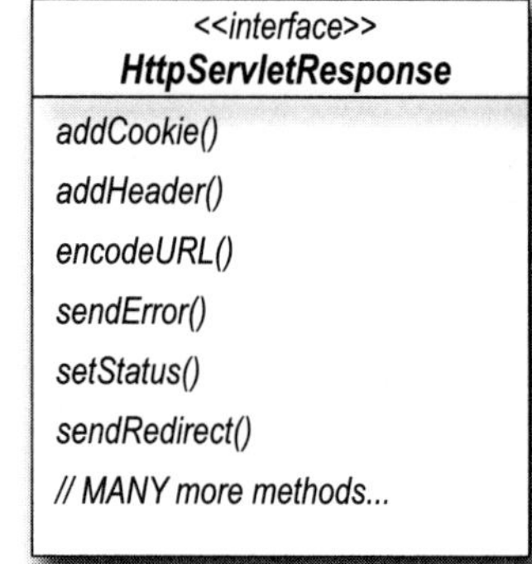

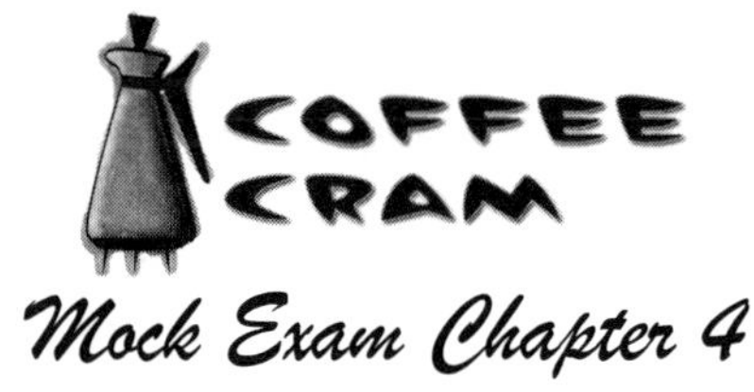

Mock Exam Chapter 4

---

1 How would servlet code from a service method (e.g., **doPost()**) retrieve the value of the "User-Agent" header from the request? (Choose all that apply.)

- ❑ A. `String userAgent = request.getParameter("User-Agent");`
- ❑ B. `String userAgent = request.getHeader("User-Agent");`
- ❑ C. `String userAgent = request.getRequestHeader("Mozilla");`
- ❑ D. `String userAgent = getServletContext().getInitParameter("User-Agent");`

---

2 Which HTTP methods are used to show the client what the server is receiving? (Choose all that apply.)

- ❑ A. GET
- ❑ B. PUT
- ❑ C. TRACE
- ❑ D. RETURN
- ❑ E. OPTIONS

---

3 Which method of **HttpServletResponse** is used to redirect an HTTP request to another URL?

- ❑ A. **sendURL()**
- ❑ B. **redirectURL()**
- ❑ C. **redirectHttp()**
- ❑ D. **sendRedirect()**
- ❑ E. **getRequestDispatcher()**

4 Which HTTP methods are NOT considered idempotent? (Choose all that apply.)

- ❑ A. GET
- ❑ B. POST
- ❑ C. HEAD
- ❑ D. PUT

5 Given **req** is a **HttpServletRequest**, which gets a binary input stream? (Choose all that apply.)

- ❑ A. `BinaryInputStream s = req.getInputStream();`
- ❑ B. `ServletInputStream s = req.getInputStream();`
- ❑ C. `BinaryInputStream s = req.getBinaryStream();`
- ❑ D. `ServletInputStream s = req.getBinaryStream();`

6 How would you set a header named "CONTENT-LENGTH" in the **HttpServletResponse** object? (Choose all that apply.)

- ❑ A. `response.setHeader(CONTENT-LENGTH,"numBytes");`
- ❑ B. `response.setHeader("CONTENT-LENGTH","numBytes");`
- ❑ C. `response.setStatus(1024);`
- ❑ D. `response.setHeader("CONTENT-LENGTH",1024);`

7 Choose the servlet code fragment that gets a binary stream for writing an image or other binary type to the **HttpServletResponse**.

- ❑ A. `java.io.PrintWriter out = response.getWriter();`
- ❑ B. `ServletOutputStream out = response.getOutputStream();`
- ❑ C.

```
java.io.PrintWriter out =
        new PrintWriter(response.getWriter());
```

- ❑ D. `ServletOutputStream out = response.getBinaryStream();`

---

8 Which methods are used by a servlet to handle form data from a client? (Choose all that apply.)

- ❑ A. **`HttpServlet.doHead()`**
- ❑ B. **`HttpServlet.doPost()`**
- ❑ C. **`HttpServlet.doForm()`**
- ❑ D. **`ServletRequest.doGet()`**
- ❑ E. **`ServletRequest.doPost()`**
- ❑ F. **`ServletRequest.doForm()`**

---

9 Which of the following methods are declared in **`HttpServletRequest`** as opposed to in **`ServletRequest`**? (Choose all that apply.)

- ❑ A. **`getMethod()`**
- ❑ B. **`getHeader()`**
- ❑ C. **`getCookies()`**
- ❑ D. **`getInputStream()`**
- ❑ E. **`getParameterNames()`**

---

10 How should servlet developers handle the **`HttpServlet`**'s **`service()`** method when extending **`HttpServlet`**? (Choose all that apply.)

- ❑ A. They should override the **`service()`** method in most cases.
- ❑ B. They should call the **`service()`** method from **`doGet()`** or **`doPost()`**
- ❑ C. They should call the **`service()`** method from the **`init()`** method.
- ❑ D. They should override at least one **`doXXX()`** method (such as **`doPost()`**).

Chapter 4 Answers

---

1 How would servlet code from a service method (e.g., **doPost()**) retrieve the value of the "User-Agent" header from the request? (Choose all that apply.) (API)

- [ ] A. `String userAgent = request.getParameter("User-Agent");`
- [x] B. `String userAgent = request.getHeader("User-Agent");`
- [ ] C. `String userAgent = request.getRequestHeader("Mozilla");`
- [ ] D. `String userAgent = getServletContext().getInitParameter("User-Agent");`

-Option B shows the correct method call passing in the header name as a String parameter.

---

2 Which HTTP methods are used to show the client what the server is receiving? (Choose all that apply.) (HF 4, HTTP methods)

- [ ] A. GET
- [ ] B. PUT
- [x] C. TRACE
- [ ] D. RETURN
- [ ] E. OPTIONS

-This method is typically used for troubleshooting, not for production.

---

3 Which method of **HttpServletResponse** is used to redirect an HTTP request to another URL? (API)

- [ ] A. `sendURL()`
- [ ] B. `redirectURL()`
- [ ] C. `redirectHttp()`
- [x] D. `sendRedirect()`
- [ ] E. `getRequestDispatcher()`

- Option D is correct, and of the methods listed, it's the only one that exists in HttpServletResponse

---

4 Which HTTP methods are NOT considered idempotent? (Choose all that apply.)

(HF 4, idempotent requests)

- ❑ A. GET
- ☑ B. POST
- ❑ C. HEAD
- ❑ D. PUT

–By design, POST is meant to convey requests to update the state of the server. In general the same update should not be applied multiple times.

---

5 Given **`req`** is a **`HttpServletRequest`**, which gets a binary input stream? (Choose all that apply.)

(API)

- ❑ A. **`BinaryInputStream s = req.getInputStream();`**
- ☑ B. **`ServletInputStream s = req.getInputStream();`**
- ❑ C. **`BinaryInputStream s = req.getBinaryStream();`**
- ❑ D. **`ServletInputStream s = req.getBinaryStream();`**

–Option B specifies the correct method and the correct return type.

---

6 How would you set a header named "CONTENT-LENGTH" in the **`HttpServletResponse`** object? (Choose all that apply.)

(API)

- ❑ A. **`response.setHeader(CONTENT-LENGTH,"numBytes");`**
- ☑ B. **`response.setHeader("CONTENT-LENGTH","numBytes");`**
- ❑ C. **`response.setStatus(1024);`**
- ❑ D. **`response.setHeader("CONTENT-LENGTH",1024);`**

–Option B shows the correct way to set an HTTP header with two String parameters, one representing the header name and the other the value.

---

7 Choose the servlet code fragment that gets a binary stream for writing an image or other binary type to the **`HttpServletResponse`**.

(API)

- ❑ A. **`java.io.PrintWriter out = response.getWriter();`**
- ☑ B. **`ServletOutputStream out = response.getOutputStream();`**
- ❑ C. **`java.io.PrintWriter out =`**
  `new PrintWriter(response.getWriter());`
- ❑ D. **`ServletOutputStream out = response.getBinaryStream();`**

–Option A is incorrect because it uses a character-oriented PrintWriter

8 Which methods are used by a servlet to handle form data from a client? (Choose all that apply.) (API)

- [ ] A. **`HttpServlet.doHead()`**
- [x] B. **`HttpServlet.doPost()`**
- [ ] C. **`HttpServlet.doForm()`**
- [ ] D. **`ServletRequest.doGet()`**
- [ ] E. **`ServletRequest.doPost()`**
- [ ] F. **`ServletRequest.doForm()`**

–Options C–F are wrong because these methods don't exist.

---

9 Which of the following methods are declared in **`HttpServletRequest`** as opposed to in **`ServletRequest`**? (Choose all that apply.) (API)

- [x] A. **`getMethod()`**
- [x] B. **`getHeader()`**
- [x] C. **`getCookies()`**
- [ ] D. **`getInputStream()`**
- [ ] E. **`getParameterNames()`**

–Options A, B, and C all relate to components of an HTTP request.

---

10 How should servlet developers handle the **`HttpServlet`**'s **`service()`** method when extending **`HttpServlet`**? (Choose all that apply.) (API)

- [ ] A. They should override the **`service()`** method in most cases.
- [ ] B. They should call the **`service()`** method from **`doGet()`** or **`doPost()`**
- [ ] C. They should call the **`service()`** method from the **`init()`** method.
- [x] D. They should override at least one **`doXXX()`** method (such as **`doPost()`**).

–Option D is correct, developers typically focus on the doGet(), and doPost() methods

5 attributes and listeners

Being a Web App

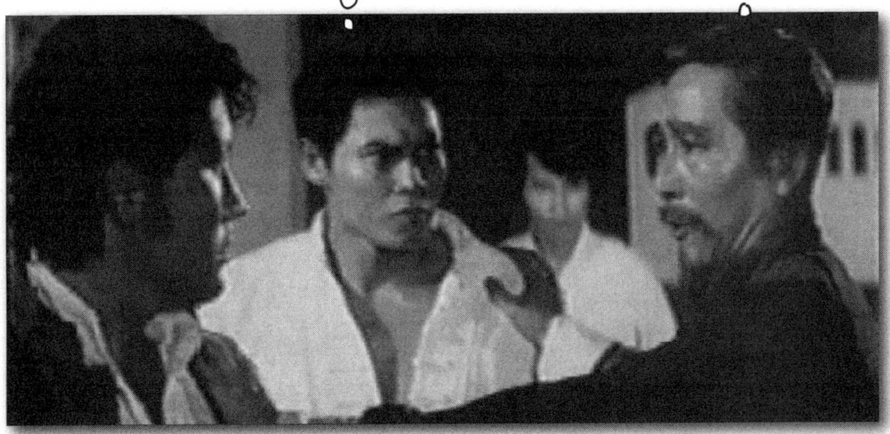

But master... he used a context attribute when he *should* have used a request attribute. He must be killed.
You must understand how the pieces of the web app interact, and you must respect the threads. If you score well on this chapter's mock exam, I will let you live.

No servlet stands alone. In today's modern web app, many components work together to accomplish a goal. You have models, controllers, and views. You have parameters and attributes. You have helper classes. But how do you tie the pieces together? How do you let components *share* information? How do you *hide* information? *How do you make information thread-safe?* Your life may depend on the answers, so, be sure you have plenty of tea when you go through this chapter. *And not that foofy herbal decaf crap.*

The Web Container Model

3.1 For the servlet and ServletContext initialization parameters: write servlet code to access initialization parameters, and create deployment descriptor elements for declaring initialization parameters.

3.2 For the fundamental servlet attribute scopes (request, session, and context): write servlet code to add, retrieve, and remove attributes; given a usage scenario, identify the proper scope for an attribute; and identify multi-threading issues associated with each scope.

3.3 *Describe the elements of the Web container request processing model: Filter, Filter chain, Request and response wrappers, and Web resource (servlet or JSP page).* ← Covered in the Filters chapter.

3.4 Describe the Web Container lifecycle event model for requests, sessions, and web applications; create and configure listener classes for each scope life cycle; create and configure scope attribute listener classes; and given a scenario, identify the proper attribute listener to use.

3.5 Describe the RequestDispatcher mechanism; write servlet code to create a request dispatcher; write servlet code to forward or include the target resource; and identify the additional request-scoped attributes provided by the container to the target resource.

Coverage Notes:

All of the objectives in this section are covered completely in this chapter, with the exception of 3.3, which is covered in the Filters chapter.

Most of what's in this chapter will come up in other parts of the book, but if you're taking the exam, THIS is the chapter where we expect you to learn and memorize the objective topics.

I want my email address to show up on the beer web page my servlet makes... but I think my email is gonna change and I don't want to have to recompile my servlet code just to change it...

Kim wants to configure his email address in the DD, not hard-code it inside the servlet class

Here's what Kim does ***not*** want in his servlet:

```
PrintWriter out = response.getWriter();
out.println("blooper@wickedlysmart.com");
```

Hard-coding the address is BAD!

What happens when his email changes? He'll have to recompile...

He'd much rather put his email address in the *Deployment Descriptor* (web.xml file) so that when he deploys his web app, his servlet can somehow "read" his email address from the DD. That way, he won't have to hard-code his address in the servlet class, and to change his email he modifies only the web.xml file, *without having to touch his servlet source code.*

Init Parameters to the rescue

You've already seen the request parameters that can come over in a doGet() or doPost(), but servlets can have initialization parameters as well.

In the DD (web.xml) file:

```
<servlet>
     <servlet-name>BeerParamTests</servlet-name>
     <servlet-class>TestInitParams</servlet-class>

     <init-param>
        <param-name>adminEmail</param-name>
        <param-value>likewecare@wickedlysmart.com</param-value>
      </init-param>

</servlet>
```

You give it a param-name and a param-value. Simple. Just make sure it's INSIDE the <servlet> element in the DD.

In the servlet code:

```
out.println(getServletConfig().getInitParameter("adminEmail"));
```

Every servlet inherits a getServletConfig() method.

The getServletConfig() method returns a... wait for it... ServletConfig. And one of its methods is getInitParameter().

You can't use servlet init parameters until the servlet is initialized

You already saw that your servlet inherits getServletConfig(), so you can call that from any method in your servlet to get a reference to a ServletConfig. Once you have a ServletConfig reference, you can call getInitParameter(). But remember, *you can't call it from your constructor!* That's too early in the servlet's life... it won't have its full servletness until the Container calls init().

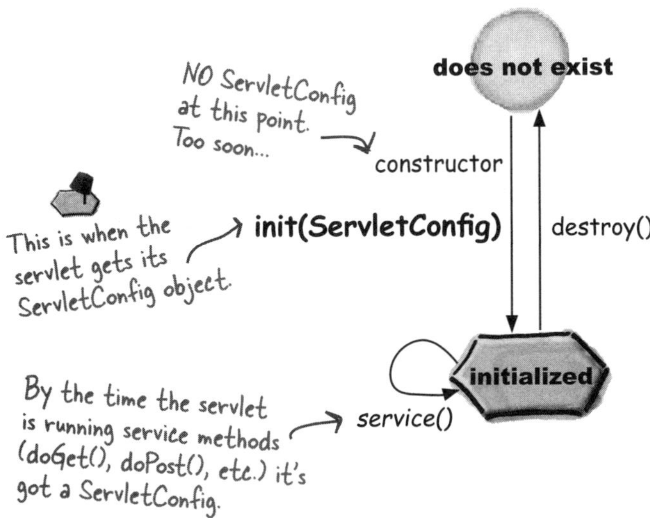

does not exist
NO ServletConfig at this point. Too soon...
constructor
This is when the servlet gets its ServletConfig object.
init(ServletConfig)
destroy()
initialized
By the time the servlet is running service methods (doGet(), doPost(), etc.) it's got a ServletConfig.
service()

When the Container initializes a servlet, it makes a unique ServletConfig for the servlet.

The Container "reads" the servlet init parameters from the DD and gives them to the ServletConfig, then passes the ServletConfig to the servlet's init() method.

there are no Dumb Questions

Q: Way back in the last chapter, you said it takes TWO things for the servlet to become a card-carrying, fez-wearing servlet. You mentioned both ServletConfig and something called ServletContext.

A: OK, yes, we'll look at the Servlet*Context* in just a few pages. For now, we care only about Servlet*Config*, because that's where you get your servlet init parameters.

Q: Wait a minute! In the last chapter you said that we could override the init() method, and nobody said a word about the ServletConfig argument!

A: We didn't mention that the init() method takes a ServletConfig because ***the one you override doesn't take one***. Your superclass includes two versions of init(), one that takes a ServletConfig and a convenience version that's a no-arg. The inherited init(ServletConfig) method calls the no-arg init() method, so the only one you need to override is the no-arg version.

There's no law that stops you from overriding the one that takes a ServletConfig, but if you DO, then you better call super.init(ServletConfig)! But there's really NO reason why you need to override the init(ServletConfig) method, since you can always *get* your ServletConfig by calling your inherited getServletConfig() method.

The servlet init parameters are read only ONCE—when the Container initializes the servlet

When the Container makes a servlet, it reads the DD and creates the name/value pairs for the ServletConfig. The Container never reads the init parameters again! Once the parameters are in the ServletConfig, they won't be read again until/unless you redeploy the servlet. *Think about that.*

1. Container reads the Deployment Descriptor for this servlet, including the servlet init parameters (<init-param>).

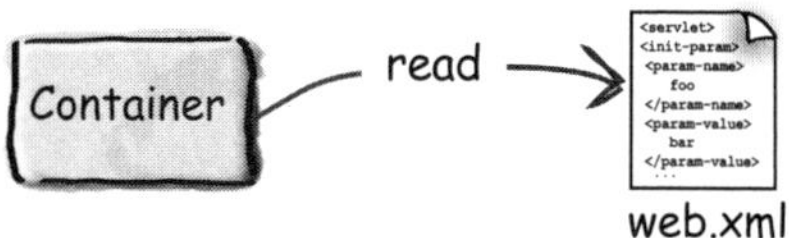

2. Container creates a new ServletConfig instance for this servlet.

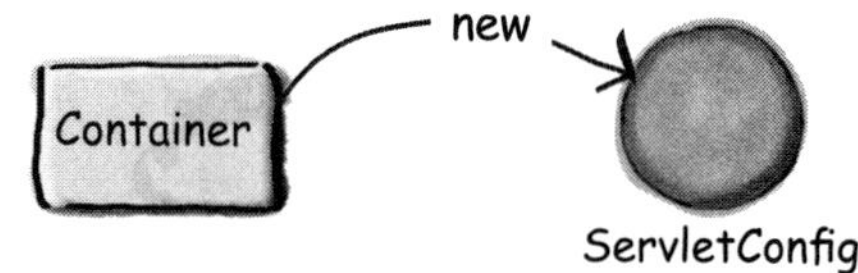

3. Container creates a name/value pair of Strings for each servlet init parameter. Assume we have only one.

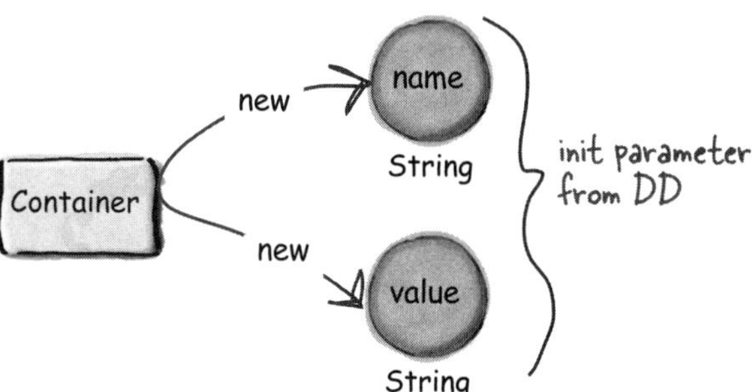

4. Container gives the ServletConfig references to the name/value init parameters.

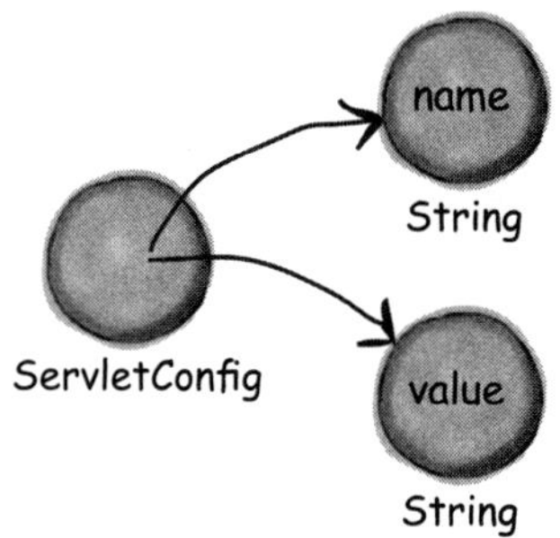

5. Container creates a new instance of the servlet class.

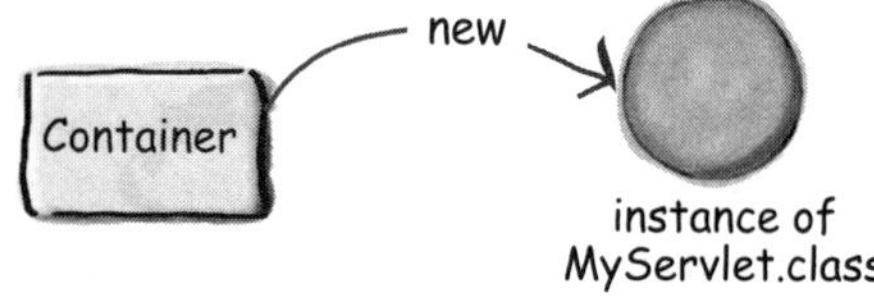

6. Container calls the servlet's init() method, passing in the reference to the ServletConfig.

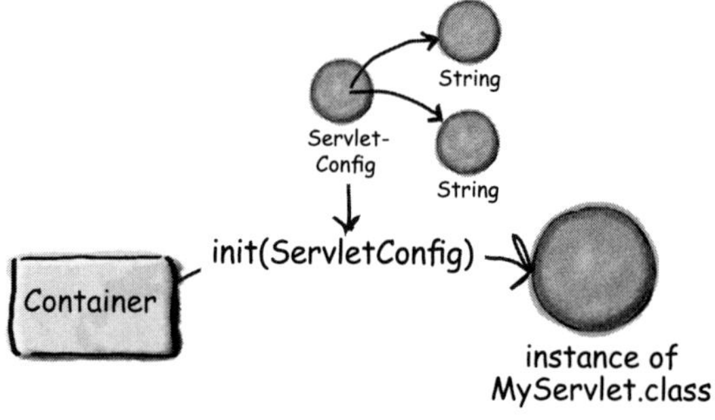

Since the Container reads the servlet init parameters only *once*, you *still* can't change your email address during the life of the servlet. So this is a dumb solution.

It's still way better than putting it in my servlet source code. All I have to do is change the xml and hit the "redeploy" button, and the new address will be in the ServletConfig.

there are no Dumb Questions

Q: So, um, where's that "redeploy" button on Tomcat?

A: With Tomcat, there *isn't* a one-button, really simple admin tool for deployment and redeployment (although there *is* an admin tool that ships with Tomcat). But think about it—what's the worst you have to do to change the servlet's init parameters? You make a quick change to the web.xml file, shut down Tomcat (bin/shutdown.sh), then restart Tomcat (bin/startup.sh). On restart, Tomcat looks in its *webapps* directory, and deploys everything it finds there.

Q: Sure it's easy to tell Tomcat to shutdown and startup, but what about the web apps that are running? They all have to go down!

A: Technically, yes. Taking your web apps down so that you can redeploy one servlet is a little harsh, especially if you have a lot of traffic on your web site. But that's why most of the production-quality Web Containers let you do a ***hot redeploy***, which means that you don't have to restart your server or take any other web apps down. In fact, Tomcat *does* include a *manager* tool that will let you deploy, undeploy, and redeploy entire web apps *without* restarting Tomcat. In a production environment, that's what you'd use. But for testing, it's easier to just restart Tomcat. Info on the management tool is at:

http://jakarta.apache.org/tomcat/tomcat-5.0-doc/manager-howto.html

But in the real world, even a hot redeploy is a Big Deal, and taking even a single app down just because the init parameter value changed can be a bad idea. If the values of your init parameters are going to change *frequently*, you're better off having your servlet methods get the values from a file or database, but this approach will mean a lot more overhead each time your servlet code runs, instead of only once during initialization.

Testing your ServletConfig

javax.servlet.ServletConfig

<<interface>> **ServletConfig**
getInitParameter(String)
Enumeration getInitParameterNames()
getServletContext()
getServletName()

Most people never use this method.

ServletConfig's main job is to give you init parameters. It can also give you a ServletContext, but we'll usually get a context in a different way, and the getServletName() method is rarely useful.

In the DD (web.xml) file:

```
<web-app xmlns="http://java.sun.com/xml/ns/j2ee"
    xmlns:xsi="http://www.w3.org/2001/XMLSchema-instance"
    xsi:schemaLocation="http://java.sun.com/xml/ns/j2ee/web-app_2_4.xsd"
    version="2.4">
  <servlet>
    <servlet-name>BeerParamTests</servlet-name>
    <servlet-class>com.example.TestInitParams</servlet-class>
    <init-param>
      <param-name>adminEmail</param-name>
      <param-value>likewecare@wickedlysmart.com</param-value>
    </init-param>
    <init-param>
      <param-name>mainEmail</param-name>
      <param-value>blooper@wickedlysmart.com</param-value>
    </init-param>
  </servlet>
  <servlet-mapping>
    <servlet-name>BeerParamTests</servlet-name>
    <url-pattern>/Tester.do</url-pattern>
  </servlet-mapping>
</web-app>
```

In a servlet class:

```
package com.example;
import javax.servlet.*;
import javax.servlet.http.*;
import java.io.*;

public class TestInitParams extends HttpServlet {

  public void doGet(HttpServletRequest request, HttpServletResponse response)
                                                   throws IOException, ServletException {
        response.setContentType("text/html");
        PrintWriter out = response.getWriter();
        out.println("test init parameters<br>");

        java.util.Enumeration e = getServletConfig().getInitParameterNames();
        while(e.hasMoreElements()) {
           out.println("<br>param name = " + e.nextElement() + "<br>");
        }
        out.println("main email is " + getServletConfig().getInitParameter("mainEmail"));
        out.println("<br>");
        out.println("admin email is " + getServletConfig().getInitParameter("adminEmail"));
     }
  }
```

Uh-oh. I just realized that in my real app I'm using JSP to render the page. So can a JSP "see" a servlet's init parameters?

How can a JSP get servlet init parameters?

A *Servlet*Config is for *servlet* configuration (it doesn't say *JSP*Config). So if you want *other* parts of your application to use the same info you put in the servlet's init parameters in the DD, you need something more.

What about the way we did it with the beer app? We passed the model info to the JSP using a request attribute...

Remember? We got the client's color choice from the request.

```
// inside the doPost() method
String color = request.getParameter("color");

BeerExpert be = new BeerExpert();
List result = be.getBrands(color);

request.setAttribute("styles", result);
```

Then we instantiated and used the MODEL to get the info we need for the VIEW.

Then we set an "attribute" in the request, and the JSP we forward the request to was able to get it.

We *could* do it this way. The request object lets you set *attributes* (think of them as a name/value pair where the value can be any object) that any other servlet or JSP that gets the request can use. That means any servlet or JSP to which the request is forwarded using a *RequestDispatcher*. We'll look at RequestDispatcher in detail at the end of this chapter, but for now all we care about is getting the data (in this case the email address) to the pieces of the web app that need it, rather than just one servlet.

Setting a request *attribute* works... but only for the JSP to which you forwarded the request

With the beer app, it made sense to store the model info for the client's request in the *request object*, because the next step was to *forward* the request to the JSP responsible for creating the view. Since that JSP needed the model data and the data was relevant to only that particular request, everything was fine.

But that doesn't help us with the email address, because we might need to use it from all over the application! There *is* a way to have a servlet read the init parameters and then store them in a place other parts of the app could use, but then we'd have to know *which* servlet would always run first when the app is deployed, and any changes to the web app could break the whole thing. No, that won't do either.

But I really want ALL the parts of my web app to have access to the email address. With init parameters, I have to configure them in the DD for every servlet, and then have all the servlets make them available for the JSPs. How boring is that? Not maintainable either. I need something more *global.*

I wonder if there's something like init parameters for the *application?*

Context init parameters to the rescue

Context init parameters work just like *servlet* init parameters, except context parameters are available to the entire webapp, not just a single servlet. So that means any servlet and JSP in the app automatically has access to the context init parameters, so we don't have to worry about configuring the DD for every servlet, and when the value changes, you only have to change it one place!

In the DD (web.xml) file:

We took the <init-param> element out of the <servlet> element.

```
<servlet>
    <servlet-name>BeerParamTests</servlet-name>
    <servlet-class>TestInitParams</servlet-class>
</servlet>

<context-param>
    <param-name>adminEmail</param-name>
    <param-value>clientheaderror@wickedlysmart.com</param-value>
</context-param>
```

You give it a param-name and param-value just like with servlet init parameters, except this time it's in the <context-param> element instead of <init-param>.

IMPORTANT!! The <context-param> is for the WHOLE app, so its not nested inside an individual <servlet> element!! Put <context-param> inside the <web-app> but OUTSIDE any <servlet> declaration.

In the servlet code:

```
out.println(getServletContext().getInitParameter("adminEmail"));
```

Every servlet inherits a getServletContext() method (and JSPs have special access to a context as well).

The getServletContext() method returns, surprisingly, a ServletContext object. And one of its methods is getInitParameter().

OR:

```
ServletContext context = getServletContext();
out.println(context.getInitParameter("adminEmail"));
```

Here we broke out the code into TWO steps—getting the ServletContext reference, and calling its getInitParameter() method.

Remember the difference between servlet init parameters and context init parameters

Here's a review of the key differences between *context* init parameters and *servlet* init parameters. Pay special attention to the fact that they're both referred to as *init* parameters, even though only *servlet* init parameters have the word "init" in the DD configuration.

Context init parameters		**Servlet init parameters**
	Deployment Descriptor	
Within the <web-app> element but NOT within a specific <servlet> element		Within the <servlet> element for each specific servlet

Context init parameters:

```
<web-app ...>
  <context-param>
    <param-name>foo</param-name>
    <param-value>bar</param-value>
  </context-param>

  <!-- other stuff including
    servlet declarations -->
</web-app>
```

Notice it doesn't say "init" anywhere in the DD for context init parameters, the way it does for servlet init parameters.

Servlet init parameters:

```
<servlet>
  <servlet-name>
     BeerParamTests
  </servlet-name>
  <servlet-class>
     TestInitParams
  </servlet-class>
  <init-param>
    <param-name>foo</param-name>
    <param-value>bar</param-value>
  </init-param>

  <!-- other stuff -->
</servlet>
```

Servlet Code

Context init parameters:

```
getServletContext().getInitParameter("foo");
```

Servlet init parameters:

```
getServletConfig().getInitParameter("foo");
```

It's the same method name!

Availability

Context init parameters: To any servlets and JSPs that are part of this web app.

Servlet init parameters: To only the servlet for which the <init-param> was configured.

(Although the servlet can choose to make it more widely available by storing it in an attribute.)

ServletConfig is one per servlet
ServletContext is one per web app

There's only one ServletContext for an entire web app, and all the parts of the web app share it. But each servlet in the app has its own ServletConfig. The Container makes a ServletContext when a web app is deployed, and makes the context available to each Servlet and JSP (which becomes a servlet) in the web app.

Web app initialization:

- Container reads the DD and creates a name/value String pair for each <context-param>.
- Container creates a new instance of ServletContext.
- Container gives the ServletContext a reference to each name/value pair of the context init parameters.
- Every servlet and JSP deployed as part of a single web app has access to that same ServletContext.

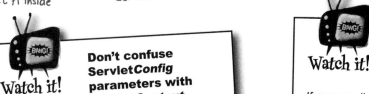

ServletContext

app-wide context init params inside

Servlet A

Servlet B

Servlet C

JSP

ServletConfig

init params for Servlet A inside

ServletConfig

init params for Servlet B inside

ServletConfig

init params for Servlet C inside

ServletConfig

Yes, JSPs are turned into first-class servlets, so they also get their own ServletConfig.

Don't confuse ServletConfig parameters with ServletContext parameters!

*You really have to keep these straight on the exam, and it's tricky. You MUST know that both Servlet**Config** and Servlet**Context** have init parameters, and both have the same getter method—getInitParameter(). BUT... you also have to know that context init parameters are set with <context-param> (not inside a <servlet> element) while servlet init parameters use <init-param> inside the individual <servlet> declarations in the DD.*

If the app is distributed, there's one ServletContext per JVM!

*If your application is distributed across multiple servers (probably in a clustered environment), your web app really COULD have more than one ServletContext. A **ServletContext is one per app, but only if the app is in a single JVM!** In a distributed environment, you'll have **one ServletContext per JVM**. Now, chances are this won't create problems, but if you have a distributed web app, you better consider the consequences of having different contexts for each JVM.*

there are no Dumb Questions

Q: What's with the inconsistent naming scheme? How come the DD elements are <*context*-param> and <*init*-param> but in the servlet code, BOTH use the getInitParameter() method?

A: They didn't ask us to help them come up with the names. If they had, of course, we'd have said it should be get*Init*Parameter() and get*Context*Parameter(), to match the XML elements in the DD. Or, they could have used different XML elements—perhaps <servlet-init-param> and <context-init-param>. But no, that would have sucked all the fun out of trying to keep them straight.

Q: Why would I ever use <init-param> anyway? Wouldn't I always want to use <context-param> so that other parts of my app could reuse the values and I won't have to duplicate XML code for every servlet declaration?

A: It all depends on which part of your app is supposed to see the value. Your application logic might require you to use a value that you want to restrict to only an individual servlet. But typically, developers find app-wide *context* init parameters a lot more helpful than servlet-specific *servlet* init parameters. Perhaps the most common use of a context parameter is storing database lookup names. You'd want all parts of your app to have access to the correct name, and when it changes, you want to change it in only one place.

Q: What happens if I give a context init parameter the same name as a servlet init parameter in the same web app?

A: The molecular-sized black hole miraculously created in a research facility in New Jersey will slip from its containment field, plummet to the earth's core, and destroy the planet.

Or maybe nothing, because there's no name space conflict since you get the parameters through two different objects (ServletContext or ServletConfig).

Q: If you modify the XML to change the value of an init parameter (either servlet or context), when does the servlet or the rest of the web app see the change?

A: ONLY when the web app is redeployed. Remember—we talked about this before—the servlet is initialized only once, at the beginning of its life, and that's when it's given its ServletConfig and ServletContext. The Container reads the values from the DD when it creates those two objects, and sets the values.

Q: Can't I get around this by setting the values at runtime? Surely there's an API that'll let me change those values dynamically...

A: No, there's not. Look in ServletContext or ServletConfig and you'll find a getter (getInitParameter()), but you won't find a setter. There's no setInitParameter().

Q: That's lame.

A: These are *init* parameters. *Init* from the Latin word *initialization*. If you think of them purely as ***deploy-time constants***, you'll have the right perspective. In fact, that's so important we're going to say it again in a bolder way:

Think of init parameters as deploy-time constants!

You can *get* them at runtime, but you can't *set* them. There's no *set*InitParameter().

Code Magnets

Rearrange the magnets to form a DD that declares a parameter that matches the servlet code:

`getServletContext().getInitParameter("foo");`

You won't use all of the magnets!

(Note: when you see <web-app ... >, remember that this is our short-cut to save space on the page. You can't deploy a web.xml file unless the <web-app> tag has all the attributes it needs.)

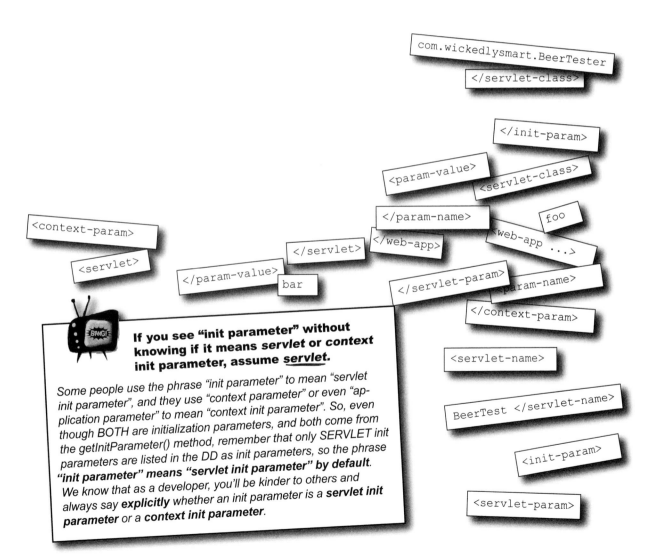

```
com.wickedlysmart.BeerTester
</servlet-class>
</init-param>
<param-value>
<servlet-class>
</param-name>
foo
<context-param>
</servlet>
</web-app>
<web-app ...>
<servlet>
</param-value>
bar
</servlet-param>
<param-name>
</context-param>
<servlet-name>
BeerTest </servlet-name>
<init-param>
<servlet-param>
```

If you see "init parameter" without knowing if it means *servlet* or *context* init parameter, assume servlet.

Some people use the phrase "init parameter" to mean "servlet init parameter", and they use "context parameter" or even "application parameter" to mean "context init parameter". So, even though BOTH are initialization parameters, and both come from the getInitParameter() method, remember that only SERVLET init parameters are listed in the DD as init parameters, so the phrase ***"init parameter" means "servlet init parameter" by default****. We know that as a developer, you'll be kinder to others and always say* ***explicitly*** *whether an init parameter is a* ***servlet init parameter*** *or a* ***context init parameter****.*

So what *else* can you do with your ServletContext?

A ServletContext is a JSP or servlet's connection to both the Container and the other parts of the web app. Here are some of the ServletContext methods. We put the ones you should know for the exam in bold.

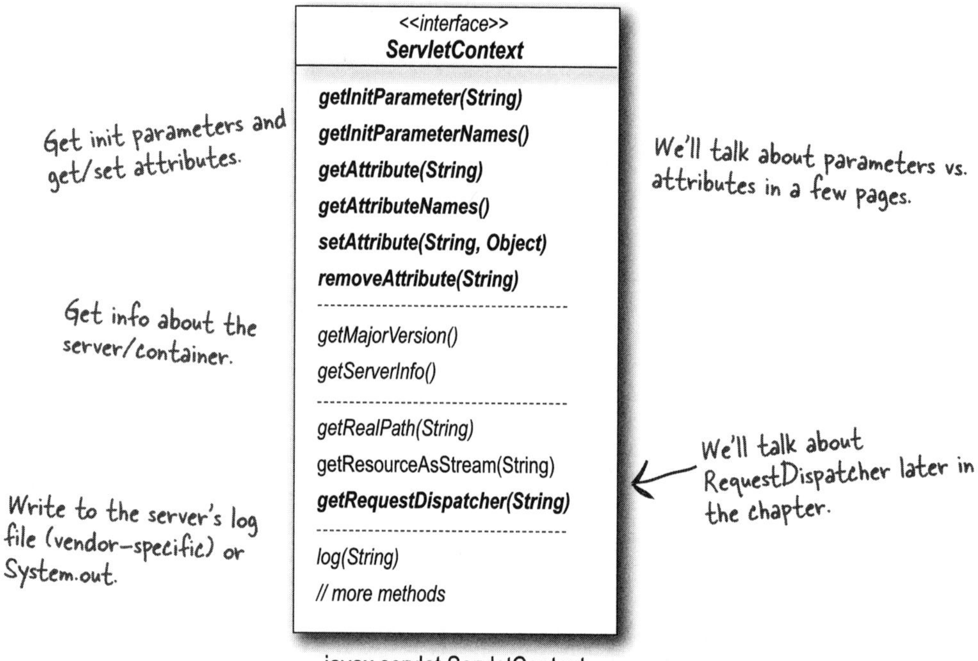

You complete me.

Before I came into your life, you were just another loser object instead of a real servlet.

Servlet

ServletContext

<<interface>>
ServletContext

Get init parameters and get/set attributes.

- ***getInitParameter(String)***
- ***getInitParameterNames()***
- ***getAttribute(String)***
- ***getAttributeNames()***
- ***setAttribute(String, Object)***
- ***removeAttribute(String)***

We'll talk about parameters vs. attributes in a few pages.

Get info about the server/container.

- *getMajorVersion()*
- *getServerInfo()*

- *getRealPath(String)*
- getResourceAsStream(String)
- ***getRequestDispatcher(String)***

We'll talk about RequestDispatcher later in the chapter.

Write to the server's log file (vendor-specific) or System.out.

- *log(String)*
- *// more methods*

javax.servlet.ServletContext

You can get a ServletContext in two different ways...

A servlet's ServletConfig object always holds a reference to the ServletContext for that servlet. So don't be fooled if you see servlet code on the exam that says:

```
getServletConfig().getServletContext().getInitParameter()
```

Not only is that legal, but it does the same thing as:

```
this.getServletContext().getInitParameter()
```

In a servlet, the only time you would NEED to go through your ServletConfig to get your ServletContext is if you're in a Servlet class that doesn't extend HttpServlet or GenericServlet (the getServletContext() method you inherit comes from GenericServlet). But the chance of ANYONE using a non-HTTP servlet is, well, asymptotically approaching zero. So just call your own getServletContext() method, but don't be dazed or confused if you see code that uses the ServletConfig to get the context.

But what if the code is inside some class that is NOT a servlet (a helper/utility class, for example)? Someone might have passed a ServletConfig to that class, and the class code would have to use getServletContext() to get a reference to the ServletContext object.

Q: How do all the parts of a web app get access to their own ServletContext?

A: For servlets, you already know: call your inherited getServletContext() method.

For JSPs it's a little different—JSPs have something called "implicit objects", and ServletContext is one of them. You'll see exactly how a JSP uses a ServletContext when we get to the JSP chapters.

Q: So you get built-in logging through your context? That sounds VERY helpful!

A: Um, no. Not unless you have a really small, simple web app. There are much better ways to do logging. The most popular, robust logging mechanism is Log4j; you can find it on the Apache site at:

`http://jakarta.apache.org/log4j`

You can also use the logging API from java.util.logging, added to J2SE in version 1.4.

It's fine to use the ServletContext log() method for simple experiments, but in a real production environment, you will almost certainly want to choose something else. There's a good reference on web app logging with and without Log4j in the *Java Servlet & JSP Cookbook* from O'Reilly.

Logging is not part of the exam objectives, but it's important. Fortunately, you'll find the APIs easy to use.

Hate to spoil your ServletContext party, but, um, those init parameters can't be anything except STRINGS! That's it! What if I want to initialize my app with a database DataSource that all the servlets can use?

What if you want an app init parameter that's a database DataSource?

Context parameters can't be anything except Strings. After all, you can't very well stuff a *Dog* object into an XML deployment descriptor. (Actually, you *could* represent a serialized object in XML, but there's no facility for this in the Servlet spec today... maybe in the future.)

What if you really want all the parts of your web app to have access to a shared database connection? You can certainly put the DataSource lookup name in a context init parameter, and that's probably the most common use of context parameters today.

But then ***who does the work of turning the String parameter into an actual DataSource reference*** that all parts of the web app can share?

You can't really put that code in a servlet, because which servlet would you choose to be The One To Lookup The DataSource And Store It In An Attribute? Do you *really* want to try to guarantee that one servlet in particular will always run first? Think about it.

FLEX YOUR MIND

How could you solve this problem?

How could you initialize a web app with an object? Assume that you need the String context init parameter in order to create that object (think about the database example).

Oh, if only there were a way to have something like a *main method* for my whole web app. Some code that always runs before ANY servlets or JSPs...

What she really wants is a *listener.*

She wants to listen for a context initialization event, so that she can get the context init parameters and ***run some code before the rest of the app can service a client.***

She needs something that can be sitting there, waiting to be notified that the app is starting up.

But which part of the app could do the work? You don't want to pick a servlet—that's not a servlet's job.

There's no problem in a plain old standalone Java app, because you've got main()! But with a servlet, what do you do?

You need *something else.* Not a servlet or JSP, but some other kind of Java object whose sole purpose in life is to initialize the app (and possibly to *un*initialize it too, cleaning up resources when it learns of the app's demise...).

She wants a ServletContextListener

We can make a separate class, not a servlet or JSP, that can listen for the two key events in a ServletContext's life—initialization (creation) and destruction. That separate class implements javax.servlet.ServletContextListener.

We need a separate object that can:

- Get notified when the context is initialized (app is being deployed).
    - Get the context init parameters from the ServletContext.
    - Use the init parameter lookup name to make a database connection.
    - Store the database connection as an attribute, so that all parts of the web app can access it.
- Get notified when the context is destroyed (the app is undeployed or goes down).
    - Close the database connection.

A ServletContextListener class:

ServletContextListener is in javax.servlet package.

A context listener is simple: implement ServletContextListener.

```
import javax.servlet.*;

public class MyServletContextListener implements ServletContextListener {

   public void contextInitialized(ServletContextEvent event) {
     //code to initialize the database connection
     //and store it as a context attribute
   }

   public void contextDestroyed(ServletContextEvent event) {
     //code to close the database connection
   }
}
```

These are the two notifications you get. Both give you a ServletContextEvent.

OK, I have a listener class. Now what do I do? Where do I put the class? Who instantiates it? How do I register for the events? How does the listener set the attribute in the right ServletContext?

FLEX YOUR MIND

What do you think the mechanism might be for making a listener be part of a specific web app?

Hint: how do you tell the Container about the *other* parts of your web app? Where might the Container discover your listener?

Tutorial: a simple ServletContextListener

Now we'll walk through the steps of making and running a ServletContextListener. This is just a simple test class so that you can see how all the pieces work together; we're not using the database connection example because you'd have to set up a database to make it work. But the steps are the same *regardless* of the code you put in your listener callback methods.

In this example, we'll turn a String init parameter into an actual object—a Dog. The listener's job is to get the context init parameter for the dog's breed (Beagle, Poodle, etc.), then use that String to construct a Dog object. The listener then sticks the Dog object into a ServletContext attribute, so that the servlet can retrieve it.

The point is that the servlet now has access to a shared application *object* (in this case a Dog), and doesn't have to read the context parameters. Whether the shared object is a Dog or a database connection doesn't matter. The key is to use the init parameters to create a single object that all parts of the app will share.

In this example, we'll put a Dog into a ServletContext.

Our Dog example:

- The listener object asks the ServletContextEvent object for a reference to the app's ServletContext.
- The listener uses the reference to the ServletContext to get the context init parameter for "breed", which is a String representing a dog breed.
- The listener uses that dog breed String to construct a Dog object.
- The listener uses the reference to the ServletContext to *set* the Dog attribute in the ServletContext.
- The tester servlet in this web app *gets* the Dog object from the ServletContext, and calls the Dog's getBreed() method.

Making and using a context listener

Maybe you're still wondering how the Container discovers and uses the listener... ***You configure a listener the same way you tell the Container about the rest of your web app—through the web.xml Deployment Descriptor!***

To listen for ServletContext events, write a listener class that implements ServletContextListener, put it in your WEB-INF/classes directory, and tell the Container by putting a <listener> element in the Deployment Descriptor.

1 Create a listener class

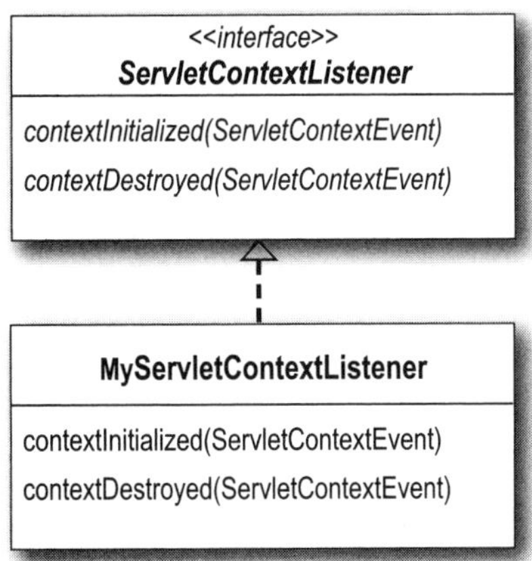

2 Put the class in WEB-INF/classes

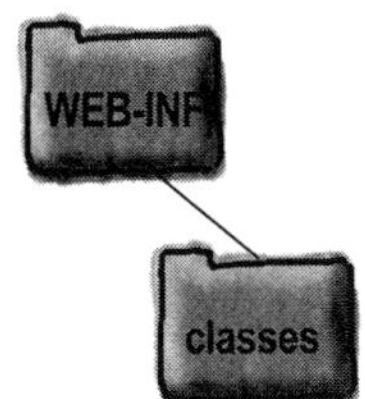

(This isn't the ONLY place it can go.... WEB-INF/classes is one of several places the Container can look for classes. We'll cover the others in the Deployment chapter.)

3 Put a <listener> element in the web.xml Deployment Descriptor

```
<listener>
  <listener-class>
     com.example.MyServletContextListener
  </listener-class>
</listener>
```

Question for you—which part of the DD does the <listener> element go into? Does it go into a <servlet> element, or just under <web-app>? Think about it.

We need three classes and one DD

For our context listener test example, we need to write the classes and the web.xml file.

For ease of testing, we'll put all of the classes in the same package: *com.example*

1 The ServletContextListener

MyServletContextListener.java

This class implements ServletContextListener, gets the context init parameters, creates the Dog, and sets the Dog as context attribute.

2 The attribute class

Dog.java

The Dog class is just a plain old Java class. Its job is to be the attribute value that the ServletContextListener instantiates and sets in the ServletContext, for the servlet to retrieve.

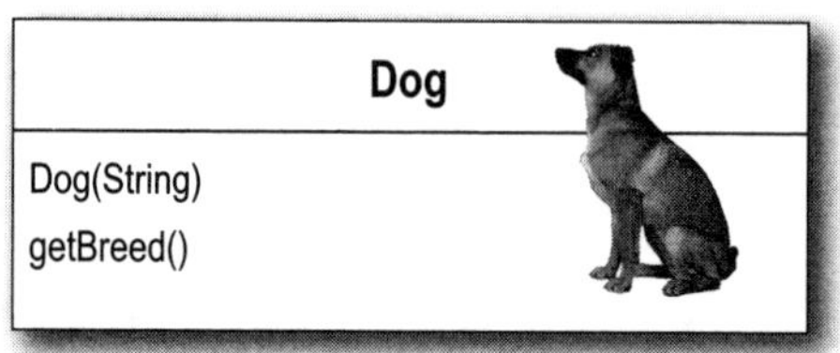

3 The Servlet

ListenerTester.java

This class extends HttpServlet. Its job is to verify that the listener worked by getting the Dog attribute from the context, invoking getBreed() on the Dog, and printing the result to the response (so we'll see it in the browser).

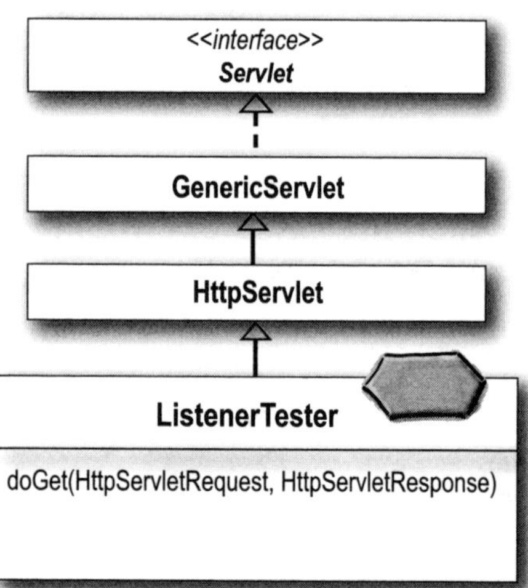

Writing the listener class

It works just like other types of listeners you might be familiar with, such as Swing GUI event handlers. Remember, all we need to do is get the context init parameters to find out the dog breed, make the Dog object, and put the Dog into the context as an attribute.

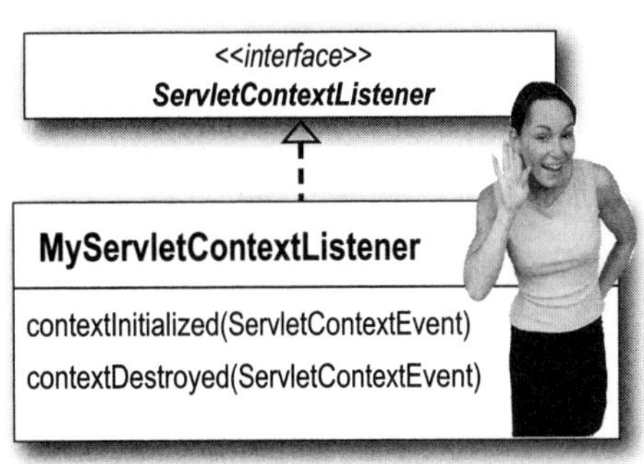


```
package com.example;

import javax.servlet.*;

public class MyServletContextListener implements ServletContextListener {

   public void contextInitialized(ServletContextEvent event) {

      ServletContext sc = event.getServletContext();

      String dogBreed = sc.getInitParameter("breed");

      Dog d = new Dog(dogBreed);

      sc.setAttribute("dog", d);
   }


  public void contextDestroyed(ServletContextEvent event) {
    // nothing to do here
  }
}
```

Implement javax.servlet.ServletContextListener.

Ask the event for the ServletContext.

Use the context to get the init parameter.

Make a new Dog.

Use the context to set an attribute (a name/object pair) that is the Dog. Now other parts of the app will be able to get the value of the attribute (the Dog).

We don't need anything here. The Dog doesn't need to be cleaned up... when the context goes away, it means the whole app is going down, including the Dog.

Writing the attribute class (Dog)

Oh yeah, we need a Dog class—the class representing the object we're going to store in the ServletContext, after reading the context init parameters.

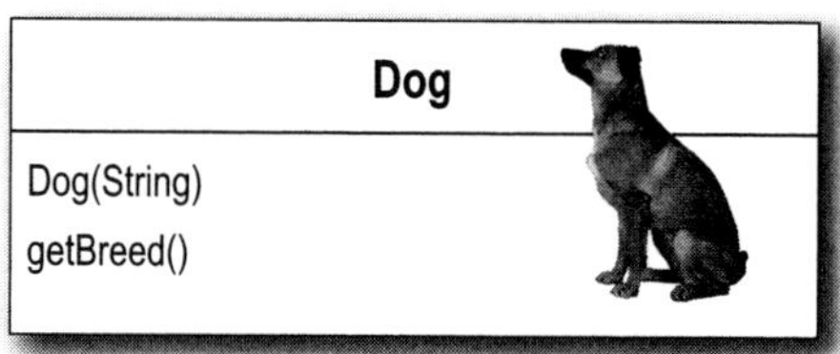


```
package com.example;

public class Dog {
   private String breed;

   public Dog(String breed) {
     this.breed = breed;
   }

   public String getBreed() {
      return breed;
   }
}
```

Nothing special here. Just a plain old Java class.

(We'll use the context init parameter as the argument for the Dog constructor.)

Our servlet will get the Dog from the context (the Dog that the listener sets as an attribute), call the Dog's getBreed() method, and print out the breed in the response so we can see it in the browser.

Q: I thought I read somewhere that servlet attributes had to be Serializable...

A: Interesting question. There are several different attribute types, and whether the attribute should be Serializable only matters with Session attributes. And the scenario in which it matters is *only* if the application is distributed across more than one JVM. We'll talk all about that in the Sessions chapter.

There's no technical *need* to have any attributes (including Session attributes) be Serializable, although you might consider making all of your attributes Serializable by default, unless you have a really good reason NOT to.

Think about it—are you really certain that nobody will ever want to use objects of that type as arguments or return values as part of a remote method call? Can you really guarantee that anyone who uses this class (Dog, in this case) will never run in a distributed environment?

So, although you aren't *required* to make any attributes Serializable, you probably *should* if you can.

Writing the servlet class

This is the class that tests the ServletContextListener. If everything is working right, by the time the Servlet's doGet() method runs for the first time, the Dog will be waiting as an attribute in the ServletContext.

HttpServlet

ListenerTester

doGet(HttpServletRequest, HttpServletResponse)

```
package com.example;

import javax.servlet.*;
import javax.servlet.http.*;
import java.io.*;

public class ListenerTester extends HttpServlet {

  public void doGet (HttpServletRequest request, HttpServletResponse response)
                                          throws IOException, ServletException {

     response.setContentType("text/html");
     PrintWriter out = response.getWriter();

     out.println("test context attributes set by listener<br>");

     out.println("<br>");

     Dog dog = (Dog) getServletContext().getAttribute("dog");

     out.println("Dog's breed is: " + dog.getBreed());
  }
}
```

Nothing special so far... just a regular servlet.

Now we get the Dog from the ServletContext. If the listener worked, the Dog will be there BEFORE this service method is called for the first time.

don't forget the cast!!

If things didn't work, THIS is where we'll find out... we'll get a big fat NullPointerException if we try to call getBreed() and there's no Dog.

getAttribute() returns type Object! You need to cast the return!

But getInitParameter() returns a String. So you must cast the return of getAttribute(), but the return of getInitParameter() can be assigned directly to a String. So... don't be fooled by bad exam code that doesn't use a cast:

Dog d = ctx.getAttribute("dog"); ← *Bad!!*

(Assume ctx is a ServletContext.)

Writing the Deployment Descriptor

Now we tell the Container that we have a listener for this app, using the <listener> element. This element is simple—it needs only the class name. That's it.

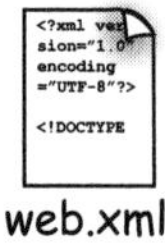

This is the web.xml file inside the WEB-INF directory for this web app.

```
<web-app xmlns="http://java.sun.com/xml/ns/j2ee"
    xmlns:xsi="http://www.w3.org/2001/XMLSchema-instance"
    xsi:schemaLocation="http://java.sun.com/xml/ns/j2ee/web-app_2_4.xsd"
    version="2.4">

  <servlet>
    <servlet-name>ListenerTester</servlet-name>
    <servlet-class>com.example.ListenerTester</servlet-class>
  </servlet>

  <servlet-mapping>
    <servlet-name>ListenerTester</servlet-name>
    <url-pattern>/ListenTest.do</url-pattern>
  </servlet-mapping>

  <context-param>
    <param-name>breed</param-name>
    <param-value>Great Dane</param-value>
  </context-param>

  <listener>
    <listener-class>
       com.example.MyServletContextListener
    </listener-class>
  </listener>

</web-app>
```

We need a context init parameter for the app. The listener needs this to construct the Dog.

Register this class as a listener. IMPORTANT: the <listener> element does NOT go inside a <servlet> element. That wouldn't work because a context listener is for a ServletContext (which means application-wide) event. The whole point is to initialize the app BEFORE any servlets are initialized.

there are no Dumb Questions

Q: Hold on... how are you telling the Container that this is a listener for ServletContext events? There doesn't seem to be an XML element for <listener-type> or anything that says what type of events this listener is for. But I noticed you have "ServletContextListener" as part of the class name—is that how the Container knows? By the naming convention?

A: No. There's no naming convention. We just did it that way to make it painfully clear what kind of a class we wrote. The Container figures it out simply by inspecting the class and noticing the listener interface (or interfaces; a listener can implement more than one listener interface).

Q: Does that mean there are other types of listeners in the servlet API?

A: Yes, there are several other types of listeners that we'll talk about in a minute.

Compile and deploy

Let's get it all working. The steps are:

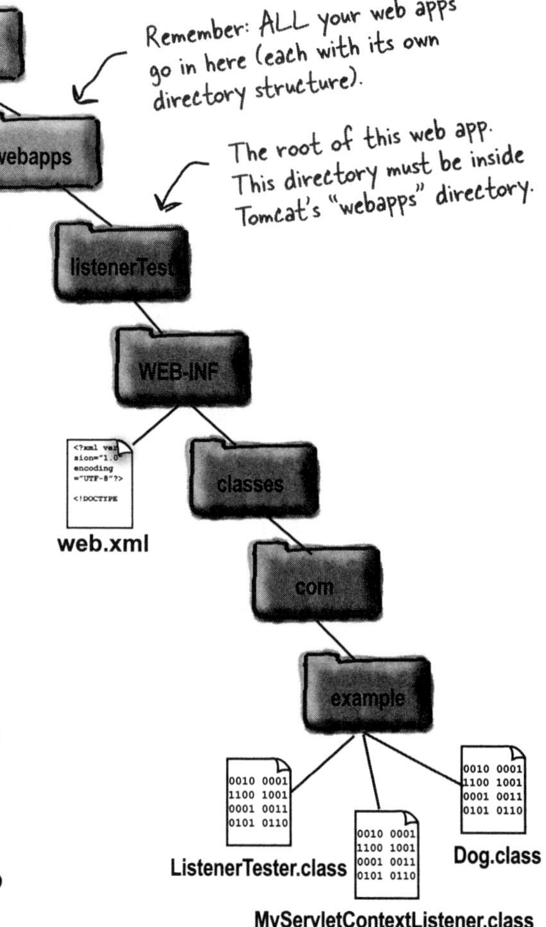
tomcat
Remember: ALL your web apps go in here (each with its own directory structure).
webapps
The root of this web app. This directory must be inside Tomcat's "webapps" directory.
listenerTest
WEB-INF
web.xml
classes
com
example
ListenerTester.class
MyServletContextListener.class
Dog.class

1. **Compile the three classes**

   They're all in the same package...

2. **Create a new web app in Tomcat**

   - Create a directory named listenerTest and place it inside the Tomcat webapps directory.
   - Create a directory named WEB-INF and place it inside the listenerTest directory.
   - Put your web.xml file in the WEB-INF directory.
   - Make a classes directory inside WEB-INF.
   - Make a directory structure inside classes that matches your package structure: a directory called com that contains example.

3. **Copy your three compiled files into your web app directory structure in Tomcat**

```
listenerTest/WEB-INF/classes/com/example/Dog.class
listenerTest/WEB-INF/classes/com/example/ListenerTester.class
listenerTest/WEB-INF/classes/com/example/MyServletContextListener.class
```

4. **Put your web.xml Deployment Descriptor into the WEB-INF directory for this web app**

```
listenerTest/WEB-INF/web.xml
```

5. **Deploy the app by shutting down and restarting Tomcat**

Try it out

Bring up your browser and let's hit the servlet directly. We didn't bother making an HTML page, so we'll access the servlet by typing in the URL from the servlet mapping in the DD (ListenTest.do).

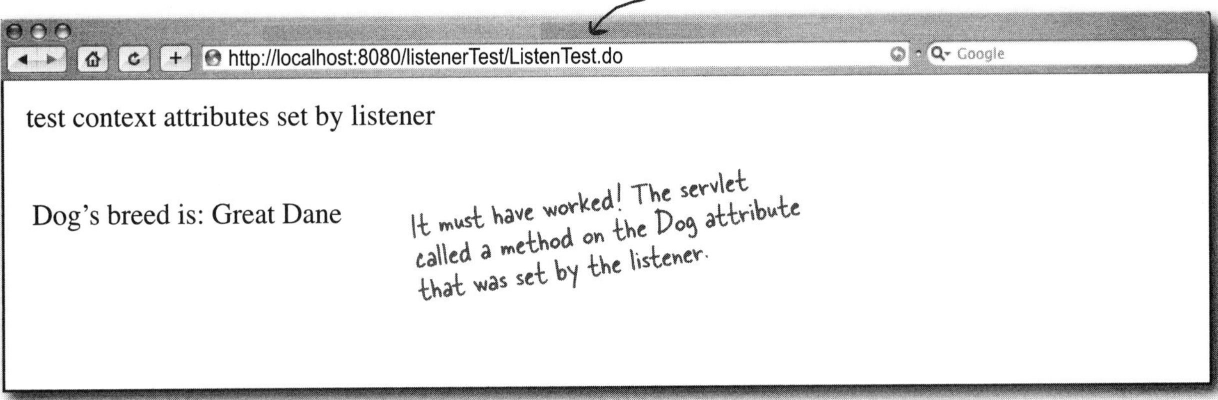
http://localhost:8080/listenerTest/ListenTest.do
Google
test context attributes set by listener
Dog's breed is: Great Dane
It must have worked! The servlet called a method on the Dog attribute that was set by the listener.

Troubleshooting

If you get a NullPointerException, you didn't get a Dog back from getAttribute(). Check the String name used in *set*Attribute() and make sure it matches the String name you're using in *get*Attribute().

Recheck your web.xml and make sure the <listener> is registered.

Try looking at the server logs and see if you can find out if the listener is actually being called.

To make it as confusing as possible, we gave everything a subtly different name. We want to make sure you're paying attention to how these names are used, and when you name everything the same, it's tough to tell how the names affect your app.

Servlet class name: ***ListenerTester.class***

Web app directory name: ***listenerTest***

URL pattern mapped to this the servlet: ***ListenTest.do***

Be careful about whether it's Listener or Listen, Tester or Test.

The full story...

Here's the scenario from start (app initialization) to finish (servlet runs). You'll see in step 11 we condensed the Servlet initialization into one big step.

1. Container reads the Deployment Descriptor for this app, including the <listener> and <context-param> elements.

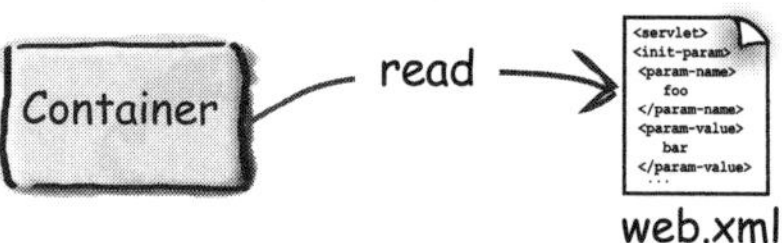

2. Container creates a new ServletContext for this application, that all parts of the app will share.

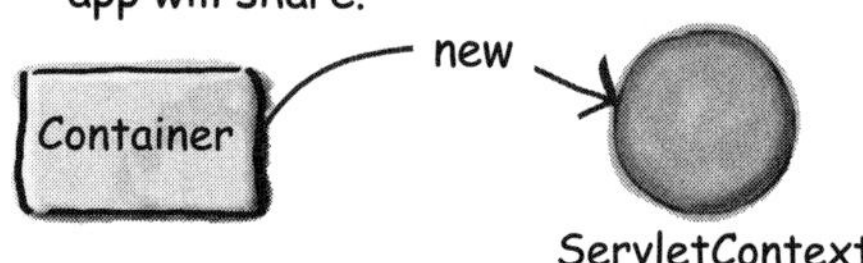

3. Container creates a name/value pair of Strings for each context init parameter. Assume we have only one.

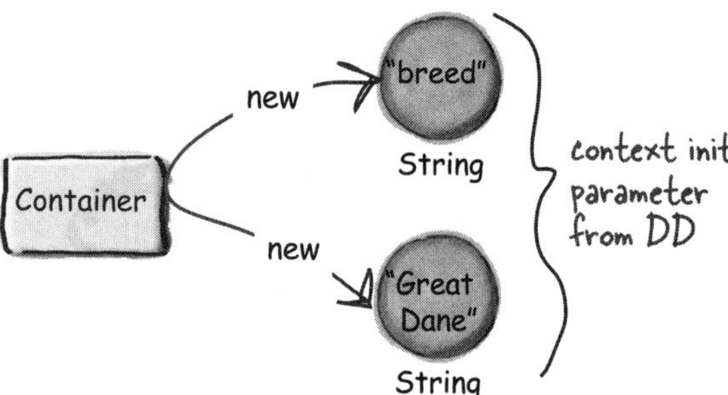

4. Container gives the ServletContext references to the name/value parameters.

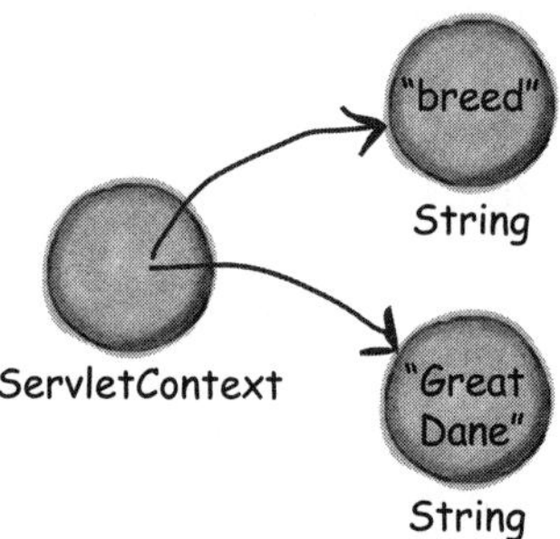

5. Container creates a new instance of the MySeveletContextListener class.

6. Container calls the listener's contextInitialized() method, passing in a new ServletContextEvent. The event object has a reference to the ServletContext, so the event-handling code can get the context from the event, and get the context init parameter from the context.

The story continues...

7. Listener asks ServletContextEvent for a reference to the ServletContext.

8. Listener asks ServletContext for the context init parameter "breed" .

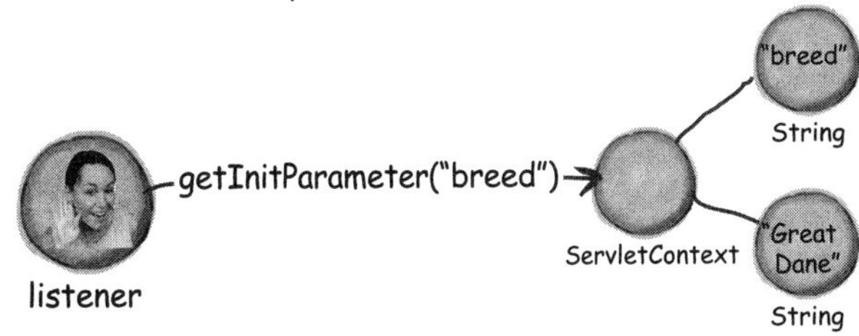

9. Listener uses the init parameter to construct a new Dog object.

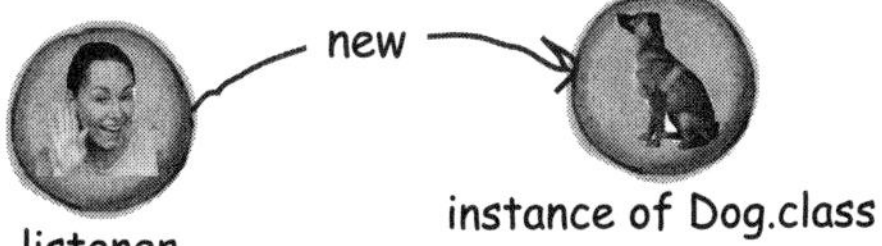

10. Listener sets the Dog as an attribute in the ServletContext.

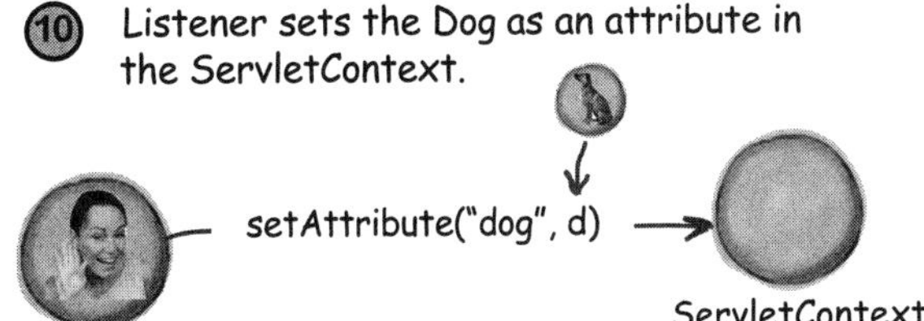

11. Container makes a new Servlet (i.e., makes a new ServletConfig with init parameters, gives the ServletConfig a reference to the ServletContext, then calls the Servlet's init() method).

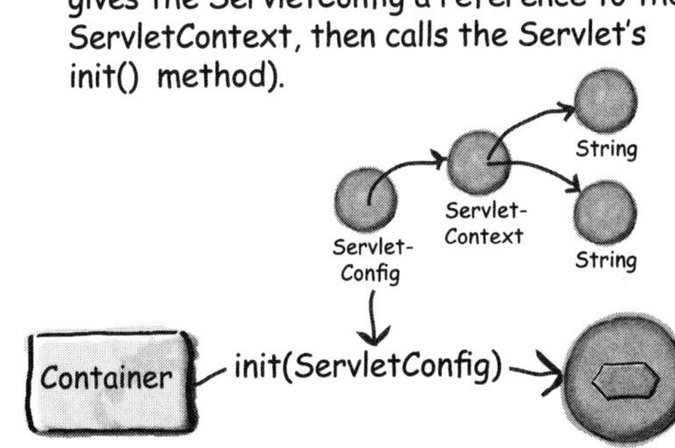

12. Servlet gets a request, and asks the ServletContext for the attribute "dog".

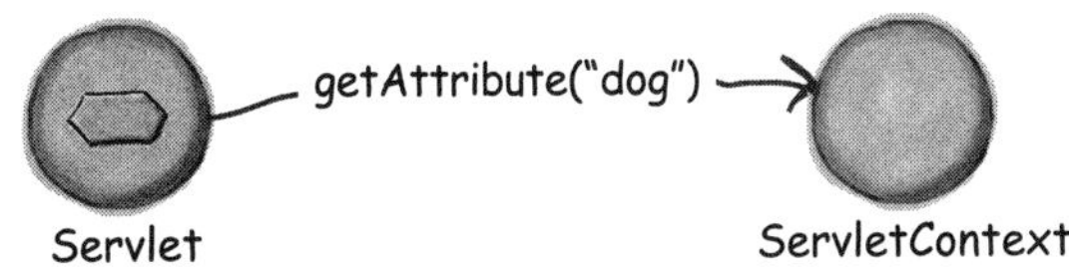

13. Servlet calls getBreed() on the Dog (and prints that to the HttpResponse).

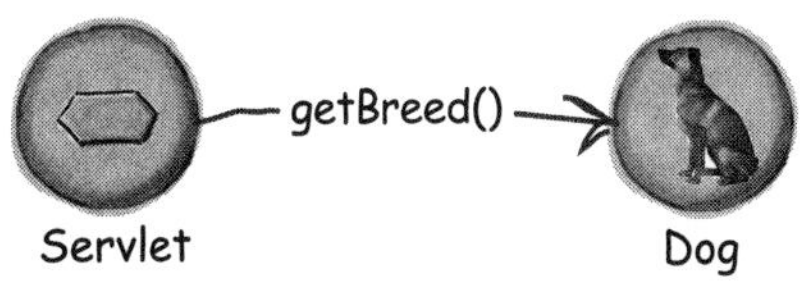

I just thought of something... since attributes *can* be set programmatically (unlike init parameters), can I listen for *attribute* events? Like if someone adds or replaces a Dog?

Listeners: not just for context events...

Where there's a *lifecycle moment,* there's usually a *listener* to hear about it. Besides context events, you can listen for events related to context *attributes,* servlet requests and attributes, and HTTP sessions and session attributes.

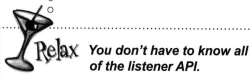

You don't have to know all of the listener API.

Other than ServletContextListener, you really don't need to memorize the methods of each of the listener interfaces. But... you DO need to know the kinds of events that you can listen for.

The exam objectives are clear: you'll be given a scenario (a developer's goal for an application) and you'll need to decide which is the right type of listener, or whether it's even POSSIBLE to be notified of that lifecycle event.

Note: we don't talk about sessions until the next chapter, so don't worry about it if you don't yet know what an HTTP session is or why you care...

Pick the Listener

Match the scenario on the left with the listener interface (at the bottom of the page) that supports that goal. Use each interface only once. *(Yes, we KNOW we haven't looked at these yet. See what you can come up with just by looking at the names. Answers are on the next page, so don't peek!)*

Scenario	Listener interface
You want to know if an attribute in a web app context has been added, removed, or replaced.	______________________
You want to know how many concurrent users there are. In other words, you want to track the active sessions.	______________________
You want to know each time a request comes in, so that you can log it.	______________________
You want to know when a request attribute has been added, removed, or replaced.	______________________
You have an attribute class (a class for an object that will be put in an attribute) and you want objects of this type to be notified when they are bound to or removed from a session.	______________________
You want to know when a session attribute has been added, removed, or replaced.	______________________

Choose from these listener interfaces.
Use each listener only once.

HttpSessionAttributeListener

ServletRequestListener

HttpSessionListener

HttpSessionBindingListener

ServletRequestAttributeListener

ServletContextAttributeListener

The eight listeners

Scenario	Listener interface	Event type
You want to know if an attribute in a web app context has been added, removed, or replaced.	javax.servlet.**ServletContextAttributeListener** *attributeAdded* *attributeRemoved* *attributeReplaced*	ServletContextAttributeEvent
You want to know how many concurrent users there are. In other words, you want to track the active sessions. (We cover sessions in detail in the next chapter).	javax.servlet.http.**HttpSessionListener** *sessionCreated* *sessionDestroyed*	HttpSessionEvent
You want to know each time a request comes in, so that you can log it.	javax.servlet.**ServletRequestListener** *requestInitialized* *requestDestroyed*	ServletRequestEvent
You want to know when a request attribute has been added, removed, or replaced.	javax.servlet.**ServletRequestAttributeListener** *attributeAdded* *attributeRemoved* *attributeReplaced*	ServletRequestAttributeEvent
You have an attribute class (a class for an object that will stored as an attribute) and you want objects of this type to be notified when they are bound to or removed from a session.	javax.servlet.http.**HttpSessionBindingListener** *valueBound* *valueUnbound*	HttpSessionBindingEvent
You want to know when a session attribute has been added, removed, or replaced.	javax.servlet.http.**HttpSessionAttributeListener** *attributeAdded* *attributeRemoved* *attributeReplaced*	HttpSessionBindingEvent Watch out for this naming inconsistency! The Event for HttpSessionAttributeListener is NOT what you expect (you expect HttpSessionAttributeEvent).
You want to know if a context has been created or destroyed.	javax.servlet.**ServletContextListener** *contextInitialized* *contextDestroyed*	ServletContextEvent
You have an attribute class, and you want objects of this type to be notified when the session to which they're bound is migrating to and from another JVM.	javax.servlet.http.**HttpSessionActivationListener** *sessionDidActivate* *sessionWillPassivate*	HttpSessionEvent It's NOT "HttpSessionActivationEvent"

The HttpSessionBindingListener

You might be confused about the difference between an HttpSession*Binding*Listener and an HttpSession*Attribute*Listener. (Well, not *you*, but someone you work with.)

A plain old HttpSession*Attribute*Listener is just a class that wants to know when *any* type of attribute has been added, removed, or replaced in a Session. But the HttpSession*Binding*Listener exists so that the attribute *itself* can find out when *it* has been added to or removed from a Session.

With *this* listener, I'm more aware of **my** role in the application. They tell **me** when ***I'm*** put into a session (or taken out).

```
package com.example;

import javax.servlet.http.*;

public class Dog implements HttpSessionBindingListener {
   private String breed;

   public Dog(String breed) {
     this.breed=breed;
   }

   public String getBreed() {
     return breed;
   }

   public void valueBound(HttpSessionBindingEvent event) {
     // code to run now that I know I'm in a session
   }

   public void valueUnbound(HttpSessionBindingEvent event) {
     // code to run now that I know I am no longer part of a session
   }
}
```

This time the Dog attribute is ALSO a Listener... listening for when the Dog itself is added or removed from a Session. (Note: binding listeners are NOT registered in the DD... it just happens automatically.)

They use the word "bound" and "unbound" to mean "added to" and "removed from".

Q: OK. I get how it works. I get that the Dog (an attribute that'll be added to a session) wants to know when it's in or out of a session. What I don't get is *WHY*.

A: If you know anything about Entity beans... then you can picture this capability as a kind of "poor man's entity bean". If you *don't* know about entity beans, you should run to your nearest book store and buy two copies of *Head First EJB* (one for you, one for your significant other so you can share special moments discussing it).

In the meantime, here's a way to think about it—imagine the Dog is a Customer class, with each active instance representing a single customer's info for name, address, order info, etc. The *real* data is stored in an underlying database. You use the database info to populate the fields of the Customer object, but the issue is *how and when do you keep the database record and the Customer info synchronized?* You know that whenever a Customer object is added to a session, it's time to refresh the fields of the Customer with this customer's data from his record in the database. So the valueBound() method is like a kick that says, "Go load me up with fresh data from the database... just in case it changed since the last time I was used." Then valueUnbound() is a kick that says, "Update the database with the value of the Customer object fields."

Remembering the Listeners

Do your best to fill in the slots in this table. Keep in mind that the listener interfaces and methods follow a consistent naming pattern (mostly).
Answers are at the end of the chapter.

Attribute listeners	
Other lifecycle listeners	
Methods in all attribute listeners (except binding listener)	
Lifecycle events related to sessions (excluding attribute-related events)	
Lifecycle events related to requests (excluding attribute-related events)	
Lifecycle events related to servlet context (excluding attribute-related events)	

What, exactly, *is* an attribute?

We saw how the ServletContext listener created a Dog object (after getting the context init parameter) and was able to stick (set) the Dog into the ServletContext as an attribute, so that other parts of the app could get it. Earlier, with the beer tutorial, we saw how the servlet was able to stick the results of the call to the model into the Request (usually HttpServletRequest) object as an attribute (so that the JSP/view could get the value).

An attribute is an object set (referred to as *bound*) into one of three other servlet API objects—ServletContext, HttpServletRequest (or ServletRequest), or HttpSession. You can think of it as simply a name/value pair (where the name is a String and the value is an Object) in a map instance variable. In reality, we don't know or care how it's actually implemented—all we really care about is the *scope* in which the attribute exists. In other words, *who* can see it and *how long* does it live.

Who can see this bulletin board? Who can get and set the attributes?

An attribute is like an object pinned to a bulletin board. Somebody stuck it on the board so that others can get it.

The big questions are: who has access to the bulletin board, and how long does it live? In other words, what is the scope of the attribute?

Attributes are not parameters!

If you're new to servlets, you might need to spend some time reinforcing the difference between *attributes* and *parameters*. Rest assured that when we created the exam we spent just that little bit of extra time trying to make sure we made attribute and parameter questions as confusing as possible.*

	Attributes	Parameters
Types	Application/context Request Session *There is no servlet-specific attribute (just use an instance variable).*	Application/context init parameters Request parameters Servlet init parameters *No such thing as session parameters!*
Method to set	setAttribute(String name, Object value)	You CANNOT *set* Application and Servlet init parameters—they're set in the DD, remember? (With Request parameters, you *can* adjust the query String, but that's different.)
Return type	Object	String ← *Big difference!*
Method to get	getAttribute(String name) *Don't forget that attributes must be cast, since the return type is Object.*	getInitParameter(String name)

*It's true. If we'd made the exam simple and straightforward and easy, you wouldn't feel that sense of pride and accomplishment from passing the exam. Making the exam difficult enough to ensure that you'd need to buy a study guide in order to pass it was never, EVER, a part of our thinking. No, *seriously*. We were just thinking of *you*.

The Three Scopes: Context, Request, and Session

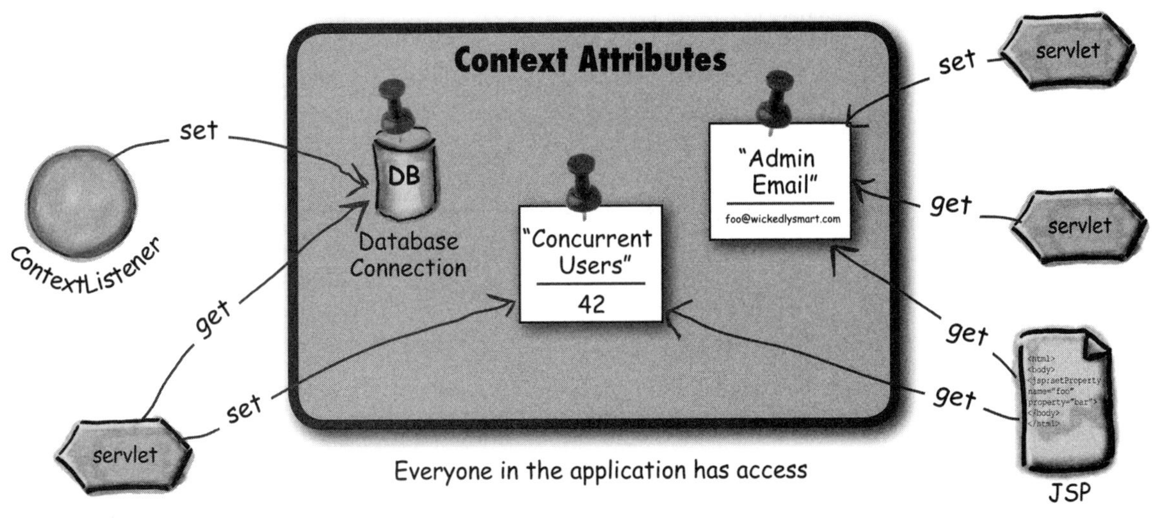

Everyone in the application has access

Accessible to only those with access to a specific HttpSession

Accessible to only those with access to a specific ServletRequest

Attribute Scope

Do your best to fill in the slots in this table. You REALLY need to understand attribute scope for the exam (and the real world) because you have to know *which* scope is the best to use for a given scenario. You'll see the answer in a few pages, but don't look ahead! If you're going to take the exam, trust us... you need to fill this out yourself by taking the time to *think it through*.

	Accessibility (who can see it)	**Scope** (how long does it live)	**What it's good for**
Context			
HttpSession			
Request			

(Note: you should think about the implications of garbage collection when you think about scope... some attributes won't be GC'd until the application is undeployed or dies. There's nothing on the exam about designing with memory management in mind, but it's something to be aware of).

Attribute API

The three attribute scopes—context, request, and session—are handled by the ServletContext, ServletRequest, and HttpSession interfaces. The API methods for attributes are exactly the same in every interface.

Object getAttribute(String name)

void setAttribute(String name, Object value)

void removeAttribute(String name)

Enumeration getAttributeNames()

Context

<<interface>>
ServletContext

getInitParameter(String)
getInitParameterNames()

getAttribute(String)
setAttribute(String, Object)
removeAttribute(String)
getAttributeNames()

getMajorVersion()
getServerInfo()

getRealPath(String)
getResourceAsStream(String)
getRequestDispatcher(String)
log(String)
// MANY more methods...

Request

<<interface>>
ServletRequest

getContextType()
getParameter()
getAttribute(String)
setAttribute(String, Object)
removeAttribute(String)
getAttributeNames()
// MANY more methods...

<<interface>>
HttpServletRequest

getContextPath()
getCookies()
getHeader(String)
getQueryString()
getSession()
// MANY more methods...

nothing related to attributes here

Session

<<interface>>
HttpSession

getAttribute(String)
setAttribute(String, Object)
removeAttribute(String)
getAttributeNames()

setMaxInactiveInterval()
getID()
getLastAccessedTime()
// MANY more methods...

The dark side of attributes...

Kim decides to test out attributes. He sets an attribute and then immediately gets the value of the attribute and displays it in the response. His doGet() looks like this:

```
public void doGet(HttpServletRequest request, HttpServletResponse response)
                                    throws IOException, ServletException {

   response.setContentType("text/html");
   PrintWriter out = response.getWriter();

   out.println("test context attributes<br>");

   getServletContext().setAttribute("foo", "22");
   getServletContext().setAttribute("bar", "42");

   out.println(getServletContext().getAttribute("foo"));
   out.println(getServletContext().getAttribute("bar"));
}
```

Here's what he sees the first time he runs it.

It's exactly what he expected.

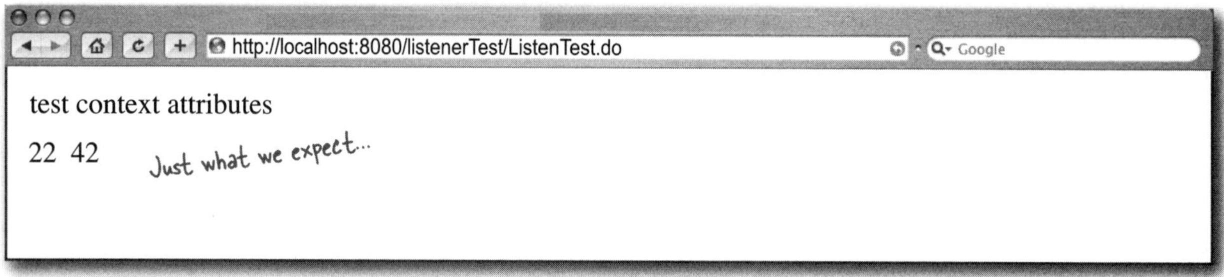

But then something goes horribly wrong...

The second time he runs it, he's shocked to see:

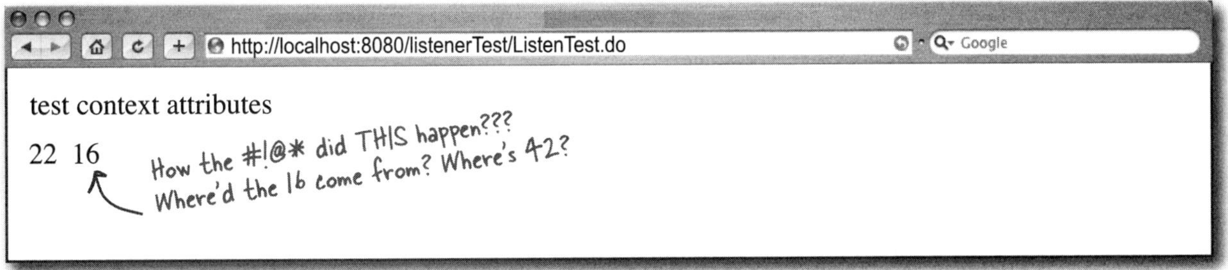
http://localhost:8080/listenerTest/ListenTest.do
Google
test context attributes
22 16
How the #!@* did THIS happen???
Where'd the 16 come from? Where's 42?

FLEX YOUR MIND

Look closely at the code, and think about what's happening. Do you see anything that could explain the problem?

You might not have enough info to solve the mystery, so here's another clue: Kim put this code in a test servlet that's part of a larger test web app. In other words, the servlet that holds this doGet() method was deployed as part of a larger app.

Now can you figure it out?

Can you think of how he might fix it?

There must be *another* servlet hitting the same context attribute...

Context scope isn't thread-safe!

That's the problem.

Remember, everyone in the app has access to context attributes, and that means multiple servlets. And ***multiple servlets means you might have multiple threads***, since requests are concurrently handled, each in a separate thread. This happens regardless of whether the requests are coming in for the same or different servlets.

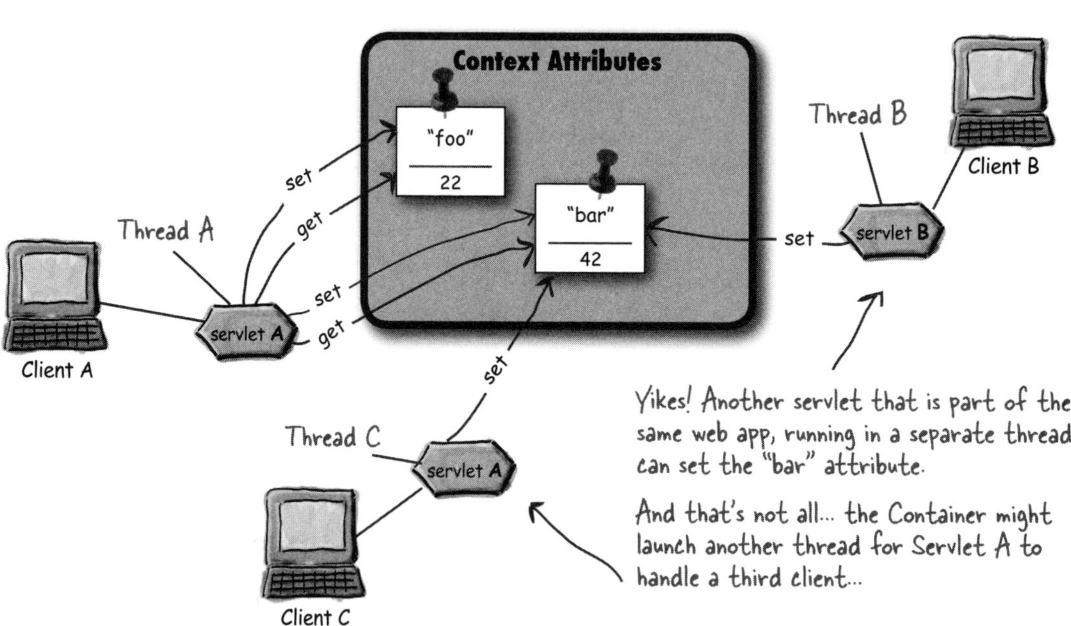

And that's not all... the Container might launch another thread for Servlet A to handle a third client...

The problem in slow motion...

Here's what happened to Kim's test servlet.

1. Servlet A sets the context attribute "foo" with a value of "22".

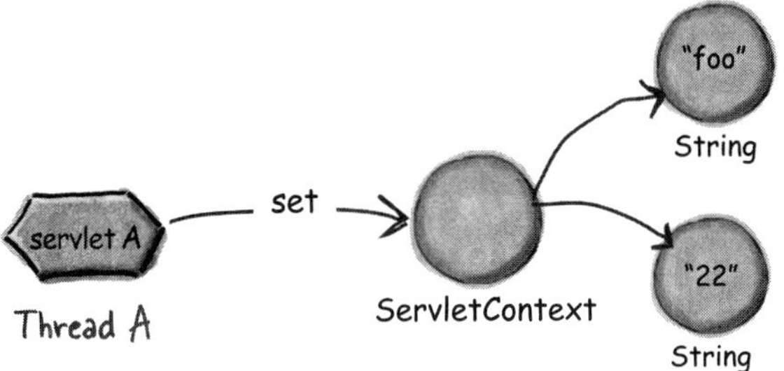

2. Servlet A sets the context attribute "bar" with a value of "42".

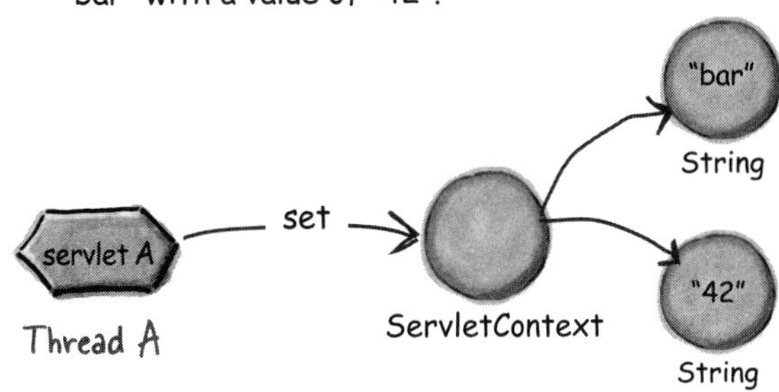

3. Thread B becomes the running thread (thread A goes back to Runnable-but-not-Running), and *sets* the context attribute "bar" with a value of "16". (The 42 is now gone.)

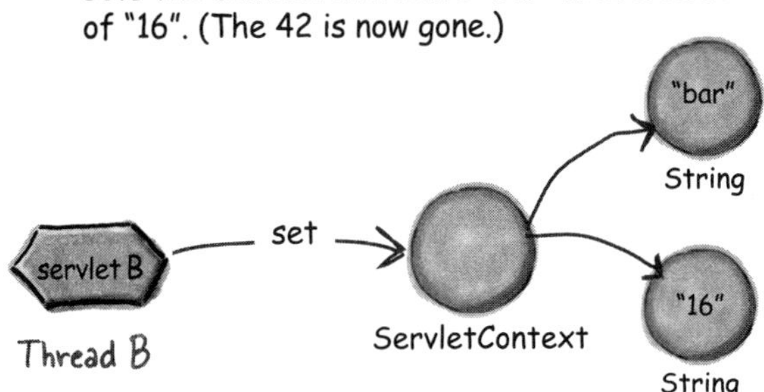

4. Thread A becomes the running thread again, and *gets* the value of "bar" and prints it to the response.

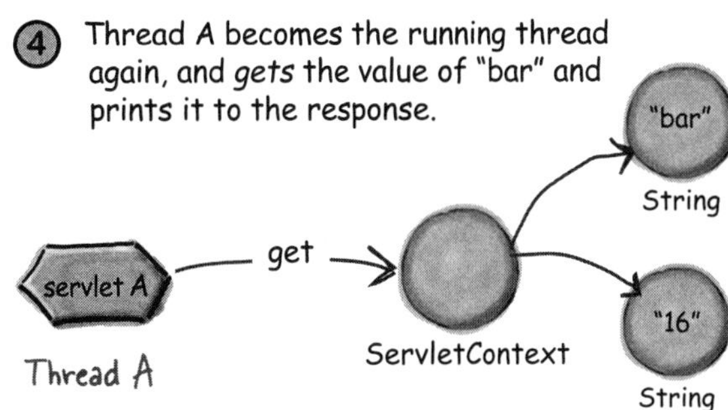


```
getServletContext().setAttribute("foo", "22");
getServletContext().setAttribute("bar", "42");

out.println(getServletContext().getAttribute("foo"));
out.println(getServletContext().getAttribute("bar"));
```

In between when servlet A set the value of "bar" and then got the value of "bar", another servlet thread snuck in and set "bar" to a different value.

So by the time servlet A printed the value of "bar", it had been changed to "16".

How do we make context attributes thread-safe?

Let's hear what some of the other developers have to say...

I'm thinking I could synchronize the doGet() method, but that doesn't really feel right. But I don't know what else to do.

Synchronizing on the doGet() means kissing your concurrency goodbye. If you synchronize doGet(), it means that servlet can handle only ONE client at a time!

Why didn't the Servlet spec developers just synchronize the get and set attribute methods in ServletContext, to make the attributes thread-safe?

Of COURSE they didn't synchronize the methods in ServletContext. Geez... that would have meant that every call to get and set an attribute would have all the synchronization overhead. What a huge waste if you don't need it. No, protecting attributes is your OWN problem... don't expect the API to save you. (I can't even believe she suggested that.)

Synchronizing the service method is a spectacularly BAD idea

OK, so we know that synchronizing the service method will kill our concurrency, but it does give you the thread protection, right? Take a look at this legal code, and decide whether it would prevent the problem Kim had with the context attribute being changed by another servlet...

```
public synchronized void doGet(HttpServletRequest request, HttpServletResponse response)
                                        throws IOException, ServletException {

    response.setContentType("text/html");
    PrintWriter out = response.getWriter();

    out.println("test context attributes<br>");

    getServletContext().setAttribute("foo", "22");
    getServletContext().setAttribute("bar", "42");

    out.println(getServletContext().getAttribute("foo"));
    out.println(getServletContext().getAttribute("bar"));
}
```

This can't work! Well, it's *legal* as a servlet, but I don't see how this will fix the problem...

What do you think? Will it fix the problem Kim had? Look back at the code and the diagrams if you're not sure.

Synchronizing the service method won't protect a context attribute!

Synchronizing the service method means that only one thread in a servlet can be running at a time... but it doesn't stop *other* servlets or JSPs from accessing the attribute!

Synchronizing the service method would stop other threads from the same servlet from accessing the context attributes, but it won't do anything to stop a completely *different* servlet.

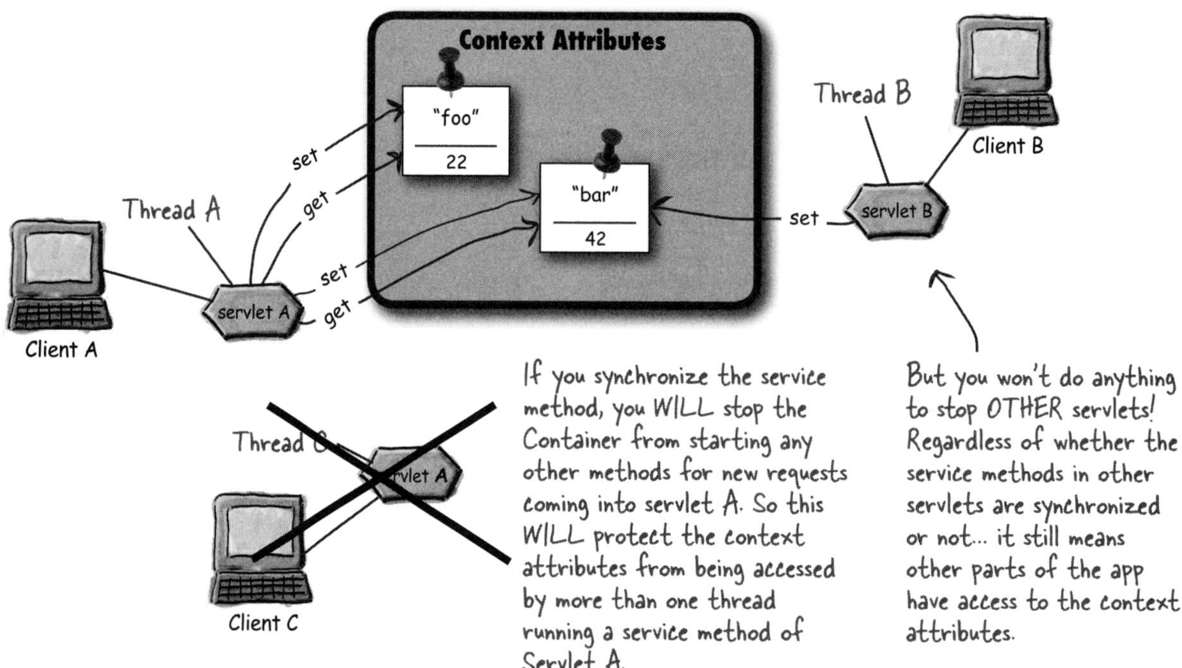

Context Attributes
"foo"
22
"bar"
42
Thread A
set
get
set
get
servlet A
Client A
Thread B
Client B
set
servlet B
Client C
If you synchronize the service method, you WILL stop the Container from starting any other methods for new requests coming into servlet A. So this WILL protect the context attributes from being accessed by more than one thread running a service method of Servlet A.
But you won't do anything to stop OTHER servlets! Regardless of whether the service methods in other servlets are synchronized or not... it still means other parts of the app have access to the context attributes.

You don't need a lock on the servlet... you need the lock on the context!

The typical way to protect the context attribute is to synchronize ON the context object itself. If everyone accessing the context has to first get the lock on the context object, then you're guaranteed that only one thread at a time can be getting or setting the context attribute. But... there's still an *if* there. It only works *if all of the other code that manipulates the same context attributes ALSO synchronizes on the ServletContext.* If code doesn't ask for the lock, then that code is still free to hit the context attributes. But if you're designing the web app, then *you* can decide to make everyone ask for the lock before accessing the attributes.

For context attributes, it won't do any good to synchronize on the Servlet, because other parts of the app will still be able to access the context!

ServletContext

```
public void doGet(HttpServletRequest request, HttpServletResponse response)
                                throws IOException, ServletException {

   response.setContentType("text/html");
   PrintWriter out = response.getWriter();

   out.println("test context attributes<br>");

   synchronized(getServletContext()) {
      getServletContext().setAttribute("foo", "22");
      getServletContext().setAttribute("bar", "42");

      out.println(getServletContext().getAttribute("foo"));
      out.println(getServletContext().getAttribute("bar"));
   }
}
```

Now we're getting the lock on the context itself!! This is the way to protect context attribute state. (You don't want synchronized(this).)

Since we have the context lock, we're assuming that once we get inside the synchronized block, the context attributes are safe from other threads until we exit the block... sort of. Safe means "safe from any other code that ALSO synchronizes on the ServletContext."

But this is the best you've got for making the context attributes as thread-safe as you can.

Expect to see lots of code about thread-safety

On the exam, you'll see plenty of code showing different strategies for making attributes thread-safe. You'll have to decide if the code works, given a particular goal. Just because the code is legal (compiles and runs), doesn't mean it'll solve the problem.

Are Session attributes thread-safe?

Think about it.

We haven't talked about HTTP sessions in detail yet (we will in the Sessions chapter), but you already know that a session is an object used to maintain conversational state with a client. The session persists *across multiple requests from the same client.* But it's still just one client we're talking about.

And if it's one client, and a single client can be in only one request at a time, doesn't that automatically mean that sessions are thread-safe? In other words, even if multiple servlets *are* involved, at any given moment there's only one request from that particular client... so there's only one thread operating on that session at a time. Right?

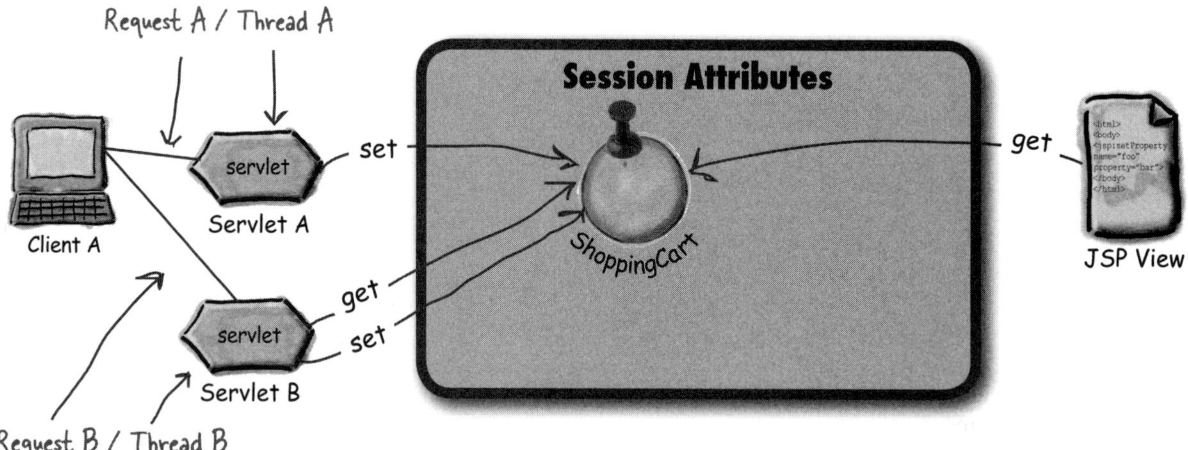

Even though both servlets can access the Session attributes in separate threads, each thread is a separate request. So it looks safe.

Unless...

Can you think of a scenario in which there *could* be more than one request *at the same time, from the same client?*

What do *you* think? Are session attributes guaranteed thread-safe?

What's REALLY true about attributes and thread-safety?

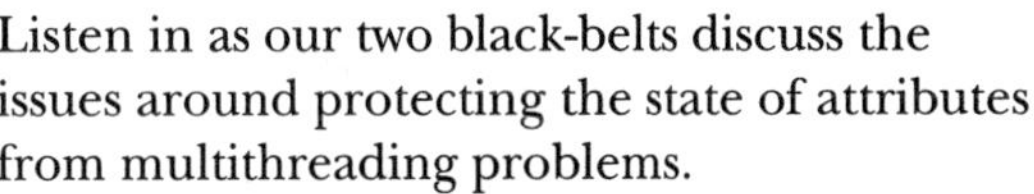

Listen in as our two black-belts discuss the issues around protecting the state of attributes from multithreading problems.

We know that context attributes are inherently NOT safe, because all pieces of the app can access context attributes, from any request (which means any thread).

Yes master. And I know that synchronizing the service method is not a solution, because although it will stop that servlet from servicing more than one request at a time, it will NOT stop *other* servlets and JSPs in the same web app from accessing the context.

Very good. Now what about ***Session*** attributes. Are *they* safe?

Yes master. They are for only *one* client, and the laws of physics prevent a client from making more than one request at a time.

You have *much* to learn, grasshopper. You do not know the truth about session attributes. Meditate on this before speaking again.

But master, I have meditated and still I do not know how one client could have more than one request...

You must think outside the Container. Color outside the lines. *Run with scissors.*

Very wise advice, master! I have it! ***The client could open a new browser window!*** So the Container can still use the same session for a client, even though it's coming from a different instance of the browser?

Yes! The Container can see the request from the second window as coming from the same session.

So Session attributes are *not* thread-safe, and they, too, must be protected. I will meditate on this...

And how would you protect these session attributes from the havoc of multiple threads?

Ah... I must synchronize the part of my code that accesses the session attributes. Just the way we did for the context attributes.

That is good, yes, but synchronize on *what?*

I must synchronize on the HttpSession!

Protect session attributes by synchronizing on the HttpSession

Look at the technique we used to protect the *context* attributes. What did we do?

You can do the same thing with session attributes, by synchronizing on the HttpSession object!

```
public void doGet(HttpServletRequest request, HttpServletResponse response)
                                      throws IOException, ServletException {

    response.setContentType("text/html");
    PrintWriter out = response.getWriter();

    out.println("test context attributes<br>");
    HttpSession session = request.getSession();

    synchronized(session) {
        session.setAttribute("foo", "22");
        session.setAttribute("bar", "42");

        out.println(session.getAttribute("foo"));
        out.println(session.getAttribute("bar"));
    }
}
```

This time, we synchronize on the HttpSession object, to protect the session attributes.

there are no Dumb Questions

Q: Isn't this overkill? Is this *really* a possibility... that a client will open another browser window?

A: Of course it is. Surely you've done this yourself without a second thought—opened a second window because you were tired of waiting for the other one to respond, or because you minimized one, or misplaced the window without realizing it, etc. The point is, you can't take the chance if you need thread-safety for your session variables. You have to know that it's quite possible for a session-scoped attribute to be used by more than one thread at a time.

Q: Isn't it a bad idea to synchronize code, because it causes a lot of overhead and hurts concurrency?

A: You should ALWAYS think carefully before synchronizing any code, because you're right—it does add some expense in checking, acquiring, and releasing locks. If you need protection, then use synchronization but remember the standard rule of all forms of locking—keep the lock for the shortest amount of time to accomplish your goal! In other words, don't synchronize the code that doesn't access the protected state. Make your synchronized block as small as possible. Get the lock, get in, get what you need, and get the heck out so the lock can release and other threads can run that code.

The evils of SingleThreadModel

Although it's not on the exam (because it's evil), you've probably heard of or even used the now-deprecated SingleThreadModel interface, so we feel compelled to mention it while simultaneously reinforcing its evilness.

The SingleThreadModel sounds good to newbies, at first glance, as a way to solve multi-threading problems. You simply have your servlet implement the SingleThreadModel interface and BOOM—as if by magic your servlet will never have more than one thread at a time running. In other words, you've reduced your servlet to a single thread. Goodbye multi-threading problems, right?

No, of course not. You already know why... implementing SingleThreadModel is no different than synchronizing the service method—all you've done is demolished your concurrency *without* protecting attribute state! Because again, even if all your servlets implement SingleThreadModel, you can still have *two* servlets (each one dutifully running only one client request thread at a time) in the same web app, accessing context attributes at the same time.

SingleThreadModel offers *nothing* but poor performance if your application has more than one component. Since it misled thousands of new developers into thinking that SingleThreadModel gave them thread-safety, it's been deprecated and the developers who use it now are subject to ridicule and humiliation.

But now you know, and *you* would never have used it anyway, since *you* already know that restricting a single servlet to a single thread protects you *only if your entire application consists of a single servlet.*

So, if you catch anybody using SingleThreadModel, revoke their Servlet license (and insist, no, *demand* that they buy a copy of this book).

Sharpen your pencil
Place a checkmark next to the things that are NOT thread-safe. (We did the first one.)
☑ Context-scoped attributes
☐ Session-scoped attributes
☐ Request-scoped attributes
☐ Instance variables in the servlet
☐ Local variables in service methods
☐ Static variables in the servlet

Only Request attributes and local variables are thread-safe!

That's it. (We include method parameters when we say "local variables"). *Everything else* is subject to manipulation by multiple threads, unless *you* do something to stop it.

there are no Dumb Questions

Q: So instance variables *aren't* thread-safe?

A: That's right. If you have multiple clients making requests on that servlet, that means multiple threads running that servlet code. And all threads have access to the servlet's instance variables, so instance variables aren't thread-safe.

Q: But they WOULD be thread-safe if you implemented the SingleThreadModel, right?

A: Yes, because you'd never have more than one thread for that servlet, so the instance variables would be thread-safe. But of course nobody would ever allow you into the servlets club ever again.

Q: I was just talking hypothetically. As in, "if someone WERE stupid enough to implement SingleThreadModel..." Not that I would ever do it. But while we're being hypothetical... if I have a friend who, say, synchronizes the service method, wouldn't that ALSO make the instance variables thread-safe?

A: Yes. But your friend would be an idiot. The effect of implementing SingleThreadModel is virtually the same as synchronizing the service method. Both can bring a web app to its knees *without protecting the session and attribute state.*

Q: But if you're not supposed to use SingleThreadModel or synchronize the service method, then how DO you make instance variables thread-safe?

A: You don't! Look at a well-written servlet, and chances are you won't *find* any instance variables. Or at least any that are non-final. (And since you're a Java programmer you know that even a final variable can still be manipulated unless it's immutable.)

So just don't use instance variables if you need thread-safe state, because all threads for that servlet can step on instance variables.

Q: Then what SHOULD you use if you need multiple instances of the servlet to share something?

A: Stop right there! You said "multiple *instances* of the servlet". We know you didn't mean that, because there is always only ONE *instance* of the servlet. *One* instance, *many* threads.

If you want all the threads to access a value, decide which attribute state makes the most sense, and store the value in an attribute. Chances are, you can solve your problems in one of two ways:

1) Declare the variable as a local variable within the service method, rather than as an instance variable.

OR

2) Use an attribute in the most appropriate scope.

Request attributes and Request dispatching

Request attributes make sense when you want some other component of the app to take over all or part of the request. Our typical, simple example is an MVC app that starts with a servlet *controller*, but ends with a JSP *view*. The controller communicates with the model, and gets back data that the view needs in order to build the response. There's no reason to put the data in a context or session attribute, since it applies *only* to this request, so we put it in the request scope.

So how do we make another part of the component take over the request? With a ***RequestDispatcher***.

```
// code in a doGet()
BeerExpert be = new BeerExpert();
ArrayList result = be.getBrands(c);

request.setAttribute("styles", result);


RequestDispatcher view =
  request.getRequestDispatcher("result.jsp");

view.forward(request, response);
```

Put model data into Request scope.

Get a dispatcher for the view JSP.

Tell JSP to take over the request, and, oh yeah, here are the Request and Response objects.

1. The Beer servlet calls the getBrands() method on the model that returns some data that the view needs.

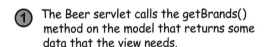

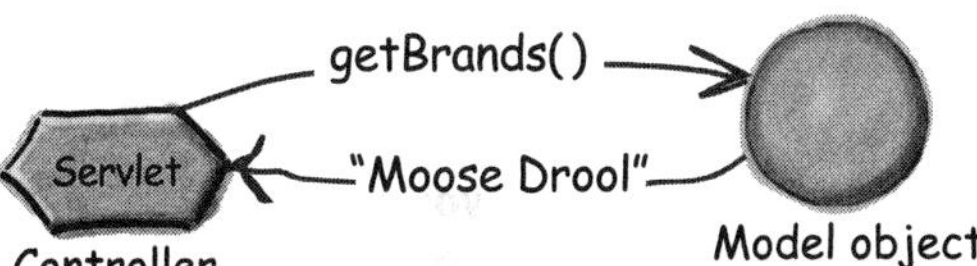

2. The servlet sets a Request attribute named "styles". (First it puts "Moose Drool" into an ArrayList.)

3. The servlet asks the HttpRequest for a RequestDispatcher, passing in a relative path to the view JSP.

4. The servlet calls forward() on the Request-Dispatcher, to tell the JSP to take over the request. (Not shown: the JSP gets the forwarded request, and gets the "styles" attribute from the Request scope.)

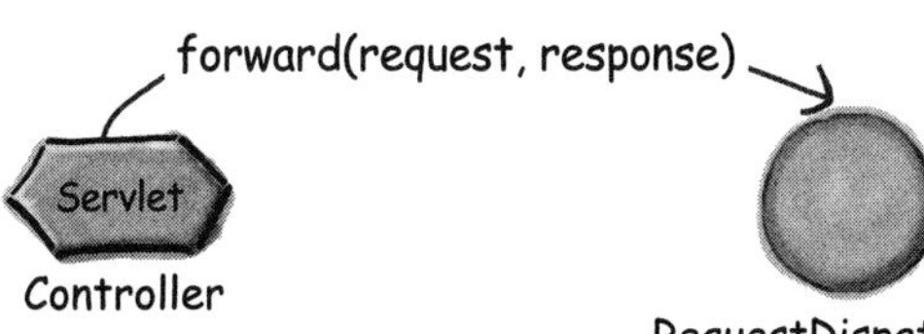

RequestDispatcher revealed

RequestDispatchers have only two methods—*forward()* and *include()*. Both take the request and response objects (which the component you're forwarding to will need to finish the job). Of the two methods, forward() is by far the most popular. It's very unlikely you'll use the include method from a controller servlet; however, behind the scenes the include method is being used by JSPs in the <jsp:include> standard action (which we'll review in chapter 8). You can get a RequestDispatcher in two ways: from the request or from the context. Regardless of where you get it, you have to tell it the web component to which you're forwarding the request. In other words, the servlet or JSP that'll take over.

<<*interface*>> ***RequestDispatcher***
forward(ServletRequest, ServletResponse) *include(ServletRequest, ServletResponse)*

javax.servlet.RequestDispatcher

Getting a RequestDispatcher from a Servlet*Request*

```
RequestDispatcher view = request.getRequestDispatcher("result.jsp");
```

The getRequestDispatcher() method in ServletRequest takes a String path for the resource to which you're forwarding the request. If the path starts with a forward slash ("/"), the Container sees that as "starting from the root of this web app". If the path does NOT start with a forward slash, it's considered *relative* to the original request. But you can't try to trick the Container into looking outside the current web app. In other words, just because you have lots of "../../../" doesn't mean it'll work if it takes you *past* the root of your current web app!

This is a relative path (because there's no initial forward slash ("/")). So in this case, the Container looks for "result.jsp" in the same logical location the request is "in". (We'll cover the details of relative paths and logical locations in the Deployment chapter.)

Getting a RequestDispatcher from a Servlet*Context*

```
RequestDispatcher view = getServletContext().getRequestDispatcher("/result.jsp");
```

Like the equivalent method in ServletRequest, this getRequestDispatcher() method takes a String path for the resource to which you're forwarding the request, EXCEPT you *cannot* specify a path relative to the current resource (the one that received this request). That means ***you must start the path with a forward slash!***

You MUST use the forward slash with the getRequestDispatcher() method of ServletContext.

Calling forward() on a RequestDispatcher

```
view.forward(request, response);
```

Simple. The RequestDispatcher you got from your context or request knows the resource you're forwarding to—the resource (servlet, JSP) you passed as the argument to getRequestDispatcher(). So you're saying, "Hey, RequestDispatcher, please forward this request to the *thing* I told you about earlier (in this case, a JSP), when I first got you. And here's the request and response, because that new thing is going to need them in order to finish handling the request."

What's wrong with this code?

What do you think? Does this RequestDispatcher code look like it will work the way you'd expect?

```
public void doGet(HttpServletRequest request, HttpServletResponse response)
                                              throws IOException, ServletException {
    response.setContentType("application/jar");
    ServletContext ctx = getServletContext();
    InputStream is = ctx.getResourceAsStream("bookCode.jar");
    int read = 0;
    byte[] bytes = new byte[1024];
    OutputStream os = response.getOutputStream();
    while ((read = is.read(bytes)) != -1) {
        os.write(bytes, 0, read);
    }
    os.flush();
    RequestDispatcher view = request.getRequestDispatcher("result.jsp");
    view.forward(request, response);
    os.close();
}
```

Assume that all this works.

You'll get a big, fat IllegalStateException!

You can't forward the request if you've already committed a response!

And by "committed a response" we mean, "sent the response to the client". Look at the code again. The big problem is:

os.flush();

That's the line that causes the response to be sent to the client, and at that point, this response is DONE. FINISHED. OVER. You can't possibly forward the request at this point, because the request is history! You've already responded, and you get only one shot at this.

So, don't be fooled if you see questions on the exam that forward a request AFTER a response is sent. The Container will throw an IllegalStateException.

Q: How come you didn't talk about the RequestDispatcher include() method?

A: It's not on the exam, for one thing. For another, we already mentioned that it's not used much in the real world. But to satisfy your curiosity, the include() method sends the request to something else (typically another servlet) to do some work ***and then comes back to the sender!*** In other words, include() means asking for *help* in handling the request, but it's not a complete hand-off. It's a *temporary*, rather than *permanent* transfer of control. With forward(), you're saying, "That's it, I'm not doing *anything* else to process this request and response." But with include(), you're saying, "I want someone else to do some things with the request and/or response, but when they're done, I want to finish handling the request and response *myself* (although I might decide to do another include or forward after that...").

Remembering the Listeners

ANSWERS

Attribute listeners	ServletRequestAttributeListener ServletContextAttributeListener HttpSessionAttributeListener
Other lifecycle listeners	ServletRequestListener ServletContextListener HttpSessionListener HttpSessionBindingListener HttpSessionActivationListener (Notice that the only difference between these and the attribute listeners is the word "Attribute" inserted in the interface name.)
Methods in all attribute listeners (except binding listener)	attributeAdded() attributeRemoved() attributeReplaced()
Lifecycle events related to sessions (excluding attribute-related events)	when the session is created, and when its destroyed sessionCreated() sessionDestroyed() (Note: there are others we'll cover in the Sessions chapter.)
Lifecycle events related to requests (excluding attribute-related events)	when the request is initialized or destroyed requestInitialized() requestDestroyed() (Notice the difference between the ~~session~~ and request events—session is sessionCreated(), request is requestInitialized().)
Lifecycle events related to servlet context (excluding attribute-related events)	when the context is initialized or destroyed contextInitialized() contextDestroyed()

Attribute Scope

ANSWERS

	Accessibility (who can see it)	Scope (how long does it live)	What it's good for
Context (NOT thread-safe!)	Any part of the web app including servlets, JSPs, ServletContextListeners, ServletContextAttribute-Listeners.	Lifetime of the ServletContext, which means life of the deployed app. If server or app goes down, the context is destroyed (along with its attributes).	Resources you want the entire application to share, including database connections, JNDI lookup names, email addresses., etc.
HttpSession (NOT thread-safe!)	Any servlet or JSP with access to this particular session. Remember, a session extends beyond a single client request to span multiple requests by the same client, which could go to different servlets.	The life of the session. A session can be destroyed programmatically or can simply time-out. (We'll go into the details in the Session Management chapter.)	Data and resources related to this client's session, not just a single request. Something that requires an ongoing conversation with the client. A shopping cart is a typical example.
Request (Thread-safe)	Any part of the application that has direct access to the Request object. That mostly means only the Servlets and JSPs to which the request is forwarded using a RequestDispatcher. Also Request-related listeners.	The life of the Request, which means until the Servlet's service() method completes. In other words, for the life of the thread (stack) handling this request.	Passing model info from the controller to the view... or any other data specific to a single client request.

Exercise

Code Magnets

ANSWERS

(configuring a context parameter in the DD)

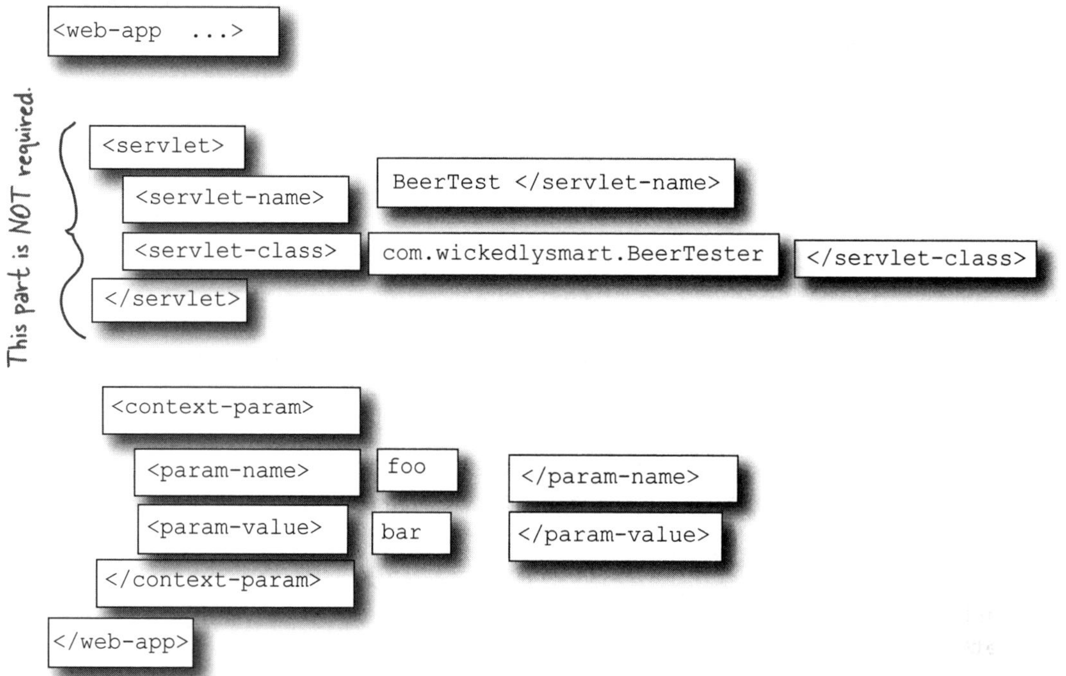
<web-app ...>
This part is NOT required.
<servlet>
<servlet-name>
BeerTest </servlet-name>
<servlet-class>
com.wickedlysmart.BeerTester
</servlet-class>
</servlet>
<context-param>
<param-name>
foo
</param-name>
<param-value>
bar
</param-value>
</context-param>
</web-app>

Not used:

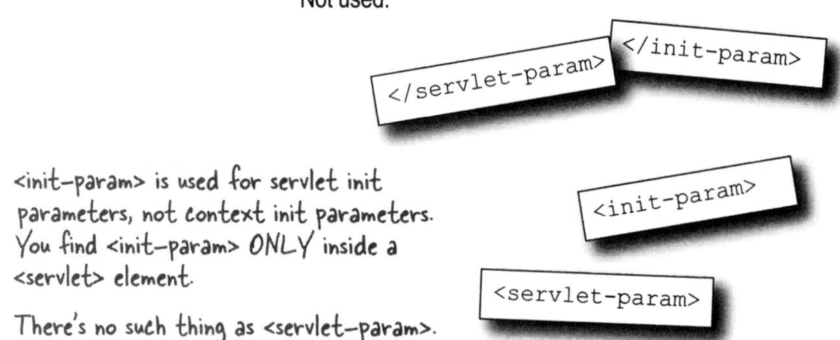
</servlet-param>
</init-param>
<init-param>
<servlet-param>

<init-param> is used for servlet init parameters, not context init parameters. You find <init-param> ONLY inside a <servlet> element.

There's no such thing as <servlet-param>.

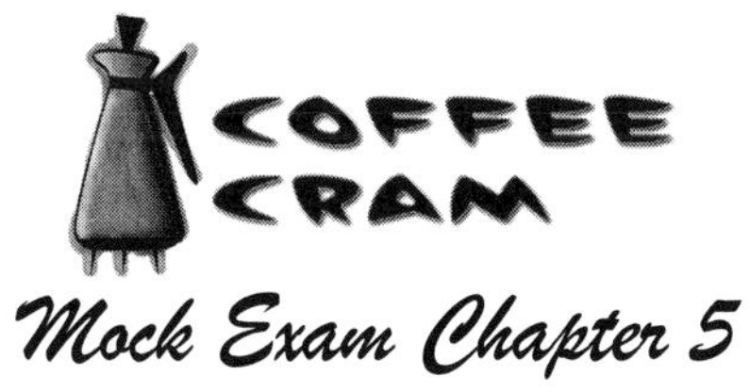

Mock Exam Chapter 5

1 When using a **RequestDispatcher**, the use of which methods can often lead to an **IllegalStateException**? (Choose all that apply.)

- ❑ A. **read**
- ❑ B. **flush**
- ❑ C. **write**
- ❑ D. **getOutputStream**
- ❑ E. **getResourceAsStream**

2 Which statements about **ServletContext** initialization parameters are true? (Choose all that apply.)

- ❑ A. They should be used for data that changes rarely.
- ❑ B. They should be used for data that changes frequently.
- ❑ C. They can be accessed using **ServletContext.getParameter()**.
- ❑ D. They can be accessed using **ServletContext.getInitParameter()**.
- ❑ E. They should be used for data that is specific to a particular servlet.
- ❑ F. They should be used for data that is applicable to an entire web application.

3 Which types define the methods **getAttribute()** and **setAttribute()**? (Choose all that apply.)

- ❑ A. **HttpSession**
- ❑ B. **ServletRequest**
- ❑ C. **ServletResponse**
- ❑ D. **ServletContext**
- ❑ E. **ServletConfig**
- ❑ F. **SessionConfig**

---

4 If a servlet is invoked using the **forward** or **include** method of **RequestDispatcher**, which methods of the servlet's request object can access the request attributes set by the container? (Choose all that apply.)

- ❑ A. **getCookies()**
- ❑ B. **getAttribute()**
- ❑ C. **getRequestPath()**
- ❑ D. **getRequestAttribute()**
- ❑ E. **getRequestDispatcher()**

---

5 Which calls provide information about initialization parameters that are applicable to an entire web application? (Choose all that apply.)

- ❑ A. **ServletConfig.getInitParameters()**
- ❑ B. **ServletContext.getInitParameters()**
- ❑ C. **ServletConfig.getInitParameterNames()**
- ❑ D. **ServletContext.getInitParameterNames()**
- ❑ E. **ServletConfig.getInitParameter(String)**
- ❑ F. **ServletContext.getInitParameter(String)**

6 Which statements about listeners are true? (Choose all that apply.)

- ❑ A. A **`ServletResponseListener`** can be used to perform an action when a servlet response has been sent.
- ❑ B. An **`HttpSessionListener`** can be used to perform an action when an **`HttpSession`** has timed out.
- ❑ C. A **`ServletContextListener`** can be used to perform an action when the servlet context is about to be shut down.
- ❑ D. A **`ServletRequestAttributeListener`** can be used to perform an action when an attribute has been removed from a **`ServletRequest`**.
- ❑ E. A **`ServletContextAttributeListener`** can be used to perform an action when the servlet context has just been created and is available to service its first request.

---

7 Which is most logically stored as an attribute in session scope?

- ❑ A. A copy of a query parameter entered by a user.
- ❑ B. The result of a database query to be returned immediately to a user.
- ❑ C. A database connection object used by all web components of the system.
- ❑ D. An object representing a user who has just logged into the system.
- ❑ E. A copy of an initialization parameter retrieved from a **`ServletContext`** object.

---

8 Given this code from an otherwise valid **HttpServlet** that has also been registered as a **ServletRequestAttributeListener**:

```
public void doGet(HttpServletRequest req,
                  HttpServletResponse res)
        throws IOException, ServletException {
  req.setAttribute("a", "b");
  req.setAttribute("a", "c");
  req.removeAttribute("a");
}
public void attributeAdded(ServletRequestAttributeEvent ev) {
  System.out.print(" A:" + ev.getName() + "->" + ev.getValue());
}
public void attributeRemoved(ServletRequestAttributeEvent ev) {
  System.out.print(" M:" + ev.getName() + "->" + ev.getValue());
}
public void attributeReplaced(ServletRequestAttributeEvent ev) {
  System.out.print(" P:" + ev.getName() + "->" + ev.getValue());
}
```

What logging output is generated?

- ❑ A. **A:a->b P:a->b**
- ❑ B. **A:a->b M:a->c**
- ❑ C. **A:a->b P:a->b M:a->c**
- ❑ D. **A:a->b P:a->b P:a->null**
- ❑ E. **A:a->b M:a->b A:a->c M:a->c**
- ❑ F. **A:a->b M:a->b A:a->c P:a->null**

---

9 When declaring a listener in the DD, which sub-elements of the **<listener>** element are required? (Choose all that apply.)

- ❑ A. **<description>**
- ❑ B. **<listener-name>**
- ❑ C. **<listener-type>**
- ❑ D. **<listener-class>**
- ❑ E. **<servlet-mapping>**

10 Which types of objects can store attributes? (Choose all that apply.)

- ❏ A. **`ServletConfig`**
- ❏ B. **`ServletResponse`**
- ❏ C. **`RequestDispatcher`**
- ❏ D. **`HttpServletRequest`**
- ❏ E. **`HttpSessionContext`**

11 Which are true? (Choose all that apply.)

- ❏ A. When a web application is preparing to shutdown, the order of listener notification is not guaranteed.
- ❏ B. When listener-friendly events occur, listener invocation order is not predictable.
- ❏ C. The container registers listeners based on declarations in the deployment descriptor.
- ❏ D. Only the container can invalidate a session.

12 Which statements about **`RequestDispatcher`** are true (where applicable, assume the **`RequestDispatcher`** was not obtained via a call to **`getNamedDispatcher()`**)? (Choose all that apply.)

- ❏ A. A **`RequestDispatcher`** can be used to forward a request to another servlet.
- ❏ B. The only method in the **`RequestDispatcher`** interface is **`forward()`**.
- ❏ C. Parameters specified in the query string used to create a **`RequestDispatcher`** are not forwarded by the **`forward()`** method.
- ❏ D. The servlet to which a request is forwarded may access the original query string by calling **`getQueryString()`** on the Http**`ServletRequest`**.
- ❏ E. The servlet to which a request is forwarded may access the original query string by calling **`getAttribute("javax.servlet.forward.query_string")`** on the **`ServletRequest`**.

13 Which statements accurately describe how many instances of a servlet the servlet container instantiates for each web application? (Choose all that apply.)

- ❑ A. If the servlet implements **`javax.servlet.SingleThreadModel`**, the container may create one instance for each request.
- ❑ B. If the servlet does not implement **`SingleThreadModel`**, the container may create multiple instances of the servlet in the same JVM.
- ❑ C. The **`<load-on-startup> web.xml`** element can determine how many instances are created.
- ❑ D. If the servlet does not implement **`SingleThreadModel`**, the container will create no more than one instance per JVM.

14 What is the recommended way to deal with servlets and thread safety?

- ❑ A. Write the servlet code to extend **`ThreadSafeServlet`**.
- ❑ B. Have the servlet implement **`SingleThreadModel`**.
- ❑ C. Log all servlet method calls.
- ❑ D. Use local variables exclusively, and if you have to use instance variables, synchronize access to them.

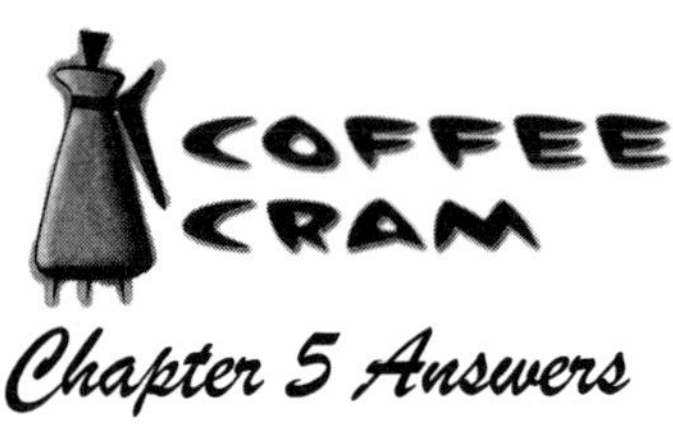

Chapter 5 Answers

1 When using a **RequestDispatcher**, the use of which methods can often lead to an **IllegalStateException**? (Choose all that apply.)

(Servlet v2.4 pg. 167)

- ❑ A. **read**
- ☑ B. **flush**
- ❑ C. **write**
- ❑ D. **getOutputStream**
- ❑ E. **getResourceAsStream**

–An IllegalStateException is caused when a response has already been 'committed' to the client (the flush method does that), and then you attempt a forward.

2 Which statements about **ServletContext** initialization parameters are true? (Choose all that apply.)

(Servlet v2.4 pg. 31)

- ☑ A. They should be used for data that changes rarely.
- ❑ B. They should be used for data that changes frequently.
- ❑ C. They can be accessed using **ServletContext.getParameter()**.
- ☑ D. They can be accessed using **ServletContext.getInitParameter()**.
- ❑ E. They should be used for data that is specific to a particular servlet.
- ☑ F. They should be used for data that is applicable to an entire web application.

–Option B is incorrect because ServletContext init parameters are only read at Container start-up time.

–Option C is incorrect because this method does not exist.

–Option E is incorrect because there is only one ServletContext object per web application.

3 Which types define the methods **getAttribute()** and **setAttribute()**? (Choose all that apply.)

(Servlet v2.4 pgs. 32, 36, 59)

- [x] A. **HttpSession**
- [x] B. **ServletRequest**
- [ ] C. **ServletResponse**
- [x] D. **ServletContext**
- [ ] E. **ServletConfig**
- [ ] F. **SessionConfig**

4 If a servlet is invoked using the **forward** or **include** method of **RequestDispatcher**, which methods of the servlet's request object can access the request attributes set by the container? (Choose all that apply.)

(Servlet v2.4 65-66)

- [ ] A. **getCookies()**
- [x] B. **getAttribute()**
- [ ] C. **getRequestPath()**
- [ ] D. **getRequestAttribute()**
- [ ] E. **getRequestDispatcher()**

-Option B is the correct method. With it you can access the container populated javax.servlet.forward.Xxx and javax.servlet.include.Xxxx attributes.

-Options C and D refer to methods that don't exist.

5 Which calls provide information about initialization parameters that are applicable to an entire web application? (Choose all that apply.)

(Servlet v2.4 pg. 32)

- [ ] A. **ServletConfig.getInitParameters()**
- [ ] B. **ServletContext.getInitParameters()**
- [ ] C. **ServletConfig.getInitParameterNames()**
- [x] D. **ServletContext.getInitParameterNames()**
- [ ] E. **ServletConfig.getInitParameter(String)**
- [x] F. **ServletContext.getInitParameter(String)**

-Options A and B are incorrect because these methods do not exist.

-Options C and E are incorrect because they provide access to servlet-specific initialization parameters.

6 Which statements about listeners are true? (Choose all that apply.)

(Servlet v2.4 pg. 80)

- [ ] A. A **ServletResponseListener** can be used to perform an action when a servlet response has been sent.
- [x] B. An **HttpSessionListener** can be used to perform an action when an **HttpSession** has timed out.
- [x] C. A **ServletContextListener** can be used to perform an action when the servlet context is about to be shut down.
- [x] D. A **ServletRequestAttributeListener** can be used to perform an action when an attribute has been removed from a **ServletRequest.**
- [ ] E. A **ServletContextAttributeListener** can be used to perform an action when the servlet context has just been created and is available to service its first request.

-Option A is incorrect because these is no ServletResponseListener interface.

-Option E is incorrect because a ServletContextListener would be used for this purpose.

7 Which is most logically stored as an attribute in session scope?

(Servlet v2.4 pg. 58)

- [ ] A. A copy of a query parameter entered by a user.
- [ ] B. The result of a database query to be returned immediately to a user.
- [ ] C. A database connection object used by all web components of the system.
- [x] D. An object representing a user who has just logged into the system.
- [ ] E. A copy of an initialization parameter retrieved from a **ServletContext** object.

-Option A is incorrect because a query parameter is more typically used immediately to perform an operation.

-Option B is incorrect because such data is typically either immediately returned or stored in request scope.

-Option C is incorrect because (since it is not specific to a particular session) it should be stored in context scope.

-Option E is incorrect because servlet context parameters should stay with the ServletContext object.

8 Given this code from an otherwise valid **HttpServlet** that has also been registered as a **ServletRequestAttributeListener**: (Servlet v2.4 pg. 199-200)

```
public void doGet(HttpServletRequest req,
                  HttpServletResponse res)
        throws IOException, ServletException {
  req.setAttribute("a", "b");
  req.setAttribute("a", "c");
  req.removeAttribute("a");
}
public void attributeAdded(ServletRequestAttributeEvent ev) {
  System.out.print(" A:" + ev.getName() + "->" + ev.getValue());
}
public void attributeRemoved(ServletRequestAttributeEvent ev) {
  System.out.print(" M:" + ev.getName() + "->" + ev.getValue());
}
public void attributeReplaced(ServletRequestAttributeEvent ev) {
  System.out.print(" P:" + ev.getName() + "->" + ev.getValue());
}
```

What logging output is generated?

- ☐ A. **A:a->b P:a->b**
- ☐ B. **A:a->b M:a->c**
- ☑ C. **A:a->b P:a->b M:a->c**
- ☐ D. **A:a->b P:a->b P:a->null**
- ☐ E. **A:a->b M:a->b A:a->c M:a->c**
- ☐ F. **A:a->b M:a->b A:a->c P:a->null**

-Tricky! The getValue method returns the OLD value of the attribute if the attribute was replaced.

9 When declaring a listener in the DD, which sub-elements of the **<listener>** element are required? (Choose all that apply.) (Servlet v2.4 section 10.4, & 13.4.9)

- ☐ A. **<description>**
- ☐ B. **<listener-name>**
- ☐ C. **<listener-type>**
- ☑ D. **<listener-class>**
- ☐ E. **<servlet-mapping>**

-The <listener-class> sub-element is the ONLY required sub-element of the <listener> element.

(API)

10 Which types of objects can store attributes? (Choose all that apply.)

- ❑ A. **ServletConfig**
- ❑ B. **ServletResponse**
- ❑ C. **RequestDispatcher**
- ☑ D. **HttpServletRequest**
- ❑ E. **HttpSessionContext**

–Options A, B, and C are invalid because these types do not store attributes.

–Option E is invalid because there is no such type.

Note: The other two types related to servlets, that can store attributes are HttpSession and ServletContext.

(Servlet v2.4 pgs. 81-84)

11 Which are true? (Choose all that apply.)

- ❑ A. When a web application is preparing to shutdown, the order of listener notification is not guaranteed.
- ❑ B. When listener-friendly events occur, listener invocation order is not predictable.
- ☑ C. The container registers listeners based on declarations in the deployment descriptor.
- ❑ D. Only the container can invalidate a session.

–Options A and B are incorrect because the container uses the DD to determine the notification order of registered listeners.

–Option D is incorrect because a servlet can invalidate a session using the HttpSession.invalidate() method.

(Servlet v2.4 pg. 65)

12 Which statements about **RequestDispatcher** are true (where applicable, assume the **RequestDispatcher** was not obtained via a call to **getNamedDispatcher()**)? (Choose all that apply.)

- ☑ A. A **RequestDispatcher** can be used to forward a request to another servlet.
- ❑ B. The only method in the **RequestDispatcher** interface is **forward()**.
- ❑ C. Parameters specified in the query string used to create a **RequestDispatcher** are not forwarded by the **forward()** method.
- ☑ D. The servlet to which a request is forwarded may access the original query string by calling **getQueryString()** on the Http**ServletRequest**.
- ☑ E. The servlet to which a request is forwarded may access the original query string by calling **getAttribute("javax.servlet.forward.query_string")** on the **ServletRequest**.

–Option B is incorrect because the interface also contains an include method.

–Option C is incorrect because such parameters are forwarded in this case.

(Servlet spec p 24)

13 Which statements accurately describe how many instances of a servlet the servlet container instantiates for each web application? (Choose all that apply.)

- [x] A. If the servlet implements **javax.servlet.SingleThreadModel**, the container may create one instance for each request.
- [ ] B. If the servlet does not implement **SingleThreadModel**, the container may create multiple instances of the servlet in the same JVM.
- [ ] C. The **<load-on-startup> web.xml** element can determine how many instances are created.
- [x] D. If the servlet does not implement **SingleThreadModel**, the container will create no more than one instance per JVM.

-Option C is incorrect because the <load-on-startup> deployment-descriptor element determines the order of instantiation, not the number of instances.

(Servlet spec p 27)

14 What is the recommended way to deal with servlets and thread safety?

- [ ] A. Write the servlet code to extend **ThreadSafeServlet**.
- [ ] B. Have the servlet implement **SingleThreadModel**.
- [ ] C. Log all servlet method calls.
- [x] D. Use local variables exclusively, and if you have to use instance variables, synchronize access to them.

-Option A and B are incorrect because ThreadSafeServlet does not exist in the Servlet API and the SingleThreadModel is deprecated in version 2.4 and not recommended..

6 session management

Conversational state

Web servers have no short-term memory. As soon as they send you a response, they forget who you are. The next time you make a request, they don't recognize you. In other words, they don't remember what you've requested in the past, and they don't remember what they've sent you in response. Nothing. Sometimes that's fine. But sometimes you need to keep conversational state with the client *across multiple requests*. A shopping cart wouldn't work if the client had to make all his choices and then checkout *in a single request*. **You'll find a surprisingly simple solution in the Servlet API.**

Session Management

4.1 Write servlet code to store objects into a session object and retrieve objects from a session object.

4.2 Given a scenario describe the APIs used to access the session object, explain when the session object was created, and describe the mechanisms used to destroy the session object, and when it was destroyed.

4.3 Using session listeners, write code to respond to an event when an object is added to a session, and write code to respond to an event when a session object migrates from one VM to another.

4.4 Given a scenario, describe which session management mechanism the Web container could employ, how cookies might be used to manage sessions, how URL rewriting might be used to manage sessions, and write servlet code to perform URL rewriting.

Coverage Notes:

All four of the exam objectives on session management are covered completely in this chapter (although some of these topics were touched on in the previous chapter). This chapter is your one chance to learn and memorize these topics, so take your time.

I want the beer app to have a back and forth *conversation* with the client... wouldn't it be cool if the user answers a question, and then the web app responds with a new question based on the answer to the previous ones?

Kim wants to keep client-specific state across multiple requests

Right now, the business logic in the model simply checks the parameter from the request and gives back a response (the *advice*). Nobody in the app remembers *anything* that went on with this client prior to the current request.

What he has NOW:

```
public class BeerExpert {
   public ArrayList getBrands(String color) {
      ArrayList brands = new ArrayList();
      if (color.equals("amber")) {
        brands.add("Jack Amber");
        brands.add("Red Moose");
      } else {
        brands.add("Jail Pale Ale");
        brands.add("Gout Stout");
      }
      return brands;
   }
}
```

We check the one incoming parameter (color) and give back the final response (an array of brands that fit that color). This isn't very smart advice...

What he WANTS:

```
public class BeerExpert {

   public NextResponse getAdvice(String answer) {
      // Process client answer by looking at
      // ALL of the client's previous answers, as well
      // as the answer from the current request.
      // if there's enough info, return final advice,
      // else, return the next question to ask
   }
}
```

The model (the business logic) has to figure out whether it has enough information to make a recommendation (in other words, to give final advice), and if it doesn't, it has to give back the next question to ask the user.

Assume the NextResponse class encapsulates the next thing to display for the user, and something that indicates whether it's the final advice recommendation or another question.

It's supposed to work like a REAL conversation...

We need some better drinks at this party. I gotta call Kim...

Dude, I'm at Joe's beach party and I am holding in my hand, as I speak, a foofy red umbrella drink...you gotta get some beer over here NOW!

Umbrella drinks? Oooooh, that's just WRONG. Good thing you called... let me ask you some questions—first, do you want something dark, amber, or pale?

Well, *I* like *dark*... but this is a wimpy-looking crowd, so I'll say *amber* to be safe.

Hmmm... I have a lot of ambers... do you care about price?

Dude... would I be working as a computer book model if I didn't need the money? OF COURSE I care about price!

No problem... I have some outsourced bitter ale I can send over.

How can he track the client's answers?

Kim's design won't work unless he can keep track of *everything* the client has already said during the conversation, not just the answer in the *current* request. He needs the servlet to get the request parameters representing the client's choices, and save it somewhere. Each time the client answers a question, the advice engine uses *all* of that client's previous answers to come up with either *another* question to ask, or a final recommendation.

What are some options?

Use a stateful session enterprise javabean

Sure, he could do that. He could have his servlet become a client to a stateful session bean, and each time a request comes in he could locate that client's stateful bean. There are a lot of little issues to work out, but yes, you can certainly use a stateful session bean to store conversational state.

But that's *way* too much overhead (over*kill*) for this app! Besides, Kim's hosting provider doesn't have a full J2EE server with an EJB Container. He's got Tomcat (a web Container) and that's it.

Use a database

This would work too. His hosting provider *does* allow access to MySQL, so he could do it. He could write the client's data to a database... but this is nearly as much of a runtime performance hit as an enterprise bean would be, possibly *more.* And way more than he needs.

Use an HttpSession

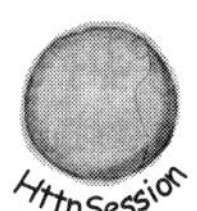

But you already knew that. We can use an HttpSession object to hold the conversational state across multiple requests. In other words, for an entire *session* with that client.

(Actually, Kim would still have to use an HttpSession even if he *did* choose another option such as a database or session bean, because if the client is a web browser, Kim still needs to match a specific client with a specific database key or session bean ID, and as you'll see in this chapter, the HttpSession takes care of that identification.)

An HttpSession object can hold conversational state across multiple requests from the same client.

In other words, it persists for an entire session with a specific client.

We can use it to store everything we get back from the client in all the requests the client makes during a session.

How sessions work

1 Diane selects "Dark" and hits the submit button.

The Container sends the request to a new thread of the BeerApp servlet.

The BeerApp thread finds the session associated with Diane, and stores her choice ("Dark") in the session as an attribute.

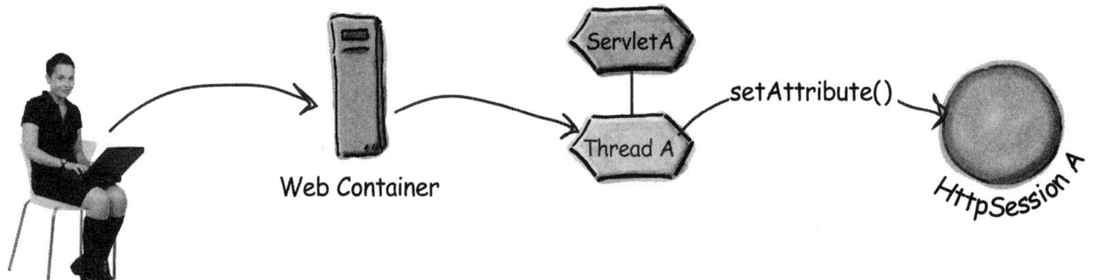

2 The servlet runs its business logic (including calls to the model) and returns a response... in this case another question, "What price range?"

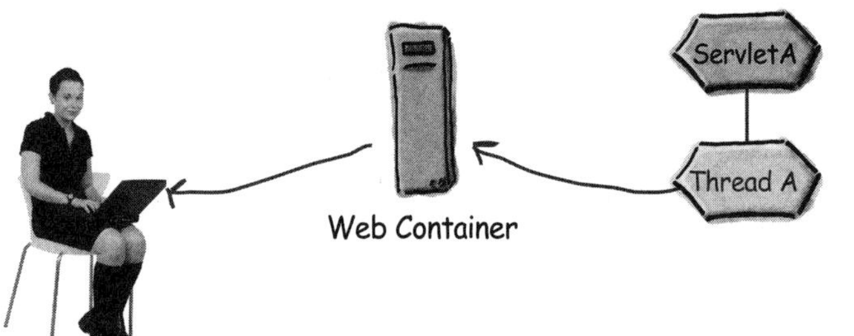

3 Diane considers the new question on the page, selects "Expensive" and hits the submit button.

The Container sends the request to a new thread of the BeerApp servlet.

The BeerApp thread finds the session associated with Diane, and stores her new choice ("Expensive") in the session as an attribute.

Same client
Same servlet
Different request
Different thread
Same session

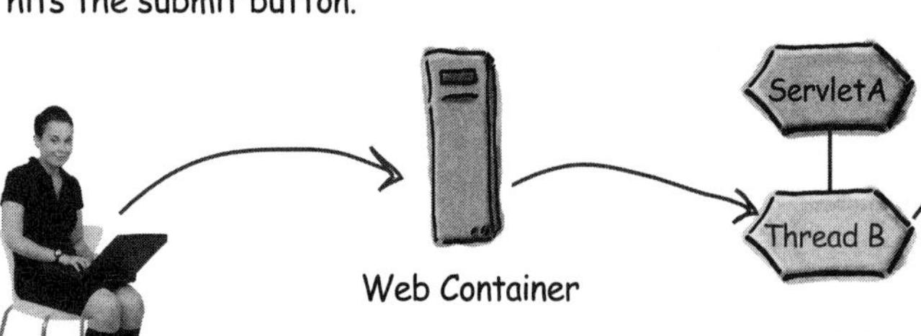

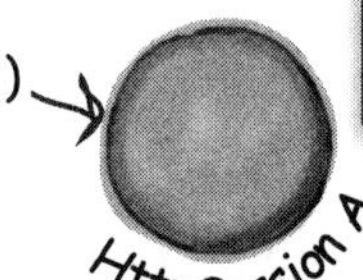

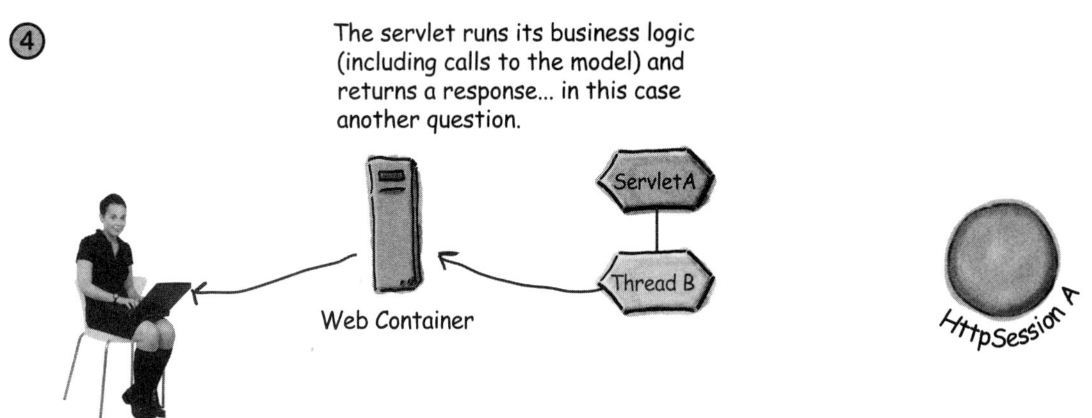
4
The servlet runs its business logic (including calls to the model) and returns a response... in this case another question.
ServletA
Thread B
Web Container
HttpSession A

Meanwhile, imagine ANOTHER client goes to the beer site...

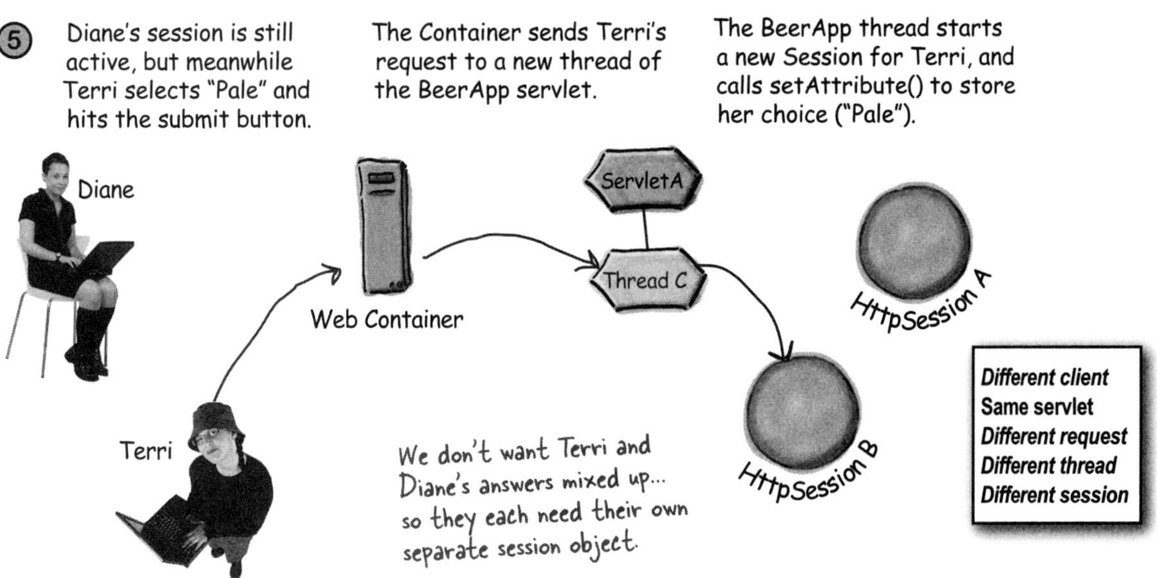
5
Diane's session is still active, but meanwhile Terri selects "Pale" and hits the submit button.
The Container sends Terri's request to a new thread of the BeerApp servlet.
The BeerApp thread starts a new Session for Terri, and calls setAttribute() to store her choice ("Pale").
Diane
ServletA
Thread C
Web Container
HttpSession A
HttpSession B
Terri
We don't want Terri and Diane's answers mixed up... so they each need their own separate session object.
Different client
Same servlet
Different request
Different thread
Different session

Terri

One problem... how does the Container know who the client is?

The HTTP protocol uses state*less* connections. The client browser makes a connection to the server, sends the request, gets the response, and closes the connection. In other words, the connection exists for only a *single* request/response.

Because the connections don't persist, the Container doesn't recognize that the client making a second request is the same client from a previous request. As far as the Container's concerned, ***each request is from a new client.***

How will the Container recognize it's Diane and not Terri? HTTP is stateless, so each request is a new connection...

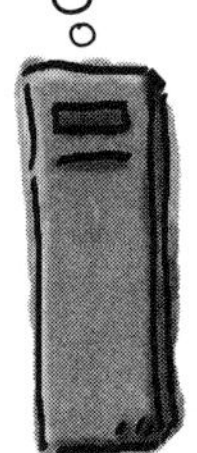

But things were going so well... I thought we had a relationship...
I'm sorry, but I don't remember you. I'm sure we shared good times together, but we'll have to start over.

there are no Dumb Questions

Q: Why can't the Container just use the IP address of the client? It's part of the request, right?

A: Oh, the Container *can* get the IP address of the request, but does that *uniquely* identify the client? If you're on a local IP network, you have a unique IP address, but chances are, that's not the IP address the outside world sees. To the server, your IP address is the address of the router, so you have the same IP address as everybody else on that network! So that wouldn't help. You'd have the same problem—the stuff Jim puts in *his* shopping cart might end up in Pradeep's cart, and vice versa. So no, IP address isn't a solution for *uniquely* identifying a specific client on the internet.

Q: Well then how about security info? If the user is logged in, and the connection is secure (HTTPS), the Container knows EXACTLY who the client is, right?

A: Yes, if the user is logged in and the connection is secure, the Container can identify the client and associate him with a session. But that's a ***big if***. Most good web site design says, "don't force the user to log in until it really matters, and don't switch on security (HTTPS) until it really matters." If your users are just browsing, even if they're adding items to a shopping cart, you probably don't want the overhead (for you or the user) of having them authenticate to the system until they decide to checkout! So, we need a mechanism to link a client to a session that doesn't require a securely authenticated client. (We'll go into security details in the... wait for it... *Security chapter.*)

The client needs a unique session ID

The idea is simple: on the client's first request, the Container generates a unique session ID and gives it back to the client with the response. ***The client sends back the session ID with each subsequent request.*** The Container sees the ID, finds the matching session, and associates the session with the request.

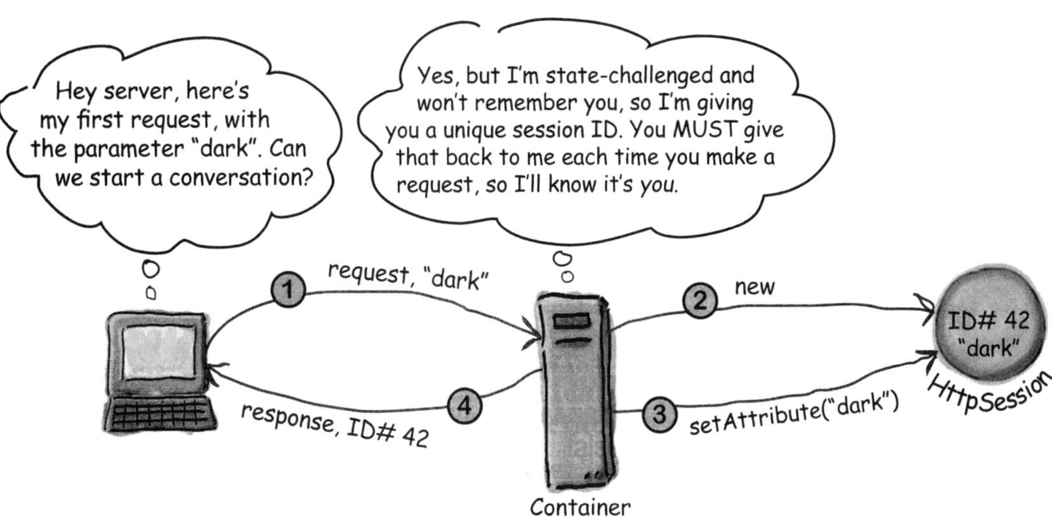

How do the Client and Container exchange Session ID info?

Somehow, the Container has to get the session ID to the client as part of the response, and the client has to send back the session ID as part of the request. The simplest and most common way to exchange the info is through *cookies*.

Cookies

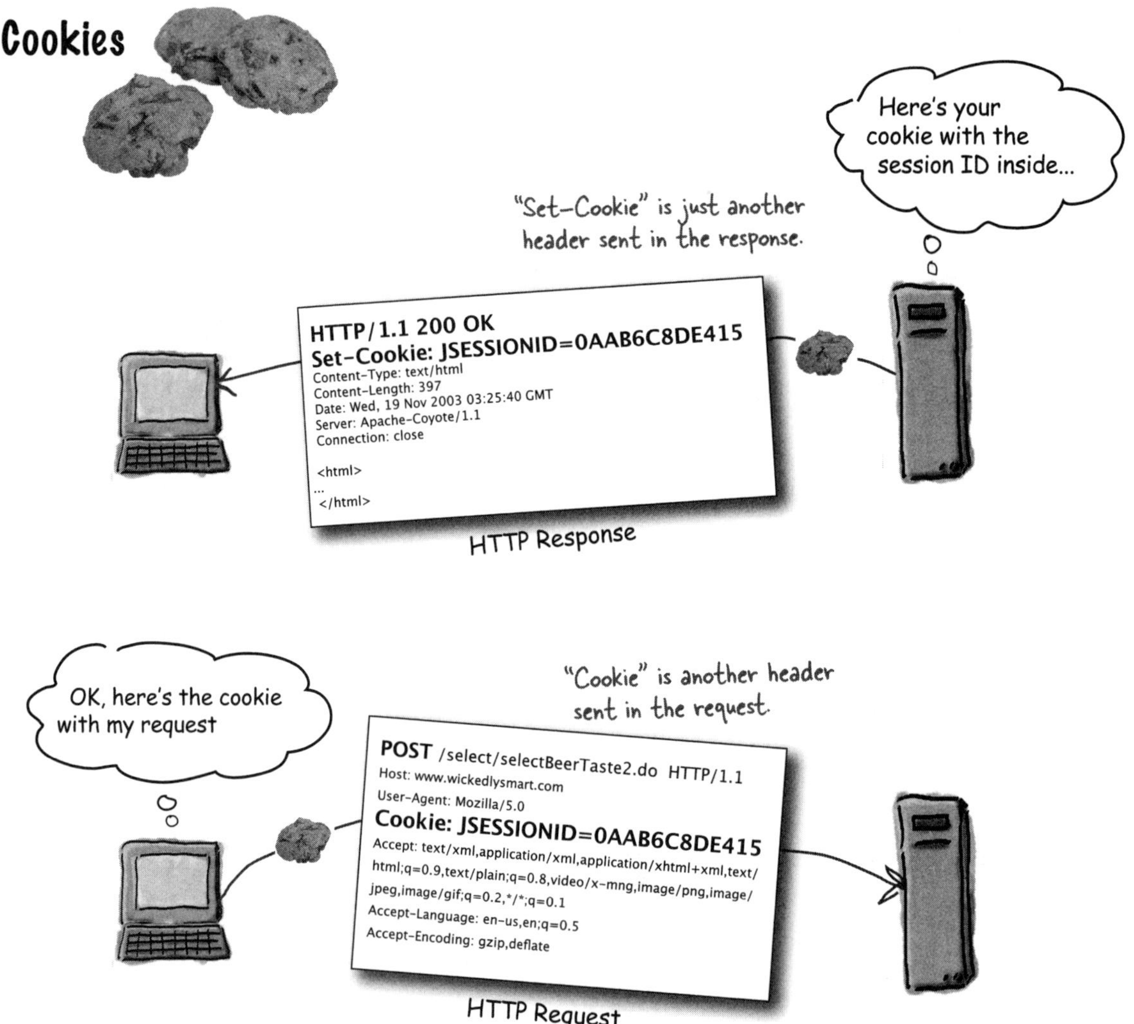

Here's your cookie with the session ID inside...
"Set-Cookie" is just another header sent in the response.
HTTP/1.1 200 OK
Set-Cookie: JSESSIONID=0AAB6C8DE415
Content-Type: text/html
Content-Length: 397
Date: Wed, 19 Nov 2003 03:25:40 GMT
Server: Apache-Coyote/1.1
Connection: close
<html>
...
</html>
HTTP Response
OK, here's the cookie with my request
"Cookie" is another header sent in the request.
POST /select/selectBeerTaste2.do HTTP/1.1
Host: www.wickedlysmart.com
User-Agent: Mozilla/5.0
Cookie: JSESSIONID=0AAB6C8DE415
Accept: text/xml,application/xml,application/xhtml+xml,text/html;q=0.9,text/plain;q=0.8,video/x-mng,image/png,image/jpeg,image/gif;q=0.2,*/*;q=0.1
Accept-Language: en-us,en;q=0.5
Accept-Encoding: gzip,deflate
HTTP Request

The best part: the Container does virtually all the cookie work!

You *do* have to tell the Container that you want to create or use a session, but the Container takes care of generating the session ID, creating a new Cookie object, stuffing the session ID into the cookie, and setting the cookie as part of the response. And on subsequent requests, the Container gets the session ID from a cookie in the request, matches the session ID with an existing session, and associates that session with the current request.

Sending a session cookie in the RESPONSE:

```
HttpSession session = request.getSession();
```

You ask the request for a session, and the Container kicks everything else into action. You don't have to do anything else!

(This method does more than just create a session, but the FIRST time you invoke it on the request, it will cause a cookie to be sent with the response. Now, there's still not guarantee the client will ACCEPT the cookie... but we're getting ahead of ourselves.)

That's it. Somewhere in your service method you ask for a session, and everything else happens *automatically.*

You don't make the new HttpSession object yourself.

You don't generate the unique session ID.

You don't make the new Cookie object.

You don't associate the session ID with the cookie.

You don't set the Cookie into the response (under the *Set-Cookie* header).

All the cookie work happens behind the scenes.

Getting the session ID from the REQUEST:

```
HttpSession session = request.getSession();
```

Whoa! The method for GETTING a session ID cookie (and matching it with an existing session) is the same as SENDING a session ID cookie. You never actually SEE the session ID yourself (although you can ask the session to give it to you).

Look familiar? Yes, it's exactly the same method used to generate the session ID and cookie for the response!

IF (the request includes a session ID cookie)

find the session matching that ID

ELSE IF (there's no session ID cookie OR there's no current session matching the session ID)

create a *new* session.

All the cookie work happens behind the scenes.

What if I want to know whether the session already existed or was just created?

Good question. The no-arg request method, getSession(), returns a session *regardless of whether there's a pre-existing session.* Since you *always* get an HttpSession instance back from that method, the only way to know if the session is new is to ***ask the session.***

```
public void doGet(HttpServletRequest request, HttpServletResponse response)
                                        throws IOException, ServletException {

    response.setContentType("text/html");
    PrintWriter out = response.getWriter();
    out.println("test session attributes<br>");

    HttpSession session = request.getSession();

    if (session.isNew()) {
       out.println("This is a new session.");
    } else {
       out.println("Welcome back!");
    }
}
```

getSession() returns a session no matter what.... but you can't tell if it's a new session unless you ask the session.

isNew() returns true if the client has not yet responded with this session ID.

Q: You get a session by calling request.getSession(), but is that the only way to get the session? Can't you get it from the ServletContext?

A: You get a session from the request object because—think about it—the session is identified by the request. When you call getSession() on the Container you're saying, "I want a session for THIS client... either the session that matches the session ID this client sent, or a new one. But in either case, *the session is for the client associated with this request.*"

But there is another way that you can get a session... from a session *event* object. Remember, a listener class isn't a servlet or JSP—it's just a class that wants to know about the events. For example, the listener might be an attribute trying to find out when it (the attribute object) was added to or removed from a session.

The event-handling methods defined by the listener interfaces related to sessions take an argument of type HttpSessionEvent, or its subclass, HttpSessionBindingEvent. And HttpSessionEvent has a getSession() method!

So, if you implement any of the four listener interfaces related to sessions (we'll get to that later in the chapter), you can access the session through the event-handling callback methods. For example, this code is from a class that implements the HttpSessionListener interface:

```
public void sessionCreated(HttpSessionEvent event) {
    HttpSession session = event.getSession();
    // event handling code
}
```

What if I want ONLY a pre-existing session?

You might have a scenario in which a servlet wants to use only a previously-created session. It might not make sense for the checkout servlet, for example, to start a *new* session.

So there's an overloaded getSession(boolean) method just for that purpose. If you don't want to create a new session, call getSession(false), and you'll get either null, or a pre-existing HttpSession.

The code below calls getSession(false), then tests whether the return value was null. If it *was* null, the code outputs a message and *then* creates a new session.

```
public void doGet(HttpServletRequest request, HttpServletResponse response)
                                        throws IOException, ServletException {

    response.setContentType("text/html");
    PrintWriter out = response.getWriter();
    out.println("test sessions<br>");

    HttpSession session = request.getSession(false);

    if (session==null) {

       out.println("no session was available");
       out.println("making one...");
       session = request.getSession();
    } else {
       out.println("there was a session!");
    }
}
```

Passing "false" means the method returns a pre-existing session, or null if there was no session associated with this client.

Now we can test for whether there was already a session (the no-arg getSession() would NEVER return null).

Here we KNOW we're making a new session.

Q: Isn't the code above just a stupid, inefficient way to do the same thing as the opposite page? In the end, you still created a new session.

A: You're right. The code above is just for testing how the two different versions of getSession() work. In the real world, the only time you'd want to use getSession(false) is if you do NOT want to create a new session. If your goal *is* to create a new session, but still respond differently if you know this is a new (versus pre-existing) session, then use the no-arg getSession() method, and simply ask the session if it's new using the HttpSession isNew() method.

Q: So it looks like getSession(true) is exactly the same as getSession()...

A: Right again. The no-arg version is a convenience for those times when you know that you always want a session, new or existing. The version that takes a boolean is useful when you know that you *don't* want a new session, or when the decision of whether to make a new session happens at runtime (and you're passing a variable into the getSession(someBoolean) method).

Gee...this all sounds nice but, uh, NEWS FLASH—anybody with half a brain disables cookies. How do you do sessions if you can't use cookies?

You <u>can</u> do sessions even if the client doesn't accept cookies, but you have to do a little more work...

We don't agree that anybody with half a brain disables cookies. In fact, most browsers *do* have cookies enabled, and everything's wonderful. ***But there's no guarantee.***

If your app *depends* on sessions, you need a different way for the client and Container to exchange session ID info. Lucky for you, the Container can handle a cookie-refusing client, but it takes a little more effort from you.

If you use the session code on the previous pages—calling getSession() on the request—the Container tries to use cookies. If cookies aren't enabled, it means the client will never join the session. In other words, ***the session's isNew() method will always return true.***

A client with cookies disabled will ignore "Set-Cookie" response headers

If a client doesn't accept cookies, you won't get an exception. No bells and sirens going off to tell you that your attempt to have a session with this client went wrong. No, it just means the client ignores your attempt to set a cookie with the session ID. In your code, if you do NOT use URL rewriting, it means that getSession() will always return a NEW session (i.e. one that always returns "true" when you call isNew() on it). The client simply never sends back a request that has a session ID cookie header.

URL rewriting: something to fall back on

If the client won't take cookies, you can use URL rewriting as a back-up. Assuming you do your part correctly, URL rewriting will *always* work—the client won't care that it's happening and won't do anything to prevent it. Remember the goal is for the client and Container to exchange session ID info. Passing cookies back and forth is the *simplest* way to exchange session IDs, but if you can't put the ID in a cookie, where can you put it? URL rewriting takes the session ID that's in the cookie and sticks it right onto the end of every URL that comes in to this app.

URL + ;jsessionid=1234567

Imagine a web page where every link has a little bit of extra info (the session ID) tacked onto the end of the URL. When the user clicks that "enhanced" link, the request goes to the Container with that extra bit on the end, and the Container simply strips off the extra part of the request URL and uses it to find the matching session.

HTTP/1.1 200 OK
Content-Length: 397
Date: Wed, 19 Nov 2003 03:25:40 GMT
Server: Apache-Coyote/1.1
Connection: close
<html>
<body>
<a href="http://www.wickedlysmart.com/BeerTest.do;jsessionid=0AAB6C8DE415">
click me
</a>
</body>
</html>
We add the session ID to the end of all the URLs in the HTML we send back in the Response.

HTTP Response

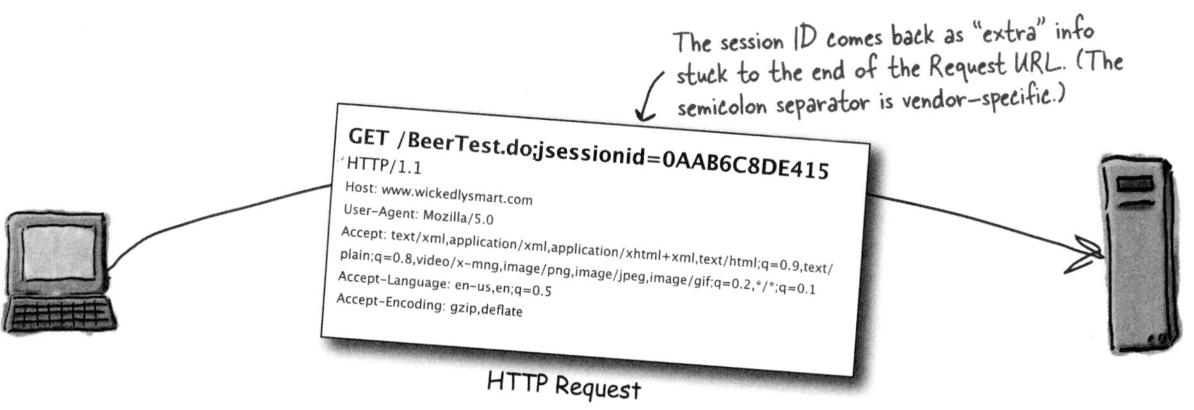

The session ID comes back as "extra" info stuck to the end of the Request URL. (The semicolon separator is vendor-specific.)
GET /BeerTest.do;jsessionid=0AAB6C8DE415
HTTP/1.1
Host: www.wickedlysmart.com
User-Agent: Mozilla/5.0
Accept: text/xml,application/xml,application/xhtml+xml,text/html;q=0.9,text/plain;q=0.8,video/x-mng,image/png,image/jpeg,image/gif;q=0.2,*/*;q=0.1
Accept-Language: en-us,en;q=0.5
Accept-Encoding: gzip,deflate

HTTP Request

URL rewriting kicks in ONLY if cookies fail, and ONLY if you tell the response to encode the URL

If cookies don't work, the Container falls back to URL rewriting, but ***only*** if you've done the extra work of encoding all the URLs you send in the response. If you want the Container to always default to using cookies first, with URL rewriting only as a last resort, you can relax. That's exactly how it works (except for the first time, but we'll get to that in a moment). But if you don't ***explicitly encode your URLs***, and the client won't accept cookies, ***you don't get to use sessions***. If you *do* encode your URLs, the Container will first attempt to use cookies for session management, and fall back to URL rewriting only if the cookie approach fails.

```
public void doGet(HttpServletRequest request, HttpServletResponse response)
                                                    throws IOException {
    response.setContentType("text/html");
    PrintWriter out = response.getWriter();
    HttpSession session = request.getSession();  <-- get a session

    out.println("<html><body>");
    out.println("<a href=\"" + response.encodeURL("/BeerTest.do") + "\">click me</a>");
    out.println("</body></html>");
}
```

Add the extra session ID info to this URL.

Q: Wait a minute... how DOES the Container know that cookies aren't working? At what point does the Container decide to use URL rewriting?

A: A really dumb Container doesn't care whether cookies work or not—the dumb Container will always attempt to send the cookie AND do URL rewriting each time, even if cookies are working. But here's how a *decent* Container handles it:

When the Container sees a call to getSession(), and the Container didn't get a session ID with the client's request, the Container now knows that it must attempt to *start* a new session with the client. At this point, the Container doesn't know if cookies will work, so with this *first* response back to the client, it tries BOTH cookies *and* URL rewriting.

Q: Why can't it try cookies *first*... and do URL rewriting on the *next* response if it doesn't get back a cookie?

A: Remember, if the Container doesn't get a session ID from the client, the Container won't even KNOW that this is the *next* request from that client. The Container won't have any way to know that it tried cookies the last time, and they didn't work. Remember, the ONLY way the Container can recognize that it has seen this client before is if the client sends a session ID!

So, when the Container sees you call request.getSession(), and realizes it needs to start a new session with this client, the Container sends the response with both a "Set-Cookie" header for the session ID, *and* the session ID appended to the URLs (assuming you used response.encodeURL()).

Now imagine the *next* request from this client—it will have the session ID appended to the request URL, but if the client accepts cookies, the request will ALSO have a session ID cookie. When the servlet calls request.getSession(), the Container reads the session ID from the request, finds the session, and thinks to itself, "This client accepts cookies, so I can *ignore* the response.encodeURL() calls. In the response, I'll send a cookie since I know that works, and there's no need for any URL rewriting, so I won't bother..."

URL rewriting works with sendRedirect()

You might have a scenario in which you want to redirect the request to a different URL, but you still want to use a session. There's a special URL encoding method just for that:

```
response.encodeRedirectURL("/BeerTest.do")
```

Q: What about all my static HTML pages... they are full of <a href> links. How do I do URL rewriting on those static pages?

A: You can't! The only way to use URL rewriting is if ALL the pages that are part of a session are dynamically-generated! You can't hard-code session ID's, obviously, since the ID doesn't exist until runtime. So, if you depend on sessions, you need URL rewriting as a fall-back strategy. And since you need URL rewriting, you have to dynamically generate the URLs in the response HTML! And that means you have to process the HTML at runtime.

Yes, this is a performance issue. So you must think very carefully about the places where sessions matter to your app, and whether sessions are critical to have or merely good to have.

URL rewriting is automatic... but only if you encode your URLs. YOU have to run all your URLs through a method of the response object—encodeURL() or encodeRedirectURL()—and the Container does everything else.

Q: You said that to use URL-rewriting, pages must be dynamically-generated, so does this mean I can do it with JSPs?

A: Yes! You can do URL-rewriting in a JSP, and there's even a simple JSTL tag that makes it easy, <c:URL>, that you'll see when you get to the chapter on using custom tags.

Q: Is URL rewriting handled in a vendor-specific way?

A: Yes, URL rewriting *is* handled in a vendor-specific way. Tomcat uses a semicolon ";" to append the *extra info* to the URL. Another vendor might use a comma or something else. And while Tomcat adds "jsessionid=" in the rewritten URL, another vendor might append only the session ID itself. The point is, whatever the Container uses as the separator is recognized by the Container when a request comes in. So when the Container sees the separator that *it* uses (in other words, the separator that *it* added during URL rewriting), it knows that everything after that is "extra info" that the Container put there. In other words, the Container knows how to recognize and parse the extra stuff *it* (the Container) appended to the URL.

URL encoding is handled by the Response!

Don't forget that the encodeURL() method is something you call on your HttpServletResponse object! You don't call it on the request, or on your context, or your session object. Just remind yourself that URL encoding is all about the response.

Don't be fooled by a request parameter "jsessionid" or a "JSESSIONID" header.

YOU don't ever use "jsessionid" yourself. If you see a "jsessionid" request parameter, somebody's doing something wrong. You should never see something like this:

```
String sessionID = request.getParameter("jsessionid");
```

← No!!

And you shouldn't see a custom "jsessionid" header in a request or response:

POST /select/selectBeerTaste.do HTTP/1.1
User-Agent: Mozilla/5.0
JSESSIONID: 0AAB6C8DE415 ← Don't do this! It's supposed to be a header!

In fact, the ONLY place a "jsessionid" belongs is inside a cookie header:

POST /select/selectBeerTaste.do HTTP/1.1
User-Agent: Mozilla/5.0
Cookie: JSESSIONID=0AAB6C8DE415 ← This is right, but you don't do it yourself.

or appended to the end of a URL as "extra info":

POST /select/selectBeerTaste.do;jsessionid=0AAB6C8DE415 ← The result of URL rewriting (you don't do this yourself either).

BULLET POINTS

- URL rewriting adds the session ID to the end of all the URLs in the HTML that you write to the response.
- The session ID then comes back with the request as "extra" info at the end of the request URL.
- URL rewriting will happen automatically if cookies don't work with the client, but you have to explicitly encode all of the URLs you write.
- To encode a URL, call response.encodeURL(aString).

```
out.println("<a href='"
  + response.encodeURL("/BeerTest.do")
  + "'>TestBeer</a>");
```

- There's no way to get automatic URL rewriting with your static pages, so if you depend on sessions, you must use dynamically-generated pages.

I REALLY don't want a bunch of stale sessions sitting around in my server taking up valuable space...
(He wants to conserve space on his machine for playing "The Sims" with the "Hot Date" expansion pack.)

Getting rid of sessions

The client comes in, starts a session, then changes her mind and leaves the site. Or the client comes in, starts a session, then her browser crashes. Or the client comes in, starts a session, and then completes the session by making a purchase (shopping cart check-out). Or her computer crashes. *Whatever.*

The point is, session objects take resources. You don't want sessions to stick around longer than necessary. Remember, the HTTP protocol doesn't have any mechanism for the server to know that the client is gone. (In distributed application terms, for those of you familiar with them— there's no *leasing.*)*

But how does the Container (or *you*) *know* when the client walked away? How does the Container *know* when the client's browser crashed? ***How does the Container know when it's safe to destroy a session?***

FLEX YOUR MIND

What are strategies you (and the Container) might use to manage the number of sessions, and eliminate unneeded sessions? What are some possible ways in which the Container could tell that a session is no longer needed?

Think about it, then look at the HttpSession API a few pages from now for clues.

*Some distributed apps use leasing as a way for the server to know when a client is gone. The client gets a lease from the server, and then must *renew* the lease at specified intervals to tell the server that the client is still alive. If the client's lease *expires*, the server knows it can destroy any resources it was holding for that client.

How we want it to work...

We'd like the Container to recognize when a session has been inactive for too long, and destroy the session. Of course we might have to fight the Container over what "too long" really means. Is 20 minutes too long? An hour? A day? (Maybe there's a way for us to tell the Container what "too long" is.)

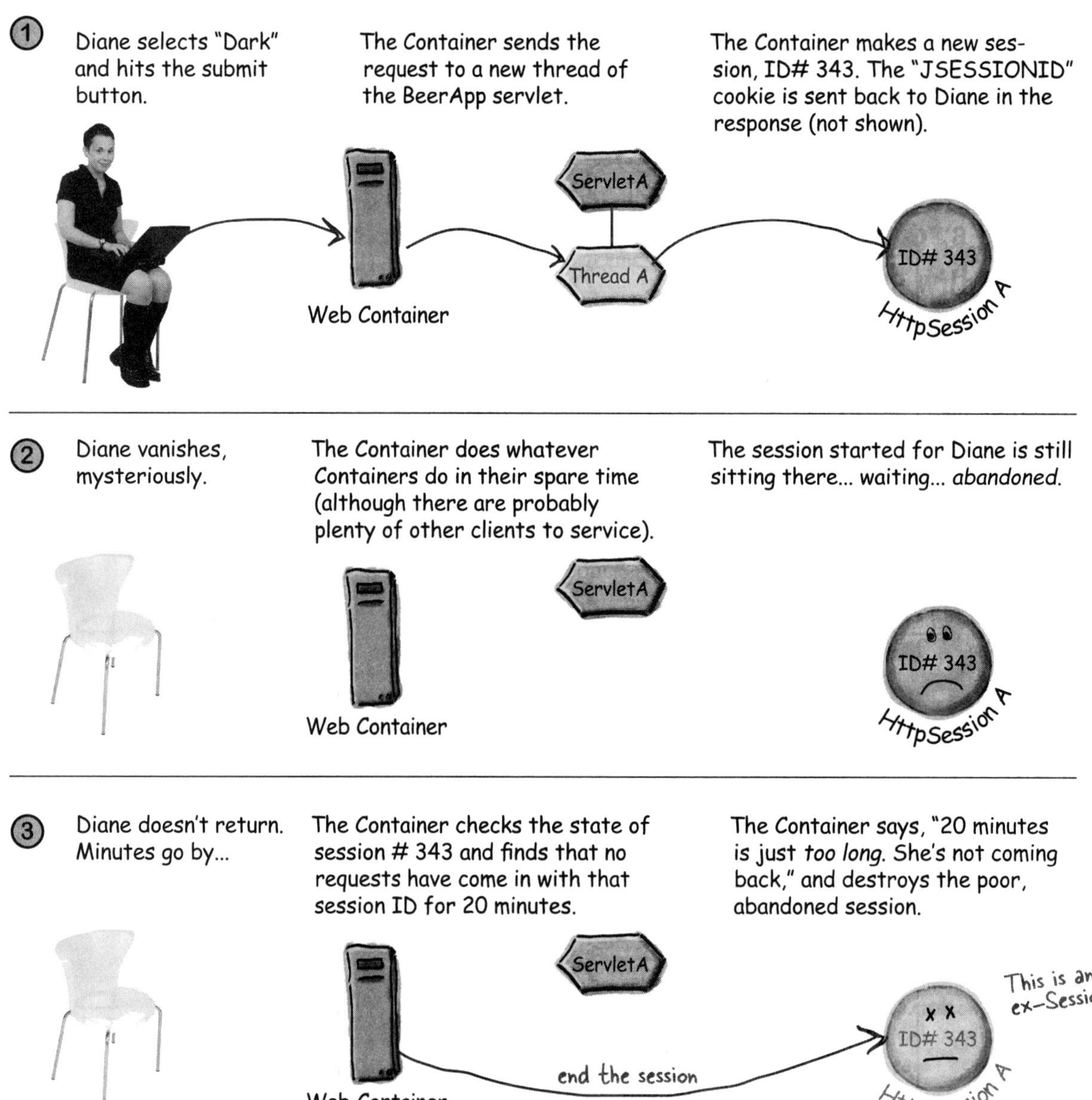

1
Diane selects "Dark" and hits the submit button.
The Container sends the request to a new thread of the BeerApp servlet.
The Container makes a new session, ID# 343. The "JSESSIONID" cookie is sent back to Diane in the response (not shown).
ServletA
Thread A
Web Container
ID# 343
HttpSession A
2
Diane vanishes, mysteriously.
The Container does whatever Containers do in their spare time (although there are probably plenty of other clients to service).
The session started for Diane is still sitting there... waiting... abandoned.
ServletA
Web Container
ID# 343
HttpSession A
3
Diane doesn't return. Minutes go by...
The Container checks the state of session # 343 and finds that no requests have come in with that session ID for 20 minutes.
The Container says, "20 minutes is just too long. She's not coming back," and destroys the poor, abandoned session.
ServletA
Web Container
end the session
ID# 343
HttpSession A
This is an ex-Session

The HttpSession interface

All you care about when you call getSession() is that you get an instance of a class that implements the HttpSession interface. It's the Container's job to create the implementation.

Once you have a session, what can you *do* with it?

Most of the time, you'll use sessions to get and set session-scoped attributes.

But there's more, of course. See if you can figure out some of the key methods for yourself (answers are on the next page, so don't turn the page!)

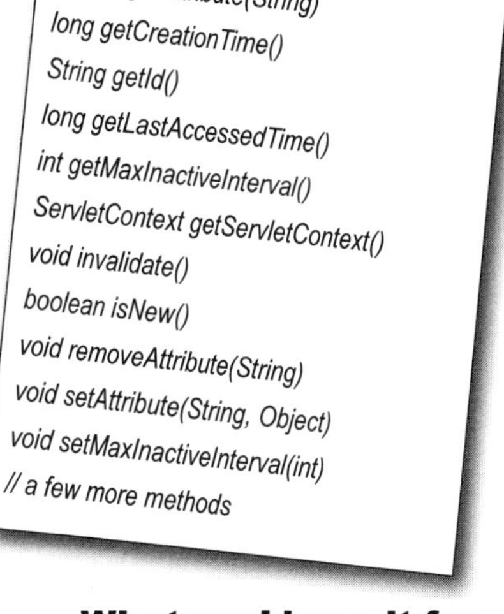

<<interface>>
javax.servlet.http.HttpSession
Object getAttribute(String)
long getCreationTime()
String getId()
long getLastAccessedTime()
int getMaxInactiveInterval()
ServletContext getServletContext()
void invalidate()
boolean isNew()
void removeAttribute(String)
void setAttribute(String, Object)
void setMaxInactiveInterval(int)
// a few more methods

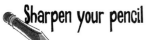

Sharpen your pencil

	What it does	**What you'd use it for**
getCreationTime()		
getLastAccessedTime()		
setMaxInactiveInterval()		
getMaxInactiveInterval()		
invalidate()		

Key HttpSession methods

You already know about the methods for attributes (getAttribute(), setAttribute(), removeAttribute()), but here are a few key ones you might need in your application (and that might be on the exam).

	What it does	**What you'd use it for**
getCreationTime()	Returns the time the session was first created.	To find out how old the session is. You might want to restrict certain sessions to a fixed length of time. For example, you might say, "Once you've logged in, you have exactly 10 minutes to complete this form..."
getLastAccessedTime()	Returns the last time the Container got a request with this session ID (in milliseconds).	To find out when a client last accessed this session. You might use it to decide that if the client's been gone a long time you'll send them an email asking if they're coming back. Or maybe you'll invalidate() the session.
setMaxInactiveInterval()	Specifies the maximum time, in seconds, that you want to allow between client requests for this session.	To cause a session to be destroyed after a certain amount of time has passed without the client making any requests for this session. This is one way to reduce the amount of stale sessions sitting in your server.
getMaxInactiveInterval()	Returns the maximum time, in seconds, that is allowed between client requests for this session.	To find out how long this session can be inactive and still be alive. You could use this to judge how much more time an inactive client has before the session will be invalidated.
invalidate()	Ends the session. This includes *unbinding* all session attributes currently stored in this session. (More on that later in this chapter.)	To kill a session if the client has been inactive or if you KNOW the session is over (for example, after the client does a shopping check-out or logs). The session instance *itself* might be recycled by the Container, but we don't care. Invalidate means the session ID no longer exists, and the attributes are removed from the session object.

FLEX YOUR MIND

Now that you've seen these methods, can you put together a strategy for eliminating abandoned sessions?

You can't be serious... does this mean that *I* have to keep track of session activity and that *I* have to destroy the stale sessions? Can't the *Container* do that?

Setting session timeout

Good news: you *don't* have to keep track of this yourself. See those methods on the opposite page? You don't have to use them to get rid of stale (inactive) sessions. The Container can do it for you.

Three ways a session can die:

- It times out
- You call invalidate() on the session object
- The application goes down (crashes or is undeployed)

1 Configuring session timeout in the DD

Configuring a timeout in the DD has virtually the same effect as calling setMaxInactiveInterval() on every session that's created.

```
<web-app ...>
  <servlet>
    ...
  </servlet>
 <session-config>
    <session-timeout>15</session-timeout>
  </session-config>
</web-app>
```

The "15" is in minutes. This says if the client doesn't make any requests on this session for 15 minutes, kill it.*

2 Setting session timeout for a *specific* session

If you want to change the session-timeout value for a particular session instance (without affecting the timeout length for any other sessions in the app):

```
session.setMaxInactiveInterval(20*60);
```

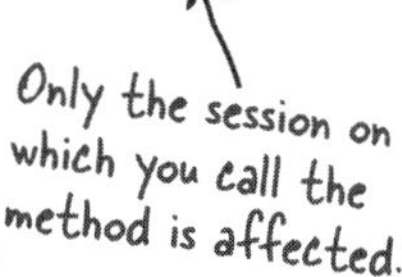

Only the session on which you call the method is affected.

The argument to the method is in seconds, so this says if the client doesn't make any requests on the session for 20 minutes, kill it.*

Timeouts in the DD are in MINUTES!

Here's a big inconsistency to watch out for... you specify timeouts in the DD using MINUTES, but if you set a timeout programmatically, you specify SECONDS!

*The session, not the client.

Code Magnets

Specify in both the DD, and programmatically, that if a session does not receive any requests for 20 minutes, it should be destroyed. We put one magnet in the servlet for you, to get started, and you might not use all magnets.

DD

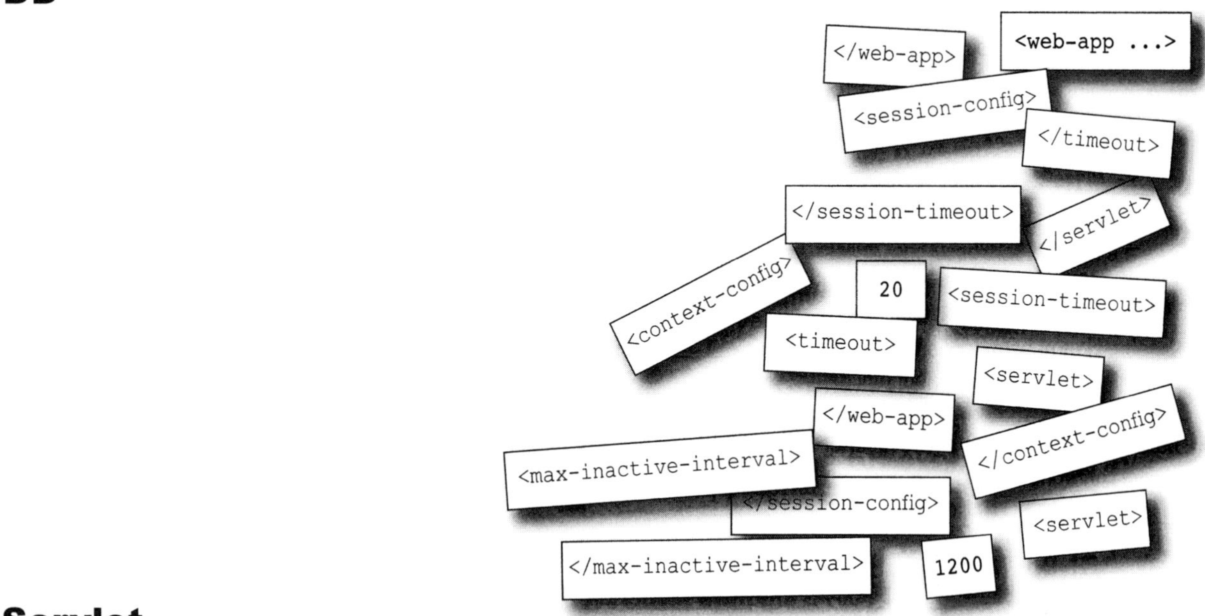

Servlet

```
public void doGet(HttpServletRequest request, HttpServletResponse response)
                                                    throws IOException {

    HttpSession

}
```

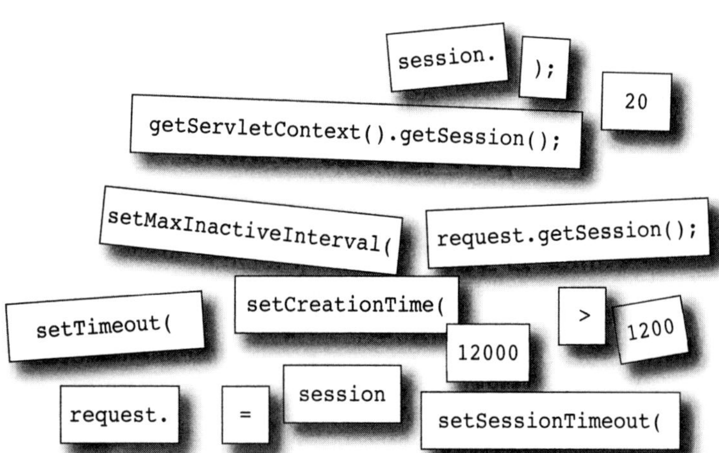

BE the Container

Each of the two listings represents code from a compiled HttpServlet. Your job is to think like the Container and determine what will happen when each of these servlets are invoked twice by the same client. Describe what happens the first and second time the same client accesses the servlet.

1

```
public void doGet(HttpServletRequest request, HttpServletResponse response)
                                                          throws IOException {
       response.setContentType("text/html");
       PrintWriter out = response.getWriter();
       HttpSession session = request.getSession();
       session.setAttribute("foo", "42");
       session.setAttribute("bar", "420");
       session.invalidate();
       String foo = (String) session.getAttribute("foo");
       out.println("Foo: " + foo);
}
```

2

```
public void doGet(HttpServletRequest request, HttpServletResponse response)
                                                          throws IOException {
       response.setContentType("text/html");
       PrintWriter out = response.getWriter();
       HttpSession session = request.getSession();
       session.setAttribute("foo", "42");
       session.setMaxInactiveInterval(0);
       String foo = (String) session.getAttribute("foo");
       if (session.isNew()) {
          out.println("This is a new session.");
       } else {
           out.println("Welcome back!");
       }

       out.println("Foo: " + foo);
}
```

Code Magnets Answers

Specify in both the DD, and programmatically, that if a session does not receive any requests for 20 minutes, it should be destroyed.

DD

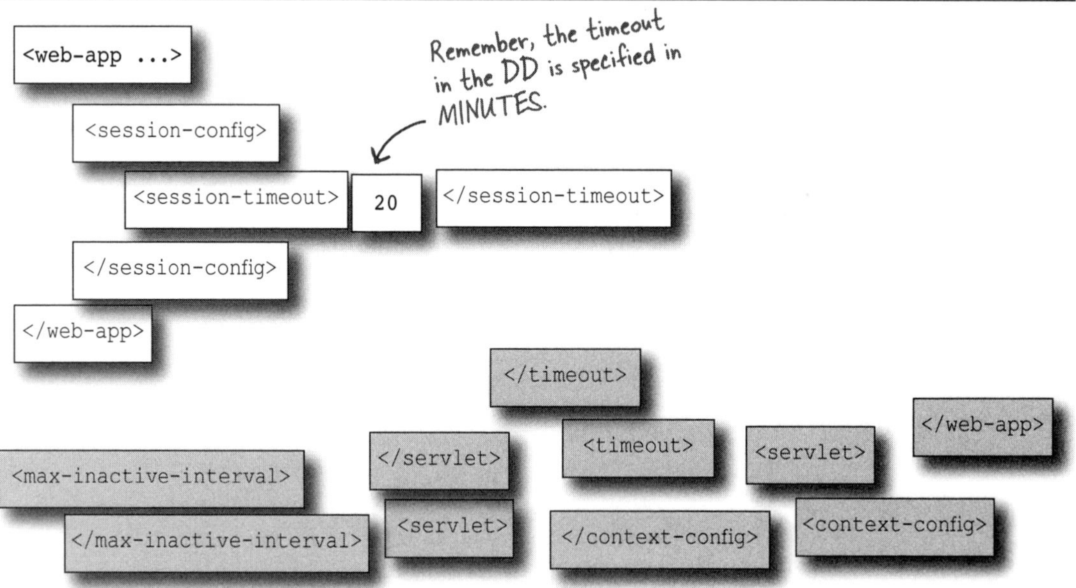
<web-app ...>
<session-config>
<session-timeout>
20
</session-timeout>
</session-config>
</web-app>
Remember, the timeout in the DD is specified in MINUTES.
</timeout>
<timeout>
<servlet>
</web-app>
<max-inactive-interval>
</servlet>
</max-inactive-interval>
<servlet>
</context-config>
<context-config>

Servlet

```
public void doGet(HttpServletRequest request, HttpServletResponse response)
                                                        throws IOException {
```

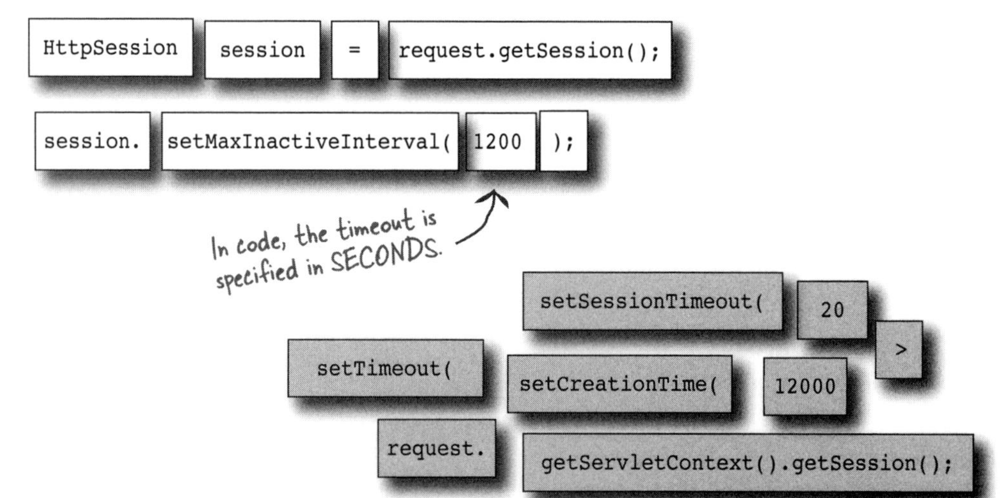
HttpSession
session
=
request.getSession();
session.
setMaxInactiveInterval(
1200
);
In code, the timeout is specified in SECONDS.
setSessionTimeout(
20
>
setTimeout(
setCreationTime(
12000
request.
getServletContext().getSession();

```
}
```

BE the Container Answers

1

```
public void doGet(HttpServletRequest request, HttpServletResponse response)
                                                            throws IOException {
     response.setContentType("text/html");
     PrintWriter out = response.getWriter();
     HttpSession session = request.getSession();
     session.setAttribute("foo", "42");
     session.setAttribute("bar", "420");
     session.invalidate();  <- here we invalidate the session

     String foo = (String)session.getAttribute("foo");

     out.println("Foo: " + foo);
}
```

Uh-oh! It's too late to call getAttribute() on the session because the session already IS invalid!

Result: a runtime exception (IllegalStateException) is thrown because you can't get an attribute AFTER the session becomes invalid.

2

```
public void doGet(HttpServletRequest request, HttpServletResponse response)
                                                            throws IOException {
     response.setContentType("text/html");
     PrintWriter out = response.getWriter();

     HttpSession session = request.getSession();
     session.setAttribute("foo", "42");
     session.setMaxInactiveInterval(0);
     String foo = (String) session.getAttribute("foo");

     if (session.isNew()) {
        out.println("This is a new session.");
     } else {
         out.println("Welcome back!");
     }
     out.println("Foo: " + foo);
}
```

Here we're causing the session to timeout IMMEDIATELY, because we're saying, "timeout after 0 seconds of inactivity".

You can't call isNew() on a session that's already been invalidated. So it's really the same problem as the code above... you can't call this method on an invalid session.

Result: a runtime exception (IllegalStateException) is thrown because you can't call isNew() on the session AFTER the session becomes invalid. Setting the maximum inactive interval to 0 means the session times out and is invalidated immediately!

Can I use cookies for other things, or are they only for sessions?

Although cookies *were* originally designed to help support session state, you *can* use custom cookies for other things. Remember, a cookie is nothing more than a little piece of data (a name/value String pair) exchanged between the client and server. The server *sends* the cookie to the client, and the client *returns* the cookie when the client makes another request.

One cool thing about cookies is that the *user* doesn't have to get involved—the cookie exchange is automatic (assuming cookies are enabled on the client, of course).

By default, a cookie lives only as long as a session; once the client quits his browser, the cookie disappears. That's how the "JSESSIONID" cookie works. ***But you can tell a cookie to stay alive even AFTER the browser shuts down.***

That way, your web app can still get the cookie information even though the session with that client is long gone. Imagine that Kim wants to display the user's name each time he returns to the beer site. So he sets the cookie the first time he receives the client's name, and if he gets the cookie back with a request, he knows not to ask for the name again. *And it doesn't matter if the user restarted his browser and hasn't been on the site for a week!*

You can use cookies to exchange name/value String pairs between the server and the client.

The server sends the cookie to the client, and the client sends it back with each subsequent request.

Session cookies vanish when the client's browser quits, but you CAN tell a cookie to persist on the client even after the browser shuts down.

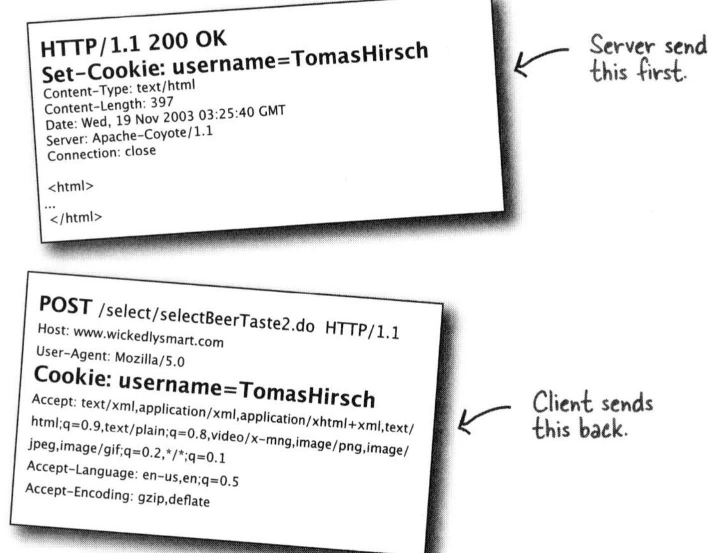

```
HTTP/1.1 200 OK
Set-Cookie: username=TomasHirsch
Content-Type: text/html
Content-Length: 397
Date: Wed, 19 Nov 2003 03:25:40 GMT
Server: Apache-Coyote/1.1
Connection: close

<html>
...
</html>
```

Server sends this first.

```
POST /select/selectBeerTaste2.do HTTP/1.1
Host: www.wickedlysmart.com
User-Agent: Mozilla/5.0
Cookie: username=TomasHirsch
Accept: text/xml,application/xml,application/xhtml+xml,text/
html;q=0.9,text/plain;q=0.8,video/x-mng,image/png,image/
jpeg,image/gif;q=0.2,*/*;q=0.1
Accept-Language: en-us,en;q=0.5
Accept-Encoding: gzip,deflate
```

Client sends this back.

Using Cookies with the Servlet API

You *can* get cookie-related headers out of the HTTP request and response, but *don't*. Everything you need to do with cookies has been encapsulated in the Servlet API in three classes: HttpServletRequest, HttpServletResponse, and Cookie.

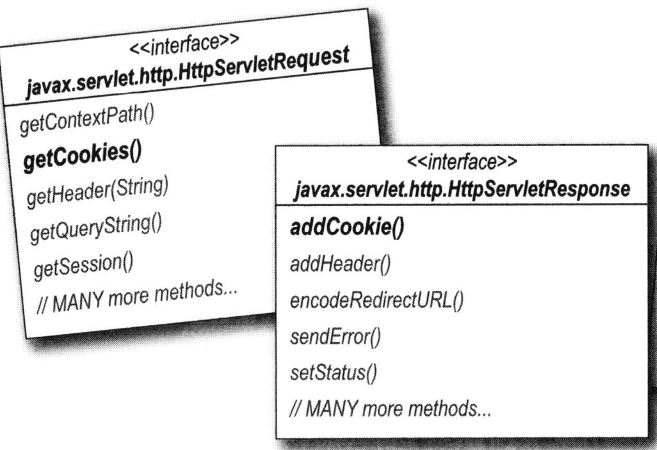

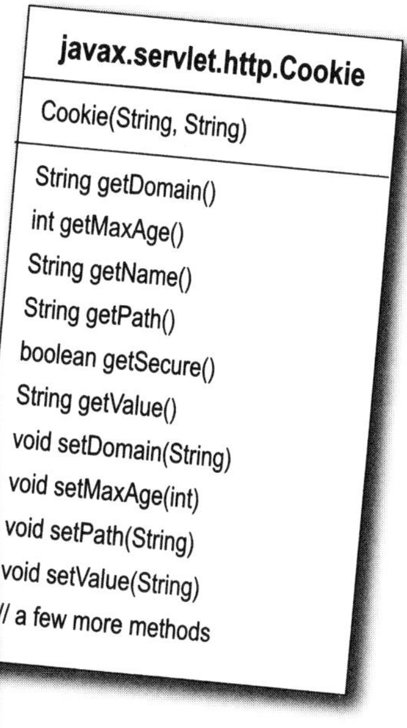

javax.servlet.http.Cookie
Cookie(String, String)
String getDomain()
int getMaxAge()
String getName()
String getPath()
boolean getSecure()
String getValue()
void setDomain(String)
void setMaxAge(int)
void setPath(String)
void setValue(String)
// a few more methods

Creating a new Cookie

```
Cookie cookie = new Cookie("username", name);
```

The Cookie constructor takes a name/value String pair.

Setting how long a cookie will live on the client

```
cookie.setMaxAge(30*60);
```

setMaxAge is defined in SECONDS. This code says "stay alive on the client for 30*60 seconds" (30 minutes). Setting max age to -1 makes the cookie disappear when the browser exits. So, if you call getMaxAge() on the "JSESSIONID" cookie, what will you get back?

Sending the cookie to the client

```
response.addCookie(cookie);
```

Getting the cookie(s) from the client request

```
Cookie[] cookies = request.getCookies();
for (int i = 0; i < cookies.length; i++) {
    Cookie cookie = cookies[i];
    if (cookie.getName().equals("username")) {
        String userName = cookie.getValue();
        out.println("Hello " + userName);
        break;
    }
}
```

There's no getCookie(String) method... you can only get cookies in a Cookie array, and then you have to loop over the array to find the one you want.

Simple custom cookie example

So, imagine that Kim wants to put up a form that asks the user to submit his name. The form calls a servlet that gets the username request parameter, and uses the name value to set a cookie in the response.

The next time this user makes a request on ANY servlet in this web app, the cookie comes back with the request (assuming the cookie is still alive, based on the cookie's maxAge value). When a servlet in the web app sees this cookie, it can put the user's name into the dynamically-generated response, and the business logic knows not to ask the user to input his name again.

This code is a simplified test version of the scenario we just described.

Servlet that creates and SETS the cookie

```
import javax.servlet.*;
import javax.servlet.http.*;
import java.io.*;

public class CookieTest extends HttpServlet {

   public void doPost(HttpServletRequest request, HttpServletResponse response)
                                             throws IOException, ServletException {

      response.setContentType("text/html");

      String name = request.getParameter("username");

      Cookie cookie = new Cookie("username", name);

      cookie.setMaxAge(30*60);

      response.addCookie(cookie);

      RequestDispatcher view = request.getRequestDispatcher("cookieresult.jsp");
      view.forward(request, response);

   }
}
```

Get the user's name submitted in the form.

Make a new cookie so store the user's name.

Keep it alive on the client for 30 minutes.

Add the cookie as a "Set-Cookie" response header.

Let a JSP make the response page.

JSP to render the view from this servlet

```
<html><body>
 <a href="checkcookie.do">click here</a>
</body></html>
```

OK, sure, there's nothing JSP-ish about this, but we hate outputting even THIS much HTML from a servlet. The fact that we're forwarding to a JSP doesn't change the cookie setting. The cookie is already in the response by the time the request is forwarded to the JSP...

Custom cookie example continued...

Servlet that GETS the cookie

```
import javax.servlet.*;
import javax.servlet.http.*;
import java.io.*;

public class CheckCookie extends HttpServlet {

   public void doGet(HttpServletRequest request, HttpServletResponse response)
                                   throws IOException, ServletException {

      response.setContentType("text/html");
      PrintWriter out = response.getWriter();

      Cookie[] cookies = request.getCookies();

      for (int i = 0; i < cookies.length; i++) {
         Cookie cookie = cookies[i];
         if (cookie.getName().equals("username")) {
            String userName = cookie.getValue();
            out.println("Hello " + userName);
            break;
         }
      }

   }
}
```

Get the cookies from the request.

Loop through the cookie array looking for a cookie named "username". If there is one, get the value and print it.

Don't confuse Cookies with headers!

*When you add a **header** to a response, you pass the name and value Strings as arguments:*

```
response.addHeader("foo", "bar");
```

*But when you add a **Cookie** to the response, you pass a Cookie object. You set the Cookie name and value in the Cookie constructor.*

```
Cookie cookie = new Cookie("name", name);
response.addCookie(cookie);
```

*And remember, too, that there's both a **set**Header() and an **add**Header() method (**add**Header **adds** a new value to an existing header, if there is one, but **set**Header **replaces** the existing value). But there's NOT a setCookie() method. There's only an **add**Cookie() method!*

Relax

You don't have to know ALL the cookie methods.

For the exam, you don't have to memorize every one of the methods in class Cookie, but you must know the request and response methods to get and add Cookies. You should also know the Cookie constructor and the getMaxAge() and setMaxAge() methods.

Key milestones for an HttpSession

Highlights of the important moments in an HttpSession object's life:

The session is created or destroyed.

Session attributes are added, removed, or replaced by other parts of the app.

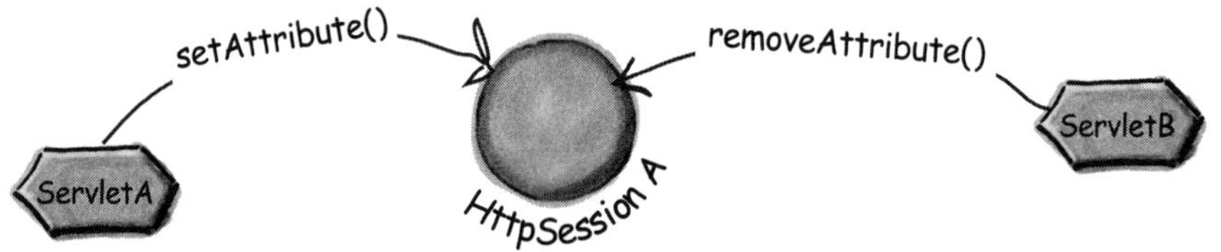

The session is passivated in one VM and activated in another within a distributed app.

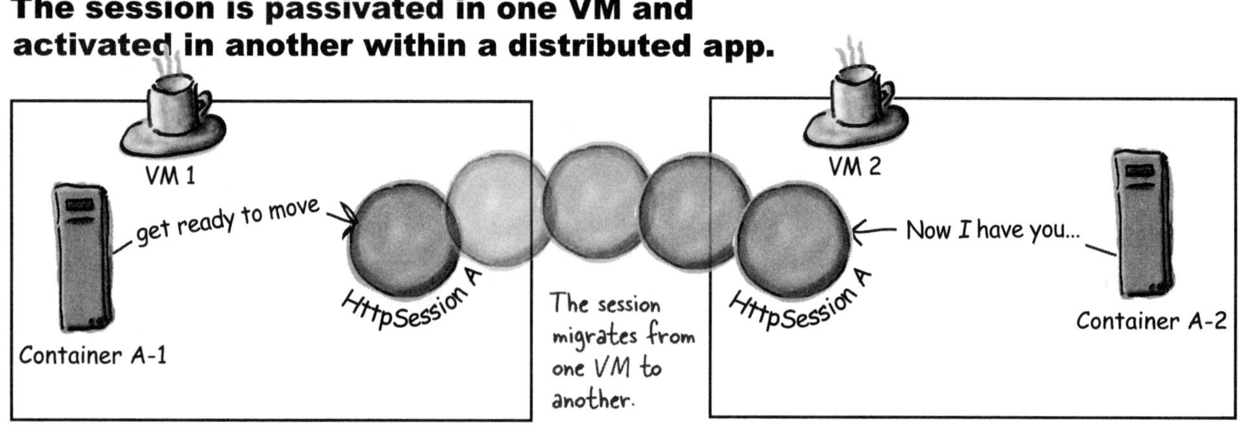

Session lifecycle Events

Milestone	**Event and Listener type**

Lifecycle

HttpSessionEvent

HttpSessionListener

The session was *created*

When the Container first creates a session. At this point, the session is still considered *new* (in other words, the client has not yet sent a request with the session ID).

The session was *destroyed*

When the Container invalidates a session (because the session timed out or some part of the application called the session's invalidate() method).

Attributes

HttpSessionBindingEvent

HttpSessionAttributeListener

An attribute was *added*

When some part of the app calls setAttribute() on the session.

An attribute was *removed*

When some part of the app calls removeAttribute() on the session.

An attribute was *replaced*

When some part of the app calls setAttribute() on the session, and the name of the attribute has already been bound to the session.

Migration

HttpSessionEvent

HttpSessionActivationListener

The session is *about* to be *passivated*

When the Container is about to migrate (move) the session into a different VM. Called *before* the session moves, so that attributes have a chance to prepare themselves for migration.

The session *has* been *activated*

When the Container has *just* migrated (moved) the session into a different VM. Called before any other part of the app can call getAttribute() on the session, so the just-moved attributes have a chance to get themselves ready for access.

Don't forget about HttpSessionBindingListener

The events on the previous page are for key moments in the life of the *session*. But the HttpSessionBindingListener is for key moments in the life of a session *attribute*. Remember from chapter 5 where we looked at how you might use this—if, for example, your attribute wants to know when it's added to a session so that it can synchronize itself with an underlying database (and update the database when it's removed from a session). Here's a little review from the previous chapter:

This listener is just so that ***I*** can find out when ***I'm*** put into a session (or taken out). It won't tell me anything about *other* session events.

```
package com.example;

import javax.servlet.http.*;

public class Dog implements HttpSessionBindingListener {
   private String breed;

   public Dog(String breed) {
     this.breed=breed;
   }

   public String getBreed() {
     return breed;
   }

   public void valueBound(HttpSessionBindingEvent event) {
     // code to run now that I know I'm in a session
   }

   public void valueUnbound(HttpSessionBindingEvent event) {
     // code to run now that I know I am no longer part of a session
   }
}
```

This listener is in the javax.servlet.http package.

This time the Dog attribute is ALSO an HttpSessionBindingListener... listening for when the Dog itself is added or removed from a Session.

The word "Bound" means someone ADDED this attribute to a session.

You can figure out what "Unbound" means.

You do NOT configure session binding listeners in the DD!

If an attribute class (like the Dog class here) implements the HttpSessionBindingListener, the Container calls the event-handling callbacks (valueBound() and valueUnbound()) when an instance of this class is added to or removed from a session. That's it. It just works. But this is NOT true for the other session-related listeners on the previous page. HttpSessionListener, HttpSessionAttributeListener, and HttpSessionActivationListener must be registered in the DD, since they're related to the session itself, rather than an individual attribute placed in the session.

Session migration

Remember from the previous chapter, we talked briefly about distributed web apps, where the pieces of the app might be replicated across multiple nodes in the network. In a clustered environment, the Container might do *load-balancing* by taking client requests and sending them out to JVMs (which may or may not be on different physical boxes, but that doesn't matter to us). The point is, the app is in multiple places.

That means each time the same client makes a request, the request could end up going to a *different* instance of the same servlet. In other words, request A for Servlet A could happen on one VM, and request B for Servlet A could end up on a different VM. So the question is, what happens to things like ServletContext, ServletConfig, and HttpSession objects?

Simple answer, important implications:

Only HttpSession objects (and their attributes) move from one VM to another.

There is one ServletContext *per VM*. There is one ServletConfig *per servlet, per VM*. ***But there is only one HttpSession object for a given session ID per web app, regardless of how many VM's the app is distributed across.***

The Beer Web App distributed across two VMs

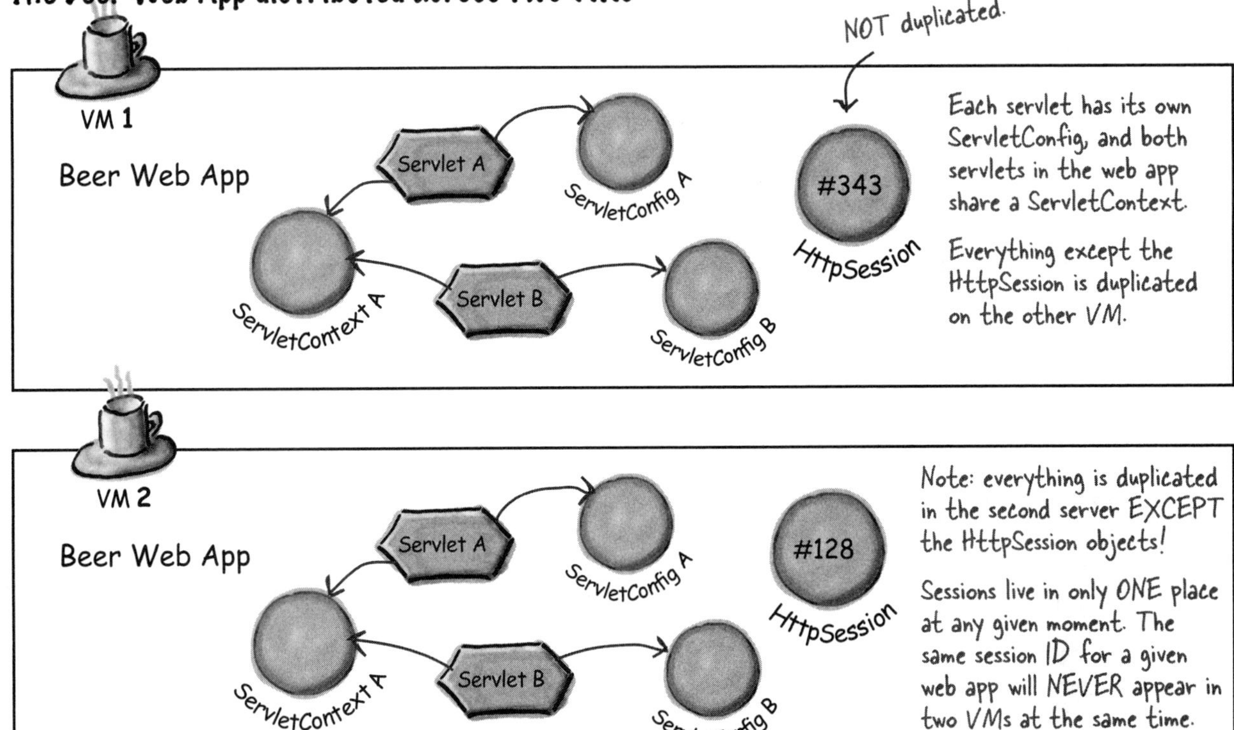
NOT duplicated.
VM 1
Beer Web App
Servlet A
ServletConfig A
#343
HttpSession
ServletContext A
Servlet B
ServletConfig B
Each servlet has its own ServletConfig, and both servlets in the web app share a ServletContext.
Everything except the HttpSession is duplicated on the other VM.
VM 2
Beer Web App
Servlet A
ServletConfig A
#128
HttpSession
ServletContext A
Servlet B
ServletConfig B
Note: everything is duplicated in the second server EXCEPT the HttpSession objects!
Sessions live in only ONE place at any given moment. The same session ID for a given web app will NEVER appear in two VMs at the same time.

Session migration in action

How an app server vendor handles clustering and web app distribution varies with each vendor, and there's no guarantee in the J2EE spec that a vendor has to support distributed apps. But the picture here gives you a high-level idea of how it works. The key point is that while other parts of the app are *replicated* on each node/VM, the session objects are *moved*. And that *is* guaranteed. In other words, if the vendor *does* support distributed apps, then the Container is *required* to migrate sessions across VMs. And that includes migrating session attributes as well.

1. Diane selects "Pale" and hits the submit button. The Load-Balancing server decides to send the request to Container **A-1** in **VM One**. The Container makes a new session, ID# 343. The "JSESSIONID" cookie is sent back to Diane in the response (not shown).

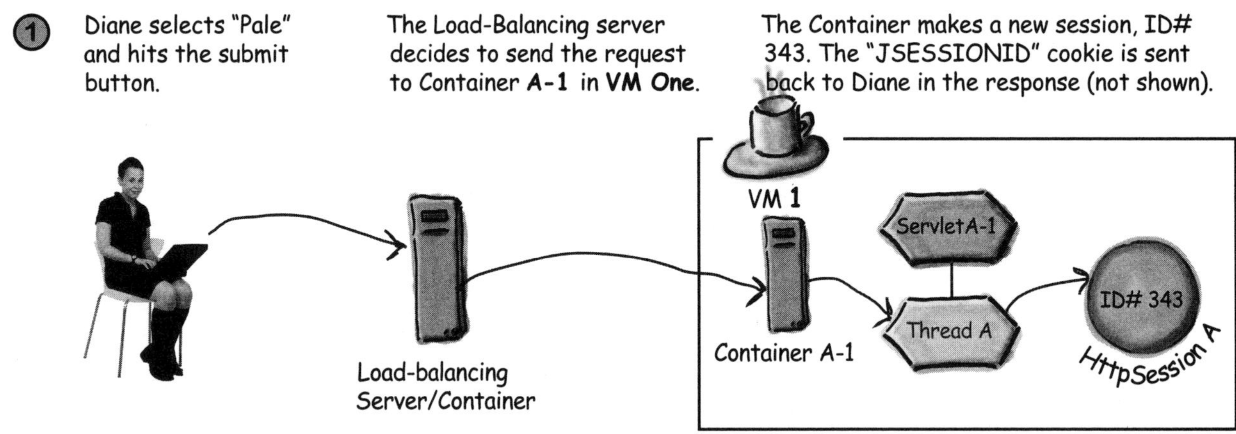

2. Diane selects "Bitter" and hits the submit button. Her request also includes the "JSESSIONID" #343. This time, the Load-Balancing server decides to send the request to Container **A-2** in **VM Two**. The Container gets the request, sees the session ID, and realizes that the session is on a different VM, VM One!

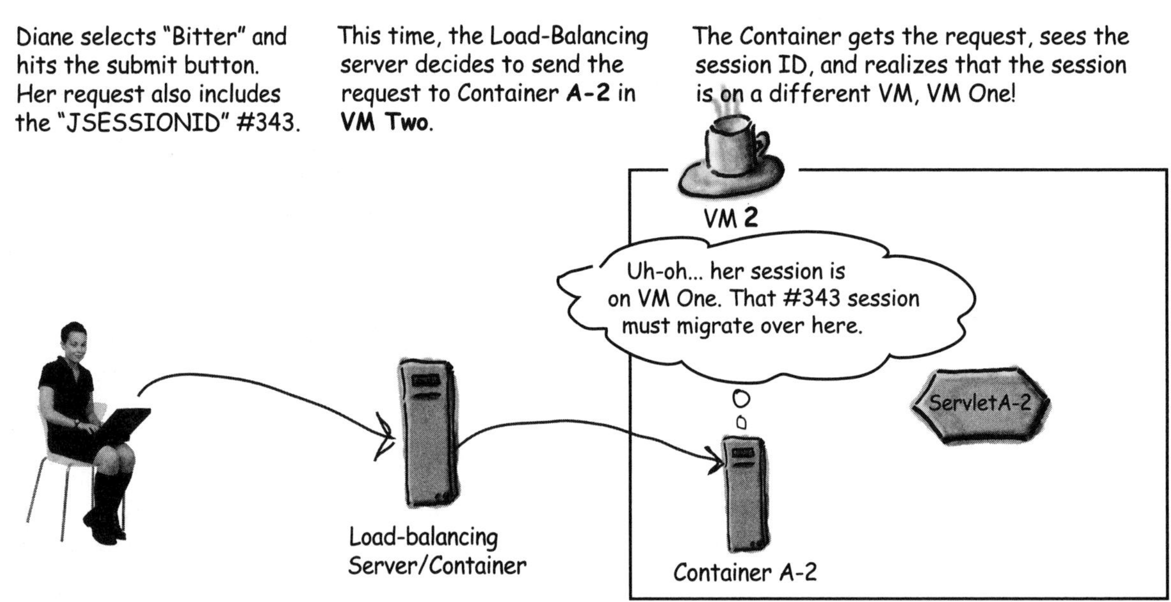

3 The session #343 migrates from VM One to VM Two. In other words, ***it no longer exists on VM One*** once it moves to VM Two.

This migration means the session was ***passivated on VM One***, and ***activated on VM Two.***

Load-balancing Server/Container

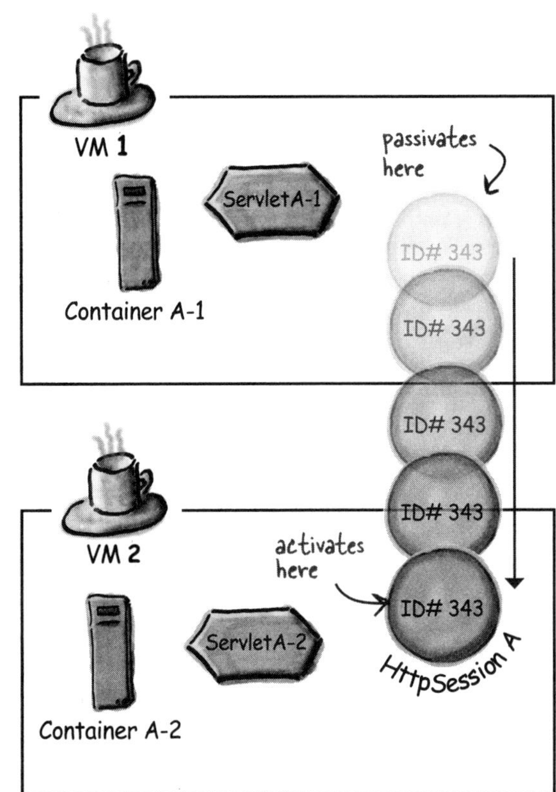

The Container makes a new thread for ServletA, and associates the new request with the recently-moved session #343.

Diane's new request is sent to the thread, and everybody is happy. Diane has no idea what happened (except for the slight delay/latency waiting for the session to move).

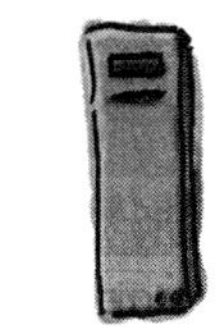

Load-balancing Server/Container

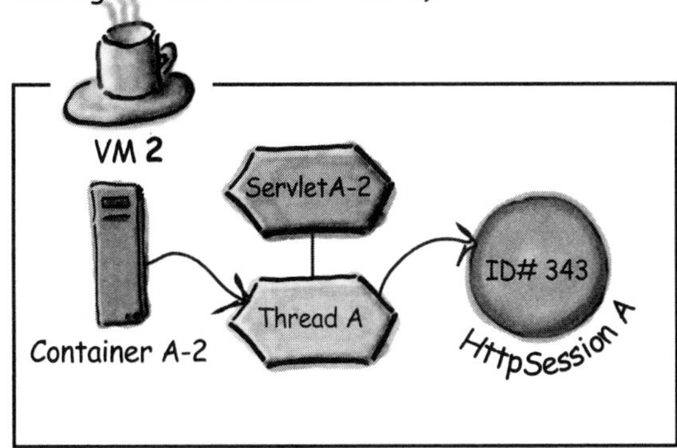

HttpSessionActivationListener lets attributes prepare for the big move...

This listener is so that as an attribute, I can find out when ***I'm*** about to be moved to a new VM as part of a session, and I can make sure my instance variables are ready...

Since it's *possible* that an HttpSession can migrate from one VM to another, the spec designers thought it would be nice if someone bothered to tell the attributes within the session that they, too, were about to move. That way the attributes can make sure they'll survive the trip.

If all your attributes are straightforward Serializable objects that don't care where they end up, you'll probably never use this listener. In fact, we're guessing 95.324% of all web apps never use this listener. But it's there if you need it, and the most likely use of this listener is to give attributes a chance to make their instance variables ready for Serialization.

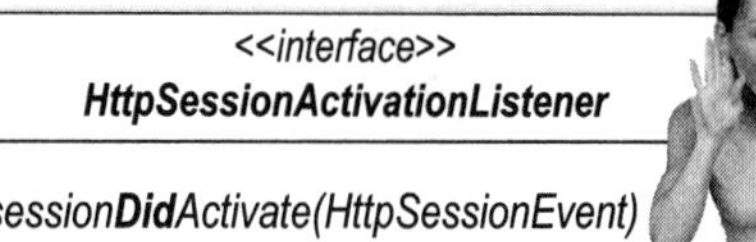

<<interface>>
HttpSessionActivationListener

*session**Did**Activate(HttpSessionEvent)*
*session**Will**Passivate(HttpSessionEvent)*

javax.servlet.http.HttpSessionActivationListener

Session migration and Serialization

Now it gets a little tricky...

A Container is required to migrate Serializable attributes (which assumes that all instance variables within the attribute are either Serializable or null).

But a Container is not required to use Serialization as the means for migrating the HttpSession object!

What does this mean to you? Simple: make sure your attribute class types are Serializable and you never have to worry about it. But if they're *not* Serializable (which could be because one of the attribute object's instance variables is not Serializable), have your attribute object class implement HttpSessionActivationListener and use the activation/passivation callbacks to work around it.

The Container is not REQUIRED to use Serialization, so there's no guarantee that readObject() and writeObject() will be called on a Serializable attribute or one of its instance variables!

If you're familiar with Serialization, you know that a class that implements Serializable can also choose to implement a writeObject() method, called by the VM whenever an object is serialized, and a readObject() method, called when an object is deserialized. A Serializable object can use these methods to, for example, set non-Serializable fields to null during Serialization (writeObject()) and then restore the fields during deserialization (readObject()). (If you're NOT familiar with the details of Serialization, don't worry about it.) But the methods won't necessarily be called during session migration! So if you need to save and restore instance variable state in your attribute, use HttpSessionActivationListener, and use the two event call-backs (sessionDidActivate() and sessionWillPassivate()) the way you'd use readObject() and writeObject().

Listener examples

Over the next three pages, pay attention to the event object types and to whether the listener is also an attribute class.

Session counter

This listener lets you keep track of the number of active sessions in this web app. Very simple.

```
package com.example;
import javax.servlet.http.*;

public class BeerSessionCounter implements HttpSessionListener {

   static private int activeSessions;

   public static int getActiveSessions() {
      return activeSessions;
   }

   public void sessionCreated(HttpSessionEvent event) {
      activeSessions++;
   }

   public void sessionDestroyed(HttpSessionEvent event) {
      activeSessions--;
   }
}
```

This class will be deployed in WEB-INF/classes like all the other web-app classes, so all servlets and other helper classes can access this method.

These methods take an HttpSessionEvent.

Configuring the listener in the DD

```
<web-app ...>
  ...
  <listener>
    <listener-class>
      com.example.BeerSessionCounter
    </listener-class>
  </listener>
</web-app>
```

FYI– this wouldn't work correctly if the app is distributed on multiple JVMs, because there is no way to keep the static variables in sync. If the class is loaded on more than one JVM, each class will have its own value for the static counter variable.

Listener examples

Attribute Listener

This listener lets you track each time any attribute is added to, removed from, or replaced in a session.

This listener uses inconsistent naming—it's an Attribute listener, but it takes a Binding event.

```
package com.example;
import javax.servlet.http.*;

public class BeerAttributeListener implements HttpSessionAttributeListener {

    public void attributeAdded(HttpSessionBindingEvent event) {

        String name = event.getName();
        Object value = event.getValue();

        System.out.println("Attribute added: " + name + ": " + value);
    }

   public void attributeRemoved(HttpSessionBindingEvent event) {
       String name = event.getName();
       Object value = event.getValue();
       System.out.println("Attribute removed: " + name + ": " + value);
   }

   public void attributeReplaced(HttpSessionBindingEvent event) {
       String name = event.getName();
       Object value = event.getValue();
       System.out.println("Attribute replaced: " + name + ": " + value);
   }

}
```

HttpSessionBindingEvent lets you get the name and value of the attribute that triggered this event.

Configuring the listener in the DD

```
<web-app ...>
  ...
   <listener>
     <listener-class>
       com.example.BeerAttributeListener
     </listener-class>
   </listener>
 </web-app>
```

Q: Hey, what the heck are you printing *to*? Where does System.out *go* in a web app?

A: Wherever this Container chooses to send it (which may or may not be configurable by you). In other words, in a vendor-specific place, often a log file. Tomcat puts the output in tomcat/logs/catalina.log. You'll have to read your server docs to find out what *your* Container does with standard output.

Listener examples

Attribute class (listening for events that affect IT)

This listener lets an attribute keep track of events that might be important to the attribute itself—when it's added to or removed from a session, and when the session migrates from one VM to another.

```
package com.example;
import javax.servlet.http.*;
import java.io.*;

public class Dog implements HttpSessionBindingListener,
                            HttpSessionActivationListener,Serializable {
   private String breed;
   // imagine more instance variables, including
   // some that are not Serializable

   // imagine constructor and other getter/setter methods

   public void valueBound(HttpSessionBindingEvent event) {
     // code to run now that I know I'm in a session
   }

   public void valueUnbound(HttpSessionBindingEvent event) {
     // code to run now that I know I am no longer part of a session
   }

   public void sessionWillPassivate(HttpSessionEvent event) {
     // code to get my non-Serializable fields in a state
     //  that can survive the move to a new VM
   }

   public void sessionDidActivate(HttpSessionEvent event) {
     // code to restore my fields... to redo whatever I undid
    // in sessionWillPassivate()
  }
}
```

Session binding events.

Session activation events (but notice that the methods take an HttpSessionEvent).

Configuring the listener in the DD

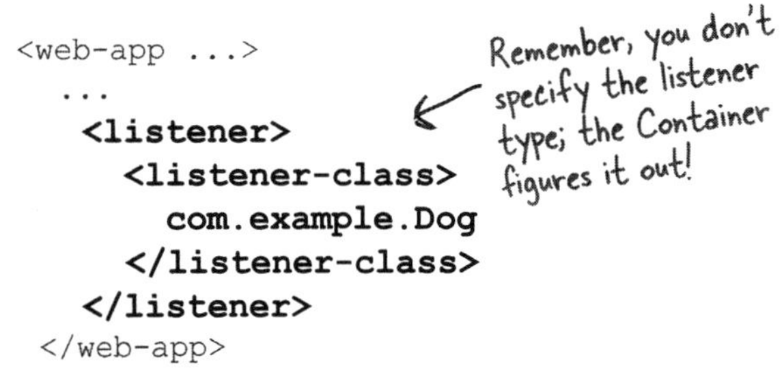

```
<web-app ...>
  ...
   <listener>
     <listener-class>
       com.example.Dog
     </listener-class>
   </listener>
 </web-app>
```

Remember, you don't specify the listener type; the Container figures it out!

HttpSessionActivationListener must be configured in the DD

This Dog class must be configured in the DD, but ONLY because it is a session activation listener! If it implemented only the HttpSessionBindingListener interface, it would NOT be configured in the DD, and the Container would simply take care of notifying it. But an HttpSessionActivationListener need not be an attribute class (although that's its most typical use).

Session-related Listeners

Scenario	Listener interface/ methods	Event type	Usually implemented by
You want to know how many concurrent users there are. In other words, you want to track the active sessions.	**HttpSessionListener** (javax.servlet.http) *sessionCreated* *sessionDestroyed*	HttpSessionEvent	☐ An attribute class ☒ Some *other* class
You want to know when a session moves from one VM to another.	**HttpSessionActivationListener** (javax.servlet.http) *sessionDidActivate* *sessionWillPassivate*	HttpSessionEvent Note: there's no specific HttpSessionActivationEvent.	☒ An attribute class ☒ Some *other* class
You have an attribute class (a class for an object that will be used as an attribute value) and you want objects of this type to be notified when they are bound to or removed from a session.	**HttpSessionBindingListener** (javax.servlet.http) *valueBound* *valueUnbound*	HttpSessionBindingEvent	☒ An attribute class ☐ Some *other* class
You want to know when any session attribute is added, removed, or replaced in a session.	**HttpSessionAttributeListener** (javax.servlet.http) *attributeAdded* *attributeRemoved* *attributeReplaced*	HttpSessionBindingEvent Note: there's no specific HttpSessionAttributeEvent.	☐ An attribute class ☒ Some *other* class

Some of the session-related events don't follow the event naming conventions!

*Http**Session**Listener methods take Http**Session**Events.*
*HttpSession**Binding**Listener methods take HttpSession**Binding**Events.*
*But HttpSession**Attribute**Listener methods take HttpSession**Binding**Events.*
*And HttpSession**Activation**Listener methods take Http**Session**Events.*
Since HttpSessionEvent and HttpSessionBindingEvent classes worked perfectly well, there was no need for the API to add two more event classes.

Session-related Event Listeners and Event Objects API overview

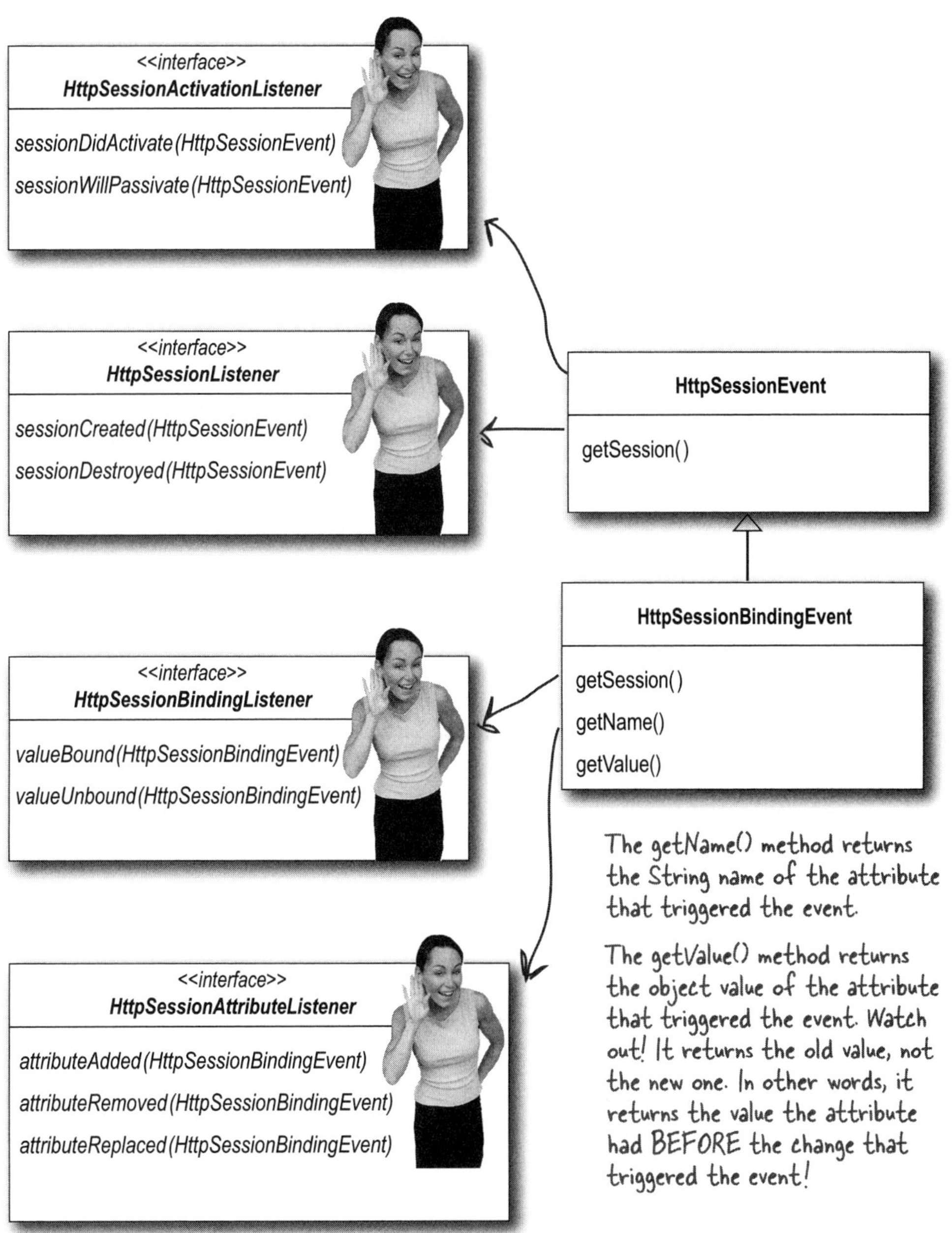

The getName() method returns the String name of the attribute that triggered the event.

The getValue() method returns the object value of the attribute that triggered the event. Watch out! It returns the old value, not the new one. In other words, it returns the value the attribute had BEFORE the change that triggered the event!

Session-related Listeners

Yes, this is almost an exact copy of the table from two pages back, so don't go there. Try to think through these listeners and put down your best guess. You can expect at least two, and as many as four questions on the exam about session listeners. Use both your memory *and* common sense to fill this out.

Scenario	**Listener interface/ methods**	**Event type**	**Usually implemented by**
You want to know when a session is created.			☐ An attribute class ☐ Some *other* class
An attribute wants to know when it has been moved into a new VM.			☐ An attribute class ☐ Some *other* class
An attribute wants to know when it has been replaced in a session.			☐ An attribute class ☐ Some *other* class
You want to be notified whenever *anything* is bound to a session.			☐ An attribute class ☐ Some *other* class

Hint: there are only two Event object types.

Mock Exam Chapter 6

---

1 Given:

```
10. public class MyServlet extends HttpServlet {
11.    public void doGet(HttpServletRequest request,
                         HttpServletResponse response)
12.           throws IOException, ServletException {
13.    // request.getSession().setAttribute("key", "value");
14.    // request.getHttpSession().setAttribute("key", "value");
15.    // ((HttpSession)request.getSession()).setAttribute("key", "value");
16.    // ((HttpSession)request.getHttpSession()).setAttribute("key", "value");
17.    }
18. }
```

Which line(s) could be uncommented without causing a compile or runtime error? (Choose all that apply.)

- ❑ A. Line 13 only.
- ❑ B. Line 14 only.
- ❑ C. Line 15 only.
- ❑ D. Line 16 only.
- ❑ E. Line 13 or line 15.
- ❑ F. Line 14 or line 16.

---

2 If a client will NOT accept a cookie, which session management mechanism could the web container employ? (Choose one.)

- ❑ A. Cookies, but NOT URL rewriting.
- ❑ B. URL rewriting, but NOT cookies.
- ❑ C. Either cookies or URL rewriting can be used.
- ❑ D. Neither cookies nor URL rewriting can be used.
- ❑ E. Cookies and URL rewriting must be used together.

3 Which statements about **HttpSession** objects are true?
(Choose all that apply.)

- ❏ A. A session whose timeout period has been set to **-1** will never expire.
- ❏ B. A session will become invalid as soon as the user closes all browser windows.
- ❏ C. A session will become invalid after a timeout period defined by the servlet container.
- ❏ D. A session may be explicitly invalidated by calling **HttpSession.invalidateSession()**.

---

4 Which of the following are NOT listener event types in the J2EE 1.4 API?
(Choose all that apply.)

- ❏ A. **HttpSessionEvent**
- ❏ B. **ServletRequestEvent**
- ❏ C. **HttpSessionBindingEvent**
- ❏ D. **HttpSessionAttributeEvent**
- ❏ E. **ServletContextAttributeEvent**

---

5 Which statements about session tracking are true?
(Choose all that apply.)

- ❏ A. URL rewriting may be used by a server as the basis for session tracking.
- ❏ B. SSL has a built-in mechanism that a servlet container could use to obtain data used to define a session.
- ❏ C. When using cookies for session tracking, there is no restriction on the name of the session tracking cookie.
- ❏ D. When using cookies for session tracking, the name of the session tracking cookie must be **JSESSIONID**.
- ❏ E. If a user has cookies disabled in their browser, the container may choose to use a **javax.servlet.http.CookielessHttpSession** object to track the user's session.

6 Given:

```
1. import javax.servlet.http.*;
2. public class MySessionListener
           implements HttpSessionListener {
3.     public void sessionCreated() {
4.         System.out.println("Session Created");
5.     }
6.     public void sessionDestroyed() {
7.         System.out.println("Session Destroyed");
8.     }
9. }
```

What is wrong with this class? (Choose all that apply.)

- ❑ A. The method signature on line 3 is NOT correct.
- ❑ B. The method signature on line 6 is NOT correct.
- ❑ C. The import statement will NOT import the **`HttpSessionListener`** interface.
- ❑ D. **`sessionCreated`** and **`sessionDestroyed`** are NOT the only methods defined by the **`HttpSessionListener`** interface.

7 Which statements about session attributes are true? (Choose all that apply.)

- ❑ A. The return type of **`HttpSession.getAttribute(String)`** is **`Object`**.
- ❑ B. The return type of **`HttpSession.getAttribute(String)`** is **`String`**.
- ❑ C. Attributes bound into a session are available to any other servlet that belongs to the same **`ServletContext`** and handles a request identified as being part of the same session.
- ❑ D. Calling **`setAttribute("keyA", "valueB")`** on an **`HttpSession`** which already holds a value for the key **`keyA`** will cause an exception to be thrown.
- ❑ E. Calling **`setAttribute("keyA", "valueB")`** on an **`HttpSession`** which already holds a value for the key **`keyA`** will cause the previous value for this attribute to be replaced with the String **`valueB`**.

8 Which interfaces define a **getSession()** method? (Choose all that apply.)

- ❑ A. **ServletRequest**
- ❑ B. **ServletResponse**
- ❑ C. **HttpServletRequest**
- ❑ D. **HttpServletResponse**

9 Given a session object **s**, and the code:

```
s.setAttribute("key", value);
```

Which listeners could be notified? (Choose one.)

- ❑ A. Only **HttpSessionListener**
- ❑ B. Only **HttpSessionBindingListener**
- ❑ C. Only **HttpSessionAttributeListener**
- ❑ D. **HttpSessionListener** and **HttpSessionBindingListener**
- ❑ E. **HttpSessionListener** and **HttpSessionAttributeListener**
- ❑ F. **HttpSessionBindingListener** and **HttpSessionAttributeListener**
- ❑ G. All three

10 Given that **req** is an **HttpServletRequest**, which snippets create a session if one doesn't exist? (Choose all that apply.)

- ❑ A. **req.getSession();**
- ❑ B. **req.getSession(true);**
- ❑ C. **req.getSession(false);**
- ❑ D. **req.createSession();**
- ❑ E. **req.getNewSession();**
- ❑ F. **req.createSession(true);**
- ❑ G. **req.createSession(false);**

11 Given a session object **s** with two attributes named **myAttr1** and **myAttr2**, which will remove both attributes from this session? (Choose all that apply.)

❑ A. **s.removeAllValues();**

❑ B. **s.removeAttribute("myAttr1");**
s.removeAttribute("myAttr2");

❑ C. **s.removeAllAttributes();**

❑ D. **s.getAttribute("myAttr1", UNBIND);**
s.getAttribute("myAttr2", UNBIND);

❑ E. **s.getAttributeNames(UNBIND);**

---

12 Which statements about **HttpSession** objects in distributed environments are true? (Choose all that apply.)

❑ A. When a session is moved from one JVM to another, any attributes stored in the session will be lost.

❑ B. When a session is moved from one JVM to another, appropriately registered **HttpSessionBindingListener** objects will be notified.

❑ C. When a session is moved from one JVM to another, appropriately registered **HttpSessionActivationListener** objects will be notified.

❑ D. When a session is moved from one JVM to another, attribute values that implement **java.io.Serializable** will be transferred to the new JVM.

---

13 Which statements about session timeouts are true? (Choose all that apply.)

❑ A. Session timeout declarations made in the DD can specify time in seconds.

❑ B. Session timeout declarations made in the DD can specify time in minutes.

❑ C. Session timeout declarations made programmatically can specify time only in seconds.

❑ D. Session timeout declarations made programmatically can specify time only in minutes.

❑ E. Session timeout declarations made programmatically can specify time in either minutes or seconds.

14 Choose the servlet code fragment that would retrieve from the request the value of a cookie named "ORA_UID"? (Choose all that apply.)

- [ ] A.
```
String value = request.getCookie("ORA_UID");
```
- [ ] B.
```
String value = request.getHeader("ORA_UID");
```
- [ ] C.
```
javax.servlet.http.Cookie[] cookies =
    request.getCookies();
String cName = null;
String value = null;
if (cookies != null){
  for (int i = 0; i < cookies.length; i++){
    cName = cookies[i].getName();
    if (cName != null &&
        cName.equalsIgnoreCase("ORA_UID")){
      value = cookies[i].getValue();
    }
  }
}
```
- [ ] D.
```
javax.servlet.http.Cookie[] cookies =
    request.getCookies();
if (cookies.length > 0){
  String value = cookies[0].getValue();
}
```

15 How would you use the `HttpServletResponse` object in a servlet to add a cookie to the client?

❑ A.
```
<context-param>
 <param-name>myCookie</param-name>
 <param-value>cookieValue</param-value>
</context-param>
```

❑ B.
```
response.addCookie("myCookie","cookieValue");
```

❑ C.
```
javax.servlet.http.Cookie newCook =
  new javax.servlet.http.Cookie("myCookie","cookieValue");
//...set other Cookie properties
response.addCookie(newCook);
```

❑ D.
```
javax.servlet.http.Cookie[] cookies = request.getCookies();
String cname = null;
if (cookies != null){
  for (int i = 0; i < cookies.length; i++){
    cName = cookies[i].getName();
    if (cName != null &&
        cName.equalsIgnoreCase("myCookie")){
      out.println( cName + ": " + cookies[i].getValue();
    }
  }
}
```

Chapter 6 Answers

---

1 Given: (Servlet Spec p. 59)

```
10. public class MyServlet extends HttpServlet {
11.   public void doGet(HttpServletRequest request,
                         HttpServletResponse response)
12.           throws IOException, ServletException {
13.   // request.getSession().setAttribute("key", "value");
14.   // request.getHttpSession().setAttribute("key", "value");
15.   // ((HttpSession)request.getSession()).setAttribute("key", "value");
16.   // ((HttpSession)request.getHttpSession()).setAttribute("key", "value");
17.   }
18. }
```

Which line(s) could be uncommented without causing a compile or runtime error? (Choose all that apply.)

- ☐ A. Line 13 only.
- ☐ B. Line 14 only.
- ☐ C. Line 15 only.
- ☐ D. Line 16 only.
- ☑ E. Line 13 or line 15.
- ☐ F. Line 14 or line 16.

–Option E is correct because both lines 13 and 15 make the correct method call. The cast to HttpSession is NOT necessary, but it does reflect the correct type, so it is valid.

---

2 If a client will NOT accept a cookie, which session management mechanism could the web container employ? (Choose one.) (Servlet v2.4 pg. 57)

- ☐ A. Cookies, but NOT URL rewriting.
- ☑ B. URL rewriting, but NOT cookies.
- ☐ C. Either cookies or URL rewriting can be used.
- ☐ D. Neither cookies nor URL rewriting can be used.
- ☐ E. Cookies and URL rewriting must be used together.

–Option B is correct because cookies CANNOT be used, but URL rewriting does NOT depend on cookies being enabled.

3 Which statements about **HttpSession** objects are true? (Choose all that apply.) (Servlet v2.4 p. 59)

- [x] A. A session whose timeout period has been set to **-1** will never expire.
- [ ] B. A session will become invalid as soon as the user closes all browser windows.
- [x] C. A session will become invalid after a timeout period defined by the servlet container.
- [ ] D. A session may be explicitly invalidated by calling **HttpSession.invalidateSession()**.

-Option B is incorrect because there is no explicit termination signal in the HTTP protocol.

-Option D is incorrect because the method that should be used is called invalidate().

4 Which of the following are NOT listener event types in the J2EE 1.4 API? (Choose all that apply.) (API)

- [ ] A. **HttpSessionEvent**
- [ ] B. **ServletRequestEvent**
- [ ] C. **HttpSessionBindingEvent**
- [x] D. **HttpSessionAttributeEvent**
- [ ] E. **ServletContextAttributeEvent**

-HttpSessionBindingEvents are used for both HttpSessionBindingListeners AND HttpSessionAttributeListeners.

5 Which statements about session tracking are true? (Choose all that apply.) (Servlet v2.4 p. 57)

- [x] A. URL rewriting may be used by a server as the basis for session tracking.
- [x] B. SSL has a built-in mechanism that a servlet container could use to obtain data used to define a session.
- [ ] C. When using cookies for session tracking, there is no restriction on the name of the session tracking cookie.
- [x] D. When using cookies for session tracking, the name of the session tracking cookie must be **JSESSIONID**.
- [ ] E. If a user has cookies disabled in their browser, the container may choose to use a **javax.servlet.http.CookielessHttpSession** object to track the user's session.

-Option C is incorrect because the specification dictates that the session tracking cookie must be JSESSIONID.

-Option E is incorrect because there is no such class.

6 Given:

(Servlet v2.4 p. 276)

```
1. import javax.servlet.http.*;
2. public class MySessionListener
           implements HttpSessionListener {
3.     public void sessionCreated() {
4.         System.out.println("Session Created");
5.     }
6.     public void sessionDestroyed() {
7.         System.out.println("Session Destroyed");
8.     }
9. }
```

What is wrong with this class? (Choose all that apply.)

- [x] A. The method signature on line 3 is NOT correct.
- [x] B. The method signature on line 6 is NOT correct.
- [ ] C. The import statement will NOT import the **HttpSessionListener** interface.
- [ ] D. **sessionCreated** and **sessionDestroyed** are NOT the only methods defined by the **HttpSessionListener** interface.

-Options A and B are correct because these methods should have an HttpSessionEvent parameter.

- Option C is incorrect because the listener is defined in the imported package.

-Option D is incorrect because these are the only two methods in this interface.

---

7 Which statements about session attributes are true? (Choose all that apply.)

(Servlet v2.4 p. 59)

- [x] A. The return type of **HttpSession.getAttribute(String)** is **Object**.
- [ ] B. The return type of **HttpSession.getAttribute(String)** is **String**.
- [x] C. Attributes bound into a session are available to any other servlet that belongs to the same **ServletContext** and handles a request identified as being part of the same session.
- [ ] D. Calling **setAttribute("keyA", "valueB")** on an **HttpSession** which already holds a value for the key **keyA** will cause an exception to be thrown.
- [x] E. Calling **setAttribute("keyA", "valueB")** on an **HttpSession** which already holds a value for the key **keyA** will cause the previous value for this attribute to be replaced with the String **valueB**.

-Option B is incorrect because the return type is Object.

-Option D is incorrect because this call will simply replace the existing value.

8 Which interfaces define a **getSession()** method? (Choose all that apply.) (Servlet v2.4 pg. 243)

- [ ] A. **ServletRequest**
- [ ] B. **ServletResponse**
- [x] C. **HttpServletRequest**
- [ ] D. **HttpServletResponse**

---

9 Given a session object **s**, and the code: (Servlet v2.4 pg. 80)

```
s.setAttribute("key", value);
```

Which listeners could be notified? (Choose one.)

- [ ] A. Only **HttpSessionListener**
- [ ] B. Only **HttpSessionBindingListener**
- [ ] C. Only **HttpSessionAttributeListener**
- [ ] D. **HttpSessionListener** and **HttpSessionBindingListener**
- [ ] E. **HttpSessionListener** and **HttpSessionAttributeListener**
- [x] F. **HttpSessionBindingListener** and **HttpSessionAttributeListener**
- [ ] G. All three

–Option F is correct because an HttpSessionAttributeListener is notified any time an attribute is added and the value object will also be notified if it implements an HttpSessionBindingListener.

---

10 Given that **req** is an **HttpServletRequest**, which snippets create a session if one doesn't exist? (Choose all that apply.) (API)

- [x] A. **req.getSession();**
- [x] B. **req.getSession(true);**
- [ ] C. **req.getSession(false);**
- [ ] D. **req.createSession();**
- [ ] E. **req.getNewSession();**
- [ ] F. **req.createSession(true);**
- [ ] G. **req.createSession(false);**

–Options A and B will each create a new session if one doesn't exist. getSession(false) returns a null if the session doesn't exist.

11 Given a session object **s** with two attributes named **myAttr1** and **myAttr2**, which will remove both attributes from this session? (Choose all that apply.) (API)

- [ ] A. `s.removeAllValues();`
- [x] B. `s.removeAttribute("myAttr1");`
  `s.removeAttribute("myAttr2");`
- [ ] C. `s.removeAllAttributes();`
- [ ] D. `s.getAttribute("myAttr1", UNBIND);`
  `s.getAttribute("myAttr2", UNBIND);`
- [ ] E. `s.getAttributeNames(UNBIND);`

-Option B is correct, removeAttribute() is the only way to remove attributes from a session object, and it removes only one attribute at a time.

12 Which statements about **HttpSession** objects in distributed environments are true? (Choose all that apply.) (Servlet v2.4 pg. 60)

- [ ] A. When a session is moved from one JVM to another, any attributes stored in the session will be lost.
- [ ] B. When a session is moved from one JVM to another, appropriately registered **HttpSessionBindingListener** objects will be notified.
- [x] C. When a session is moved from one JVM to another, appropriately registered **HttpSessionActivationListener** objects will be notified.
- [x] D. When a session is moved from one JVM to another, attribute values that implement **java.io.Serializable** will be transferred to the new JVM.

-Option A is incorrect because serializable attributes will be transferred.

-Option B is incorrect since attributes remain bound to the session.

13 Which statements about session timeouts are true? (Choose all that apply.) (API)

- [ ] A. Session timeout declarations made in the DD can specify time in seconds.
- [x] B. Session timeout declarations made in the DD can specify time in minutes.
- [x] C. Session timeout declarations made programmatically can specify time only in seconds.
- [ ] D. Session timeout declarations made programmatically can specify time only in minutes.
- [ ] E. Session timeout declarations made programmatically can specify time in either minutes or seconds.

-In the DD, using the <session-timeout> element, only minutes can be specified, using HttpSession's setMaxInactiveInterval() only seconds can be specified.

14 Choose the servlet code fragment that would retrieve from the request the value of a cookie named "ORA_UID"? (Choose all that apply.) (API)

- [ ] A. `String value = request.getCookie("ORA_UID");`

  – Option A refers to a method that doesn't exist.

- [ ] B. `String value = request.getHeader("ORA_UID");`

- [x] C.

```
javax.servlet.http.Cookie[] cookies =
    request.getCookies();
String cName = null;
String value = null;
if (cookies != null){
  for (int i = 0; i < cookies.length; i++){
    cName = cookies[i].getName();
    if (cName != null &&
          cName.equalsIgnoreCase("ORA_UID")){
      value = cookies[i].getValue();
    }
  }
}
```

  – Option C gets a Cookie array using request.getCookies(), then checks for a Cookie of a specified name.

- [ ] D.

```
javax.servlet.http.Cookie[] cookies =
      request.getCookies();
if (cookies.length > 0){
  String value = cookies[0].getValue();
}
```

  – Option D only looks at the first Cookie in the array.

15 How would you use the **HttpServletResponse** object in a servlet to add a cookie to the client? (API)

❑ A.
```
<context-param>
  <param-name>myCookie</param-name>
  <param-value>cookieValue</param-value>
</context-param>
```

❑ B. `response.addCookie("myCookie","cookieValue");`

-Option B is not correct because the addCookie method takes a Cookie object, not Strings..

☑ C.
```
javax.servlet.http.Cookie newCook =
  new javax.servlet.http.Cookie("myCookie","cookieValue");
//...set other Cookie properties
response.addCookie(newCook);
```

❑ D.
```
javax.servlet.http.Cookie[] cookies = request.getCookies();
String cname = null;
if (cookies != null){
  for (int i = 0; i < cookies.length; i++){
    cName = cookies[i].getName();
    if (cName != null &&
        cName.equalsIgnoreCase("myCookie")){
      out.println( cName + ": " + cookies[i].getValue();
    }
  }
}
```

-Option D is not correct because it shows servlet code retrieving, not creating, a cookie.

Being a JSP

He doesn't know a *directive* from a *scriptlet*, but HE gets the corner office and the Aeron and the twice-a-week massage? I've had it.

Relax... when he fails the exam, we BOTH know what will happen. I just hope they don't get blood on the Aeron...

A JSP becomes a servlet. A servlet that *you* don't create. The Container looks at your JSP, translates it into Java source code, and compiles it into a full-fledged Java servlet class. But you've got to know what happens when the code you write in the JSP is turned into Java code. You *can* write Java code in your JSP, but should you? And if you don't write Java code, then what *do* you write? How does it translate into Java code? In this chapter, we'll look at six different kinds of JSP elements—each with its own purpose and, yes, *unique syntax*. You'll learn how, why, and what to write in your JSP. Perhaps more importantly, you'll learn what *not* to write in your JSP.

The JSP Technology Model

Coverage Notes:

6.1 Identify, describe, or write JSP code for the following elements: (a) template text, (b) scripting elements (comments, directives, declarations, scriptlets, and expressions), (c) standard and custom actions, and (d) expression language elements.

Most is covered in this chapter, but the details behind (c) standard and custom actions, and (d) expression language elements are covered in later chapters.

6.2 Write JSP code that uses the directives: (a) *page* (with attributes *import*, *session*, *contentType*, and *isELIgnored*), (b) *include*, and (c) *taglib*.

The page directive is covered in this chapter, but include and taglib are covered in later chapters.

6.3 *Write a JSP Document (XML-based document) that uses the correct syntax.*

Not covered here; refer to the chapter on Deployment.

6.4 Describe the purpose and event sequence of the JSP page lifecycle: (1) JSP page translation, (2) JSP page compilation, (3) load class, (4) create instance, (5) call the jspInit method, (6) call the _jspService method, and (7) call the jspDestroy method.

All covered in this chapter. (Hint: these will be some of the most no-brainer questions on the real exam, once you've learned the fundamentals in this chapter.)

6.5 Given a design goal, write JSP code using the appropriate implicit objects: (a) request, (b) response, (c) out, (d) session, (e) config, (f) application, (g) page, (h) pageContext, and (i) exception.

All covered in this chapter, although you're expected to already know what most of them mean based on the previous two chapters.

6.6 Configure the deployment descriptor to declare one or more tag libraries, deactivate the evaluation language, and deactivate the scripting language.

We cover everything here except declaring tag libraries. That's covered in the chapter on Using JSTL.

6.7 *Given a specific design goal for including a JSP segment in another page, write the JSP code that uses the most appropriate inclusion mechanism (the include directive or the jsp:include standard action).*

Not covered here; refer to the next chapter (Scriptless JSPs).

In the end, a JSP is just a servlet

Your JSP eventually becomes a full-fledged servlet running in your web app. It's a lot like any other servlet, except that the servlet class is written *for* you—by the Container.

The Container takes what you've written in your JSP, ***translates*** it into a servlet class source (.java) file, then ***compiles*** that into a Java servlet class. After that, it's just servlets all the way down, and the servlet runs in exactly the same way it would if you'd written and compiled the code yourself. In other words, the Container loads the servlet class, instantiates and initializes it, makes a separate thread for each request, and calls the servlet's service() method.

The most important point for this chapter is simply: what role does your JSP code play in the final servlet class?

In other words, *where* do the elements in the JSP end up in the source code of the generated servlet?

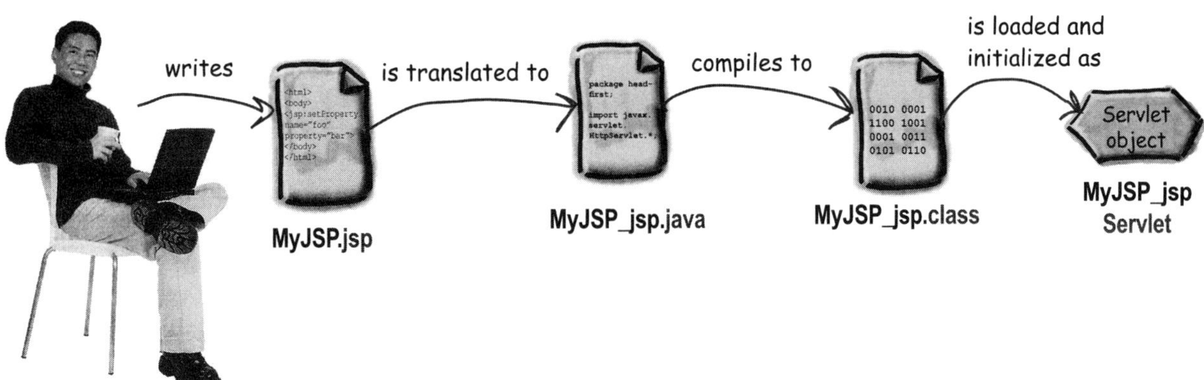

Some of the questions we'll answer in this chapter include:

- Where does each part of your JSP file end up in the servlet source code?
- Do you have access to the "servletness" of your JSP page? For example, does a JSP have a concept of a ServletConfig or ServletContext?
- What are the types of elements you can put in a JSP?
- What's the syntax for the different elements in a JSP?
- What's the lifecycle of a JSP, and can you step into the middle of it?
- How do the different elements in a JSP interact in the final servlet?

Making a JSP that displays how many times it's been accessed

Pauline wants to use JSPs in her web apps—she's *really* sick of writing HTML into a servlet's PrintWriter println().

She decides to learn JSPs by making a simple dynamic page that prints the number of times the page has been requested. She understands that you can put regular old Java code in a JSP using a ***scriptlet***—which just means Java code within a <% ... %> tag.

I know I can put Java code in the JSP, so I'll make a static method in a Counter class to hold the access count static variable, and then I'll call that method from the JSP...

BasicCounter.jsp

```
<html>
<body>
The page count is:
<%
  out.println(Counter.getCount());
%>
</body>
</html>
```

The "out" object is implicitly there. Everything between <% and %> is a scriptlet, which is just plain old Java.

Counter.java

```
package foo;

public class Counter {
   private static int count;
   public static synchronized int getCount()     {
      count++;
      return count;
   }
}
```

Plain old Java helper class.

She deploys and tests it

It's trivial to deploy and test. The only tricky part is making sure that the Counter class is available to the JSP, and that's easy—just be sure the Counter class is in the WEB-INF/ classes directory of the web app. She accesses the JSP directly in the browser at: **http://localhost:8080/testJSP1/BasicCounter.jsp**

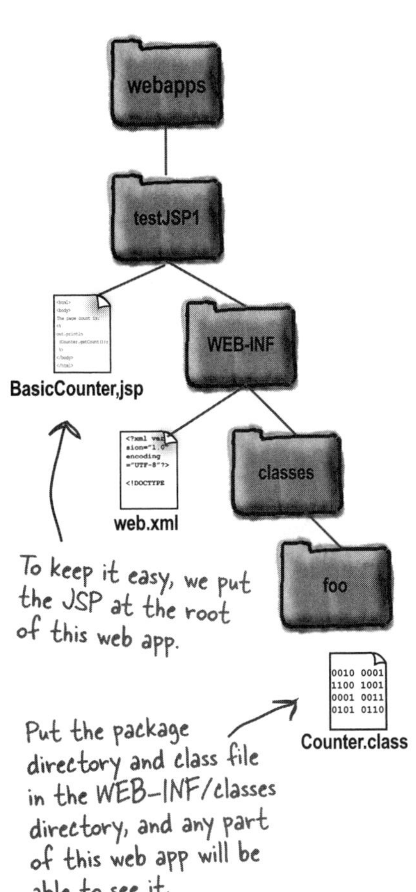

HTTP Status 500 -
The server encountered an internal error () that prevented it from fulfilling this request.

An error occurred at line: 1 in the jsp file: /BasicCounter.jsp

[javac] Compiling 1 source file
/Users/kathy/Applications2/jakarta-tomcat-5.0.19/work/Catalina/localhost/testJSP1/org/apache/jsp/BasicCounter_jsp.java:45: cannot resolve symbol
symbol : variable Counter

org.apache.jasper.compiler.DefaultErrorHandler.javacError(DefaultErrorHandler.java:127)
org.apache.jasper.compiler.ErrorDispatcher.javacError(ErrorDispatcher.java:351)
org.apache.jasper.compiler.Compiler.generateClass(Compiler.java:415)
org.apache.jasper.compiler.Compiler.compile(Compiler.java:458)
org.apache.jasper.compiler.Compiler.compile(Compiler.java:439)
org.apache.jasper.JspCompilationContext.compile(JspCompilationContext.java:553)
org.apache.jasper.servlet.JspServletWrapper.service(JspServletWrapper.java:291)
org.apache.jasper.servlet.JspServlet.serviceJspFile(JspServlet.java:301)
org.apache.jasper.servlet.JspServlet.service(JspServlet.java:248)

Can you figure out what's wrong?

webapps
testJSP1
WEB-INF
BasicCounter,jsp
web.xml
classes
foo
Counter.class
To keep it easy, we put the JSP at the root of this web app.
Put the package directory and class file in the WEB-INF/classes directory, and any part of this web app will be able to see it.

What she expected:

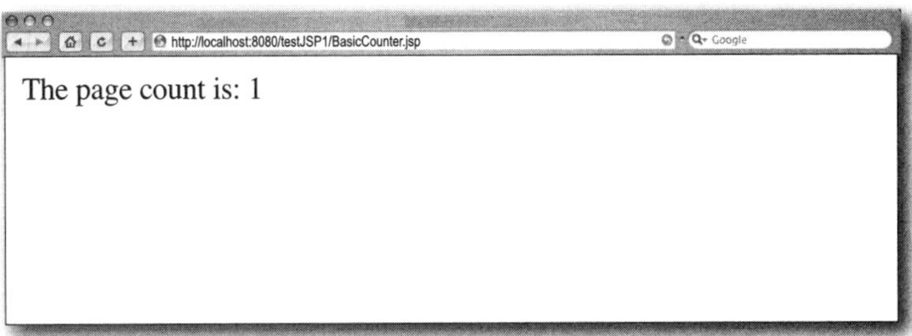

What she got:

The JSP doesn't recognize the Counter class

The Counter class is in the *foo* package, but there's nothing in the JSP to acknowledge that. It's the same thing that happens to you with any other Java code, and you know the rule: import the package or use the fully-qualified class name in your code.

I guess you have to use the fully-qualified class name inside JSPs. That makes sense, since all JSPs are turned into plain old Java servlet code by the Container. But I sure wish you could put *imports* into your JSP code...

Counter.java

```
package foo;

public class Counter {
   private static int count;
   public static int getCount() {
       count++;
       return count;
   }
}
```

JSP code *was*:

```
<% out.println(Counter.getCount()); %>
```

JSP code *should be*:

```
<% out.println(foo.Counter.getCount()); %>
```

Now it'll work.

But you CAN put
import statements in
a JSP... you just need
a directive.

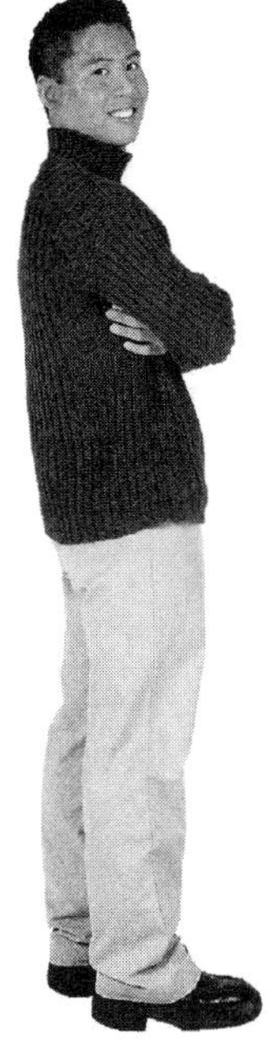

Use the page directive to import packages

A *directive* is a way for you to give special instructions to the Container at page translation time. Directives come in three flavors: ***page***, ***include***, and ***taglib***. We'll look at the include and taglib directives in later chapters, but for now all we care about is the ***page*** directive, because it's the one that lets you *import.*

To import a *single* package:

```
<%@ page import="foo.*" %>

<html>
<body>
The page count is:
<%
  out.println(Counter.getCount());
%>
</body>
</html>
```

This is a page directive with an import attribute.

(Notice there's no semicolon at the end of a directive.)

Scriptlets are normal Java, so all statements in a scriptlet must end in a semicolon!

To import *multiple* packages:

```
<%@ page import="foo.*,java.util.*" %>
```

Use a comma to separate the packages.
The quotes go around the entire list of packages!

Notice what's different between the Java code that prints the counter and the page directive?

The Java code is between angle brackets with percent signs: <% and %>. But the directive adds an additional character to the start of the element—the @ sign!

If you see JSP code that starts with <%@, *you know it's a directive.* (We'll get into more details about the page directive later in the book.)

But then Kim mentions "expressions"

Just when you thought it was safe, Kim notices the scriptlet with an out.println() statement. This is JSP, folks. Part of the whole point of JSP is to *avoid* println()! That's why there's a JSP *expression* element—it automatically prints out whatever you put between the tags.

You don't need to say **out.println()** in a JSP! Just use an **expression**...

***Scriptlet* code:**

```
<%@ page import="foo.*" %>
<html>
<body>
The page count is:
<% out.println(Counter.getCount()); %>
</body>
</html>
```

***Expression* code:**

```
<%@ page import="foo.*" %>
<html>
<body>
The page count is now:
<%= Counter.getCount() %>
</body>
</html>
```

The expression is shorter—we don't need to explicitly do the print...

Notice what's different between the tag for the scriptlet code and the tag for the expression? The *scriptlet* code is between angle brackets with percent signs: **<%** and **%>**. But the *expression* adds an additional character to the start of the element—an *equals* sign (=).

So far we've seen three different JSP element types:

Scriptlet:	<% %>
Directive:	<%@ %>
Expression:	<%= %>

HELLO! If you're gonna tell us how to improve our code, you could AT LEAST get the Java syntax right... **there's no frickin' semicolon at the end of that expression!**

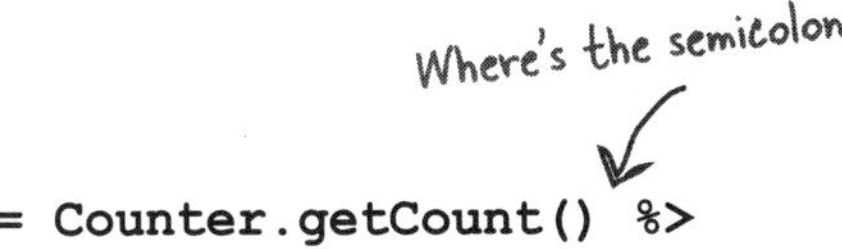

Where's the semicolon?

```
<%= Counter.getCount() %>
```

Expressions become the argument to an out.print()

In other words, the Container takes *everything* you type between the <%= and %> and puts it in as the argument to a statement that prints to the implicit response PrintWriter *out.*

When the Container sees *this:*

```
<%= Counter.getCount() %>
```

It turns it into *this:*

```
out.print(Counter.getCount());
```

If you *did* put a semicolon in your expression:

```
<%= Counter.getCount(); %>
```

That would be bad. It would mean *this*:

```
out.print(Counter.getCount(););
```

Yikes!! This will never compile.

NEVER end an *expression* with a semicolon!

<%= neverPutASemicolonInHere %>

<%= becauseThisIsAnArgumentToPrint() %>

there are no Dumb Questions

Q: Well, if you're supposed to use expressions INSTEAD of putting out.println() into a scriptlet, then why is the implicit "out" there?

A: You probably won't use the implicit out variable from within your JSP page, but you might pass it to something *else*... some other object that's part of your app that does not have direct access to the output stream for the response.

Q: In an expression, what happens if the method doesn't return anything?

A: You'll get an error!! You cannot, MUST NOT use a method with a void return type as an expression. The Container is smart enough to figure out that ***there won't be anything to print if the method has a void return type!***

Q: Why does the import directive start with the word "page"? Why is it <%@ page import...%> instead of just <%@ import... %>.

A: Good question! Rather than having a whole big pile of different directives, the JSP spec has just three JSP directives, but the directives can have attributes. What you called "the import directive" is actually "the import attribute of the page directive".

Q: What are the other attributes for the page directive?

A: Remember, the page directive is about giving the Container information it needs when translating your JSP into a servlet. The attributes we care about (besides import) are session, contentType, and isELIgnored (we'll come back to these later in the chapter).

Sharpen your pencil

Decide which of the following expressions are and are not valid, and why. We haven't covered every example here, so make your best guess based on what you know about how expressions work. (Answers are later in this chapter so do this NOW.)

Valid? (Check if valid, and if not, explain why not.)

- ☐ <%= 27 %>
- ☐ <%= ((Math.random() + 5)*2); %>
- ☐ <%= "27" %>
- ☐ <%= Math.random() %>
- ☐ <%= String s = "foo" %>
- ☐ <%= new String[3] %>
- ☐ <% = 42*20 %>
- ☐ <%= 5 > 3 %>
- ☐ <%= false %>
- ☐ <%= new Counter() %>

Kim drops the final bombshell...

You don't even NEED the Counter class... you can do the whole thing in the JSP.

Hmmm... I know the JSP turns into a servlet, so maybe I could declare a count variable in a scriptlet and that would turn into a variable in the servlet. Would that work?

What she tried:

```
<html>
<body>
<% int count=0; %>
The page count is now:
<%= ++count %>
</body>
</html>
```

Will it *compile*?

Will it *work*?

Declaring a variable in a scriptlet

The variable declaration is *legal*, but it didn't quite work the way Pauline hoped.

What she tried:

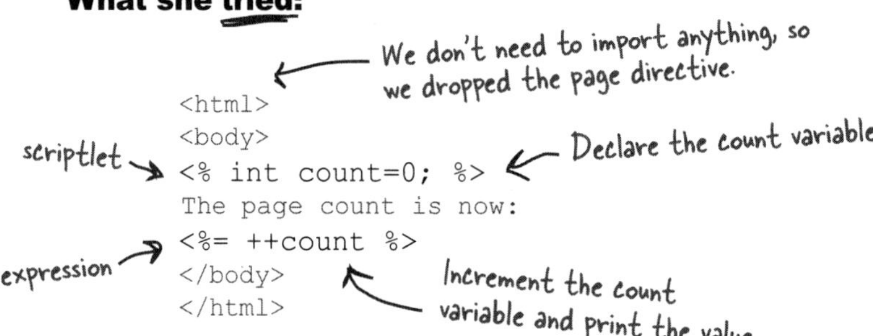

We don't need to import anything, so we dropped the page directive.
<html>
<body>
scriptlet
<% int count=0; %>
Declare the count variable.
The page count is now:
expression
<%= ++count %>
</body>
</html>
Increment the count variable and print the value.

What she got the first time she hit the page:

What she got the second, third, and every other time she hit the page:

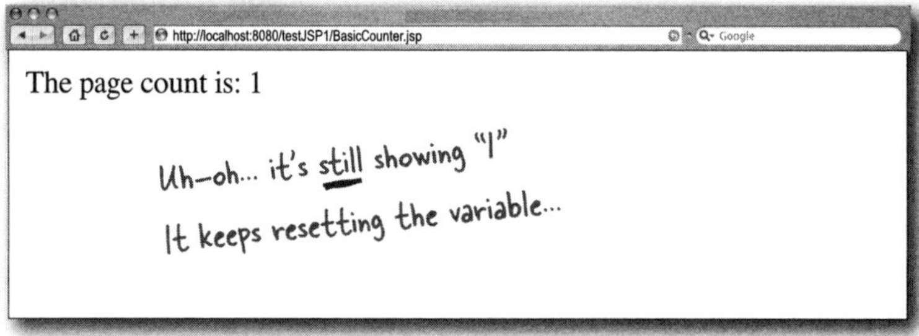

What REALLY happens to your JSP code?

You *write* a JSP, but it *becomes* a servlet. The only way to really tell what's happening is to look at what the Container does to your JSP code. In other words, how does the Container *translate* your JSP into a servlet?

Once you know where different JSP elements land in the servlet's class file, you'll find it much easier to know how to structure your JSP.

The servlet code on this page is *not* the real code generated by the Container—we simplified it down to the essential parts. The Container-generated servlet file is, well, *uglier.* The real generated servlet source code is slightly harder to read, but we will look at the real thing in a few pages. For now, though, all we care about is *where* in the servlet class our JSP code actually ends up.

This JSP:

```
<html><body>            →
<% int count=0; %>      →
The page count is now:  →
<%= ++count %>          →
</body></html>          →
```

Becomes this servlet:

```
public class basicCounter_jsp extends SomeSpecialHttpServlet {

  public void _jspService(HttpServletRequest request,
      HttpServletResponse response)throws java.io.IOException,
                                           ServletException {

     PrintWriter out = response.getWriter();
     response.setContentType("text/html");
     out.write("<html><body>");
     int count=0;
     out.write("The page count is now:");
     out.print( ++count );
     out.write("</body></html>");

  }
}
```

The Container puts all the code into a generic service method. Think of it as a catch-all combo doGet/doPost.

ALL scriptlet and expression code lands in a service method.

That means variables declared in a scriptlet are always LOCAL variables!

Note: if you want to see the generated servlet code from Tomcat, look in yourTomcatHomeDir/work/Catalina/yourServerName/yourWebAppName/org/apache/jsp. (The underlined names will change depending on your system and your web app.)

Don't tell me—there must be *another* kind of JSP element for declaring **instance** variables instead of *local* variables...

We need another JSP element...

Declaring the count variable in a scriptlet meant that the variable was reinitialized each time the service method ran. Which means ***it was reset to 0 with each request.*** We need to somehow make count an *instance* variable.

So far we've looked at directives, scriptlets, and expressions. ***Directives*** are for special instructions to the Container, ***scriptlets*** are just plain old Java that lands as-is within the generated servlet's service method, and the result of an ***expression*** always becomes the argument to a print() method.

But there's another JSP element called a ***declaration.***

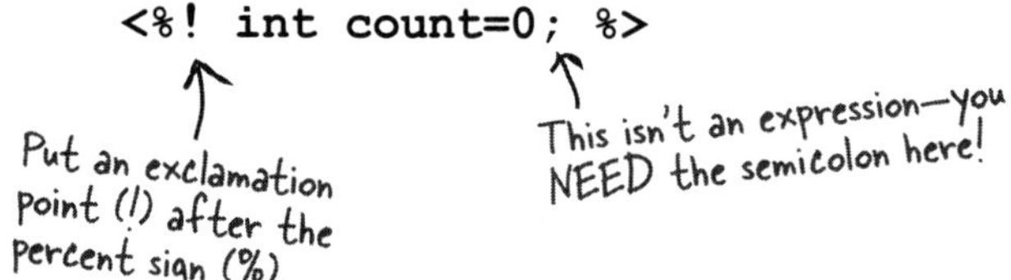

```
<%! int count=0; %>
```


Put an exclamation point (!) after the percent sign (%).
This isn't an expression—you NEED the semicolon here!

JSP declarations are for declaring members of the generated servlet class. ***That means both variables and methods!*** In other words, anything between the <%! and %> tag is added to the class *outside* the service method. That means you can declare both static and instance variables and methods.

JSP Declarations

A JSP declaration is always defined *inside* the class but *outside* the service (or any other) method. It's that simple—declarations are for static and instance variables and methods. (In theory, yes, you could define other members including inner classes, but 99.9999% of the time you'll use declarations for methods and variables.) The code below solves Pauline's problem; now the counter keeps incrementing each time a client requests the page.

Variable Declaration

This JSP:

```
<html><body>
<%! int count=0; %>
The page count is now:
<%= ++count %>
</body></html>
```

Becomes this servlet:

```
public class basicCounter_jsp extends HttpServlet {

  int count=0;

  public void _jspService(HttpServletRequest request,
    HttpServletResponse response)throws java.io.IOException {

      PrintWriter out = response.getWriter();
      response.setContentType("text/html");
      out.write("<html><body>");
      out.write("The page count is now:");
      out.print( ++count );
      out.write("</body></html>");
  }
}
```

This time, we're incrementing an instance variable instead of a local variable.

Method Declaration

This JSP:

```
<html>
<body>
<%! int doubleCount() {
      count = count*2;
      return count;
    }
%>
<%! int count=1; %>
The page count is now:
<%= doubleCount() %>
</body>
</html>
```

Becomes this servlet:

```
public class basicCounter_jsp extends HttpServlet {

  int doubleCount() {
     count = count*2;
     return count;
  }
  int count=1;

  public void _jspService(HttpServletRequest request,
    HttpServletResponse response)throws java.io.IOException {
      PrintWriter out = response.getWriter();
      response.setContentType("text/html");
      out.write("<html><body>");
      out.write("The page count is now:");
      out.print( doubleCount() );
      out.write("</body></html>");
  }
}
```

The method goes in just the way you typed it in your JSP.

It's Java, so no problem with forward-referencing (declaring the variable AFTER you used it in a method).

Time to see the REAL generated servlet

We've been looking at a super-simplified version of the servlet the Container actually creates from your JSP. There's no need to look at the Container-generated code during development, but you can use it to help *learn*. Once you've seen what the Container does with the different elements of a JSP, you shouldn't need to ever look at the Container-generated .java source files. Some vendors won't *let* you see the generated Java source, and keep only the compiled .class files.

Don't be intimidated when you see parts of the API that you don't recognize. Most of the class and interface types are vendor-specific implementations you shouldn't care about.

What the Container does with your JSP

- Looks at the ***directives***, for information it might need during translation.

- Creates an HttpServlet subclass.

  For Tomcat 5, the generated servlet extends:

  `org.apache.jasper.runtime.HttpJspBase`

- If there's a *page directive* with an ***import*** attribute, it writes the import statements at the top of the class file, just below the package statement.

  For Tomcat 5, the package statement (*which you don't care about*) is:

  `package org.apache.jsp;`

- If there are ***declarations***, it writes them into the class file, usually just below the class declaration and before the service method. Tomcat 5 declares one static variable and one instance method of its own.

- Builds the **service** method. The service method's actual name is `_jspService()`. It's called by the servlet superclass' overridden service() method, and receives the HttpServletRequest and HttpServletResponse. As part of building this method, the Container declares and initializes all the ***implicit objects***. (You'll see more implicit objects when you turn the page.)

- Combines the plain old HTML (called template text), ***scriptlets***, and ***expressions*** into the service method, formatting everything and writing it to the PrintWriter response output.

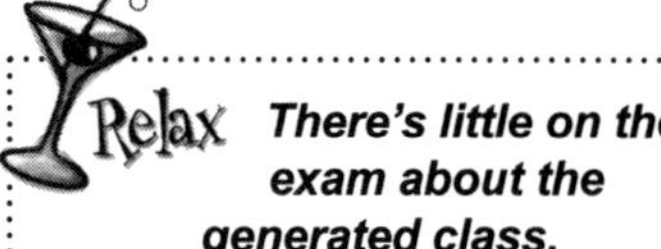

There's little on the exam about the generated class.

We've been showing generated code so that you can understand how the JSP is translated into servlet code. But you don't need to know the details about how a particular vendor does it, or what the generated code actually looks like. All you need to know is the behavior of each element type (scriptlet, directive, declaration, etc.) in terms of how that element works inside the generated servlet. You need to know, for example, that your scriptlet can use implicit objects, and you need to know the Servlet API type of the implicit objects. But you do NOT need to know the code used to make those objects available.

The only other thing you need to know about the generated code are the three JSP lifecycle methods: jspInit(), jspDestroy, and _jspService(). (They're covered later in this chapter.)

Tomcat 5 generated class

```
<html><body>
<%! int count=0; %>
The page count is now:
<%= ++count %>
</body></html>
```

```
package org.apache.jsp;
import javax.servlet.*;
import javax.servlet.http.*;
import javax.servlet.jsp.*;

public final class BasicCounter_jsp extends org.apache.jasper.runtime.HttpJspBase
                    implements org.apache.jasper.runtime.JspSourceDependent {

  int count=0;
  private static java.util.Vector _jspx_dependants;

  public java.util.List getDependants() {
    return _jspx_dependants;
  }

  public void _jspService(HttpServletRequest request, HttpServletResponse response)
                              throws java.io.IOException, ServletException {
    JspFactory _jspxFactory = null;
    PageContext pageContext = null;
    HttpSession session = null;
    ServletContext application = null;
    ServletConfig config = null;
    JspWriter out = null;
    Object page = this;
    JspWriter _jspx_out = null;
    PageContext _jspx_page_context = null;

    try {
      _jspxFactory = JspFactory.getDefaultFactory();
      response.setContentType("text/html");
      pageContext = _jspxFactory.getPageContext(this, request, response,
                  null, true, 8192, true);
      _jspx_page_context = pageContext;
      application = pageContext.getServletContext();
      config = pageContext.getServletConfig();
      session = pageContext.getSession();
      out = pageContext.getOut();
      _jspx_out = out;
      out.write("\r<html>\r<body>\r");
      out.write("\rThe page count is now: \r");
      out.print( ++count );
      out.write("\r</body>\r</html>\r");
    } catch (Throwable t) {
      if (!(t instanceof SkipPageException)){
        out = _jspx_out;
        if (out != null && out.getBufferSize() != 0)
          out.clearBuffer();
        if (_jspx_page_context != null) _jspx_page_context.handlePageException(t);
      }
    } finally {
      if (_jspxFactory != null) _jspxFactory.releasePageContext(_jspx_page_context);
    }
  }
}
```

If you have page directive imports, they'll show up here (we didn't have any imports for this JSP).

The Container puts YOUR declarations (things inside <%! %> tags) and any of its own below the class declaration.

The Container declares a bunch of its own local variables, including those that represent the "implicit objects" your code might need, like "out" and "request".

Now it tries to initialize the implicit objects.

And it tries to run and output your JSP HTML, scriptlet, and expression code.

Of course things might go wrong...

The out variable isn't the only implicit object...

When a Container translates the JSP into a servlet, the beginning of the service method is a pile of ***implicit object*** declarations and assignments.

With implicit objects, you can write a JSP knowing that your code is going to be part of a servlet. In other words, you can take advantage of your servletness, even though you're not *directly* writing a servlet class yourself.

Think back to chapters 4, 5, and 6. What were some of the important objects you used? How did your servlet get servlet init parameters? How did your servlet get context init parameters? How did your servlet get a session? How did your servlet get the parameters submitted by the client in a form?

These are just a few of the reasons your JSP might need to use some of what's available to a servlet. All of the implicit objects map to something from the Servlet/JSP API. The *request* implicit object, for example, is a reference to the ***HttpServletRequest*** object passed to the service method by the Container.

API	Implicit Object
JspWriter	out
HttpServletRequest	request
HttpServletResponse	response
HttpSession	session
ServletContext	application
ServletConfig	config
JspException	exception
PageContext	pageContext
Object	page

Which of these represent the attribute scopes of request, session, and application? (OK, pretty obvious). But now there's a NEW fourth scope, "page-level", and page-scoped attributes are stored in pageContext.

This implicit object is only available to designated "error pages". (You'll see that later in the book.) ← exception

pageContext ← A PageContext encapsulates other implicit objects, so if you give some helper object a PageContext reference, the helper can use that reference to get references to the OTHER implicit objects and attributes from all scopes.

Q: What's the difference between a JspWriter and a PrintWriter I get from an HttpServletResponse?

A: The JspWriter is not in the class hierarchy of PrintWriter, so you can't use it in place of a PrintWriter. But it has most of the same print methods, except it adds some buffering capabilities.

Each of the listings is from a JSP. Your job is to figure out what will happen when the Container tries to turn the JSP into a servlet. Will the Container be able to translate your JSP into legal, compilable servlet code? If not, why not? If so, what happens when a client accesses the JSP?

1

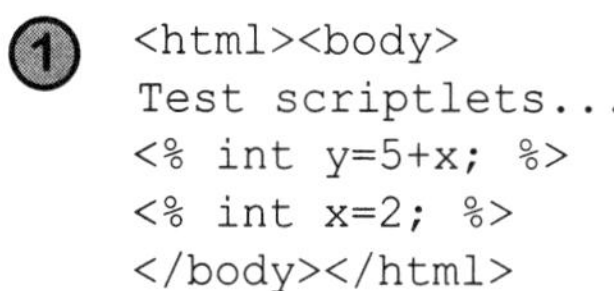

```
<html><body>
Test scriptlets...
<% int y=5+x; %>
<% int x=2; %>
</body></html>
```

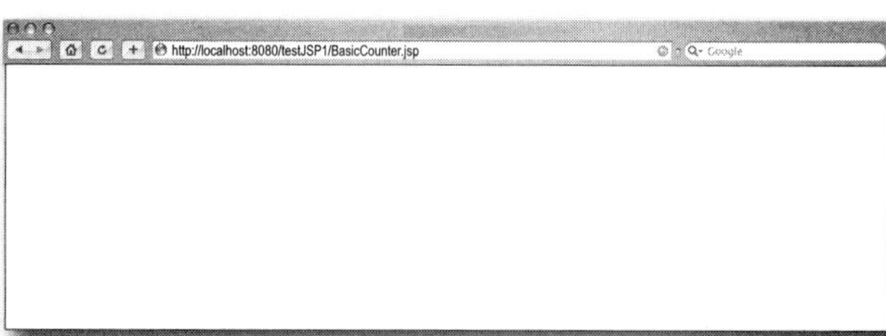

2

```
<%@ page import="java.util.*" %>
<html><body>
Test scriptlets...
<% ArrayList list = new ArrayList();
   list.add(new String("foo"));
%>
<%= list.get(0)  %>
</body></html>
```

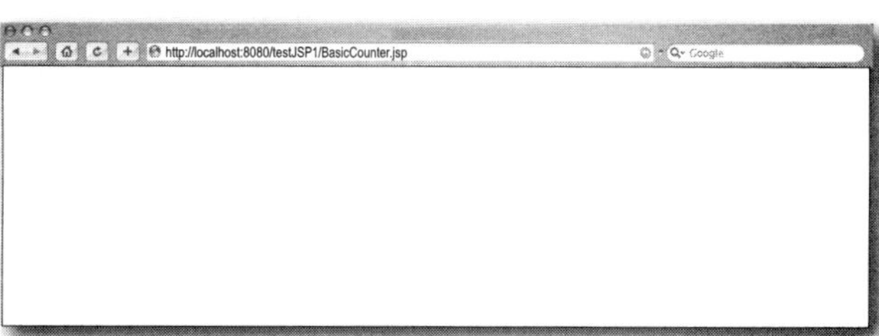

3

```
<html><body>
Test scriptlets...
<%! int x = 42; %>
<% int x = 22; %>
<%= x %>
</body></html>
```

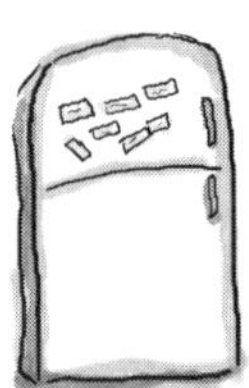

Mock Exam Magnets

Study the scenario (and everything else on this page), then place the magnets on the JSP to make a legal file that would produce the correct result. You don't have to use any magnet more than once, and you won't use all of the magnets. This exercise assumes there's a servlet (which you don't need to see) that takes the initial request, binds an attribute into the request scope, and forwards to the JSP you're creating.

(Note: we called this "Mock Exam Magnets" instead of "Code Magnets" because the exam is FULL of Drag and Drop questions like this one.)

Design Goal

Create a JSP that will produce this:

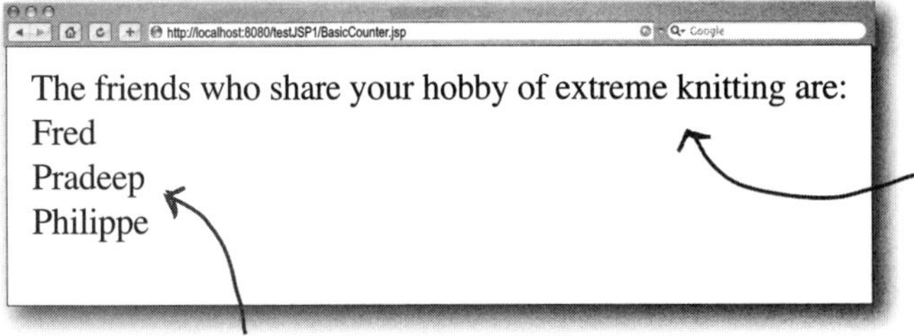

The text "extreme knitting" comes from a form request *parameter*. You'll need to get that parameter from your JSP. A servlet will get the request first (and then forward the request to your JSP) but that doesn't change the way you get the parameter in your JSP.

The three names come from an **ArrayList** request *attribute* called "names". You'll need to *get* the attribute from the request object. Assume a servlet got this request and set an attribute in request scope.

The HTML form

```
<html><body>
<form method="POST"

   action="HobbyPage.do">
   Choose a hobby:<p>

   <select name="hobby" size="1">
     <option>horse skiing
     <option>extreme knitting
     <option>alpine scuba
     <option>speed dating
   </select>
  <br><br>
  <center>
    <input type="SUBMIT">
  </center>
 </form>
</body></html>
```

This goes to a servlet that sets the request attribute then forwards the request to the JSP you're writing.

Important tips and clues

- The request attribute is of type java.util.ArrayList.
- The implicit variable for the HttpServletRequest object is named *request*, and you can use it within scriptlets or expressions, but *not* within directives or declarations. Whatever you can do with a request object in a servlet, you do inside your JSP.
- A JSP's servlet method can process request parameters, because remember, your code is going to be inside a servlet's service method. You don't have to worry about which of the HTTP methods (GET or POST) was used in the request.

We've put a few lines in for you. The code you put in this JSP MUST work with the code that's already here. When you're done, it should be compilable and produce the result on the opposite page (you must ASSUME that there's already a working servlet that first gets the request, sets the request attribute "names", and forwards the request to this JSP).

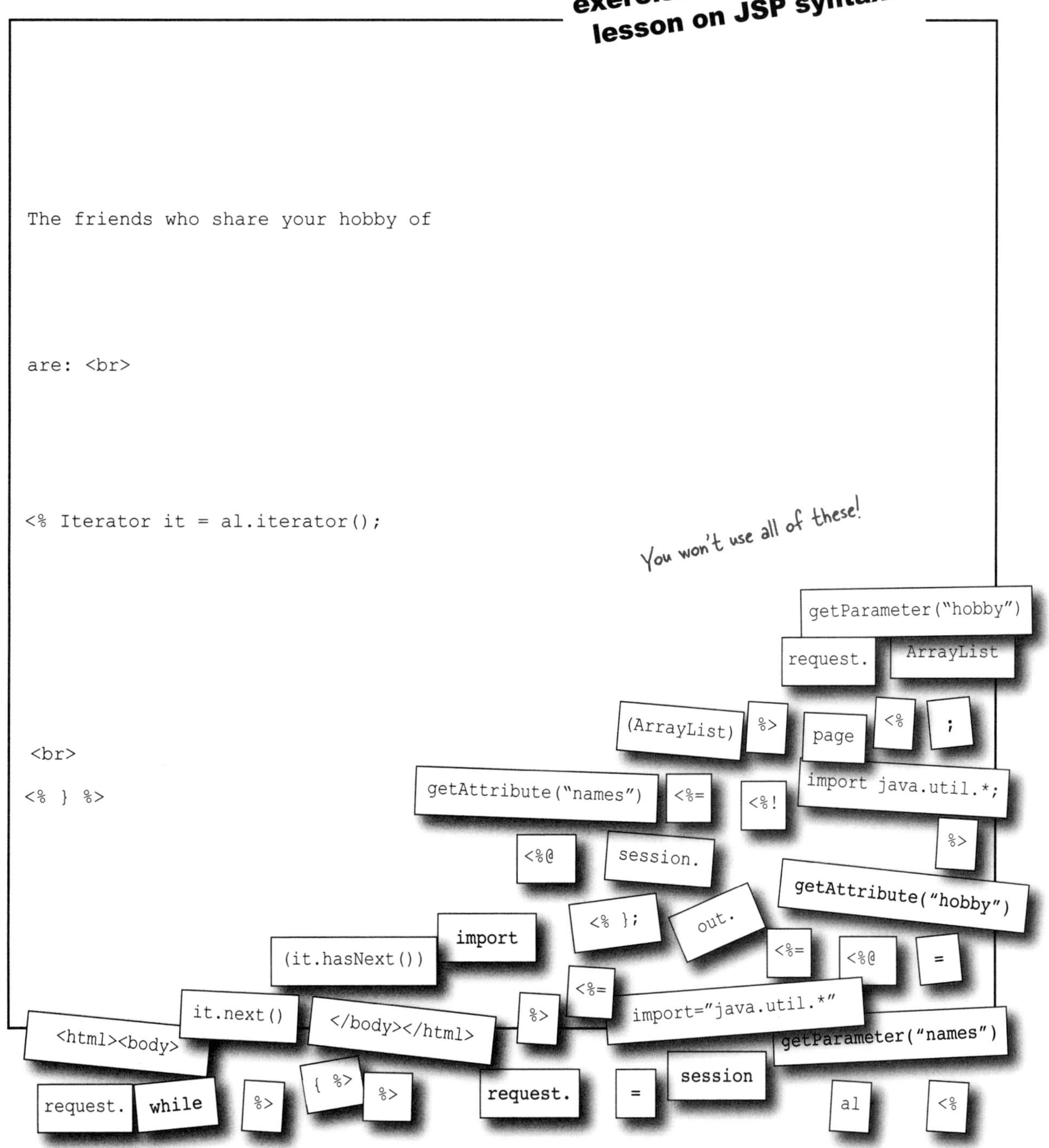

BE the Container

Answers

#2 is straightforward and works. #1 is a fundamental Java language issue (using a local variable before it's declared), and #3 also demonstrates a fundamental Java language issue—what happens when you have an instance and local variable with the same name. So you see... if you translate the JSP code into servlet Java code, you'll have no trouble figuring out the result. Once your JSP stuff is inside a servlet, <u>it's just Java</u>.

1

```
<html><body>
Test scriptlets...
<% int y=5+x; %>
<% int x=2; %>
</body></html>
```

This won't compile! It's exactly like writing a method with:

```
void foo() {
   int y = 5 + x;
   int x = 2;
}
```

You're trying to use variable 'x' BEFORE it's defined. The Java language doesn't allow that, and the Container won't bother to rearrange the order of your scriptlet code.

2

```
<%@ page import="java.util.*" %>
<html><body>
Test scriptlets...
<% ArrayList list = new ArrayList();
   list.add(new String("foo"));
%>
<%= list.get(0)  %>
</body></html>
```

http://localhost:8080/testJSP1/BasicCounter.jsp

Test scriptlets... foo

No problems; prints the first (and only) object in the ArrayList.

3

```
<html><body>
Test scriptlets...
<%! int x = 42; %>
<% int x = 22; %>
<%= x %>
</body></html>
```

The scriptlet declares a local variable "x" (that hides the instance variable x) so if you want to print the instance variable x (42) instead of the local variable x (22), change the expression to: <%= this.x %>

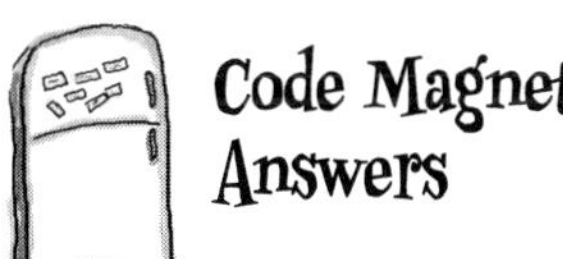

Code Magnets Answers

If your answer looks a little different, but you still think it should work—try it! You'll have to make the servlet that takes the form request, sets an attribute, and forwards (dispatches) the request to the JSP.

We need the import page directive because of ArrayList and Iterator.

```
The friends who share your hobby of
```

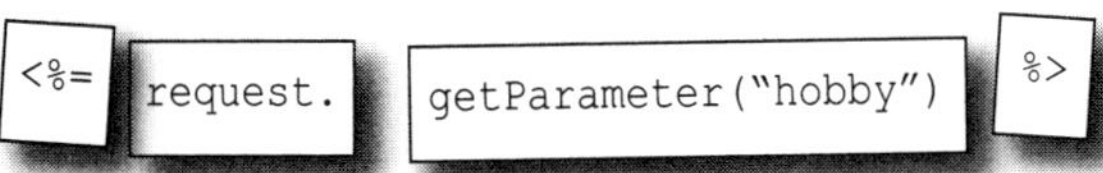


```
are: <br>
```

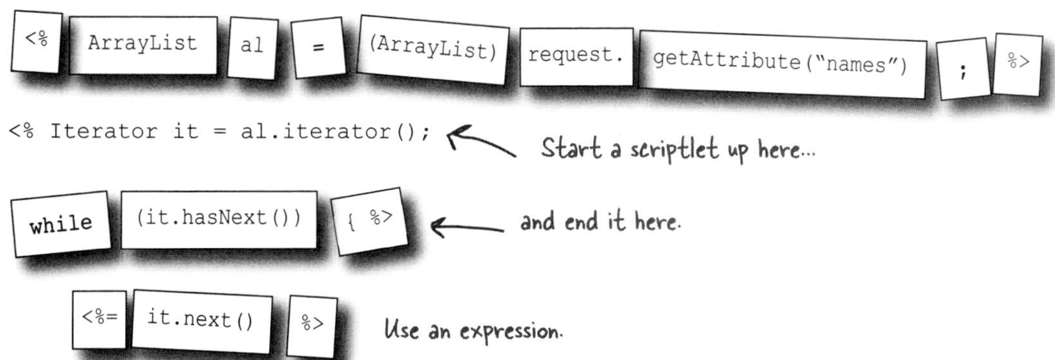

Start a scriptlet up here...

and end it here.

Use an expression.

```
<br>

<% } %>
```

Finish the while loop block! (If you forget this, it won't compile).

```
</body></html>
```

A comment...

Yes, you can put comments in your JSP. If you're a Java programmer with very little HTML experience, you might find yourself typing:

// this is a comment

without thinking twice. But if you do, then unless it's within a scriptlet or declaration tag, you'll end up DISPLAYING that to the client as part of the response. In other words, to the Container, those two slashes are just more template text, like "Hello" or "Email is:".

You can put two different types of comments in a JSP:

- **<!-- HTML comment -->**

  The Container just passes this straight on to the client, where the browser interprets it as a comment.

- **<%-- JSP comment --%>**

  These are for the page developers, and just like Java comments in a Java source file, they're stripped out of the translated page. If you're typing a JSP and want to put in comments about what you're doing, the way you'd use comments in a Java source file, use a JSP comment.
  If you want comments to stay as part of the HTML response to the client (although the browser will hide them from the client's view), use an HTML comment.

Sharpen your pencil
ANSWERS

Valid and Invalid Expressions

Valid?

☑ <%= 27 %>
All primitive literals are fine.

☐ <%= ((Math.random() + 5)*2); %>
NO! The semicolon can't be here.

☑ <%= "27" %>
String literal is fine.

☑ <%= Math.random() %>
Yes, the method returns a double.

☐ <%= String s = "foo" %>
NO! You can't have a variable declaration here.

☑ <%= new String[3] %>
Yes, because the new String array is an object, and ANY object can be sent to a println() statement.

☐ <% = 42*20 %>
NO! The arithmetic is fine, but there's a space between the % and the =. It can't be <% =, it must be <%= .

☑ <%= 5 > 3 %>
Sure, this resolves to a boolean, so it prints 'true'.

☑ <%= false %>
We already said primitive literals are fine.

☑ <%= new Counter() %>
No problem. This is just like the String[]... it prints the result of the object's toString() method.

API for the generated servlet

The Container generates a class from your JSP that implements the HttpJspPage interface. This is the only part of the generated servlet's API that you need to know. You don't care that in Tomcat, for example, your generated servlet extends:

```
org.apache.jasper.runtime.HttpJspBase
```

All you need to know about are the three key methods:

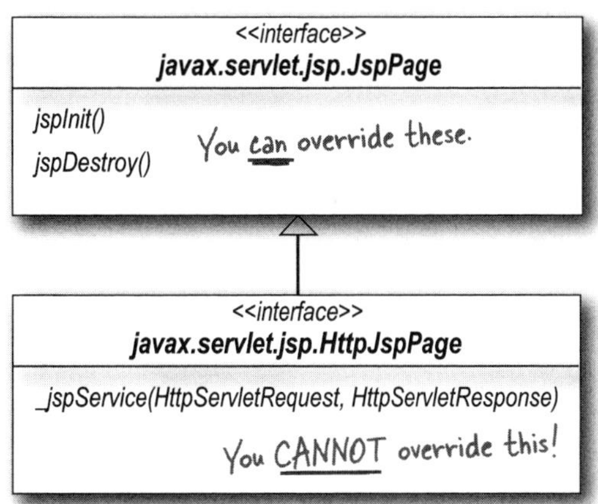

➤ jspInit()

This method is called from the init() method.
You can override this method. (Can you figure out *how*?)

➤ jspDestroy()

This method is called from the servlet's destroy() method.
You can override this method as well.

➤ _jspService()

This method is called from the servlet's service() method, which means it runs in a separate thread for each request. The Container passes the Request and Response objects to this method.
You can't override this method! You can't do ANYTHING with this method yourself (except write code that goes inside it), and it's up to the Container vendor to take your JSP code and fashion the _jspService() method that uses it.

Note the underscore at the front of the _jspService() method

It's NOT in front of the other two methods, jspInit() and jspDestroy(). Think of it this way, the underscore in front of the method means "don't touch!"
So, no underscore in front of the name means you can override. But if there IS an underscore in front of the method name, you must NOT try to override it!

Lifecycle of a JSP

You write the ***.jsp*** file.

The ***Container*** writes the ***.java*** file for the servlet your JSP becomes.

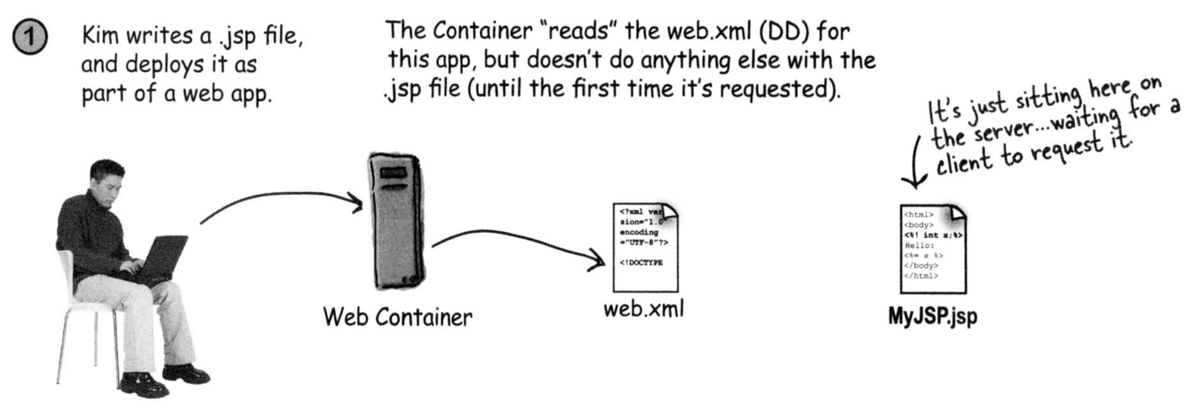

1
Kim writes a .jsp file, and deploys it as part of a web app.
The Container "reads" the web.xml (DD) for this app, but doesn't do anything else with the .jsp file (until the first time it's requested).
It's just sitting here on the server...waiting for a client to request it.
JSP syntax errors are caught in this phase.
Java language/syntax errors are caught here.
Web Container
MyJSP_jsp.class
web.xml
MyJSP.jsp

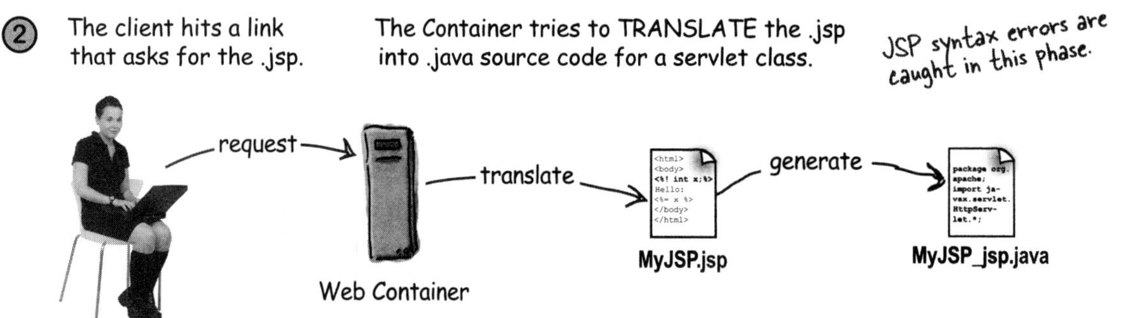

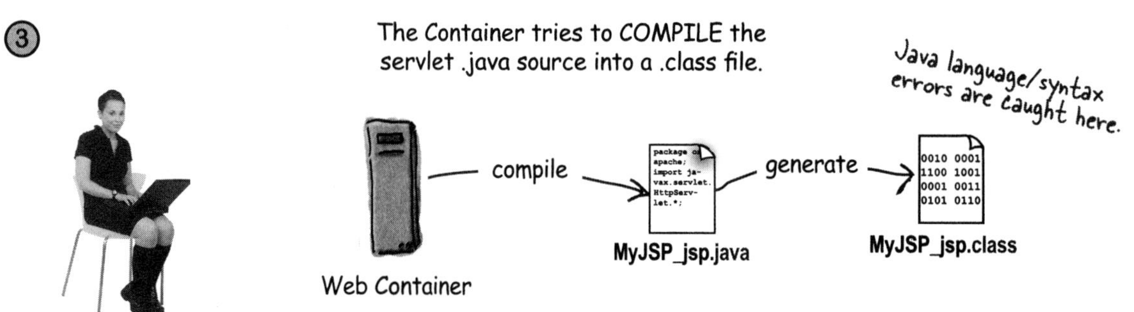

The client hits a link that asks for the .jsp.

JSP lifecycle continued...

4 The Container LOADS the newly-generated servlet class.

5 The Container instantiates the servlet and causes the servlet's jspInit() method to run.

The object is now a full-fledged servlet, ready to accept client requests.

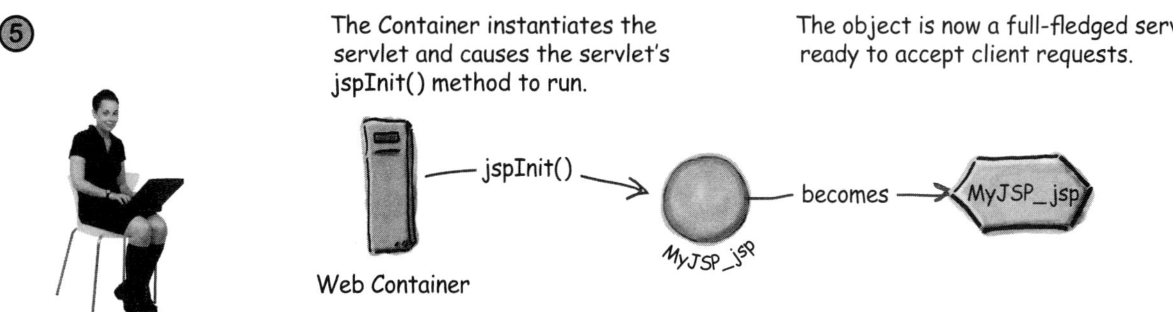

6 The Container creates a new thread to handle this client's request, and the servlet's _jspService() method runs.

Everything that happens after this is just plain old servlet request-handling.

Eventually the servlet sends a response back to the client (or forwards the request to another web app component).

Wow. I am truly impressed. I would never have guessed that they could make requesting a JSP take just as much overhead as calling a method on an EJB. I'm thinking the client has to wait, what, *five minutes* for all that translating, compiling, and initializing?

Translation and compilation happens only ONCE

When you deploy a web app with a JSP, the whole translation and compilation step happens only once in the JSP's life. Once it's been translated and compiled, it's just like any other servlet. And just like any other servlet, once that servlet has been loaded and initialized, the only thing that happens at request time is creation or allocation of a thread for the service method. So the picture on the previous two pages is for only *the first request.*

Q: OK, so that means only the first client to ask for the JSP takes the big hit. But there MUST be a way to configure the server to pre-translate and compile...right?

A: Although it's only the first client that has to wait, most Container vendors DO give you a way to ask for the whole translation/compilation thing to happen in advance, so that even the first request happens like any other servlet request.

But watch out—it's vendor-dependent and not guaranteed. There IS a mention in the JSP spec (JSP 11.4.2) of a suggested protocol for JSP precompilation. You make a request for the JSP appending a query string "?jsp_precompile", and the Container might (if it chooses) do the translation/compilation right then instead of waiting for the first real request.

If the JSP turns into a servlet, I wonder if I can configure servlet init parameters... and while I'm at it, I wonder if I can override the servlet's init() method...

Sharpen your pencil

Think about these questions. Flip back through earlier pages (and chapters) if you need to, but don't turn the page until you've done this.

Yes, you CAN get servlet init parameters from a servlet, the questions are:

1) How would you *retrieve* them in your code? (Big, huge, gravel-hauling hint: pretty close to the same way you retrieve them in a "normal" servlet. From which object do you normally get servlet init parameters? Is that object available to your JSP code?)

2) How/where would you *configure* the servlet init parameters?

3) Suppose you *do* want to override the init() method... how would you do it? Is there something else you can do that'll give you the same result?

Initializing your JSP

You *can* do servlet initialization stuff in your JSP, but it's *slightly* different from what you do in a regular servlet.

Configuring servlet init parameters

You configure servlet init params for your JSP virtually the same way you configure them for a normal servlet. The only difference is that you have to add a <jsp-file> element within the <servlet> tag.

```
<web-app ...>
  ...
   <servlet>
     <servlet-name>MyTestInit</servlet-name>
     <jsp-file>/TestInit.jsp</jsp-file>
     <init-param>
       <param-name>email</param-name>
       <param-value>ikickedbutt@wickedlysmart.com</param-value>
     </init-param>
   </servlet>
  ...
</web-app>
```

This is the only line that's different from a regular servlet. It basically says, "apply everything in this <servlet> tag to the servlet created from this JSP page..."

Overriding jspInit()

Yes, it's that simple. If you implement a **jspInit()** method, the Container calls this method at the beginning of this page's life as a servlet. It's called from the servlet's init() method, so by the time this method runs there is a ServletConfig and ServletContext available to the servlet. That means you can call getServletConfig() and getServletContext() from within the jspInit() method.

This example uses the jspInit() method to retrieve a servlet init parameter (configured in the DD), and uses the value to set an application-scoped attribute.

Override the jspInit() method using a declaration.

```
<%!
  public void jspInit() {

    ServletConfig sConfig = getServletConfig();

    String emailAddr = sConfig.getInitParameter("email");

    ServletContext ctx = getServletContext();

    ctx.setAttribute("mail", emailAddr);
  }
%>
```

You're in a servlet, so you can call your inherited getServletConfig() method!

This is EXACTLY what you'd do in a normal servlet.

Get a reference to the ServletContext and set an application-scope attribute.

Attributes in a JSP

The example on the opposite page shows the JSP setting an application-scoped attribute using a method declaration that overrides jspInit(). But most of the time you'll be using one of the four *implicit objects* to get and set attributes corresponding to the four attribute scopes available in a JSP.

Yes, four. Remember, in addition to the standard servlet request, session, and application (context) scopes, a JSP adds a fourth scope—page scope—that you get from a pageContext object.

You usually won't need (or care about) page scope unless you're developing custom tags, so we won't say any more about it until the custom tags chapter.

	In a servlet	**In a JSP (using implicit objects)**
Application	**getServletContext()**.setAttribute("foo", barObj);	**application**.setAttribute("foo", barObj);
Request	**request**.setAttribute("foo", barObj);	**request**.setAttribute("foo", barObj);
Session	**request.getSession()**.setAttribute("foo", barObj);	**session**.setAttribute("foo", barObj);
Page	Does not apply!	**pageContext**.setAttribute("foo", barObj);

But this isn't the whole story! In a JSP, there's *another* way to get and set attributes at *any* scope, using only the pageContext implicit object. Turn the page and find out how...

There's no such thing as "context" scope... even though attributes in application scope are bound to the ServletContext object.

*The naming convention might trick you into thinking that attributes stored in the Servlet**Context** are... **context** scope. But there's no such thing. Remember, when you see "Context", think "application". But there's an inconsistency between the servlet and JSP names used to get app-scoped attributes—in a servlet, you say:*

```
getServletContext().getAttribute("foo")
```

but in a JSP you say:

```
application.getAttribute("foo")
```

Using PageContext for attributes

You can use a PageContext reference to get attributes from any scope, including the page scope for attributes bound to the PageContext.

The methods that work with other scopes take an int argument to indicate the scope. Although the attribute access methods come from JspContext, you'll find the constants for the scopes inside the PageContext class.

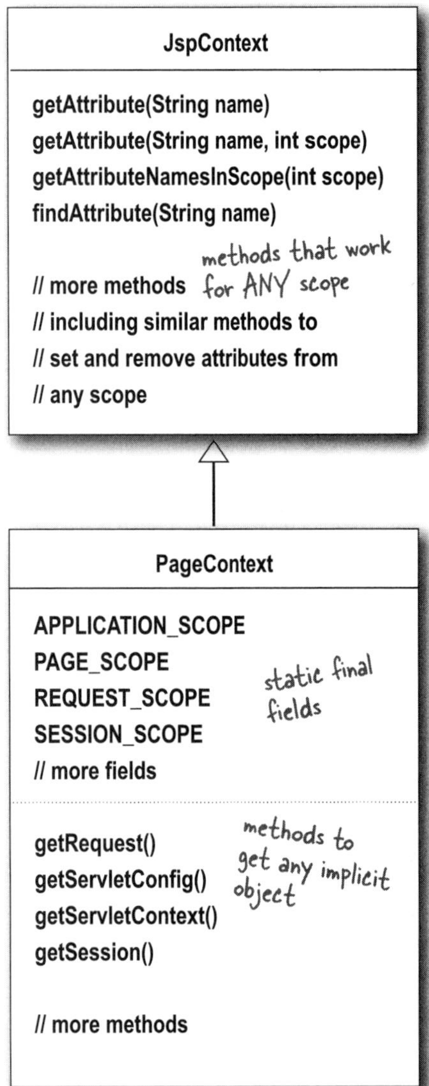

Examples using pageContext to get and set attributes

pageContext getAttribute(String) is for page scope

There are TWO overloaded getAttribute() methods you can call on pageContext: a one-arg that takes a String, and a two-arg that takes a String and an int. The one-arg version works just like all the others—it's for attributes bound TO the pageContext object. But the two-arg version can be used to get an attribute from ANY of the four scopes.

Setting a *page*-scoped attribute

```
<% Float one = new Float(42.5); %>
<% pageContext.setAttribute("foo", one); %>
```

Getting a *page*-scoped attribute

```
<%= pageContext.getAttribute("foo") %>
```

Using the pageContext to set a *session*-scoped attribute

```
<% Float two = new Float(22.4); %>
<% pageContext.setAttribute("foo", two, PageContext.SESSION_SCOPE); %>
```

Using the pageContext to get a *session*-scoped attribute

```
<%= pageContext.getAttribute("foo", PageContext.SESSION_SCOPE) %>
```

(Which is identical to: `<%= session.getAttribute("foo") %>`)

Using the pageContext to get an *application*-scoped attribute

```
Email is:
<%= pageContext.getAttribute("mail", PageContext.APPLICATION_SCOPE) %>
```

Within a JSP, the code above is identical to:

```
Email is:
<%= application.getAttribute("mail") %>
```

Using the pageContext to find an attribute when you don't *know* the scope

```
<%= pageContext.findAttribute("foo") %>
```

find it where?

Where does the findAttribute() method look? It looks first in the page context, so if there's a "foo" attribute with page context scope, then calling *find*Attribute(String name) on a PageContext works just like calling *get*Attribute(String name) on a PageContext. But if there's no "foo" attribute, the method starts looking in other scopes, from most restricted to least restricted scope —in other words, first request scope, then session, then finally application scope. ***The first one it finds with that name wins.***

While we're on the subject... let's talk more about the three *directives*

We already looked at the directive used for getting import statements into the generated servlet class made from your JSP. That was a *page* directive (one of the three directive types) with an *import* attribute (one of 13 attributes of the page directive). We'll take a quick look now at the others, although some won't be covered in detail until later chapters, and some won't be covered in detail *at all* in this book, because they're rarely used.

1 The page directive

```
<%@ page import="foo.*" session="false" %>
```

Defines page-specific properties such as character encoding, the content type for this page's response, and whether this page should have the implicit session object. A page directive can use up to thirteen different attributes (like the import attribute), although only four attributes are covered on the exam.

2 The taglib directive

```
<%@ taglib tagdir="/WEB-INF/tags/cool"  prefix="cool" %>
```

Defines tag libraries available to the JSP. We haven't talked about using custom tags and standard actions yet, so this might not make any sense at this point. Just go with it for now...we have two whole chapters on tag libraries coming up soon.

3 The include directive

```
<%@ include file="wickedHeader.html" %>
```

Defines text and code that gets added into the current page at translation time. This lets you build reusable chunks (like a standard page heading or navigation bar) that can be added to each page without having to duplicate all that code in each JSP.

Q: I'm confused... this page heading says ,"while we're on the subject..." but I don't see how *directives* have anything to do with pageContext and attributes.

A: They don't, not really. We just said that to cover a ~~bad~~ ~~pathetic~~ nonexistent transition between two unrelated topics. We *hoped* nobody would notice, but NO...you just couldn't let it go, could you?

Attributes to the *page* directive

Of the 13 page directive attributes in the JSP 2.0 spec, only *four* are covered on the exam. You do NOT have to memorize the entire list; just get a feel for what you can do. (We'll look at the *isELIgnored* and the two error-related attributes in later chapters.)

POSSIBLY on the exam

import Defines the Java import statements that'll be added to the generated servlet class. You get some imports for free (by default): *java.lang* (duh), *javax.servlet*, *javax.servlet.http*, and *javax.servlet.jsp*.

isThreadSafe Defines whether the generated servlet needs to implement the SingleThreadModel, which, as you know, is a Spectacularly Bad Thing. The default value is..."true", which means, "My app is thread safe, so I do NOT need to implement SingleThreadModel, which I know is inherently evil." The only reason to specifiy this attribute is if you need to set the attribute value to "false", which means that you want the generated servlet to use the SingleThreadModel, ***but you never will.***

contentType Defines the MIME type (and optional character encoding) for the JSP response. *You know the default.*

isELIgnored Defines whether EL expressions are ignored when this page is translated. We haven't talked about EL yet; that's coming in the next chapter. For now, just know that you might choose to ignore EL syntax in your page, and this is one of the two ways you can tell the Container.

isErrorPage Defines whether the current page represents *another* JSP's error page. The default value is "false", but if it's true, the page has access to the implicit *exception* object (which is a reference to the offending Throwable). If false, the implicit exception object is not available to the JSP.

errorPage Defines a URL to the resource to which uncaught Throwables should be sent. If you define a JSP here, then *that* JSP will have an **isErrorPage="true"** attribute in *its* page directive.

NOT on the exam

language Defines the scripting language used in scriptlets, expressions, and declarations. Right now, the only possible value is "java", but the attribute is here because isn't it just like those spec developers to be thinking of the future, when other languages might be used.

extends Defines the superclass of the class this JSP will become. You won't use this unless you REALLY know what you're doing—it overrides the class hierarchy provided by the Container.

session Defines whether the page will have an implicit *session* object. The default value is "true".

buffer Defines how buffering is handled by the implicit *out* object (reference to the JspWriter).

autoFlush Defines whether the buffered output is flushed automatically. The default value is "true".

info Defines a String that gets put into the translated page, just so that you can *get* it using the generated servlet's inherited getServletInfo() method.

pageEncoding Defines the character encoding for the JSP. The default is "ISO-8859-1" (unless the contentType attribute already defines a character encoding, or the page uses XML Document syntax).

This is SUCH a nice chapter with a VERY lovely look at how to put Java code in a JSP, but, um, look at this company-wide memo I just got.

Interoffice Memo from the CTO

URGENT

Effective immediately, anyone caught using scriptlets, expressions, or declarations in their JSP code will be suspended without pay until such time as it can be determined whether the programmer was fully responsible or simply trying to maintain some OTHER idiot's code.

If, in fact, the determination is made that the programmer is, in fact, responsible, the company will go ahead and, in fact, terminate the employee.

Rick Forester
Chief Technology Officer

"Remember: there is no "I" in TEAM."

"Write your code as if the next guy* to maintain it is a homicidal maniac who knows where you live."

[*Note to HR: we use "guy" in its non-gender specific form.]

Scriptlets considered harmful?

Is it true? *Could* there be a downside to putting all this Java into your JSP? After all, isn't that the whole frickin' POINT to a JSP? So that you write your Java in what is essentially an HTML page as opposed to writing HTML in a Java class?

Some people believe (OK, technically a *lot* of people including the JSP and Servlet spec teams) that it's *bad practice* to put all this Java into your JSP.

Why? Imagine you've been hired to build a big web site. Your team includes a small handful of back-end Java programmers, and a huge group of "web designers"—graphic artists and page creators who use Dreamweaver and Photoshop to build fabulous-looking web pages. These are not *programmers* (well, except for the ones who still think HTML is "coding").

Aspiring actors working as web designers while waiting for their big showbiz break.

Two questions—WHY are
you making us learn it, and WHAT is
the alternative? What the f*** else
IS there besides HTML if you can't
put scriptlets, declarations, and
expressions in your JSP?

There didn't used to BE an alternative.

That means there are already *mountains* of JSP files brimming with Java code stuck in every conceivable spot in the page, nestled between scriptlet, expression, and declaration tags. It's out there and there isn't anything anyone can do to change the past. So that means you've got to know how to *read* and *understand* these elements, and how to *maintain* pages written with them (unless you're given the chance to massively refactor the app's JSPs).

Secretly, we think there's still a place for some of this–nothing beats a little Java in a JSP for quickly testing something out on your server. But for the most part, you don't want to use this for real, production pages.

The reason this is all on the exam is because the *alternatives* are still fairly new, so most of the pages out there today are still "old-school". ***For the time being, you still have to be able to work with it!*** At some point, when the new Java-free techniques hit critical mass, the objectives from this chapter will probably drop off the exam, and we'll all breathe a collective sigh at the death of Java-in-JSPs.

But today is not that day.

(Note to parents and teachers: the four-letter word implied in this thought bubble, that starts with "f", followed by three asterisks, is NOT what you think. It was just a word that we found too funny to include without distracting the reader, so we bleeped it out. Because it's funny. Not *bad*.)

Oh if only there were a way in a JSP to use simple tags that cause Java methods to run, without having to put actual Java code into the page.

EL: the answer to, well, *everything*.

Or *almost* everything. But certainly an answer to two big complaints about putting actual Java into a JSP:

1) Web page designers shouldn't have to know Java.

2) Java code in a JSP is hard to change and maintain.

EL stands for "Expression Language", and it became officially part of the spec beginning with JSP 2.0 spec. EL is nearly always a much simpler way to do some of the things you'd normally do with scriptlets and expressions.

Of course right now you're thinking, "But if I want my JSP to use custom methods, how can I declare and write those methods if I can't use Java?"

Ahhhh... writing the actual functionality (method code) is *not* the purpose of EL. The purpose of EL is to offer a simpler way to *invoke* Java code—but the code itself belongs *somewhere else.* That means in a regular old Java class that's either a JavaBean, a class with static methods, or something called a Tag Handler. In other words, you don't write method code into your JSP when you're following today's Best Practices. You write the Java method *somewhere else,* and *call* it using EL.

Sneak peek at EL

The entire next chapter is on EL, so we won't go into details here. The only reason we're covering it is because it's yet another kind of element (with its own syntax) that goes in a JSP, and the exam objectives for this chapter include recognizing everything that can go into a JSP.

An EL expression ALWAYS looks like this: ${something}

In other words, the expression is ALWAYS enclosed in curly braces, and prefixed with a dollar ($) sign.

This EL expression:

```
Please contact: ${applicationScope.mail}
```

Is the same as this Java expression:

```
Please contact: <%= application.getAttribute("mail") %>
```

there are no Dumb Questions

Q: Not to be all negative, but I'm not sure I see an earth-shattering difference between the EL and the Java expression. Sure, it's a little shorter, but is that worth a whole new scripting language and JSP coding approach?

A: You SO haven't seen the full benefit of EL yet. The differences will become obvious in the next chapter when we dive in. But you must remember that to a Java programmer, EL is NOT neccessarily a dramatic development advantage. In fact, to a Java programmer it simply means "one more thing (with its own syntax and everything) to learn, when, hey, I already KNOW Java..."

But it's not always about *you*. EL is *much* easier for a non-Java programmer to learn and get up to speed in. And for a Java programmer, it is still much easier to maintain a scriptless page.

Yes, it's still something to learn. It doesn't let web page designers completely off the hook, but you'll soon see that it's more intuitive and natural for a web designer to use EL. For now, in this chapter, you simply need to be able to *recognize* EL when you see it. And don't worry at this point about recognizing whether the expression itself is valid—all we care about now is that you can pick out an EL expression in a JSP page.

And just HOW do you expect me to get my programmers to stop using scripting elements in their JSPs?

Easy—you *can* put an element in the DD that disables all scripting elements!

Using <scripting-invalid>

It's simple—you can make it invalid for a JSP to have scripting elements (scriptlets, Java expressions, or declarations) by putting a <scripting-invalid> tag in the DD:

```
<web-app ...>
 ...
  <jsp-config>
     <jsp-property-group>
     <url-pattern>*.jsp</url-pattern>
     <scripting-invalid>
        true
      </scripting-invalid>
    </jsp-property-group>
  </jsp-config>
 ...
</web-app>
```

This disables scripting elements for ALL JSPs in the app (because we used the wildcard *.jsp as the URL pattern.)

Watch out—you might have seen other books or articles show a page directive that disables scripting. In a *draft* version of the 2.0 spec, there was a page directive attribute:

<%@ page isScriptingEnabled="false" %>

This does not work! The isScriptingEnabled attribute is no longer in the JSP spec!

but it was removed from the final spec!!

The ***only*** way to invalidate scripting now is through the <scripting-invalid> DD tag.

You can choose to ignore EL

Yes, EL is a good thing that's going to save the world as we know it. But sometimes you might want to disable it. Why?

Think back to when the *assert* keyword was added to the Java language with version 1.4. Suddenly the formerly unreserved and perfectly legal identifier "assert" *meant* something to the compiler. So if you had, say, a variable named *assert*, you were screwed. Except that J2SE version 1.4 came with assertions disabled by default. If you knew you were writing (or recompiling) code that didn't use *assert* as an identifier, then you could choose to enable assertions.

So it's kind of the same thing with disabling EL—if you happened to have template text (plain old HTML or text) in your JSP that included something that looked like EL (${something}), you'd be in Big Trouble if you couldn't tell the Container to just ignore anything that appears to be EL and instead treat it like any other unprocessed text. Except there's one big difference between EL and assertions:

El is enabled by default!

If you want EL-looking things in your JSP to be ignored, you have to say so explicitly, either through a page directive or a DD element.

Putting <el-ignored> in the DD

```
<web-app ...>
  ...
   <jsp-config>
      <jsp-property-group>
      <url-pattern>*.jsp</url-pattern>
      <el-ignored>
         true
       </el-ignored>
     </jsp-property-group>
   </jsp-config>
  ...
</web-app>
```

The page directive takes priority over the DD setting!

If there's a conflict between the <el-ignored> setting in the DD and the isELIgnored page directive attribute, the directive always wins! That lets you specify the default behavior in the DD, but override it for a specific page using a page directive.

Using the isELIgnored page directive attribute

```
<%@ page isELIgnored="true" %>
```

The page directive attribute starts with "is", but the DD tag doesn't!

Watch out for the naming inconsistency!

The DD tag is <el-ignored>, so one might reasonably think that the page directive attribute would be, oh, maybe elIgnored? But no, one would be wrong if one jumped to the natural conclusion. The DD and directive for ignoring EL do not match! Don't be fooled by <is-el-ignored> .

But wait... there's still *another* JSP element we haven't seen: actions

So far, you've seen five different types of elements that can appear in a JSP: scriptlets, directives, declarations, Java expressions, and EL expressions.

But we haven't seen ***actions.*** They come in two flavors: *standard* and...*not.*

Standard Action:

```
<jsp:include page="wickedFooter.jsp" />
```

Other Action:

```
<c:set var="rate" value="32" />
```

For now, don't worry about what these do or how they work, just recognize an action when you see the syntax in a JSP. Later, we'll go into the details.

Although that's misleading, because there are some actions that aren't considered *standard actions*, but which are still part of a now-standard library. In other words, you'll later learn that some of the non-standard (the objectives refer to them as *custom*) actions are... standard, but yet they still aren't considered "standard actions". Yes, that's right—they're standardized non-standard custom actions. Doesn't that just clear it right up for you?

In a later chapter when we get to "using tags", we'll have a slightly richer vocabulary with which to talk about this in more detail, so relax. **For now, all we care about is recognizing an action when you see it in a JSP!**

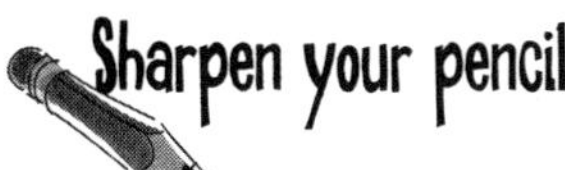

Look at the syntax for an action, and compare it to the syntax for the other kinds of JSP elements. Then answer this:

1) What are the differences between an action element and a scriptlet?

---

2) How will you recognize an action when you see it?

Evaluation Matrix

Think about what happens when each of these settings (or combination of settings) occurs. You'll see the answers when you turn the page, so do this one NOW.

① EL Evaluation

Place a checkmark in the evaluated column if the settings would cause the EL expressions to be evaluated, OR place a checkmark in the ignored column if EL will be treated like other template text. No row will have two checkmarks, of course.

DD configuration <el-ignored>	page directive isELIgnored	evaluated	ignored
unspecified	unspecified		
false	unspecified		
true	unspecified		
false	false		
false	true		
true	false		

② Scripting validity

Place a checkmark in the evaluated column if the settings would cause the scripting expressions to be evaluated, OR place a checkmark in the error column if scripting will cause a translation error.

DD configuration <scripting-invalid>	evaluated	error
unspecified		
true		
false		

JSP Element Magnets

Match the JSP element with its label by placing the JSP snippet in the box with the label representing that element type. Remember, you'll have Drag and Drop questions on the real exam similar to this exercise, so don't skip it!

JSP element type

- directive
- declaration
- EL expression
- scriptlet
- expression
- action

JSP snippet

Drag these over and drop them onto the matching label.

```
<% Float one = new Float(42.5); %>

<%! int y = 3; %>

<%@ page import="java.util.*" %>

<jsp:include file="foo.html" />

<%= pageContext.getAttribute("foo") %>

email: ${applicationScope.mail}
```

JSP Element Magnets: the Sequel

You know what they're called, but do you remember ***where they go in the generated servlet***? Of course you do. But this is just a little reinforcement/practice before we move on to a different chapter and topic.
(Put the element in the box corresponding to where that element's generated code will go in the servlet class file. Note that the magnet itself does not represent the ACTUAL code that will be generated.

```
[                    ]

public final class BasicCounter_jsp extends org.apache.jasper.runtime.HttpJspBase
                        implements org.apache.jasper.runtime.JspSourceDependent {

  [                    ]

  public void _jspService(HttpServletRequest request, HttpServletResponse response)
                                  throws java.io.IOException, ServletException {

     ...

        [                    ]

        [                    ]

        [                    ]

     ...
  }

}
```

The order of these three magnets does not matter.

```
<%= request.getAttribute("foo") %>
email: ${applicationScope.mail}
<%@ page import="java.util.*" %>
<% Float one = new Float(42.5); %>
<%! int y = 3; %>
```

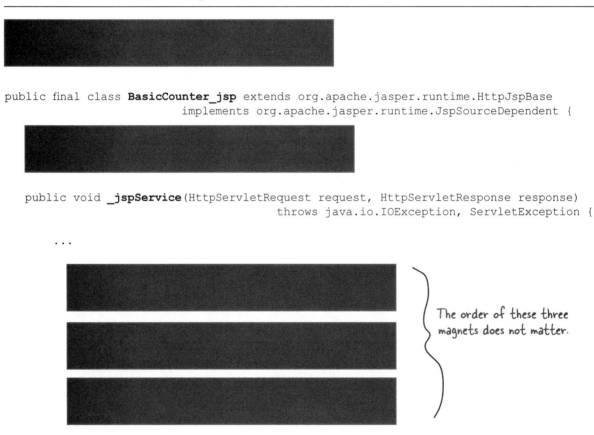

Evaluation Matrix ANSWERS

① EL Evaluation

DD configuration <el-ignored>	page directive isELIgnored	evaluated	ignored
unspecified	unspecified	✓	
false	unspecified	✓	
true	unspecified		✓
false	false	✓	
false	true		✓
true	false	✓	

② Scripting validity

DD configuration <scripting-invalid>	evaluated	error
unspecified	✓	
true		✓
false	✓	

JSP Element Magnets

ANSWERS

```
<%@ page import="java.util.*" %>
```

directive

```
<%! int y = 3; %>
```

declaration

```
email: ${applicationScope.mail}
```

EL expression

```
<% Float one = new Float(42.5); %>
```

scriptlet

```
<%= pageContext.getAttribute("foo") %>
```

expression

```
<jsp:include file="foo.html" />
```

action

The word "expression" by itself means "scripting expression" NOT "EL expression".

Of course the word "expression" is overloaded for JSP elements. If you see the word "expression" or "scripting expression" it means the same thing—an expression using Java language syntax:
<%= foo.getName() %>
The only time the word "expression" refers to EL is if you specifically see "EL" in the descriptions or label! So, always assume that the default for the word "expression" is "scripting/Java expression", not EL.

JSP Element Magnets: the Sequel

ANSWERS

```
<%@ page import="java.util.*" %>
```

A page directive with an import attribute turns into a Java import statement.

```
public final class BasicCounter_jsp extends org.apache.jasper.runtime.HttpJspBase
                    implements org.apache.jasper.runtime.JspSourceDependent {

    <%! int y = 3; %>
```

Declarations are for MEMBER declarations, so they go inside the class and outside any method.

```
  public void _jspService(HttpServletRequest request, HttpServletResponse response)
                              throws java.io.IOException, ServletException {

     ...

        <%= request.getAttribute("foo") %>
```

Expressions turn into print() statements in the service method.

```
        <% Float one = new Float(42.5); %>
```

Scriptlets go inside the service method.

```
        email: ${applicationScope.mail}
```

EL expressions go inside the service method.

```
     ...
  }
}
```

(Note: the order of these three things doesn't matter.)

NOTE: remember that the JSP code doesn't actually GO into the servlet like this... it's all translated into Java language code. This exercise is just to show you in what part of the generated class these elements GO, but we're not showing you the actual generated code the elements are translated into. For example, the declaration goes from <%! int y = 3; %> to just int y = 3;

Mock Exam Chapter 7

1 Given this DD element:

```
<jsp-property-group>
   <url-pattern>*.jsp</url-pattern>
   <el-ignored>true</el-ignored>
</jsp-property-group>
```

What does the element accomplish? (Choose all that apply.)

- ❑ A. All files with the specified extension mapping should be treated by the JSP container as well-formed XML files.
- ❑ B. All files with the specified extension mapping should have any Expression Language code evaluated by the JSP container.
- ❑ C. By default, all files with the specified extension mapping should NOT have any Expression Language code evaluated by the JSP container.
- ❑ D. Nothing, this tag is NOT understood by the container.
- ❑ E. Although this tag is legal, it is redundant, because the container behaves this way by default.

---

2 Which directives specify an HTTP response that will be of type "image/svg"? (Choose all that apply.)

- ❑ A. **<%@ page type="image/svg" %>**
- ❑ B. **<%@ page mimeType="image/svg" %>**
- ❑ C. **<%@ page language="image/svg" %>**
- ❑ D. **<%@ page contentType="image/svg" %>**
- ❑ E. **<%@ page pageEncoding="image/svg" %>**

3 Given this JSP:

```
<%@ page import="java.util.*" %>
<html><body> The people who like
<%= request.getParameter("hobby") %>
are: <br>
<% ArrayList al = (ArrayList) request.getAttribute("names"); %>
<% Iterator it = al.iterator();
   while (it.hasNext()) { %>
     <%= it.next() %>
<br>
<% } %>
</body></html>
```

Which types of code are used in this JSP? (Choose all that apply.)

- ❑ A. EL
- ❑ B. directive
- ❑ C. expression
- ❑ D. template text
- ❑ E. scriptlet

4 Which statements about `jspInit()` are true? (Choose all that apply.)

- ❑ A. It has access to a `ServletConfig`.
- ❑ B. It has access to a `ServletContext`.
- ❑ C. It is only called once.
- ❑ D. It can be overridden.

5 Which types of objects are available to the **jspInit()** method? (Choose all that apply.)

- ❑ A. **ServletConfig**
- ❑ B. **ServletContext**
- ❑ C. **JspServletConfig**
- ❑ D. **JspServletContext**
- ❑ E. **HttpServletRequest**
- ❑ F. **HttpServletResponse**

6 Given:

```
<%@ page isELIgnored="true" %>
```

What is the effect? (Choose all that apply.)

- ❑ A. Nothing, this **page** directive is NOT defined.
- ❑ B. The directive turns off the evaluation of Expression Language code by the JSP container in all of the web application's JSPs.
- ❑ C. The JSP containing this directive should be treated by the JSP container as a well-formed XML file.
- ❑ D. The JSP containing this directive should NOT have any Expression Language code evaluated by the JSP container.
- ❑ E. This page directive will only turn off EL evaluation if the DD declares a **<el-ignored>true</el-ignored>** element with a URL pattern that includes this JSP.

7 Which statement concerning JSPs is true? (Choose one.)

- ❑ A. Only **jspInit()** can be overridden.
- ❑ B. Only **jspDestroy()** can be overridden.
- ❑ C. Only **_jspService()** can be overridden.
- ❑ D. Both **jspInit()** and **jspDestroy()** can be overridden.
- ❑ E. **jspInit()**, **jspDestroy()**, and **_jspService()** can all be overridden.

8 Which JSP lifecycle step is out of order?

- ❑ A. Translate the JSP into a servlet.
- ❑ B. Compile servlet source code.
- ❑ C. Call `_jspService()`
- ❑ D. Instantiate the servlet class.
- ❑ E. Call `jspInit()`
- ❑ F. Call `jspDestroy()`

---

9 Which are valid JSP implicit variables? (Choose all that apply.)

- ❑ A. `stream`
- ❑ B. `context`
- ❑ C. `exception`
- ❑ D. `listener`
- ❑ E. `application`

---

10 Given a request with two parameters: one named “first” represents a user’s first name and another named “last” represents his last name.

Which JSP scriptlet code outputs these parameter values?

❑ A.
```
<% out.println(request.getParameter("first"));
   out.println(request.getParameter("last")); %>
```

❑ B.
```
<% out.println(application.getInitParameter("first"));
   out.println(application.getInitParameter("last")); %>
```

❑ C.
```
<% println(request.getParameter("first"));
   println(request.getParameter("last")); %>
```

❑ D.
```
<% println(application.getInitParameter("first"));
   println(application.getInitParameter("last")); %>
```

---

11 Given:

```
11. Hello ${user.name}!
12. Your number is <c:out value="${user.phone}"/>.
13. Your address is <jsp:getProperty name="user" property="addr" />
14. <% if (user.isValid()) {%>You are valid!<% } %>
```

Which statements are true? (Choose all that apply.)

- ❏ A. Lines 11 and 12 (and no others) contain examples of EL elements.
- ❏ B. Line 14 is an example of scriptlet code.
- ❏ C. None of the lines in this example contain template text.
- ❏ D. Lines 12 and 13 include examples of JSP standard actions.
- ❏ E. Line 11 demonstrates an invalid use of EL.
- ❏ F. All four lines in this example would be valid in a JSP page.

---

12 Which JSP expression tag will print the context initialization parameter named "javax.sql.DataSource"?

- ❏ A. `<%= application.getAttribute("javax.sql.DataSource") %>`
- ❏ B. `<%= application.getInitParameter("javax.sql.DataSource") %>`
- ❏ C. `<%= request.getParameter("javax.sql.DataSource") %>`
- ❏ D. `<%= contextParam.get("javax.sql.DataSource") %>`

---

13 Which statements about disabling scripting elements are true? (Choose all that apply.)

- ❏ A. You can't disable scripting via the DD.
- ❏ B. You can only disable scripting at the application level.
- ❏ C. You can disable scripting programmatically by using the **isScriptingEnabled** page directive attribute.
- ❏ D. You can disable scripting via the DD by using the **<scripting-invalid>** element.

---

14 In sequence, what are the Java types of the following JSP implicit objects: **application**, **out**, **request**, **response**, **session**?

- ❑ A. **java.lang.Throwable**
  java.lang.Object
  java.util.Map
  java.util.Set
  java.util.List

- ❑ B. **javax.servlet.ServletConfig**
  java.lang.Throwable
  java.lang.Object
  javax.servlet.jsp.PageContext
  java.util.Map

- ❑ C. **javax.servlet.ServletContext**
  javax.servlet.jsp.JspWriter
  javax.servlet.ServletRequest
  javax.servlet.ServletResponse
  javax.servlet.http.HttpSession

- ❑ D. **javax.servlet.ServletContext**
  java.io.PrintWriter
  javax.servlet.ServletConfig
  java.lang.Exception
  javax.servlet.RequestDispatcher

---

15 Which is an example of the syntax used to import a class in a JSP?

- ❑ A. `<% page import="java.util.Date" %>`
- ❑ B. `<%@ page import="java.util.Date" @%>`
- ❑ C. `<%@ page import="java.util.Date" %>`
- ❑ D. `<% import java.util.Date; %>`
- ❑ E. `<%@ import file="java.util.Date" %>`

Chapter 7 Answers

1 Given this DD element: (JSP v2.0 pg 1-87)

```
<jsp-property-group>
   <url-pattern>*.jsp</url-pattern>
   <el-ignored>true</el-ignored>
</jsp-property-group>
```

What does the element accomplish? (Choose all that apply.)

☐ A. All files with the specified extension mapping should be treated by the JSP container as well-formed XML files.

☐ B. All files with the specified extension mapping should have any Expression Language code evaluated by the JSP container.

☑ C. By default, all files with the specified extension mapping should NOT have any Expression Language code evaluated by the JSP container.

☐ D. Nothing, this tag is NOT understood by the container.

☐ E. Although this tag is legal, it is redundant, because the container behaves this way by default.

-Option C turns off the evaluating of EL expressions by a JSP 2.0 container and by default the container does evaluate EL.

2 Which directives specify an HTTP response that will be of type "image/svg"? (Choose all that apply.) (JSP v2.0 section 1.10.1)

☐ A. <%@ page type="image/svg" %>

☐ B. <%@ page mimeType="image/svg" %>

☐ C. <%@ page language="image/svg" %>

☑ D. <%@ page contentType="image/svg" %>

☐ E. <%@ page pageEncoding="image/svg" %>

-Option D is the correct syntax for this directive.

3 Given this JSP: (JSP v2.0 section 1)

```
1.  <%@ page import="java.util.*" %>
2.  <html><body> The people who like
3.  <%= request.getParameter("hobby") %>
4.  are: <br>
5.  <% ArrayList al = (ArrayList) request.getAttribute("names"); %>
6.  <% Iterator it = al.iterator();
7.     while (it.hasNext()) { %>
8.       <%= it.next() %>
9.  <br>
10. <% } %>
11. </body></html>
```

Which types of code are used in this JSP? (Choose all that apply.)

- [ ] A. EL
- [x] B. directive
- [x] C. expression
- [x] D. template text
- [x] E. scriptlet

–There's no EL in this JSP. There's a directive on line 1, expressions on lines 3 and 8, template text all over (like line 2), and of course scripting elements.

4 Which statements about **`jspInit()`** are true? (Choose all that apply.) (JSP v2.0 section 11.2.1)

- [x] A. It has access to a **`ServletConfig`**.
- [x] B. It has access to a **`ServletContext`**.
- [x] C. It is only called once.
- [x] D. It can be overridden.

5 Which types of objects are available to the **jspInit()** method? (Choose all that apply.) (JSP v2.0 section 11.2.1)

- [x] A. `ServletConfig`
- [x] B. `ServletContext`
- [ ] C. `JspServletConfig`
- [ ] D. `JspServletContext`
- [ ] E. `HttpServletRequest`
- [ ] F. `HttpServletResponse`

–JSPs turn into plain old servlets, so they have access to the plain old ServletConfig and ServletContext objects... and it's just a little early in the lifecycle to be talking about requests and responses.

---

6 Given: (JSP v2.0 pg 1-49)

```
<%@ page isELIgnored="true" %>
```

What is the effect? (Choose all that apply.)

- [ ] A. Nothing, this **page** directive is NOT defined.
- [ ] B. The directive turns off the evaluation of Expression Language code by the JSP container in all of the web application's JSPs.
- [ ] C. The JSP containing this directive should be treated by the JSP container as a well-formed XML file.
- [x] D. The JSP containing this directive should NOT have any Expression Language code evaluated by the JSP container.
- [ ] E. This page directive will only turn off EL evaluation if the DD declares a **<el-ignored>true</el-ignored>** element with a URL pattern that includes this JSP.

–Option B is incorrect because the directive only affects the enclosing JSP.

---

7 Which statement concerning JSPs is true? (Choose one.) (JSP v2.0 section 11)

- [ ] A. Only **jspInit()** can be overridden.
- [ ] B. Only **jspDestroy()** can be overridden.
- [ ] C. Only **_jspService()** can be overridden.
- [x] D. Both **jspInit()** and **jspDestroy()** can be overridden.
- [ ] E. **jspInit()**, **jspDestroy()**, and **_jspService()** can all be overridden.

–Remember the underscore is your clue that a method can't be overridden.

8 Which JSP lifecycle step is out of order?

(JSP v2.0 section 11)

❑ A. Translate the JSP into a servlet.

❑ B. Compile servlet source code.

☑ C. Call `_jspService()`

-The _jspService method can never be called before jspInit.

❑ D. Instantiate the servlet class.

❑ E. Call `jspInit()`

❑ F. Call `jspDestroy()`

9 Which are valid JSP implicit variables? (Choose all that apply.)

(JSP v2.0 section 1.8.3)

❑ A. `stream`

❑ B. `context`

☑ C. `exception`

❑ D. `listener`

☑ E. `application`

-Options A, B, and D don't exist as implicit objects created by the container for JSPs.

10 Given a request with two parameters: one named "first" represents a user's first name and another named "last" represents his last name.

(JSP v2.0 pg 1-41)

Which JSP scriptlet code outputs these parameter values?

☑ A.
```
<% out.println(request.getParameter("first"));
   out.println(request.getParameter("last")); %>
```

-Option A uses the "out" implicit object and its println() method.

❑ B.
```
<% out.println(application.getInitParameter("first"));
   out.println(application.getInitParameter("last")); %>
```

❑ C.
```
<% println(request.getParameter("first"));
   println(request.getParameter("last")); %>
```

-Options C and D are missing the "out" implicit object.

❑ D.
```
<% println(application.getInitParameter("first"));
   println(application.getInitParameter("last")); %>
```

---

11 Given:

(JSP v2.0 pg. 1-10)

```
11. Hello ${user.name}!
12. Your number is <c:out value="${user.phone}"/>.
13. Your address is <jsp:getProperty name="user" property="addr" />
14. <% if (user.isValid()) {%>You are valid!<% } %>
```

Which statements are true? (Choose all that apply.)

- [x] A. Lines 11 and 12 (and no others) contain examples of EL elements.
- [x] B. Line 14 is an example of scriptlet code.
- [ ] C. None of the lines in this example contain template text.

  -Option C is incorrect because all four lines include template text.
- [ ] D. Lines 12 and 13 include examples of JSP standard actions.

  -Option D is incorrect because line 12 does not include a JSP standard action.
- [ ] E. Line 11 demonstrates an invalid use of EL.

  -Option E is incorrect because the EL in line 11 is valid.
- [x] F. All four lines in this example would be valid in a JSP page.

---

12 Which JSP expression tag will print the context initialization parameter named "javax.sql.DataSource"?

(JSP v2.0 pg 1-41)

- [ ] A. <%= application.getAttribute("javax.sql.DataSource") %>
- [x] B. <%= application.getInitParameter("javax.sql.DataSource") %>
- [ ] C. <%= request.getParameter("javax.sql.DataSource") %>
- [ ] D. <%= contextParam.get("javax.sql.DataSource") %>

-Option B shows the correct use of the application implicit object.

---

13 Which statements about disabling scripting elements are true? (Choose all that apply.)

(JSP v2.0 section 3.3.3)

- [ ] A. You can't disable scripting via the DD.
- [ ] B. You can only disable scripting at the application level.
- [ ] C. You can disable scripting programmatically by using the **isScriptingEnabled** page directive attribute.
- [x] D. You can disable scripting via the DD by using the **<scripting-invalid>** element.

-You can only disable scripting elements through the DD. The <jsp-property-group> element allows you to disable scripting in selective JSPs by specifying URL patterns to be disabled.

14 In sequence, what are the Java types of the following JSP implicit objects: **application**, **out**, **request**, **response**, **session**?

(JSP v2.0 pg 1-41)

- ❑ A. **java.lang.Throwable**
  java.lang.Object
  java.util.Map
  java.util.Set
  java.util.List
- ❑ B. **javax.servlet.ServletConfig**
  java.lang.Throwable
  java.lang.Object
  javax.servlet.jsp.PageContext
  java.util.Map
- ☑ C. **javax.servlet.ServletContext**
  javax.servlet.jsp.JspWriter
  javax.servlet.ServletRequest
  javax.servlet.ServletResponse
  javax.servlet.http.HttpSession
- ❑ D. **javax.servlet.ServletContext**
  java.io.PrintWriter
  javax.servlet.ServletConfig
  java.lang.Exception
  javax.servlet.RequestDispatcher

-Option C shows the Java type of each implicit object.

15 Which is an example of the syntax used to import a class in a JSP?

(JSP v2.0 pg. 1-44)

- ❑ A. **<% page import="java.util.Date" %>**
- ❑ B. **<%@ page import="java.util.Date" @%>**
- ☑ C. **<%@ page import="java.util.Date" %>**
- ❑ D. **<% import java.util.Date; %>**
- ❑ E. **<%@ import file="java.util.Date" %>**

-Options A & D are invalid because only Java statements may be included within <% ... %> tags.

-Option C is the only example that shows the correct syntax.

-Option E is invalid because there is no import directive.

8 scriptless JSP

Script-free pages

Everything in my life is better since I stopped using scriptlets. I'm taller, I've added four pounds of lean muscle mass, and my knitting has *really* improved.
That's wonderful. But you know all technologies have trade-offs... you used to have hair.

Lose the scripting. Do your web page designers really have to know Java? Is that fair? Do they expect server-side Java programmers to be, say, graphic designers? And even if it's just *you* on the team, do you really want a pile of bits and pieces of Java code in your JSPs? Can you say, "maintenance nightmare"? Writing scriptless pages is not just *possible*, it's become much *easier* and more flexible with the new JSP 2.0 spec, thanks to the new Expression Language (EL). Patterned after JavaScript and XPATH, web designers feel right at home with EL, and you'll like it too (once you get used to it). But there are some traps... EL *looks* like Java, but isn't. Sometimes EL behaves differently than if you used the same syntax in Java, so pay attention!

Building JSP pages using the Expression Language (EL) and Standard Actions

Coverage Notes:

All of the objectives in this section are covered completely in this chapter. And it's a big one. Take your time in this chapter; there's a lot of picky details to go through.

7.1 Write a code snippet using top-level variables in the EL. This includes the following implicit variables: pageScope, requestScope, sessionScope, and applicationScope; param and paramValues; header and headerValues; cookies; and initParam.

7.2 Write a code snippet using the following EL operators: property access (the . operator), collection access (the [] operator).

7.3 Write a code snippet using the following EL operators: aritmetic operators, relational operators, and logical operators.

7.4 For EL functions: Write a code snippet using an EL function; identify or create the TLD file structure used to declare an EL function; and identify or create a code example to define an EL function.

8.1 Given a design goal, create a code snippet using the following standard actions: jsp:useBean (with attributes: 'id', 'scope', 'type', and 'class'), jsp:getProperty, and jsp: setProperty (with all attribute combinations).

8.2 Given a design goal, create a code snippet using the following standard actions: jsp:include, jsp:forward, and jsp:param.

6.7 Given a specific design goal for including a JSP segment in another page, write the JSP code that uses the most appropriate inclusion mechanism (the include directive or the <jsp:include> standard action).

In this chapter, we cover BOTH include mechanisms: <jsp:include> from objective 8.2, and the include page directive from objective 6.7 (most of the objectives in section 6 were covered in the previous chapter on JSPs).

Our MVC app depends on attributes

Remember in the original MVC beer app, the Servlet *controller* talked to the *model* (Java class with business logic), then *set* an attribute in the request scope before forwarding to the JSP *view.*

The JSP had to *get* the attribute from the request scope, and use it to render a response to send back to the client. Here's a quick, simplified look at how the attribute goes from controller to view (just imagine the servlet talks to the model):

Servlet (controller) code

```
public void doPost(HttpServletRequest request, HttpServletResponse response)
                                        throws IOException, ServletException {

    String name = request.getParameter("userName");
    request.setAttribute("name", name);

    RequestDispatcher view = request.getRequestDispatcher("/result.jsp");
    view.forward(request, response);
}
```

Use the request parameter from the form to set a request-scoped attribute that the JSP will use.

Forward the request to the view.

JSP (view) code

```
<html><body>
Hello
<%= request.getAttribute("name") %>
</body></html>
```

Use a scripting expression to get the attribute and print it to the response.

(Remember: scripting expressions are ALWAYS the argument to the out.print() method.)

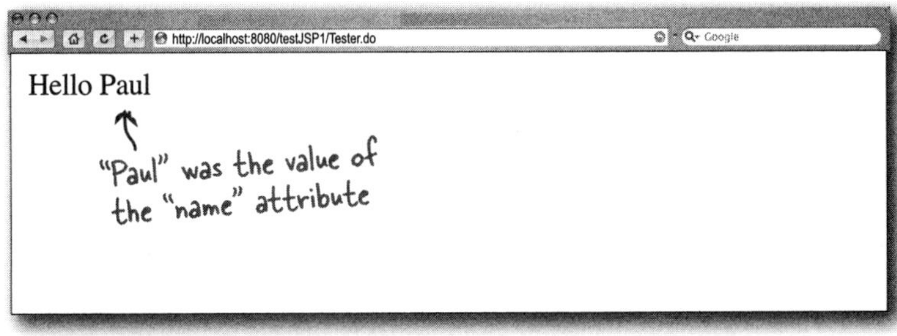
http://localhost:8080/testJSP1/Tester.do
Hello Paul
"Paul" was the value of the "name" attribute

But what if the attribute is not a String, but an instance of Person?

And not just a Person, but a Person with a "name" property. We're using the term "property" in the non-enterprise JavaBean* way—the Person class has a getName() and setName() method pair, which in the JavaBean spec means Person has a property called "name". Don't forget that the "name" property means a change in case for the first letter, "n". In other words, the name of the property is what you get when you strip off the prefix "get" and "set", and make the first character after that lower case. So, getName/setName becomes *name*.

A simple JavaBean.

foo.Person
public String getName() public void setName(String)

We can tell from the getter/setter pair that Person has a property called "name" (note the lowercase "n").

Servlet code

```
public void doPost(HttpServletRequest request, HttpServletResponse response)
                                      throws IOException, ServletException {

   foo.Person p = new foo.Person();
   p.setName("Evan");
   request.setAttribute("person", p);

   RequestDispatcher view = request.getRequestDispatcher("result.jsp");
   view.forward(request, response);
}
```

JSP code

```
<html><body>
Person is: <%= request.getAttribute("person") %>
</body></html>
```

What does getAttribute() return?

What we WANT:

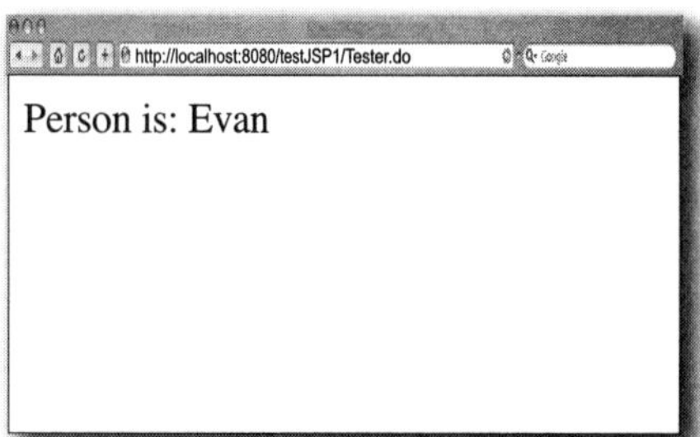

What we GOT:

http://localhost:8080/testJSP1/Tester.do

Person is: foo.Person@512d66

Oh... obviously the expression just called the attribute's default toString() method...

*We'll talk about JavaBeans in a few pages, but for now, just know that it's a plain old Java class that has getters and setters that follow a naming convention.

We need more code to get the Person's name

Sending the result of getAttribute() to print/write statement doesn't give us what we want—it just runs the object's toString() method. And since class Person doesn't override its inherited Object.toString(), well, you know what happens. But we want to print the Person's *name.*

JSP code

```
<html><body>

<% foo.Person p = (foo.Person) request.getAttribute("person"); %>
Person is: <%= p.getName() %>

</body></html>
```

Print the result of getName().

OR using an expression

```
<html><body>
Person is:
<%= ((foo.Person) request.getAttribute("person")).getName() %>

</body></html>
```

What we GOT:

But then we remember that MEMO...

The one that can be summarized as "*Use Scripting and Die*"

We need a different approach.

Person is a JavaBean, so we'll use the bean-related standard actions

With a couple of standard actions, we can eliminate all the scripting code in our JSP (remember: scripting code includes declarations, scriptlets, and expressions) and still print out the value of the person attribute's *name* property. Don't forget that *name* is not an attribute—only the *person* object is an attribute. The name property is simply the thing returned from a Person's getName() method.

Without standard actions (using scripting)

The way we've been doing it.

```
<html><body>

<% foo.Person p = (foo.Person) request.getAttribute("person"); %>
Person is: <%= p.getName() %>

</body></html>
```

With standard actions (no scripting)

NO Java code here! No scripting, just two standard action tags.

```
<html><body>
<jsp:useBean id="person"  class="foo.Person" scope="request" />
Person created by servlet: <jsp:getProperty name="person"  property="name" />
</body></html>
```

Deconstructing <jsp:useBean> and <jsp:getProperty>

All we really wanted was the functionality of <jsp:getProperty> because we wanted only to display the value of the person's "name" property. But how does the Container know what "person" means? If we had only the <jsp:getProperty> tag in the JSP, it's almost like using an undeclared variable—the name "person". The Container usually has no idea what you're talking about, unless you FIRST put a <jsp:useBean> into the page. The <jsp:useBean> is a way of declaring and initializing the actual bean object you're using in <jsp:getProperty>.

Declare and initialize a bean attribute with <jsp:useBean>

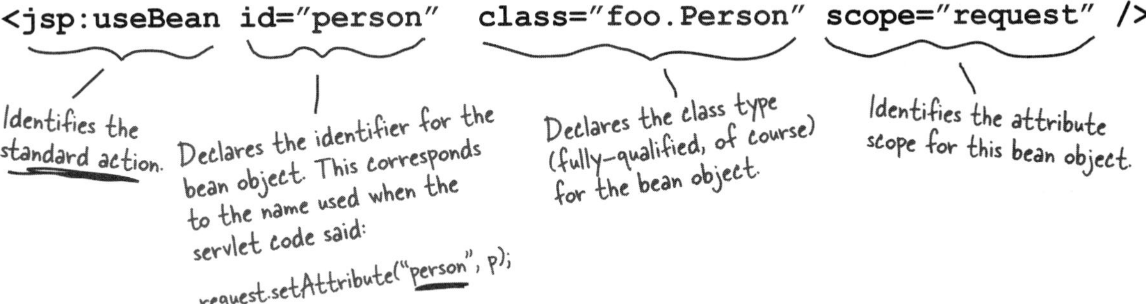
<jsp:useBean id="person" class="foo.Person" scope="request" />
Identifies the standard action.
Declares the identifier for the bean object. This corresponds to the name used when the servlet code said:
request.setAttribute("person", p);
Declares the class type (fully-qualified, of course) for the bean object.
Identifies the attribute scope for this bean object.

Get a bean attribute's property value with <jsp:getProperty>

```
<jsp:getProperty name="person" property="name" />
```

Identifies the standard action.

Identifies the actual bean object. This will match the "id" value from the <jsp:useBean> tag.

Identifies the property name (in other words, the thing with the getter and setter in the bean class).

Note: this "name" property has nothing to do with the name="person" part of this tag. The property is called "name" simply because of the way the Person class is defined.

<jsp:useBean> can also CREATE a bean!

If the <jsp:useBean> can't find an attribute object named "person", it can make one! It's kind of the way request.getSession() (or getSession(true)) works—it first searches for an existing thing, but if it doesn't find one, it creates one.

Look at the code from the generated servlet, and you'll see what's happening—there's an *if* test in there! It checks for a bean based on the values of ***id*** and ***scope*** in the tag, and if it doesn't get one, it makes an instance of the class specified in ***class***, assigns the object to the ***id*** variable, then sets it as an attribute in the ***scope*** you defined in the tag.

This *tag*

```
<jsp:useBean id="person"  class="foo.Person" scope="request" />
```

Turns into this *code* in the _jspService() method

```
foo.Person person = null;

synchronized (request) {

  person = (foo.Person)_jspx_page_context.getAttribute("person", PageContext.REQUEST_SCOPE);

  if (person == null){

     person = new foo.Person();

     _jspx_page_context.setAttribute("person", person, PageContext.REQUEST_SCOPE);
  }
}
```

Declare a variable based on the value of id. This variable is what lets other parts of your JSP (including other bean tags) refer to that variable.

Tries to get the attribute at the scope you defined in the tag, and assigns the result to the id variable.

BUT, if there was NOT an attribute with that name at that scope...

Make one, and assign it to the id variable.

Finally, set the new object as an attribute at the scope you defined.

This could be a bad thing—I don't WANT to have a bean that doesn't have its property values set! If the Container makes a bean using that tag, the bean won't have property values...

You can use <jsp:setProperty>

But you already knew that where there's a *get* there's usually a *set*. The <jsp:**set**Property> tag is the third and final bean standard action. It's simple to use:

```
<jsp:useBean id="person"  class="foo.Person" scope="request" />
<jsp:setProperty name="person" property="name" value="Fred" />
```

That's worse! NOW it means that if the bean already existed, my JSP will reset the existing bean's property value! I want to set the property on only the NEW beans...

<jsp:useBean> can have a body!

If you put your setter code (<jsp:setProperty>) *inside* the body of <jsp:useBean>, ***the property setting is conditional!*** In other words, the property values will be set *only* if a *new* bean is created. If an existing bean with that *scope* and *id* are found, the body of the tag will never run, so the property won't be reset from your JSP code.

With a <jsp:useBean > body, you can have code that runs conditionally... ONLY if the bean attribute can't be found and a new bean is created.

```
<jsp:useBean id="person" class="foo.Person" scope="page" >

    <jsp:setProperty name="person" property="name" value="Fred" />

</jsp:useBean >
```

There's no slash!

This is the body.

Any code inside the body of <jsp:useBean > is CONDITIONAL. It runs ONLY if the bean isn't found and a new one is created.

Finally we close off the tag. Everything between the opening and closing tags is the body.

Q: Why didn't they just let you specify arguments to the constructor of the bean? Why do you have to go through the extra trouble of setting values anyway?

A: The simple answer is this: beans can't HAVE constructors with arguments! Well, as a Java *class*, they can, but when an object is going to be treated as a bean, Bean Law states that ONLY the bean's public, no-arg constructor will be called. End of story. In fact if you do NOT have a public no-arg constructor in your bean class, this whole thing will fail anyway.

Q: What the heck is Bean Law?

A: The law according to the creakingly-ancient JavaBeans specification. We're talking JavaBeans—NOT *Enterprise* JavaBeans (EJB) which is completely unrelated. (Go figure.)The plain old non-enterprise JavaBeans spec defines what it takes for a class to be a JavaBean. Although the spec actually gets pretty complex, the only things you need to know for using beans with JSP and servlets are these few rules (we're showing only those that apply to what we're doing with servlets and JSPs):

1) You MUST have a public, no-arg constructor.

2) You MUST name your public getter and setter methods starting with "get" (or "is", for a boolean) and "set", followed by the same word. (get**Foo**(), set**Foo**()). The property name is derived from stripping off the "get" and "set", and changing the first character of what's left to lowercase.

3) The setter argument type and the getter return type MUST be identical. This defines the property type.

int getFoo()   void setFoo(***int*** foo)

4) The property name and type are derived from the getters and setters and NOT from a member in the class. For example, just because you have a private int foo variable does NOT mean a thing in terms of properties. You can name your variables whatever you like. The "foo" property name comes from the *methods*. In other words, you have a property simply because you have a getter and setter. How you implement them is up to you.

5) For use with JSPs, the property type SHOULD be a type that is either a String or a primitive. If it isn't, it can still be a legal bean, but you won't be able to rely only on standard actions, and you might have to use scripting.

Generated servlet when <jsp:useBean> has a body

It's simple. The Container puts the extra property-setting code inside the *if* test.

Code in _jspService() WITH the <jsp:useBean> body

```
foo.Person person = null;

person = (foo.Person) _jspx_page_context.getAttribute("person", PageContext.PAGE_SCOPE);

if (person == null){

   person = new foo.Person();

   _jspx_page_context.setAttribute("person", person, PageContext.PAGE_SCOPE);

   org.apache.jasper.runtime.JspRuntimeLibrary.introspecthelper(
        _jspx_page_context.findAttribute("person"), "name", "Fred", null, null, false);

}
```

Declare the reference variable.

Look for an existing attribute with the name and scope from the tag.

If there isn't one, make a new instance.

Bind the new bean object to the specified scope.

THIS is the part that's new. It's here ONLY when useBean has a body.

You were expecting:

person.setName("Fred");

but that's what this code does. Except it uses a generic property-setting method that takes the attribute, the property, and the value as arguments. The end result is still the same: ultimately it invokes setName() on the Person object.

(Remember you aren't expected to know the Tomcat implementation code...only the end result.)

Can you make polymorphic bean references?

When you write a <jsp:useBean>, the *class* attribute determines the class of the new *object* (if one is created). It also determines the type of the *reference* variable used in the generated servlet.

The way it is NOW in the JSP

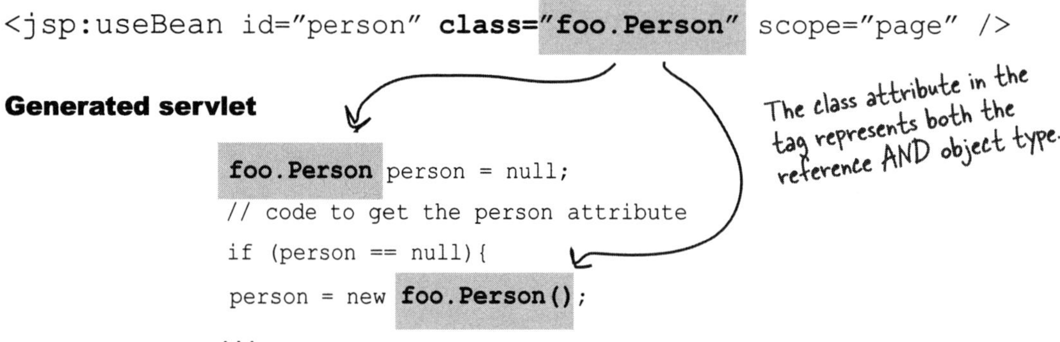
<jsp:useBean id="person" class="foo.Person" scope="page" />
Generated servlet
foo.Person person = null;
// code to get the person attribute
if (person == null){
person = new foo.Person();
...
The class attribute in the tag represents both the reference AND object type.

But... what if we want the reference type to be *different* from the actual object type? We'll change the Person class to make it *abstract*, and make a concrete subclass Employee. Imagine we want the *reference* type to be Person, and the new *object* type to be Employee.

```
package foo;

public abstract class Person {
   private String name;

   public void setName(String name) {
      this.name=name;
   }

   public String getName() {
      return name;
   }
}
```

```
package foo;

public class Employee extends Person {
    private int empID;

    public void setEmpID(int empID) {
       this.empID = empID;
    }

    public int getEmpID() {
       return empID;
    }
}
```

Adding a type attribute to <jsp:useBean>

With the changes we just made to the Person class, we're in trouble if the attribute can't be found:

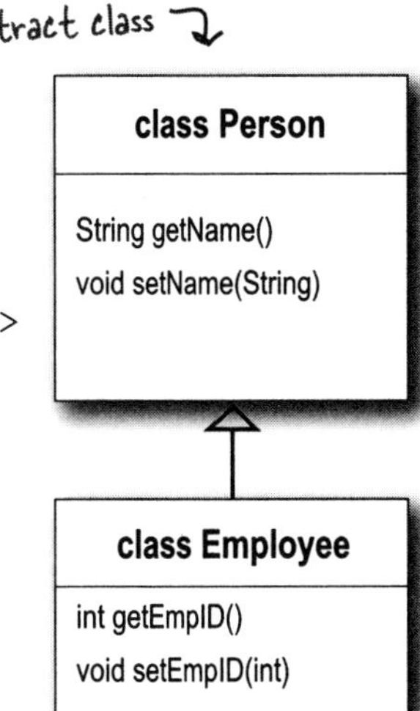

Our original JSP

```
<jsp:useBean id="person" class="foo.Person" scope="page"/>
```

Has this result

```
java.lang.InstantiationException: foo.Person
```

Because the Container tries to:

```
new foo.Person();
```

Person is now abstract! Obviously, you can't make one, but the Container still tries, based on the class attribute in the tag.

We need to make the *reference* variable type Person, and the *object* an instance of class Employee. Adding a type attribute to the tag lets us do that.

Our new JSP with a *type*

```
<jsp:useBean id="person" type="foo.Person" class="foo.Employee"  scope="page">
```

Generated servlet

```
foo.Person person = null;
// code to get the person attribute
if (person == null){
person = new foo.Employee();
...
```

Now the reference type is the abstract Person and the object type is the concrete Employee.

Type can be a class type, abstract type, or an interface—anything that you can use as a declared reference type for the class type of the bean object. You can't violate Java typing rules, of course. If the *class* type can't be assigned to the *reference* type, you're screwed. So that means the *class* must be a subclass or concrete implementation of the *type.*

Using *type* without *class*

What happens if we declare a *type*, but not a *class*? Does it matter if the type is abstract or concrete?

no class, just type

JSP

```
<jsp:useBean id="person" type="foo.Person" scope="page"/>
```

Result if the person attribute already exists in "page" scope

It works perfectly.

Result if the person attribute does NOT exist in "page" scope

WON'T WORK!!

```
java.lang.InstantiationException: bean person not found within scope
```

If type is used without class, the bean must already exist.

If class is used (with or without type) the class must NOT be abstract, and must have a public no-arg constructor.

Q: In your example, "foo.Person" is an abstract type, so of COURSE it can't be instantiated. What if you change the type to "foo.Employee"? Will it use the type for both the reference AND the object type?

A: NO! It never works. If the Container discovers that the bean doesn't exist, and it sees only a type attribute without a class, it knows that you've given it only HALF of what it needs—the *reference* type but not the *object* type. In other words, *you haven't told it what to make a new instance of!*

There is no fallback rule that says, "If you can't find the object, go ahead and use the type for BOTH the reference and the object." No, that is NOT how it works.

Bottom line: if you use type without class, you better make CERTAIN that the bean is already stored as an attribute, at the *scope* and with the *id* you put in the tag.

The scope attribute defaults to "page"

If you don't specify a scope in either the <jsp:useBean> or <jsp:getProperty> tags, the Container uses the default of "page".

This

```
<jsp:useBean id="person" class="foo.Employee" scope="page"/>
```

Is the same as *this*

```
<jsp:useBean id="person" class="foo.Employee"/>
```

Don't confuse type with class!

Check out this code:

```
<jsp:useBean id="person" type="foo.Employee" class="foo.Person"/>
```

Be prepared to recognize that this will NEVER work! You'll get a big fat:

```
org.apache.jasper.JasperException: Unable to compile class for JSP
foo.Person is abstract; cannot be instantiated
          Person = new foo.Person();
```

Be SURE that you remember:

type == *reference* type
class == *object* type

Or to put it another way:

type is what you DECLARE (can be abstract)
***class* is what you INSTANTIATE (must be concrete)**
type x = new *class*()

Now, you're probably thinking, "Well DUH—class is always a class while type doesn't have to be—type can be an interface. So of COURSE they used "class" to represent things that must ALWAYS be a class, and "type" for things that can be interfaces as well." And you'd be right. But you're also thinking, "Of course, not EVERYTHING in the spec has the most intuitive and obvious name, so I better be sure." Sometimes (like security <auth-constraint>), the name of a thing is the opposite of what it actually is. But in this case, class is class, and type is... type.

BE the Container

Look at this standard action:

```
<jsp:useBean id="person" type="foo.Employee" >
   <jsp:setProperty name="person" property="name" value="Fred" />
</jsp:useBean >
Name is: <jsp:getProperty name="person"  property="name" />
```

abstract class

Person
String getName() void setName(String)

Employee
int getEmpID() void setEmpID(int)

concrete class

(Both classes are in package "foo".)

Now imagine that a servlet does some work and then forwards the request to the JSP that has the code above.
Figure out what the JSP code above would do for each of the three different servlet code examples. (The answers are at the end of the chapter.)

1. What happens if the servlet code looks like:

```
foo.Person p = new foo.Employee();
p.setName("Evan");
request.setAttribute("person", p);
```

2. What happens if the servlet code looks like:

```
foo.Person p = new foo.Person();
p.setName("Evan");
request.setAttribute("person", p);
```

I just thought of something... suppose we aren't using a servlet controller, and the HTML form action goes straight to the JSP... is there a way I can use the request parameters to set a bean property, WITHOUT using scripting?

Going straight from the request to the JSP without going through a servlet...

Imagine this is our form:

```
<html><body>

<form action="TestBean.jsp">
  name: <input type="text" name="userName">
  ID#: <input type="text" name="userID">
  <input type="submit">
 </form>

</body></html>
```

The request goes STRAIGHT to the JSP.

We know we can do it with a combination of standard actions and scripting:

```
<jsp:useBean id="person" type="foo.Person" class="foo.Employee"/>
<% person.setName(request.getParameter("userName")); %>
```

We can even do it with scripting INSIDE a standard action:

```
<jsp:useBean id="person" type="foo.Person" class="foo.Employee">

<jsp:setProperty name="person" property="name"
              value="<%= request.getParameter("userName") %>" />
</jsp:useBean>
```

Yes, you ARE seeing an expression INSIDE the <jsp:setProperty> tag (which happens to be inside the body of a <jsp:useBean> tag)
And yes, it DOES look bad.

The param attribute to the rescue

It's so simple. You can send a request parameter straight into a bean, without scripting, using the *param* attribute.

The param attribute lets you set the value of a bean property to the value of a request parameter. JUST by naming the request parameter!

Inside TestBean.jsp

```
<jsp:useBean id="person" type="foo.Person" class="foo.Employee">
    <jsp:setProperty name="person" property="name" param="userName" />
</jsp:useBean>
```

```
<html><body>

<form action="TestBean.jsp">
  name: <input type="text" name="userName">
  ID#: <input type="text" name="userID">
  <input type="submit">
 </form>

</body></html>
```

The param value "userName" comes from the name attribute of the form's input field.

But wait! It gets even better...

And all you have to do is make sure your form *input field name* (which becomes the request parameter name) is the same as the *property name* in your bean. Then in the <jsp:setProperty> tag, you don't have to specify the *param* attribute. If you name the *property* but don't specify a *value* or *param*, you're telling the Container to get the value from a *request parameter* with a matching name.

If we change the HTML so that the input field name matches the property name:

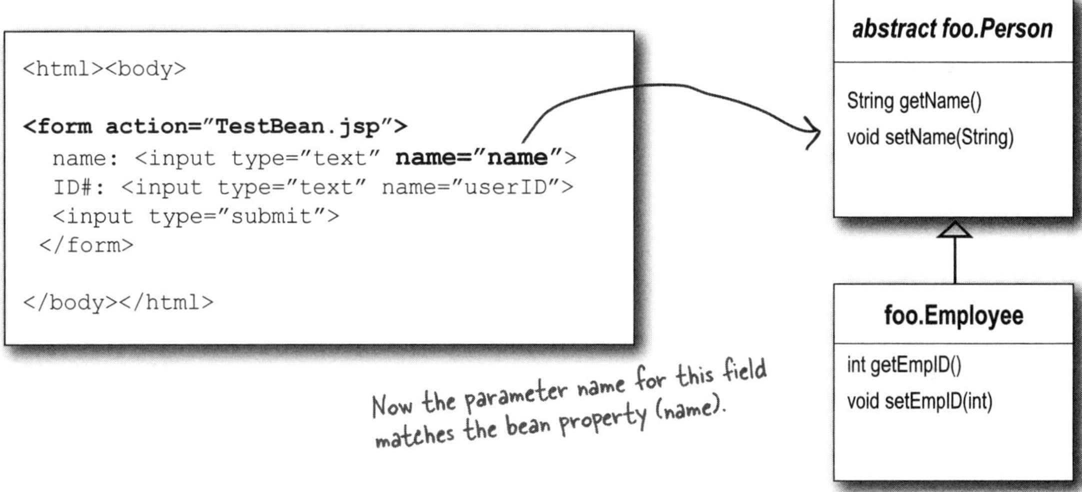

<html><body>
<form action="TestBean.jsp">
name: <input type="text" name="name">
ID#: <input type="text" name="userID">
<input type="submit">
</form>
</body></html>
abstract foo.Person
String getName()
void setName(String)
foo.Employee
int getEmpID()
void setEmpID(int)
Now the parameter name for this field matches the bean property (name).

We get to do THIS

```
<jsp:useBean id="person" type="foo.Person" class="foo.Employee">
    <jsp:setProperty name="person" property="name"  />
</jsp:useBean>
```

We didn't specify ANY value!

If the request parameter name matches the bean property name, you don't need to specify a value in the <jsp:setProperty> tag for that property.

If you can stand it, it gets even BETTER...

Watch what happens if you make ALL the request parameter names match the bean property names. The *person* bean (which is an instance of foo. Employee) actually has two properties—name and empID.

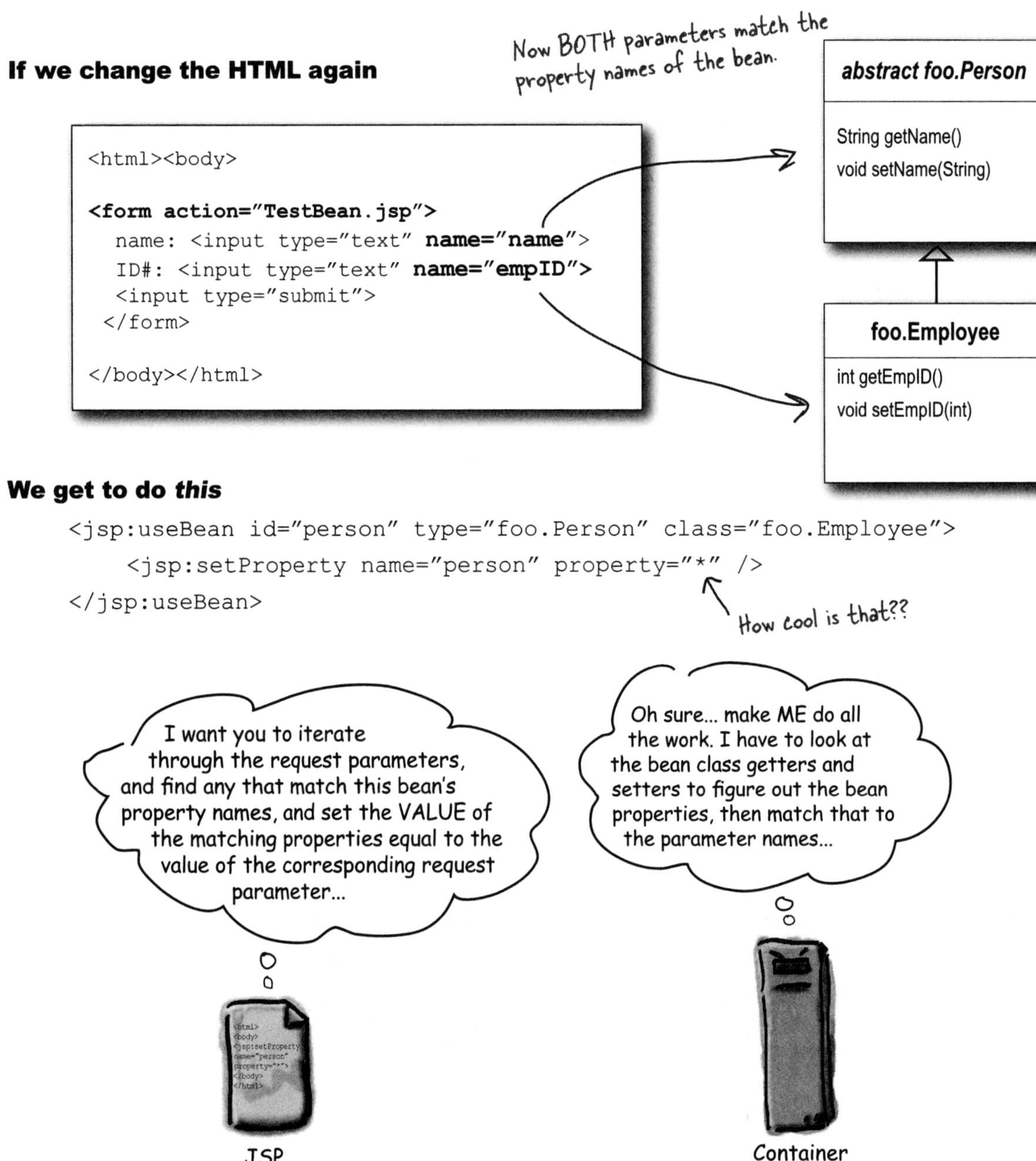
If we change the HTML again
Now BOTH parameters match the property names of the bean.
<html><body>
<form action="TestBean.jsp">
name: <input type="text" name="name">
ID#: <input type="text" name="empID">
<input type="submit">
</form>
</body></html>
abstract foo.Person
String getName()
void setName(String)
foo.Employee
int getEmpID()
void setEmpID(int)
We get to do this
<jsp:useBean id="person" type="foo.Person" class="foo.Employee">
<jsp:setProperty name="person" property="*" />
</jsp:useBean>
How cool is that??
I want you to iterate through the request parameters, and find any that match this bean's property names, and set the VALUE of the matching properties equal to the value of the corresponding request parameter...
Oh sure... make ME do all the work. I have to look at the bean class getters and setters to figure out the bean properties, then match that to the parameter names...
JSP
Container

Bean tags convert primitive properties automatically

If you're familiar with JavaBeans from any earlier lifetime, this is no surprise to you. JavaBean properties *can* be *anything*, but if they're Strings or primitives, all the coercing is done for you.

That's right—you don't have to do the parsing and conversion yourself

abstract foo.Person

String getName()
void setName(String)

foo.Employee

int getEmpID()
void setEmpID(int)

If we make the type *Employee* (instead of *Person*)

```
<html><body>

   <jsp:useBean id="person" type="foo.Employee" class="foo.Employee" >
       <jsp:setProperty name="person" property="*"  />
   </jsp:useBean>

   Person is: <jsp:getProperty name="person" property="name" />
   ID is: <jsp:getProperty name="person" property="empID" />

</body></html>
```

Now the generated servlet will say:
Employee person = new Employee(); instead of:
Person person = new Employee();

It all works

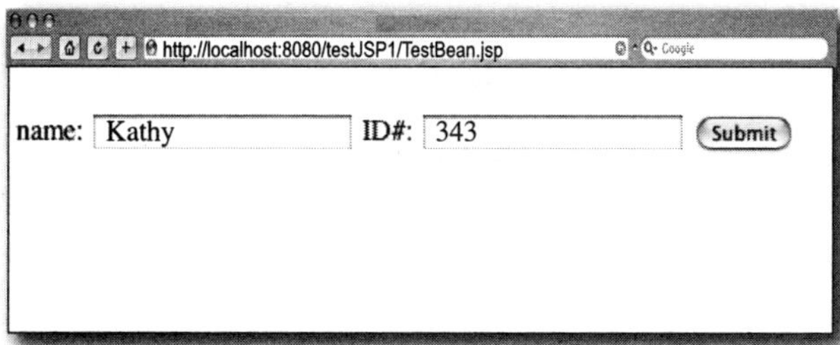

The <jsp:setProperty> action takes the String request parameter, converts it to an int, and passes that int to the bean's setter method for that property.

there are no Dumb Questions

Q: OK, I'm thinking that the Container code is doing some kind of Integer.parseInt("343"), so wouldn't you get a NumberFormatException if the user doesn't type in something that can be parsed to an int? Like, what if the user types "three" in the employee ID field?

A: Good catch. Yes, something will definitely go wrong if the request parameter for the empID property can't be parsed into an int. You need to validate the contents of that field, to make sure it contains only numeric characters. You could send the form data to a servlet first, instead of sending it straight to the JSP. But if you're committed to going from the form straight to the JSP, and you don't want scripting, just use JavaScript in the HTML form to check the field *before* sending the request. If you're not familiar with JavaScript (which of course has virtually NOTHING to do with Java), it's a simple scripting language that's processed on the client side. In other words, by the browser. A quick Google search on "JavaScript validate input field" should turn up some scripts you can use to stop users from entering, say, anything but numbers into an input field.

Q: If a bean property doesn't have to be a String or a primitive, then HOW can you *set* the property without scripting? The value attribute of the tag is always a String, right?

A: It is *possible* (but potentially a *lot* of extra work) to create a special class, called a custom property editor, that supports the bean. It takes your String value and figures out how to parse that into something that can be used to set a more complex type. This is part of the JavaBeans spec, though, not the JSP spec. Also, if the value attribute in the <jsp:setProperty> tag is an *expression* rather than a String literal, then IF that expression evaluates to an object that's compatible with bean property type, then it will probably work. If you pass in an expression that evaluates to a Dog, for example, the Person bean's setDog(Dog) method will be called. But think about it—this means the Dog object must already exist. Anyway, you're way better off NOT trying to construct new things in your JSP! Trying to get away with constructing and setting even marginally complex data types is gonna be tough without scripting. (And none of that is on the exam).

Watch it!

Automatic String-to-primitive conversion does NOT work if you use scripting!! It fails even if an expression is INSIDE the <jsp:setProperty> tag.

If you use the <jsp:setProperty> standard action tag with the property wildcard, OR just a property name without a value or param attribute (which means the property name matches the request parameter name), OR you use a param attribute to indicate the request parameter whose value should be assigned to the bean's property, OR you type a literal value, the automatic conversion from String to int works. Each of these examples converts automatically:

```
<jsp:setProperty name="person" property="*" />
<jsp:setProperty name="person" property="empID"  />
<jsp:setProperty name="person" property="empID" value="343" />
<jsp:setProperty name="person" property="empID" param="empID" />
```

These all work!

BUT... if you use scripting, the automatic conversion does NOT work:

This does NOT work!

```
<jsp:setProperty name="person" property="empID" value="<%= request.getParameter("empID")%>"/>
```

```
org.apache.jasper.JasperException: Unable to compile class for JSP
Generated servlet error:
setEmpID(int) in foo.Employee cannot be applied to (java.lang.String)
Person.setEmpID(request.getParameter("empID"));
```

Whew! I am just SO relieved at how much *easier* it is to use those tags instead of scripting. The benefits to me are staggeringly obvious.

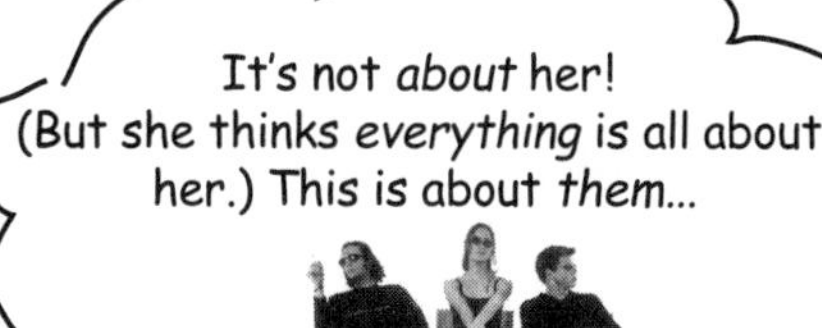

It's not *about* her! (But she thinks *everything* is all about her.) This is about *them*...

The bean standard action tags are more natural to a non-programmer.

Once again, the benefit of using tags over scripting is more about the web page designers than about *you* (the Java programmer). Although even Java programmers find that tags are easier to maintain than hard-coded Java scripting elements. With the bean-related tags, the designer needs only the basic identification info (attribute name, scope, and property name). True, they *do* have to know the fully-qualified class name, but as far as the web page designer knows—it's just a name with dots (.) in it. The web designer doesn't need any knowledge of what's really behind it, and they can think of beans as simply *records with fields.* You tell the designers the record (the class and the identifier) and the fields (the properties).

Still, the bean standard actions aren't as elegant as they could be.

And that's why this isn't the end of the story on scriptless pages. Read on...

But what if the property is something OTHER than a String or primitive?

We know how easy it is to print an *attribute* when the attribute itself is a String. Then we made an attribute that was a non-String object (a Person bean instance). But we didn't want to print the *attribute* (person)—we wanted to print a *property* of the attribute (in our example, the person's *name* and *empID*). That worked fine, because the standard actions can handle String *and* primitive properties. So, we know that standard actions can deal with an attribute of any type, as long as all the attribute's *properties* are Strings or primitives.

But what if they're not? What if the bean has a property that is *not* a String or primitive? What if the property is yet another Object type? An Object type *with properties of its own?*

What if what we really want is to print a property of that property?

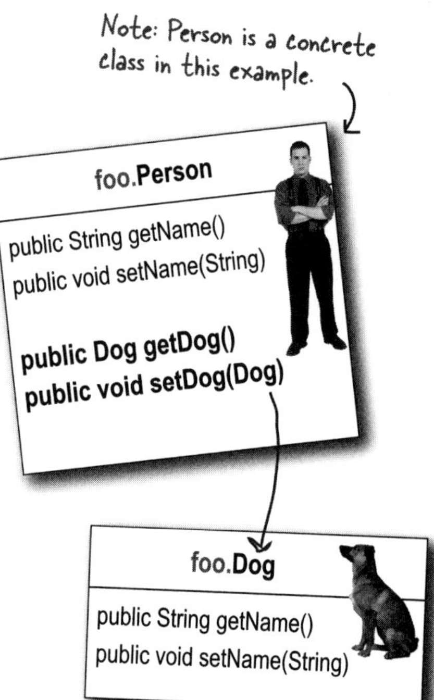

Person has a String "name" property.
Person has a Dog "dog" property.
Dog has a String "name" property.

What if we want to print the *name* of the Person's *dog*?

Servlet code

```
public void doPost(HttpServletRequest request, HttpServletResponse response)
                                        throws IOException, ServletException {

    foo.Person p = new foo.Person();
    p.setName("Evan");

    foo.Dog dog = new foo.Dog();
    dog.setName("Spike");
    p.setDog(dog);

    request.setAttribute("person", p);

    RequestDispatcher view = request.getRequestDispatcher("result.jsp");
    view.forward(request, response);
}
```

This time we make a Dog, give it a name, and call setDog() on the Person.

Now that the Person has a Dog value for its "dog" property, we set the Person (just the Person) as a request attribute.

Trying to display the property of the property

We know we can do it with scripting, but can we do it with the bean standard actions? What happens if we put "dog" as the property in the <jsp:getProperty> tag?

Without standard actions (using scripting)

This works perfectly... but we had to use scripting.

```
<html><body>

<%=  ((foo.Person) request.getAttribute("person")).getDog().getName() %>

</body></html>
```

With standard actions (no scripting)

```
<html><body>
<jsp:useBean id="person"  class="foo.Person" scope="request" />
Dog's name is: <jsp:getProperty name="person"  property="dog" />
</body></html>
```

But what's the value of "dog"?

What we WANT

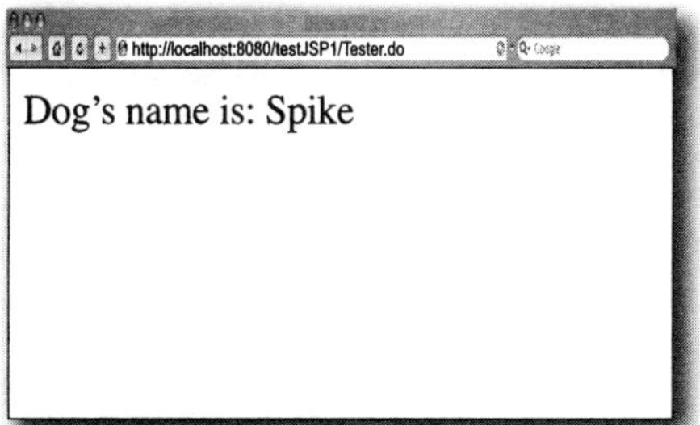

What we GOT

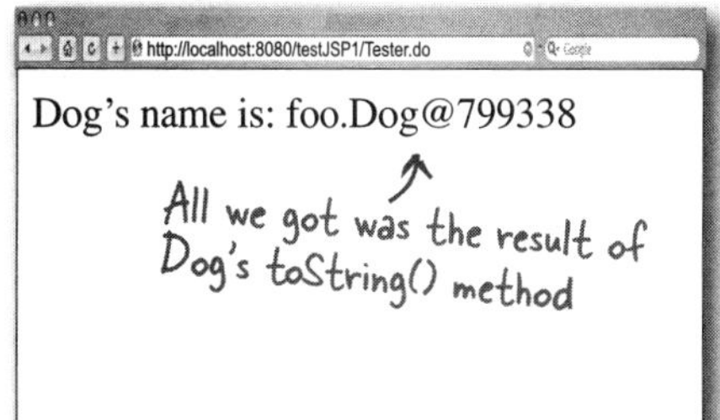

You can't say: property="dog.name"

There's no combination of the bean standard actions that'll work given the original servlet code, because the Dog is not an attribute! Dog is a property of the attribute, so you can display the Dog, but you can't navigate to the *name* property of the *Dog* property of the *Person* attribute.
The <jsp:getProperty> lets you access *only* the properties of the bean attribute. There's no capability for nested properties, where you want a property of a *property*, rather than a property of the *attribute*.

Expression Language (EL) saves the day!

Yes, just in time to save us, the JSP Expression Language (EL) was added to the JSP 2.0 spec, releasing us from the tyranny of scripting.

Look how beautifully simple our JSP is now...

JSP code *without* scripting, using EL

```
<html><body>

Dog's name is: ${person.dog.name}

</body></html>
```

This is it! We didn't even declare what person means... it just knows.

EL makes it easy to print nested properties... in other words, properties of properties!

This:

```
${person.dog.name}
```

Replaces *this*:

```
<%=  ((foo.Person) request.getAttribute("person")).getDog().getName()  %>
```

You don't need to know EVERYTHING about EL.

The exam doesn't expect you to be a complete EL being. Everything you might typically use, or be tested on, is covered in the next few pages. So, if you want to study the EL spec, knock yourself out. Just so you're clear that WE didn't tell you to do that.

Deconstructing the JSP Expression Language (EL)

The syntax and range of the language are dirt simple. The tricky part is that some of EL looks like Java, but behaves differently. You'll see when we get to the [] operator in a moment. So you'll find things that wouldn't work in Java but will work in EL, and vice-versa. Just don't try to map Java language/syntax rules onto EL, and you'll be fine. For the next few pages, think of EL as a way to access Java objects *without using Java.*

EL expressions are ALWAYS within curly braces, and prefixed with the dollar sign

```
${person.name}
```

The first named variable in the expression is either an implicit object or an attribute.

```
${firstThing.secondThing}
```

EL IMPLICIT OBJECT OR **ATTRIBUTE**

EL IMPLICIT OBJECT:

All these are map objects:

- **pageScope**
- **requestScope**
- **sessionScope**
- **applicationScope**
- **param**
- **paramValues**
- **header**
- **headerValues**
- **cookie**
- **initParam**

pageContext

Of all the implicit objects, only pageContext is not a map. It's an actual reference to the pageContext object! (And the pageContext is a JavaBean.)

Note: EL implicit objects are not the same as the implicit objects available to JSP scripting, except for pageContext.

ATTRIBUTE:

- **in page scope**
- **in request scope**
- **in session scope**
- **in application scope**

If the first thing in the EL expression is an attribute, it can be the name of an attribute stored in any of the four available scopes.

(Java reminder: a map is a collection that holds key/value pairs, like Hashtable and HashMap.)

Using the dot (.) operator to access properties and map values

The first variable is either an implicit object or an attribute, and the thing to the *right* of the dot is either a map *value* (if the first variable is a map) or a bean *property* if the first variable is an attribute that's a JavaBean.

① **If the expression has a variable followed by a dot, the left-hand variable MUST be a Map or a bean.**

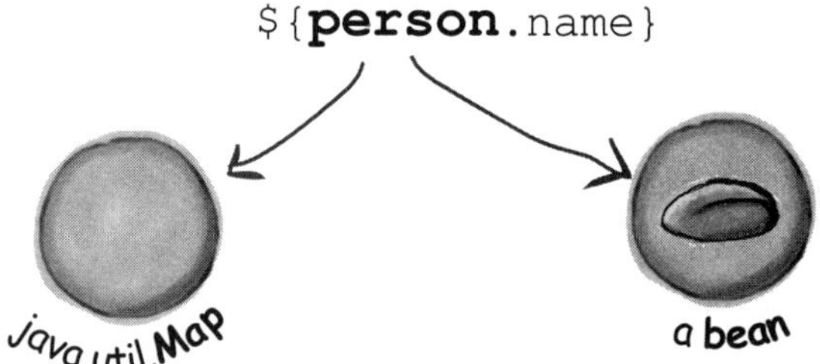

When the variable is on the left side of the dot, it's either a Map (something with keys) or a bean (something with properties).

This is true regardless of whether the variable is an implicit object or an attribute.

The pageContext implicit object is a bean—it has getter methods. All other implicit objects are Maps.

② **The thing to the *right* of the dot MUST be a Map key or a bean property.**

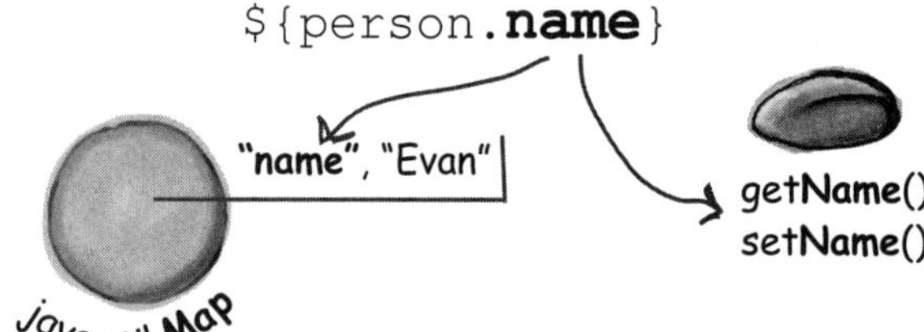

③ **And the thing on the *right* must follow normal Java naming rules for identifiers.**

* Must start with a letter, _, or $.
* After the first character, you can include numbers.
* Can't be a Java keyword.

The [] operator is like the dot only way better

The dot operator works only when the thing on the right is a bean property or map key for the thing on the left. That's it. But the [ ] operator is a lot more powerful and flexible...

This:

```
${person["name"]}
```

Is the same as *this*:

```
${person.name}
```

The simple dot operator version works because *person* is a bean, and *name* is a property of *person*.

But what if *person* is an *array*?

Or what if *person* is a *List*?

Or what if *name* is something that can't be expressed with the normal Java naming rules?

That doesn't look better. That just looks like more work, adding brackets and quotes...

The [ ] gives you more options...

When you use the dot operator, the thing on the left can be only a Map or a bean, and the thing on the right must follow Java naming rules for identifiers. But with the [ ], the thing on the left can also be a List or an array (of any type). That also means the thing on the right can be a number, or anything that resolves to a number, or an identifier that doesn't fit the Java naming rules. For example, you might have a Map key that's a String with dots in the name ("com.foo.trouble").

1. ***If* the expression has a variable followed by a bracket [ ], the left-hand variable can be a Map, a bean, a List, or an array.**

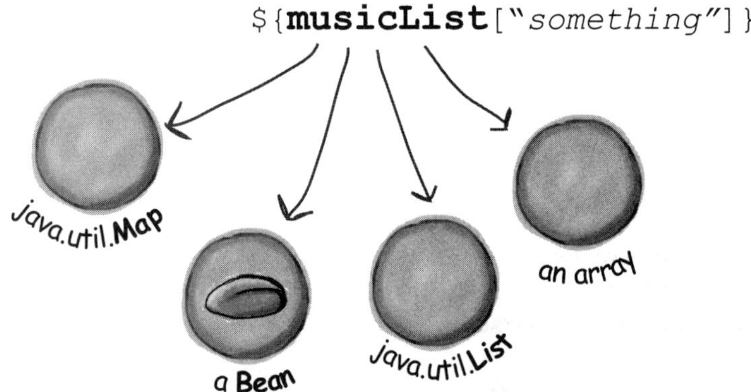

2. **If the thing *inside* the brackets is a String literal (i.e., in quotes), it can be a Map key or a bean property, or an index into a List or array.**

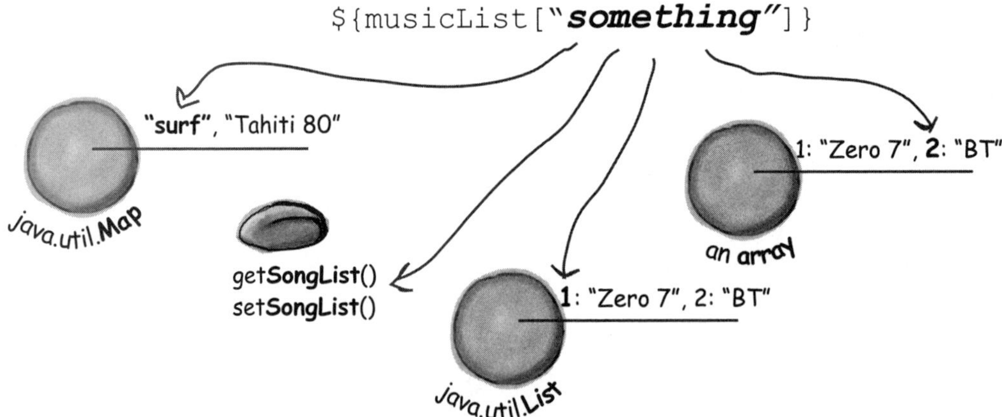

Using the [] operator with an array

In a Servlet

```
String[] favoriteMusic = {"Zero 7", "Tahiti 80", "BT", "Frou Frou"};
request.setAttribute("musicList", favoriteMusic);
```

In a JSP

```
Music is:  ${musicList}
```

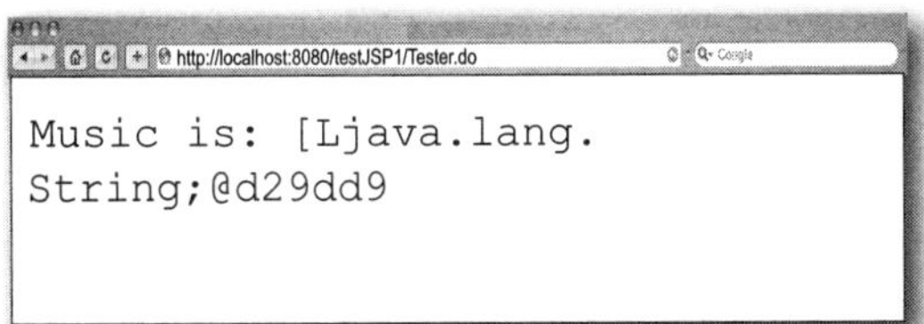

Makes sense... calls toString() on the array.

```
First song is: ${musicList[0]}
```

duh..

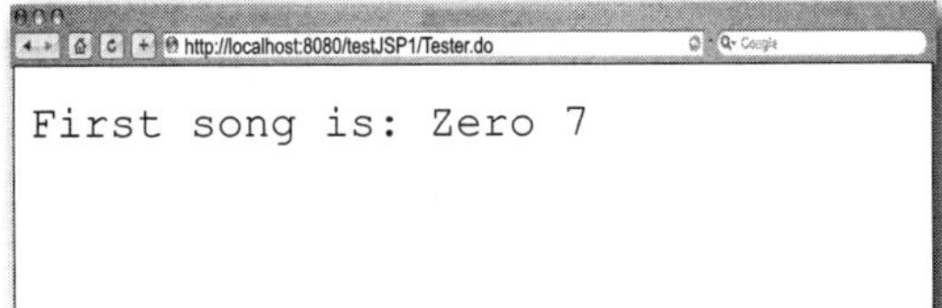


```
Second song is: ${musicList["1"]}
```

WTF???

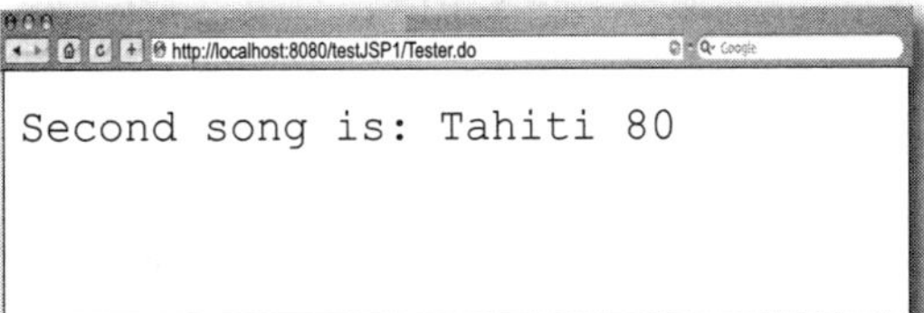

This is a joke, right? Or else there's more than punch in this drink... I could SWEAR that those are quotes around the array index, and that's just not right, dude...

A String index is coerced to an int for arrays and Lists

The EL for accessing an *array* is the same as the EL for accessing a *List*.

Remember folks, this is NOT Java. In EL, the [ ] operator is NOT the array access operator. No, it's just called the [ ] operator. (We swear, look it up in the spec—it has no name! Just the symbol [ ]. Like Prince, kind of.) If it DID have a name, it would be the array/List/Map/bean Property access operator.

In a Servlet

```
java.util.ArrayList favoriteFood = new java.util.ArrayList();
favoriteFood.add("chai ice cream");
favoriteFood.add("fajitas");
favoriteFood.add("thai pizza");
favoriteFood.add("anything in dark chocolate");
request.setAttribute("favoriteFood", favoriteFood);
```

In a JSP

```
Foods are: ${favoriteFood}
```

Obviously ArrayList has a nice overridden toString().

http://localhost:8080/testJSP1/Tester.do

Foods are: [chai ice cream, fajitas, thai pizza, anything in dark chocolate]

```
First food is ${favoriteFood[0]}
```

right

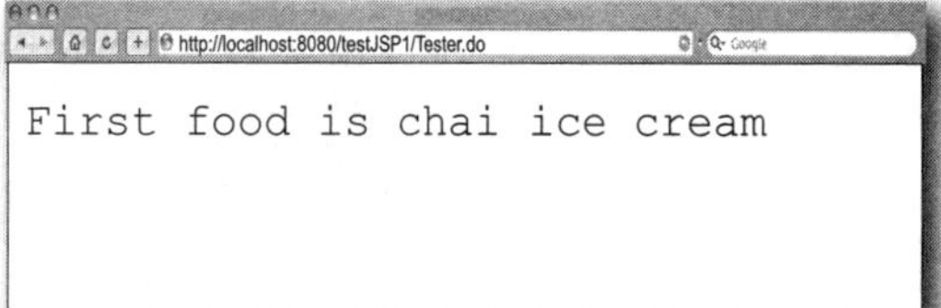


```
Second food is ${favoriteFood["1"]}
```

Very, very weird, but OK... if that's the way it works, I'll have to get used to it.

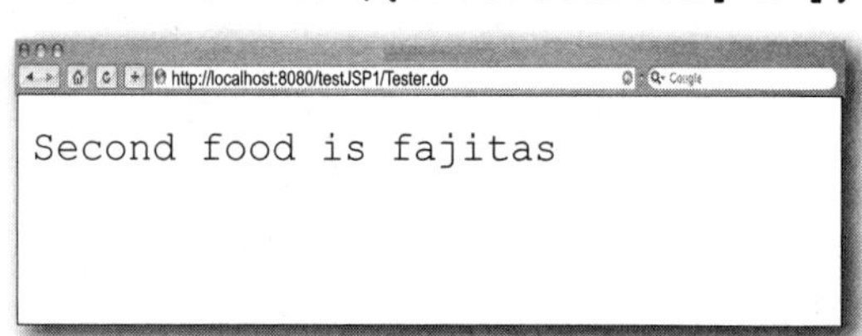

If the thing to the left of the bracket is an array or a List, and the index is a String literal, the index is coerced to an int.

This would NOT work:

`${favoriteFood["one"]}`

Because "one" can't be turned into an int. You'll get an error if the index can't be coerced.

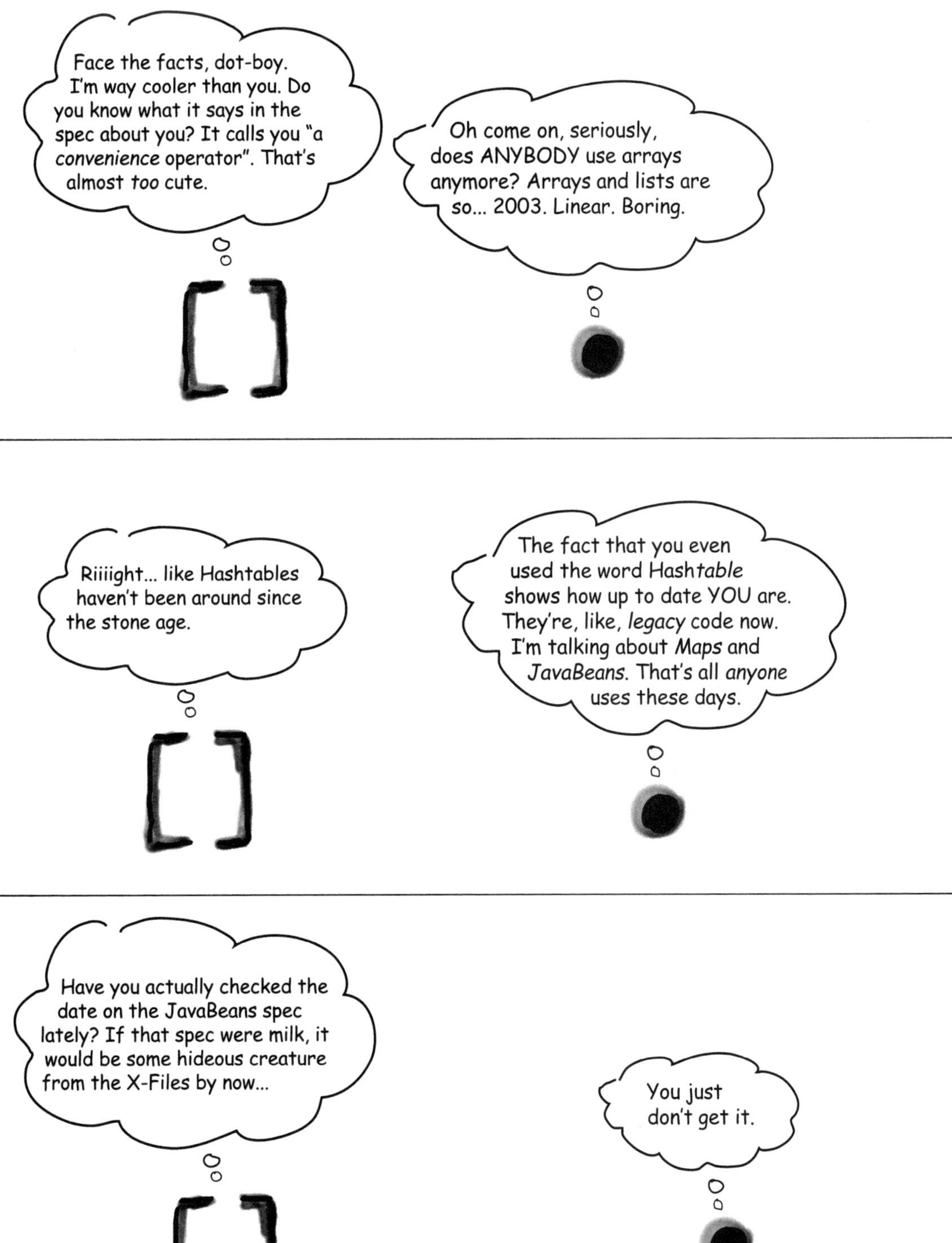
Face the facts, dot-boy. I'm way cooler than you. Do you know what it says in the spec about you? It calls you "a *convenience* operator". That's almost *too* cute.
Oh come on, seriously, does ANYBODY use arrays anymore? Arrays and lists are so... 2003. Linear. Boring.
Riiiight... like Hashtables haven't been around since the stone age.
The fact that you even used the word Hash*table* shows how up to date YOU are. They're, like, *legacy* code now. I'm talking about *Maps* and *JavaBeans*. That's all *anyone* uses these days.
Have you actually checked the date on the JavaBeans spec lately? If that spec were milk, it would be some hideous creature from the X-Files by now...
You just don't get it.

For beans and Maps you can use either operator

For JavaBeans and Maps, you can use either the [] operator or the convenient **dot** operator. Just think of map keys the same way you think of property names in a bean.

You ask for the key or property name, and you get back the value of the key or property.

In a Servlet

```
java.util.Map musicMap = new java.util.HashMap();
musicMap.put("Ambient", "Zero 7");
musicMap.put("Surf", "Tahiti 80");
musicMap.put("DJ", "BT");
musicMap.put("Indie", "Travis");
request.setAttribute("musicMap", musicMap);
```

Make a Map, put some String keys and objects in it, then make it a request attribute.

In a JSP

Ambient is: **${musicMap.Ambient}**

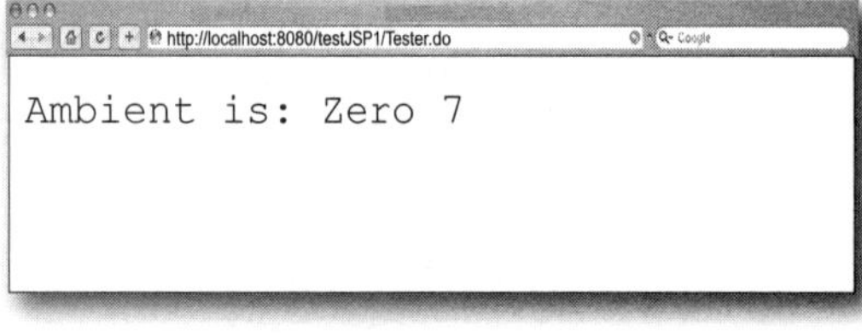

Both expressions use Ambient as the key into a Map (since musicMap is a Map!).

Ambient is: **${musicMap["Ambient"]}**

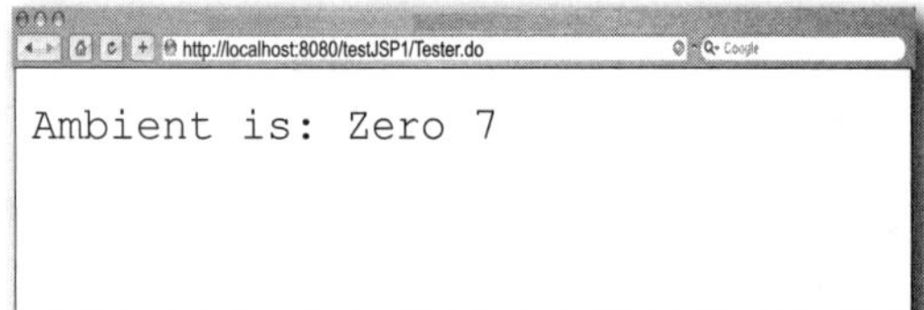

If it's NOT a String literal, it's evaluated

If there are no quotes inside the brackets, the Container evaluates what's inside the brackets by searching for an attribute bound under that name, and substitutes the value of the attribute. (If there is an implicit object with the same name, the implicit object will always be used.)

```
Music is: ${musicMap[Ambient]}
```

Without quotes around Ambient, this does NOT work!! Since there's no bound attribute named "Ambient", the result comes back null..

Find an attribute named "Ambient". Use the VALUE of that attribute as the key into the Map, or return null.

In a servlet

```
java.util.Map musicMap = new java.util.HashMap();
musicMap.put("Ambient", "Zero 7");
musicMap.put("Surf", "Tahiti 80");
musicMap.put("DJ", "BT");
musicMap.put("Indie", "Frou Frou");

request.setAttribute("musicMap", musicMap);

request.setAttribute("Genre", "Ambient");
```

This *DOES* work in a JSP

```
Music is ${musicMap[Genre]}  --evaluates to-->  Music is ${musicMap["Ambient"]}
```

because there IS a request attribute named "Genre" with a value of "Ambient", and "Ambient" is a key into musicMap.

This does *NOT* work in a JSP (given the servlet code)

```
Music is ${musicMap["Genre"]}  --doesn't change-->  Music is ${musicMap["Genre"]}
```

because there IS no key in musicMap named "Genre". With the quotes around it, the Container didn't try to evaluate it and just assumed it was a literal key name.

This is a valid EL expression, but it doesn't do what we wanted.

You can use nested expressions inside the brackets

It's expressions all the way down in EL. You nest expressions to any arbitrary level. In other words, you can put a complex expression inside a complex expression inside a... (it keeps going). And the expressions are evaluated from the inner most brackets out.

This part will seem completely intuitive to you, because it's no different than nesting Java code within parens. The tricky part is to watch out for quotes vs. *no* quotes.

In a servlet

```
java.util.Map musicMap = new java.util.HashMap();
musicMap.put("Ambient", "Zero 7");
musicMap.put("Surf", "Tahiti 80");
musicMap.put("DJ", "BT");
musicMap.put("Indie", "Frou Frou");
request.setAttribute("musicMap", musicMap);

String[] musicTypes = {"Ambient", "Surf", "DJ", "Indie"};
request.setAttribute("MusicType", musicTypes);
```

This DOES work in a JSP

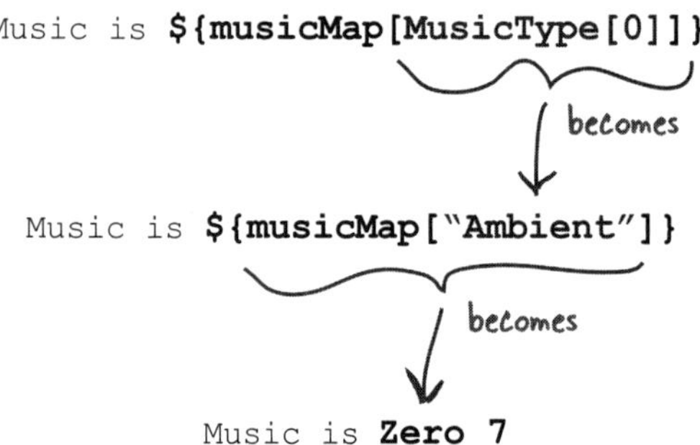

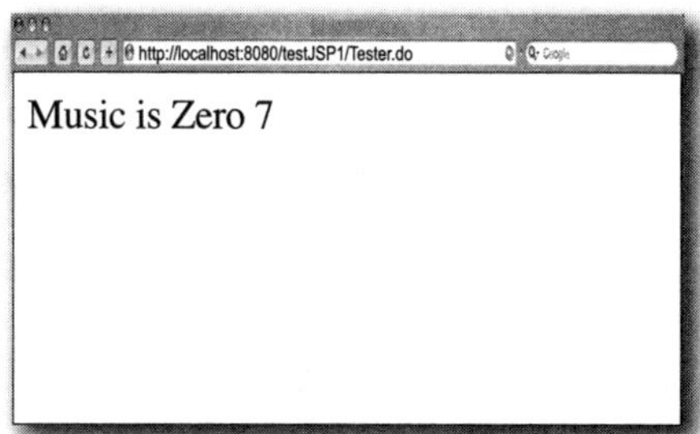

You can't do ${foo.1}

With beans and Maps, you can use the dot operator, but only if the thing you type after the dot is a legal Java identifer.

This

```
${musicMap.Ambient}
```

works

Is the same as *this*

```
${musicMap["Ambient"]}
```

works

But *this*

```
${musicList["1"]}
```

CANNOT be turned into *this*

```
${musicList.1}
```

NO! NO! NO!

If you wouldn't use it for a variable name in your Java code, DON'T put it after the dot.

Sharpen your pencil

What prints?

Given the servlet code below, figure out what would print (or if there'd be an error, just write, you know, "error"). Answers are at the bottom of the next page.

```
java.util.ArrayList nums = new java.util.ArrayList();
nums.add("1");
nums.add("2");
nums.add("3");
request.setAttribute("numbers", nums);
String[] favoriteMusic = {"Zero 7", "Tahiti 80", "BT", "Frou Frou"};
request.setAttribute("musicList", favoriteMusic);
```

1. `${musicList[numbers[0]]}`

2. `${musicList[numbers[0]+1]}` (We'll talk more about EL operators in a few pages.)

3. `${musicList[numbers["2"]]}`

4. `${musicList[numbers[numbers[1]]]}`

Code Magnets

Don't be surprised if you find something like this on the exam (except in the real exam it'll look... uglier).

Study the three classes on the page, and the servlet code on the opposite page, then construct the code magnets to make the EL that'll produce the response shown in the browser. (Turn the page for the answers, but not until you DO THIS, especially if you're going to take the exam.)

foo.Toy

```
package foo;
public class Toy {
  private String name;
  public void setName(String name) {
    this.name=name;
  }
  public String getName() {
    return name;
  }
}
```

foo.Person

```
package foo;
public class Person {
  private Dog dog;
  private String name;
  public void setDog(Dog dog) {
    this.dog=dog;
  }
  public Dog getDog() {
    return dog;
  }
  public void setName(String name) {
    this.name=name;
  }
  public String getName() {
    return name;
  }
}
```

foo.Dog

```
package foo;
public class Dog {
  private String name;
  private Toy[ ] toys;
  public void setName(String name) {
    this.name=name;
  }
  public String getName() {
    return name;
  }
  public void setToys(Toy[] toys) {
    this.toys=toys;
  }
  public Toy[ ] getToys() {
    return toys;
  }
}
```

Answers to Sharpen on previous page: 1) Tahiti 80 2) BT 3) Frou Frou 4) Frou Frou

Servlet code

```
foo.Person p = new foo.Person();
p.setName("Leelu");
foo.Dog d = new foo.Dog();
d.setName("Clyde");
foo.Toy t1 = new foo.Toy();
t1.setName("stick");
foo.Toy t2 = new foo.Toy();
t2.setName("neighbor's cat");
foo.Toy t3 = new foo.Toy();
t3.setName("Barbie™ doll head");
d.setToys(new foo.Toy[]{t1, t2, t3});
p.setDog(d);
request.setAttribute("person", p);
```

Compose the EL for this output:

http://localhost:8080/testJSP1/Tester.do

```
Leelu's dog Clyde's toys are: stick,
neighbor's cat, and a Barbie™ doll
head
```

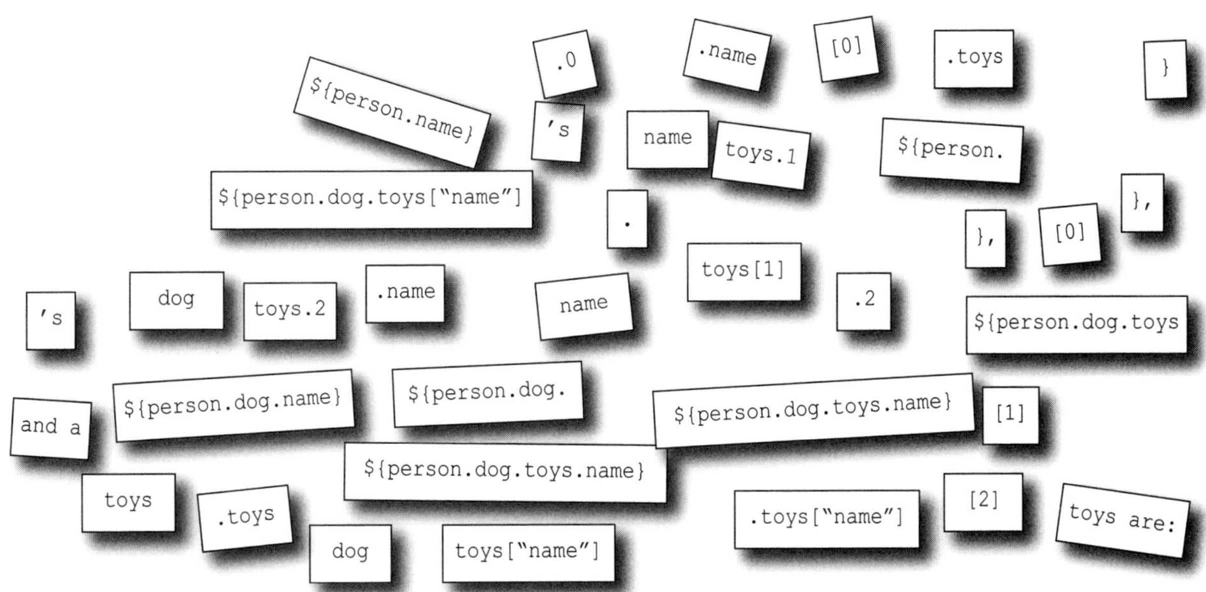

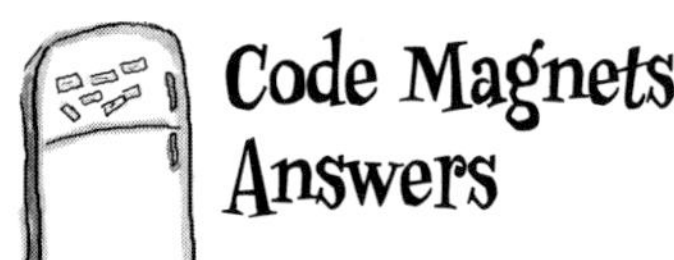

Code Magnets Answers

This is not the ONLY way to produce the output, but it's the only way using this set of magnets. Bonus exercise: write the EL expressions a little differently (forget the magnets), but print the same result.

Servlet code

```
foo.Person p = new foo.Employee();
p.setName("Leelu");
foo.Dog d = new foo.Dog();
d.setName("Clyde");
foo.Toy t1 = new foo.Toy();
t1.setName("stick");
foo.Toy t2 = new foo.Toy();
t2.setName("neighbor's cat");
foo.Toy t3 = new foo.Toy();
t3.setName("Barbie™ doll head");
d.setToys(new foo.Toy[]{t1, t2, t3});
p.setDog(d);
request.setAttribute("person", p);
```

Compose the EL for this output:

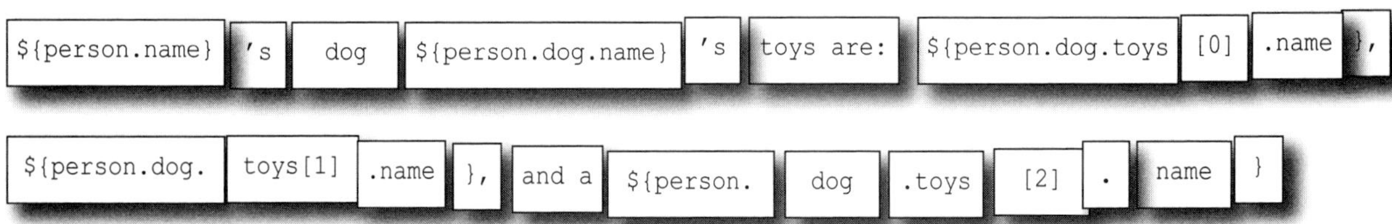


```
${person.name}'s dog ${person.dog.name}'s toys are: ${person.dog.toys[0].
name}, ${person.dog.toys[1].name}, and a ${person.dog.toys[2].name}
```

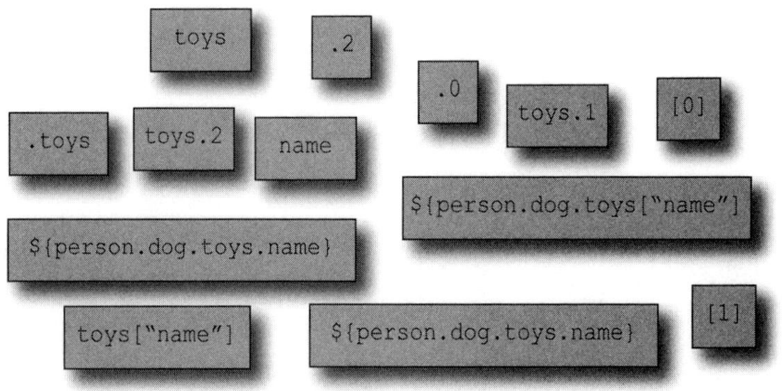

Remember that my HTML form action goes straight to the JSP... is there a way I can use the request parameters just using EL?

The EL implicit objects

Remember, EL has some implicit objects. But these are not the same as the JSP implicit objects (except for one, pageContext). Here's a quick list; we'll look at some of them in more detail on the next few pages. You'll notice that all but one (pageContext again), are simple Maps—name/value pairs.

pageScope
requestScope
sessionScope
applicationScope

A Map of the scope attributes.

param
paramValues

Maps of the request parameters.

header
headerValues

Maps of the request headers.

cookie — Ooohhhh... this is a tough one... could it be a Map of... cookies?

initParam — A Map of the context init parameters (NOT servlet init parameters!)

pageContext — The only thing that is NOT a Map. This is the real deal—an actual reference to the pageContext object, which you can think of as a bean. Look in the API for the PageContext getter methods.

Request parameters in EL

Piece of cake. The param implicit object is fine when you know you have only one parameter for that particular parameter name. Use paramValues when you might have more than one parameter value for a given parameter name.

In the HTML form

```
<form action="TestBean.jsp">
  Name: <input type="text" name="name">
  ID#: <input type="text" name="empID">

  First food: <input type="text" name="food">
  Second food: <input type="text" name="food">

  <input type="submit">
</form>
```

The "name" and "empID" will each have a single value. But the "food" parameter could have two values, if the user fills in both fields before hitting the submit button...

Remember, param is just a Map of parameter names and values. The things to the right of the dot come from the names specified in the input fields of the form.

In the JSP

```
Request param name is: ${param.name} <br>

Request param empID is: ${param.empID} <br>

Request param food is: ${param.food} <br>

First food request param: ${paramValues.food[0]} <br>
Second food request param: ${paramValues.food[1]} <br>

Request param name: ${paramValues.name[0]}
```

Even though there might be multiple values for the "food" parameter, you can still use the single param implicit object, but you'll get only the first value.

In the client's browser (client fills in the form and hits the submit button)

The response

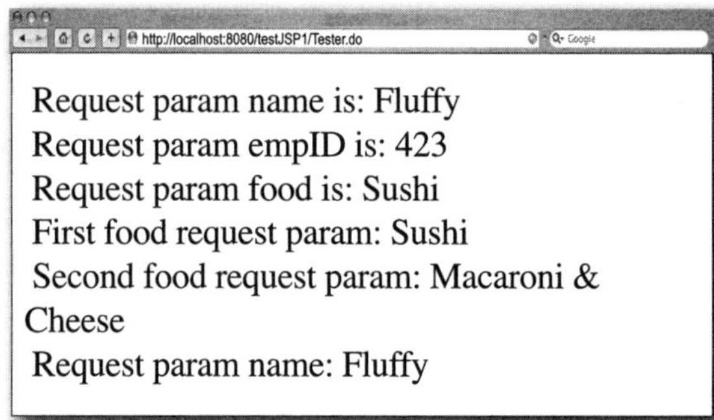

http://localhost:8080/testJSP1/Tester.do
Request param name is: Fluffy
Request param empID is: 423
Request param food is: Sushi
First food request param: Sushi
Second food request param: Macaroni & Cheese
Request param name: Fluffy

What if you want more information from the request?

What if you want, say, the server host information that comes with the "host" header in the request? If you look in the HttpServletRequest API, you can see a getHeader(String) method. We know that if we pass "host" to the getHeader() method, we'll get back something like: "localhost:8080" (because that's where the web server is).

Getting the "host" header

We know we can do it with *scripting*

```
Host is: <%= request.getHeader("host") %>
```

But with EL, we've got the header implicit object

```
Host is: ${header["host"]}

Host is: ${header.host}
```

The header implicit object keeps a Map of all the headers. Use either access operator to pass in the header name and the value of that header will print. (Note: there's also a headerValues implicit object for headers with multiple values. It works just like paramValues.)

Getting the HTTP request method

Uh-oh. This is a little trickier... there's a method in the HttpServletRequest API for getMethod(), that returns GET, POST, etc. But how do I get it using EL?

We know we can do it with *scripting*

```
Method is: <%= request.getMethod() %>
```

But with EL, *this* will NOT work

```
Method is: ${request.method}
```

NO! NO! NO! There IS no implicit request object!

And *this* will NOT work

```
Method is: ${requestScope.method}
```

NO! NO! NO! There IS an implicit requestScope, but it's NOT the request object itself.

Can you figure out how to do it?
Hint: look at the other implicit objects.

The requestScope is NOT the request object

The implicit requestScope is just a Map of the request scope attributes, not the request object itself! What you want (the HTTP method) is a *property* of the request object, not an attribute at request scope. In other words, you want something that comes from calling a getter method on the request object (if we treat the request object like a bean).

But there is no request implicit object, only requestScope! What to do?

You need something else...

Use requestScope to get request ATTRIBUTES, not request PROPERTIES. For request properties, you need to go through pageContext.

Use pageContext to get to everything else...

```
Method is: ${pageContext.request.method}
```

***pageContext* has a *request* property**
***request* has a *method* property**

Don't confuse the Map *scope* objects with the objects to which the attributes are bound.

It's so easy to think that, say, applicationScope is a reference to ServletContext, since that's where application-scoped attributes are bound. But just as with requestScope and the request object, the scope Map for application-scoped attributes is just that—a Map of attributes, and nothing more. You can't treat it like a Servlet Context, so don't expect to get ServletContext properties back from the applicationScope implicit object!

If EL looks through all the scopes anyway, why would I ever use one of the scope implicit objects? The only thing I can think of is a naming conflict, but I wonder if there might be another reason...

Scope implicit objects can save you

If all you need is to print the name of a *person*, and you really don't care what scope the *person* is in (or, you do care, but you know there's only *one* person out of all four scopes), you just use:

```
${person.name}
```

Or, if you're worried about a potential naming conflict, you can be explicit about which person you want:

```
${requestScope.person.name}
```

But is there another reason you might have to preface the attribute with the implicit scope object? Other than to control...scoping?

Think about this scenario: if you have a name that's not in quotes in brackets [ ], that means it MUST adhere to Java naming rules, right? Here, we're OK, because person is a perfectly legal Java variable name. But that's because somewhere, someone said,

```
request.setAttribute("person", p);
```

But an attribute name is a String!

Strings don't follow Java variable name rules!

That means someone *could* say:

```
request.setAttribute("foo.person", p);
```

And then you'd be in trouble, because THIS won't work:

NO! This is certainly legal, but the Container just thinks that "foo" is an attribute somewhere, with a "person" property. But the Container never finds a "foo" attribute.

```
${foo.person.name}
```

But you'll be so thankful for scope objects, because using a scope object lets you switch to the [ ] operator, that can take String names that don't conform to Java naming rules.

Perfect! Using the requestScope object gives us a way to put the attribute name in quotes.

```
${requestScope["foo.person"].name}
```

Getting Cookies and init params

We've looked at all the implicit objects except cookies and init params, so here we are. And yes, any of the implicit objects can show up on the exam.

Printing the value of the "userName" Cookie

This is kind of a pain, because the request object does NOT have a getCookie(cookieName) method! We have to get the whole Cookie array and iterate through it ourselves.

We know we can do it with *scripting*

```
<% Cookie[] cookies = request.getCookies();

for (int i = 0; i < cookies.length; i++) {
   if ((cookies[i].getName()).equals("userName")) {
      out.println(cookies[i].getValue());
   }
} %>
```

But with EL, we've got the Cookie implicit object

```
${cookie.userName.value}
```

WAY easier. Just give it the name, and the value comes back from the Map of Cookie names/values.

Printing the value of a context init parameter

We have to configure the parameter in the DD

Remember. this is how you configure context (app-wide) parameters. These are NOT the same as servlet init params.

```
<context-param>
    <param-name>mainEmail</param-name>
    <param-value>likewecare@wickedlysmart.com</param-value>
 </context-param>
```

We know we can do it with *scripting*

```
email is: <%= application.getInitParameter("mainEmail") %>
```

And with EL, it's even easier

```
email is: ${initParam.mainEmail}
```

The EL initParam is NOT for params configured using <init-param> !

Here's what's confusing: servlet init params are configured using <init-param> while context params use <context-param> but the EL implicit "initParam" is for **context** *params! Had they consulted us, we would have suggested that the spec designers might consider naming this variable, oh, "contextParam"... but once again, they forgot to ask us.*

EL is wonderful... but sometimes I need *functionality*, not just attribute or property values. If only there were a way to have an EL expression call a Java method that returns a value...then I would be happy.

She doesn't know about EL functions

When you need a little extra help from, say, a Java method, but you don't want scripting, you can use an EL function. It's an easy way to write a simple EL expression that calls a static method in a plain old Java class that you write. Whatever the method returns is used in the expression. It does take a tiny bit more work to configure things, but functions give you a lot more...*functionality*.

Imagine you want your JSP to roll dice

You've decided it would be awesome to have a web-based dice-rolling service. That way, instead of hunting around behind desks and in the sofa cushions for *real* dice, a user could just go to your web page, click on the virtual dice, and voila! They roll! (Of course, you have no idea that a Google search will probably bring up, oh, about 4,420 sites that do this.)

1 Write a Java class with a public static method.

This is just a plain old Java class. The method MUST be public and static, and it can have arguments. It should (but isn't required to) have a non-void return type. After all, the whole point is to call this from a JSP and get something back that you can use as part of the expression or to print out.

Put the class file in the /WEB-INF/classes directory structure (matching the appropriate package directory structure, just like you would with any other class).

2 Write a Tag Library Descriptor (TLD) file.

For an EL function, the TLD provides a mapping between the Java class that *defines* the function and the JSP that *calls* the function. That way, the function name and the actual method name can be different. You might be stuck with a class with a really stupid method name, for example, and maybe you want to provide a more obvious or intuitive name to page designers using EL. No problem—the TLD says, "This is the Java class, this is the method *signature* for the function (including return type) and this is the *name* we'll use in EL expressions". In other words, the *name* used in EL doesn't have to be the same as the actual method name, and the TLD is where you map that.

Put the TLD file inside the /WEB-INF directory. Name it with a .tld extension. (There are other places the TLD can go; we'll talk about that in the next two chapters.)

3 Put a taglib directive in your JSP.

The taglib directive tells the Container, "I'm going to use this TLD, and in the JSP, when I want to use a function from this TLD, I'm going to prefix it with this name..." In other words, it lets you define the namespace. You can use functions from more than one TLD, and even if the functions have the same name, that's OK. The taglib directive is kind of like giving all your functions fully-qualified names. You invoke the function by giving both the function name AND the TLD prefix. The prefix can be anything you like.

4 Use EL to invoke the function.

This is the easy part. You just call the function from an expression using ${prefix:name()}.

The function class, the TLD, and the JSP

The class with the function

```
package foo;

public class DiceRoller {
   public static int rollDice() {
      return (int) ((Math.random() * 6) + 1);
   }
}
```

The function method MUST be public AND static.

The Tag Library Descriptor (TLD) file

```
<?xml version="1.0" encoding="ISO-8859-1" ?>

<taglib xmlns="http://java.sun.com/xml/ns/j2ee"
xmlns:xsi="http://www.w3.org/2001/XMLSchema-instance"
xsi:schemaLocation="http://java.sun.com/xml/ns/j2ee/web-
jsptaglibrary_2_0.xsd" version="2.0">

<tlib-version>1.2</tlib-version>
<uri>DiceFunctions</uri>
  <function>
     <name>rollIt</name>
     <function-class>foo.DiceRoller</function-class>
     <function-signature>
          int rollDice()
     </function-signature>
  </function>

</taglib>
```

Do NOT worry about all the stuff inside the <taglib ...> tag. We'll talk more about TLDs in the next two chapters.

The uri in the taglib directive tells the Container the name of the TLD (which does NOT have to be the name of the FILE!), which the Container needs so it knows which method to call when the JSP invokes the EL function.

The JSP

```
<%@ taglib prefix="mine" uri="DiceFunctions"%>

<html><body>

${mine:rollIt()}

</body></html>
```

The prefix "mine" is just the nickname we'll use inside THIS page, so that we can tell one TLD from another (in case you DO have more than one).

The function name rollIt() comes from the <name> in the TLD, not from anything in the actual Java class.

Deploying an app with static functions

The only thing that's new here is the "myFunctions.tld" file. It has to be somewhere within WEB-INF or one of its subdirectories (unless it's deployed in a JAR file, but we'll talk about that later in the book). Here, because this app is so simple, we have both the DD (web.xml) and the TLD (myFunctions.tld) at the top level of WEB-INF, but you *could* organize them into subdirectories.

The key point is that the class with the static function MUST be available to the app, so... for now, you know that putting it inside WEB-INF/classes will work. And remember that in the *taglib* directive in the JSP, we specified a URI that matches the URI declared in the TLD. For now, think of the URI as simply ***whatever you decided to name the TLD.*** It's just a name. In the next chapter on using custom tags, we'll go into all the details about TLDs and URIs.

```
<%@ taglib prefix="mine" uri="DiceFunctions"%>
```

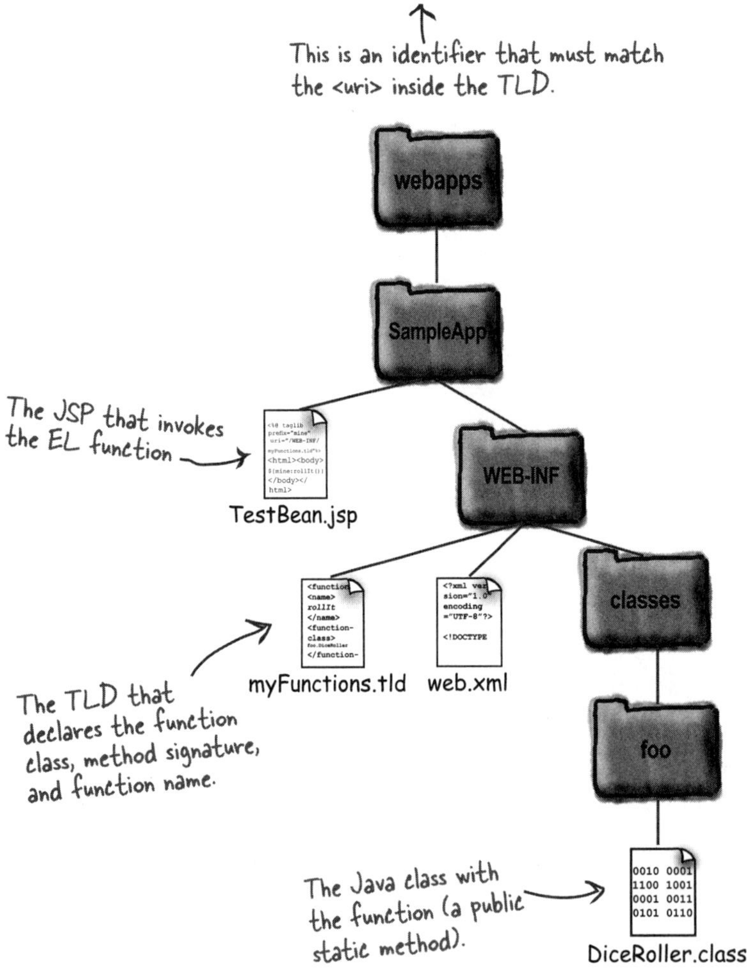

This is an identifier that must match the <uri> inside the TLD.

webapps

SampleApp

The JSP that invokes the EL function

TestBean.jsp

WEB-INF

The TLD that declares the function class, method signature, and function name.

myFunctions.tld

web.xml

classes

foo

The Java class with the function (a public static method).

DiceRoller.class

The class with the function (the public static method) must be available to the web app just like servlet, bean, and listener classes. That means somewhere in WEB-INF/classes...

Put the TLD file somewhere under WEB-INF, and make sure the taglib directive in the JSP includes a uri attribute that matches the <uri> element in the TLD.

there are no Dumb Questions

Q: A regular scriptlet expression MUST return something. If you say <%= foo.getFoo() %>, getFoo() must NOT have a void return type. (At least that's what you said earlier.) So I'm thinking it's the same with EL functions?

A: No! It's NOT the same with EL functions, although just about everybody finds that... surprising. Think about this—if you're calling an EL function that doesn't return anything, then you're calling it *just for its side effects!* Given that part of the goal for EL is to reduce the amount of logic in a JSP (a JSP supposed to be the VIEW!), invoking an EL function just for its side effects doesn't sound like a good idea.

Q: How did the Container find the TLD? The URI doesn't match the path or file name of the TLD. Was this a miracle?

A: Just the question we were hoping someone would ask. Yes, you're right—we never *did* tell the Container exactly where to find the real TLD file. When the app is deployed, the Container searches through WEB-INF and its subdirectories (or in JAR files within WEB-INF/lib) looking for .tld files. When it finds one, it reads the URI and creates a map that says, "The TLD with *this* URI is actually *this* file at *this* location..." There's a little more to the story that we'll cover in the next chapter.

Q: Can an EL function have arguments?

A: Definitely. Just remember in the TLD to specify the fully-qualified class name (unless it's a primitive) for each argument. A function that takes a Map would be:

```
<function-signature>
    int rollDice(java.util.Map)
</function-signature>
```

Watch it!

The METHOD name is not the same as the FUNCTION name!

Memorize the relationships between the class, the TLD, and the JSP. Most importantly, remember that the METHOD name does NOT have to match the FUNCTION name. What you use in EL to invoke the function must match the <name> element in the <function> declaration in the TLD. The element for <function-signature> is there to tell the Container which method to call when the JSP uses the <name>.

And the only place the class name appears (besides the class declaration itself) is in the <function-class> element.

Oh, and while we're here... did you notice that everything in the <function> tag has the word <function> in it EXCEPT for the <name> tag? So, don't be fooled by this:

```
<function>
   <function-name>rollIt</function-name>
   <function-class>
       foo.DiceRoller</function-class>
   <function-signature>
       int rollDice()
   </function-signature>
</function>
```

NO!!

The correct tag for the function name is <name>!

```
<function>
   <name>rollIt</name>
   <function-class>
       foo.DiceRoller</function-class>
   <function-signature>
       int rollDice()
   </function-signature>
</function>
```

Good!

And a few other EL operators...

You probably won't (and *shouldn't*) do calculations and logic from EL. Remember, a JSP is the View, and the View's job is to render the response, not to make Big Important Decisions or do Big Processing. If you need real functionality, that's normally the job of the Controller and Model. For lesser functionality, you've got custom tags (including the JSTL tags) and EL functions.

But... for little things, sometimes a little arithmetic or a simple boolean test might come in handy. So, with that perspective, here's a look at the most useful EL artithmetic, relational, and logical operators.

Arithmetic (5)

Addition:	**+**
Subtraction:	**-**
Multiplication:	*****
Division:	**/** *and* **div**
Remainder:	**%** *and* **mod**

By the way... you CAN divide by zero in EL—you get INFINITY, not an error.

But you CANNOT use the Remainder operator against a zero—you'll get an exception.

Logical (3)

AND:	**&&** *and* **and**
OR:	**||** *and* **or**
NOT:	**!** *and* **not**

Relational (6)

Equals:	**==** *and* **eq**
Not equals:	**!=** *and* **ne**
Less than:	**<** *and* **lt**
Greater than:	**>** *and* **gt**
Less than or equal to:	**<=** *and* **le**
Greater than or equal to:	**>=** *and* **ge**

Watch it!

Don't use EL reserved words as identifiers!

You can already see 11 of them on this page—the alternate "words" for the relational, logical and some arithmetic operators. But there are a few more:

true	*a boolean literal*
false	*the OTHER boolean literal*
null	*It means... null*
instanceof	*(this is reserved for "the future")*
empty	*an operator to see if something is null or empty (eg. ${empty A}) returns true if A is null or empty (you'll see this in action a little later in the chapter)*

Sharpen your pencil

Look at the servlet code, then figure out what prints next to each EL expression. You'll have to guess in a few places, since we haven't covered every possible rule. This exercise will help you figure out how EL behaves. Hint: EL is flexible and forgiving. Another hint: the actual nine answers are printed at the bottom of this page upside down, but they are NOT in any order. But if you really need help, at least you'll have the nine answers, and you can use elimination to figure out where they all go.

Given this servlet code:

```
String num = "2";
request.setAttribute("num", num);
Integer i = new Integer(3);
request.setAttribute("integer", i);
java.util.ArrayList list = new java.util.ArrayList();
list.add("true");
list.add("false");
list.add("2");
list.add("10");
request.setAttribute("list", list);
```

What prints for each of these?

Assume that the Dog bean class and rollIt() function are both available.

```
__________  ${num > 3}

__________  ${integer le 12}

__________  ${requestScope[integer] ne 4 and 6 le num || false}

__________  ${list[0] || list["1"] and true}

__________  ${num > integer}

__________  ${num == integer-1}


            <jsp:useBean class="foo.Dog" id="myDog" >
               <jsp:setProperty name="myDog" property="name"  value="${list[1]}" />
            </jsp:useBean>

__________  ${myDog.name and true}

__________  ${42 div 0}

__________  ${mine:rollIt() le 0}
```

false false false false false
true true true Infinity

Given this servlet code:

```
String num = "2";
request.setAttribute("num", num);
Integer i = new Integer(3);
request.setAttribute("integer", i);
java.util.ArrayList list = new java.util.ArrayList();
list.add("true");
list.add("false");
list.add("2");
list.add("10");
request.setAttribute("list", list);
```

What prints for each of these?

false `${num > 3}` — The "num" attribute was found, and its value "2" coerced to an int.

true `${integer le 12}` — Even better! The Integer value was converted to its primitive value, and then compared.

false `${requestScope[integer] ne 4 and 6 le num || false}`

true `${list[0] || list["1"] and true}`

false `${num > integer}`

true `${num == integer-1}` — Watch out for using = instead of ==. There is NO = in EL.

See if you can figure out the precedence rules for when you don't use parens. It's very intuitive (left to right), and you should have NO problems with precedence on the exam.

```
<jsp:useBean class="foo.Dog" id="myDog" >
   <jsp:setProperty name="myDog" property="name"  value="${list[1]}" />
</jsp:useBean>
```

Yes, you can use EL inside a tag!

false `${myDog.name and true}`

Infinity `${42 div 0}`

false `${mine:rollIt() le 0}`

If you remember the rollIt() code, it always returns a number greater than zero.

EL handles null values gracefully

A key design decision the developers of EL came up with is to handle null values without throwing exceptions. Why? Because they figured "it's better to show a partial, incomplete page than to show the user an error page."

Assume that there is *not* an attribute named "foo", but there IS an attribute named "bar", but that "bar" does not have a property or key named "foo".

EL	What prints
`${foo}`	
`${foo[bar]}`	
`${bar[foo]}`	
`${foo.bar}`	
`${7 + foo}`	7
`${7 / foo}`	Infinity
`${7 - foo}`	7
`${7 % foo}`	Exception is thrown
`${7 < foo}`	false
`${7 == foo}`	false
`${foo == foo}`	true
`${7 != foo}`	true
`${true and foo}`	false
`${true or foo}`	true
`${not foo}`	true

Nothing prints out for these expressions. If you say "The value is: ${foo}." You'll just see "The value is."

In arithmetic expressions, EL treats the unknown variable as "zero".

In logical expressions, EL treats the unknown variable as "false".

EL is null-friendly. It handles unknown or null values so that the page still displays, even if it can't find an attribute/property/key with the name in the expression.

In arithmetic, EL treats the null value as "zero".

In logical expressions, EL treats the null value as "false".

JSP Expression Language (EL) review

BULLET POINTS

- EL expressions are always within curly braces, and prefixed with a dollar($) sign ${expression} .
- The first named variable in the expression is either an implicit object or an attribute in one of the four scopes (page, request, session, or application).
- The dot operator lets you access values by using a Map key or a bean property name, for example ${foo.bar} gives you the value of *bar*, where *bar* is the name of Map key into the Map *foo*, or *bar* is the property of bean *foo*. Whatever comes to the right of the dot operator must follow normal Java naming rules for identifiers! (In other words, must start with a letter, underscore, or dollar sign, can include numbers after the first character, but nothing else, etc.)
- You can NEVER put anything to the right of the dot that wouldn't be legal as a Java identifier. For example, you can't say ${foo.1}.
- The [ ] operator is more powerful than the dot, because it lets you access arrays and Lists, *and* you can put other expressions including named variables within the brackets, *and* you can nest them to any level you can stand.
- For example, if musicList is an ArrayList, you can access the first value in the list by saying ${musicList[0]} OR ${musicList["0"]}. EL doesn't care if you put quotes around the list index.
- If what's inside the brackets is not in quotes, the Container evaluates it. If it is in quotes, and it's not an index into an array or List, the Container sees it as the literal name of a property or key.
- All but one of the EL implicit objects are Maps. From the Map implicit objects you can get attributes from any of the four scopes, request parameter values, header values, cookie values, and context init parameters. The non-map implicit object is pageContext, which is a reference to... the PageContext object.
- Don't confuse the implicit EL scope objects (Maps of the attributes) with the objects to which the attributes are bound. In other words, don't confuse the ***requestScope*** implicit object with the actual JSP implicit ***request*** object. The only way to access the request object is by going through the pageContext implicit object. (Although some of what you might want from the request is already available through other EL implicit objects, including *param/paramValues*, *header/headerValues*, and *cookie*.)
- EL functions allow you to call a public static method in a plain old Java class. The function name does not have to match the actual method name! For example, ${foo:rollIt()} does not mean that there must be a method named rollIt() in a class that has a function.
- The function name (e.g. rollIt()) is mapped to a real static method using a TLD (Tag Library Descriptor) file. Declare a function using the <function> element, including the <name> of the function (rollIt()), the fully-qualified <function-class>, and the <function-signature> which includes the return type as well as the method name and argument list.
- To use a function in a JSP, you must declare the namespace using a taglib directive. Put a prefix attribute in the taglib directive to tell the Container the TLD in which the function you're calling can be found. Example:

```
<%@ taglib prefix="mine"
           uri="/WEB-INF/foo.tld"%>
```

Hey, have you guys noticed that they haven't even *mentioned*, like, the ONE thing that's most important to a web site designer?
Yeah. I haven't heard ONE thing about using layout templates. The *last* thing I want to do is put the same navigation bar code into all 235 of my JSPs... what if it *changes*?
Hmmmm.... I always thought the important thing was to make sure you don't end up on *webpagesthatsuck.com*.

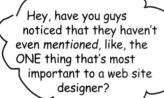

Of COURSE we'll talk about layout templates. If ANYONE knows about reusable components it's a Java programmer.

Reusable template pieces

You have headers on every page on your web site. They're always the same. You have the same footer on every page as well. How stupid would it be to code in the same header and footer tags into every JSP in your web app?

If you're thinking like a Java programmer (which of course you are), you know that doing that is about as un-OO as it gets. The thought of all that duplicate code probably makes you feel a little sick. What happens when the site designer makes, oh, a tiny little *change* to the header or footer?

You have to propagate the change everywhere.

Relax. There's a mechanism for handling this in a JSP—it's called ***include***. You write your JSP in the usual way, except that instead of putting the reusable stuff explicitly into the JSP you're authoring, you instead tell the Container to *include* the other file into the existing page, at the location you select. It's kind of like saying:

<html><body>

<!-- insert the header file here -->

Welcome to our site...

blah blah blah more stuff here...

<!-- insert the footer file here -->

</body></html>

In this section we'll look at two different include mechanisms: the include *directive* and the <jsp:include/> *standard action.*

The include directive

The include directive tells the Container one thing: *copy* everything in the *included* file and *paste* it into *this* file, right ***here***...

Standard header file ("Header.jsp")

We want this HTML content on every page in our web app.

```
<html><body>

<img src="images/Web-Services.jpg" > <br>
<em><strong>We know how to make SOAP suck less.</strong></em> <br>

</body></html>
```

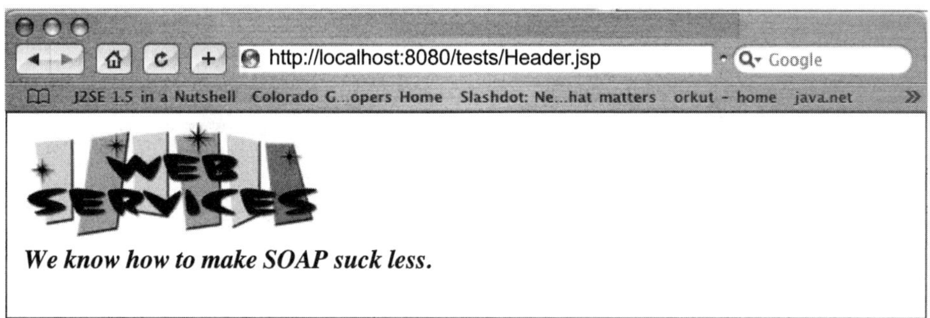

A JSP from the web app ("Contact.jsp")

```
<html><body>

<%@ include file="Header.jsp"%>

<br>
<em>We can help.</em> <br><br>
Contact us at: ${initParam.mainEmail}
</body></html>
```

This says "Insert the complete Header.jsp file into this point in THIS page, then keep going with the rest of this JSP..."

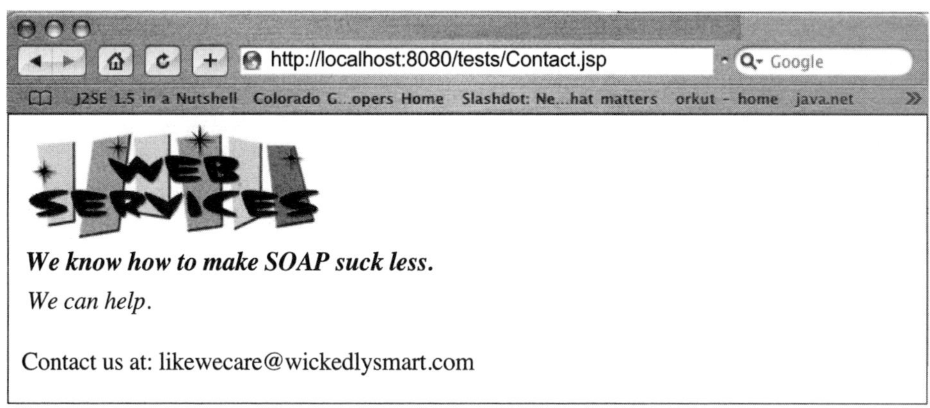

The <jsp:include> standard action

The <jsp:include> standard action *appears* to do the same thing as the include standard action.

Standard header file ("Header.jsp")

```
<html><body>

<img src="images/Web-Services.jpg" > <br>
<em><strong>We know how to make SOAP suck less.</strong></em> <br>

</body></html>
```

This is what we want on EVERY page.

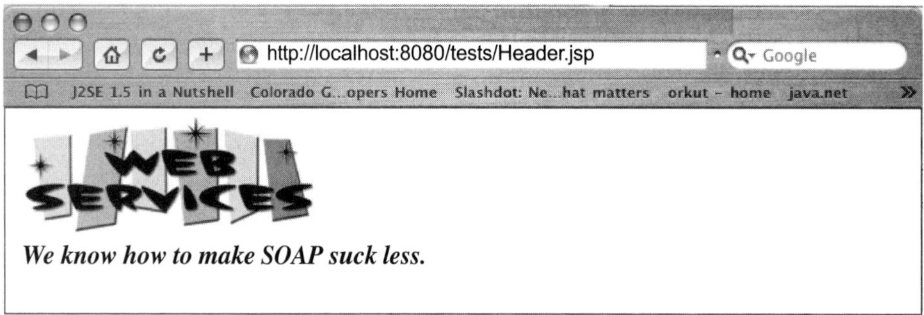

A JSP from the web app ("Contact.jsp")

```
<html><body>

<jsp:include page="Header.jsp" />

<br>
<em>We can help.</em> <br><br>
Contact us at: ${initParam.mainEmail}
</body></html>
```

This says "Insert the response of Header.jsp file into this point in THIS page, then keep going with the rest of this JSP..."

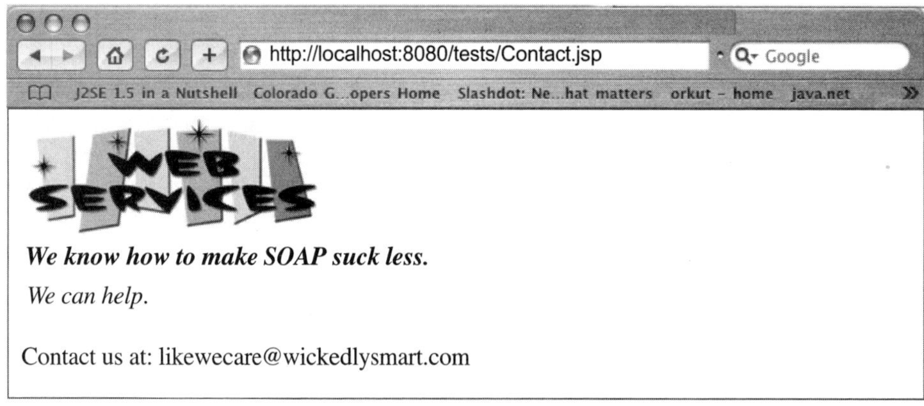

They're NOT the same underneath...

The <jsp:include /> standard action and the include directive look the same, and often give the same result, but take a look at the generated servlets. We took this code directly out of the _jspService() method from Tomcat's generated servlet code...

Generated servlet code for the header file

```
out.write("\r<html>\r<body>\r<img src=\"images/Web-Services.jpg\" >
     <br>\r<em><strong>We know how to make SOAP suck less.</strong></em> <br>\r\r
     </body>\r</html>\r");
```

Simple... it just does the output.

Generated servlet for the JSP using the include directive

```
out.write("<html><body>\r");
```

This part in bold is EXACTLY the same as the Header.jsp page generates.

```
out.write("\r<html>\r<body>\r<img src=\"images/Web-Services.jpg\" >
     <br>\r<em><strong>We know how to make SOAP suck less.</strong></em> <br>\r\r
     </body>\r</html>\r");

out.write("\r<br>\r\r\r<em>We can help.</em> <br><br>\r\rContact us at: ");
out.write((java.lang.String) org.apache.jasper.runtime.PageContextImpl.
     proprietaryEvaluate("${initParam.mainEmail}", java.lang.String.class,
     (PageContext)_jspx_page_context, null, false));

out.write("\r\r\r</body></html>");
```

The include directive just takes the contents of the "Header.jsp" file and places it into the "Contact.jsp" page BEFORE it does the translation!

Generated servlet for the JSP using the <jsp:include /> standard action

```
out.write("<html><body>\r");
```

This is different! The original Header.jsp file is NOT inside the generated servlet. Instead, it's some kind of runtime call...

```
org.apache.jasper.runtime.JspRuntimeLibrary.include(request, response,
                                                 "Header.jsp", out, false);

out.write("\r<br>\r\r\r<em>We can help.</em> <br><br>\r\rContact us at: ");
out.write((java.lang.String) org.apache.jasper.runtime.PageContextImpl.
       proprietaryEvaluate("${initParam.mainEmail}", java.lang.String.class,
       (PageContext)_jspx_page_context, null, false));

out.write("\r\r\r</body></html>");
```

The include directive happens at translation time <jsp:include> happens at runtime

With the include *directive*, there is NO difference between you opening your JSP page and pasting in the contents of "Header.jsp". In other words, it really is just as though you duplicated the code from the header file into your other JSP. Except the Container does it at translation time for you, so that you don't have to duplicate the code everywhere. You can write all your pages with an include directive, and the Container will go through the trouble of copying the header code into each JSP before translating and compiling the generated servlet.

But <jsp:include> is a completely different story. Rather than copying in the source code from "Header.jsp", the include standard action inserts the *response* of "Header.jsp", at runtime. The key to <jsp:include> is that the Container is creating a RequestDispatcher from the page attribute and applying the include() method. The dispatched/included JSP executes against the same request and response objects, within the same thread.

The include directive inserts the SOURCE of "Header.jsp", at translation time.

But the <jsp:include /> standard action inserts the RESPONSE of "Header.jsp", at runtime.

Q: So why wouldn't you always use <jsp:include>? That way you can guarantee you'll always have the latest content.

A: Think about it. There's an extra performance hit with every <jsp:include>. With the directive, on the other hand, the hit happens only once—when the including page is translated. So if you're pretty sure that once you go to production the included file won't change, the directive might be the way to go. Of course there's still the tradeoff that the generated servlet class is a little larger when you use the directive.

Q: I tried this with Tomcat— I made a static HTML file, and included it with the directive. Then I changed the HTML file, without redeploying or anything, and the output from the JSP reflected the difference! So if that's the case, then why ever use <jsp:include >?

A: Ahhh... you have a friendly Container (like Tomcat 5). Yes, most of the newer Containers have a way of detecting when the included files have changed, and they do retranslate the including file and everything's great. The problem is that this is NOT GUARANTEED BY THE SPEC! So if you write your code to depend on it, your app won't necessarily be portable to other Containers.

The include directive at first request

With the include ***directive***, the Container has a lot of work to do, but *only* on the first request. From the second request on, there's no extra runtime overhead.

1

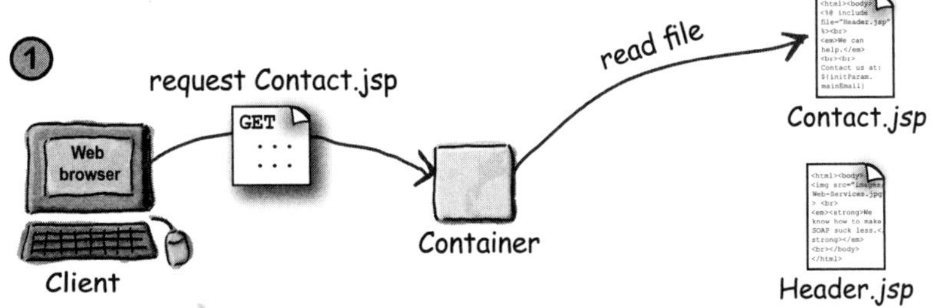

The client makes a request for Contact.jsp, which has not been translated. The Container reads the Contact.jsp page to start the translation process.

2

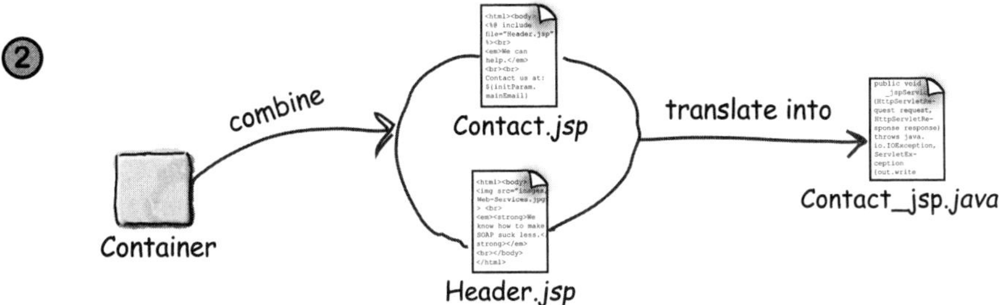

The container sees the include directive, and combines the source code of Header.jsp and Contact.jsp, and creates/translates that into a Java source file for the generated servlet.

3

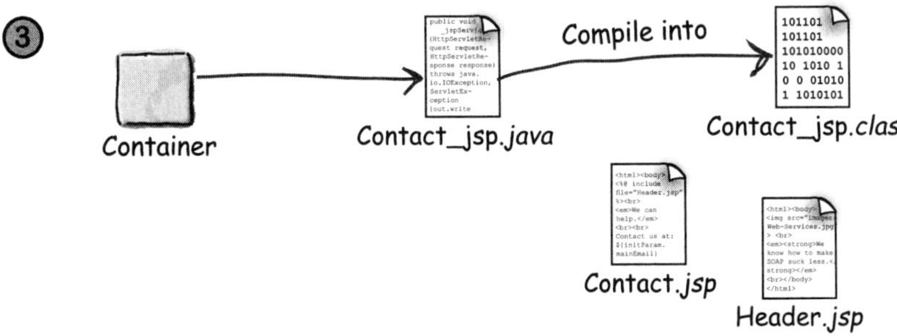

The Container compiles the translated source file into a servlet class. It's just like any other servlet at this point, and the previous step never has to happen again, unless Contact.jsp changes (or, if your Container is smart and can tell that the included *Header*.jsp has changed).

4

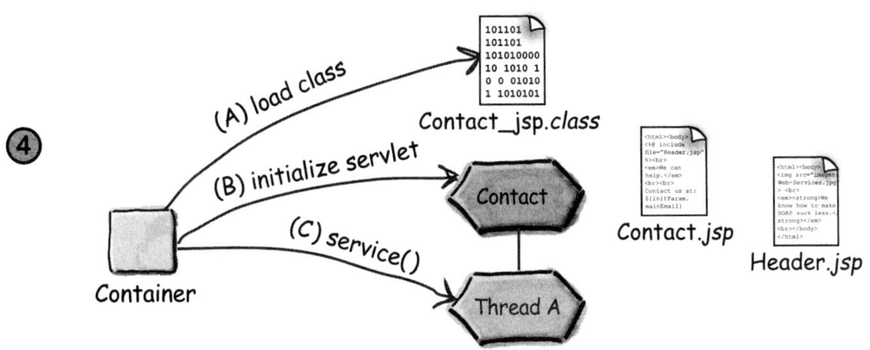

To complete the request, the Container loads the newly-compiled class, initializes a servlet (instantiates the servlet then calls init() on the new object), allocates a thread for the request, and calls the _jspService() method. From the second request on, the Container does only step (C): allocates a thread and calls the _jspService() method.

The <jsp:include> standard action at first request

With the include standard action, there's less work at translation time, and more work with each request, especially if the included file is a JSP.

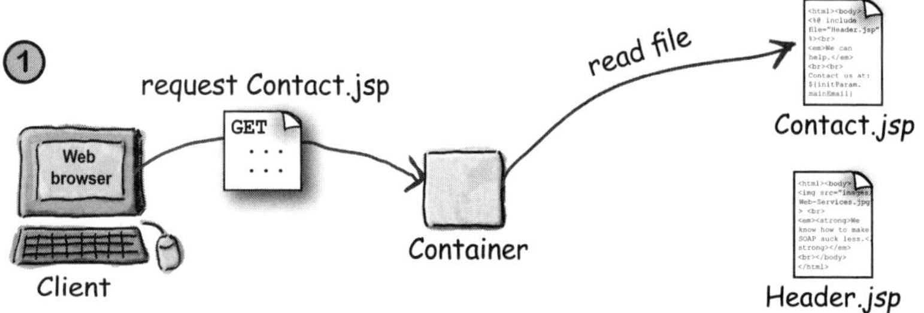

The client makes a request for Contact.jsp, which has not been translated. The Container reads the Contact.jsp page to start the translation process.

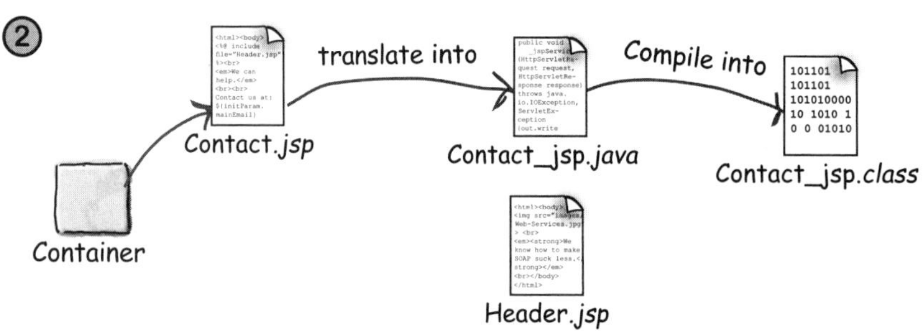

The container sees the include standard action, and uses that to insert a method call in the generated servlet code that—at runtime—will dynamically combine the response from Header.jsp into the response from Contact.jsp. The Container generates servlets for both JSP files. (This is not dictated by the spec, so we're showing only an example of how it *could* work.)

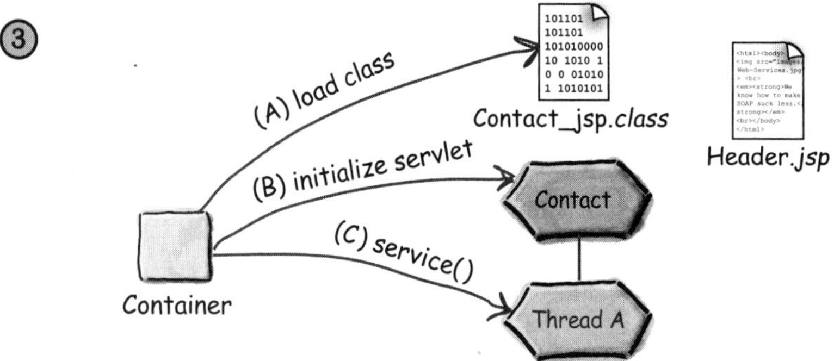

The Container compiles the translated source file into a servlet class. It's just like any other servlet at this point. The generated servlet class file is loaded into the Container's JVM and is initialized. Next, the Container allocates a thread for the request and calls the JSP's _jspService() method.

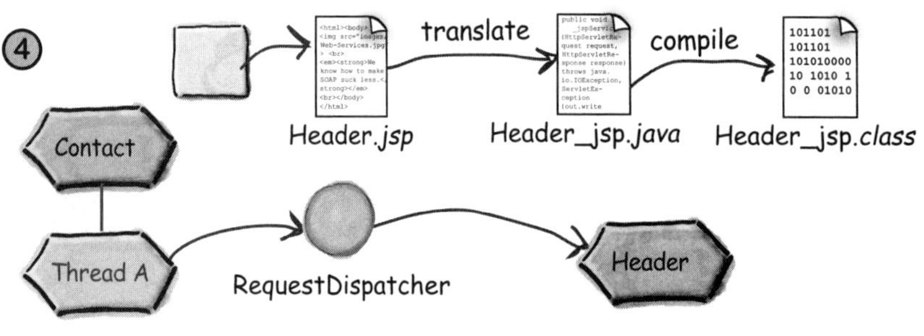

The Contact servlet hits the method that does the dynamic include, and something vendor-specific happens! All we care about is that the response generated by the Header servlet is combined with the response from the Contact servlet (at the appropriate place). (NOT SHOWN: at some point the Header.jsp is translated and compiled, then the generated servlet class is loaded and initialized.)

The attribute names are different for the include directive and <jsp:include/>

Memorize this! Look at the attributes for the two include mechanisms... what's different?

```
<%@ include file="Header.jsp"%>

<jsp:include page="Header.jsp" />
```

*Yep. The directive attribute is **file** but the standard action attribute is **page**! To help you remember, the include directive <%@ include **file**="foo.jsp"> is used only at **translation** time (as with all directives). And when translating, the Container cares only about **files**—.jsp to .java, and .java to .class.*
*But the <jsp:include **page**="foo.jsp"> standard action, as with all standard actions, is executed at **request** time, when the Container cares about **pages** to be executed.*

Q: Can the included JSP have its own dynamic content? In your examples, the Header.*jsp* might as well have been a static Header.*html* page.

A: It's a JSP, so yes it can be dynamic (but you're right—in our example we could have made the header a static HTML page and it would have worked in exactly the same way). There are a few limitations, though: an included page CANNOT change the response status code or set headers (which means it can't call, say, addCookies()). You won't get an error if the included JSP tries to do things it can't—you just won't get what you asked for.

Q: But if the included thing is dynamic, and you're using the static include directive, does that mean that the dynamic stuff is evaluated only once?

A: Let's say you include a JSP that has an EL expression that calls the *rollIt* function that generates a random number. Remember, with the include directive, that EL expression is simply copied into the includING JSP. So each time that page is accessed, the EL expression runs and a new random number is generated. Burn this in: ***with the include directive, the source of the included thing becomes PART of the page with the include directive.***

The include directive is position-sensitive!

*And it's the ONLY directive whose position in the JSP actually matters. With a **page** directive, for example, you can put it anywhere in the page, although by convention most people put page directives at the top.*

But the include directive tells the Container exactly WHERE to insert the source from the included file! For example, if you're including both a header and a footer, it might look something like this:

```
<html><body>

<%@ include file="Header.html"%> <br>

<em>We can help.</em> <br><br>

Contact us at: ${initParam.mainEmail} <br>

<%@ include file="Footer.html"%>

</body></html>
```

This has to be at the bottom of your JSP (before the closing tags), if that's where you want the stuff from Footer.html to appear. Remember, everything from the JSP plus the two included files is combined into one big page, and THE ORDER MATTERS!

And, yes, the <jsp:include> is of course ALSO position-sensitive, but that's more obvious than with the page directive.

HELLO! Did you actually LOOK at the generated servlet code for the include directive? You've got nested HTML and BODY tags! That's wrong *and* stupid.

Uh-oh. She's right...

Think about what we did. We made a page for the header, "Header.jsp". It was a nice JSP all on its own, complete with its opening and closing HTML and BODY tags. Then we made the "Contact.jsp" and it, too, had nice opening and closing tags. Well, didn't we say that *everything* in the included file is pasted (virtually) into the page with the include? ***That means everything.***

The code below, from the generated servlet, will NOT work in all browsers. It worked in ours because we got lucky.

```
out.write("<html><body>\r");

out.write("\r<html>\r<body>\r
            <img src=\"images/Web-Services.jpg\" >
            <br>r<em><strong>We know how to make SOAP
            suck less.</strong></em> <br>\r\r
            </body>\r</html>\r");

out.write("\r<br>\r\r\r<em>We can help.</em>
            <br><br>\r\rContact us at: ");
out.write((java.lang.String) org.apache.jasper.runtime.
            PageContextImpl.proprietaryEvaluate("${initParam.
            mainEmail}", java.lang.String.class,
            (PageContext)_jspx_page_context, null, false));

out.write("\r\r\r</body></html>");
```

Yikes!!

Do NOT put opening and closing HTML and BODY tags within your reusable pieces!

Design and write your layout template chunks (like headers, nav bars, etc.) assuming they will be included in some OTHER page.

Don't expect ME to strip out your redundant opening and closing tags.

The way we SHOULD have done it

Here we took the opening and closing tags out of the included files. This *does* mean that the included files can no longer generate valid HTML pages on their own; they now *depend* on being included in something bigger. Something with <html><body> and </body></html> tags. But that's the point—you're designing these reusable chunks so that you can compose complete layouts from smaller pieces, without duplicating the code by hand. These reusable chunks aren't *meant* to live on their own.

① The Header file ("Header.jsp")

```
<img src="images/Web-Services.jpg" > <br>
<em><strong>We know how to make SOAP suck less.</strong></em> <br>
```

② Contact.jsp

```
<html><body>

<%@ include file="Header.jsp"%> <br>

<em>We can help.</em> <br><br>
Contact us at: ${initParam.mainEmail}

<%@ include file="Footer.html"%>

</body></html>
```

Notice we took out all the HTML and BODY tags from the included files.

③ The Footer file ("Footer.html")

```
<a href="index.html">home page</a>
```

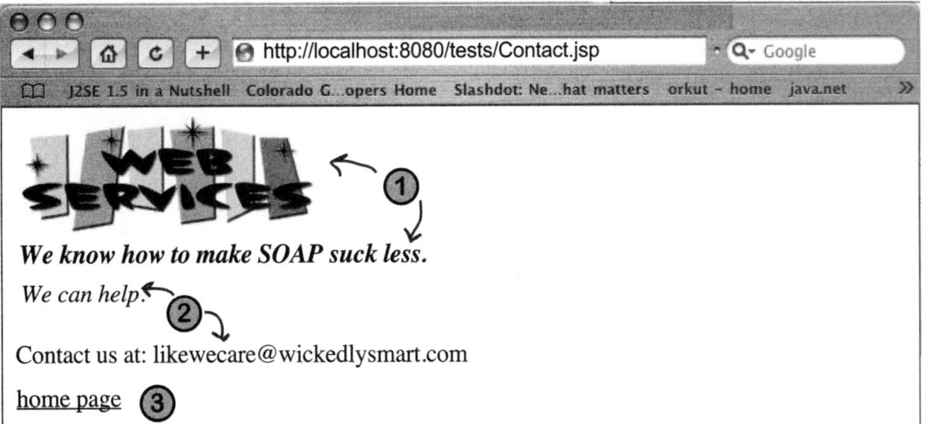

Note: this idea of stripping out the opening and closing tags applies to BOTH include mechanisms— <jsp:include> and the include directive.

Customizing the included content with <jsp:param>

OK, so you've got a header that's supposed to appear the same way on every page. But what if you want to customize part of the header? What if you want, say, a context-sensitive subtitle that's part of the header, but that changes depending on the page?

You have a couple options.

The dumb way: put the subtitle information into the main page, as, say, the first thing in your page after the include for the header.

The smarter way: pass the subtitle information as a new request parameter to the included page!

Why that's cool: if the subtitle information is supposed to be part of the header, but it's a part that changes, you still want the header part of the template to make the decision about how that subtitle should appear in the final page. In other words, let the person who designed the header decide how the subtitle should be rendered!

JSP that does the include

```
<html><body>

<jsp:include page="Header.jspf" >

   <jsp:param name="subTitle" value="We take the sting out of SOAP." />

</jsp:include>

<br>
<em>Web Services Support Group.</em> <br><br>
Contact us at: ${initParam.mainEmail}
</body></html>
```

Look... no closing slash!

<jsp:include> can have a BODY, so that you add (or replace) request parameters that the included thing can use.

The included header that USES the new param ("Header.jspf")

```
<img src="images/Web-Services.jpg" > <br>
<em><strong>${param.subTitle}</strong></em> <br>
```

To the included file, the param set with <jsp:param> is just like any OTHER request parameter. Here we're using EL to get it.

Note: this idea of params doesn't make any sense with the include directive (which is not dynamic), so it applies ONLY to the <jsp:include> standard action.

This got me thinking... if I can include one JSP in another, what if I wanted to forward from one JSP to another? If the client gets to my page and hasn't logged in, I want to send him to a *different* page...

The <jsp:forward> standard action

You CAN forward from one JSP to another. Or from one JSP to a servlet. Or from one JSP to any other resource in your web app.

Of course, you don't usually *want* to do this in production, because if you're using MVC, the View is supposed to be the View! And the View has no business doing control logic. In other words, it shouldn't be the View's job to figure out if the guy is logged in or not—someone *else* should have made that decision (the Controller), before deciding to forward to the View.

But let's suspend all that good MVC judgement for the time being, and see how we *could* do it, if we *were* to forward *from* a JSP page to something else.

Why bother if you'll never do it? Well, you *might* one day stumble on a problem where <jsp:forward> *is* a useful solution. More importantly, like a lot of what's in the book (and the exam), the use of <jsp:forward> ***is out there.*** Lurking in gazillions of JSPs that you might one day find yourself maintaining (or ideally *refactoring*).

A conditional forward...

So imagine you're a JSP and you assume you're being called from a request that includes a *userName* parameter. Since you're counting on that parameter, you want to first check that the *userName* parameter isn't null. If it's not, no problem—finish the response. But if the *userName* parameter *is* null, you want to stop right here and turn the whole request over to something *else*—like a different JSP that will ask for the *userName*.

For now, we know we can do it with scripting:

JSP with a conditional forward (Hello.jsp)

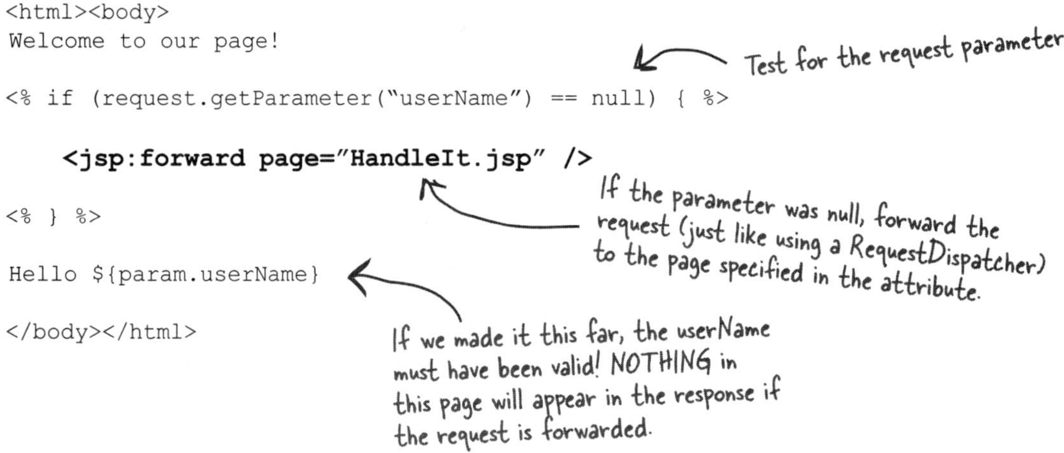

<html><body>
Welcome to our page!
Test for the request parameter
<% if (request.getParameter("userName") == null) { %>
<jsp:forward page="HandleIt.jsp" />
If the parameter was null, forward the request (just like using a RequestDispatcher) to the page specified in the attribute.
<% } %>
Hello ${param.userName}
</body></html>
If we made it this far, the userName must have been valid! NOTHING in this page will appear in the response if the request is forwarded.

JSP to which the request is forwarded (HandleIt.jsp)

```
<html><body>
We're sorry... you need to log in again.

<form action="Hello.jsp" method="get">
Name: <input name="userName" type="text">
<input name="Submit" type="submit">
</form>

</body></html>
```

This is just a plain old page that gets the request parameter input from the user and then requests the JSP we were just on... Hello.jsp.

How it runs...

The *first* time you request the Hello.jsp, the JSP does the conditional test, discovers there's no value for userName, and forwards to the HandleIt.jsp. Assuming the user types a name into the name input field, the *second* request won't do the forward, since the userName request parameter has a non-null value.

First request for Hello.jsp

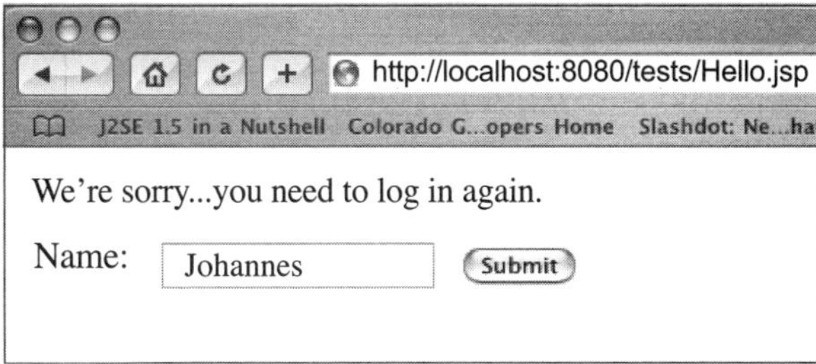

Wait a minute... what happened to the words "Welcome to our page!"? They're in the Hello.jsp *before* the forward happens...so why don't they show up on the first request?

Second request for Hello.jsp

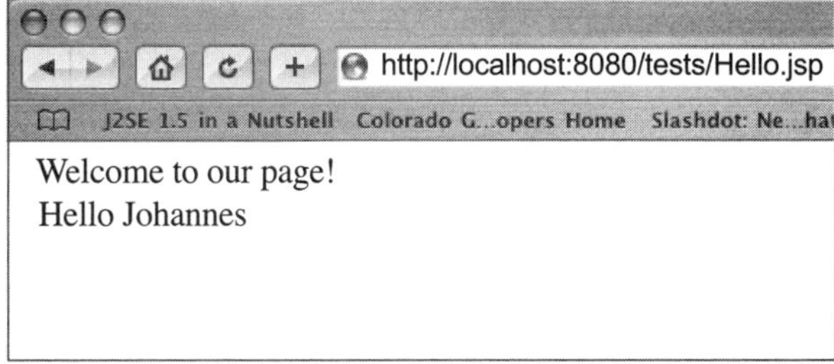

How come the "Welcome to our page!" text didn't print out the first time?

With <jsp:forward>, the buffer is cleared BEFORE the forward

When a forward happens, the resource to which the request is forwarded starts with a clear response buffer! In other words, anything written to the response before the forward happens is thrown out.

NOTHING you write before the forward will appear if the forward happens.

there are no Dumb Questions

Q: This makes sense if the page is buffered... because what you write is sent to the buffer, and the Container just clears the buffer. But what if you commit the response BEFORE you do the forward? Like, what happens if you write something and then call flush() on the out object?

A: OK, we know you're just asking this out of intellectual curiosity since it would be a phenomenally stupid and pointless thing to do. But you know that.

But you *also* know that weird things can still be on the exam, since your too-lazy-to-learn-it co-worker might just put something this crazy into his code, in which case you better get used to it.

You can probably think through the answer, though. If you write something like:

```
<html><body>

Welcome to our page!

<% out.flush(); %>

<% if (request.getParameter("userName") == null) {
%>
    <jsp:forward page="HandleIt.jsp" /> <% } %>
Hello ${param.userName}
</body></html>
```

The Container dutifully commits (sends) "Welcome to our page!" as the response and *then* the Container sees the forward. Uh-oh. ***Too late.*** And an IllegalStateException happens.

Except nobody will *see* the exception! The client just sees "Welcome to our page!"... *and nothing else*. The forward throws an exception but it's too late for the Container to take back the response, so the client sees what was flushed, and that's it. The forward doesn't happen, the rest of the current page doesn't happen. End of story for that page. So ***never do a flush-and-forward!***

I don't understand how we ended with a scriptlet. I was TOLD there would be no scripting in this chapter. If only there were a way to do a conditional test without having to go back to scripting...

She doesn't know about JSTL tags

When you need more functionality, something beyond what you can get with the standard actions or EL, you don't have to resort to scripting. In the next chapter, you'll learn how to use the JSP Standard Tag Library 1.1 (JSTL 1.1) to do just about everything you'll ever need, using a combination of tags and EL. Here's a sneak peek of how to do our conditional forward *without scripting*.

```
<%@ taglib prefix="c" uri="http://java.sun.com/jsp/jstl/core" %>
<html><body>
Welcome to our page!

<c:if test="${empty param.userName}" >
  <jsp:forward page="HandleIt.jsp" />
</c:if>

Hello ${param.userName}
</body></html>
```

Declare a taglib directive that names the library where the tags live.

This replaces the scriptlet if test

By the way... you probably won't be able to run this yet because you don't have JSTL in your web app. We'll do that in the next chapter.

Bean-related standard action review

- The <jsp:useBean> standard action defines a variable that holds a reference to either an *existing* bean attribute or, if the bean doesn't already exist, a *new* bean.
- The <jsp:useBean> MUST have an "id" attribute which declares the variable name that'll be used in this JSP to refer to the bean.
- If you don't include a "scope" attribute with <jsp:useBean>, the scope defaults to *page* scope.
- The "class" attribute is optional, and it declares the class type that will be used if a new bean is created. The type must be public, non-abstract, and have a public no-arg constructor.
- If you put a "type" attribute in <jsp:useBean>, it must be a type to which the bean can be cast.
- If you have a "type" attribute but do NOT have a "class" attribute, the bean must already exist, since you haven't specified the class type that should be instantiated for the new bean.
- The <jsp:useBean> tag can have a body, and anything in the body runs ONLY if a new bean is created as a result of <jsp:useBean> (which means that no bean with that "id" was found in the specified (or default) scope).
- The main purpose of the body of <jsp:useBean> is to set the new bean's properties, using <jsp:setProperty>.
- <jsp:setProperty> must have a name attribute (which will match the "id" from <jsp:useBean>), and a "property" attribute. The "property" attribute must be either an actual property name or the wildcard "*".
- If you don't include a "value" attribute, the Container will set the property value only if there's a request parameter with a name that matches the property name. If you use the wildcard (*) for the "property" attribute, the Container will set the value of all properties that have a matching request parameter name. (Other properties won't be affected.)
- If the request parameter name is different from the property name but you want to set the value of the property equal to the request parameter value, you can use the "param" attribute in the <jsp:setProperty> tag.
- If you specify a "type" attribute in <jsp:useBean>, you can set properties in <jsp:setProperty> ONLY on properties of the "type", but NOT on properties that exist only in the actual "class" type. (In other words, polymorphism and normal Java type rules apply.)
- Property values can be Strings or primitives, and the <jsp:setProperty> standard action will do the conversions automatically.

The include review

BULLET POINTS

- You can build a page with reusable components using one of two include mechanisms—the include *directive* or the <jsp:include> *standard action*.
- The include *directive* does the include at translation time, only once. So the include *directive* is considered the appropriate mechanism for including content that isn't likely to change after deployment.
- The include *directive* essentially copies everything from within the included file and pastes it into the page with the include. The Container combines all the included files and compiles just one file for the generated servlet. At runtime, the page with the include runs exactly as though you had typed all the source into one file yourself.
- The <jsp:include> *standard action* includes the response of the included page into the original page at runtime. So the include *standard action* is considered appropriate for including content that may be updated after deployment, while the include *directive* is not.
- Either mechanism can include dynamic elements (JSP code with EL expressions, for example) as well as static HTML pages.
- The include *directive* is the only position-sensitive directive; the included content is inserted into the page at the exact location of the directive.
- The attributes for the include *directive* and the include *standard action* are inconsistently named—the *directive* uses "file" as the attribute while the *standard action* uses a "page" attribute.
- In your reusable components, be sure to strip out the opening and closing tags. Otherwise, the generated output will have nested opening and closing tags, which not all browsers can handle. Design and construct your reusable pieces knowing that they'll be included/inserted into something else.
- You can customize an included file by setting (or replacing) a request parameter using the <jsp:param > standard action inside the body of a <jsp:include>.
- We didn't show it in this chapter, but the <jsp:param> can be used inside the body of a <jsp:forward> tag as well.
- The ONLY places where a <jsp:param> makes sense are within a <jsp:include> or a <jsp:forward> standard action.
- If the param name used in <jsp:param> already has a value as a request parameter, the new value will overwrite the previous one. Otherwise, a new request parameter is added to the request.
- The included resource has some limitations: it cannot change the response status code or set headers.
- The <jsp:forward> standard action forwards the request (just like using a RequestDispatcher) to another resource from the same web app.
- When a forward happens, the response buffer is cleared first! The resource to which the request was forwarded gets to start with a clean output. So anything written to the response *before* the forward will be thrown away.
- If you commit the response *before* the forward (by calling out.flush(), for example), the client will be sent whatever was flushed, but that's it. The forward won't happen, and the rest of the original page won't be processed.

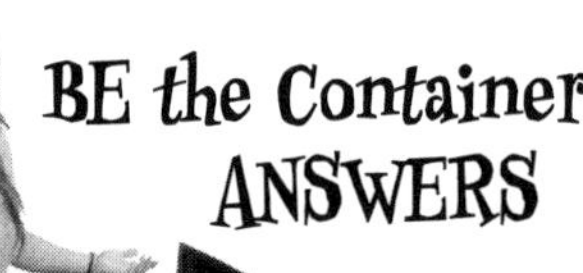

BE the Container ANSWERS

Look at this standard action:

Note: this has a type but no class, and it does NOT specify scope, which means it uses "page".

```
<jsp:useBean id="person" type="foo.Employee" >
  <jsp:setProperty name="person" property="name" value="Fred" />
</jsp:useBean >
Name is: <jsp:getProperty name="person"  property="name" />
```

The body will NEVER run! It's pointless to put a body inside a <jsp:useBean > tag if you have only a type and no class! Remember, the tag body executes ONLY if a new bean is created, which can never happen when only a type (but no class) is declared in the tag.

If we made it this far, we'll print "Evan".

1. What happens if the servlet code looks like:

```
foo.Person p = new foo.Employee();
p.setName("Evan");
request.setAttribute("person", p);
```

FAILS at request time! The "person" attribute is stored at request scope, so the <jsp:useBean > tag won't work since it specifies only a type. The Container KNOWS that if you have only a type specified, there MUST be an existing bean attribute of that name and scope.

2. What happens if the servlet code looks like:

```
foo.Person p = new foo.Person();
p.setName("Evan");
request.setAttribute("person", p);
```

Actually, this servlet fails to compile. We cheated a little, since on this question it isn't "Be the Container", it's more like "Be the COMPILER". foo.Person is now abstract, so we can't instantiate the foo.Person.

abstract

Person
String getName() void setName(String)

Employee
int getEmpID() void setEmpID(int)

Both classes are in the package "foo".

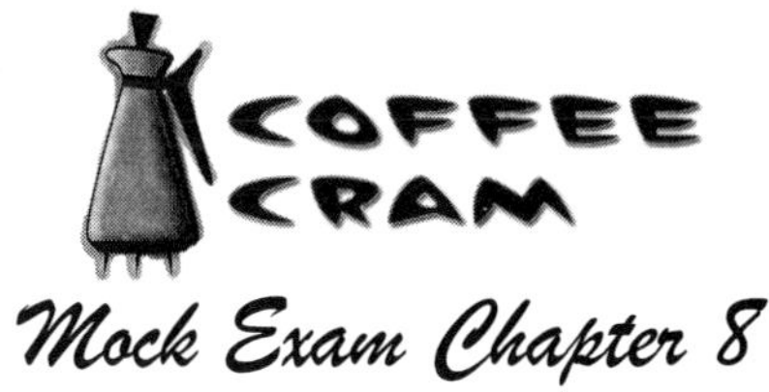

Mock Exam Chapter 8

---

1 Given an HTML form that uses checkboxes to allow a user to select multiple values for a parameter called, **hobbies**.

Which EL expressions evaluate to the first value of the **hobbies** parameter? (Choose all that apply.)

- ❑ A. **${param.hobbies}**
- ❑ B. **${paramValue.hobbies}**
- ❑ C. **${paramValues.hobbies[0]}**
- ❑ D. **${paramValues.hobbies[1]}**
- ❑ E. **${paramValues[hobbies][0]}**
- ❑ F. **${paramValues[hobbies][1]}**

---

2 Given that a web application stores the webmaster email address in the servlet context initialization parameter called **master-email**.

Which retrieves that value? (Choose all that apply.)

- ❑ A. **<a href='mailto:${initParam.master-email}'>**
email me</a>
- ❑ B. **<a href='mailto:${contextParam.master-email}'>**
email me</a>
- ❑ C. **<a href='mailto:${initParam['master-email']}'>**
email me</a>
- ❑ D. **<a href='mailto:${contextParam['master-email']}'>**
email me</a>

3 Given the following Java class:

```
package com.mycompany;
public class MyFunctions {
  public static String hello(String name) {
    return "Hello "+name;
  }
}
```

This class represents the handler for a function that is part of a tag library.

```
<%@ taglib uri="http://mycompany.com.tags" prefix="comp" %>
```

Which Tag Library Descriptor entry defines this custom function so that it can be used in an EL expression?

❑ A.

```
<taglib>
  ...
  <tag>
    <name>Hello</name>
    <tag-class>com.mycompany.MyFunctions</tag-class>
    <body-content>JSP</body-content>
  </tag>
</taglib>
```

❑ B.

```
<taglib>
  ...
  <function>
    <name>Hello</name>
    <function-class>com.mycompany.MyFunctions</function-class>
    <function-signature>java.lang.String hello(java.lang.String)
         </function-signature>
  </function>
</taglib>
```

❑ C.

```
<web-app>
  ...
  <servlet>
    <servlet-name>hello</servlet-name>
    <servlet-class>com.mycompany.MyFunctions</servlet-class>
  </servlet>
</web-app>
```

❑ D.

```
<taglib>
  ...
  <function>
    <name>Hello</name>
    <function-class>com.mycompany.MyFunctions</function-class>
    <function-signature>hello(java.lang.String)</function-signature>
  </function>
</taglib>
```

---

4 Given:

```
package com.example;
public class TheBean {
  private int value;
  public TheBean() { value = 42; }
  public int getValue() { return value; }
  public void setValue(int v) { value = v; }
}
```

Assuming no instances of **TheBean** have been created yet, which JSP standard action statements create a new instance of this bean and store it in the request scope? (Choose all that apply.)

❑ A. `<jsp:useBean name="myBean"`
`type="com.example.TheBean" />`

❑ B. `<jsp:makeBean name="myBean"`
`type="com.example.TheBean" />`

❑ C. `<jsp:useBean id="myBean"`
`class="com.example.TheBean"`
`scope="request" />`

❑ D. `<jsp:makeBean id="myBean"`
`class="com.example.TheBean"`
`scope="request" />`

---

5 Given a Model 1 architecture in which a JSP page handles all of the controller functions, that JSP controller needs to dispatch the request to another JSP page.

Which standard action code will perform this dispatch?

❑ A. `<jsp:forward page="view.jsp" />`

❑ B. `<jsp:forward file="view.jsp" />`

❑ C. `<jsp:dispatch page="view.jsp" />`

❑ D. `<jsp:dispatch file="view.jsp" />`

---

6 Given:

```
11. <% java.util.List list = new java.util.ArrayList();
12.     list.add("a");
13.     list.add("2");
14.     list.add("c");
15.     request.setAttribute("list", list);
16.     request.setAttribute("listIdx", "1");
17. %>
18. <%-- insert code here --%>
```

Which, inserted at line 18, are valid and evaluate to **c** ? (Choose all that apply.)

- ❏ A. `${list.2}`
- ❏ B. `${list[2]}`
- ❏ C. `${list.listIdx+1}`
- ❏ D. `${list[listIdx+1]}`
- ❏ E. `${list['listIdx' + 1]}`
- ❏ F. `${list[list[listIdx]]}`

---

7 Which statements about the **.** (dot) and **[]** EL operators are true? (Choose all that apply.)

- ❏ A. `${foo.bar}` is equivalent to `${foo[bar]}`
- ❏ B. `${foo.bar}` is equivalent to `${foo["bar"]}`
- ❏ C. `${foo["5"]}` is valid syntax if **foo** is a **Map**
- ❏ D. `${header.User-Agent}` is equivalent to `${header[User-Agent]}`
- ❏ E. `${header.User-Agent}` is equivalent to `${header["User-Agent"]}`
- ❏ F. `${foo[5]}` is valid syntax if **foo** is a **List** or an array

8 Given a JSP page with the line:

`${101 % 10}`

What will be displayed?

- ❑ A. `1`
- ❑ B. `10`
- ❑ C. `1001`
- ❑ D. `101 % 10`
- ❑ E. `{101 % 10}`

---

9 Given:

```
${param.firstname}
${param.middlename}
${param.lastname}
${paramValues.lastname[0]}
```

Which describes the output produced by this portion of a JSP page when passed the query string `?firstname=John&lastname=Doe`?

- ❑ A. `John Doe`
- ❑ B. `John Doe Doe`
- ❑ C. `John null Doe`
- ❑ D. `John null Doe Doe`
- ❑ E. A null pointer exception will be thrown.

---

10 Which show valid usage of EL implicit variables? (Choose all that apply.)

- ❑ A. `${cookies.foo}`
- ❑ B. `${initParam.foo}`
- ❑ C. `${pageContext.foo}`
- ❑ D. `${requestScope.foo}`
- ❑ E. `${header["User-Agent"]}`
- ❑ F. `${requestDispatcher.foo}`
- ❑ G. `${pageContext.request.requestURI}`

11 Which are true about the **<jsp:useBean>** standard action? (Choose all that apply.)

- ❑ A. The **id** attribute is optional.
- ❑ B. The **scope** attribute is required.
- ❑ C. The **scope** attribute is optional and defaults to **request**.
- ❑ D. Either the **class** or **type** attributes may be specified, but at least one.
- ❑ E. It is valid to include both the **class** attribute and the **type** attribute, even if their values are NOT the same.

12 How would you include dynamic content in a JSP, similar to a server-side include (SSI)? (Choose all that apply.)

- ❑ A. `<%@ include file="/segments/footer.jspf" %>`
- ❑ B. `<jsp:forward page="/segments/footer.jspf" />`
- ❑ C. `<jsp:include page="/segments/footer.jspf" />`
- ❑ D.

```
RequestDispatcher dispatcher
    = request.getRequestDispatcher("/segments/footer.jspf");
  dispatcher.include(request,response);
```

13 In an HTML page with a rich, graphical layout, which JSP standard action can be used to import an image file into the JSP page?

- ❑ A. `<jsp:image page="logo.png" />`
- ❑ B. `<jsp:image file="logo.png" />`
- ❑ C. `<jsp:include page="logo.png" />`
- ❑ D. `<jsp:include file="logo.png" />`
- ❑ E. This CANNOT be done using a JSP standard action.

14 Given:

```
package com.example;
public class MyFunctions {
  public static String repeat(int x, String str) {
    // method body
  }
}
```

and given the JSP:

```
1. <%@ taglib uri="/WEB-INF/myfuncts" prefix="my" %>
2. <%-- insert code here --%>
```

Which, inserted at line 2 in the JSP, is a valid EL function invocation?

- ❑ A. `${repeat(2, "420")}`
- ❑ B. `${repeat("2", "420")}`
- ❑ C. `${my:repeat(2, "420")}`
- ❑ D. `${my:repeat("2", "420")}`
- ❑ E. A valid invocation CANNOT be determined.

---

15 Given:

```
public class MyBean {
  private java.util.Map params;
  private java.util.List objects;
  private String name;
  public java.util.Map getParams() { return params; }
  public String getName() { return name; }
  public java.util.List getObjects() { return objects; }
}
```

Which will cause errors (assume that an attribute named **`mybean`** can be found, and is of type **`MyBean`**)? (Choose all that apply.)

- ❑ A. `${mybean.name}`
- ❑ B. `${mybean["name"]}`
- ❑ C. `${mybean.objects.a}`
- ❑ D. `${mybean["params"].a}`
- ❑ E. `${mybean.params["a"]}`
- ❑ F. `${mybean["objects"].a}`

16

Given a JSP page:

```
1. The user has sufficiently logged in or out:
2.    ${param.loggedIn or param.loggedOut}.
```

If the request includes the query string "**loggedOut=true**", what will be this statement's displayed value?

- ❑ A. **The user has sufficiently logged in or out: false.**
- ❑ B. **The user has sufficiently logged in or out: true.**
- ❑ C. **The user has sufficiently logged in or out: ${param. loggedIn or param.loggedOut}.**
- ❑ D. **The user has sufficiently logged in or out: param. loggedIn or param.loggedOut.**
- ❑ E. **The user has sufficiently logged in or out: or true.**

17

Which about EL access operators are true? (Choose all that apply.)

- ❑ A. Anywhere the **.** (dot) operator is used, the **[]** could be used instead.
- ❑ B. Anywhere the **[]** operator is used, the**.** (dot)could be used instead.
- ❑ C. If the **.** (dot) operator is used to access a bean property but the property doesn't exist, then a runtime exception is thrown.
- ❑ D. There are some situations where the**.** (dot)operator must be used and other situations where the **[]** operator must be used.

18

The following code fragment appears in a JSP page:

```
<jsp:include page="/jspf/header.html"/>
```

The JSP page is part of a web application with the context root **myapp**.

Given that the application's top level directory is **myapp**, what is the path to the **header.html** file?

- ❑ A. **/header.html**
- ❑ B. **/jspf/header.html**
- ❑ C. **/myapp/jspf/header.html**
- ❑ D. **/includes/jspf/header.html**

Chapter 8 Answers

1 Given an HTML form that uses checkboxes to allow a user to select multiple values for a parameter called, **`hobbies`**.

(JSP. v2.0 sections 2.2.3)

Which EL expressions evaluate to the first value of the **`hobbies`** parameter? (Choose all that apply.)

- ☑ A. **`${param.hobbies}`**
- ☐ B. **`${paramValue.hobbies}`**
- ☑ C. **`${paramValues.hobbies[0]}`**
- ☐ D. **`${paramValues.hobbies[1]}`**
- ☐ E. **`${paramValues[hobbies][0]}`**
- ☐ F. **`${paramValues[hobbies][1]}`**

-Option B is incorrect because there is no "paramValue" implicit variable.

-Option D is incorrect, arrays are 0 indexed.

-Options E and F have incorrect syntax.

---

2 Given that a web application stores the webmaster email address in the servlet context initialization parameter called **`master-email`**.

(JSP v2.0 sections 2.2.3 and 2.3.4)

Which retrieves that value? (Choose all that apply.)

- ☐ A. **`<a href='mailto:${initParam.master-email}'> email me</a>`**
- ☐ B. **`<a href='mailto:${contextParam.master-email}'> email me</a>`**
- ☑ C. **`<a href='mailto:${initParam['master-email']}'> email me</a>`**
- ☐ D. **`<a href='mailto:${contextParam['master-email']}'> email me</a>`**

-Option A is trying to subtract email from master

-Option B, there is no contextParam implicit variable

-Option D, there is no contextParam implicit variable

3 Given the following Java class:

(JSP v2.0 section 2.6.3)

```
package com.mycompany;
public class MyFunctions {
  public static String hello(String name) {
    return "Hello "+name;
  }
}
```

This class represents the handler for a function that is part of a tag library.

```
<%@ taglib uri="http://mycompany.com.tags" prefix="comp" %>
```

Which Tag Library Descriptor entry defines this custom function so that it can be used in an EL expression?

❑ A.

```
<taglib>
  ...
  <tag>
    <name>Hello</name>
    <tag-class>com.mycompany.MyFunctions</tag-class>
    <body-content>JSP</body-content>
  </tag>
</taglib>
```

☑ B.

```
<taglib>
  ...
  <function>
    <name>Hello</name>
    <function-class>com.mycompany.MyFunctions</function-class>
    <function-signature>java.lang.String hello(java.lang.String)
         </function-signature>
  </function>
</taglib>
```

-Option B uses the correct syntax.

❑ C.

```
<web-app>
  ...
  <servlet>
    <servlet-name>hello</servlet-name>
    <servlet-class>com.mycompany.MyFunctions</servlet-class>
  </servlet>
</web-app>
```

❑ D.

```
<taglib>
  ...
  <function>
    <name>Hello</name>
    <function-class>com.mycompany.MyFunctions</function-class>
    <function-signature>hello(java.lang.String)</function-signature>
  </function>
</taglib>
```

-Option D is incorrect because the function signature is incomplete

---

4 Given:

(JSP v2.0 section 5.1)

```
package com.example;
public class TheBean {
  private int value;
  public TheBean() { value = 42; }
  public int getValue() { return value; }
  public void setValue(int v) { value = v; }
}
```

Assuming no instances of **TheBean** have been created yet, which JSP standard action statements create a new instance of this bean and store it in the request scope? (Choose all that apply.)

☐ A. **<jsp:useBean name="myBean"**
type="com.example.TheBean" />

-Option A is invalid because the type attribute is NOT used to create a new instance and the scope attribute must be specified (or defaults to page).

☐ B. **<jsp:makeBean name="myBean"**
type="com.example.TheBean" />

-Option B is invalid for all of the above reasons plus jsp:makeBean is NOT a real tag.

☑ C. **<jsp:useBean id="myBean"**
class="com.example.TheBean"
scope="request" />

☐ D. **<jsp:makeBean id="myBean"**
class="com.example.TheBean"
scope="request" />

-Option D is invalid because jsp:makeBean is NOT a real tag.

---

5 Given a Model 1 architecture in which a JSP page handles all of the controller functions, that JSP controller needs to dispatch the request to another JSP page.

(JSP v2.0 section 5.5)

Which standard action code will perform this dispatch?

☑ A. **<jsp:forward page="view.jsp" />**

-Option A is correct (pg 1-110).

☐ B. **<jsp:forward file="view.jsp" />**

-Option B is invalid because the forward action has no file attribute.

☐ C. **<jsp:dispatch page="view.jsp" />**

☐ D. **<jsp:dispatch file="view.jsp" />**

-Options C and D are invalid because there is no dispatch action.

(JSP v2.0 section 2.3.4)

6 Given:

```
11. <% java.util.List list = new java.util.ArrayList();
12.     list.add("a");
13.     list.add("2");
14.     list.add("c");
15.     request.setAttribute("list", list);
16.     request.setAttribute("listIdx", "1");
17. %>
18. <%-- insert code here --%>
```

Which, inserted at line 18, are valid and evaluate to **c** ? (Choose all that apply.)

- [ ] A. `${list.2}`
- [x] B. `${list[2]}`
- [ ] C. `${list.listIdx+1}`
- [x] D. `${list[listIdx+1]}`
- [ ] E. `${list['listIdx' + 1]}`
- [x] F. `${list[list[listIdx]]}`

–Options A and C are incorrect because the dot operator cannot be used with a primitive.

–Option E is incorrect because ('listIdx' + 1) becomes a String.

(JSP v2.0 pg. 1-69)

7 Which statements about the **.** (dot) and **[]** EL operators are true? (Choose all that apply.)

- [ ] A. `${foo.bar}` is equivalent to `${foo[bar]}`

  –Option A is incorrect because it should be foo["bar"].

- [x] B. `${foo.bar}` is equivalent to `${foo["bar"]}`
- [x] C. `${foo["5"]}` is valid syntax if **foo** is a **Map**
- [ ] D. `${header.User-Agent}` is equivalent to `${header[User-Agent]}`
- [ ] E. `${header.User-Agent}` is equivalent to `${header["User-Agent"]}`

  –Options D and E are incorrect because of the dash in User-Agent. Only header["User-Agent"] will work.

- [x] F. `${foo[5]}` is valid syntax if **foo** is a **List** or an array

---

8 Given a JSP page with the line: (JSP v2.0 pg. 1-71)

`${101 % 10}`

What will be displayed?

- [x] A. `1` —Option A is correct. The modulus operator returns the remainder of a division operation.
- [ ] B. `10`
- [ ] C. `1001`
- [ ] D. `101 % 10`
- [ ] E. `{101 % 10}`

---

9 Given: (JSP v2.0 pg 1-67 and pg 1-79)

```
10. ${param.firstname}
11. ${param.middlename}
12. ${param.lastname}
13. ${paramValues.lastname[0]}
```

Which describes the output produced by this portion of a JSP page when passed the query string `?firstname=John&lastname=Doe`?

- [ ] A. `John Doe` —Option A is invalid because line 13 prints the user's last name as well.
- [x] B. `John Doe Doe`
- [ ] C. `John null Doe` —Options C and D are invalid because line 11 results in printing nothing rather than "null".
- [ ] D. `John null Doe Doe`
- [ ] E. A null pointer exception will be thrown.

---

10 Which show valid usage of EL implicit variables? (Choose all that apply.) (JSP v2.0 pg. 1-66)

- [ ] A. `${cookies.foo}` —Option A is incorrect because the variable is "cookie".
- [x] B. `${initParam.foo}`
- [ ] C. `${pageContext.foo}` —Option C is incorrect because pageContext is NOT a Map and it doesn't have a "foo" property.
- [x] D. `${requestScope.foo}`
- [x] E. `${header["User-Agent"]}`
- [ ] F. `${requestDispatcher.foo}` —Option F is incorrect because this is NOT an implicit object.
- [x] G. `${pageContext.request.requestURI}`

(JSP v2.0 pgs. 1-103 and pg. 1-104)

11 Which are true about the **<jsp:useBean>** standard action? (Choose all that apply.)

- ❑ A. The **id** attribute is optional.
- ❑ B. The **scope** attribute is required.
- ❑ C. The **scope** attribute is optional and defaults to **request**.
- ☑ D. Either the **class** or **type** attributes may be specified, but at least one.
- ☑ E. It is valid to include both the **class** attribute and the **type** attribute, even if their values are NOT the same.

–Option A is incorrect because id is required.

–Options B and C are incorrect because scope is optional and defaults to page.

(JSP v2.0 section 5.4)

12 How would you include dynamic content in a JSP, similar to a server-side include (SSI)? (Choose all that apply.)

- ❑ A. `<%@ include file="/segments/footer.jspf" %>`
- ❑ B. `<jsp:forward page="/segments/footer.jspf" />`
- ☑ C. `<jsp:include page="/segments/footer.jspf" />`
- ❑ D.

```
RequestDispatcher dispatcher
    = request.getRequestDispatcher("/segments/footer.jspf");
dispatcher.include(request,response);
```

–Option A is incorrect because it uses an include directive, which is for static includes that happen at translation time.

–Option D would be correct if it was a scriptlet: it functionally does the same thing as option C, but its syntax is only used by servlets.

(JSP v2.0 section 5.4)

13 In an HTML page with a rich, graphical layout, which JSP standard action can be used to import an image file into the JSP page?

- ❑ A. `<jsp:image page="logo.png" />`
- ❑ B. `<jsp:image file="logo.png" />`
- ❑ C. `<jsp:include page="logo.png" />`
- ❑ D. `<jsp:include file="logo.png" />`
- ☑ E. This CANNOT be done using a JSP standard action.

–Options A and B are invalid because there is no image standard action.

–Option C is invalid, not because the syntax of the include action is wrong, but because it does not make sense to import the binary data of the image file into the JSP content.

–Option D is invalid because the include action does not take a file attribute.

This is a tricky question because it is NOT possible to import the contents of any binary file into a JSP page, which generates an HTML response.

14 Given: (JSP v2.0 section 2.6)

```
package com.example;
public class MyFunctions {
  public static String repeat(int x, String str) {
    // method body
  }
}
```

and given the JSP:

```
1. <%@ taglib uri="/WEB-INF/myfuncts" prefix="my" %>
2. <%-- insert code here --%>
```

Which, inserted at line 2 in the JSP, is a valid EL function invocation?

- [ ] A. `${repeat(2, "420")}`
- [ ] B. `${repeat("2", "420")}`
- [ ] C. `${my:repeat(2, "420")}`
- [ ] D. `${my:repeat("2", "420")}`
- [x] E. A valid invocation CANNOT be determined.

–Option E is correct. The necessary mapping information is NOT known.

---

15 Given: (JSP v2.0 pg. 1-68)

```
public class MyBean {
  private java.util.Map params;
  private java.util.List objects;
  private String name;
  public java.util.Map getParams() { return params; }
  public String getName() { return name; }
  public java.util.List getObjects() { return objects; }
}
```

Which will cause errors (assume that an attribute named **mybean** can be found, and is of type **MyBean**)? (Choose all that apply.)

- [ ] A. `${mybean.name}`
- [ ] B. `${mybean["name"]}`
- [x] C. `${mybean.objects.a}`
- [ ] D. `${mybean["params"].a}`
- [ ] E. `${mybean.params["a"]}`
- [x] F. `${mybean["objects"].a}`

–Options C and F will cause errors. "a" is NOT a List property, and since "objects" is NOT a Map, a lookup won't be performed (as opposed to D and E).

16 Given a JSP page:

```
1. The user has sufficiently logged in or out:
2.    ${param.loggedIn or param.loggedOut}.
```

(JSP v2.0 pgs 1-66 and 1-73)

If the request includes the query string "**loggedOut=true**", what will be this statement's displayed value?

- [ ] A. **The user has sufficiently logged in or out: false.**
- [x] B. **The user has sufficiently logged in or out: true.**
- [ ] C. **The user has sufficiently logged in or out: ${param. loggedIn or param.loggedOut}.**
- [ ] D. **The user has sufficiently logged in or out: param. loggedIn or param.loggedOut.**
- [ ] E. **The user has sufficiently logged in or out: or true.**

-Option B is correct because the EL expression using "or" will return true if either loggedIn or loggedOut is true.

17 Which about EL access operators are true? (Choose all that apply.)

(JSP v2.0 pg. 1-69)

- [x] A. Anywhere the **.** (dot) operator is used, the **[]** could be used instead.
- [ ] B. Anywhere the **[]** operator is used, the**.** (dot)could be used instead.
- [ ] C. If the **.** (dot) operator is used to access a bean property but the property doesn't exist, then a runtime exception is thrown.
- [ ] D. There are some situations where the**.** (dot)operator must be used and other situations where the **[]** operator must be used.

-Option B is incorrect because only the [] will work when accessing a) Lists and arrays, and b) Maps whose keys are not well-formed.

-Option D is incorrect because the dot operator can always be converted to the [] operator.

18 The following code fragment appears in a JSP page:

```
<jsp:include page="/jspf/header.html"/>
```

(JSP v2.0 section 5.4)

The JSP page is part of a web application with the context root **myapp**.

Given that the application's top level directory is **myapp**, what is the path to the **header.html** file?

- [ ] A. **/header.html**
- [ ] B. **/jspf/header.html**
- [x] C. **/myapp/jspf/header.html**
- [ ] D. **/includes/jspf/header.html**

-The path /jspf/header.html when used as the value of the <jsp:include> action's page attribute is relative to the web application, so a leading back slash ("/") means "begin at the application's top level."

9 using JSTL

Custom tags are powerful

You mean, I spent all this time writing scriptlets for the things I *can't* do with EL and standard actions, when I *could* have used JSTL?

Sometimes you need more than EL or standard actions.

What if you want to loop through the data in an array, and display one item per row in an HTML table? You *know* you could write that in two seconds using a for loop in a scriptlet. But you're trying to get away from scripting. No problem. When EL and standard actions aren't enough, you can use *custom tags*. They're as easy to use in a JSP as standard actions. Even better, someone's already written a pile of the ones you're most likely to need, and bundled them into the JSP Standard Tag Library (JSTL). In *this* chapter we'll learn to *use* custom tags, and in the next chapter we'll learn to create our own.

Building JSP pages using tag libraries

9.1 Describe the syntax and semantics of the 'taglib' directive: for a standard tag library, for a library of Tag Files.

9.2 Given a design goal, create the custom tag structure to support that goal.

9.3 Identify the tag syntax and describe the action semantics of the following JSP Standard Tag Library (JSTL v1.1) tags: (a) core tags: out, set, remove, and catch, (b) conditional tags: if, choose, when, and otherwise, (c) iteration tags: forEach, and (d) URL-related: url.

Coverage Notes:

All of the objectives in this section are covered in this chapter, although some of the content is covered again in the next chapter (Developing Custom Tags).

Installing the JSTL 1.1

The JSTL 1.1 is NOT part of the JSP 2.0 specification! Having access to the Servlet and JSP API's doesn't mean you have access to JSTL.

Before you can use JSTL, you need to put two files, "jstl.jar" and "standard.jar" into the WEB-INF/lib directory of your web app. That means each web app needs a copy.

In Tomcat 5, the two files are already in the example applications that ship out-of-the-box with Tomcat, so all you need to do is copy them from one directory and put them into your own app's WEB-INF/lib directory.

Copy the files from the Tomcat examples at:

webapps/jsp-examples/WEB-INF/lib/jstl.jar
webapps/jsp-examples/WEB-INF/lib/standard.jar

And place it in your own web app's WEB-INF/lib directory.

There's got to be a way to iterate through a collection in a JSP...*without* scripting. I want to show one element per row in a table...

EL and standard actions are limited

What happens when you bump into a brick wall? You can go back to scripting, of course—but you know that's not the path.

Developers usually want *way* more standard actions or—even better—the ability to create their *own* actions.

That's what ***custom tags*** are for. Instead of saying <jsp:setProperty>, you want to do something like <my:doCustomThing>. And you can.

But it's not that easy to create the support code that goes behind the tag. For the JSP page creator, custom tags are much easier to use than scripting. For the Java programmer, however, building the custom tag *handler* (the Java code invoked when a JSP uses the tag) is tougher.

Fortunately, there's a standard library of custom tags known as the **JSP Standard Tag Library** (JSTL 1.1). Given that your JSP shouldn't be doing a bunch of business logic anyway, you might find that the JSTL (combined with EL) is all you'll ever need. Still, there could be times when you need something from, say, a custom tag library developed specifically for your company.

In *this* chapter, you'll learn how to use the core JSTL tags, as well as custom tags from other libraries. In the *next* chapter, we'll learn how to actually build the classes that handle calls to the custom tags, so that you can develop your own.

Looping without scripting

Imagine you want something that loops over a collection (say, an array of catalog items), pulls out one element at a time, and prints that element in a dynamically-generated table row. You can't possibly hard-code the complete table—you have no idea how many rows there will be at runtime, and of course you don't know the values in the collection. The <c:forEach> tag is the answer. This does require a very slight knowledge of HTML tables, but we've included notes here for those who aren't familiar with the topic.

By the way, on the exam you *are* expected to know how to use <c:forEach> with tables.

Servlet code

```
...
String[] movieList = {"Amelie", "Return of the King", "Mean Girls"};
request.setAttribute("movieList", movieList);
...
```

Make a String[] of movie names, and set the array as a request attribute.

What you want

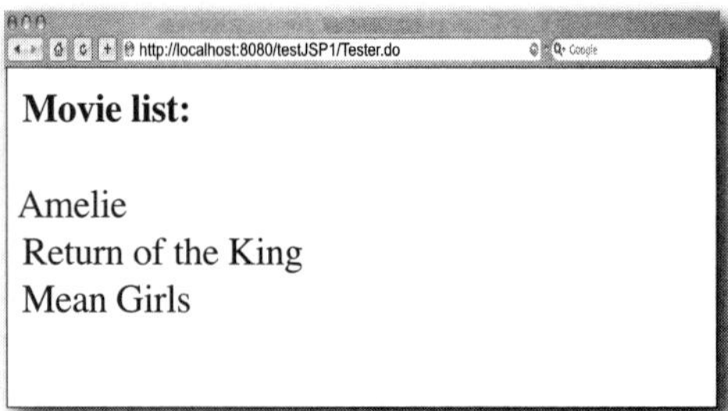

In a JSP, *with* scripting

```
<table>
<% String[] items = (String[]) request.getAttribute("movieList");
   String var=null;
   for (int i = 0; i < items.length; i++) {
      var = items[i];
 %>
  <tr><td><%= var %></td></tr>
  <% } %>
</table>
```

<c:forEach>

The <c:forEach> tag from the JSTL is perfect for this—it gives you a simple way to iterate over arrays and collections.

JSP code

(We'll talk about this taglib directive later in the chapter.)

```
<%@ taglib prefix="c" uri="http://java.sun.com/jsp/jstl/core" %>
<html><body>
<strong> Movie list:</strong>
<br><br>

<table>

  <c:forEach var="movie" items="${movieList}" >

     <tr>

        <td>${movie}</td>

     </tr>

  </c:forEach>

</table>

</body></html>
```

Loops through the entire array (the "movieList" attribute) and prints each element in a new row. (This table has just one column per row.)

Crash refresher on HTML tables

<tr> stands for Table Row.

<td> stands for Table Data.

```
<table>
```

<tr>	**<td>**data for this cell**</td>**	**<td>**data for this cell**</td>**	**<td>**data for this cell**</td>**	</tr>
<tr>	**<td>**data for this cell**</td>**	**<td>**data for this cell**</td>**	**<td>**data for this cell**</td>**	</tr>
<tr>	**<td>**data for this cell**</td>**	**<td>**data for this cell**</td>**	**<td>**data for this cell**</td>**	</tr>

```
</table>
```

Tables are pretty straightforward. They've got *cells*, arranged into *rows* and *columns*, and the data goes inside the cells. The trick is telling the table how many rows and columns you want.

Rows are defined with the <tr> (Table Row) tag, and columns are defined with the <td> (Table Data) tag. The number of rows comes from the number of <tr> tags, and the number of columns comes from the number of <td> tags you put inside the <tr></tr> tags.

Data to print/display goes only inside the <td> </td> tags!

Deconstructing <c:forEach>

The <c:forEach> tag maps nicely into a for loop—the tag repeats the *body* of the tag *for each* element in the collection (and we use "collection" here to mean either an array or Collection or Map or comma-delimited String).

The key feature is that the tag assigns each element in the collection to the variable you declare with the *var* attribute.

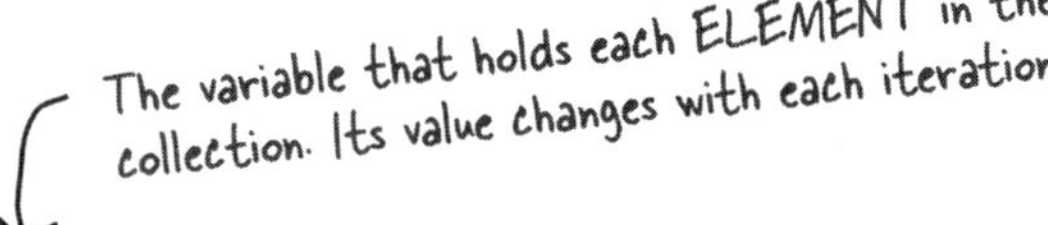

The variable that holds each ELEMENT in the collection. Its value changes with each iteration.

The <c:forEach> tag

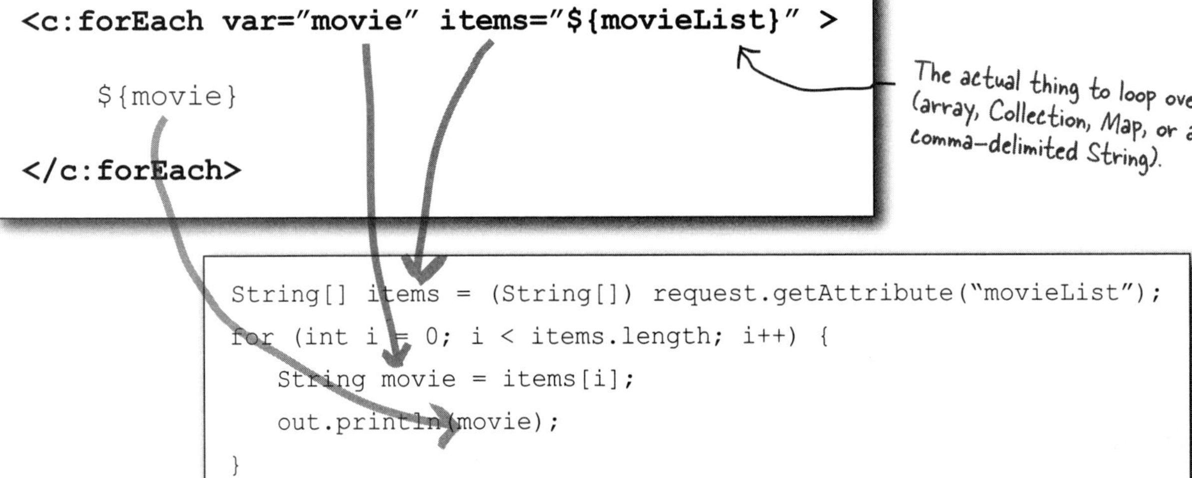

Getting a loop counter with the optional varStatus attribute

varStatus makes a new variable that holds an instance of javax.servlet.jsp.jstl.core.LoopTagStatus.

```
<table>
  <c:forEach var="movie" items="${movieList}" varStatus="movieLoopCount" >
     <tr>
         <td>Count: ${movieLoopCount.count}</td>
     </tr>
     <tr>
         <td>${movie} <br><br></td>
     </tr>
  </c:forEach>
</table>
```

Helpfully, the LoopTagStatus class has a count property that gives you the current value of the iteration counter. (Like the "i" in a for loop.)

http://localhost:8080/testJSP1/Tester.do

Count: 1
Amelie

Count: 2
Return of the King

Count: 3
Mean Girl

You can even nest <c:forEach> tags

What if you have something like a collection of collections? An array of arrays? You can nest <c:forEach> tags for more complex table structures. In this example, we put String arrays into an ArrayList, then make the ArrayList a request attribute. The JSP has to loop through the ArrayList to get each String array, then loop through each String array to print the actual elements of the array.

Servlet code

```
String[] movies1 = {"Matrix Revolutions", "Kill Bill", "Boondock Saints"};
String[] movies2 = {"Amelie", "Return of the King", "Mean Girls"};
java.util.List movieList = new java.util.ArrayList();
movieList.add(movies1);
movieList.add(movies2);
request.setAttribute("movies", movieList);
```

JSP code

```
<table>

  <c:forEach var="listElement" items="${movies}" >

    <c:forEach var="movie" items="${listElement}" >
      <tr>
        <td>${movie}</td>
      </tr>
    </c:forEach>

  </c:forEach>

</table>
```

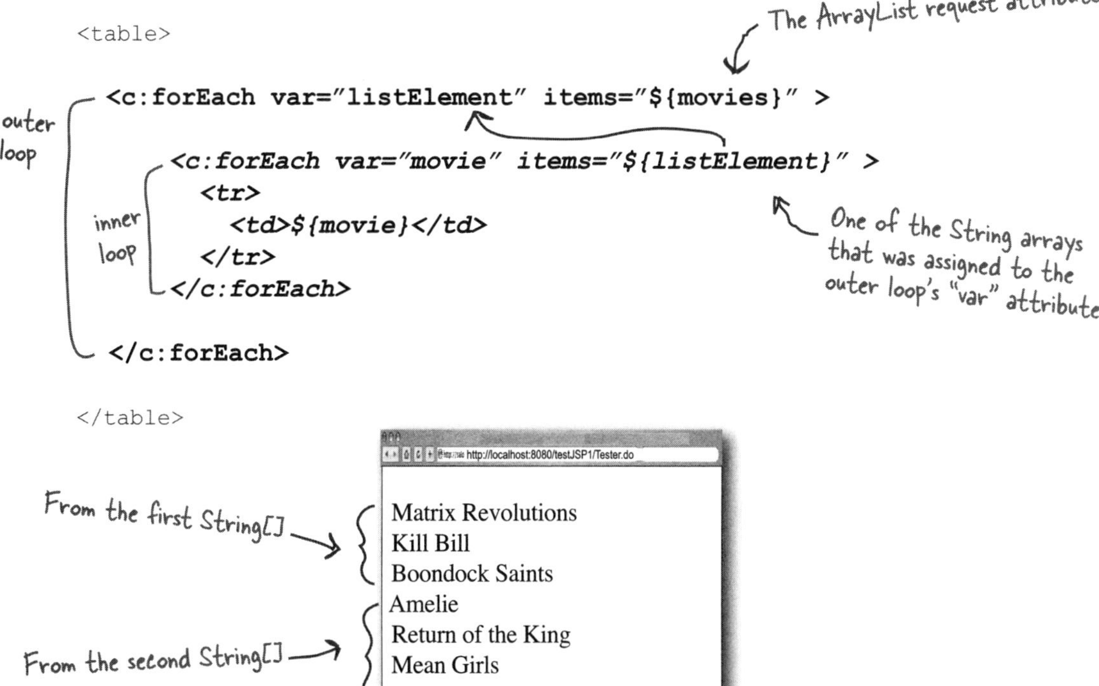

there are no Dumb Questions

Q: How did you know that the "varStatus" attribute was an instance of whatever that was, and how did you know that it has a "count" property?

A: Ahhhh... we looked it up.

It's all there in the JSTL 1.1 spec. If you don't have the spec already, go download it NOW (the intro of this book tells you where to get the specs covered on the exam). It is THE reference for all the tags in the JSTL, and tells you all the possible attributes, whether they're optional or required, the attribute type, and any other details on how you use the tag.

Everything you need to know about these tags (for the exam) is in this chapter. But some of the tags have a few more options than we cover here, so you might want to have a look in the spec.

Q: Since you know more than you're telling about this tag... does it give you a way to change the iteration steps? In a real Java for loop, I don't have to do i++, I can do i +=3, for example, to get every third element instead of every element...

A: Not a problem. The <c:forEach> tag has optional attributes for *begin*, *end* (in case you want to iterate over a subset of the collection), and *step* if you want to skip over some elements.

Q: Is the "c" in <c:forEach> a required prefix?

A: Well, *some* prefix is required, of course; all tags and EL functions must have a prefix to give the Container the namespace for that tag or function name. But you don't HAVE to name the prefix "c". It's just the standard convention for the set of tags in JSTL known as "**c**ore". We recommend using something *other* than "c" as a prefix, whenever you want to totally confuse the people you work with.

Watch it!

The "var" variable is scoped to ONLY the tag!

That's right, tag scope. No this isn't a full-fledged scope to which you can bind attributes like the other four—page, request, session, and application. Tag scope simply means that the variable was declared INSIDE a loop.

And you already know what that means in Java terms. You'll see that for most other tags, a variable set with a "var" attribute will be visible to whatever scope you specifically set (using an optional "scope" attribute), OR, the variable will default to page scope.

So don't be fooled by code that tries to use the variable somewhere BELOW the end of the <c:forEach> body tag!

```
<c:forEach var="foo" items="${fooList}" >
     ${foo}      ← OK
</c:forEach>

${foo}   ← NO!! The "foo" variable is out of scope!
```

It might help to think of tag scope as being just like block scope in plain old Java code. An example is the for loop you all know and love:

```
for (int i = 0; i < items.length; i++) {
   x + i;
}
doSomething(i);      NO!! The "i" variable is out of scope!
```

Doing a conditional include with <c:if>

Imagine you have a page where users can view comments from other users. And imagine that members can also post comments, but non-member guests cannot. **You want *everyone* to get the same page, but you want *members* to "see" more things on the page.** You want a conditional <jsp:include > and of course, you don't want to do it with scripting!

What members see:

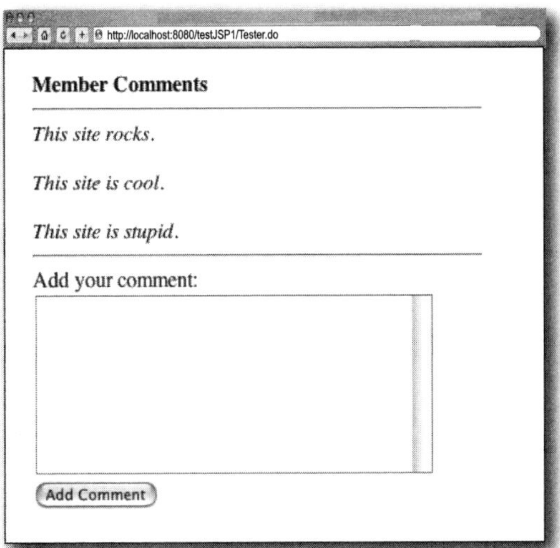

What NON-members see:

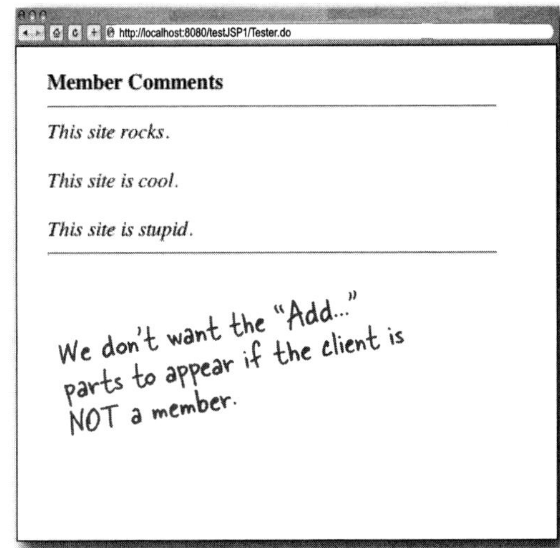

JSP code

```
<%@ taglib prefix="c" uri="http://java.sun.com/jsp/jstl/core" %>
<html><body>
<strong>Member Comments</strong> <br>
<hr>${commentList}<hr>

<c:if test="${userType eq 'member' }" >
   <jsp:include page="inputComments.jsp"/>
</c:if>
</body></html>
```

Assume a servlet somewhere set the userType attribute, based on the user's login information.

Yes, those are SINGLE quotes around 'member'. Don't forget that you can use EITHER double or single quotes in your tags and EL.

Included page ("inputComments.jsp")

```
<form action="commentsProcess.jsp" method="post">
Add your comment: <br>
<textarea name="input" cols="40" rows="10"></textarea> <br>
<input name="commentSubmit" type="button" value="Add Comment">
</form>
```

But what if you need an *else?*

What if you want to do *one* thing if the condition is true, and a *different* thing if the condition is false? In other words, what if we want to show either one thing *or* the other, but *nobody* will see both? The <c:if> on the previous page worked fine because the logic was: *everybody* sees the first part, and then if the test condition is true, show a little extra.

But now imagine this scenario: you have a car sales web site, and ***you want to customize the headline that shows up on each page, based on a user attribute*** set up earlier in the session. Most of the page is the same regardless of the user, but each user sees a customized *headline*—one that best fits the user's personal motivation for buying. (We are, after all, trying to sell him a car and become obscenely wealthy.) At the beginning of the session, a form asks the user to choose what's most important...

Imagine a web site for a car company. The first page asks the user what he feels is most important.

Just like a good salesman, the pages that talk about features of the car will customize the presentation based on the user's preference, so that each feature of the car looks like it was made with HIS personal needs in mind...

At the beginning of the session:

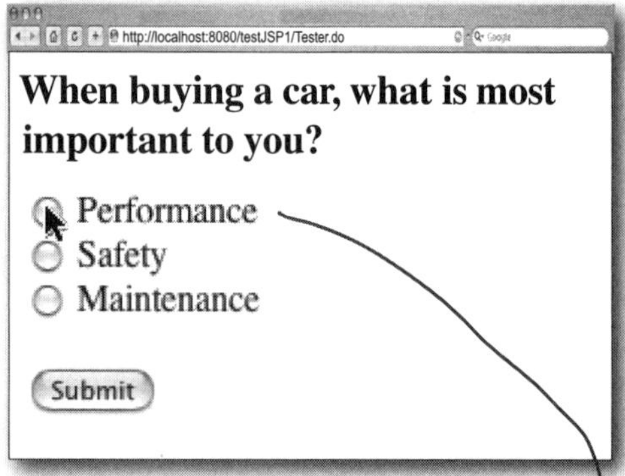

Somewhere later in the session:

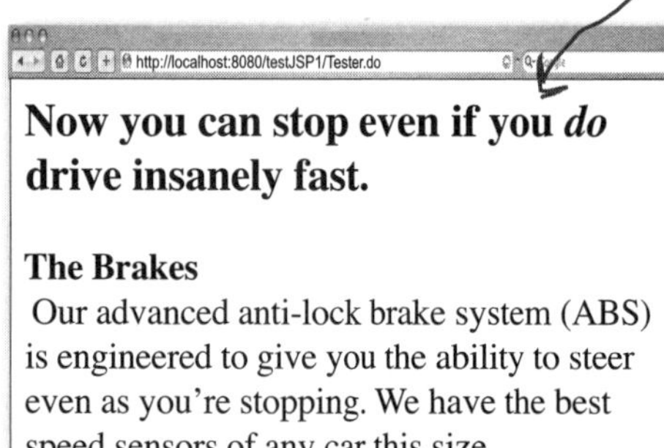

The user's page is customized a little, to fit his interests...

The <c:if> tag won't work for this

There's no way to do exactly what we want using the <c:if> tag, because ***it doesn't have an "else"***. We can almost do it, using something like:

JSP using <c:if>, but it doesn't work right...

```
<c:if test="${userPref=='performance'}" >
    Now you can stop even if you <em>do</em> drive insanely fast..
</c:if>
<c:if test="${userPref=='safety'}" >
    Our brakes won't lock up no matter how bad a driver you are.
</c:if>
<c:if test="${userPref=='maintenance'}" >
    Lost your tech job? No problem--you won't have to service these brakes
    for at least three years.
</c:if>
```

But what happens if userPref doesn't match any of these? There's no way to specify the default headline?

```
<!-- continue with the rest of the page that EVERYONE should see  -->
```

The <c:if> won't work unless we're CERTAIN that we'll never need a default value. What we really need is kind of an if/else construct:*

JSP *with* scripting, and it does what we want

Assume "userPref" was set somewhere earlier in the session.

```
<html><body><h2>
<% String pref = (String) session.getAttribute("userPref");
   if (pref.equals("performance")) {
       out.println("Now you can stop even if you <em>do</em> drive insanely fast.");
   } else if (pref.equals("safety")) {
       out.println("Our brakes won't lock up, no matter how bad a driver you are. ");
   } else if (pref.equals("maintenance")) {
       out.println(" Lost your tech job? No problem--you won't have to service these
brakes for at least three years.");
   } else {
       // userPref doesn't match those, so print the default headline
       out.println("Our brakes are the best.");
  } %>
</h2><strong>The Brakes</strong> <br>
Our advanced anti-lock brake system (ABS) is engineered to give you the ability to
steer even as you're stopping. We have the
best speed sensors of any car this size. <br>
</body></html>
```

*Yes, we agree with you—there's nearly *always* a better approach than chained if tests. But you're just gonna have to suspend disbelief long enough to learn how this all works....

I will **CHOOSE** you **WHEN** you are ready to give up your obsession with Pilates. **OTHERWISE**, I'll have to go with Kenny for the synchronized swim team.

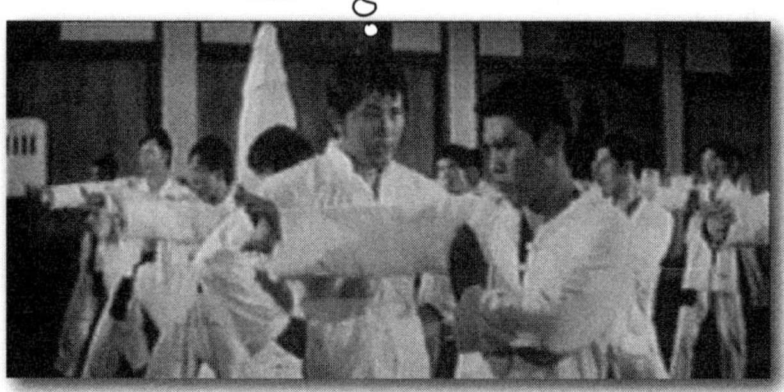

The <c:choose> tag and its partners <c:when> and <c:otherwise>

No more than ONE of these four bodies (including the <c:otherwise>) will run.

(It's not like a switch statement-- there's no fall-through.)

```
<c:choose>
    <c:when test="${userPref == 'performance'}">
        Now you can stop even if you <em>do</em> drive insanely fast.
    </c:when>

    <c:when test="${userPref == 'safety'}">
        Our brakes will never lock up, no matter how bad a driver you are.
    </c:when>

    <c:when test="${userPref == 'maintenance'}">
        Lost your tech job? No problem--you won't have to service these brakes
for at least three years.
    </c:when>

    <c:otherwise>
        Our brakes are the best.
    </c:otherwise>
</c:choose>
<!-- the rest of the page goes here... -->
```

If none of the <c:when> tests are true, the <c:otherwise> runs as a default.

Note: the <c:choose> tag is NOT required to have a <c:otherwise> tag.

The <c:set> tag... so much cooler than <jsp:setProperty>

The <jsp:setProperty> tag can do only one thing—set the property of a bean.

But what if you want to set a value in a Map? What if you want to make a *new* entry in a Map? Or what if you simply want to create a new request-scoped attribute?

You get all that with <c:set>, but you have to learn a few simple rules. Set comes in two flavors: ***var*** and ***target***. The *var* version is for setting attribute variables, the *target* version is for setting bean properties or Map values. Each of the two flavors comes in two variations: with or without a body. The <c:set> body is just another way to put in the *value*.

Setting an attribute variable var with <c:set>

1 With NO body

If there's NOT a session-scoped attribute named "userLevel", this tag creates one (assuming the value attribute is not null).

```
<c:set var="userLevel" scope="session" value="Cowboy" />
```

The scope is optional; var is required. You MUST specify a value, but you have a choice between putting in a value attribute or putting the value in the tag body (see #2 below).

value doesn't have to be a String...

```
<c:set var="Fido" value="${person.dog}" />
```

If ${person.dog} evaluates to a Dog object, then "Fido" is of type Dog.

2 WITH a body

Remember, no slash here when the tag has a body.

```
<c:set var="userLevel" scope="session" >
     Sheriff, Bartender, Cowgirl
</c:set>
```

The body is evaluated and used as the value of the variable.

If the *value* evaluates to null, the variable will be REMOVED! That's right, *removed*.

*Imagine that for the value (either in the body of the tag or using the value attribute), you use ${person.dog}. If ${person.dog} evaluates to null (meaning there is no **person**, or person's **dog** property is null, then if there IS a variable attribute with a name "Fido", that attribute will be removed! (If you don't specify a scope, it will start looking at page, then request, etc.). This happens even if the "Fido" attribute was originally set as a String, or a Duck, or a Broccoli.*

Using <c:set> with beans and Maps

This flavor of <c:set> (with its two variations—with and without a body) works for only two things: bean properties and Map values. That's it. You can't use it to add things to lists or arrays. It's simple—you give it the object (a bean or Map), the property/key name, and the value.

Setting a target property or value with <c:set>

1 With NO body

If target is a bean, set the value of the property "dogName".

```
<c:set target="${PetMap}" property="dogName" value="Clover" />
```

target must NOT be null!!

If target is a Map, set the value of a key named "dogName".

2 WITH a body

Don't put the "id" name of the attribute here!

```
<c:set target="${person}" property="name" >
  ${foo.name}
</c:set>
```

No slash... watch for this on the exam.

The body can be a String or expression.

The "target" must evaluate to the OBJECT! You don't type in the String "id" name of the bean or Map attribute!

This is a huge gotcha. In the <c:set > tag, the "target" attribute in the tag seems like it should work just like "id" in the <jsp:setProperty >. Even the "var" attribute in the other version of <c:set> takes a String literal that represents the name of the scoped attribute. BUT... it doesn't work this way with "target"!
With the "target" attribute, you do NOT type in the String literal that represents the name under which the attribute was bound to the page, scope, etc. No, the "target" attribute needs a value that resolves to the REAL THING. That means an EL expression or a scripting expression (<%= %>), or something we haven't seen yet: <jsp:attribute>.

Key points and gotchas with <c:set>

Yes, <c:set> is easy to use, but there are a few deal-breakers you have to remember...

- You can never have BOTH the "var" and "target" attributes in a <c:set>.
- "Scope" is optional, but if you don't use it the default is *page* scope.
- If the "value" is null, the attribute named by "var" will be removed!
- If the attribute named by "var" does not exist, it'll be created, but only if "value" is not null.
- If the "target" expression is null, the Container throws an exception.
- The "target" is for putting in an expression that resolves to the Real Object. If you put in a String literal that represents the "id" name of the bean or Map, it won't work. In other words, "target" is not for the attribute *name* of the bean or Map—it's for the actual attribute *object*.
- If the "target" expression is not a Map or a bean, the Container throws an exception.
- If the "target" expression is a bean, but the bean does not have a property that matches "property", the Container throws an exception. But be careful, because the EL expression by itself will NOT cause an exception if the property doesn't exist. So even though: ${fooBean.notAProperty} won't cause an exception by itself (it just returns null), if that *same* "notAProperty" is the value of a "target" attribute, the Container throws an exception.

there are no Dumb Questions

Q: Why would I use the body version instead of the no-body version? It looks like they both do exactly the same thing.

A: That's because they DO... do the same thing. The body version is just for convenience when you want more room for the value. It might be a long and complex expression, for example, and putting it in the body makes it easier to read.

Q: If I don't specify a scope, does that mean it will find attributes that are ONLY within page scope, or does it do a search beginning with page scope?

A: If you don't use the optional "scope" attribute in the tag, and you're using "var" or "target", the Container will search scopes in the order in which you've come to expect—page, then request, then session, then application (context).

If you use the "var" version without a scope, and the Container can't find an attribute of that name in any of the four scopes, the Container makes a new one in page scope.

Q: Why is the word "attribute" so overloaded? It means both "the things that go inside tags" and "the things that are bound to objects in one of the four scopes." So you end up with an attribute of a tag whose value is an attribute of the page and...

A: We hear you. But that's what they're called. Once again, nobody asked US. We would have called the bound objects something like, oh, "bound objects".

I can't believe you have to use <c:set> to *remove* an attribute. That feels wrong.

<c:remove> just makes sense

We agree with Dick—using a *set* to *remove* something feels wrong. (But remember, *set* does a *remove* only when you pass in a null value.)

The <c:remove> tag is intuitive and simple:

```
<%@ taglib prefix="c" uri="http://java.sun.com/jsp/jstl/core" %>
<html><body>

   <c:set var="userStatus" scope="request" value="Brilliant" />

   userStatus: ${userStatus} <br>

   <c:remove var="userStatus" scope="request" />

   userStatus is now: ${userStatus}

</body></html>
```

The var attribute MUST be a String literal! It can't be an expression!!

The scope is optional, and like always—page is the default scope.

http://localhost:8080/testJSP1/Tester.do

userStatus: Brilliant
userStatus is now:

The value of userStatus was removed, so nothing prints when the EL expression is used AFTER the remove.

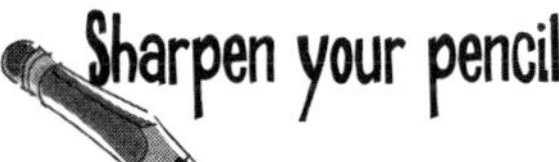

Test your Tag memory

If you're studying for the exam, don't skip this one.
The answers are at the end of the chapter.

1. Fill in the name of the optional attribute.

```
<c:forEach var="movie" items="${movieList}" [          ]="foo"  >
   ${movie}
</c:forEach>
```

2. Fill in the missing attribute name.

```
<c:if [          ]="${userPref=='safety'}" >
    Maybe you should just walk...
</c:if>
```

3. Fill in the missing attribute name.

```
<c:set var="userLevel" scope="session"  [          ]="foo" />
```

4. Fill in the missing tag names (two different tag types), and the missing attribute name.

```
<c:choose>
    <c:[          ] [          ]="${userPref == 'performance'}">
        Now you can stop even if you <em>do</em> drive insanely fast.
    </c:[          ] >
    <c:[                    ] >
        Our brakes are the best.
    </c:[                    ] >
</c:choose>
```

With <c:import>, there are now THREE ways to include content

So far, we've used two different ways to add content from another resource into a JSP. But there's yet *another* way, using JSTL.

① The include *directive*

```
<%@ include file="Header.html" %>
```

Static: adds the content from the value of the *file* attribute to the current page at ***translation*** time.

② The <jsp:include> *standard action*

```
<jsp:include page="Header.jsp" />
```

Dynamic: adds the content from the value of the *page* attribute to the current page at ***request*** time.

Unlike the other two includes, the <c:import> url can be from outside the web Container!

③ The <c:import> JSTL tag

```
<c:import url="http://www.wickedlysmart.com/skyler/horse.html" />
```

Dynamic: adds the content from the value of the *URL* attribute to the current page, at ***request*** time. It works a lot like <jsp:include>, but it's more powerful and flexible.

Do NOT confuse <c:import> (a type of include) with the "import" attribute of the page directive (a way to put a Java import statement in the generated servlet).

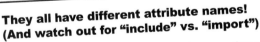

They all have different attribute names! (And watch out for "include" vs. "import")

Each of the three mechanisms for including content from another resource into your JSP uses a different word for the attribute. The include directive uses ***file****, the <jsp:include> uses* ***page****, and the JSTL <c:import> tag uses* ***url****. This makes sense, when you think about it... but you do have to memorize all three. The directive was originally intended for static layout templates, like HTML headers. In other words, a "file". The <jsp:include> was intended more for dynamic content coming from JSPs, so they named the attribute "page" to reflect that. The attribute for <c:import> is named for exactly what you give it—a URL! Remember, the first two "includes" can't go outside the current Container, but <c:import>* ***can****.*

<c:import> can reach OUTSIDE the web app

With <jsp:include> or the include directive, you can include only pages that are part of the current web app. But now with <c:import>, you have the option to pull in content from *outside* the Container. This simple example shows a JSP on Server A importing the contents of a URL on Server B. At request time, the HTML chunk in the imported file is added to the JSP. The imported chunk uses a reference to an image that is *also* on Server B.

Server A, the JSP doing the import

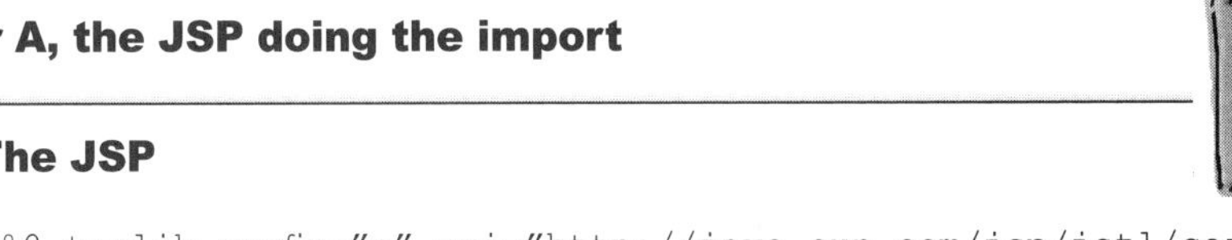

The JSP

```
<%@ taglib prefix="c" uri="http://java.sun.com/jsp/jstl/core" %>
<html><body>

  <c:import url="http://www.wickedlysmart.com/skyler/horse.html" />

  <br>
  This is my horse.

</body></html>
```

(Don't forget: as with other include mechanisms, the thing you import should be an HTML fragment and NOT a complete page with opening and closing <html><body> tags.)

Server B, the imported content

The imported file

```
<img src="http://www.wickedlysmart.com/skyler/horse.gif">
```

"horse.html" and "horse.gif" are both on Server B, a completely different web server from the one with the JSP.

The response

The horse is coming from a completely different web server than the page that contains the text.

Customizing the thing you include

Remember in the previous chapter when we did a <jsp:include> to put in the layout header (a graphic with some text), but we wanted to customize the subtitle used in the header? We used <jsp:param> to make that happen...

① The JSP with the <jsp:include>

```
<html><body>

<jsp:include page="Header.jsp">

   <jsp:param name="subTitle" value="We take the sting out of SOAP." />

</jsp:include>

<br>
<em>Welcome to our Web Services Support Group.</em> <br><br>
Contact us at: ${initParam.mainEmail}
</body></html>
```

② The included file ("Header.jsp")

```
<img src="images/Web-Services.jpg" > <br>

<em><strong>${param.subTitle}</strong></em>
<br>
```

Doing the same thing with <c:param>

Here we accomplish the same thing we did on the previous page, but using a combination of <c:import> and <c:param>. You'll see that the structure is virtually identical to the one we used with standard actions.

1 The JSP with the <jsp:include>

```
<%@ taglib prefix="c" uri="http://java.sun.com/jsp/jstl/core" %>
<html><body>

<c:import url="Header.jsp" >

   <c:param name="subTitle" value="We take the sting out of SOAP." />

</c:import>

<br>
<em>Welcome to our Web Services Support Group.</em> <br><br>

Contact us at: ${initParam.mainEmail}

</body></html>
```

No slash, because NOW the tag has a body...

2 The included file ("Header.jsp")

```
<img src="images/Web-Services.jpg" > <br>

<em><strong>${param.subTitle}</strong></em>
<br>
```

This page doesn't change at all. It doesn't care HOW the parameter got there, as long as it's there.

Sorry to change the subject here... but I just noticed a HUGE problem with JSPs! How can you guarantee session tracking from a JSP... without using scripting?

Session tracking happens automatically with JSPs, unless you explicitly disable it with a page directive that has a session attribute that says session="false".

He missed the point... I said "guarantee". My real question is--if the client doesn't support cookies, how can I get URL rewriting to happen? How can I get the session ID added to the URLs in my JSP?

Ahhh... he obviously doesn't know about the <c:url> tag. It does URL rewriting automatically.

<c:url> for all your hyperlink needs

Remember way back in our old servlet days when we wanted to use a session? First we had to *get* the session (either the existing one or a new one). At that point, the Container knows that it's supposed to associate the client from this request with a particular session ID. The Container *wants* to use a cookie—it wants to include a unique cookie with the response, and then the client will send that cookie back with each subsequent request. Except one problem... the client might have a browser with cookies disabled. Then what?

The Container will, automatically, fall back to URL rewriting if it doesn't get a cookie from the client. But with servlets, you STILL have to encode your URLs. In other words, *you* still have to tell the Container to "append the jsessionid to the end of this particular URL..." for each URL where it matters. Well, you can do the same thing from a JSP, using the <c:url> tag.

URL rewriting from a servlet

```
public void doGet(HttpServletRequest request, HttpServletResponse response)
                                          throws IOException, ServletException {
    response.setContentType("text/html");
    PrintWriter out = response.getWriter();
    HttpSession session = request.getSession();

    out.println("<html><body>");
    out.println("<a href=\"" + response.encodeURL("/BeerTest.do") + "\">click</a>");
    out.println("</body></html>");
}
```

Add the extra session ID info to this URL.

URL rewriting from a JSP

```
<%@ taglib prefix="c" uri="http://java.sun.com/jsp/jstl/core" %>
<html><body>

This is a hyperlink with URL rewriting enabled.

<a href="<c:url value='/inputComments.jsp' />">Click here</a>

</body></html>
```

This adds the jsessionid to the end of the "value" relative URL (if cookies are disabled).

What if the URL needs encoding?

Remember that in an HTTP GET request, the parameters are appended to the URL as a query string. For example, if a form on an HTML page has two text fields—first name and last name—the request URL will stick the parameter names and values on to the end of the request URL. But...an HTTP request won't work correctly if it contains *unsafe* characters (although most modern browsers will try to compensate for this).

If you're a web developer, this is old news, but if you're new to web development, you need to know that URLs often need to be *encoded.* URL encoding means replacing the unsafe/reserved characters with other characters, and then the whole thing is decoded again on the server side. For example, spaces aren't allowed in a URL, but you can substitute a plus sign "+" for the space. The problem is, <c:url> does NOT automatically encode your URLs!

Using <c:url> with a query string

Remember, the <c:url> tag does URL rewriting, but *not* URL encoding!

```
<c:set var="last" value="Hidden Cursor" />
<c:set var="first" value="Crouching Pixels"/>

<c:url value="/inputComments.jsp?first=${first}&last=${last}" var="inputURL" />

The URL using params is: ${inputURL} <br>
```

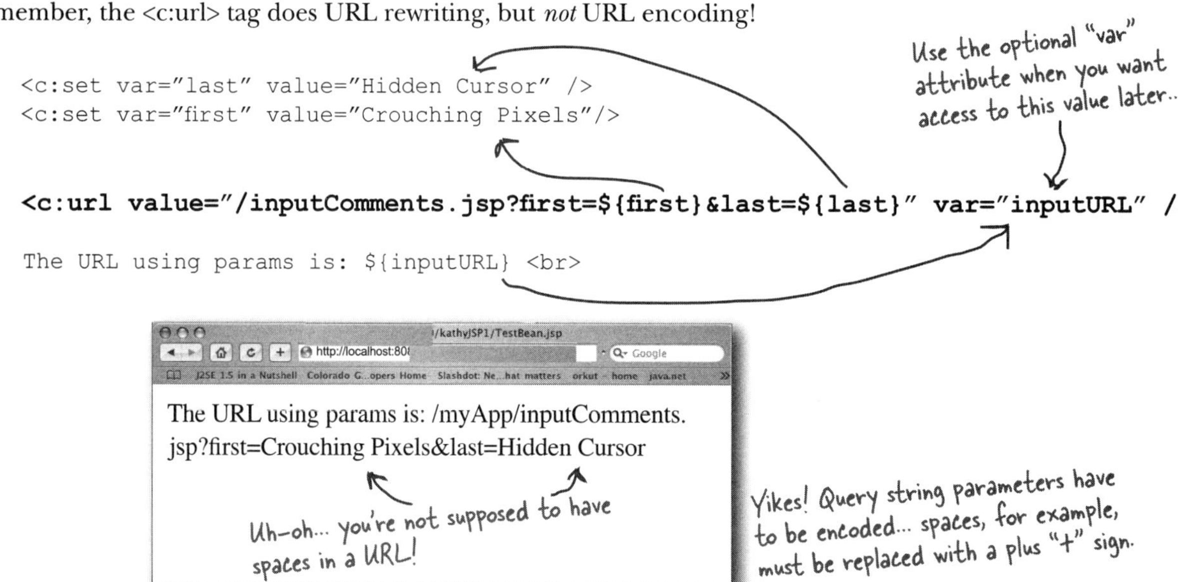

Use the optional "var" attribute when you want access to this value later...
/kathyJSP1/TestBean.jsp
http://localhost:80
Google
The URL using params is: /myApp/inputComments.jsp?first=Crouching Pixels&last=Hidden Cursor
Uh-oh... you're not supposed to have spaces in a URL!
Yikes! Query string parameters have to be encoded... spaces, for example, must be replaced with a plus "+" sign.

Using <c:param> in the body of <c:url>

This solves our problem! Now we get both URL rewriting and URL encoding.

```
<c:url value="/inputComments.jsp" var="inputURL" >
   <c:param name="firstName" value="${first}" />
   <c:param name="lastName" value="${last}" />
</c:url>
```

no slash

Now we're safe, because <c:param> takes care of the encoding!

Now the URL looks like this:

```
/myApp/inputComments.jsp?firstName=Crouching+Pixels&lastName=Hidden+Cursor
```

I'm interrupting this JSTL talk for a few moments to talk about your error-handling. We're about to do something that might cause an exception...

You do NOT want your clients to see this:

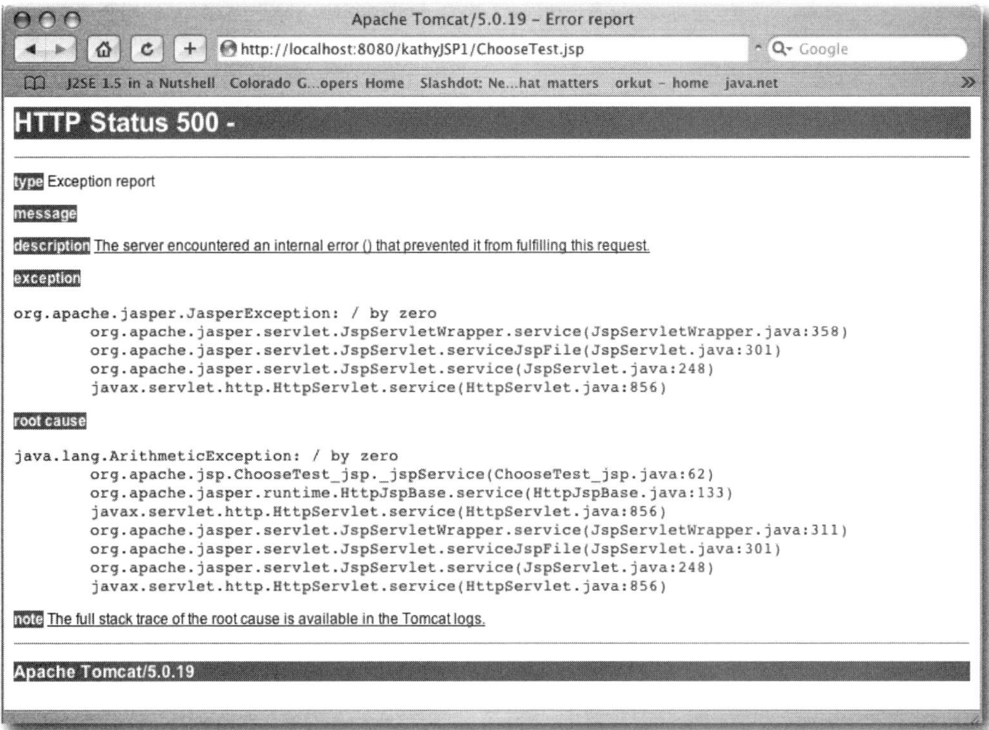

Apache Tomcat/5.0.19 - Error report
http://localhost:8080/kathyJSP1/ChooseTest.jsp
Google
J2SE 1.5 in a Nutshell Colorado G...opers Home Slashdot: Ne...hat matters orkut - home java.net
HTTP Status 500 -
type Exception report
message
description The server encountered an internal error () that prevented it from fulfilling this request.
exception
org.apache.jasper.JasperException: / by zero
org.apache.jasper.servlet.JspServletWrapper.service(JspServletWrapper.java:358)
org.apache.jasper.servlet.JspServlet.serviceJspFile(JspServlet.java:301)
org.apache.jasper.servlet.JspServlet.service(JspServlet.java:248)
javax.servlet.http.HttpServlet.service(HttpServlet.java:856)
root cause
java.lang.ArithmeticException: / by zero
org.apache.jsp.ChooseTest_jsp._jspService(ChooseTest_jsp.java:62)
org.apache.jasper.runtime.HttpJspBase.service(HttpJspBase.java:133)
javax.servlet.http.HttpServlet.service(HttpServlet.java:856)
org.apache.jasper.servlet.JspServletWrapper.service(JspServletWrapper.java:311)
org.apache.jasper.servlet.JspServlet.serviceJspFile(JspServlet.java:301)
org.apache.jasper.servlet.JspServlet.service(JspServlet.java:248)
javax.servlet.http.HttpServlet.service(HttpServlet.java:856)
note The full stack trace of the root cause is available in the Tomcat logs.
Apache Tomcat/5.0.19

Make your own error pages

The guy surfing your site doesn't want to see your stack trace. And he's not too thrilled to get a standard "404 Not Found", either.

You can't prevent *all* errors, of course, but you can at least give the user a friendlier (and more attractive) error response page. You can design a custom page to handle errors, then use the page directive to configure it.

The designated ERROR page ("errorPage.jsp")

```
<%@ page isErrorPage="true" %>

<html><body>
<strong>Bummer.</strong>
<img src="images/bummerGuy.jpg">
</body></html>
```

Confirms for the Container, "Yes, this IS an officially-designated error page."

The BAD page that throws an exception ("badPage.jsp")

```
<%@ page errorPage="errorPage.jsp" %>

<html><body>
About to be bad...
<% int x = 10/0; %>
</body></html>
```

Tells the Container, "If something goes wrong here, forward the request to errorPage.jsp".

What happens when you request "badPage.jsp"

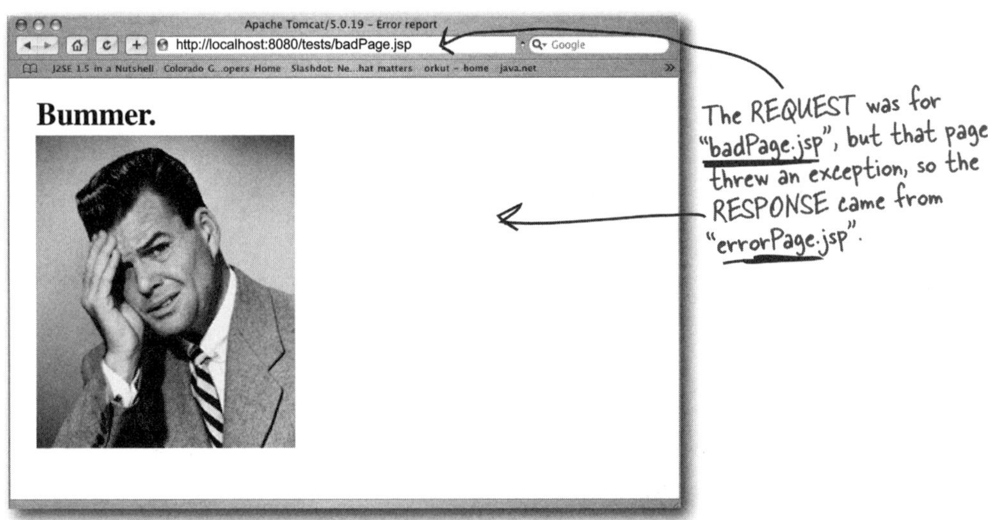

The REQUEST was for "badPage.jsp", but that page threw an exception, so the RESPONSE came from "errorPage.jsp".

It will take me FOREVER to put page directives in all my JSPs, to specify the error page to use. And what if I want a different error page depending on the error? If only there were a way to configure error pages for the whole web app...

She doesn't know about the <error-page> DD tag.

You can declare error pages in the DD for the entire web app, and you can even configure *different* error pages for different exception types, or HTTP error code types (404, 500, etc.).

The Container uses <error-page> configuration in the DD as the default, but if a JSP has an explicit *errorPage* page directive, the Container uses the directive.

Configuring error pages in the DD

You can declare error pages in the DD based on either the <exception-type> or the HTTP status <error-code> number. That way you can show the client different error pages specific to the type of the problem that generated the error.

Declaring a catch-all error page

This applies to everything in your web app—not just JSPs. You can override it in individual JSPs by adding a page directive with an *errorPage* attribute.

```
<error-page>
  <exception-type>java.lang.Throwable</exception-type>
  <location>/errorPage.jsp</location>
</error-page>
```

Declaring an error page for a more explicit exception

This configures an error page that's called only when there's an ArithmeticException. If you have both this declaration and the catch-all above, any exception other than ArithmeticException will still end up at the "errorPage.jsp".

```
<error-page>
  <exception-type>java.lang.ArithmeticException</exception-type>
  <location>/arithmeticError.jsp</location>
</error-page>
```

Declaring an error page based on an HTTP status code

This configures an error page that's called only when the status code for the response is "404" (file not found).

```
<error-page>
  <error-code>404</error-code>
  <location>/notFoundError.jsp</location>

</error-page>
```

The <location> MUST be relative to the web-app root/context, which means it MUST start with a slash. (This is true regardless of whether the error page is based on <error-code> or <exception-type>.)

Error pages get an extra object: exception

An error page is essentially the JSP that *handles* the exception, so the Container gives the page an extra object for the *exception*. You probably won't want to show the exception to the user, but you've got it. In a scriptlet, you can use the implicit object *exception*, and from a JSP, you can use the EL implicit object ${pageContext.exception}. The object is type java.lang.Throwable, so in a script you can call methods, and with EL you can access the *stackTrace* and *message* properties.

Note: the exception implicit object is available ONLY to error pages with an explicitly-defined page directive:

<%@ page isErrorPage="true" %>

In other words, configuring an error page in the DD is not enough to make the Container give that page the implicit exception object!

A more explicit ERROR page ("errorPage.jsp")

```
<%@ page  isErrorPage="true" %>

<html><body>
<strong>Bummer.</strong><br>

You caused a ${pageContext.exception} on the server.<br>

<img src="images/bummerGuy.jpg">
</body></html>
```

What happens when you request "badPage.jsp"

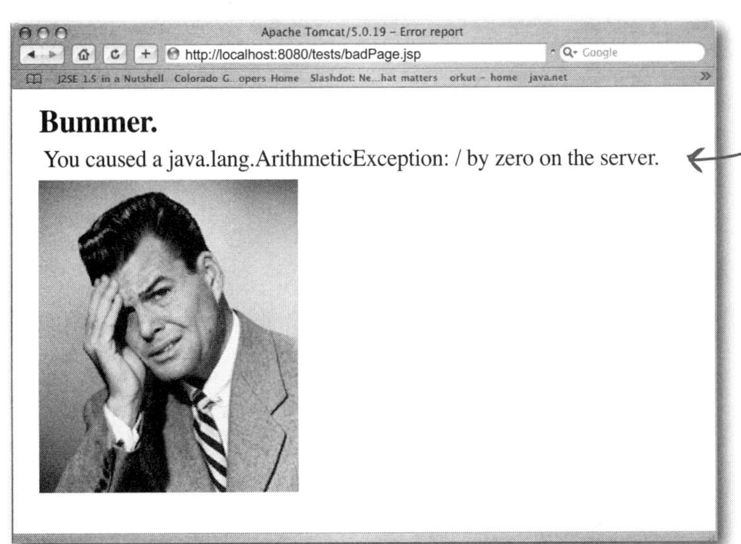

This time, you get more details. You probably won't show this to the user...we just did this so you could see it.

What if I think there's an exception I might be able to recover from in a JSP? What if there are some errors I want to catch myself?

The <c:catch> tag. Like try/catch...*sort of*

If you have a page that invokes a risky tag, but you think you can recover, there's a solution. You can do a kind of try/catch using the <c:catch> tag, to wrap the risky tag or expression. Because if you don't, and an exception is thrown, your default error handling will kick in and the user will get the error page declared in the DD. The part that might feel a little strange is that the <c:catch> serves as both the try *and* the catch—there's no separate *try* tag. You wrap the risky EL or tag calls or whatever in the body of a <c:catch>, and the exception is caught right there. But you can't assume it's exactly like a catch block, either, because once the exception occurs, control jumps to the end of the <c:catch> tag body (more on that in a minute).

```
<%@ taglib prefix="c" uri="http://java.sun.com/jsp/jstl/core" %>
<%@ page errorPage="errorPage.jsp" %>
<html><body>

About to do a risky thing: <br>

<c:catch>

    <% int x = 10/0; %>

</c:catch>

If you see this, we survived.

</body></html>
```

This scriptlet will DEFINITELY cause an exception... but we caught it instead of triggering the error page.

If this prints out, then we KNOW we made it past the exception (which in this example, means we successfully caught the exception).

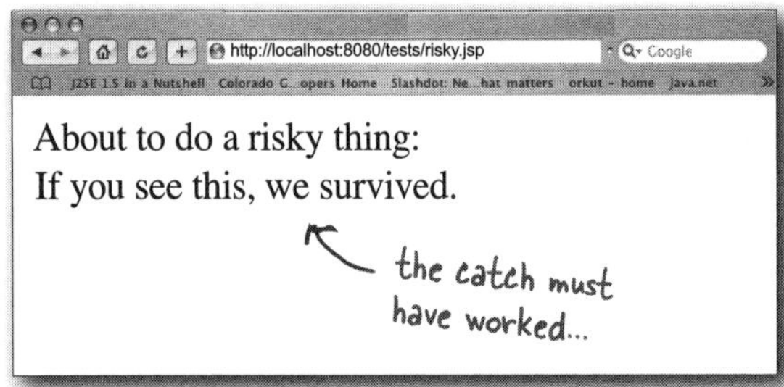
http://localhost:8080/tests/risky.jsp
About to do a risky thing:
If you see this, we survived.
the catch must have worked...

But how do I get access to the Exception object? The one that was actually thrown? Since this isn't an actual error page, the implicit exception object doesn't work here.

You can make the exception an attribute

In a real Java try/catch, the catch argument is the exception object. But with web app error handling, remember, *only officially-designated error pages get the exception object.* To any other page, the exception just isn't there. So this does *not* work:

```
<c:catch>
    Inside the catch...
    <% int x = 10/0; %>
</c:catch>

Exception was: ${pageContext.exception}
```

Won't work because this isn't an official error page, so it doesn't get the exception object.

Using the "var" attribute in <c:catch>

Use the optional *var* attribute if you want to access the exception after the end of the <c:catch> tag. It puts the exception object into the page scope, under the name *you* declare as the value of *var.*

```
<%@ taglib prefix="c" uri="http://java.sun.com/jsp/jstl/core" %>
<%@ page errorPage="errorPage.jsp" %>
<html><body>

About to do a risky thing: <br>

<c:catch var="myException">

    Inside the catch...
    <% int x = 10/0; %>
</c:catch>

<c:if test="${myException != null}">
   There was an exception:  ${myException.message} <br>
</c:if>

We survived.
</body></html>
```

This creates a new page-scoped attribute named "myException", and assigns the exception object to it.

Now there's an attribute myException, and since it's a Throwable, it has a "message" property (because Throwable has a getMessage() method).

Flow control works in a <c:catch> the way it does in a *try* block—NOTHING runs inside the <c:catch> body *after* the exception.

In a regular Java try/catch, once the exception occurs, the code BELOW that point in the ***try*** *block never executes—control jumps directly to the catch block. With the <c:catch> tag, once the exception occurs, two things happen:*

1) If you used the optional "var" attribute, the exception object is assigned to it.

2) Flow jumps to ***below*** *the body of the <c:catch> tag.*

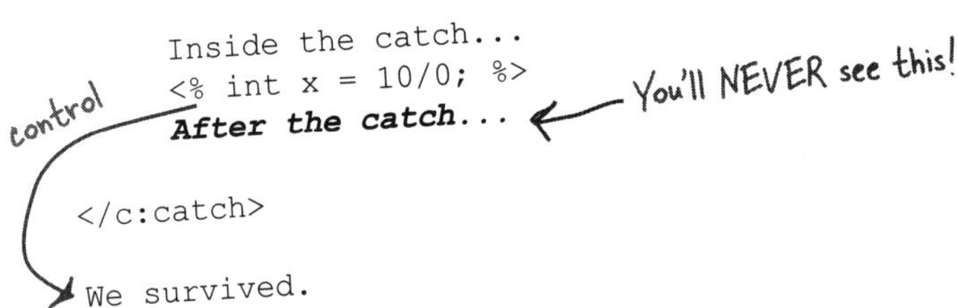


```
<c:catch>

    Inside the catch...
    <% int x = 10/0; %>
    After the catch...

</c:catch>

We survived.
```

Be careful about this. If you want to use the "var" exception object, you must wait until AFTER you get to the end of the <c:catch> body. In other words, there is simply no way to use any information about the exception WITHIN the <c:catch> tag body.

It's tempting to think of a <c:catch> tag as being just like a normal Java code catch block, but it isn't. A <c:catch> acts more like a ***try*** *block, because it's where you put the risky code. Except it's like a try that never needs (or has) a catch or finally block. Confused? The point is—learn this tag for exactly what it is, rather than mapping it into your existing knowledge of how a normal try/catch works. And on the exam, if you see code within the <c:catch> tag that is below the point at which the exception is thrown, don't be fooled.*

What if you need a tag that's NOT in JSTL?

The JSTL is huge. Version 1.1 has *five* libraries—four with custom *tags*, and one with a bunch of *functions* for String manipulation. The tags we cover in this book (which happen to be the ones you're expected to know for the exam) are for the generic things you're most likely to need, but it's possible that between all five libraries, you'll find everything you might ever need. On the next page, we'll start looking at what happens when the tags below aren't enough.

The "Core" library

General-purpose

`<c:out>`

`<c:set>`

`<c:remove>`

`<c:catch>`

Conditional

`<c:if>`

`<c:choose>`

`<c:when>`

`<c:otherwise>`

URL related

`<c:import>`

`<c:url>`

`<c:redirect>`

`<c:param>`

Iteration

`<c:forEach>`

`<c:forTokens>`

We didn't cover this one... it lets you iterate over tokens where YOU give it the delimiter. Works a lot like StringTokenizer. We also didn't cover <c:redirect> and <c:out>, but that gives you a wonderful excuse to get the JSTL docs.

The "Formatting" library

Internationalization

`<fmt:message>`

`<fmt:setLocale>`

`<fmt:bundle>`

`<fmt:setBundle>`

`<fmt:param>`

`<fmt:requestEncoding>`

Formatting

`<fmt:timeZone>`

`<fmt:setTimeZone>`

`<fmt:formatNumber>`

`<fmt:parseNumber>`

`<fmt:parseDate>`

The "SQL" library

Database access

`<sql:query>`

`<sql:update>`

`<sql:setDataSource>`

`<sql:param>`

`<sql:dateParam>`

The "XML" library

Core XML actions

`<x:parse>`

`<x:out>`

`<x:set>`

XML flow control

`<x:if>`

`<x:choose>`

`<x:when>`

`<x:otherwise>`

`<x:forEach>`

Transform actions

`<x:transform>`

`<x:param>`

Relax

Only the "core" library is covered on the exam.

The "core" library (which by convention we always prefix with "c") is the only JSTL library covered on the exam. The rest are specialized, so we don't go into them. But you should at least know that they're available. The XML transformation tags, for example, could save your life if you have to process RSS feeds. Writing your own custom tags can be a pain, so make sure before you write one that you're not reinventing the wheel.

Using a tag library that's NOT from the JSTL

Creating the code that goes *behind* a tag (in other words, the Java code that's invoked when you put the tag in your JSP) isn't trivial. We have a whole chapter (the next one) devoted to developing your own custom tag handlers. But the last part of this chapter is about how to *use* custom tags. What happens, for example, if someone hands you a custom tag library they created for your company or project? How do you know what the tags are and how to use them? With JSTL, it's easy—the JSTL 1.1 specification *documents* each tag, including how to use each of the required and optional attributes.

But not every custom tag will come so nicely packaged and well-documented. You have to know how to figure out a tag even if the documentation is weak or nonexistent, and, one more thing—you have to know how to *deploy* a custom tag library.

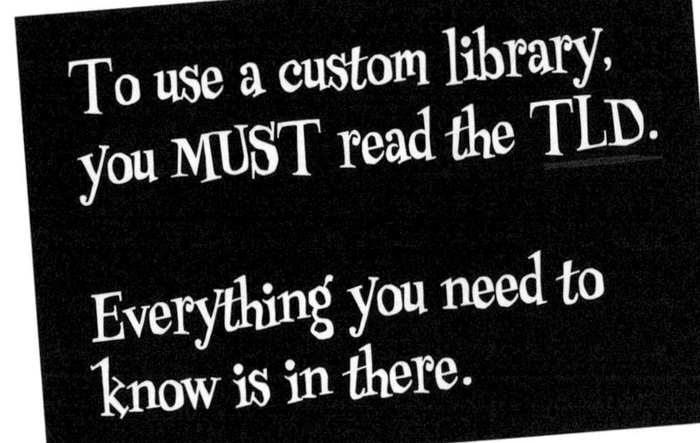

To use a custom library, you MUST read the TLD.
Everything you need to know is in there.

Main things you have to know:

① The tag name and syntax

The tag has a *name*, obviously. In <c:set>, the tag *name* is *set*, and the *prefix* is *c*. You can use any prefix you want, but the *name* comes from the TLD. The syntax includes things like required and optional attributes, whether the tag can have a body (and if so, what you can put there), the type of each attribute, and whether the attribute can be an expression (vs. a literal String).

② The library URI

The URI is a unique identifier in the Tag Library Descriptor (TLD). In other words, it's a unique name for the tag library the TLD describes. The URI is what you put in your taglib directive. It's what tells the Container how to identify the TLD file within the web app, which the Container needs in order to map the tag name used in the JSP to the Java code that runs when you use the tag.

Making sense of the TLD

The TLD describes two main things: custom tags, and EL functions. We used one when we made the dice rolling function in the previous chapter, but we had only a <function> element in the TLD. Now we have to look at the <tag> element, which can be more complex. Besides the function we declared earlier, the DD below describes one tag, *advice.*

```
<?xml version="1.0" encoding="ISO-8859-1" ?>
<taglib xmlns="http://java.sun.com/xml/ns/j2ee"
xmlns:xsi="http://www.w3.org/2001/XMLSchema-instance"
xsi:schemaLocation="http://java.sun.com/xml/ns/j2ee/web-jsptaglibrary_2_0.xsd"
version="2.0">

    <tlib-version>0.9</tlib-version>

    <short-name>RandomTags</short-name>
    <function>
       <name>rollIt</name>
       <function-class>foo.DiceRoller</function-class>
       <function-signature>int rollDice()</function-signature>
    </function>

   <uri>randomThings</uri>

   <tag>

      <description>random advice</description>

      <name>advice</name>

      <tag-class>foo.AdvisorTagHandler</tag-class>

      <body-content>empty</body-content>

      <attribute>

         <name>user</name>

         <required>true</required>

         <rtexprvalue>true</rtexprvalue>

      </attribute>

   </tag>
</taglib>
```

This is the version of the XML schema that you use for JSP 2.0. Don't memorize it... just copy it into your <taglib> element.

MANDATORY (the tag, not the value)— the developer puts it in to declare the version of the tag library.

MANDATORY; mainly for tools to use..

The EL function we used in the last chapter.

The unique name we use in the taglib directive!

Optional, but a really good idea...

REQUIRED! This is what you use inside the tag (example: <my:advice>).

REQUIRED! This is how the Container knows what to call when someone uses the tag in a JSP.

REQUIRED! This says that the tag must NOT have anything in the body.

If your tag has attributes, then one <attribute> element per tag attribute is required.

This says you MUST put a "user" attribute in the tag.

This says the "user" attribute can be a **r**un**t**ime **expr**ession **value** (i.e. doesn't have to be a String literal).

Using the custom "advice" tag

The "advice" tag is a simple tag that takes one attribute—the user name—and prints out a piece of random advice. It's simple enough that it *could* have been just a plain old EL function (with a static method getAdvice(String name)), but we made it a simple tag to show you how it all works...

The TLD elements for the advice tag

```
<taglib ...>
...
<uri>randomThings</uri>
<tag>
    <description>random advice</description>
    <name>advice</name>
    <tag-class>foo.AdvisorTagHandler</tag-class>
    <body-content>empty</body-content>

   <attribute>
      <name>user</name>
      <required>true</required>
      <rtexprvalue>true</rtexprvalue>
   </attribute>

</tag>
</taglib ...>
```

This is the same tag you saw on the previous page, but without the annotations.

JSP that uses the tag

```
<html><body>

<%@ taglib prefix="mine" uri="randomThings"%>

Advisor Page<br>

<mine:advice user="${userName}" />

</body></html>
```

The uri matches the <uri> element in the TLD.

It's OK to use EL here, because the <rtexprevalue> in the TLD is set to "true" for the user attribute. (Assume the "userName" attribute already exists.)

The TLD says the tag can't have a body, so we made it an empty tag (which means the tag ends with a slash).

Each library you use in a page needs its own taglib directive with a unique prefix.

The custom tag handler

This simple tag handler extends SimpleTagSupport (a class you'll see in the next chapter), and implements two key methods: doTag(), the method that does the actual work, and setUser(), the method that accepts the attribute value.

Java class that does the tag work

```
package foo;
import javax.servlet.jsp.JspException;
import javax.servlet.jsp.tagext.SimpleTagSupport;
import java.io.IOException;

public class AdvisorTagHandler extends SimpleTagSupport {

    private String user;

    public void doTag() throws JspException, IOException {
       getJspContext().getOut().write( "Hello " + user + " <br>" );
       getJspContext().getOut().write( "Your advice is: " + getAdvice() );
    }

    public void setUser(String user) {
       this.user=user;
    }

    String getAdvice() {
       String[] adviceStrings = {"That color's not working for you.",
              "You should call in sick.", "You might want to rethink that haircut."};
       int random = (int) (Math.random() * adviceStrings.length);
       return adviceStrings[random];
    }
}
```

SimpleTagSupport implements things we need in custom tags.

The Container calls doTag() when the JSP invokes the tag using the name declared in the TLD.

The Container calls this method to set the value from the tag attribute. It uses JavaBean property naming conventions to figure out that a "user" attribute should be sent to the setUser() method.

Our own internal method.

Custom tag handlers don't use custom method names!

With EL functions, you created a Java class with a static method, named the method whatever you wanted, then used the TLD to map the actual method <function-signature> to the function <name>. But with custom tags, the method name is ALWAYS ***doTag()****, so you never declare the method name for a custom tag. Only functions use a method signature declaration in the TLD!*

Pay attention to <rtexprvalue>

The <rtexprvalue> is especially important because it tells you whether the value of the attribute is evaluated at translation or runtime. If the <rtexprvalue> is false, or the <rtexprvalue> isn't defined, you can use only a String literal as that attribute's value!

If you see this:

```
<attribute>
    <name>rate</name>
    <required>true</required>
    <rtexprvalue>false</rtexprvalue>
</attribute>
```

OR this:

```
<attribute>
    <name>rate</name>
    <required>true</required>

</attribute>
```

If there's no <rtexprvalue>, the default value is false.

Then you know THIS WON'T WORK!

```
<html><body>
  <%@ taglib prefix="my" uri="myTags"%>

  <my:handleIt rate="${currentRate}" />
</body></html>
```

NO! This must NOT be an expression... it must be a String literal.

Q: You still didn't answer the question about how you know what type the attribute is...

A: We'll start with the easy one. If the <rtexprvalue> is false (or not there at all), then the attribute type can be ONLY a String literal. But if you can use an expression, then you have to hope that it's either dead obvious from the tag description and attribute name, OR that the developer included the optional <type> subelement of the <attribute> element. The <type> takes a fully-qualified class name for the type. Whether the TLD declares the type or not, the Container expects the type of the expression to match the type of argument in the tag handler's setter method for that attribute. In other words, if the tag handler has a setDog(Dog) method for the "dog" attribute, then the value of your expression for that attribute better evaluate to a Dog object! (Or something that can be implicitly assigned to a Dog reference type.)

<rtexprvalue> is NOT just for EL expressions

You can use ***three*** kinds of expressions for the value of an attribute (or tag body) that allows runtime expressions.

1. **EL expressions**

```
<mine:advice user="${userName}" />
```

2. **Scripting expressions**

```
<mine:advice user='<%= request.getAttribute("username") %>' />
```

It has to be an expression, not just a scriplet. So it must have the "=" sign in there and no semicolon on the end.

3. **<jsp:attribute> standard actions**

```
<mine:advice>
   <jsp:attribute name="user">${userName}</jsp:attribute>
</mine:advice>
```

What is this?? I thought this tag didn't have a body...

<jsp:attribute> lets you put attributes in the BODY of a tag, even when the tag body is explicitly declared "empty" in the TLD!!

The <jsp:attribute> is simply an alternate way to define attributes to a tag. The key point is, there must be only ONE <jsp:attribute> for EACH attribute in the enclosing tag. So if you have a tag that normally takes three attributes IN the tag (as opposed to in the body), then inside the body you'll now have three <jsp:attribute> tags, one for each attribute. Also notice that the <jsp:attribute> has an attribute of its own, ***name****, where you specify the name of the outer tag's attribute for which you're setting a value. There's a little more about this on the next page...*

What can be in a tag body

A tag can have a body *only* if the <body-content> element for this tag is not configured with a value of ***empty***. The <body-content> element can be one of either three or four values, depending on the type of tag.

```
<body-content>empty</body-content>
```

The tag must NOT have a body.

```
<body-content>scriptless</body-content>
```

The tag must NOT have scripting elements (scriptlets, scripting expressions, and declarations), but it CAN have template text and EL and custom and standard actions.

```
<body-content>tagdependent</body-content>
```

The tag body is treated as plain text, so the EL is NOT evaluated and tags/actions are not triggered.

```
<body-content>JSP</body-content>
```

The tag body can have anything that can go inside a JSP.

THREE ways to invoke a tag that can't have a body

Each of these are acceptable ways to invoke a tag configured in the TLD with <body-content>**empty**</body-content>.

1 An *empty* tag

```
<mine:advice user="${userName}" />
```

When you put a slash in the opening tag, you don't use a closing tag.

2 A tag with *nothing* between the opening and closing tags

```
<mine:advice user="${userName}"> </mine:advice>
```

We have an opening and closing tag, but NOTHING in between.

3 A tag with only <jsp:attribute> tags between the opening and closing tags

```
<mine:advice>
   <jsp:attribute name="user">${userName}</jsp:attribute>
</mine:advice>
```

The <jsp:attribute> tag is the ONLY thing you can put between the opening and closing tags of a tag with a <body-content> of empty! It's just an alternate way to put the attributes in, but <jsp:attribute> tags don't count as "body content".

The tag handler, the TLD, and the JSP

The tag handler developer creates the TLD to tell both the Container and the JSP developer how to use the tag. A JSP developer doesn't care about the <tag-class> element in the TLD; that's for the Container to worry about. The JSP developer cares most about the uri, the tag name, and the tag syntax. Can the tag have a body? Does this attribute have to be a String literal, or can it be an expression? Is this attribute optional? What type does the expression need to evaluate to?

Think of the TLD as **the API for custom tags**. You have to know how to call it and what arguments it needs.

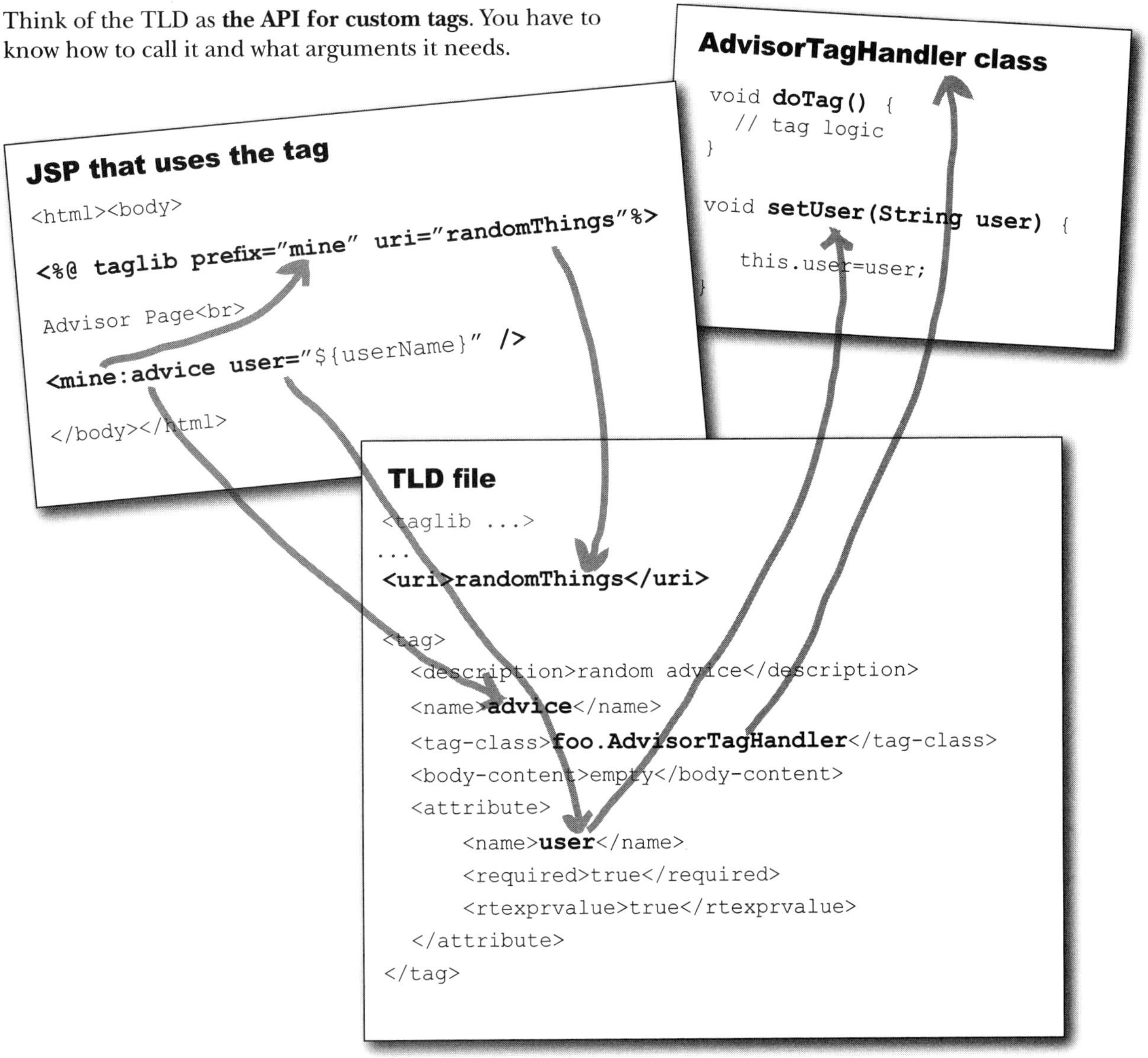

These three pieces—the tag handler class, the TLD, and the JSP are all you need to deploy and run a web app that uses the tag.

JSP that uses the tag

```
<html><body>

<%@ taglib prefix="mine" uri="randomThings"%>

Advisor Page<br>

<mine:advice user="${userName}" />

</body></html>
```

AdvisorTagHandler class

```
void doTag() {
  // tag logic
}

void setUser(String user) {

   this.user=user;
}
```

TLD file

```
<taglib ...>
...
<uri>randomThings</uri>

<tag>
  <description>random advice</description>
  <name>advice</name>
  <tag-class>foo.AdvisorTagHandler</tag-class>
  <body-content>empty</body-content>
  <attribute>
      <name>user</name>
      <required>true</required>
      <rtexprvalue>true</rtexprvalue>
  </attribute>
</tag>
```

The taglib <uri> is just a name, not a location

The <uri> element in the TLD is a unique name for the tag library. That's it. It does NOT need to represent any actual location (path or URL, for example). It simply has to be a name—*the same name you use in the taglib directive.*

"But," you're asking, "how come with the JSTL it gives the full URL to the library?" The taglib directive for the JSTL is:

```
<%@ taglib prefix="c" uri="http://java.sun.com/jsp/jstl/core" %>
```

This LOOKS like a URL to a web resource, but it's not. It's just a name that happens to be formatted as a URL.

The web Container doesn't normally try to *request* something from the uri in the taglib directive. It doesn't need to use the uri as a *location*! If you type that as a URL into your browser, you'll be redirected to a different URL, one that has *information* about JSTL. The Container could care less that this particular uri happens to also be a valid URL (the whole "http://..." thing). It's just the convention Sun uses for the uri, to help ensure that it's a unique name. Sun could have named the JSTL uri "java_foo_tags" and it would have worked in exactly the same way. ***All that matters is that the <uri> in the TLD and the uri in the taglib directive match!***

As a developer, though, you do want to work out a scheme to give your libraries unique <uri> values, because <uri> names need to be *unique* for any given web app. You can't, for example, have two TLD files in the same web app, with the same <uri>. So, the domain name convention is a good one, but you don't necessarily need to use that for all of your in-house development.

Having said all that, there *is* one way in which the uri could be used as a location, but it's considered a really bad practice—if you don't specify a <uri> inside the TLD, the Container will attempt to use the uri attribute in the taglib directive as a path to the actual TLD. But to hard-code the location of your TLD is obviously a bad idea, so just pretend you don't know it's possible.

The Container looks for a match between the <uri> in the TLD and the uri value in the taglib directive. The uri does NOT have to be the location of the actual tag handler!

The Container builds a map

Before JSP 2.0, the developer had to specify a mapping between the <uri> in the TLD and the actual location of the TLD file. So when a JSP page had a taglib directive like this:

```
<%@ taglib prefix="mine" uri="randomThings"%>
```

The Deployment Descriptor (web.xml) had to tell the Container where the TLD file with a matching <uri> was located. You did that with a <taglib> element in the DD.

The OLD (before JSP 2.0) way to map a taglib uri to a TLD file

```
<web-app>
...
  <jsp-config>
    <taglib>
      <taglib-uri>randomThings</taglib-uri>
      <taglib-location>/WEB-INF/myFunctions.tld</taglib-location>
    </taglib>
  </jsp-config>
</web-app>
```

In the DD, map the <uri> in the TLD to an actual path to a TLD file.

The NEW (JSP 2.0) way to map a taglib uri to a TLD file

No <taglib> entry in the DD!

The Container automatically builds a map between TLD files and <uri> names, so that when a JSP invokes a tag, the Container knows exactly where to find the TLD that describes the tag.

How? By looking through a specific set of locations where TLDs are allowed to live. When you deploy a web app, as long as you put the TLD in a place the Container will search, the Container will find the TLD and build a map for that tag library.

If you *do* specify an explicit <taglib-location> in the DD (web.xml), a JSP 2.0 Container will use it! In fact, when the Container begins to build the <uri>-to-TLD map, the Container will look *first* in your DD to see if you've made any <taglib> entries, and if you have, it'll use those to help construct the map. ***For the exam, you're expected to know about <taglib-location>, even though it's no longer required for JSP 2.0.***

So the next step is for us to see where the Container looks for TLDs, and also where it looks for the tag handler *classes* declared in the TLDs.

Four places the Container looks for TLDs

The Container searches in several places to find TLD files—you don't need to do anything except make sure your TLDs are in one of the right locations.

1. **Directly inside WEB-INF**
2. **Directly inside a sub-directory of WEB-INF**
3. **Inside the META-INF directory inside a JAR file that's inside WEB-INF/lib**
4. **Inside a sub-directory of META-INF inside a JAR file that's inside WEB-INF/lib**

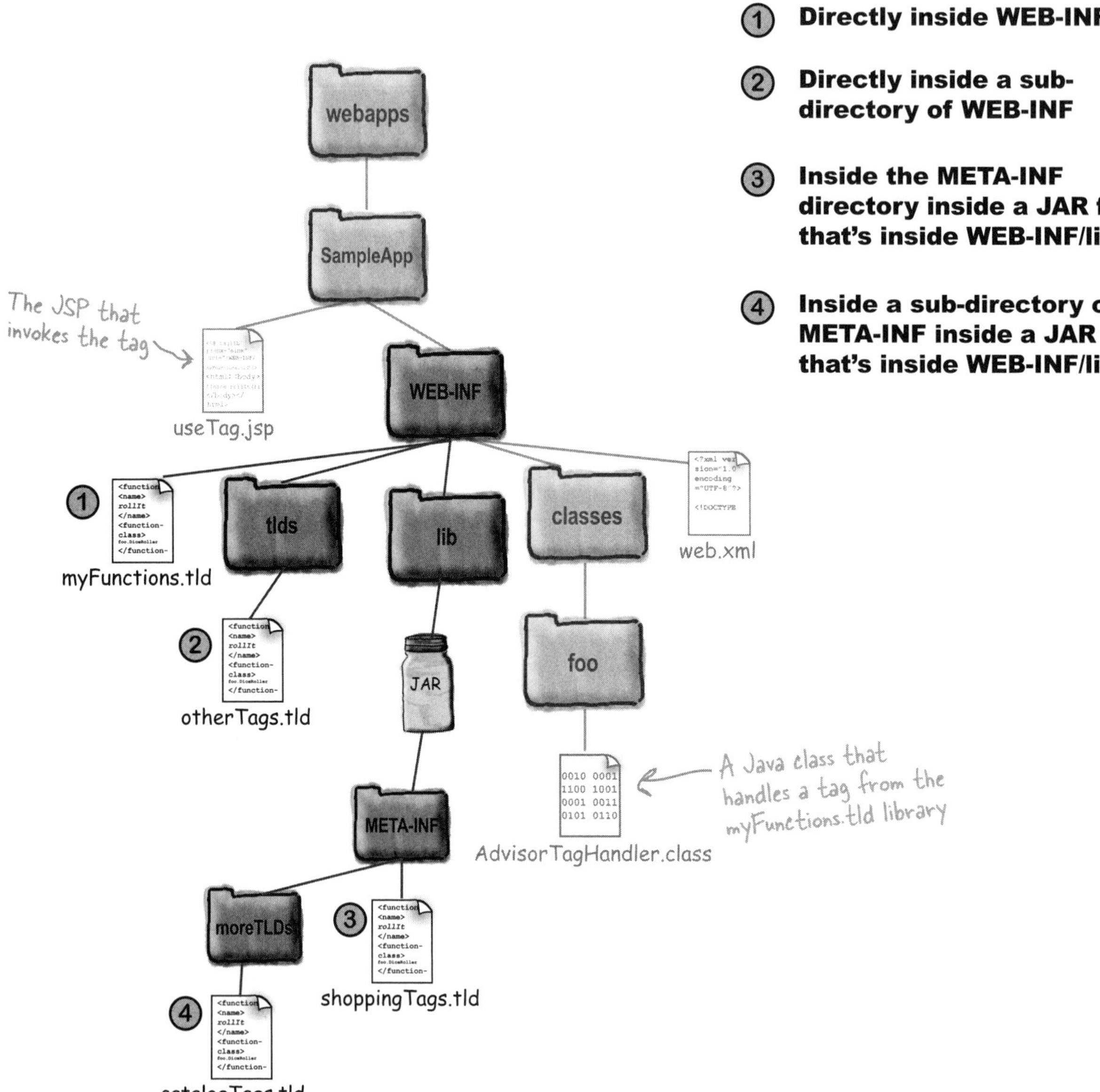

When a JSP uses more than one tag library

If you want to use more than one tag library in a JSP, do a separate taglib directive for each TLD. There a few issues to keep in mind...

- Make sure the taglib uri names are unique. In other words, don't put in more than one directive with the same uri value.

- Do NOT use a prefix that's on the reserved list.
  The reserved prefixes are:
  - **jsp:**
  - **jspx:**
  - **java:**
  - **javax:**
  - **servlet:**
  - **sun:**
  - **sunw:**

Sharpen your pencil

Empty tags

Write in examples of the THREE different ways to invoke a tag that must have an empty body.
(Check your answers by looking back through the chapter. No, we're not going to tell you the page number.)

1. ______________________________

2. ______________________________

3. ______________________________

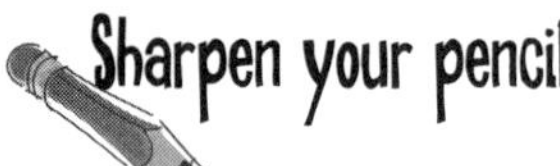

How the JSP, the TLD, and the bean attribute class relate

Fill in the spaces based on the information that you can see in the TLD. Draw arrows to indicate where the different pieces of information are tied together. In other words, for each blank, show exactly where you found the information needed to fill in the blank.

AdvisorTagHandler class

```
void doTag() {
  // tag logic
}

void set______(String x) {

   // code here
}
```

JSP that uses the tag

```
<html><body>

<%@ taglib prefix="mine" uri="________________"%>

Advisor Page<br>

<________:__________   ________="${foo}" />

</body></html>
```

TLD file

```
<taglib ...>
...
<uri>randomThings</uri>

<tag>
  <description>random advice</description>
  <name>advice</name>
  <tag-class>foo.AdvisorTagHandler</tag-class>
  <body-content>empty</body-content>
  <attribute>
     <name>user</name>
     <required>true</required>
     <rtexprvalue>________</rtexprvalue>
  </attribute>
</tag>
```

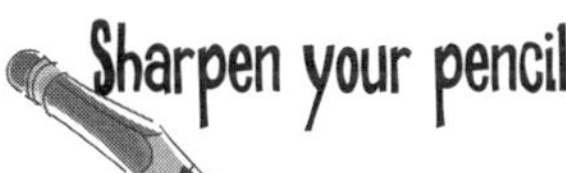

Test your Tag memory ANSWERS

The attribute that names the loop counter variable.

1. Fill in the name of the optional attribute.

```
<c:forEach var="movie" items="${movieList}" varStatus ="foo" >
   ${movie}
</c:forEach>
```

2. Fill in the missing attribute name.

```
<c:if test ="${userPref=='safety'}" >
    Maybe you should just walk...
</c:if>
```

The <c:set> tag must have a value, but you could choose to put the value in the body of the tag instead of as an attribute.

3. Fill in the missing attribute name.

```
<c:set var="userLevel" scope="session" value ="foo" />
```

4. Fill in the missing tag names (two different tag types), and the missing attribute name.

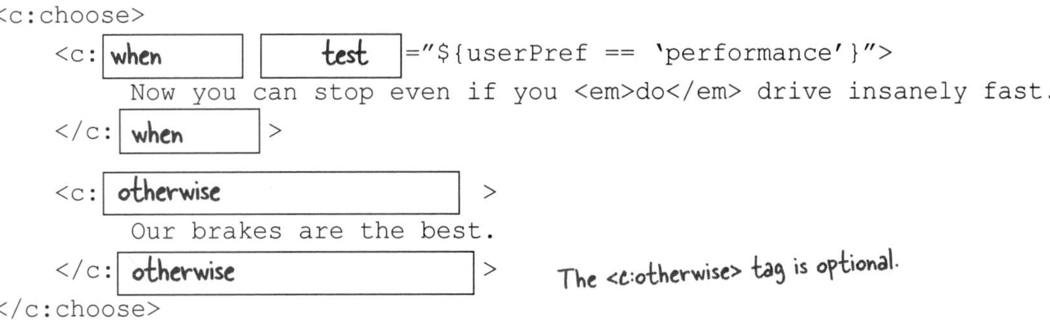

```
<c:choose>
    <c:when test ="${userPref == 'performance'}">
        Now you can stop even if you <em>do</em> drive insanely fast.
    </c:when >

    <c:otherwise >
        Our brakes are the best.
    </c:otherwise >
</c:choose>
```

The <c:otherwise> tag is optional.

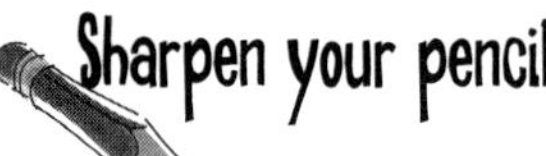

How the JSP, the TLD, and the bean attribute class relate ANSWERS

AdvisorTagHandler class

```
void doTag() {
  // tag logic
}

void setUser(String user) {

   this.user=user;
}
```

JSP that uses the tag

```
<html><body>

<%@ taglib prefix="mine" uri="randomThings"%>

Advisor Page<br>

<mine:advice  user="${userName}" />


</body></html>
```

TLD file

```
<taglib ...>
...
<uri>randomThings</uri>

<tag>
  <description>random advice</description>
  <name>advice</name>
  <tag-class>foo.AdvisorTagHandler</tag-class>
  <body-content>empty</body-content>
  <attribute>
     <name>user</name>
     <required>true</required>
     <rtexprvalue>true</rtexprvalue>

  </attribute>
</tag>
```

Mock Exam Chapter 9

1 Which is true about TLD files?

- ❑ A. TLD files may be placed in any subdirectory of **`WEB-INF`**.
- ❑ B. TLD files are used to configure JSP environment attributes, such as **`scripting-invalid`**.
- ❑ C. TLD files may be placed in the **`META-INF`** directory of the WAR file.
- ❑ D. TLD files can declare both Simple and Classic tags, but TLD files are NOT used to declare Tag Files.

2 Assuming the standard JSTL prefix conventions are used, which JSTL tags would you use to iterate over a collection of objects? (Choose all that apply.)

- ❑ A. **`<x:forEach>`**
- ❑ B. **`<c:iterate>`**
- ❑ C. **`<c:forEach>`**
- ❑ D. **`<c:forTokens>`**
- ❑ E. **`<logic:iterate>`**
- ❑ F. **`<logic:forEach>`**

3 A JSP page contains a **taglib** directive whose **uri** attribute has the value **myTags**. Which deployment descriptor element defines the associated TLD?

❑ A.
```
<taglib>
    <uri>myTags</uri>
    <location>/WEB-INF/myTags.tld</location>
</taglib>
```

❑ B.
```
<taglib>
    <uri>myTags</uri>
    <tld-location>/WEB-INF/myTags.tld</tld-location>
</taglib>
```

❑ C.
```
<taglib>
    <tld-uri>myTags</tld-uri>
    <tld-location>/WEB-INF/myTags.tld</tld-location>
</taglib>
```

❑ D.
```
<taglib>
    <taglib-uri>myTags</taglib-uri>
    <taglib-location>/WEB-INF/myTags.tld</taglib-location>
</taglib>
```

4 A JavaBean **Person** has a property called **address**. The value of this property is another JavaBean **Address** with the following string properties: **street1**, **street2**, **city**, **stateCode** and **zipCode**. A controller servlet creates a session-scoped attribute called **customer** that is an instance of the **Person** bean.

Which JSP code structures will set the **city** property of the **customer** attribute to the **city** request parameter? (Choose all that apply.)

❑ A.
```
${sessionScope.customer.address.city = param.city}
```

❑ B.
```
<c:set target="${sessionScope.customer.address}"
       property="city" value="${param.city}" />
```

❑ C.
```
<c:set scope="session" var="${customer.address}"
       property="city" value="${param.city}" />
```

❑ D.
```
<c:set target="${sessionScope.customer.address}"
       property="city">
   ${param.city}
</c:set>
```

5 Which **<body-content>** element combinations in the TLD are valid for the following JSP snippet? (Choose all that apply.)

```
<my:tag1>
  <my:tag2 a="47" />
  <% a = 420; %>
  <my:tag3>
    value = ${a}
  </my:tag3>
</my:tag1>
```

❑ A. tag1 body-content is **empty**
tag2 body-content is **JSP**
tag3 body-content is **scriptless**

❑ B. tag1 body-content is **JSP**
tag2 body-content is **empty**
tag3 body-content is **scriptless**

❑ C. tag1 body-content is **JSP**
tag2 body-content is **JSP**
tag3 body-content is **JSP**

❑ D. tag1 body-content is **scriptless**
tag2 body-content is **JSP**
tag3 body-content is **JSP**

❑ E. tag1 body-content is **JSP**
tag2 body-content is **scriptless**
tag3 body-content is **scriptless**

6 Assuming the appropriate **taglib** directives, which are valid examples of custom tag usage? (Choose all that apply.)

❑ A. `<foo:bar />`

❑ B. `<my:tag></my:tag>`

❑ C. `<mytag value="x" />`

❑ D. `<c:out value="x" />`

❑ E. `<jsp:setProperty name="a" property="b" value="c" />`

7 Given the following scriptlet code:

```
<select name='styleId'>
<% BeerStyle[] styles = beerService.getStyles();
   for ( int i=0; i < styles.length; i++ ) {
     BeerStyle style = styles[i]; %>
  <option value='<%= style.getObjectID() %>'>
    <%= style.getTitle() %>
  </option>
<% } %>
</select>
```

Which JSTL code snippet produces the same result?

❑ A.
```
<select name='styleId'>
  <c:for array='${beerService.styles}'>
    <option value='${item.objectID}'>${item.title}</option>
  </c:for>
</select>
```

❑ B.
```
<select name='styleId'>
  <c:forEach var='style' items='${beerService.styles}'>
    <option value='${style.objectID}'>${style.title}</option>
  </c:forEach>
</select>
```

❑ C.
```
<select name='styleId'>
  <c:for var='style' array='${beerService.styles}'>
    <option value='${style.objectID}'>${style.title}</option>
  </c:for>
</select>
```

❑ D.
```
<select name='styleId'>
  <c:forEach var='style' array='${beerService.styles}'>
    <option value='${style.objectID}'>${style.title}</option>
  </c:for>
</select>
```

Chapter 9 Answers

1 Which is true about TLD files?

(JSP v2.0 pgs 3-16, 1-160)

- [x] A. TLD files may be placed in any subdirectory of **WEB-INF**.
- [ ] B. TLD files are used to configure JSP environment attributes, such as **scripting-invalid**.

  -Option B is invalid because TLD files configure tag handlers not the JSP environment.

- [ ] C. TLD files may be placed in the **META-INF** directory of the WAR file.

  -Option C is invalid because TLD files are not recognized in the META-INF of the WAR file.

- [ ] D. TLD files can declare both Simple and Classic tags, but TLD files are NOT used to declare Tag Files.

  -Option D is invalid because Tag Files may be declared in a TLD (but it is rare).

---

2 Assuming the standard JSTL prefix conventions are used, which JSTL tags would you use to iterate over a collection of objects? (Choose all that apply.)

(JSTL v1.1 pg. 42)

- [ ] A. **<x:forEach>** -Option A is incorrect as this is the tag used for iterating over XPath expressions.
- [ ] B. **<c:iterate>** -Option B is incorrect because no such tag exists.
- [x] C. **<c:forEach>**
- [ ] D. **<c:forTokens>** -Option D is incorrect because this tag is used for iterating over tokens within a single string.
- [ ] E. **<logic:iterate>**
- [ ] F. **<logic:forEach>**

-Options E and F are incorrect because the prefix 'logic' is not a standard JSTL prefix (this prefix is typically used by tags in the Jakarta Struts package).

3 A JSP page contains a **taglib** directive whose **uri** attribute has the value **myTags**. Which deployment descriptor element defines the associated TLD? (JSP v2.0 pgs 3-12,13)

- ☐ A.
```
<taglib>
    <uri>myTags</uri>
    <location>/WEB-INF/myTags.tld</location>
</taglib>
```

- ☐ B.
```
<taglib>
    <uri>myTags</uri>
    <tld-location>/WEB-INF/myTags.tld</tld-location>
</taglib>
```

- ☐ C.
```
<taglib>
    <tld-uri>myTags</tld-uri>
    <tld-location>/WEB-INF/myTags.tld</tld-location>
</taglib>
```

- ☑ D.
```
<taglib>
    <taglib-uri>myTags</taglib-uri>
    <taglib-location>/WEB-INF/myTags.tld</taglib-location>
</taglib>
```

– Option D specifies valid tag elements.

4 A JavaBean **Person** has a property called **address**. The value of this property is another JavaBean **Address** with the following string properties: **street1**, **street2**, **city**, **stateCode** and **zipCode**. A controller servlet creates a session-scoped attribute called **customer** that is an instance of the **Person** bean. (JSTL v1.1 pg 4-28)

Which JSP code structures will set the **city** property of the **customer** attribute to the **city** request parameter? (Choose all that apply.)

- ☐ A.
```
${sessionScope.customer.address.city = param.city}
```

–Option A is invalid because EL does not permit assignment.

- ☑ B.
```
<c:set target="${sessionScope.customer.address}"
       property="city" value="${param.city}" />
```

- ☐ C.
```
<c:set scope="session" var="${customer.address}"
       property="city" value="${param.city}" />
```

–Option C is invalid because the var attribute does not accept a runtime value, nor does it work with the property attribute.

- ☑ D.
```
<c:set target="${sessionScope.customer.address}"
       property="city">
   ${param.city}
</c:set>
```

5 Which **<body-content>** element combinations in the TLD are valid for the following JSP snippet? (Choose all that apply.)

(JSP v2.0 Appendix JSP.C specifically pgs 3-21 and 3-30)

```
<my:tag1>
  <my:tag2 a="47" />
  <% a = 420; %>
  <my:tag3>
    value = ${a}
  </my:tag3>
</my:tag1>
```

–Tag1 includes scripting code so it must have at least 'JSP' body-content. Tag2 is only shown as an empty tag, but it could also contain 'JSP' or 'scriptless' body-content. Tag3 contains no scripting code so it may have either 'JSP' or 'scriptless' body-content.

- [ ] A. tag1 body-content is **empty**
  tag2 body-content is **JSP**
  tag3 body-content is **scriptless**

  –Option A is invalid because tag1 cannot be 'empty'.

- [x] B. tag1 body-content is **JSP**
  tag2 body-content is **empty**
  tag3 body-content is **scriptless**

- [x] C. tag1 body-content is **JSP**
  tag2 body-content is **JSP**
  tag3 body-content is **JSP**

- [ ] D. tag1 body-content is **scriptless**
  tag2 body-content is **JSP**
  tag3 body-content is **JSP**

  –Option D is invalid because tag1 cannot be 'scriptless'.

- [x] E. tag1 body-content is **JSP**
  tag2 body-content is **scriptless**
  tag3 body-content is **scriptless**

---

6 Assuming the appropriate **taglib** directives, which are valid examples of custom tag usage? (Choose all that apply.)

(JSP v2.0 section 7)

- [x] A. `<foo:bar />`
- [x] B. `<my:tag></my:tag>`
- [ ] C. `<mytag value="x" />`

  –Option C is invalid because there is no prefix.

- [x] D. `<c:out value="x" />`
- [ ] E. `<jsp:setProperty name="a" property="b" value="c" />`

–Option E is invalid because this is an example of a JSP standard action, not a custom tag.

7 Given the following scriptlet code:

(JSTL v1.1 pg 6-48)

```
<select name='styleId'>
<% BeerStyle[] styles = beerService.getStyles();
   for ( int i=0; i < styles.length; i++ ) {
     BeerStyle style = styles[i]; %>
  <option value='<%= style.getObjectID() %>'>
    <%= style.getTitle() %>
  </option>
<% } %>
</select>
```

Which JSTL code snippet produces the same result?

- [ ] A.
```
<select name='styleId'>
  <c:for array='${beerService.styles}'>
    <option value='${item.objectID}'>${item.title}</option>
  </c:for>
</select>
```

- [x] B.
```
<select name='styleId'>
  <c:forEach var='style' items='${beerService.styles}'>
    <option value='${style.objectID}'>${style.title}</option>
  </c:forEach>
</select>
```

-Option B is correct because it uses the proper JSTL tag/attribute names.

- [ ] C.
```
<select name='styleId'>
  <c:for var='style' array='${beerService.styles}'>
    <option value='${style.objectID}'>${style.title}</option>
  </c:for>
</select>
```

- [ ] D.
```
<select name='styleId'>
  <c:forEach var='style' array='${beerService.styles}'>
    <option value='${style.objectID}'>${style.title}</option>
  </c:for>
</select>
```

10 custom tag development

When even JSTL is not enough...

Sometimes JSTL and standard actions aren't enough.

When you need something custom, and you don't want to go back to scripting, you can write your *own* tag handlers. That way, your page designers can use your *tag* in their pages, while all the *hard* work is done behind the scenes in your tag handler *class*. But there are three different ways to build your own tag handlers, so there's a lot to learn. Of the three, two were introduced with JSP 2.0 to make your life easier (Simple Tags and Tag Files). But you still have to learn about ***Classic*** tags for that ridiculously rare occasion when neither of the other two will do what you want. Custom tag development gives you virtually unlimited power, if you can learn to wield it...

Building a Custom Tag Library

10.1 Describe the semantics of the "Classic" custom tag event model when each event method (doStartTag(), doAfterBody(), and doEndTag()) is executed, and explain what the return value for each event method means; and write a tag handler class.

10.2 Using the PageContext API, write tag handler code to access the JSP implicit variables and access web application attributes.

10.3 Given a scenario, write tag handler code to access the parent tag and an arbitrary tag ancestor.

10.4 Describe the semantics of the "Simple" custom tag event model when the event method (doTag()) is executed; write a tag handler class; and explain the constraints on the JSP content within the tag.

10.5 Describe the semantics of the Tag File model; describe the web application structure for tag files; write a tag file; and explain the constraints on the JSP content in the body of the tag.

Coverage Notes:

Although objective 10.1 doesn't explicitly mention the lifecycle methods associated with BodyTag (doInitBody() and setBodyContext()), you can expect to see them on the exam! Everything you need to know related to Classic tags is covered in this chapter, including things you might not infer from objective 10.1.

Objective 10.2 (PageContext API) is covered only very briefly in this chapter, because most of what you need to know about the PageContext API has already been covered earlier in the book. Virtually all of this objective is about using PageContext to access implicit variables and scoped attributes, both covered in the "Scriptless JSP" chapter, although we do provide a one-page summary again in this chapter.

I like the idea of having reusable chunks, but <jsp:include> and <c:import> aren't perfect. There's no standard for directories to put the included files in, the JSP is hard to read, and the fact that you make new request parameters to send something to the included file feels wrong...

Includes and imports can be messy

Using <jsp:include> or <c:import> lets you add reusable chunks of content, dynamically, to your pages. And you can even customize how the included file behaves by setting new request parameters that the included file can use.

Sure, it works fine. But should you really have to create new *request parameters* just to give the included file some customizing information?

Aren't request parameters supposed to represent form data sent *from the client* as part of the request? While there might be good reasons to add or change request parameters in your app, using them to send something to the included file isn't the cleanest approach.

Until JSP 2.0, there wasn't a standard way to deploy included files—you could put the included pieces just about anywhere in the web app. And a JSP with a bunch of <jsp:include> or <c:import> tags isn't the easiest thing to read. Wouldn't it be better if the tag itself told you something about the thing being included? Wouldn't it be nice to say something like:

<x:logoHeader> or <x:navBar>

You know where this is going...

Tag Files: like *include*, only better

With Tag Files, you can invoke reusable content using a custom tag instead of the generic <jsp:include> or <c:import>. You can think of Tag Files as a kind of "tag handler lite", because they let page developers create custom tags, without having to write a complicated Java tag handler class, but Tag Files are really just glorified *includes.*

Simplest way to make and use a Tag File

1. **Take an included file (like "Header.jsp") and rename it with a .tag extension.**

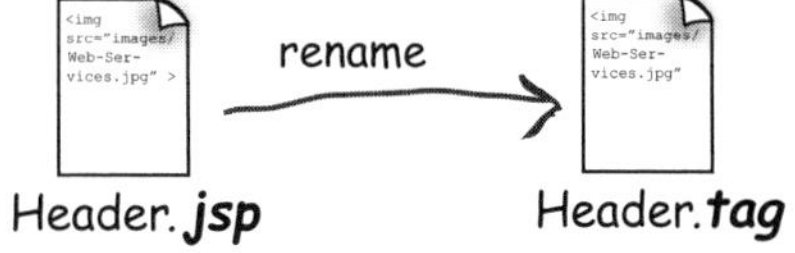


```
<img src="images/Web-Services.jpg" > <br>
```

This is the entire file... remember, we stripped out the opening and closing <html> and <body> tags, so they won't be duplicated in the final JSP.

2. **Put the tag file ("Header.tag") in a directory named "tags" inside the "WEB-INF" directory.**

3. **Put a taglib directive (with a *tagdir* attribute) in the JSP, and invoke the tag.**

```
<%@ taglib prefix="myTags" tagdir="/WEB-INF/tags" %>

<html><body>

<myTags:Header/>

Welcome to our site.
</body></html>
```

Use the "tagdir" attribute in the taglib directive, instead of the "uri" we use with TLDs for tag libraries.

The name of the tag is simply the name of the tag file! (minus the .tag extension)

So instead of:

<jsp:include page="Header.jsp"/>

we now have:

<myTags:Header/>

But how do you send it parameters?

When we included a file using <jsp:include>, we used the <jsp:param> tag inside the <jsp:include> to pass information to the included file. To refresh your memory on how it works with <jsp:include>:

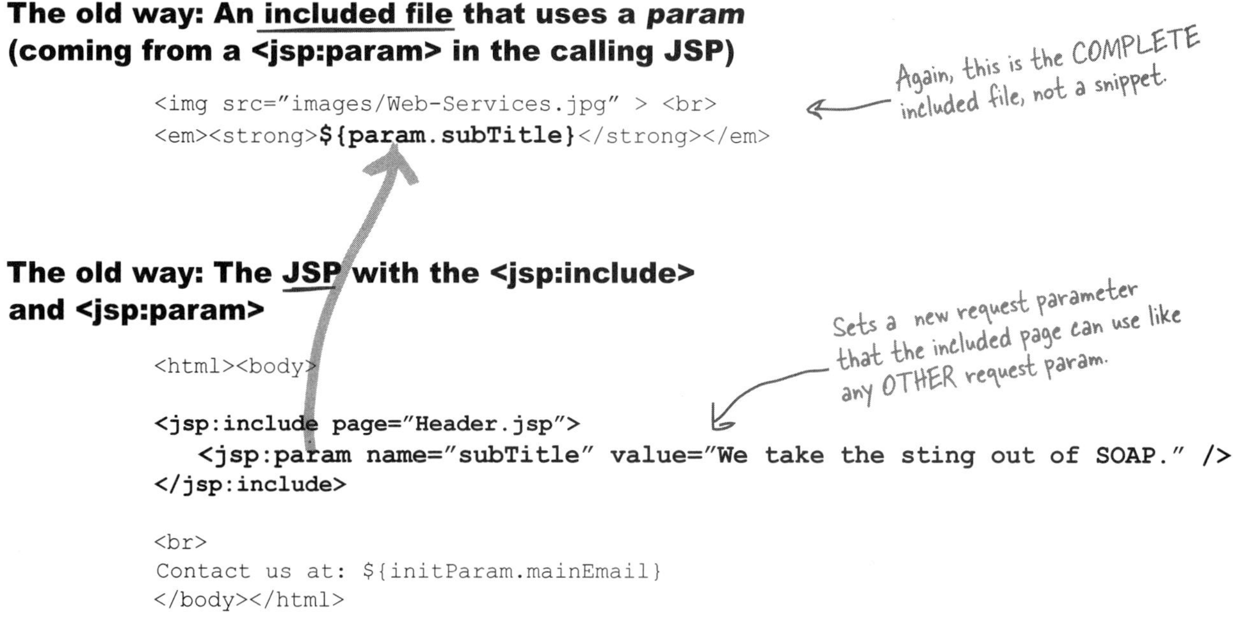

The old way: An included file that uses a *param* (coming from a <jsp:param> in the calling JSP)

```
<img src="images/Web-Services.jpg" > <br>
<em><strong>${param.subTitle}</strong></em>
```

Again, this is the COMPLETE included file, not a snippet.

The old way: The JSP with the <jsp:include> and <jsp:param>

```
<html><body>

<jsp:include page="Header.jsp">
   <jsp:param name="subTitle" value="We take the sting out of SOAP." />
</jsp:include>

<br>
Contact us at: ${initParam.mainEmail}
</body></html>
```

Sets a new request parameter that the included page can use like any OTHER request param.

The result

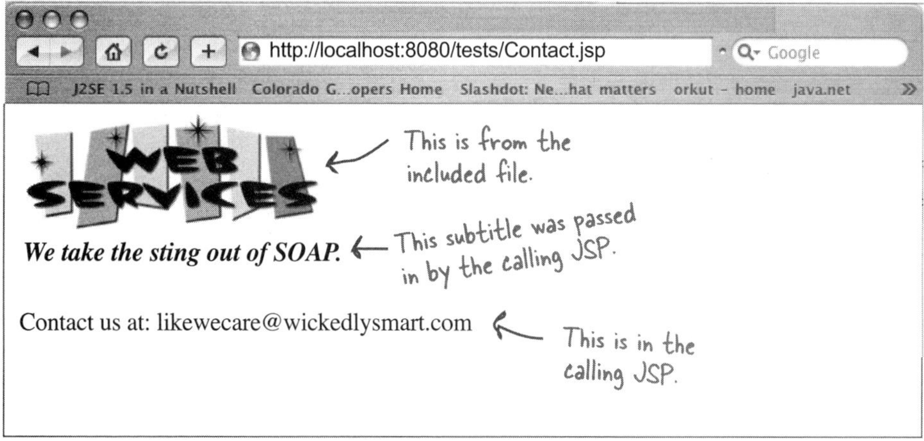
http://localhost:8080/tests/Contact.jsp
Google
J2SE 1.5 in a Nutshell
Colorado G...opers Home
Slashdot: Ne...hat matters
orkut - home
java.net
WEB SERVICES
This is from the included file.
We take the sting out of SOAP.
This subtitle was passed in by the calling JSP.
Contact us at: likewecare@wickedlysmart.com
This is in the calling JSP.

To a Tag File, you don't send request parameters, you send tag attributes!

You invoke a Tag File with a tag, and tags can have attributes. So it's only natural that the Tag File developer might want to invoke the tag with attributes... attributes that get sent to the Tag File.

Invoking the tag from the JSP

Before ***(using <jsp:param> to set a request parameter)***

```
<jsp:include page="Header.jsp">
   <jsp:param name="subTitle" value="We take the sting out of SOAP." />
</jsp:include>
```

After ***(using a Tag with an attribute)***

```
<myTags:Header subTitle="We take the String out of SOAP" />
```

Using the attribute in the Tag File

Before ***(using a request param value)***

```
<em><strong>${param.subTitle}</strong></em>
```

After ***(using a Tag File attribute)***

```
<em><strong>${subTitle}</strong></em> <br>
```

This is inside the actual Tag File (in other words, the included file).

All tag attributes have TAG scope. That's right, just the tag. Once the tag is closed, the tag attributes go out of scope!

You have to be clear about these—the <jsp:include> <jsp:param> value goes in as a request parameter. That's not the same as a request-scoped attribute, remember. The name/value pair for the <jsp:param> looks to the web-app as though it came in with a form submission. That's one of the reasons we DON'T like using it—the value you meant to pass ONLY to the included file, ends up visible to any component in the web app that is a part of this request (such as servlets or JSPs to which the request is forwarded).

But the nice, clean thing about tag attributes for Tag Files is that they're scoped to the tag itself. Just be sure you know the implications. This will NOT work:

```
<%@ taglib prefix="myTags" tagdir="/WEB-INF/tags" %>
<html><body>
<myTags:Header subTitle="We take the String out of SOAP" />
<br>
${subTitle}
</body></html>
```

This won't work! The attribute is out of scope.

Wait...something's not right here. How does the person writing the JSP even KNOW that the tag has that attribute? Where's the TLD that describes the attribute type?

Aren't tag attributes declared in the TLD?

With custom tags, including the JSTL, the tag attributes are defined in the TLD. Remember? This is the TLD from the custom <my:advice> tag from the last chapter:

```
<tag>
    <description>random advice</description>
    <name>advice</name>
    <tag-class>foo.AdvisorTagHandler</tag-class>
    <body-content>empty</body-content>

    <attribute>
        <name>user</name>
        <required>true</required>
        <rtexprvalue>true</rtexprvalue>
    </attribute>
</tag>
```

So, these are the things the developer who is using a tag needs to know. What's the attribute name? Is it optional or required? Can it be an expression, or must it be only a String literal?

But while you do specify *custom tag* attributes in a TLD, you do NOT specify *tag file* attributes in a TLD!

That means we still have a problem—how does the page developer *know* what attributes the tag accepts and/or requires? *Turn the page...*

Tag Files use the attribute directive

There's a shiny new type of directive, and it's just for Tag Files. Nothing else can use it. It's just like the <attribute> sub-element in the <tag> section of the TLD for a custom tag.

Inside the Tag File *(Header.tag)*

This means the attribute is not optional.

It can be a String literal OR an expression.

```
<%@ attribute  name="subTitle" required="true" rtexprvalue="true" %>

<img src="images/Web-Services.jpg" > <br>
<em><strong>${subTitle}</strong></em> <br>
```

Inside the JSP that uses the tag

```
<%@ taglib prefix="myTags" tagdir="/WEB-INF/tags" %>
<html><body>
<myTags:Header subTitle="We take the String out of SOAP" />

<br>
Contact us at: ${initParam.mainEmail}
</body></html>
```

What happens if you do NOT have the attribute when you use the tag

```
<myTags:Header />
```

You can't do this... you can't leave out the subTitle attribute because the tag file's attribute directive says required="true".

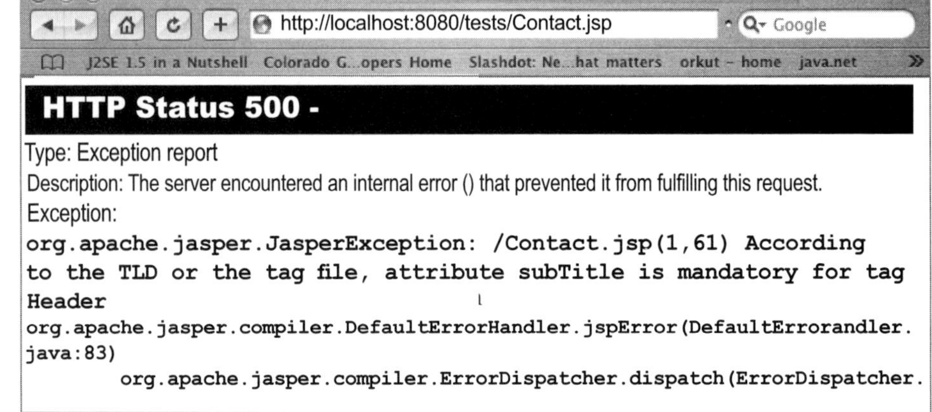
http://localhost:8080/tests/Contact.jsp
Google
J2SE 1.5 in a Nutshell
Colorado G...opers Home
Slashdot: Ne...hat matters
orkut - home
java.net
HTTP Status 500 -
Type: Exception report
Description: The server encountered an internal error () that prevented it from fulfilling this request.
Exception:
org.apache.jasper.JasperException: /Contact.jsp(1,61) According to the TLD or the tag file, attribute subTitle is mandatory for tag Header
org.apache.jasper.compiler.DefaultErrorHandler.jspError(DefaultErrorandler.java:83)
org.apache.jasper.compiler.ErrorDispatcher.dispatch(ErrorDispatcher.

When an attribute value is really big

Imagine you have a tag attribute that might be as long as, say, a paragraph. Sticking that in the opening tag could get ugly. So, you can choose to put content in the body of the tag, and then use that as a kind of attribute.

This time we'll take the subTitle attribute *out* of the tag, and instead make it the *body* of the <myTags:Header> tag.

Trust me on this. Sometimes it's good to have a BODY.

Inside the Tag File (*Header.tag*)

We no longer need the attribute directive!

```
<img src="images/Web-Services.jpg" > <br>
<em><strong><jsp:doBody/></strong></em> <br>
```

This says, "Take whatever is in the body of the tag used to invoke this tag file, and stick it here."

Inside the JSP that uses the tag

```
<%@ taglib prefix="myTags" tagdir="/WEB-INF/tags" %>
<html><body>

<myTags:Header>
   We take the sting out of SOAP. OK, so it's not Jini,<br>
   but we'll help you get through it with the least<br>
   frustration and hair loss.
</myTags:Header>

<br>
Contact us at: ${initParam.mainEmail}
</body></html>
```

Now we just give the tag a body, instead of putting all this as the value of an attribute in the opening tag.

But we're back to the same problem we had before—without a TLD, where do you declare the body-content type?

Declaring body-content for a Tag File

The only way to declare body-content type for a Tag File is with another new Tag File directive, the ***tag* directive**. The *tag* directive is the Tag File equivalent of the *page* directive in a JSP page, and it has a lot of the same attributes plus an important one you *won't* find in *page* directive—***body-content.***

For a custom tag, the <body-content> element inside the <tag> element of a TLD is mandatory! But a Tag File does *not* have to declare <body-content> if the default—*scriptless*—is acceptable. A value of ***scriptless*** means you can't have scripting elements. And scripting elements, remember, are *scriptlets* (<% ... %>), scriptlet *expressions* (<%= ... %>), and *declarations* (<%! ... %>).

In fact, ***Tag File bodies are never allowed to have scripting***, so it's not an option. But you *can* declare body-content (using the tag directive with a body-content attribute) if you want one of the other two options, *empty* or *tagdependent.*

You CANNOT use scripting code in the body of a Tag File tag!

The body-content of a Tag File defaults to "scriptless", so you don't have to declare body-content unless you want one of the OTHER two options: "empty" (nothing in the tag body) or "tagdependent" (treats the body as plain text).

Inside the Tag File with a *tag* directive *(Header.tag)*

```
<%@ attribute name="fontColor" required="true" %>

<%@ tag body-content="tagdependent" %>

<img src="images/Web-Services.jpg" > <br>
<em><strong><font color="${fontColor}"><jsp:doBody/></font></strong></em> <br>
```

This means the body-content will be treated like plain text, which means EL, tags, and scripts will NOT be evaluated. The only other legal values here are "empty" or "scriptless" (the default).

Inside the JSP that uses the tag

```
<%@ taglib prefix="myTags" tagdir="/WEB-INF/tags" %>
<html>

<myTags:Header fontColor="#660099">
   We take the sting out of SOAP. OK, so it's not Jini,<br>
   but we'll help you get through it with the least<br>
   frustration and hair loss.
</myTags:Header>

<br>
Contact us at: ${initParam.mainEmail}
</body></html>
```

"fontColor" is declared with an attribute directive in the Tag File.

The type for this body-content is declared in the Tag File using a tag directive with a body-content attribute.

Where the Container looks for Tag Files

The Container searches for tag files in four locations A tag file MUST have a TLD if it's deployed in a JAR, but if it's put directly into the web app (in "WEB-INF/tags" or a sub-directory), it does not *need* a TLD.

1. **Directly inside *WEB-INF/tags***
2. **Inside a sub-directory of *WEB-INF/tags***
3. **Inside the *META-INF/tags* directory inside a JAR file that's inside *WEB-INF/lib***
4. **Inside a sub-directory of *META-INF/tags* inside a JAR file that's inside *WEB-INF/lib***
5. ***IF the tag file is deployed in a JAR, there MUST be a TLD for the tag file.***

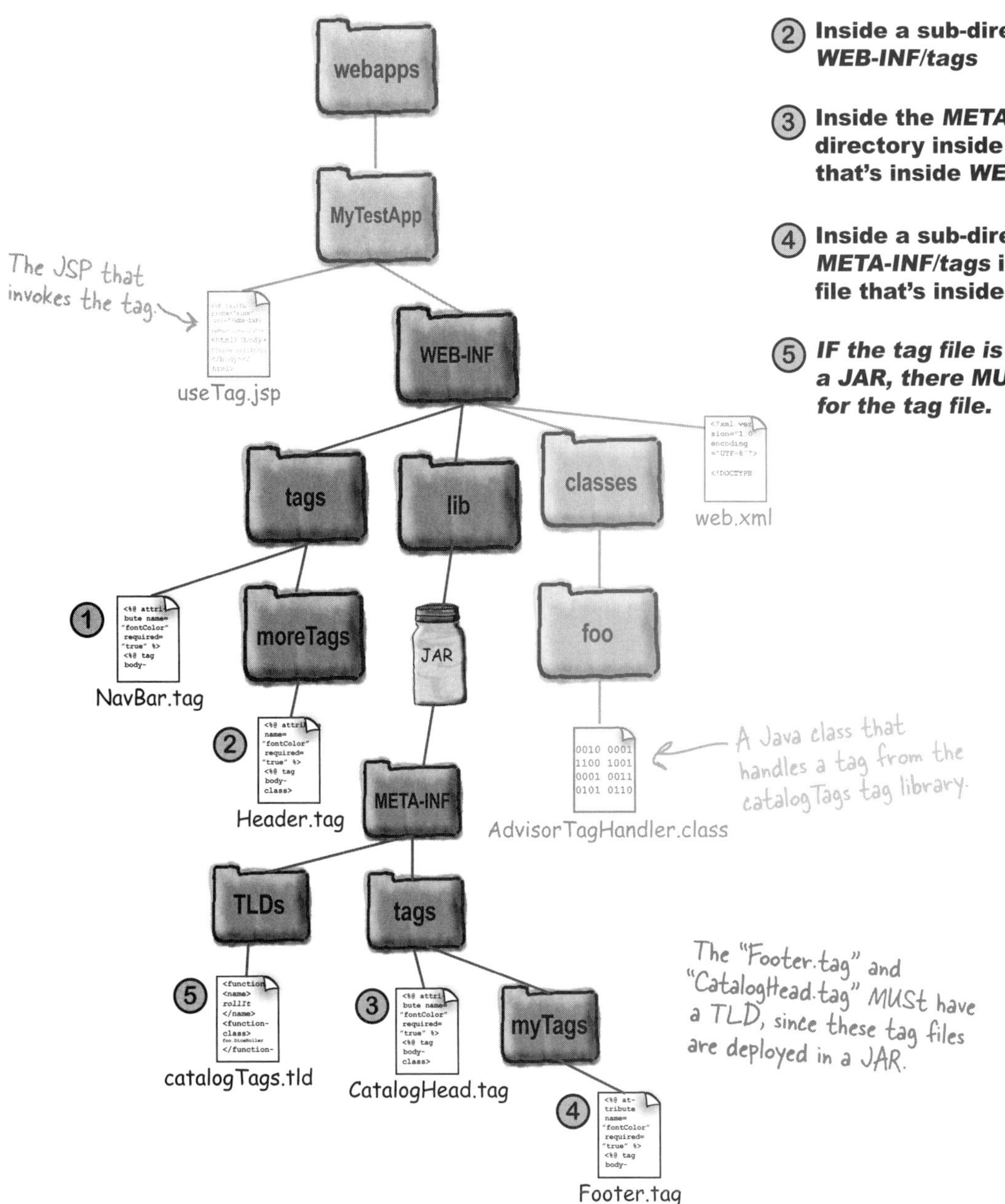

there are no Dumb Questions

Q: Does the Tag File have access to the request and response implicit objects?

A: Yes! Remember, even though it's a .tag file, it's gonna end up as part of a JSP. You can use the implicit *request* and *response* objects (if you do *scripting*... the normal EL implicit objects are always there as well), and you have access to a JspContext as well.

You don't have a ServletContext, though—a Tag File uses a ***JspContext*** instead of a ***ServletContext***.

Q: I thought on the opposite page you just said we could not do scripting in a Tag File!

A: No, that's not exactly what we said. You *can* do scripting in a Tag *File*, but you *can't* do scripting inside the *body* of the tag used to invoke the Tag File.

Q: Can you combine Tag Files and TLDs for custom tags in the same directory?

A: Yes. In fact, if you make a TLD that references your Tag Files, the Container will consider both Tag Files and custom tags mentioned in the *same* TLD as *belonging to the same library.*

Q: Hold on—I thought you said Tag Files didn't have a TLD? Isn't that why you have to use an attribute directive? Since you can't declare the attribute in a TLD?

A: Trick question. If you deploy your Tag Files in a JAR, they MUST have a TLD that describes their location. But it doesn't describe attribute, body-content, etc. The TLD entries for a Tag File describe *only* the location of the actual Tag File.

The TLD for a Tag File looks like this:

```
<taglib ....>
   <tlib-version>1.0</tlib-version>
   <uri>myTagLibrary</uri>
    <tag-file>
        <name>Header</name>
         <path>/META-INF/tags/Header.tag</path>
    </tag-file>
</taglib>
```

Notice that declaring a <tag-file> is quite different from declaring an actual <tag>.

Q: Why did they do it this way? Wouldn't it be so much simpler to just have custom tags and Tag Files declared the same way in a TLD? But NO... instead they had to come up with this whole other thing where you have to use new directives for defining the attributes and body-content. So, why *are* tags and Tag Files done differently?

A: On one hand, yes, it would have been simpler if custom tags and Tag Files were declared in the same way, using a TLD. The question is, simpler for *whom*? For a custom tag developer, sure. But Tag Files were added to the spec with someone *else* in mind—*page designers*.

Tag Files give non-Java developers a way to build custom tags *without* writing a Java class to handle the tag's functionality. And not having to build a TLD for the Tag File just makes life easier for the Tag File developer. (Remember, Tag Files *do* need a TLD if the Tag File is deployed in the JAR, but a non-Java programmer might not be using JARs anyway.)

The bottom line: custom tags *must* have a TLD, but Tag Files can declare attributes and body-content directly inside the Tag File, and need TLDs *only* if the Tag File is in a JAR.

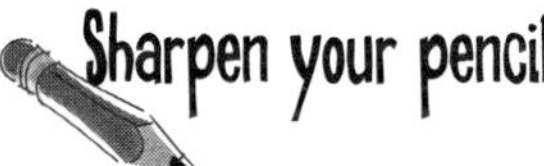

Memorizing Tag Files

Before we move on to a new topic, make sure you can write one yourself (answers are at the end of the chapter).

1. Fill in what would you must put into a Tag File to declare that the Tag has one required attribute, named "title", that can use an EL expression as the value of the attribute.

2. Fill in what would you must put into a Tag File to declare that the Tag must NOT have a body.

3. Draw a Tag File document in each of the locations where the Container will look for Tag Files.

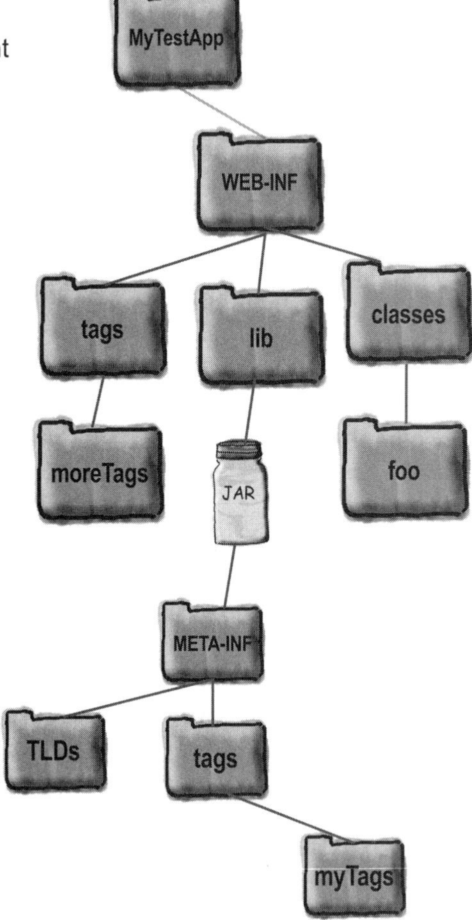

When you need more than Tag Files... Sometimes you need Java

Tag Files are fine when you're doing an *include*—when all you need to handle the tag you can do from *another* JSP (renamed with a .tag extension and with the appropriate directives added). But sometimes you need more. Sometimes you need good old Java code, and you don't want to do it from scriptlets, since that's what you're trying to prevent by using tags.

When you need Java, you need a custom tag *handler*. A tag *handler*, as opposed to a tag *file*, is simply a Java class that does the work of the tag. It's a little like an EL function, except much more powerful and flexible. Where EL functions are nothing more than static methods, a tag handler class has access to tag attributes, the tag body, and even the page context so it can get scoped attributes and the request and response.

Custom tag handlers come in two flavors: *Classic* and *Simple*. Classic tags were all you had in the previous version of JSP, but with JSP 2.0, a new and *much* simpler model was added. You'll have a hard time coming up with reasons to use the classic model when you need a custom tag handler, because the simple model (especially combined with JSTL and tag files) can handle nearly anything you'd want to do. But we can't dump the classic model for two reasons, and these two reasons are why you still have to learn it for the exam:

1) Like scripting, *Classic tag handlers are out there*, and you might need to read and support them, even if you never *create* one yourself.

2) There are those rare scenarios for which a classic tag handler is the best choice. This is pretty obscure, though. So point #1 is by far the most important reason to learn about Classic tags.

Tag files implement the tag functionality with another page (using JSP).

Tag handlers implement the tag functionality with a special Java class.

Tag handlers come in two flavors: Simple and Classic.

Making a Simple tag handler

For the simplest of Simple tags, the process is...*simple.*

1 Write a class that extends SimpleTagSupport

```
package foo;
import javax.servlet.jsp.tagext.SimpleTagSupport;
// more imports needed

public class SimpleTagTest1 extends SimpleTagSupport {
   // tag handler code here
}
```

2 Implement the doTag() method

```
public void doTag() throws JspException, IOException {
   getJspContext().getOut().print("This is the lamest use of a custom tag");
}
```

The doTag() method declares an IOException, so you don't have to wrap the print in a try/catch.

3 Create a TLD for the tag

```
<taglib ...>
  <tlib-version>1.2</tlib-version>
  <uri>simpleTags</uri>
  <tag>
     <description>worst use of a custom tag</description>
     <name>simple1</name>
     <tag-class>foo.SimpleTagTest1</tag-class>
     <body-content>empty</body-content>
  </tag>
</taglib>
```

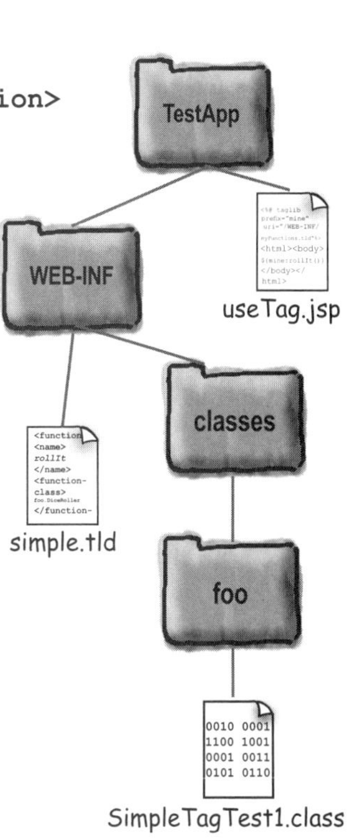

4 Deploy the tag handler and TLD

Put the TLD in WEB-INF, and put the tag handler inside WEB-INF/classes, using the package directory structure, of course. In other words, tag handler classes go in the same place all other web app Java classes go.

4 Write a JSP that *uses* the tag

```
<%@ taglib prefix="myTags" uri="simpleTags" %>
<html><body>
<myTags:simple1/>
</body></html>
```

A Simple tag with a body

If the tag needs a body, the TLD <body-content> needs to reflect that, and you need a special statement in the doTag() method.

The JSP that uses the tag

```
<%@ taglib prefix="myTags" uri="simpleTags" %>
<html><body>
Simple Tag 2:

<myTags:simple2>
   This is the body
</myTags:simple2>

</body></html>
```

This time, we invoke the tag WITH a body...

The tag handler class

```
package foo;
import javax.servlet.jsp.JspException;
import javax.servlet.jsp.tagext.SimpleTagSupport;
import java.io.IOException;

public class SimpleTagTest2 extends SimpleTagSupport {

    public void doTag() throws JspException, IOException {
        getJspBody().invoke(null);
    }
}
```

This says, "Process the body of the tag and print it to the response". The null argument means the output goes to the response rather than some OTHER writer you pass in.

The TLD for the tag

```
<?xml version="1.0" encoding="ISO-8859-1" ?>
<taglib xmlns="http://java.sun.com/xml/ns/j2ee"
xmlns:xsi="http://www.w3.org/2001/XMLSchema-instance"
xsi:schemaLocation="http://java.sun.com/xml/ns/j2ee/web-jsptaglibrary_2_0.xsd" ver-
sion="2.0">

  <tlib-version>1.2</tlib-version>
  <uri>simpleTags</uri>
  <tag>
     <description>marginally better use of a custom tag</description>
     <name>simple2</name>
     <tag-class>foo.SimpleTagTest2</tag-class>
     <body-content>scriptless</body-content>
  </tag>
</taglib>
```

This says the tag can have a body, but the body cannot have scripting (scriptlets, scripting expressions, or declarations).

The Simple tag API

A Simple tag handler must implement the SimpleTag interface. The easiest way to do that is to extend SimpleTagSupport and override just the method you need, doTag(). You don't *have* to use SimpleTagSupport, but we reckon 99.999999% of simple tag developers *do*.

JspTag interface
(javax.servlet.jsp.tagext.JspTag)

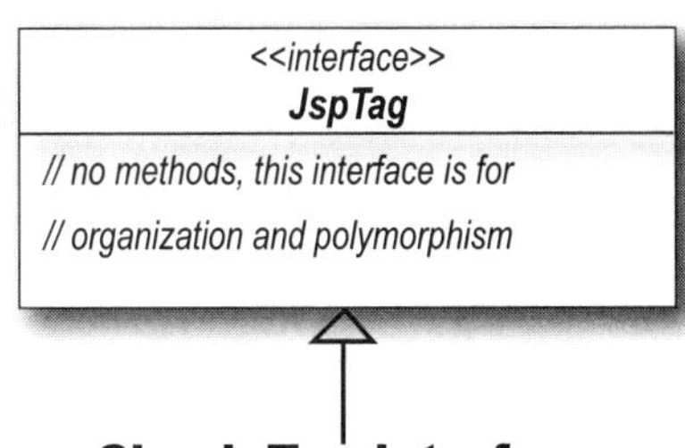

SimpleTag interface
(javax.servlet.jsp.tagext.SimpleTag)

<<interface>>
SimpleTag

void doTag()
JspTag getParent()
void setJspBody(JspFragment)
void setJspContext(JspContext)
void setParent(JspTag parent)

These are the lifecycle methods... the Container calls these whenever a tag is invoked. Can you guess the order in which these methods are called?

SimpleTagSupport
(javax.servlet.jsp.tagext.SimpleTagSupport)

You extend this!

SimpleTagSupport

void doTag()
JspTag findAncestorWithClass (JspTag, Class)
JspFragment getJspBody()
JspContext getJspContext()
JspTag getParent()
void setJspBody(JspFragment)
void setJspContext(JspContext)
void setParent(JspTag parent)

SimpleTagSupport implements the methods of SimpleTag (but the doTag() doesn't do anything, so you must override it in your tag handler). It also adds three more convenience methods, including the most useful one—getJspBody().

The life of a Simple tag handler

When a JSP invokes a tag, a new instance of the tag handler class is instantiated, two or more methods are called on the handler, and when the doTag() method completes, the handler object goes away. (In other words, these handler objects are *not* reused.)

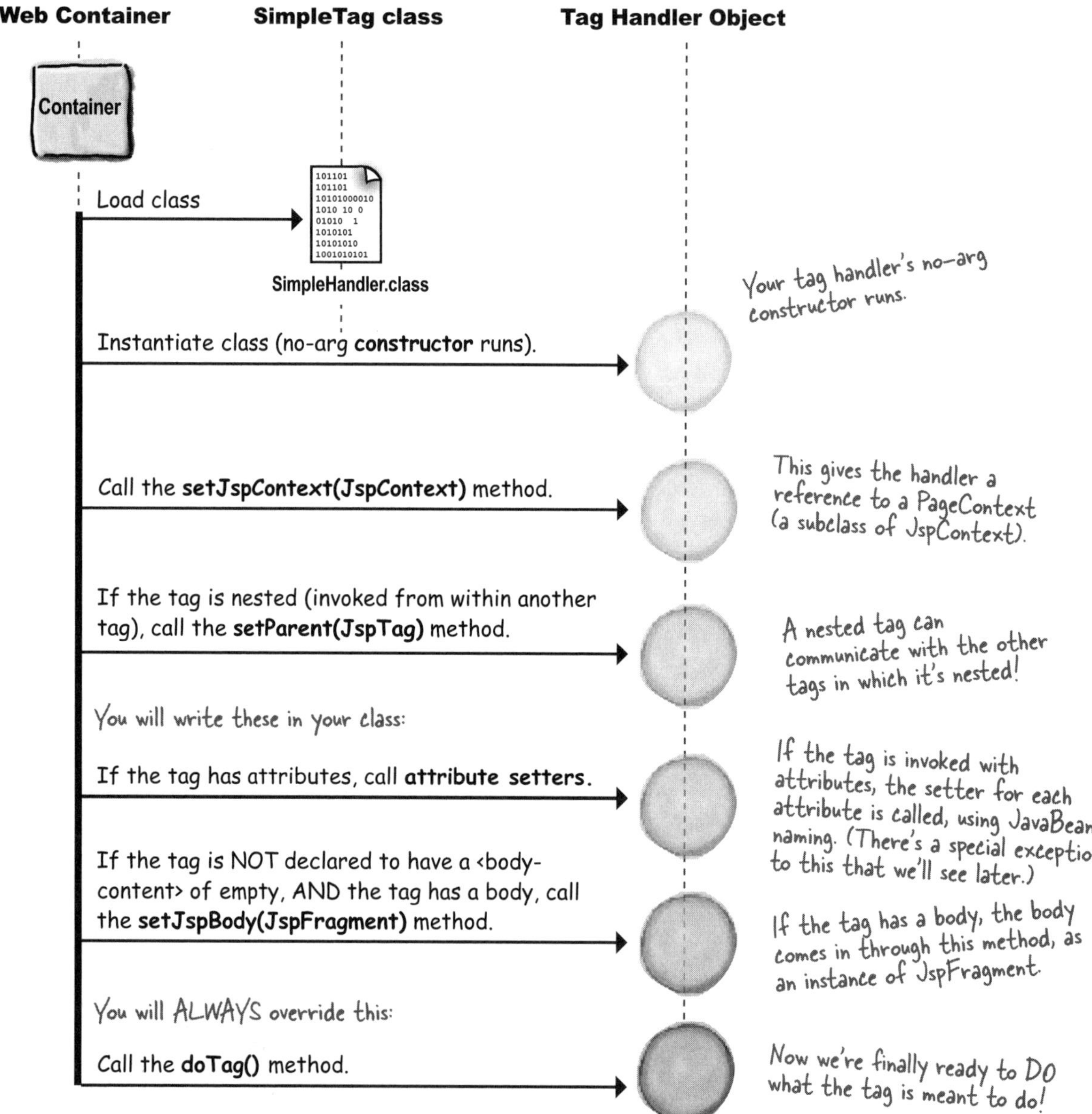
Web Container
SimpleTag class
Tag Handler Object
Container
Load class
SimpleHandler.class
Your tag handler's no-arg constructor runs.
Instantiate class (no-arg constructor runs).
Call the setJspContext(JspContext) method.
This gives the handler a reference to a PageContext (a subclass of JspContext).
If the tag is nested (invoked from within another tag), call the setParent(JspTag) method.
A nested tag can communicate with the other tags in which it's nested!
You will write these in your class:
If the tag has attributes, call attribute setters.
If the tag is invoked with attributes, the setter for each attribute is called, using JavaBean naming. (There's a special exception to this that we'll see later.)
If the tag is NOT declared to have a <body-content> of empty, AND the tag has a body, call the setJspBody(JspFragment) method.
If the tag has a body, the body comes in through this method, as an instance of JspFragment.
You will ALWAYS override this:
Call the doTag() method.
Now we're finally ready to DO what the tag is meant to do!

BE the Container

Look at each of the TLD/JSP pairs. Assume that the tag handler prints the body of the tag. Then answer the following questions about each one... what's the result? If it works, what prints out? Which methods in the custom tag class are invoked?

1

```
<tag>
    <description></description>
    <name>simple</name>
    <tag-class>foo.SimpleTagTest</tag-class>
    <body-content>empty</body-content>
</tag>
```

```
Simple Tag:
<myTags:simple>
  This is the body of the tag
</myTags:simple>
```

What do you see in the browser?

If it works, which SimpleTag lifecycle methods are called in the handler?

- ☐ *void doTag()*
- ☐ *JspTag getParent()*
- ☐ *void setJspBody()*
- ☐ *void setJspContext()*
- ☐ *void setParent()*

2

```
<tag>
    <description></description>
    <name>simple</name>
    <tag-class>foo.SimpleTagTest</tag-class>
    <body-content>scriptless</body-content>
</tag>
```

```
Simple Tag:
<myTags:simple>
  ${2*3}
</myTags:simple>
```

What do you see in the browser?

If it works, which SimpleTag lifecycle methods are called in the handler?

- ☐ *void doTag()*
- ☐ *JspTag getParent()*
- ☐ *void setJspBody()*
- ☐ *void setJspContext()*
- ☐ *void setParent()*

BE the Container

Answers

1

```
<tag>
    <description></description>
    <name>simple</name>
    <tag-class>foo.SimpleTagTest</tag-class>
    <body-content>empty</body-content>
</tag>
```

```
Simple Tag:
<myTags:simple>
   This is the body of the tag
</myTags:simple>
```

What do you see in the browser?

It doesn't work because it is supposed to have an empty body.

```
org.apache.jasper.JasperException: /simpleTag1.jsp(1,76)
According to TLD, tag myTags:simple must be empty, but is not
```

If it works, which SimpleTag lifecycle methods are called in the handler?

None, because it doesn't work.

- ☐ *void doTag()*
- ☐ *JspTag getParent()*
- ☐ *void setJspBody()*
- ☐ *void setJspContext()*
- ☐ *void setParent()*

2

```
<tag>
    <description></description>
    <name>simple</name>
    <tag-class>foo.SimpleTagTest</tag-class>
    <body-content>scriptless</body-content>
</tag>
```

```
Simple Tag:
<myTags:simple>
   ${2*3}
</myTags:simple>
```

What do you see in the browser?

Simple Tag: 6

If it works, which SimpleTag lifecycle methods are called in the handler?

- ☑ *void doTag()*
- ☐ *JspTag getParent()*
- ☑ *void setJspBody()*
- ☑ *void setJspContext()*
- ☐ *void setParent()*

The setParent() method is called only when the tag is invoked from WITHIN another tag. Since this tag was not nested, setParent() is NOT called.

What if the tag body uses an expression?

Imagine you have a tag with a body that uses an EL expression for an attribute. Now imagine that the attribute doesn't exist at the time you invoke the tag! In other words, the tag *body* depends on the tag *handler* to set the attribute. The example doesn't do anything very useful, but it's here to show you how it works in preparation for a bigger example.

The JSP tag invocation

```
<myTags:simple3>
   Message is: ${message}
</myTags:simple3>
```

At the point where the tag is invoked, "message" is NOT a scoped attribute! If you took this expression out of the tag, it would return null.

The tag handler doTag() method

```
public void doTag() throws JspException, IOException {
   getJspContext().setAttribute("message", "Wear sunscreen.");
   getJspBody().invoke(null);
}
```

The tag handler sets an attribute and THEN invokes the body.

Sharpen your pencil

Imagine you have a tag that looks like this:

```
<table>
<myTags:simple4>
  <tr><td>${movie}</td></tr>
</myTags:simple4>
</table>
```

Imagine that the tag handler has access to an array of String movie names, and you want to print one row for each movie name in the array. In the browser, you'll see something like:

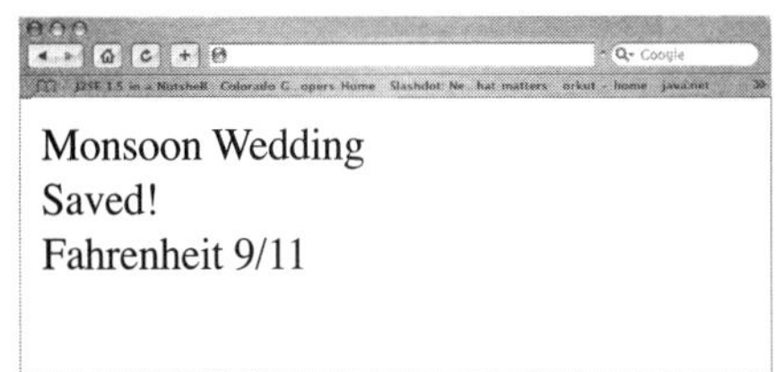

Write the tag handler doTag() method to support that goal.

```
public void doTag() throws JspException,
                                IOException {



}
```

A tag with dynamic row data: iterating the body

In this example, the EL expression in the body of the tag represents a single value in a collection, and the goal is to have the tag generate one row for each element in the collection. It's simple—the doTag() method simply does the work in a loop, invoking the body on each iteration of the loop.

The JSP tag invocation

```
<table>
  <myTags:simple4>
    <tr><td>${movie}</td></tr>
  </myTags:simple4>
</table>
```

The movie attribute doesn't exist at the time the tag is invoked. It will be set by the tag handler, and the body will be called repeatedly.

The tag handler doTag() method

```
String[] movies = {"Monsoon Wedding", "Saved!", "Fahrenheit 9/11"};

public void doTag() throws JspException, IOException {
   for(int i = 0; i < movies.length; i++) {
      getJspContext().setAttribute("movie", movies[i]);
      getJspBody().invoke(null);
   }
}
```

Set the attribute value to be the next element in the array.

Invoke the body again.

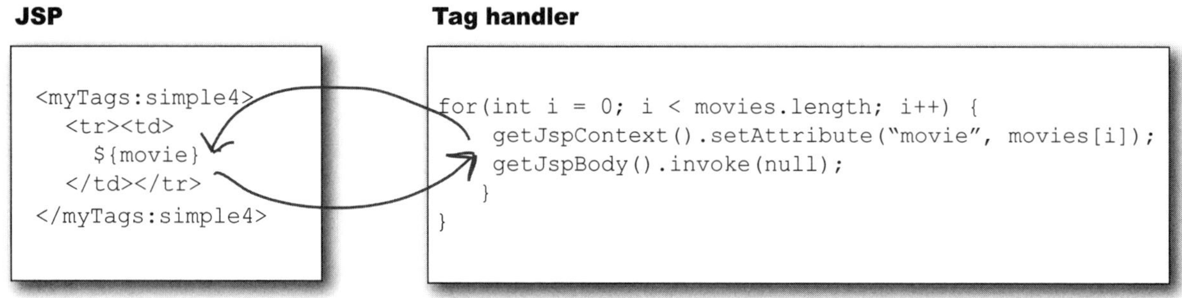
JSP
<myTags:simple4>
<tr><td>
${movie}
</td></tr>
</myTags:simple4>
Tag handler
for(int i = 0; i < movies.length; i++) {
getJspContext().setAttribute("movie", movies[i]);
getJspBody().invoke(null);
}
}

Each loop of the Tag handler resets the "movie" attribute value and calls getJspBody().invoke() again.

A Simple tag with an attribute

If the tag needs an attribute, you declare it in the TLD, and provide a bean-style setter method in the tag handler class for each attribute. If the tag invocation includes attributes, the Container invokes a setter method for each attribute.

The JSP tag invocation

```
<table>
  <myTags:simple5  movieList="${movieCollection}">
    <tr>
      <td>${movie.name}</td>
      <td>${movie.genre}</td>
    </tr>
  </myTags:simple5>
</table>
```

It's just an attribute like any other tag attribute. It doesn't matter that it's a Simple Tag handler taking care of the tag.

We're not showing the imports...

The tag handler class

```
public class SimpleTagTest5 extends SimpleTagSupport {

  private List movieList;

    public void setMovieList(List movieList) {
        this.movieList=movieList;
    }

    public void doTag() throws JspException, IOException {
        Iterator i = movieList.iterator();
        while(i.hasNext()) {
            Movie movie = (Movie) i.next();
            getJspContext().setAttribute("movie", movie);
            getJspBody().invoke(null);
        }
    }
}
```

Declare a variable to hold the attribute.

Write a bean-style setter method for the attribute. The method name MUST match the attribute name in the TLD (minus the "set" prefix and changing the case of the first letter).

The TLD for the tag

```
<tag>
   <description>takes an attribute and iterates over body</description>
   <name>simple5</name>
   <tag-class>foo.SimpleTagTest5</tag-class>
   <body-content> scriptless </body-content>
   <attribute>
       <name>movieList</name>
       <required>true</required>
       <rtexprvalue>true</rtexprvalue>
   </attribute>
</tag>
```

Use a regular <tag> <attribute> declaration in the TLD, just like other custom tags (with the exception of Tag Files).

What exactly IS a JspFragment?

A JspFragment is an object that represents JSP code. Its sole purpose in life is to be invoked. In other words, it's something that's meant to *run* and generate *output*. The body of a tag that invokes a simple tag handler is encapsulated in the JspFragment object, then sent to the tag handler in the setJspBody() method.

The crucial thing you must remember about JspFragment is that it must NOT contain any scripting elements! It can contain template text, standard and custom actions, and EL expressions, but no scriptlets, declarations, or scripting expressions.

One cool thing is that since it's an object, you can even pass the fragment around to other helper objects. And *those* objects, in turn, can get information from it by invoking the JspFragment's *other* method—getJspContext(). And of course once you've got a context, you can ask for attributes. So the getJspContext() method is really a way for the tag body to get information to other objects.

Most of the time, though, you'll use JspFragment simply to output the body of the tag to the response. You might, however, want to get access to the *contents* of the body. Notice that JspFragment doesn't have an access method like getContents() or getBody(). You can *write* the body to something, but you can't directly *get* the body. If you *do* want access to the body, you can use the argument to the invoke() method to pass in a java.io.Writer, then use methods on that Writer to process the contents of the tag body.

For the exam, and real life, this is probably all you will ever need to know about the details of JspFragment, so we won't spend any more time on it in the book.

JspFragment
JspContext getJspContext() void invoke(java.io.Writer)

The invoke() method takes a Writer... pass null to send the body to the response output, or a Writer if you want direct access to the actual body contents.

The invoke() method takes a java.io.Writer. If you want the body to be written to the response output, pass null to the invoke method.

Most of the time, that's what you'll do. But if you want access to the actual contents of the body, you can pass in a Writer, then use that Writer to process the body in some way.

SkipPageException: stops processing the page...

Imagine you're in a page that invokes the tag, and the tag depends on specific request attributes (that it gets from the JspContext available to the tag handler).

Now imagine the tag can't find the attributes it needs, and that the tag knows the rest of the page will never work if the tag can't succeed. What do you do? You could have the tag throw a JspException, and that would kill the page... but what if it's only the *rest* of the page that won't work? In other words, what if you still want the *first* part of the page—the part of the page that's evaluated *before* the tag invocation—to still appear as the response, but you don't want the response to include anything still left to be processed *after* the tag throws an exception?

No problem. That's exactly why SkipPageException exists.

The tag handler doTag() method

```
public void doTag() throws JspException, IOException {
   getJspContext().getOut().print("Message from within doTag().<br>");
   getJspContext().getOut().print("About to throw a SkipPageException");
   if (thingsDontWork) {
     throw new SkipPageException();
   }
}
```

At this point, we decided that the rest of the tag AND the rest of the page should stop. Only the part of the page and the tag BEFORE the exception will appear in the response.

The JSP that invokes the tag

```
<%@ taglib prefix="myTags" uri="simpleTags" %>
<html><body>
About to invoke a tag that throws SkipPageException <br>
<myTags:simple6/>
<br>Back in the page after invoking the tag.
</body></html>
```

The tag handled in the doTag() method above (that throws SkipPageException).

What is the result if the *thingsDontWork* test is true?

Fill in what you'll see in the browser:

SkipPageException shows everything up to the point of the exception

Everything in the doTag() method up to the point of the SkipPageException still shows up in the response. But after the exception, anything still left in either the tag or the page won't be evaluated.

In the JSP

```
<%@ taglib prefix="myTags" uri="simpleTags" %>
<html><body>
About to invoke a tag that throws SkipPageException <br>
<myTags:simple6/>

<br>Back in the page after invoking the tag.

</body></html>
```

This doesn't print out!

http://localhost:8080/tests/badTag.jsp

About to invoke a tag that throws SkipPageException

Message from within doTag().

About to throw a SkipPageException

In the tag handler

```
public void doTag() throws JspException, IOException {
    getJspContext().getOut().print("Message from within doTag().<br>");
    getJspContext().getOut().print("About to throw a SkipPageException");
    if (thingsDontWork) {
      throw new SkipPageException();
    }
}
```

But what happens when the tag is invoked from an included page?

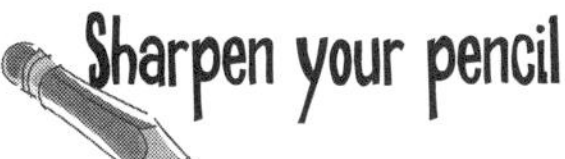

Look at the code below and figure out what prints when you bring up PageA.
Hint: look in the API for javax.servlet.jsp.SkipPageException.

Fill in what you'll see in the browser:

PageA JSP that includes PageB

```
<html><body>
  This is page (A) that includes another page (B). <br>
  Doing the include now:<br>
  <jsp:include page="badTagInclude.jsp" />
  <br>Back in page A after the include...
</body></html>
```

PageB (the included file) JSP that invokes the bad tag

```
<%@ taglib prefix="myTags" uri="simpleTags" %>
This is page B that invokes the tag that throws SkipPageException.
Invoking the tag now:<br>
<myTags:simple6/>
<br>Still in page B after the tag invocation...
```

The tag handler doTag() method

```
public void doTag() throws JspException, IOException {
   getJspContext().getOut().print("Message from within doTag().<br>");
   getJspContext().getOut().print("About to throw a SkipPageException");
   throw new SkipPageException();
}
```

SkipPageException stops only the page that directly invoked the tag

If the page that invokes the tag was included from some other page, only the page that invokes the tag stops processing! The original page that did the include keeps going after the SkipPageException.

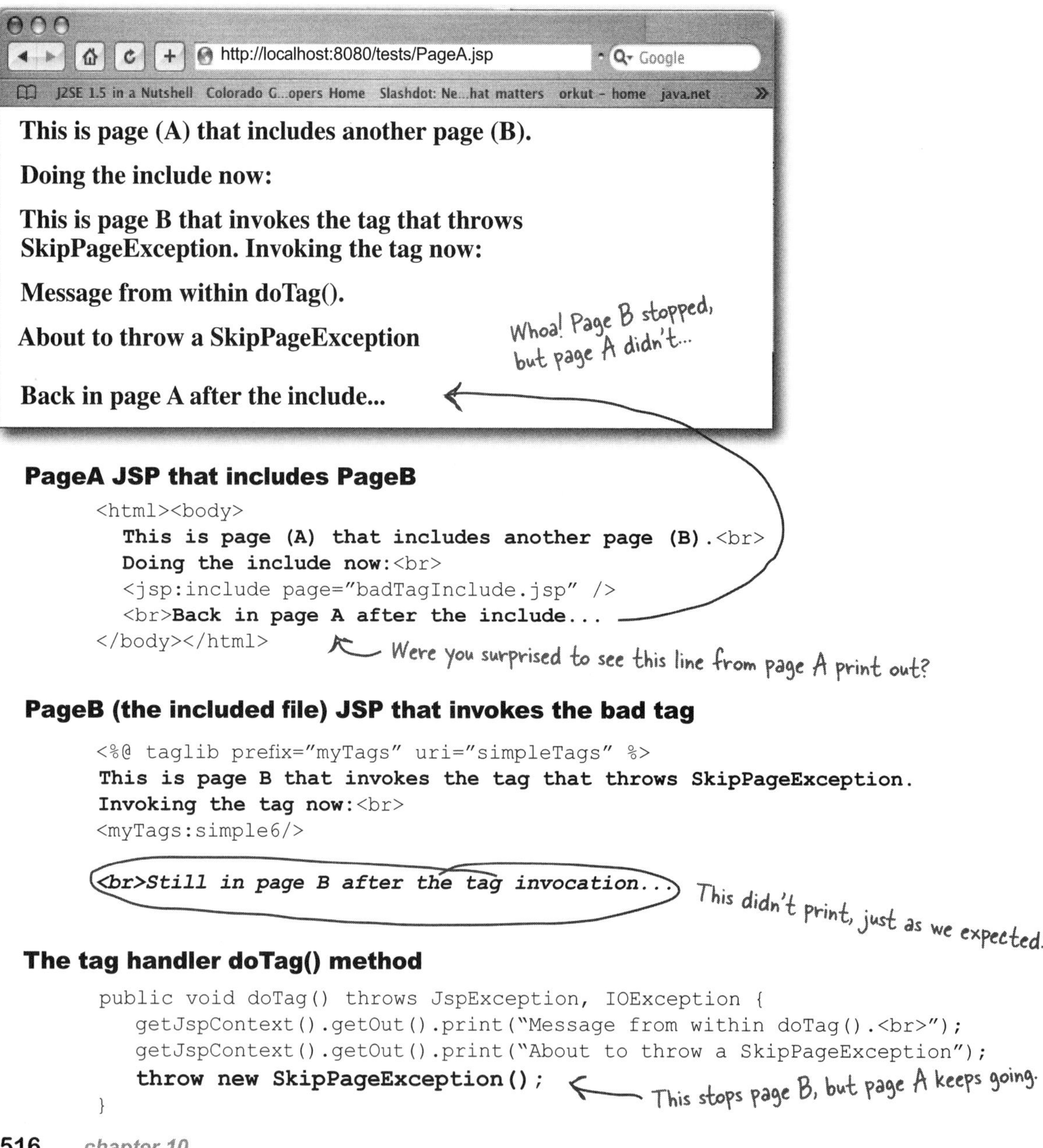

http://localhost:8080/tests/PageA.jsp
This is page (A) that includes another page (B).
Doing the include now:
This is page B that invokes the tag that throws SkipPageException. Invoking the tag now:
Message from within doTag().
About to throw a SkipPageException
Back in page A after the include...
Whoa! Page B stopped, but page A didn't...
Were you surprised to see this line from page A print out?
This didn't print, just as we expected.
This stops page B, but page A keeps going.

PageA JSP that includes PageB

```
<html><body>
  This is page (A) that includes another page (B).<br>
  Doing the include now:<br>
  <jsp:include page="badTagInclude.jsp" />
  <br>Back in page A after the include...
</body></html>
```

PageB (the included file) JSP that invokes the bad tag

```
<%@ taglib prefix="myTags" uri="simpleTags" %>
This is page B that invokes the tag that throws SkipPageException.
Invoking the tag now:<br>
<myTags:simple6/>

<br>Still in page B after the tag invocation...
```

The tag handler doTag() method

```
public void doTag() throws JspException, IOException {
   getJspContext().getOut().print("Message from within doTag().<br>");
   getJspContext().getOut().print("About to throw a SkipPageException");
   throw new SkipPageException();
}
```

there are no Dumb Questions

Q: What happens to a SimpleTag handler after it completes doTag()? Does the Container keep it around and reuse it?

A: No. SimpleTag handlers are never reused! Each tag handler instance takes care of a single invocation. So you never have to worry, for example, that instance variables in a SimpleTag handler won't have the correct initial values. A SimpleTag handler object will always be initialized before any of its methods are called.

Q: Do the attribute methods in a SimpleTag handler have to be of a type that can be automatically converted to and from a String? In other words, are you stuck with just primitives and String values?

A: Weren't you paying attention a few pages back? The attribute we sent to the SimpleTag handler was an ArrayList of movies. So that would be "no", to answer your question. But... if the attribute (which you can think of as a *property* if you think of the SimpleTag handler as a bean) is NOT a String or primitive, then the <rtexprvalue> value in the TLD had better be set to true. Because that's the only way you can set an attribute value for something that can't be expressed as a String in the tag. In other words, you can't send a Dog into the tag if you're forced to represent the Dog as a String literal. But if you can use an expression for the value of the attribute, then that expression can evaluate to whatever object type you need to match the argument to the handler's corresponding setter method.

Q: In a SimpleTag handler, if the tag is declared to have a body but it is invoked using an empty tag (since there's no way to say that a body is required), is the setJspBody() still invoked?

A: No! The setJspBody() is invoked ONLY if these two things are true:

1) The tag is NOT declared in the TLD to have an empty body.

2) The tag is invoked with a body.

That means that even if the tag is declared to have a non-empty body, the setJspBody() method will not be called if the tag is invoked in either of these two ways:

<foo:bar /> (empty tag)

<foo:bar></foo:bar> (no body).

- Tag Files implement tag functionality using a *page*, while tag handlers implement tag functionality using a Java tag handler *class*.
- Tag handlers come in two types: ***Classic*** and ***Simple*** (Simple tags and Tag Files were added in JSP 2.0).
- To make a Simple tag handler, extend **SimpleTagSupport** (which implements the **SimpleTag** interface).
- To deploy a Simple tag handler, you must create a TLD that describes the tag using the same <tag> element used by JSTL and other custom tag libraries.
- To use a Simple tag with a body, make sure the TLD <tag> for this tag does not declare <body-content> empty. Then call **getJspBody().invoke()** to cause the body to be processed.
- The **SimpleTagSupport** class includes implementation methods for everything in the **SimpleTag** interface, plus three convenience methods including **getJspBody()**, which you can use to get access to the contents of the body of the tag.
- The Simple tag lifecycle: ***Simple tags are never reused by the Container***, so each time a tag is invoked, the tag handler is instantiated, and its setJspContext() method is invoked. If the tag is called from within another tag, the setParent() method is called. If the tag is invoked with attributes, a bean-style setter method is invoked for each attribute. If the tag is invoked with a body (assuming its TLD does NOT declare it to have an empty body), the setJspBody() method is invoked. Finally, the doTag() method is invoked, and when it completes, the tag handler instance is destroyed.
- The ***setJspBody() method will be invoked ONLY if the tag is actually called with a body***. If the tag is invoked without a body, either with an empty tag <my:tag/> or with nothing between the opening and closing tags <my:tag></my:tag>, the setJspBody() method will NOT be called. Remember, if the tag has a body, the TLD must reflect that, and the <body-content> must not have a value of "empty".
- The Simple tag's doTag() method can set an attribute used by the body of the tag, by calling getJspContext().setAttribute() followed by getJspBody().invoke().
- The ***doTag() method declares a JspException and an IOException,*** so you can write to the JspWriter without wrapping it in a try/catch.
- You can iterate over the body of a Simple tag by invoking the body (getJspBody().invoke()) in a loop.
- If the tag has an attribute, declare the attribute in the TLD using an <attribute> element, and ***provide a bean-style setter method in the tag handler class.*** When the tag is invoked, the setter method will be called *before* doTag().
- The getJspBody() method returns a JspFragment, which has two methods: **invoke(java.io.Writer)**, and **getJspContext()** that returns a JspContext the tag handler can use to get access to the PageContext API (to get access to implicit variables and scoped attributes).
- Passing *null* to invoke() writes the evaluated body to the response output, but you can pass another Writer in if you want direct access to the body contents.
- Throw a **SkipPageException** if you want the current page to stop processing. If the page that invoked the tag was included from another page, the including page keeps going even though the included page stops processing from the moment the exception is thrown.

It's just wonderful that JSP spec designers gave us Simple Tags and Tag Files, but, um, they waited until AFTER my company wrote about 10 million custom tags using the Classic model...

You still have to know about Classic tag handlers

You might get lucky. Maybe the place you work is starting out with JSP 2.0, and can use Tag Files and SimpleTag handlers from the start.

That *could* happen.

But it probably won't. Chances are, you're working (or will work in the future) somewhere that's been using JSPs since the pre-2.0 days, using the Classic tag model for writing custom tag handlers.

You probably need to at least be able to read the source code for a Classic tag handler. You might be called on to maintain or refactor a Classic tag handler class.

But even if you don't ever have to read or write a Classic tag handler, they're still covered (very lightly) by one of the exam objectives. Be grateful—on the previous version of the exam you might have seen at least seven or eight Classic tag handler questions on the exam. Today, exam candidates will see only a couple of questions on Classic tag handlers.

Tag handler API

Everything in a grey box is from the original (Classic) tag model for custom tag handlers.

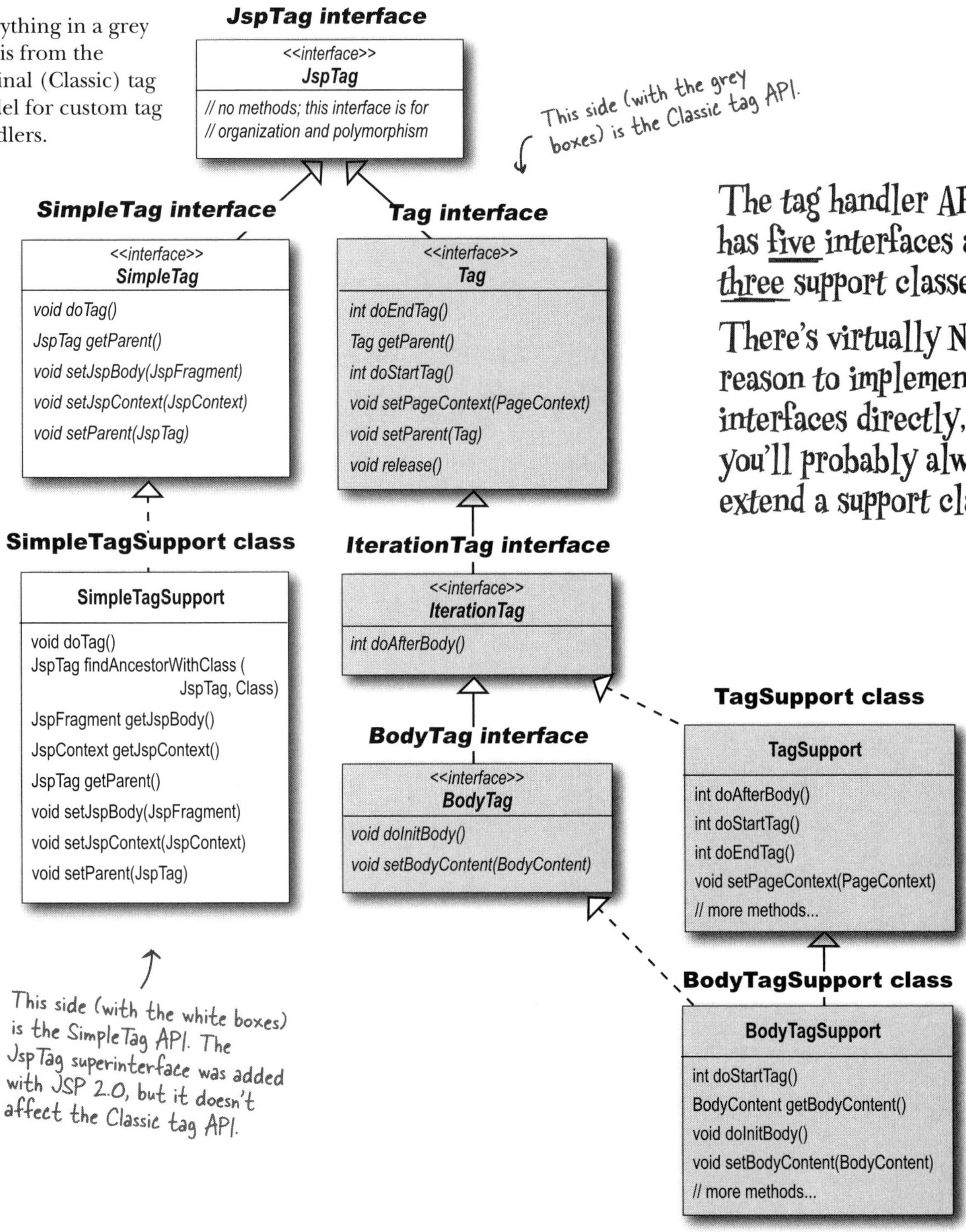

JspTag interface

<<interface>>
JspTag

// no methods; this interface is for
// organization and polymorphism

This side (with the grey boxes) is the Classic tag API.

SimpleTag interface

<<interface>>
SimpleTag

void doTag()
JspTag getParent()
void setJspBody(JspFragment)
void setJspContext(JspContext)
void setParent(JspTag)

Tag interface

<<interface>>
Tag

int doEndTag()
Tag getParent()
int doStartTag()
void setPageContext(PageContext)
void setParent(Tag)
void release()

The tag handler API has five interfaces and three support classes.

There's virtually NO reason to implement the interfaces directly, so you'll probably always extend a support class.

SimpleTagSupport class

SimpleTagSupport

void doTag()
JspTag findAncestorWithClass (JspTag, Class)
JspFragment getJspBody()
JspContext getJspContext()
JspTag getParent()
void setJspBody(JspFragment)
void setJspContext(JspContext)
void setParent(JspTag)

IterationTag interface

<<interface>>
IterationTag

int doAfterBody()

BodyTag interface

<<interface>>
BodyTag

void doInitBody()
void setBodyContent(BodyContent)

TagSupport class

TagSupport

int doAfterBody()
int doStartTag()
int doEndTag()
void setPageContext(PageContext)
// more methods...

BodyTagSupport class

BodyTagSupport

int doStartTag()
BodyContent getBodyContent()
void doInitBody()
void setBodyContent(BodyContent)
// more methods...

This side (with the white boxes) is the SimpleTag API. The JspTag superinterface was added with JSP 2.0, but it doesn't affect the Classic tag API.

A very small Classic tag handler

This example is so basic that it's not much different from a SimpleTag handler's doTag() method. In fact the differences won't become painful until you try to process a tag with a body (but you'll just have to wait for that).

A JSP that invokes a Classic tag

```
<%@ taglib prefix="mine" uri="KathyClassicTags" %>
<html><body>
  Classic Tag One:<br>
  <mine:classicOne />
</body></html>
```

This tag uses a Classic tag handler. But to the JSP, it looks just like any other tag invocation.

The TLD <tag> element for the Classic tag

```
<tag>
   <description>ludicrous use of a Classic tag</description>
   <name>classicOne</name>
   <tag-class>foo.Classic1</tag-class>
   <body-content>empty</body-content>
</tag>
```

There's no way to know for certain that this <tag> is handled by a Classic tag handler, unless you know that foo.Classic1 class implements the Tag interface (instead of SimpleTag). We could completely replace the foo.Classic1 code to have it use a SimpleTag, and the TLD would not change.

The Classic tag handler

```
package foo;
import javax.servlet.jsp.*;
import javax.servlet.jsp.tagext.*;
import java.io.*;

public class Classic1 extends TagSupport {

    public int doStartTag() throws JspException {

       JspWriter out = pageContext.getOut();

        try {
          out.println("classic tag output");
        } catch(IOException ex) {
           throw new JspException("IOException- " + ex.toString());
        }

       return SKIP_BODY;
    }
}
```

By extending TagSupport, we're implementing both Tag and IterationTag. Here we're overriding only one method, doStartTag().

The methods declare JspException, but NOT an IOException! (The SimpleTag doTag() declares IOException.)

Classic tags inherit a pageContext member variable from TagSupport (in contrast to the getJspContext() method of SimpleTag).

Here we must use a try/catch, because we can't declare the IOException.

We have to return an int to tell the Container what to do next. Much more on this coming up...

A Classic tag handler with TWO methods

This example overrides both the doStartTag() and doEndTag() methods, although it could accomplish the same output all within doStartTag(). The point of doEndTag() is that it's called *after* the body is evaluated. We don't show the TLD here, because it's virtually identical to the previous one, except for some of the names. The tag is declared to have no attributes, and an empty body.

A JSP that invokes a Classic tag

```
<%@ taglib prefix="mine" uri="KathyClassicTags" %>
<html><body>
  Classic Tag Two:<br>
  <mine:classicTwo />
</body></html>
```

The Classic tag handler

We won't show the package or imports unless we add something from a new package.

```
public class Classic2 extends TagSupport {
    JspWriter out;

    public int doStartTag() throws JspException {
        out = pageContext.getOut();
        try {
          out.println("in doStartTag()");
        } catch(IOException ex) {
           throw new JspException("IOException- " + ex.toString());
        }
        return SKIP_BODY;
    }

    public int doEndTag() throws JspException {
       try {
          out.println("in doEndTag()");
        } catch(IOException ex) {
           throw new JspException("IOException- " + ex.toString());
        }
      return EVAL_PAGE;
   }
}
```

SKIP_BODY: This says, "Don't evaluate the body if there is one-- just go straight to the doEndTag() method."

EVAL_PAGE: This says, "Evaluate the rest of the page" (as opposed to SKIP_PAGE, which would be just like throwing a SkipPageException from a SimpleTag handler).

Classic Tag Two:

in doStartTag() in doEndTag()

When a tag has a body: comparing Simple vs. Classic

Now it starts to look different from a SimpleTag. Remember, SimpleTag bodies are evaluated when (and if) you want by calling invoke() on the JspFragment that encapsulates the body. But in Classic tags, ***the body is evaluated in between the doStartTag() and doEndTag() methods!*** Both of the examples below have the exact same behavior.

The JSP that uses the tag

```
<%@ taglib prefix="myTags" uri="myTags" %>
<html><body>
  <myTags:simpleBody>
     This is the body
  </myTags:simpleBody>
</body></html>
```

A SimpleTag handler class

```
// package and imports
public class SimpleTagTest extends SimpleTagSupport {
    public void doTag() throws JspException, IOException {
        getJspContext().getOut().print("Before body.");
        getJspBody().invoke(null); <— This causes the body to be evaluated.
        getJspContext().getOut().print("After body.");
    }
}
```

A Classic tag handler that does the same thing

```
// package and imports
public class ClassicTest extends TagSupport {
   JspWriter out;

   public int doStartTag() throws JspException {
      out = pageContext.getOut();
      try {
        out.println("Before body.");
      } catch(IOException ex) {
         throw new JspException("IOException- " + ex.toString());
      }
      return EVAL_BODY_INCLUDE;   <— THIS is what causes the body to be
    }                                  evaluated in a Classic tag handler!

   public int doEndTag() throws JspException {
      try {
        out.println("After body.");
      } catch(IOException ex) {
         throw new JspException("IOException- " + ex.toString());
      }
      return EVAL_PAGE;
   }
}
```

But how do you loop over the body? It looks like doStartTag() is called too early, and doEndTag() is too late, and I don't have any way to keep re-invoking the body evaluation...

Simple tag

```
// package and imports
public class SimpleTagTest extends SimpleTagSupport {
  public void doTag() throws JspException, IOException {
     for(int i = 0; i < 3, i++) {
       getJspBody().invoke(null);
     }
  }
}
```

It's easy to loop the body of a Simple tag; you just keep calling invoke() on the body, from within doTag().

Classic tag

```
// package and imports
public class ClassicTest extends TagSupport {

    public int doStartTag() throws JspException {
       return EVAL_BODY_INCLUDE;
    }
```

But where do you loop over the body, if the body is evaluated in between the methods instead of IN a method like doTag()?

```
    public int doEndTag() throws JspException {
       return EVAL_PAGE;
  }
}
```

Classic tags have a different lifecycle

Simple tags are simple—it's all about doTag(). But with classic tags, there's a do*Start*Tag() and a do*End*Tag(). And that brings up an interesting problem—when and how is the body evaluated? There's no doBody() method, but there *is* a **do*After*Body()** method that's called *after* the body is evaluated and before the doEndTag() runs.

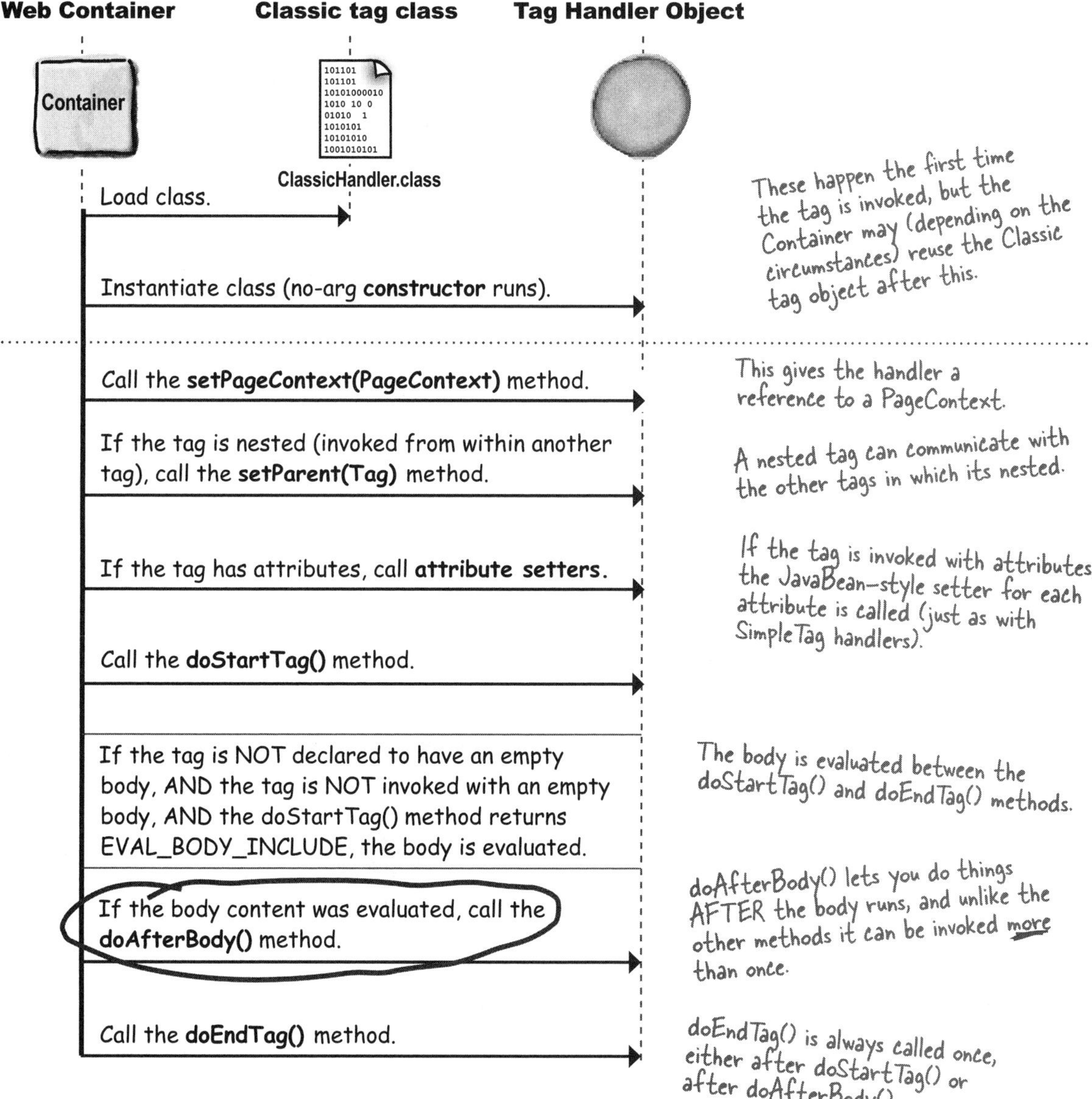

Web Container
Classic tag class
Tag Handler Object
Container
101101
101101
10101000010
1010 10 0
01010 1
1010101
10101010
1001010101
ClassicHandler.class
Load class.
Instantiate class (no-arg constructor runs).
These happen the first time the tag is invoked, but the Container may (depending on the circumstances) reuse the Classic tag object after this.
Call the setPageContext(PageContext) method.
This gives the handler a reference to a PageContext.
If the tag is nested (invoked from within another tag), call the setParent(Tag) method.
A nested tag can communicate with the other tags in which its nested.
If the tag has attributes, call attribute setters.
If the tag is invoked with attributes, the JavaBean-style setter for each attribute is called (just as with SimpleTag handlers).
Call the doStartTag() method.
If the tag is NOT declared to have an empty body, AND the tag is NOT invoked with an empty body, AND the doStartTag() method returns EVAL_BODY_INCLUDE, the body is evaluated.
The body is evaluated between the doStartTag() and doEndTag() methods.
If the body content was evaluated, call the doAfterBody() method.
doAfterBody() lets you do things AFTER the body runs, and unlike the other methods it can be invoked more than once.
Call the doEndTag() method.
doEndTag() is always called once, either after doStartTag() or after doAfterBody().

The Classic lifecycle depends on return values

The doStartTag() and doEndTag() methods return an int. That int tells the Container what to do next. With doStartTag(), the question the Container asks is, "Should I evaluate the body?" (assuming there is one, and assuming the TLD doesn't declare the body as empty).

With doEndTag(), the Container asks, "Should I keep evaluating the rest of the calling page?" The return values are represented by constants declared in the Tag and IterationTag interfaces.

Possible return values when you extend TagSupport

doStartTag()

```
SKIP_BODY
EVAL_BODY_INCLUDE
```

doAfterBody()

```
SKIP_BODY
EVAL_BODY_AGAIN
```

doEndTag()

```
SKIP_PAGE
EVAL_PAGE
```

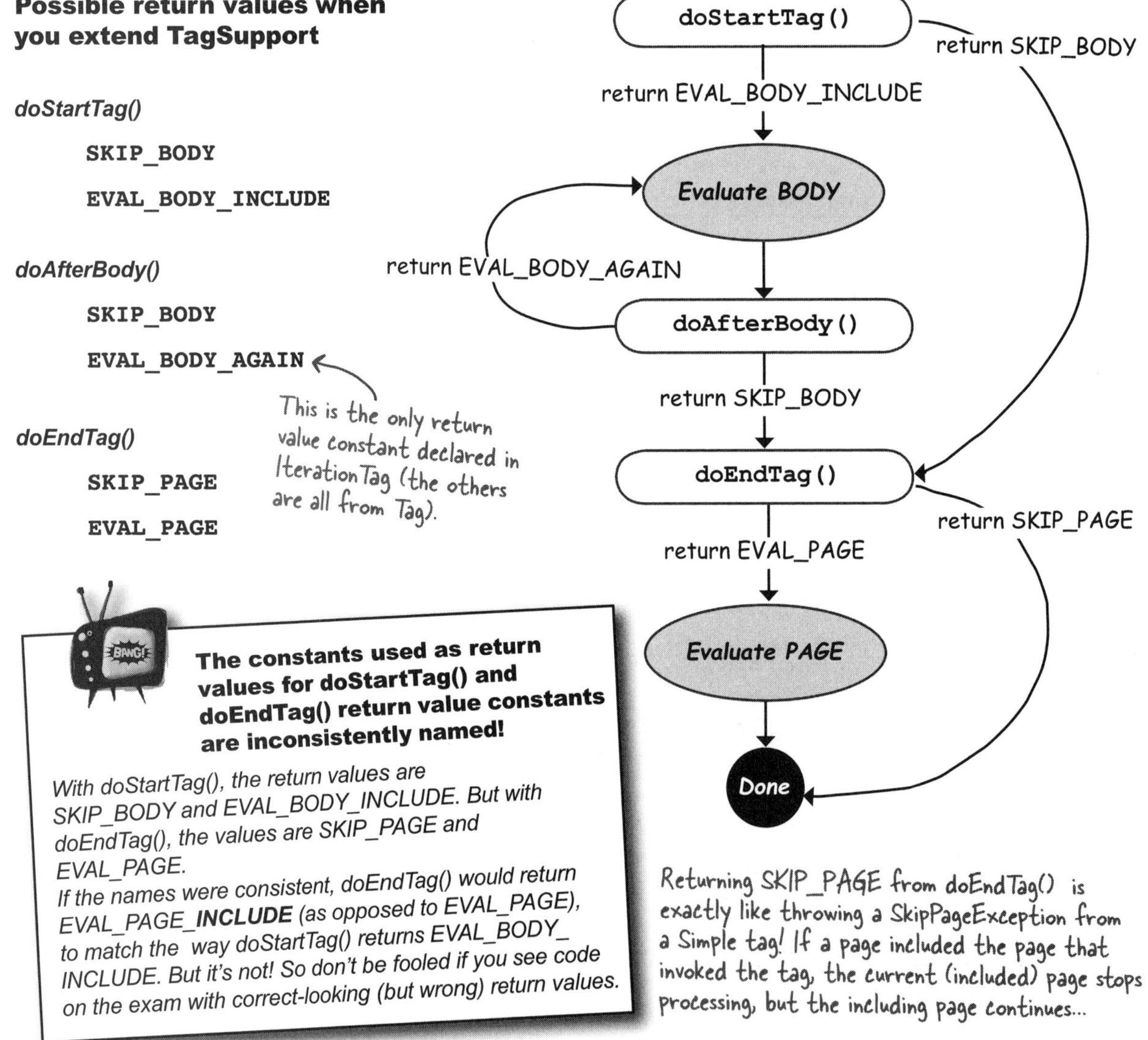

This is the only return value constant declared in IterationTag (the others are all from Tag).
doStartTag()
return SKIP_BODY
return EVAL_BODY_INCLUDE
Evaluate BODY
return EVAL_BODY_AGAIN
doAfterBody()
return SKIP_BODY
doEndTag()
return SKIP_PAGE
return EVAL_PAGE
Evaluate PAGE
Done
BANG!
Returning SKIP_PAGE from doEndTag() is exactly like throwing a SkipPageException from a Simple tag! If a page included the page that invoked the tag, the current (included) page stops processing, but the including page continues...

The constants used as return values for doStartTag() and doEndTag() return value constants are inconsistently named!

With doStartTag(), the return values are SKIP_BODY and EVAL_BODY_INCLUDE. But with doEndTag(), the values are SKIP_PAGE and EVAL_PAGE.
*If the names were consistent, doEndTag() would return EVAL_PAGE_**INCLUDE** (as opposed to EVAL_PAGE), to match the way doStartTag() returns EVAL_BODY_INCLUDE. But it's not! So don't be fooled if you see code on the exam with correct-looking (but wrong) return values.*

IterationTag lets you repeat the body

When you write a tag handler that extends TagSupport, you get all the lifecycle methods from the Tag interface, plus the one method from IterationTag—doAfterBody(). Without doAfterBody(), you can't iterate over the body because doStartTag() is too early, and doEndTag() is too late. But with doAfterBody(), your return value tells the Container whether it should repeat the body again (EVAL_BODY_AGAIN) or call the doEndTag() method (SKIP_BODY).

Tag interface

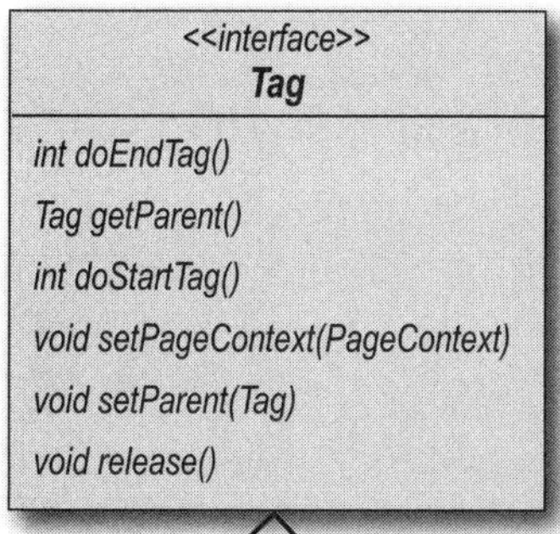

IterationTag interface

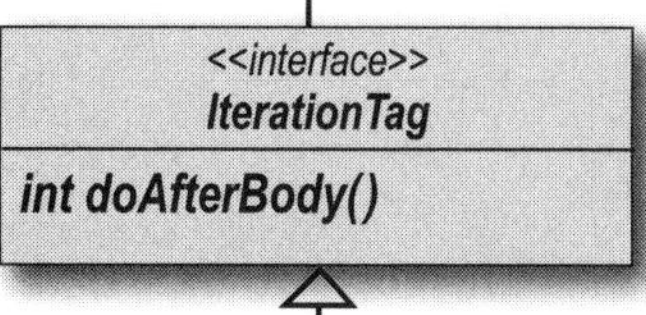

TagSupport class

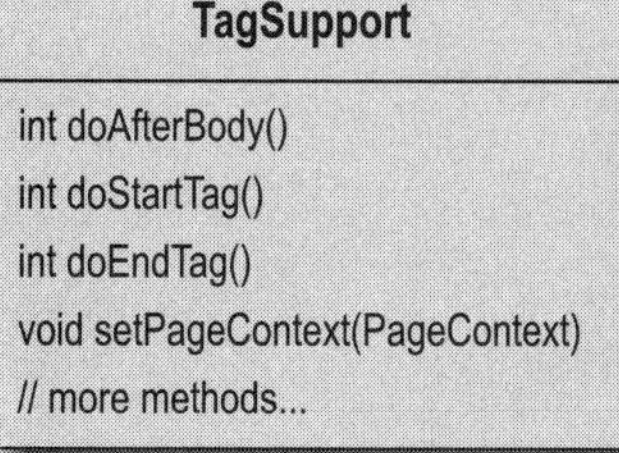

Sharpen your pencil

Try to implement the same functionality of this SimpleTag doTag() in a Classic tag handler. Assume the TLD is configured to allow body content.

```
public void doTag() throws JspException, IOException {
   String[] movies = {"Spiderman", "Saved!", "Amelie"};
   for(int i = 0; i < movies.length; i++) {
      getJspContext().setAttribute("movie", movies[i]);
      getJspBody().invoke(null);
   }
}
```

```
// package and imports
public class MyIteratorTag extends TagSupport {

   public int doStartTag() throws JspException {

   public int doAfterBody() throws JspException {

   public int doEndTag() throws JspException {

}
```

BE the Container

Look at the legal tag handler code below and figure out whether it would give you the result shown, given the JSP tag invocation listed below. This is also the same result produced by the ClassicTag handler from the previous page. Yes, we're answering the Sharpen Your Pencil with yet another exercise...

The tag handler class

```
// package and imports
public class MyIteratorTag extends TagSupport {
    String[] movies= new String[] {"Spiderman", "Saved!", "Amelie"};
    int movieCounter;

    public int doStartTag() throws JspException {
        movieCounter=0;

        return EVAL_BODY_INCLUDE;
    }
    public int doAfterBody() throws JspException {

        if (movieCounter < movies.length) {
           pageContext.setAttribute("movie", movies[movieCounter]);
           movieCounter++;
           return EVAL_BODY_AGAIN;
        } else {
         return SKIP_BODY;
        }
    }
    public int doEndTag() throws JspException {
        return EVAL_PAGE;
    }
}
```

JSP that invokes the tag

```
<%@ taglib prefix="mine" uri="KathyClassicTags" %>
<html><body>
  <table border="1">
    <mine:iterateMovies>
      <tr><td>${movie}</td></tr>
    </mine:iterateMovies>
  </table>
</body></html>
```

Desired result

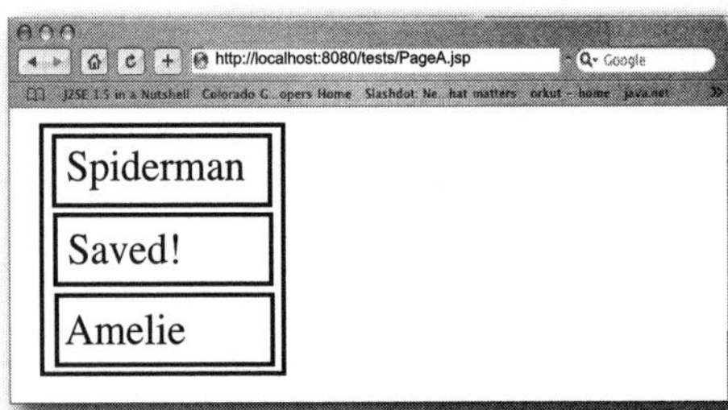

Default return values from TagSupport

If you don't override the TagSupport lifecycle methods that return an integer, be aware of the default values the TagSupport method implementations return. The TagSupport class assumes that your tag doesn't have a body (by returning SKIP_BODY) from doStartTag()), and that if you DO have a body that's evaluated, you want it evaluated only once (by returning SKIP_BODY from doAfterBody()). It also assumes that you want the rest of the page to evaluate (by returning EVAL-PAGE from doEndtag()).

Default return values when you don't override the TagSupport method implementation

doStartTag()

```
SKIP_BODY
EVAL_BODY_INCLUDE
```

doAfterBody()

```
SKIP_BODY
EVAL_BODY_AGAIN
```

doEndTag()

```
SKIP_PAGE
EVAL_PAGE
```

The TagSupport class assumes your tag doesn't have a body, or that if the body IS evaluated, that the body should be evaluated only ONCE.

It also assumes that you always want the rest of the page to be evaluated.

doStartTag() and doEndTag() run exactly once.

You really must know this lifecycle for the exam. Don't forget that doStartTag() and doEndTag() are always called, and they're called only once, regardless of anything else that happens. But doAfterBody() can run from 0 to many times, depending on the return value of doStartTag() and previous doAfterBody() calls.

You MUST override doStartTag() if you want the tag body to be evaluated!!

Think about it! The default return value from doStartTag() is SKIP_BODY, so if you want the body of your tag evaluated, and you extend TagSupport, you MUST override doStartTag() if for no other reason than to return EVAL_BODY_INCLUDE.
With doAfterBody(), it should be obvious that if you want to iterate over the body, you have to override that method as well, since its return value is SKIP_BODY.

BE the Container Answer

Desired result

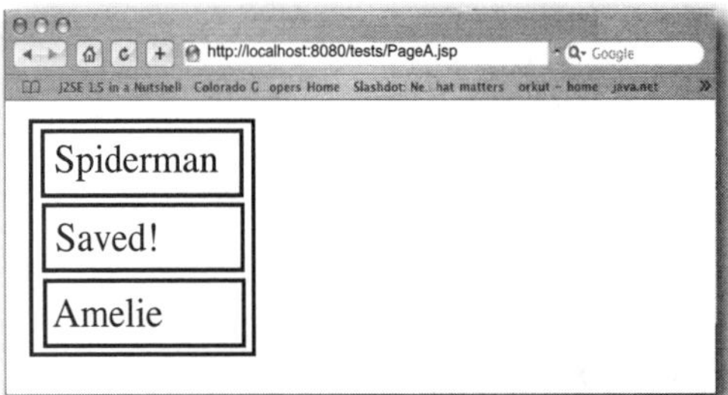

Actual result (unless you add the two lines highlighted below)

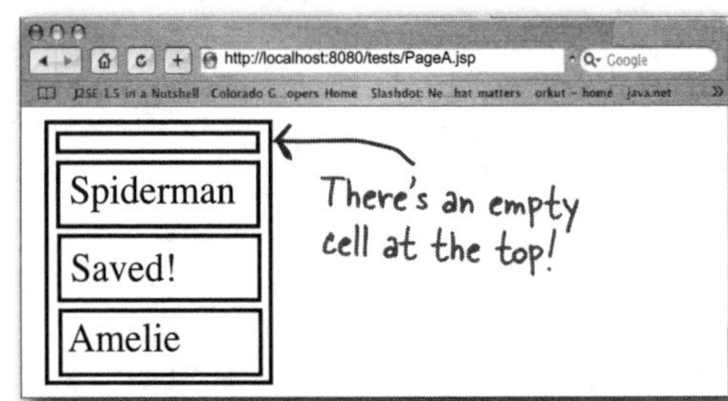

The tag handler class

```
public class MyIteratorTag extends TagSupport {
    String[] movies= new String[] {"Spiderman", "Saved!", "Amelie"};
    int movieCounter;

    public int doStartTag() throws JspException {
       movieCounter=0;

       pageContext.setAttribute("movie", movies[movieCounter]);
       movieCounter++;
       return EVAL_BODY_INCLUDE;
    }

    public int doAfterBody() throws JspException {
       if (movieCounter < movies.length) {
          pageContext.setAttribute("movie", movies[movieCounter]);
          movieCounter++;
          return EVAL_BODY_AGAIN;
       } else {
         return SKIP_BODY;
       }
    }
    public int doEndTag() throws JspException {
       return EVAL_PAGE;
    }
}
```

You MUST add these two lines to produce the correct response.

This doAfterBody() method was correct, but it runs only AFTER the body has already been processed once! Without the two extra lines in doStartTag(), the body is processed once without there being a movie attribute, so you get the empty cell.

JSP that invokes the tag

```
<%@ taglib prefix="mine" uri="KathyClassicTags" %>
<html><body>
  <table border="1">
    <mine:iterateMovies>
      <tr><td>${movie}</td></tr>
    </mine:iterateMovies>
  </table>
</body></html>
```

there are no Dumb Questions

Q: This seems stupid—there's duplicate code in doStartTag() and doAfterBody().

A: Yes, there's duplicate code. In this case, if you're implementing TagSupport, and you want to set values the body can use, then you MUST set those attribute values in doStartTag(). You can't wait until doAfterBody(), because by the time you get to doAfterBody(), the body has already been processed once.

Yes, it's kind of stupid. Which is why SimpleTag is so much better. Of course if you were writing the code, you'd make a private method in your tag handler... say, setMovie(), and you'd call that method from both doStartTag() and doAfterBody(). But it's still an awkward approach.

The Container can reuse Classic tag handlers!

Watch out—this is completely different from SimpleTag handlers, which are definitely NOT reused. That means you have to be very careful about instance variables—you should reset them in doStartTag().

The Tag interface does have a release() method, but that's called only when the tag handler instance is about to be removed by the Container. So don't assume that release() is a way to reset the tag handler's state in between tag invocations!

Q: WHY are you setting the instance variable value for *movieCounter* INSIDE the doStartTag() method? Why can't you just initialize it when you declare it?

A: Yikes! Unlike SimpleTag handlers, which are never reused, a Classic tag handler can be pooled and reused by the Container. That means you'd better reset your instance variable values with each new tag invocation (which means in doStartTag()). Otherwise, this code works the first time, but the next time a JSP invokes it, the *movieCounter* variable will still have its last value, instead of 0!

But what if you DO need access to the body contents?

You'll probably find that most of the time the lifecycle methods from the Tag and IterationTag interfaces, as provided by TagSupport, are enough. Between the three key methods (doStartTag(), doAfterBody(), and doEndTag()), you can do just about anything.

Except...you don't have direct access to the *contents* of the body. If you need access to the actual body contents, so that you can, say, use it in an expression or perhaps filter or alter it in some way, then extend BodyTagSupport instead of TagSupport, and you'll have access to the BodyTag interface methods.

Extending BodyTagSupport gives you two more lifecycle methods from the BodyTag interface–setBodyContent() and doInitBody(). You can use these to do something with the actual CONTENTS of the body of the tag used to invoke the handler.

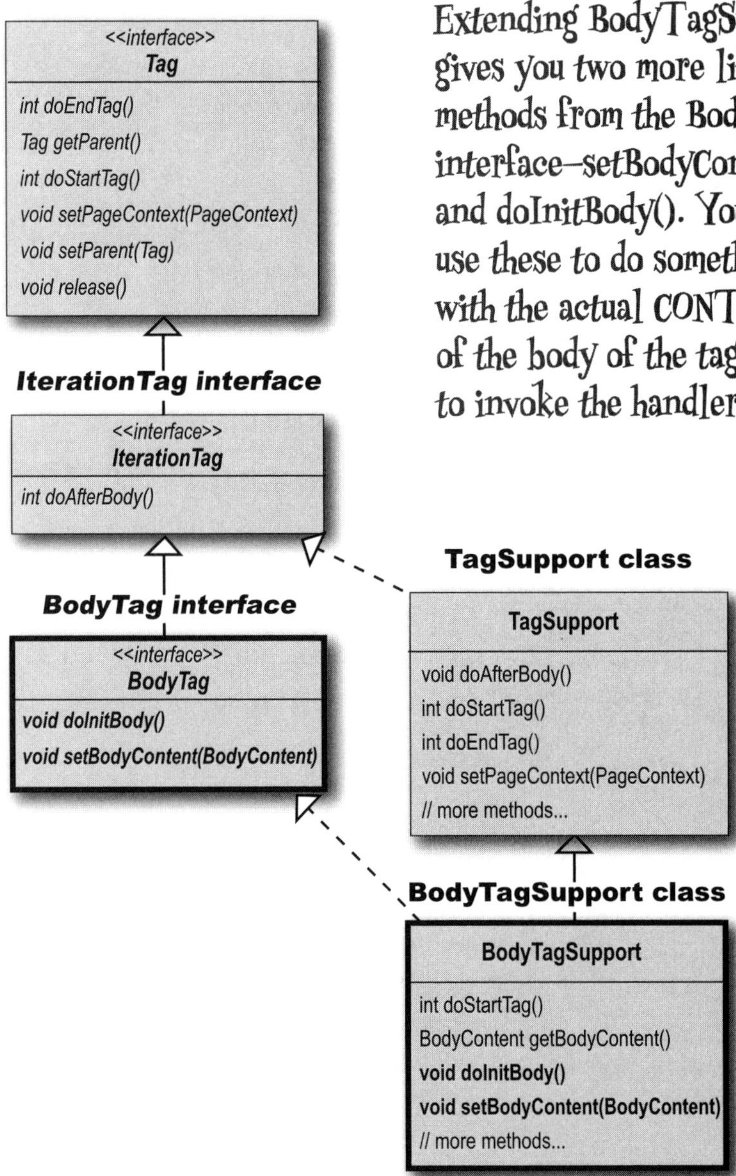

With BodyTag, you get two new methods

When you implement BodyTag (by extending BodyTagSupport), you get two more lifecycle methods—setBodyContent() and doInitBody(). You also get one new return value for doStartTag(), EVAL_BODY_BUFFERED. That means there are now *three* possible return values for doStartTag(), instead of the *two* you get when you extend TagSupport.

Lifecycle for a tag that implements BodyTag (directly or by extending BodyTagSupport)

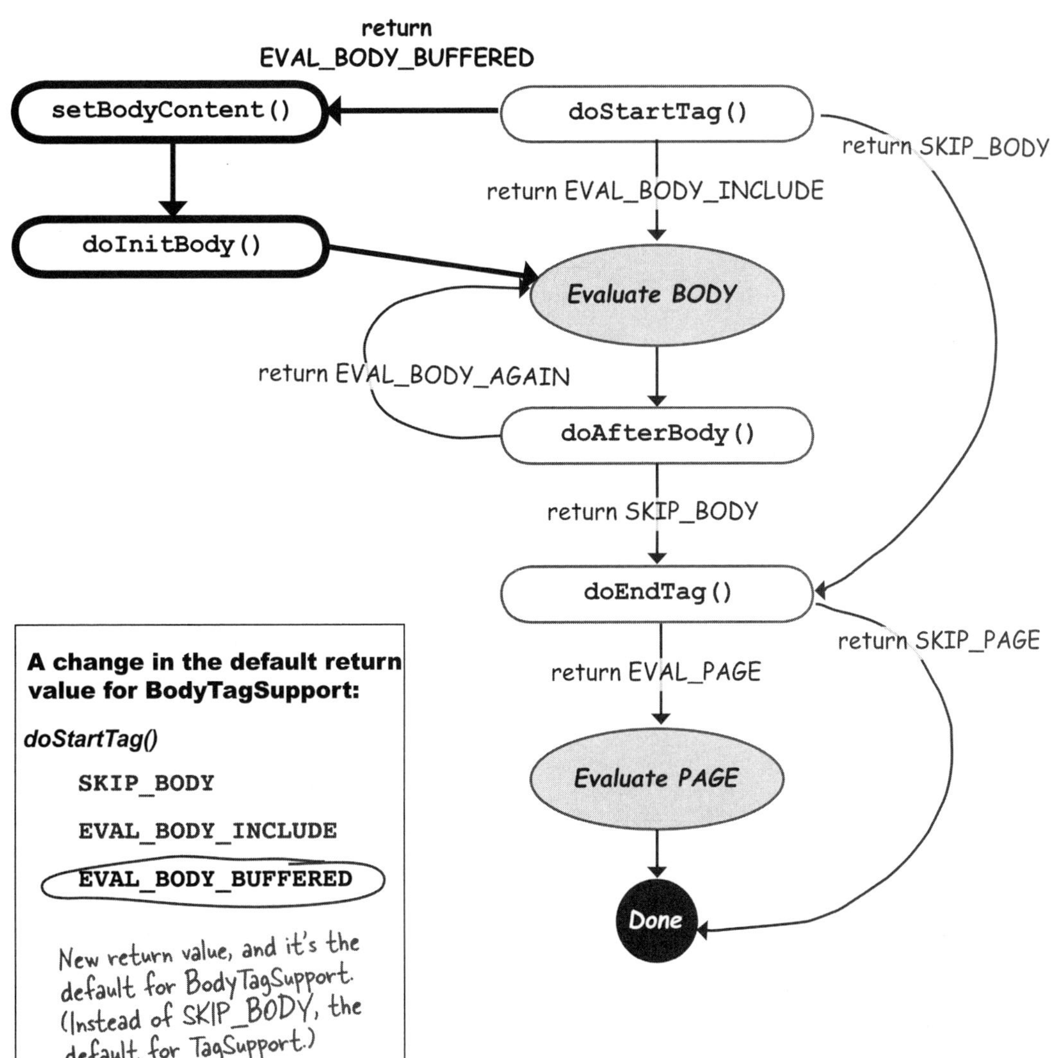

With BodyTag, you can buffer the body

The BodyContent argument to setBodyContent() is actually a type of java.io.Writer. (Yes, it's OK to find that disturbing from an OO perspective.) But that means you can process the body by, say, chaining it to another IO stream or getting the raw bytes.

Q: What happens if I return EVAL_BODY_BUFFERED even though the invoking tag is empty?

A: The setBodyContent() and doInitBody() method will not be called if the tag invoking the handler is empty! And by empty, we mean that the tag was invoked using an empty tag <my:tag /> or with no content between the opening and closing tags <my:tag><my:tag>.

The Container knows there's no body this time, and it just skips to the doEndTag() method, so this is usually not a problem.

Unless the TLD declares the tag to have an empty body! If the TLD says <body-content>empty</body-content>, you don't have a choice, and you must NOT return EVAL_BODY_BUFFERED or EVAL_BODY_INCLUDE from doStartTag().

Q: What about attributes in a Classic tag? Are they handled the same way as with Simple tags?

A: Yes, on the sequence diagram for both Simple tag handlers and Classic tag handlers, there was a place where bean-style setter methods are called for each attribute. This happens before a Simple tag's doTag() or a Classic tag's doStartTag(). In other words, tag attributes work in exactly the same way for both Classic and Simple tags, including the way in which they're declared in the TLD.

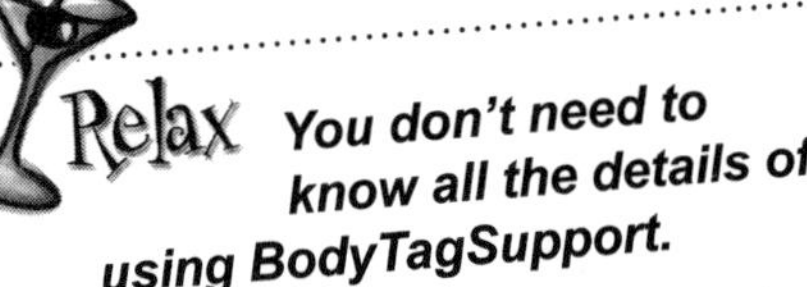

You don't need to know all the details of using BodyTagSupport.

For the exam (and probably for the rest of your JSP-development life), you need to know the lifecycle for BodyTagSupport, and how it differs from TagSupport. You need to know, for example, that if you do NOT extend BodyTagSupport or implement BodyTag, then you must NOT return EVAL_BODY_BUFFERED from doStartTag(). And you should know the two new methods from the BodyTag interface, but that's about it.

If the TLD for a tag declares an empty body, doStartTag() MUST return SKIP_BODY!

That might be obvious, but it means you have to be careful to keep your tag handler and TLD in sync. So, if you declare a tag in the TLD to have <body-content>empty</body-content>, then there is absolutely NO point in implementing BodyTag (or extending BodyTagSupport). That also means there is no point in implementing IterationTag, but you get that automatically by extending TagSupport.

The point is, you need to return SKIP_BODY from doStartTag() if your TLD declares an empty body for the tag, even IF you implement IterationTag or BodyTag.

Lifecycle methods for Classic tag methods

Fill in the chart below. We've covered *almost* everything you need to do this correctly, but you'll have to guess in a few places. (Don't turn the page!)

	BodyTagSupport	TagSupport
doStartTag() *possible* return values		
default return value from the implementation class		
Number of times it can be called (per tag invocation from a JSP)		
doAfterBody() *possible* return values		
default return value from the implementation class		
Number of times it can be called (per tag invocation from a JSP)		
doEndTag() *possible* return values		
default return value from the implementation class		
Number of times it can be called (per tag invocation from a JSP)		
doInitBody() and setBodyContent() Circumstances under which they can be called, and number of times per tag invocation.		

Lifecycle return values for Classic tag methods

You're expected to know all of this for the exam!

	BodyTagSupport	TagSupport
doStartTag() *possible* return values	SKIP_BODY EVAL_BODY_INCLUDE EVAL_BODY_BUFFERED	SKIP_BODY EVAL_BODY_INCLUDE
default return value from the implementation class	EVAL_BODY_BUFFERED	SKIP_BODY
Number of times it can be called (per tag invocation from a JSP)	Exactly once	Exactly once
doAfterBody() *possible* return values	SKIP_BODY EVAL_BODY_AGAIN	SKIP_BODY EVAL_BODY_AGAIN
default return value from the implementation class	SKIP_BODY	SKIP_BODY
Number of times it can be called (per tag invocation from a JSP)	Zero to many	Zero to many
doEndTag() *possible* return values	SKIP_PAGE EVAL_PAGE	SKIP_PAGE EVAL_PAGE
default return value from the implementation class	EVAL_PAGE	EVAL_PAGE
Number of times it can be called (per tag invocation from a JSP)	Exactly once	Exactly once
doInitBody() and setBodyContent() Circumstances under which they can be called, and number of times per tag invocation.	Exactly once, and ONLY if doStartTag() returns EVAL_BODY_BUFFERED	NEVER!

What if you have tags that work together?

Imagine this scenario...you have a <mine:Menu> tag that builds a custom navigation bar. It needs menu items. So you use a <mine:MenuItem> tag nested within the <mine:Menu> tag, and the menu tag gets ahold (somehow) of the menu items and uses those items to build the navigation bar.

```
<mine:Menu >
   <mine:MenuItem itemValue="Dogs" />
   <mine:MenuItem itemValue="Cats" />
   <mine:MenuItem itemValue="Horses" />
</mine:Menu>
```

The Menu tag needs the attribute values from the nested MenuItem tags...

The big question is, how do the tags talk to one another? In other words, how does the Menu tag (the enclosing tag) get the attribute values from the MenuItems (the inner/nested tags)?

Nested tags are used in several places in the JSTL; the <c:choose> tag, with its nested <c:when> and <c:otherwise> tags, is a good example. And you might need to use "cooperating tags" (that's how the spec says it) in your own custom development as well.

Fortunately, there's a mechanism for getting info to and from outer and inner tags, regardless of the depth of nesting. That means you can get info from a deeply nested tag out to not just the tag's immediate enclosing tag, but to any arbitrary tag up the tag nesting hierarchy.

Sharpen your pencil

Look at the Tag API, review the previous tag handler code, and think about how cooperating tags might get info to and from one another.

<<interface>> **Tag**
int doEndTag()
Tag getParent()
int doStartTag()
void setPageContext(PageContext)
void setParent(Tag)
void release()

A Tag can call its Parent Tag

Both SimpleTag and Tag have a getParent() method. The getParent() in Tag returns a *Tag*, but the getParent() in SimpleTag returns an instance of *JspTag*. We'll see the implications of those return types in a minute.

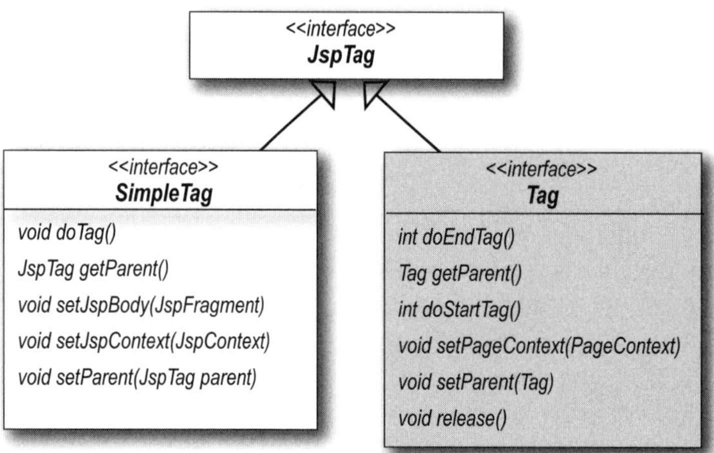

A nested tag can access its parent (enclosing) tag

```
<mine:OuterTag>
   <mine:InnerTag />
</mine:OuterTag>
```

In this relationship, "OuterTag" is the parent of "InnerTag".

Getting the parent tag in a Classic tag handler

```
public int doStartTag() throws JspException {

    OuterTag parent = (OuterTag) getParent();
    // do something with it
    return EVAL_BODY_INCLUDE;
}
```

Don't forget to cast it!

Getting the parent tag in a Simple tag handler

```
public void doTag() throws JspException, IOException {
    OuterTag parent = (OuterTag) getParent();
    // do something with it
}
```

Again, don't forget the cast.

It's exactly the same as in a Classic tag handler.

Find out just how deep the nesting goes...

You can walk your way *up* the ancestor tag chain by continuing to call getParent() on whatever is returned by getParent(). Because getParent() returns either another tag (on which you can call getParent()), or null.

In a JSP

```
<mine:NestedLevel>
  <mine:NestedLevel>
   <mine:NestedLevel/>
  </mine:NestedLevel>
</mine:NestedLevel>
```

In a Classic tag handler

```
package foo;
import javax.servlet.jsp.*;
import javax.servlet.jsp.tagext.*;
import java.io.*;
public class NestedLevelTag extends TagSupport {
   private int nestLevel = 0;

   public int doStartTag() throws JspException {
       nestLevel = 0;
       Tag parent = getParent();   // Call the inherited getParent() method.

       while (parent!=null) {      // If it's null, then we're at the top level, and we don't have a parent.
            parent = parent.getParent();
            nestLevel++;           // But if it's not null, get the parent of the parent we just got, and increment the counter.
         }
       }

       try {
         pageContext.getOut().println("<br>Tag nested level: " + nestLevel);
       } catch(IOException ex) {
            throw new JspException("IOException- " + ex.toString());
       }
       return EVAL_BODY_INCLUDE;
   }
}
```

Result

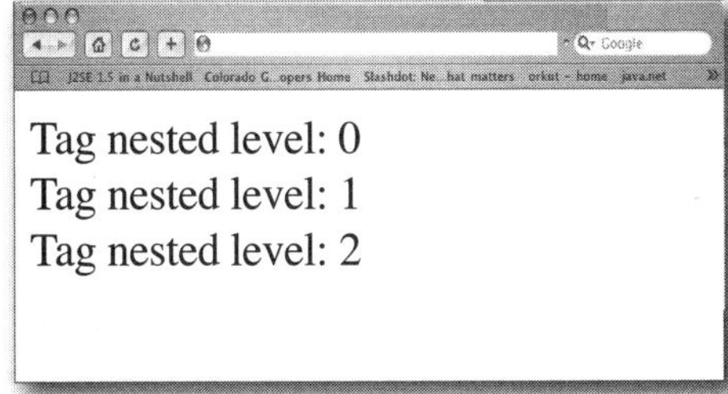

Simple tags can have Classic parents

This is not a problem, because a SimpleTag's getParent() returns type JspTag, and Classic tags and Simple tags now share the JspTag super interface. Actually, *Classic* tags can have *Simple* parents, but it takes a slight hack to make that work because you can't cast a SimpleTag to the Tag return value of the Tag interface getParent(). We won't go into how to access a Simple tag parent from a Classic child tag*, but all you need to know for the exam (and almost certainly real web app life) is that by using getParent(), a Classic tag can access Classic tag parents, and a Simple tag can access either a Classic or Simple parent.

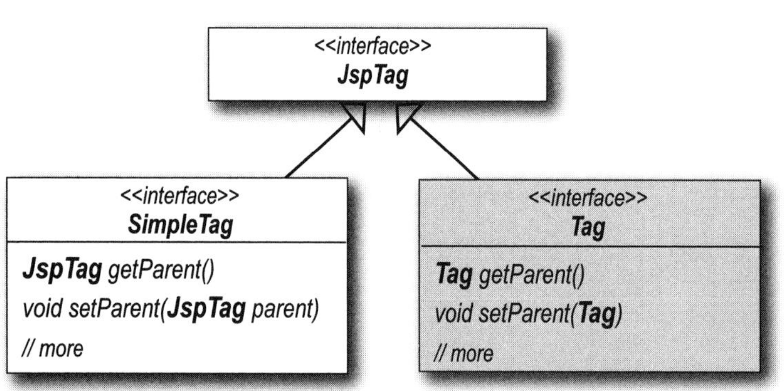

Using the getParent() method, a Classic tag can access Classic tag parents, and a Simple tag can access either a Classic or Simple parent.

In a JSP

```
<mine:ClassicParent name="ClassicParentTag">
   <mine:SimpleInner />
</mine:ClassicParent>
```

What if the child (SimpleInner) wants access to the parent's "name" attribute?

In the SimpleInner tag handler

```
public void doTag() throws JspException, IOException {
   MyClassicParent parent = (MyClassicParent) getParent();
   getJspContext().getOut().print("Parent attribute is: " + parent.getName());
}
```

It's OK for a SimpleTag to ask for a Classic parent...

Once you have a parent, you can call methods on it like any other Java object, so you can get attributes of the parent tag!

In the ClassicParent tag handler

```
public class MyClassicParent extends TagSupport {
   private String name;
   public void setName(String name) {
      this.name=name;
   }
   public String getName() {
      return name;
   }
   public int doStartTag() throws JspException {
      return EVAL_BODY_INCLUDE;
   }
}
```

Provide a getter method for the attribute, so that the child tag can get the attribute value.

If you return SKIP_BODY, the inner tag will never be processed!

*If you're really curious, look at the TagAdapter class in the J2EE 1.4 API.

You can walk up, but you can't walk down...

There's a getParent() method, but there's no getChild(). Yet the scenario we showed earlier was for an outer <my:Menu> tag that needed access to its nested <my:MenuItem> tags. What can we do? How can the parent tag get information about the child tags, when a child can get a reference to the parent, but the parent can't ask for a reference to the child?

That is so sad...
It's tragic. My child can find me, his parent, but I have no way to find my child! I just have to wait for him to call ME...

Sharpen your pencil

How could a parent tag get attribute values from a child tag? Describe how you would implement the functionality of the cooperating Menu and MenuItem tags.

Getting info from child to parent

We have two main ways in which tags can cooperate with one another:

1) The child tag needs info (like an attribute value) from its parent tag.

2) The parent tag needs info from each of its child tags.

We've already seen how the first scenario works—the child tag gets a reference to its parent using getParent(), then calls getter methods on the parent. But what happens when the parent needs info from the child? We have to do the same thing. In other words, if the parent needs info from the child, it's the child's job to give it to the parent!

Since there's no automatic mechanism for the parent to find out about its child tags, you simply have to use the same design approach to get info to the parent *from* the child as you do to get info from the parent *to* the child. You get a reference to the parent tag, and call methods. Only instead of getters, this time you'll call some kind of *set* or *add* method.

In a JSP

```
<%@ taglib prefix="mine" uri="KathyClassicTags" %>
<html><body>

<mine:Menu >
   <mine:MenuItem itemValue="Dogs" />
   <mine:MenuItem itemValue="Cats" />
   <mine:MenuItem itemValue="Horses" />
</mine:Menu>

</body></html>
```

Result

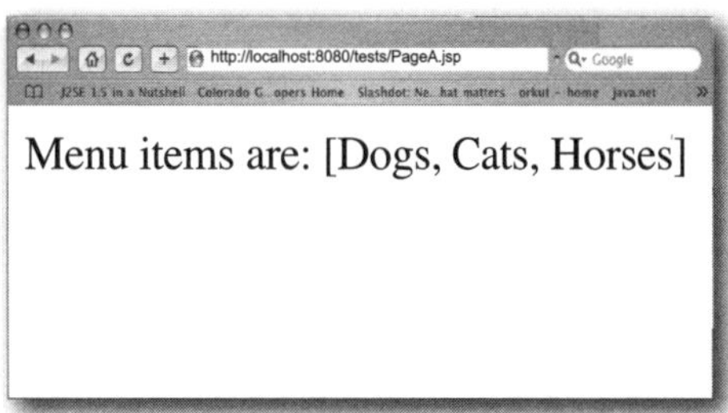

In this example we didn't actually DO anything with the menu items except prove that we got them, but you can imagine that you might use the items to build a navigation bar, for example...

Menu and MenuItem tag handlers

In the child tag: MenuItem

```
public class MenuItem extends TagSupport {
    private String itemValue;

    public void setItemValue(String value) {
       itemValue=value;
    }

    public int doStartTag() throws JspException {
       return EVAL_BODY_INCLUDE;
    }

    public int doEndTag() throws JspException {
       Menu parent = (Menu) getParent();
       parent.addMenuItem(itemValue);
       return EVAL_PAGE;
    }
}
```

MenuItem has an attribute declared in the TLD for the itemValue. This is the value we need to send to the parent tag...

Simple—get a reference to the parent tag and call its addMenuItem() method.

In the parent tag: Menu

```
public class Menu extends TagSupport {
   private ArrayList items;

   public void addMenuItem(String item) {
       items.add(item);
   }

   public int doStartTag() throws JspException {
       items = new ArrayList();

       return EVAL_BODY_INCLUDE;
   }

   public int doEndTag() throws JspException {
       try {
          pageContext.getOut().println("Menu items are: " + items);
       } catch(Exception ex) {
           throw new JspException("Exception: " + ex.toString());
       }
       // imagine complex menu-building code here...
       return EVAL_PAGE;
    }
}
```

This is NOT an attribute setter method! This method exists ONLY so that a child tag can tell the parent tag about the child's attribute value. (It's called in between doStartTag() and doEndTag().)

Don't forget to reset the ArrayList in doStartTag(), since the tag handler might be reused by the Container.

If you do not return EVAL_BODY_INCLUDE, the child tag's will never be processed!

Getting an arbitrary ancestor

There is another mechanism you can use if you want to, say, skip some nesting levels and go straight to a grandparent or something even further up the tag nesting hierarchy. The method is in both TagSupport and SimpleTagSupport (although they have slightly different behavior), and it's called findAncestorWithClass().

Getting an immediate parent using getParent()

```
OuterTag parent = (OuterTag) getParent();
```

Getting an arbitrary ancestor using findAncestorWithClass()

```
WayOuterTag ancestor = (WayOuterTag) findAncestorWithClass(this, WayOuterTag.class);
```

```
findAncestorWithClass(this, WayOuterTag.class);
```

starting tag (this) — the class of the tag you want (WayOuterTag.class)

The Container walks the tag nesting hierarchy until it finds a tag that's an instance of this class. It returns the *first* one, so there's no way to say "skip the *first* tag you see that's an instance of WayOuterTag.class and give me the *second* instance instead..." So if you really know for a fact that you wanted the second instance of a tag ancestor of that type, you'll just have to get the return value of findAncestorWithClass(), and then call getParent() or findAncestorWithClass() on *it.*

You will not be tested on any details of using findAncestorWithClass(). All you need to know for the exam is that it exists!

Key differences between Simple and Classic tags

	Simple tags	Classic tags
Tag interfaces		
Support implementation classes		
Key lifecycle methods that YOU might implement		
How you write to the response output		
How you access implicit variables and scoped attributes from a support implementation		
How you cause the body to be processed		
How you cause the current page evaluation to STOP		

Key differences between Simple and Classic tags

	Simple tags	Classic tags
Tag interfaces	SimpleTag (extends JspTag)	Tag (extends JspTag) IterationTag (extends Tag) BodyTag (extends IterationTag)
Support implementation classes	SimpleTagSupport (implements SimpleTag)	TagSupport (implements IterationTag) BodyTagSupport (extends TagSupport, implements BodyTag)
Key lifecycle methods that YOU might implement	doTag()	doStartTag() doEndTag() doAfterBody() (and for BodyTag— doInitBody() and setBodyContent())
How you write to the response output	getJspContext().getOut().println (no try/catch needed because SimpleTag methods declare IOException)	pageContext.getOut().println (wrapped in a try/catch because Classic tag methods do NOT declare the IOException!)
How you access implicit variables and scoped attributes from a support implementation	With the getJspContext() method that returns a JspContext (which is usually a PageContext)	With the pageContext implicit variable--NOT a method like it is with SimpleTag!
How you cause the body to be processed	getJspBody().invoke(null)	Return EVAL_BODY_INCLUDE from doStartTag(), or EVAL_BODY_BUFFERED if the class implements BodyTag.
How you cause the current page evaluation to STOP	Throw a SkipPageException	Return SKIP_PAGE from doEndTag()

Using the PageContext API for tag handlers

This page is just a review from what you saw in the Script-free JSPs chapter, but it comes up again here because it's crucial for a tag handler. A tag handler class, remember, is *not* a servlet or a JSP, so it doesn't have automatic access to a bunch of implicit objects. But it does get a reference to a PageContext, and with it, it can get to all kinds of things it might need.

Remember that while Simple tags get a reference to a JspContext and Classic tags get a reference to a PageContext, the Simple tag's JspContext is usually a PageContext instance. So if your Simple tag handler needs access to PageContext-specific methods or fields, you'll have to cast it from a JspContext to the PageContext it really is on the heap.

JspContext

getAttribute(String name)
getAttribute(String name, int scope)
getAttributeNamesInScope(int scope)
findAttribute(String name)
getOut()

// more methods including similar
// methods to set and remove attributes
// from any scope

PageContext

APPLICATION_SCOPE
PAGE_SCOPE
REQUEST_SCOPE
SESSION_SCOPE
// more fields

static fields

getRequest()
getServletConfig()
getServletContext()
getSession()

// more methods

methods to get any implicit object

The one-arg getAttribute(String) is for page scope ONLY!

There are TWO overloaded getAttribute() methods you can call on pageContext: a one-arg that takes a String, and a two-arg that takes a String and an int. The one-arg version works just like all the others—it's for attributes bound TO the pageContext object. But the two-arg version can be used to get an attribute from ANY of the four scopes.

findAttribute() looks in EACH scope starting with PAGE_SCOPE.

You can expect to be tested on this!! The difference between getAttribute(String) and findAttribute(String) can be dramatic—the getAttribute(String) method looks ONLY in page scope, while the findAttribute(STRING) will search all four scopes to find a matching attribute, in the order of page, request, session, and application. It returns the first one it finds that matches the findAttribute(String) argument.

Memorizing Tag Files

ANSWERS

1. Fill in what would you must put into a Tag File to declare that the Tag has one required attribute, named "title", that can use an EL expression as the value of the attribute.

```
<%@ attribute name="title" required="true" rtexprvalue="true" %>
```

2. Fill in what would you must put into a Tag File to declare that the Tag must NOT have a body.

```
<%@ tag body-content="empty" %>
```

3. Draw a Tag File document in each of the locations where the Container will look for Tag Files.

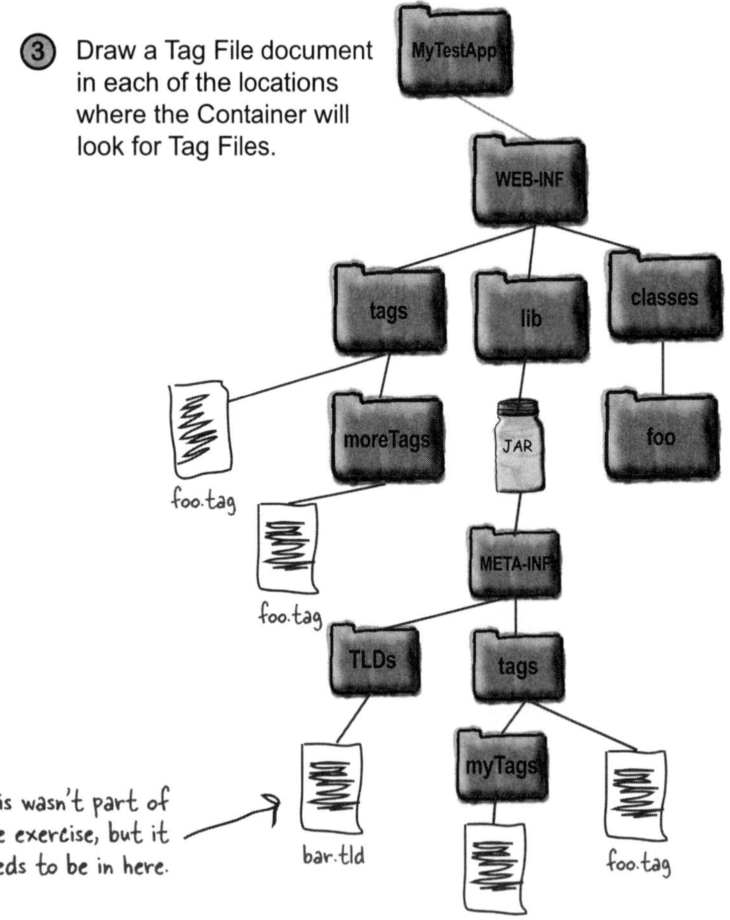

Directly inside *WEB-INF/tags*

Inside a sub-directory of *WEB-INF/tags*

Inside the *META-INF/tags* directory inside a JAR file that's inside *WEB-INF/lib*

Inside a sub-directory of *META-INF/tags* inside a JAR file that's inside *WEB-INF/lib*

IF the tag file is deployed in a JAR, there MUST be a TLD for the tag file.

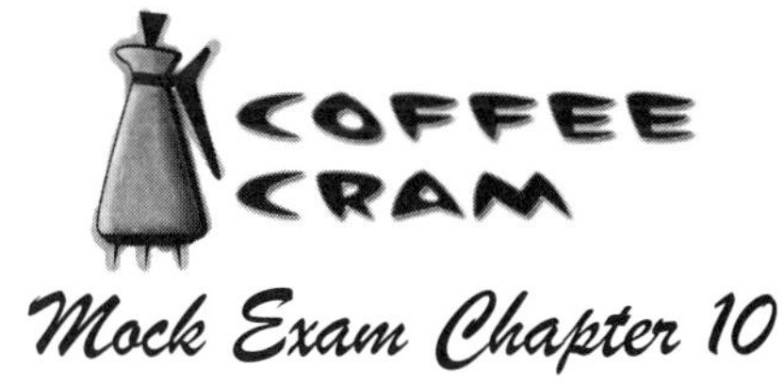

Mock Exam Chapter 10

---

1 How can a Classic tag handler instruct the container to ignore the remainder of the JSP that invoked the tag?
(Choose all that apply.)

- ❑ A. The **doEndTag()** method should return **Tag.SKIP_BODY**.
- ❑ B. The **doEndTag()** method should return **Tag.SKIP_PAGE**.
- ❑ C. The **doStartTag()** method should return **Tag.SKIP_BODY**.
- ❑ D. The **doStartTag()** method should return **Tag.SKIP_PAGE**.

---

2 Which directives and/or standard actions are applicable ONLY within tag files? (Choose all that apply.)

- ❑ A. **tag**
- ❑ B. **page**
- ❑ C. **jsp:body**
- ❑ D. **jsp:doBody**
- ❑ E. **jsp:invoke**
- ❑ F. **taglib**

3 Given a JSP page:

```
<my:tag1>
   <my:tag2>
      <my:tag3 />
   </my:tag2>
</my:tag1>
```

The tag handler for **my:tag1** is **Tag1Handler** and extends TagSupport. The tag handler for **my:tag2** is **Tag2Handler** and extends SimpleTagSupport. The tag handler for **my:tag3** is **Tag3Handler** and extends TagSupport.

Which is true? (Choose all that apply.)

❑ A. **Tag3Handler** CANNOT access the instance of **Tag1Handler** because Simple tags do NOT support access to the tag parent.

❑ B. Only Classic tags are considered in composing the parent/child tag hiearchy; therefore, **Tag3Handler** may use the **getParent** method only once to gain access to the instance of **Tag1Handler**.

❑ C. **Tag3Handler** may use the **getParent** method twice to gain access to the instance of **Tag1Handler**.

❑ D. Only BodyTag handlers can access the parent/child tag hiearchy; therefore, **Tag3Handler** CANNOT gain access to the instance of **Tag1Handler**.

---

4 Which Simple tag mechanism will tell a JSP page to stop processing?

❑ A. Return **SKIP_PAGE** from the **doTag** method.

❑ B. Return **SKIP_PAGE** from the **doEndTag** method.

❑ C. Throw a **SkipPageException** from the **doTag** method.

❑ D. Throw a **SkipPageException** from the **doEndTag** method.

5 Which are true about the Classic tag model? (Choose all that apply.)

- ❑ A. The **`Tag`** interface can only be used to create empty tags.
- ❑ B. The **`SKIP_PAGE`** constant is a valid return value of the **`doEndTag`** method.
- ❑ C. The **`EVAL_BODY_BUFFERED`** constant is a valid return value of the **`doAfterBody`** method.
- ❑ D. The **`Tag`** interface only provides two values for the return value of the **`doStartTag`** method: **`SKIP_BODY`** and **`EVAL_BODY`**.
- ❑ E. There are three tag interfaces **`Tag`**, **`IterationTag`**, and **`BodyTag`**, but only two built-in base classes: **`TagSupport`**, and **`BodyTagSupport`**.

---

6 Which about the **`findAncestorWithClass`** method are true? (Choose all that apply.)

- ❑ A. It requires one parameter: A **`Class`**.
- ❑ B. It is a static method in the **`TagSupport`** class.
- ❑ C. It is a non-static method in the **`TagSupport`** class.
- ❑ D. It is NOT defined by any of the standard JSP tag interfaces.
- ❑ E. It requires two parameters: A **`Tag`** and a **`Class`**.
- ❑ F. It requires one parameter: A **`String`** representing the name of the tag to be found.
- ❑ G. It requires two parameters: A **`Tag`** and a **`String`**, representing the name of the tag to be found.

---

7 Which must be true if you want to use dynamic attributes for a Simple tag handler? (Choose all that apply.)

- ❑ A. Your Simple tag must NOT declare any static tag attributes.
- ❑ B. Your Simple tag must use the **`<dynamic-attributes>`** element in the TLD.
- ❑ C. Your Simple tag handler must implement the **`DynamicAttributes`** interface.
- ❑ D. Your Simple tag should extend the **`DynamicSimpleTagSupport`** class, which provides default support for dynamic attributes.
- ❑ E. Your Simple tag CANNOT be used with the **`jsp:attribute`** standard action, because this action works only with static attributes.

---

8 Which is true about tag files? (Choose all that apply.)

- ❑ A. A tag file may be placed in any subdirectory of **`WEB-INF`**.
- ❑ B. A tag file must have the file extension of **`.tag`** or **`.tagx`**.
- ❑ C. A TLD file must be used to map the symbolic tag name to the actual tag file.
- ❑ D. A tag file may NOT be placed in a JAR file in the **`WEB-INF/lib`** directory.

9 Given:

```
10. public class BufTag extends BodyTagSupport {
11.   public int doStartTag() throws JspException {
12.     // insert code here
13.   }
14. }
```

Assume that the tag has been properly configured to allow body content.

Which, if inserted at line 12, would cause the JSP code **<mytags:mytag>BodyContent</mytags:mytag>** to output **BodyContent**?

- ❑ A. `return SKIP_BODY;`
- ❑ B. `return EVAL_BODY_INCLUDE;`
- ❑ C. `return EVAL_BODY_BUFFERED;`
- ❑ D. `return BODY_CONTENT;`

---

10 Which about **doAfterBody()** is true? (Choose all that apply.)

- ❑ A. **doAfterBody()** is only called on tags that extend **TagSupport**.
- ❑ B. **doAfterBody()** is only called on tags that extend **IterationTagSupport**.
- ❑ C. Assuming no exceptions occur, **doAfterBody()** is always called after **doStartTag()** for any tag that implements **IterationTag**.
- ❑ D. Assuming no exceptions occur, **doAfterBody()** is called after **doStartTag()** for any tag that implements **IterationTag** and returns **SKIP_BODY** from **doStartTag()**.
- ❑ E. Assuming no exceptions occur, **doAfterBody()** is called after **doStartTag()** for any tag that implements **IterationTag** and returns **EVAL_BODY_INCLUDE** from **doStartTag()**.

11 Given a JSP page:

```
<%@ taglib prefix="my" uri="/WEB-INF/myTags.tld" %>
<my:tag1>
  <%-- JSP content --%>
</my:tag1>
```

The tag handler for **my:tag1** is **Tag1Handler** and extends TagSupport.

What happens when the instance of **Tag1Handler** calls the **getParent** method? (Choose all that apply.)

- ❑ A. A **JspException** is thrown.
- ❑ B. The **null** value is returned.
- ❑ C. A **NullPointerException** is thrown.
- ❑ D. An **IllegalStateException** is thrown.

---

12 Which is true about the lifecycle of a Simple tag? (Choose all that apply.)

- ❑ A. The **release** method is called after the **doTag** method.
- ❑ B. The **setJspBody** method is always called before the **doTag** method.
- ❑ C. The **setParent** and **setJspContext** methods are called immediately before the tag attributes are set.
- ❑ D. The **JspFragment** of the tag body is invoked by the Container before the tag handler's **doTag** method is called. This value, a **BodyContent** object, is passed to the tag handler using the **setJspBody** method.

13 Given:

```
10. public class ExampleTag extends TagSupport {
11.   private String param;
12.   public void setParam(String p) { param = p; }
13.   public int doStartTag() throws JspException {
14.     // insert code here
15.     // more code here
16.   }
17. }
```

Which, inserted at line 14, would be guaranteed to assign the value of the request-scoped attribute **param** to the local variable **p**? (Choose all that apply.)

- ❑ A. `String p = findAttribute("param");`
- ❑ B. `String p = request.getAttribute("param");`
- ❑ C. `String p = pageContext.findAttribute("param");`
- ❑ D. `String p = getPageContext().findAttribute("param");`
- ❑ E. `String p = pageContext.getRequest().getAttribute("param");`

14 Which are valid method calls on a **PageContext** object? (Choose all that apply.)

- ❑ A. `getAttributeNames()`
- ❑ B. `getAttribute("key")`
- ❑ C. `findAttribute("key")`
- ❑ D. `getSessionAttribute()`
- ❑ E. `getAttributesScope("key")`
- ❑ F. `findAttribute("key", PageContext.SESSION_SCOPE)`
- ❑ G. `getAttribute("key", PageContext.SESSION_SCOPE)`

---

15 Which is the most efficient **`JspContext`** method to call to access an attribute that is known to be in application scope?

❏ A. **`getPageContext()`**

❏ B. **`getAttribute(String)`**

❏ C. **`findAttribute(String)`**

❏ D. **`getAttribute(String, int)`**

❏ E. **`getAttributesScope("key")`**

❏ F. **`getAttributeNamesInScope(int)`**

---

16 What is the best strategy, when implementing a custom tag, for finding the value of an attribute whose scope is unknown?

❏ A. Check all scopes with a single **`pageContext.getAttribute(String)`** call.

❏ B. Check all scopes with a single **`pageContext.findAttribute(String)`** call.

❏ C. Check each scope with calls to **`pageContext.getAttribute(String, int)`**.

❏ D. Call **`pageContext.getRequest().getAttribute(String)`**, then call **`pageContext.getSession().getAttribute(String)`**, and so on.

❏ E. None of these will work.

17 Given a tag, **simpleTag**, whose handler is implemented using the Simple tag model and a tag, **complexTag**, whose handler is implemented using the Classic tag model. Both tags are declared to be non-empty in the TLD.

Which JSP code snippets are valid uses of these tag? (Choose all that apply.)

❑ A.
```
<my:simpleTag>
  <my:complexTag />
</my:simpleTag>
```

❑ B.
```
<my:simpleTag>
  <%= displayText %>
</my:simpleTag>
```

❑ C.
```
<my:simpleTag>
  <%@ include file="/WEB-INF/web/common/headerMenu.html" %>
</my:simpleTag>
```

❑ D.
```
<my:simpleTag>
  <my:complexTag>
    <% i++; %>
  </my:complexTag>
</my:simpleTag>
```

18 Which are true about the Tag File model? (Choose all that apply.)

❑ A. Each tag file must have a corresponding entry in a TLD file.

❑ B. All directives allowed in JSP pages are allowed in Tag Files.

❑ C. All directives allowed in Tag Files are allowed in JSP pages.

❑ D. The **<jsp:doBody>** standard action can only be used in Tag Files.

❑ E. The allowable file extensions for Tag Files are **.tag** and **.tagx**.

❑ F. For each attribute declared and specified in a Tag File, the container creates a page-scoped attribute with the same name.

19 Which are valid in tag files? (Choose all that apply.)

❑ A. `<jsp:doBody />`

❑ B. `<jsp:invoke fragment="frag" />`

❑ C. `<%@ page import="java.util.Date" %>`

❑ D.
```
<%@ variable name-given="date"
      variable-class="java.util.Date" %>
```

❑ E.
```
<%@ attribute name="name" value="blank"
      type="java.lang.String" %>
```

20 Which returns the enclosing tag when called from within a tag handler class? (Choose all that apply.)

❑ A. `getParent()`

❑ B. `getAncestor()`

❑ C. `findAncestor()`

❑ D. `getEnclosingTag()`

21 Given a web application structure:

```
/WEB-INF/tags/mytags/tag1.tag
/WEB-INF/tags/tag2.tag
/WEB-INF/tag3.tag
/tag4.tag
```

Which tags could be used by an appropriate **taglib** directive? (Choose all that apply.)

❑ A. `tag1.tag`

❑ B. `tag2.tag`

❑ C. `tag3.tag`

❑ D. `tag4.tag`

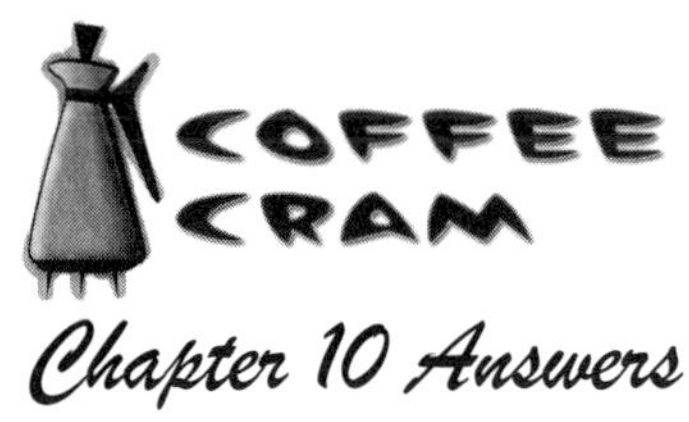

Chapter 10 Answers

---

1 How can a Classic tag handler instruct the container to ignore the remainder of the JSP that invoked the tag? (Choose all that apply.)

(JSP v2.0 pg 2-56)

- ❑ A. The **doEndTag()** method should return **Tag.SKIP_BODY**.
  -Option A is invalid because this is not a valid return value for doEndTag().
- ☑ B. The **doEndTag()** method should return **Tag.SKIP_PAGE**.
- ❑ C. The **doStartTag()** method should return **Tag.SKIP_BODY**.
  -Option C is invalid because it only causes the body of the tag to be skipped.
- ❑ D. The **doStartTag()** method should return **Tag.SKIP_PAGE**.
  -Option D is invalid because this is not a valid return value for doStartTag().

---

2 Which directives and/or standard actions are applicable ONLY within tag files? (Choose all that apply.)

(JSP v2.0 8.5 (pg 1-179)
JSP v2.0 section 5.11
JSP v2.0 section 5.12
JSP v2.0 section 5.13)

- ☑ A. **tag** -Option A is valid (pg 1-179).
- ❑ B. **page** -Option B is invalid because the page directive is never allowed in a tag file (pg 1-179).
- ❑ C. **jsp:body** -Option C is invalid because the jsp:body action can appear in EITHER a tag file or JSP.
- ☑ D. **jsp:doBody** - Option D is valid (pg 1-121).
- ☑ E. **jsp:invoke** -Option E is valid (pg 1-119).
- ❑ F. **taglib** -Option F is invalid because the taglib directive can appear in EITHER a tag file or JSP.

3 Given a JSP page:

(JSP v2.0 SimpleTagSupport API pg 2-86
JSP v2.0 TagSupport API pg 2-64)

```
<my:tag1>
  <my:tag2>
    <my:tag3 />
  </my:tag2>
</my:tag1>
```

The tag handler for **my:tag1** is **Tag1Handler** and extends TagSupport. The tag handler for **my:tag2** is **Tag2Handler** and extends SimpleTagSupport. The tag handler for **my:tag3** is **Tag3Handler** and extends TagSupport.

Which is true? (Choose all that apply.)

☐ A. **Tag3Handler** CANNOT access the instance of **Tag1Handler** because Simple tags do NOT support access to the tag parent.

-Option A is invalid because Simple tags do have a getParent method.

☐ B. Only Classic tags are considered in composing the parent/child tag hiearchy; therefore, **Tag3Handler** may use the **getParent** method only once to gain access to the instance of **Tag1Handler**.

-Option B is invalid because Simple tags do participate in the parent/child tag hierarchy along with Classic tags.

☑ C. **Tag3Handler** may use the **getParent** method twice to gain access to the instance of **Tag1Handler**.

☐ D. Only BodyTag handlers can access the parent/child tag hiearchy; therefore, **Tag3Handler** CANNOT gain access to the instance of **Tag1Handler**.

-Option D is invalid because every JspTag has access to its parent tag.

4 Which Simple tag mechanism will tell a JSP page to stop processing?

(JSP v2.0 section 13.6.1)

☐ A. Return **SKIP_PAGE** from the **doTag** method.

-Option A is invalid because the doTag method dies return a value.

☐ B. Return **SKIP_PAGE** from the **doEndTag** method.

-Option B is invalid because a Simple tag does not have the doEndTag event method.

☑ C. Throw a **SkipPageException** from the **doTag** method.

☐ D. Throw a **SkipPageException** from the **doEndTag** method.

-Option D is invalid because a Simple tag does not have the doEndTag event method.

5 Which are true about the Classic tag model? (Choose all that apply.)

(JSP v2.0 sections 13.1 and 13.2)

- [ ] A. The **Tag** interface can only be used to create empty tags.

-Option A is invalid because the Tag interface can support tags with a body, but you can't iterate or gain access to the body content.

- [x] B. The **SKIP_PAGE** constant is a valid return value of the **doEndTag** method.

- [ ] C. The **EVAL_BODY_BUFFERED** constant is a valid return value of the **doAfterBody** method.

-Option C is invalid because doAfterBody can only return SKIP_BODY or EVAL_BODY_AGAIN.

- [ ] D. The **Tag** interface only provides two values for the return value of the **doStartTag** method: **SKIP_BODY** and **EVAL_BODY**.

-Option D is invalid because doStartTag returns SKIP_BODY and EVAL_BODY_INCLUDE.

- [x] E. There are three tag interfaces **Tag**, **IterationTag**, and **BodyTag**, but only two built-in base classes: **TagSupport**, and **BodyTagSupport**.

---

6 Which about the **findAncestorWithClass** method are true? (Choose all that apply.)

(JSP v2.0 pg. 2-64)

- [ ] A. It requires one parameter: A **Class**.
- [x] B. It is a static method in the **TagSupport** class.
- [ ] C. It is a non-static method in the **TagSupport** class.

-Option C is invalid because the method is static.

- [x] D. It is NOT defined by any of the standard JSP tag interfaces.
- [x] E. It requires two parameters: A **Tag** and a **Class**.
- [ ] F. It requires one parameter: A **String** representing the name of the tag to be found.

-Options A and F are invalid because the method takes two parameters.

- [ ] G. It requires two parameters: A **Tag** and a **String**, representing the name of the tag to be found.

-Option G is invalid because the second argument is a Class.

7 Which must be true if you want to use dynamic attributes for a Simple tag handler? (Choose all that apply.)

(JSP v2.0 section 13.3 pgs 2-74,75)

- ❑ A. Your Simple tag must NOT declare any static tag attributes.

-Option A is invalid because you can have both static and dynamic attributes in a Simple tag.

- ☑ B. Your Simple tag must use the **`<dynamic-attributes>`** element in the TLD.

- ☑ C. Your Simple tag handler must implement the **`DynamicAttributes`** interface.

- ❑ D. Your Simple tag should extend the **`DynamicSimpleTagSupport`** class, which provides default support for dynamic attributes.

-Option D is invalid because there is no such helper class in the built-in APIs.

- ❑ E. Your Simple tag CANNOT be used with the **`jsp:attribute`** standard action, because this action works only with static attributes.

-Option E is invalid because you are allowed to use the jsp:attribute action with dynamic tags.

---

8 Which is true about tag files? (Choose all that apply.)

(JSP v2.0 section 8.4)

- ❑ A. A tag file may be placed in any subdirectory of **`WEB-INF`**.

-Option A is invalid because tag files must be placed under the WEB-INF/tags directory.

- ☑ B. A tag file must have the file extension of **`.tag`** or **`.tagx`**.

-Option B is correct (pg 1-176, 8.4.1).

- ❑ C. A TLD file must be used to map the symbolic tag name to the actual tag file.

-Option C is invalid because tag files may be discovered by the container in several well-known locations. This container feature is optional.

- ❑ D. A tag file may NOT be placed in a JAR file in the **`WEB-INF/lib`** directory.

9 Given: (JSP v2.0 pg. 2-68)

```
10. public class BufTag extends BodyTagSupport {
11.   public int doStartTag() throws JspException {
12.     // insert code here
13.   }
14. }
```

Assume that the tag has been properly configured to allow body content.

Which, if inserted at line 12, would cause the JSP code **<mytags:mytag>BodyContent</mytags:mytag>** to output **BodyContent**?

- ❑ A. **return SKIP_BODY;**
- ☑ B. **return EVAL_BODY_INCLUDE;**
- ❑ C. **return EVAL_BODY_BUFFERED;**
- ❑ D. **return BODY_CONTENT;**

-Option A is invalid because it causes the body of the tag to be skipped.

- Option C is invalid because it directs the body of the tag to a buffer which this tag does not process.

-Option D is invalid because this is not a valid return code.

10 Which about **doAfterBody()** is true? (Choose all that apply.) (JSP v2.0 pg. 1-152)

- ❑ A. **doAfterBody()** is only called on tags that extend **TagSupport**.

-Option A is invalid because doAfterBody() can be called on any tag that implements the IteratorTag interface.

- ❑ B. **doAfterBody()** is only called on tags that extend **IterationTagSupport**.

-Option B is invalid because there is no such class.

- ❑ C. Assuming no exceptions occur, **doAfterBody()** is always called after **doStartTag()** for any tag that implements **IterationTag**.
- ❑ D. Assuming no exceptions occur, **doAfterBody()** is called after **doStartTag()** for any tag that implements **IterationTag** and returns **SKIP_BODY** from **doStartTag()**.

-Options C and D are invalid because doAfterBody() is only called when doStartTag() returns EVAL_BODY_INCLUDE.

- ☑ E. Assuming no exceptions occur, **doAfterBody()** is called after **doStartTag()** for any tag that implements **IterationTag** and returns **EVAL_BODY_INCLUDE** from **doStartTag()**.

11 Given a JSP page:

(JSP v2.0 TagSupport API pg 2-64)

```
<%@ taglib prefix="my" uri="/WEB-INF/myTags.tld" %>
<my:tag1>
  <%-- JSP content --%>
</my:tag1>
```

The tag handler for **`my:tag1`** is **`Tag1Handler`** and extends TagSupport.

What happens when the instance of **`Tag1Handler`** calls the **`getParent`** method? (Choose all that apply.)

☐ A. A **`JspException`** is thrown.

☑ B. The **`null`** value is returned.

☐ C. A **`NullPointerException`** is thrown.

☐ D. An **`IllegalStateException`** is thrown.

-Option B is the correct answer. The getParent method does not throw any exceptions.

12 Which is true about the lifecycle of a Simple tag? (Choose all that apply.)

(JSP v2.0 section 13.6 pgs 2-80/83)

☐ A. The **`release`** method is called after the **`doTag`** method.

-Option A is invalid because a Simple tag has no release method.

☐ B. The **`setJspBody`** method is always called before the **`doTag`** method.

-Option B is invalid because the setJspBody is not called if the Simple tag is an empty tag.

☑ C. The **`setParent`** and **`setJspContext`** methods are called immediately before the tag attributes are set.

☐ D. The **`JspFragment`** of the tag body is invoked by the Container before the tag handler's **`doTag`** method is called. This value, a **`BodyContent`** object, is passed to the tag handler using the **`setJspBody`** method.

-Option D is invalid because the fragment is invoked by the doTag implementation, NOT before the doTag is called.

13 Given: (JSP v2.0 pg 2-27)

```
10. public class ExampleTag extends TagSupport {
11.   private String param;
12.   public void setParam(String p) { param = p; }
13.   public int doStartTag() throws JspException {
14.     // insert code here
15.     // more code here
16.   }
17. }
```

Which, inserted at line 14, would be guaranteed to assign the value of the request-scoped attribute **param** to the local variable **p**? (Choose all that apply.)

❑ A. `String p = findAttribute("param");` –Option A is invalid because there is no such method.

❑ B. `String p = request.getAttribute("param");` –Option B is invalid because there is no request instance variable.

❑ C. `String p = pageContext.findAttribute("param");` –Option C is invalid because an attribute in page scope would be found before checking request scope.

❑ D. `String p = getPageContext().findAttribute("param");` –Option D is invalid because there is no getPageContext() method.

☑ E. `String p = pageContext.getRequest().getAttribute("param");`

14 Which are valid method calls on a **PageContext** object? (Choose all that apply.) (JSP v2.0 pg. 2-23)

❑ A. `getAttributeNames()`

☑ B. `getAttribute("key")`

☑ C. `findAttribute("key")`

❑ D. `getSessionAttribute()`

☑ E. `getAttributesScope("key")`

❑ F. `findAttribute("key", PageContext.SESSION_SCOPE)`

☑ G. `getAttribute("key", PageContext.SESSION_SCOPE)`

–Options A and D are invalid because there are no methods with these names.

–Option F is invalid because findAttribute() does not have a scope parameter.

15 Which is the most efficient **JspContext** method to call to access an attribute that is known to be in application scope? (JSP v2.0 pg. 2-23)

- ❑ A. **getPageContext()** -Option A is invalid because there is no such method.
- ❑ B. **getAttribute(String)** -Option B is invalid because this method only looks in page scope.
- ❑ C. **findAttribute(String)** -Option C is invalid because this method would be less efficient than Option D because it first checks the other three scopes.
- ☑ D. **getAttribute(String, int)**
- ❑ E. **getAttributesScope("key")** -Option E is invalid because it would be only the first step in a process that would be much less efficient than Option D.
- ❑ F. **getAttributeNamesInScope(int)** -Option F is invalid because no such method exists.

16 What is the best strategy, when implementing a custom tag, for finding the value of an attribute whose scope is unknown? (JSP v2.0 pg. 2-23)

- ❑ A. Check all scopes with a single **pageContext.getAttribute(String)** call. -Option A is invalid because this method only checks the page scope.
- ☑ B. Check all scopes with a single **pageContext.findAttribute(String)** call.
- ❑ C. Check each scope with calls to **pageContext.getAttribute(String, int)**.
- ❑ D. Call **pageContext.getRequest().getAttribute(String)**, then call **pageContext.getSession().getAttribute(String)**, and so on.
- ❑ E. None of these will work.

-Options C and D are invalid because they are less efficient than simply calling findAttribute().

17 Given a tag, **simpleTag**, whose handler is implemented using the Simple tag model and a tag, **complexTag**, whose handler is implemented using the Classic tag model. Both tags are declared to be non-empty in the TLD.

(JSP v2.0 7.1.6 pg 1-156)

Which JSP code snippets are valid uses of these tag? (Choose all that apply.)

☑ A.
```
<my:simpleTag>
   <my:complexTag />
</my:simpleTag>
```

-Option A is correct; a Simple tag may include a Complex tag in the body as long as that tag contains no scripting code.

❑ B.
```
<my:simpleTag>
   <%= displayText %>
</my:simpleTag>
```

-Option B is invalid because simple tags cannot have a body that includes a JSP expression tag.

☑ C.
```
<my:simpleTag>
   <%@ include file="/WEB-INF/web/common/headerMenu.html" %>
</my:simpleTag>
```

-Option C is correct because the include directive is processed before the body of the simpleTag is converted into a JspFragment; however, the included content must also be non-scripting (which is why this example includes an HTML segment).

❑ D.
```
<my:simpleTag>
   <my:complexTag>
     <% i++; %>
   </my:complexTag>
</my:simpleTag>
```

-Option D is not invalid because of the complexTag usage (as in Option A), but because the complexTag body has scripting code in it.

---

18 Which are true about the Tag File model? (Choose all that apply.)

(JSP v2.0 pg. 1-173)

❑ A. Each tag file must have a corresponding entry in a TLD file.

-Option A is invalid because tag files need only to be placed in the appropriate location in order to be used.

❑ B. All directives allowed in JSP pages are allowed in Tag Files.

-Option B is invalid because the page directive is not available in Tag Files.

❑ C. All directives allowed in Tag Files are allowed in JSP pages.

-Option C is invalid because the tag, attribute, and variable directives are not available in JSP pages.

☑ D. The **<jsp:doBody>** standard action can only be used in Tag Files.

☑ E. The allowable file extensions for Tag Files are **.tag** and **.tagx**.

☑ F. For each attribute declared and specified in a Tag File, the container creates a page-scoped attribute with the same name.

19 Which are valid in tag files? (Choose all that apply.) (JSP v2.0 pg. 1-174)

- [x] A. `<jsp:doBody />`
- [x] B. `<jsp:invoke fragment="frag" />`
- [ ] C. `<%@ page import="java.util.Date" %>`
- [x] D. `<%@ variable name-given="date" variable-class="java.util.Date" %>`
- [ ] E. `<%@ attribute name="name" value="blank" type="java.lang.String" %>`

-Option C is invalid because the page directive is not valid in tag files.

-Option E is invalid because there is no value attribute defined for the attribute directive.

20 Which returns the enclosing tag when called from within a tag handler class? (Choose all that apply.) (JSP v2.0 pg. 2-53)

- [x] A. `getParent()`
- [ ] B. `getAncestor()`
- [ ] C. `findAncestor()`
- [ ] D. `getEnclosingTag()`

-Option A is correct; it is the only one of the methods shown that exists.

21 Given a web application structure: (JSP v2.0 pg. 1-176)

```
/WEB-INF/tags/mytags/tag1.tag
/WEB-INF/tags/tag2.tag
/WEB-INF/tag3.tag
/tag4.tag
```

Which tags could be used by an appropriate **`taglib`** directive? (Choose all that apply.)

- [x] A. `tag1.tag`
- [x] B. `tag2.tag`
- [ ] C. `tag3.tag`
- [ ] D. `tag4.tag`

-Options C and D are invalid because tag files must be placed under the /WEB-INF/tags directory or a subdirectory of /WEB-INF/tags.

Deploying your web app

I'm proud of you father! Your deployment descriptor looks perfect—you've configured error pages, welcome files, servlet mappings... but I'm not sure our clients will appreciate the subtle irony of your ".die" and ".kickass" extensions...
Well? How does it look?

Finally, your web app is ready for prime time. Your pages are polished, your code is tested and tuned, and your deadline was two weeks ago. But where does everything go? So many directories, so many rules. What do *you* name your directories? What does the *client* think they're named? What does the client actually request, and how does the Container know where to look? How do you make certain that you don't accidentally leave out a directory when you move the whole web app to a different machine? What happens if the client requests a *directory* instead of a specific *file*? How do you configure the DD for error pages, welcome files, and MIME types? It's not as bad as it sounds...

Web Application Deployment

Coverage Notes:

2.1 Construct the file and directory structure of a web application that may contain (a) static content, (b) JSP pages, (c) servlet classes, (d) the deployment descriptor, (e) tag libraries, (f) JAR files, and (g) Java class files. Describe how to protect resource files from HTTP access.

This objective has been covered throughout the book in other chapters, so most of the content in this chapter related to this objective is either for review or to look at something in a little more detail.

2.2 Describe the purpose and semantics for each of the following deployment descriptor elements: error-page, init-param, mime-mapping, servlet, servlet-class, servlet-mapping, servlet-name, and welcome-file.

2.3 Construct the correct structure for each of the following deployment descriptor elements: error-page, init-param, mime-mapping, servlet, servlet-class, servlet-name, and welcome-file.

Objectives 2.2 and 2.3 focus mainly on picky XML tag details related to the Deployment Descriptor. While this is probably the least fun part of the book (and the exam), most of this content is easy to understand and it's just a matter of memorizing the tags.
There is one tricky part, though, and we'll spend most of our time on it—servlet mapping.

2.4 Explain the purpose of a WAR file and describe the contents of a WAR file and how one may be constructed.

6.3 Write a JSP Document (XML-based syntax) that uses the correct syntax.

*We decided to stick this objective into this chapter for two reasons: 1) most of this chapter has to do with XML, and 2) we didn't want to add anything else into the JSP chapters. We decided it was better for you to concentrate more on the syntax and behavior of all the other parts of JSP, rather than also worrying about the XML versions of everything. But now that you're, you know, an **expert**... we figure you can handle it.*

The Joy of Deployment

We've covered most of the fun stuff, but now it's time for a more detailed look at deployment.

In this chapter, you need to think about three main issues:

1 Where do YOU put things in the web app?

Where do you put static resources? JSP pages? Servlet class files? JavaBean class files? Listener class files? Tag Files? Tag handler classes? TLDs? JAR files? The web.xml DD? Where do you put things that you don't want the Container to serve? (In other words, which parts of the web app are protected from direct client access?) Where do you put "welcome" files?

2 Where will the CONTAINER look for things in the web app?

Where will the Container look when the client requests an HTML page? A JSP page? A servlet? Something that doesn't exist as an actual file (like, BeerTest.**do**)? Where will the Container look for tag handler classes? Where will the Container look for TLDs? Tag Files? JAR files? The Deployment Descriptor? Other classes my servlets depend on? Where does the Container look for "welcome" files ? (Obviously, once you know all of this, then everything in number "1" becomes a no-brainer.)

3 How does the CLIENT request things in the web app?

What does the client type into the browser to access an HTML page? A JSP page? A servlet? Something that doesn't actually exist as a file? In which places can the client make a direct request, and in which places is the client restricted from direct access to a resource? What happens if the client types in a path to only a directory, not a specific file?

What goes where in a web app

In several chapters of this book, we've looked at the locations in which the various files must be placed. In the chapter on custom tags, for example, you saw that Tag Files must be deployed in /WEB-INF/tags or a subdirectory, or in a JAR file under /META-INF/tags or a subdirectory. If you put a Tag File anywhere else, the Container will either ignore it or treat it as static content ready to be served.

The Servlet and JSP specs have a lot of picky rules about where things go, and you really do need to know most of them. Since we've already covered most of this in one way or another, we use these first few pages as a test of your memory and understanding. Don't skip it! Treat these next few pages as practice exam questions!

there are no Dumb Questions

Q: Why should I have to know where everything goes... isn't that what deployment tools are for? Or even an ANT build script?

A: If you're lucky, you're using a J2EE deployment tool that lets you point and click your way through a series of wizard screens. Then your Container uses that info to build the XML Deployment Descriptor (web.xml), build out the necessary directory structures, and copy your files into the appropriate locations. But even if you *are* lucky, don't you think you need to know what the tool is doing? You might need to tweak what the tool does. You might need to troubleshoot. You might switch to a different vendor that doesn't have an automated deployment tool.

A lot of developers use a build tool like ANT, but even then, you still need to tell ANT what to do.

Q: But I just got an ANT build script off the internet, and it's already configured to do it all for me.

A: Again, that's great—but you still need to know what's really happening. If you're completely at the mercy of your tool, you're in trouble if something goes wrong. Knowing how to structure a web app is like knowing how to change a tire—maybe you'll never need to do it yourself, but if it's 3:00 AM and you're in the middle of nowhere, isn't it nice to know you *can*?

And for those of you taking the exam, well, *you* don't have a choice. Virtually everything in this chapter is covered on the exam.

Name the directories

Write the correct directory names in, given the files shown within those directories. Everything in here has been covered in an earlier chapter, but don't worry if you haven't completely memorized them all yet. *This* is the chapter where you have to *burn it in*.

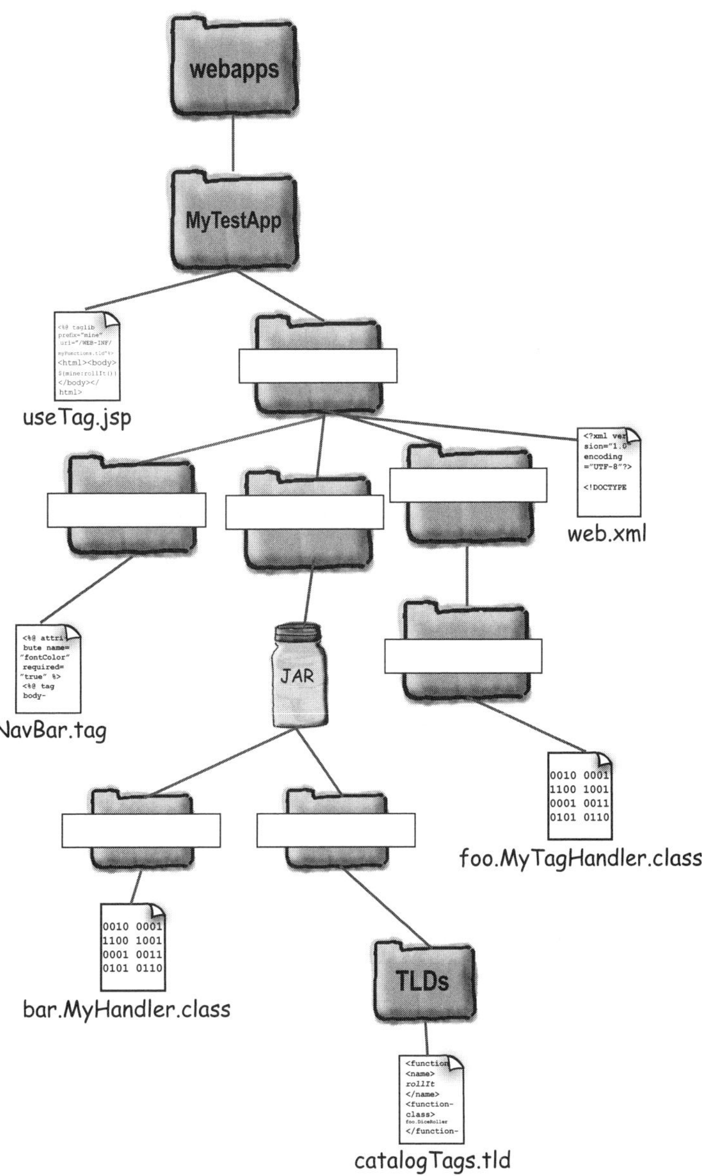

Draw the directory and file structure

Look at the following web app description and draw a directory structure that supports that web app. Be sure to include the files too. There may be more than one way to structure this; we recommend using the simplest (i.e. least number of directories) to organize it.

Application name: Dating

Static content and JSPs: welcome.html, signup.jsp, search.jsp

Servlets: dating.Enroll.class, dating.Search.class

Custom tag handler class: tagClasses.TagOne.class

TLD: DatingTags.tld

JavaBeans: dating.Client.class

DD: web.xml

Support JAR files: DatingJar.jar

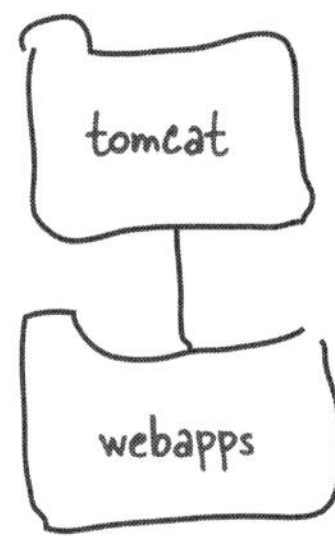

BE the Container

What's wrong with this deployment? There are several things here that do not follow the Servlet or JSP specification for where they should be placed. Assume that all files have the correct names and extensions.

List everything that's wrong with this picture:

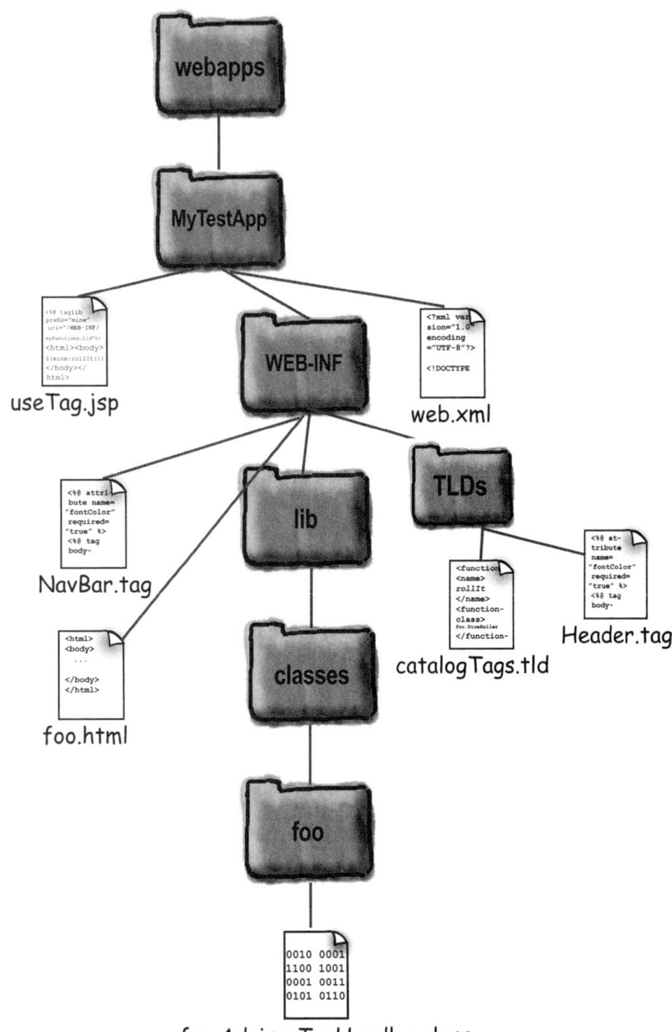

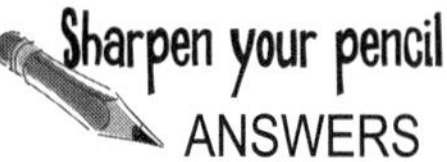

Name the directories

To deploy a web app successfully, you MUST follow this structure. WEB-INF must be immediately under the application context ("MyTestApp" in this example). The "classes" directory must be immediately inside "WEB-INF". The package structure for the classes must be immediately inside "classes". The "lib" directory must be immediately inside "WEB-INF", and the JAR file must be immediately inside "lib". The "META-INF" directory must be immediately inside the JAR, and TLD files in a JAR must be somewhere under "META-INF" (they can be in any subdirectory, and "TLDs" is not required as a directory name). TLDs that are NOT in a JAR must be somewhere under "WEB-INF". Tag Files (files with a .tag or .tagx extension) must be *somewhere* under "WEB-INF/tags" (unless they're deployed in a JAR, in which case they must be somewhere under "META-INF/tags").

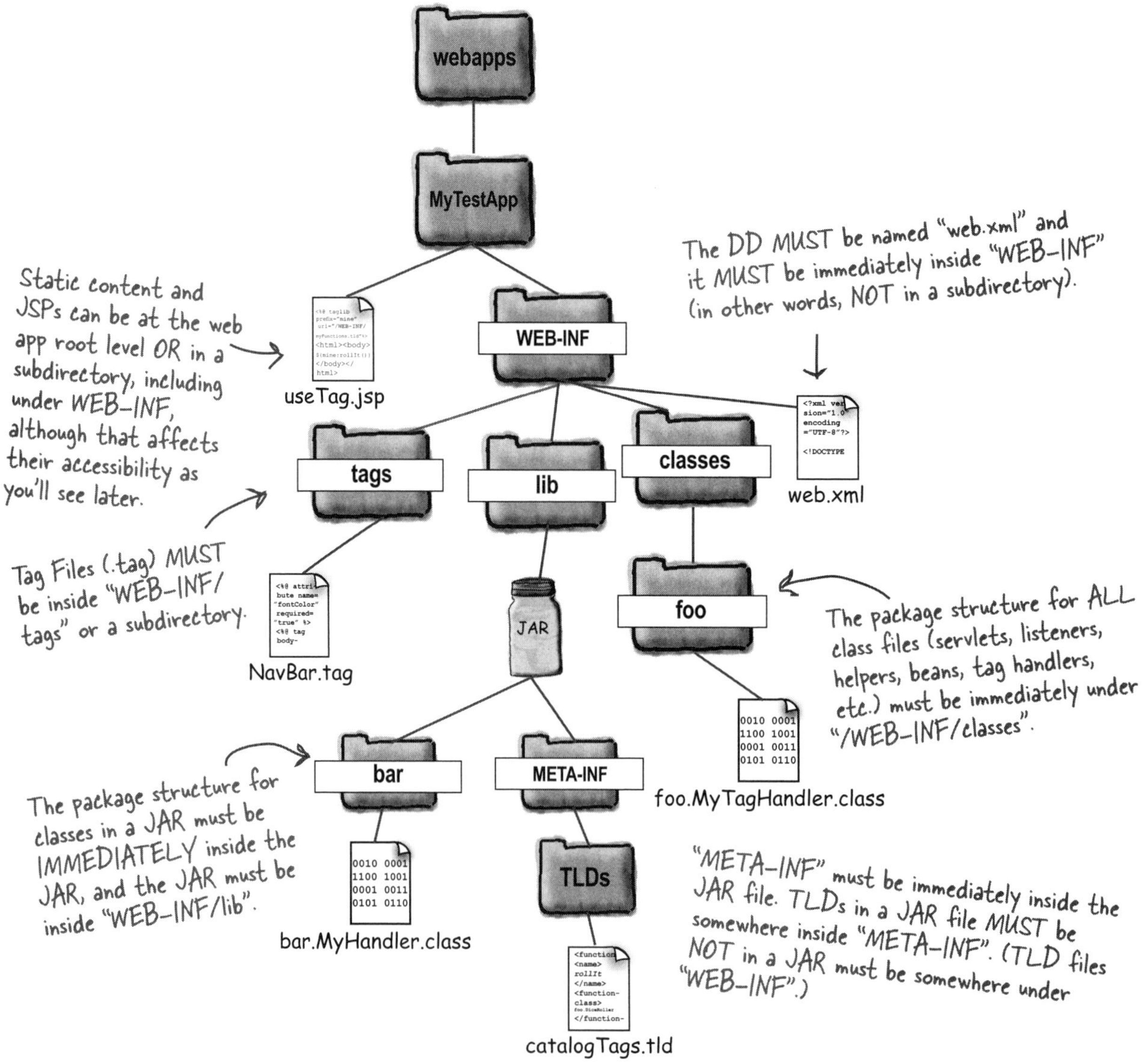

webapps

MyTestApp

useTag.jsp

WEB-INF

web.xml

tags

lib

classes

NavBar.tag

JAR

foo

foo.MyTagHandler.class

bar

META-INF

bar.MyHandler.class

TLDs

catalogTags.tld

Static content and JSPs can be at the web app root level OR in a subdirectory, including under WEB-INF, although that affects their accessibility as you'll see later.

The DD MUST be named "web.xml" and it MUST be immediately inside "WEB-INF" (in other words, NOT in a subdirectory).

Tag Files (.tag) MUST be inside "WEB-INF/tags" or a subdirectory.

The package structure for ALL class files (servlets, listeners, helpers, beans, tag handlers, etc.) must be immediately under "/WEB-INF/classes".

The package structure for classes in a JAR must be IMMEDIATELY inside the JAR, and the JAR must be inside "WEB-INF/lib".

"META-INF" must be immediately inside the JAR file. TLDs in a JAR file MUST be somewhere inside "META-INF". (TLD files NOT in a JAR must be somewhere under "WEB-INF".)

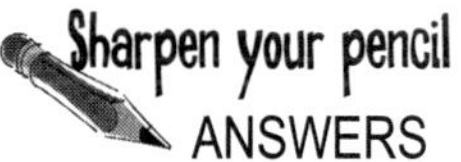

ANSWERS

Draw the directory and file structure

The only things that could be different in this picture are 1) the static content and JSPs could be in a subdirectory under “Dating”, or *hidden* under “WEB-INF” and 2) the DatingTags.tld could be in a subdirectory of WEB-INF.

Application name: Dating

Static content and JSPs: welcome.html, signup.jsp, search.jsp

Servlets: dating.Enroll class, dating.Search class

Custom tag handler class: tagClasses.TagOne class

TLD: DatingTags.tld

JavaBeans class: dating.Client class

DD: web.xml

Support JAR files: DatingJar.jar

BE the Container

Answers

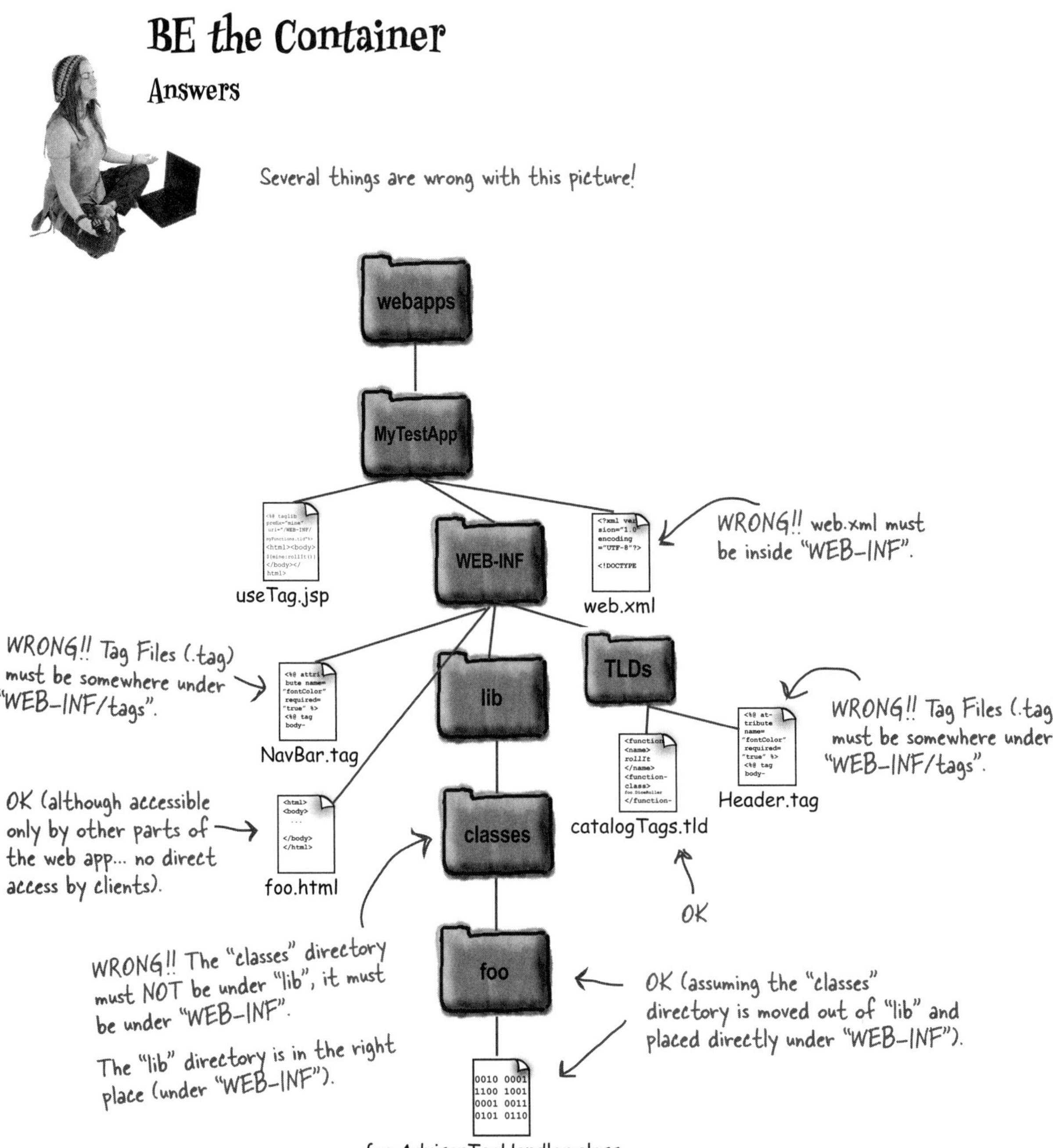

What she really wants is a WAR file

The directory structure of a web app is intense. And everything has to be in exactly the right place. Moving a web app can hurt.

But there's a solution, called a WAR file, which stands for **W**eb **AR**chive. And if that sounds suspiciously like a JAR file (**J**ava **AR**chive), that's because a WAR *is* a JAR. A JAR with a *.war* extension instead of *.jar*.

WAR files

A WAR file is simply a snapshot of your web app structure, in a nice portable, compressed form (it's really just a JAR file). You jar up your entire web app structure (minus the web app context directory—the one that's *above* WEB-INF), and give it a .war extension. But that does leave one problem—if you don't include the specific web app directory (BeerApp, for example), how does the Container know the name/context of this web app?

That depends on your Container. ***In Tomcat, the name of the WAR file becomes the web app name!*** Imagine you deploy BeerApp as a normal directory structure under tomcat/webapps/BeerApp. To deploy it as a WAR file, you jar up everything in the BeerApp directory (but not the BeerApp directory itself), then name the resulting JAR file ***BeerApp.war***. Then you drop the BeerApp.war file into the tomcat/webapps directory. That's it. Tomcat unpacks the WAR file, and creates the web app context directory using the name of the WAR file. But again, *your* Container may handle WAR deployment and naming differently. What matters to us here is what's required by the spec, and the answer is—it makes almost no difference whether the app is deployed in or out of a WAR! In other words, you still need WEB-INF, web.xml, etc. Everything on the previous pages applies.

Almost everything. There is one thing you can do when you use a WAR file that you can't do when you deploy without one—***declare library dependencies.***

In a WAR file, you can declare library dependencies in the META-INF/MANIFEST.MF file, which gives you a *deploy-time* check for whether the Container can find the packages and classes your app depends on. That means you don't have to wait until a resource is requested before the whole thing blows up because the Container doesn't have a particular class in its classpath that the requested resource needs.

Don't be fooled by questions about WAR files... the rules don't change!

Quick quiz: do you still need a file named "web.xml" if you deploy as a WAR? Of course. Do you still need a "WEB-INF" directory if you deploy as a WAR? Of course. Do you still need to put classes in a "classes" directory under "WEB-INF"? Of course. You get the idea. The rules don't change just because you put your app in a WAR! The only significant difference is that a WAR file will have a "META-INF" directory under the web app context (a peer to the "WEB-INF" directory).

What a deployed WAR file looks like

When you deploy a web app into Tomcat by putting the WAR file into the webapps directory, Tomcat unpacks it, creates the context directory (***MyTestApp*** in this example), and the only new thing you'll see is the META-INF directory (with the MANIFEST.MF file) inside. You will probably *never* put anything into the META-INF directory yourself, so you'll probably never care whether your app is deployed as a WAR unless you do need to specify library dependencies in the MANIFEST.MF file.

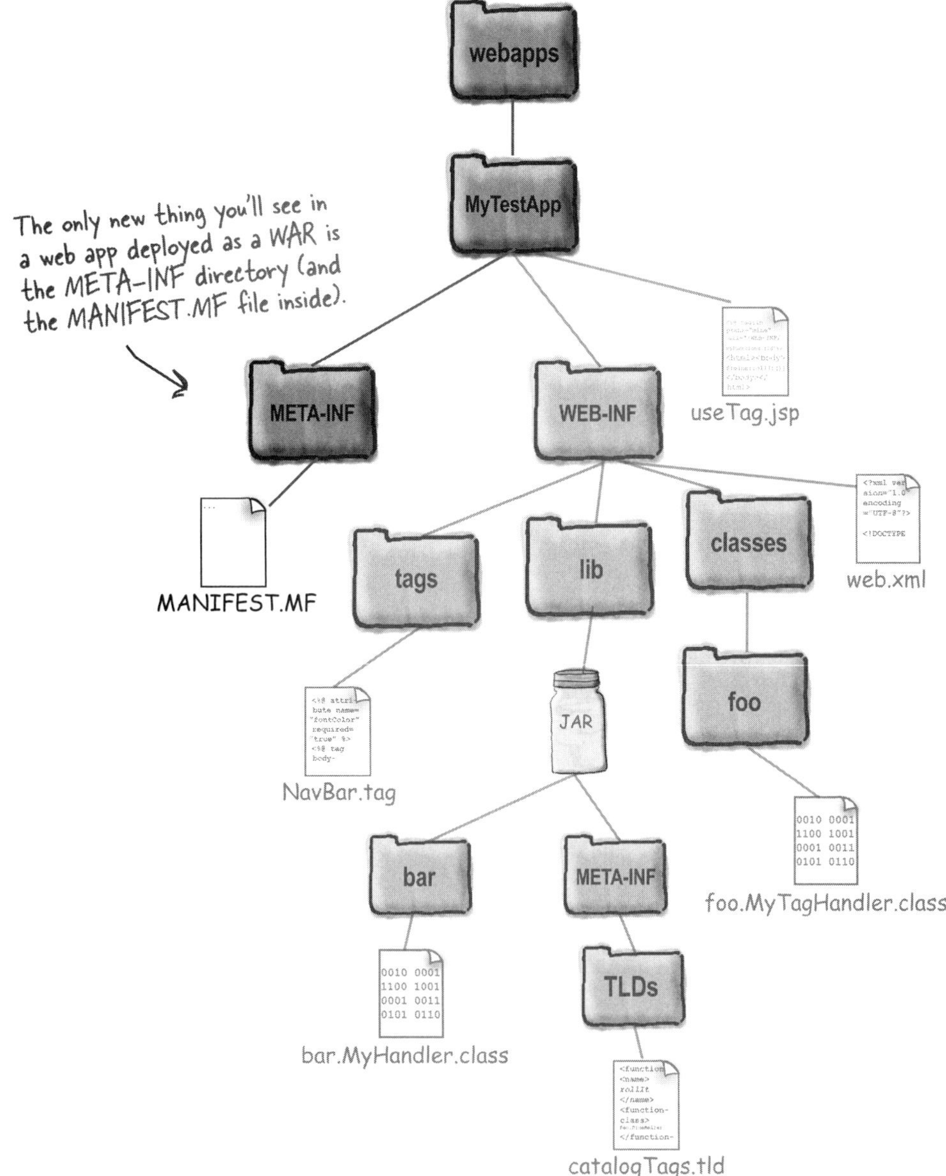

Making static content and JSPs directly accessible

When you deploy static HTML and JSPs, you can choose whether to make them directly accessible from outside the web app. By *directly accessible*, we mean that a client can enter the path to the resource into his browser, and the server will return the resource. But you can prevent direct access by putting files under WEB-INF or, if you're deploying as a WAR file, under META-INF.

This is a directly accessible path in the web app.

Valid request

`http://www.wickedlysmart.com/MyTestApp/register/signUp.jsp`

No! Nothing under WEB-INF can be directly accessed.

Invalid request (produces "404 Not Found" error)

`http://www.wickedlysmart.com/MyTestApp/WEB-INF/process.jsp`

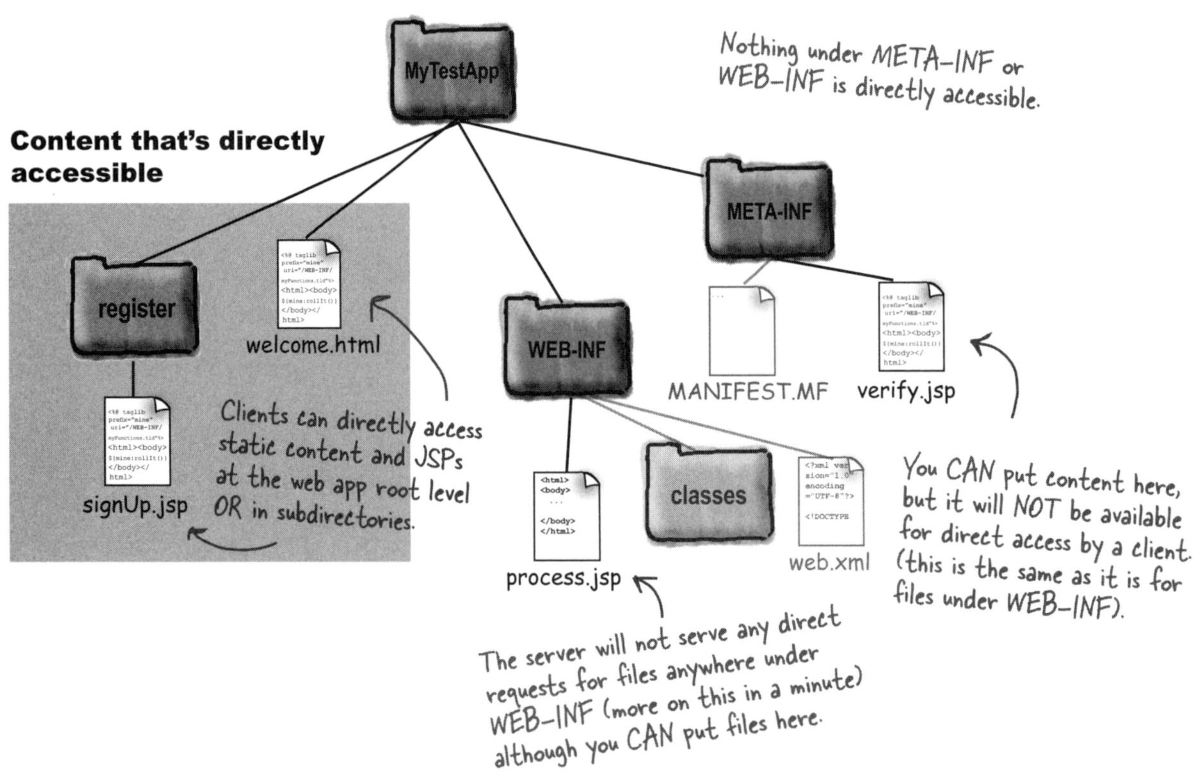
MyTestApp
Nothing under META-INF or WEB-INF is directly accessible.
Content that's directly accessible
META-INF
register
welcome.html
WEB-INF
MANIFEST.MF
verify.jsp
signUp.jsp
Clients can directly access static content and JSPs at the web app root level OR in subdirectories.
classes
You CAN put content here, but it will NOT be available for direct access by a client. (this is the same as it is for files under WEB-INF).
process.jsp
web.xml
The server will not serve any direct requests for files anywhere under WEB-INF (more on this in a minute) although you CAN put files here.

If the server gets a client request for anything under WEB-INF or META-INF, the Container MUST respond with a 404 NOT FOUND error!

there are no Dumb Questions

Q: If you can't serve content from WEB-INF or META-INF, what's the point of putting pages there??!!

A: Think about that. You have Java classes and class members with package-level (default) access, right? These are classes and members not available to the "public", but meant for internal use by other classes and members that are publicly exposed. It's the same way for these non-accessible static content and JSPs. By putting them under WEB-INF (or, with a WAR file, META-INF), you're protecting them from any direct access, while still allowing other parts of the web app to use them.

You might, for example, want to forward to or include a file while making sure that no client can directly request it. Chances are, if you want to protect a resource from direct access, you'll use WEB-INF and not META-INF, but for the exam, you have to know that the rules apply to both.

Q: What about a META-INF directory inside a *JAR* file inside WEB-INF/lib? Does that have the same protection as META-INF inside the *WAR* file?

A: Well... yes. But the fact that the content is in META-INF is not the point. In this case, you're talking about a JAR file inside the lib directory inside WEB-INF. And *anything* in WEB-INF is protected from direct access! So, it doesn't matter *where* under WEB-INF the content is, it's still protected. When we say that META-INF is protected, we're really talking about META-INF inside a WAR file, because the META-INF inside WEB-INF/lib JAR files is always protected anyway by virtue of being under WEB-INF.

Q: On an earlier page you mentioned putting library dependencies in the META-INF/MANIFEST.MF file. Are you required to do that? Isn't everything in the WEB-INF/lib jar files and the WEB-INF/classes directory automatically on the classpath for this application?

A: Yes, classes you deploy *in/with* the web app, by using the WEB-INF/classes directory or a JAR in WEB-INF/lib, are available and you don't have to do or say anything. They just work. But... you might have a Container with optional packages on its classpath, and maybe you're depending on some of those packages. Or maybe you're depending on a particular *version* of a library! The MANIFEST.MF file gives you a place to tell the Container about the optional libraries you must have access to. If the Container can't provide them, it won't let you successfully deploy the application. Which is a lot better than if you deploy and then find out later, at request time, when you get some horrible (or worse—subtle) runtime error.

Q: How does the Container access the content inside JAR files in WEB-INF/lib?

A: The Container automatically puts the JAR file into its classpath, so *classes* for servlets, listeners, beans, etc. are available exactly as they are if you put the classes (in their correct package directory structure, of course) within the WEB-INF/classes directory. In other words, it doesn't matter whether the classes are in or out of a JAR as long as they're in the right locations.

Keep in mind, though, that the Container will always look for classes in the WEB-INF/classes directory *before* it looks inside JAR files in WEB-INF/lib.

Q: OK, that explains class files, but what about other kinds of files? What if I need to access a text file that's deployed in a JAR in WEB-INF/lib?

A: This is different. If your web app code needs direct access to a resource (text file, JPEG, etc.) that's inside a JAR, you need to use the getResource() or getResourceAs Stream() methods of the classloader—this is just plain old J2SE, not specific to servlets.

Now, you might recognize those two methods (getResource() and getResourceAsStream()), because they exist also in the ServletContext API. The difference is, the methods inside ServletContext work only for resources within the web app that are *not* deployed within a JAR file. (For the exam, you need to know that you *can* use the standard J2SE mechanism for getting resources from JAR files, but you do *not* need to know any details.)

How servlet mapping REALLY works

You've seen examples of servlet mapping in the Deployment Descriptors we've used in earlier chapters, beginning with the tutorial.

Every servlet mapping has two parts—the <servlet> element and the <servlet-mapping> element. The <servlet> defines a servlet name and class, and the <servlet-mapping> defines the URL pattern that maps to a servlet name defined somewhere else in the DD.

```
<web-app xmlns="http://java.sun.com/xml/ns/j2ee"
    xmlns:xsi="http://www.w3.org/2001/XMLSchema-instance"
    xsi:schemaLocation="http://java.sun.com/xml/ns/j2ee/web-app_2_4.xsd"
    version="2.4">

  <servlet>
    <servlet-name>Beer</servlet-name>
    <servlet-class>com.example.BeerSelect</servlet-class>
  </servlet>

  <servlet-mapping>
    <servlet-name>Beer</servlet-name>
    <url-pattern>/Beer/SelectBeer.do</url-pattern>
  </servlet-mapping>

</web-app>
```

This name is mainly for use in other parts of the DD. It is NOT something the client will know about.

When a request comes in that looks like this, the Container finds the matching <servlet-name> in a <servlet> element, to know which class is responsible for handling the request.

If the client request comes in for "/Beer/SelectBeer.do", that refers to the servlet named "Beer".

And I see that there is a <servlet> with that <servlet-name>, "Beer", and it tells me which servlet class will handle this request.

<web-app ...
<servlet>
...
</servlet>
<servlet-mapping>
...
</servlet-mapping>
</web-app>

web.xml

Container

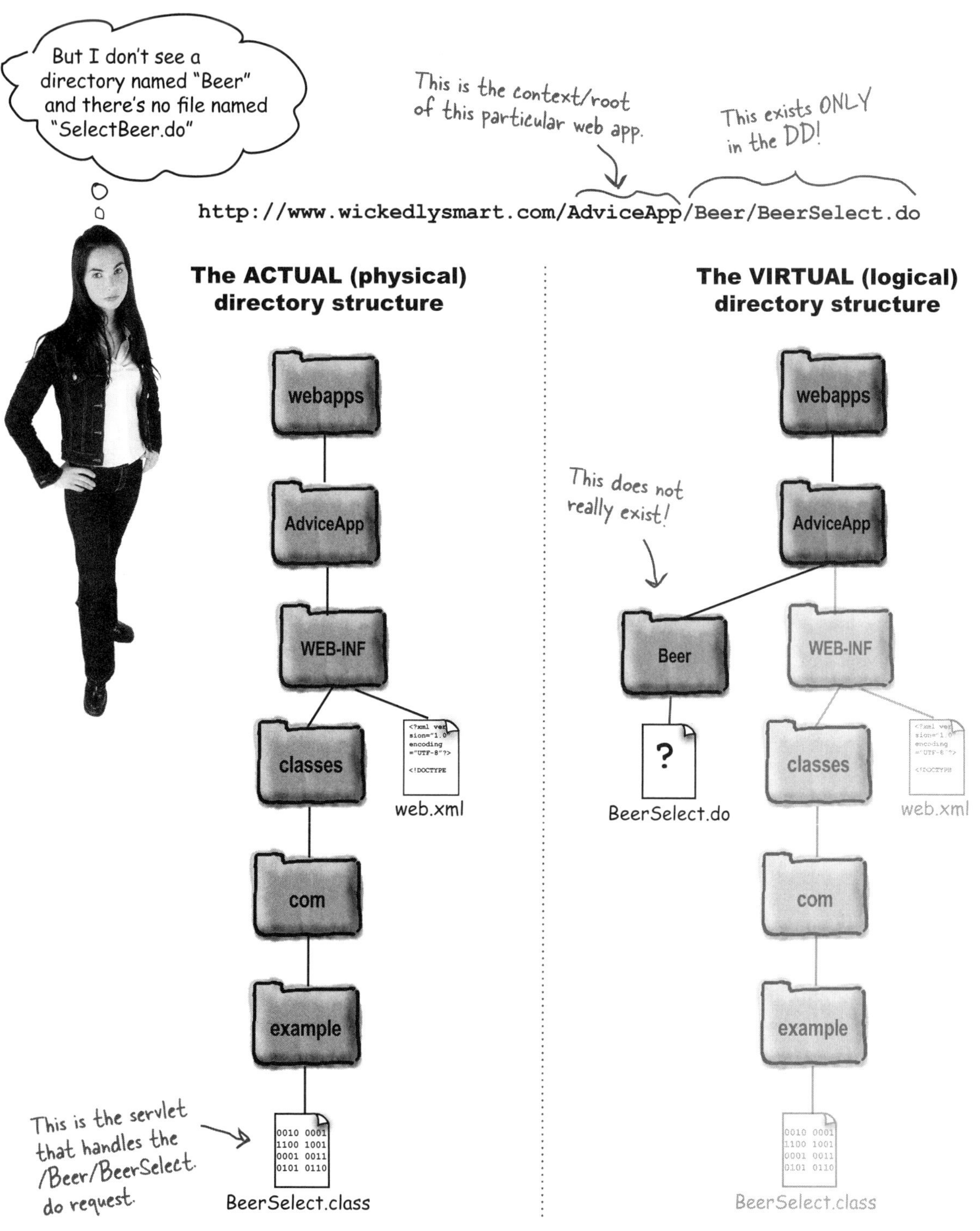

But I don't see a directory named "Beer" and there's no file named "SelectBeer.do"
This is the context/root of this particular web app.
This exists ONLY in the DD!
http://www.wickedlysmart.com/AdviceApp/Beer/BeerSelect.do
The ACTUAL (physical) directory structure
webapps
AdviceApp
WEB-INF
classes
web.xml
com
example
This is the servlet that handles the /Beer/BeerSelect.do request.
BeerSelect.class
The VIRTUAL (logical) directory structure
webapps
AdviceApp
This does not really exist!
Beer
?
BeerSelect.do
WEB-INF
classes
web.xml
com
example
BeerSelect.class

Servlet mappings can be "fake"

The URL pattern you put into a servlet mapping can be completely made-up. Imaginary. Fake. Just a logical name you want to give clients. Clients who have no business knowing *anything* about the *real* physical structure of your web app.

With servlet mappings, you have two structures to organize: the *real* physical directory and file structure in which your web app resources live, and the *virtual/logical* structure.

The THREE types of <url-pattern> elements

1 EXACT match

```
<url-pattern>/Beer/SelectBeer.do</url-pattern>
```

MUST begin with a slash (/).

Can have an extension, but it's not required.

2 DIRECTORY match

```
<url-pattern>/Beer/*</url-pattern>
```

MUST begin with a slash (/).

This can be a virtual OR real directory.

Always ends with a slash/asterisk (/*).

3 EXTENSION match

```
<url-pattern>*.do</url-pattern>
```

MUST begin with an asterisk (*) (NEVER with a slash).

After the asterisk, it MUST have a dot extension (.do, .jsp, etc.).

The virtual/logical structure exists simply because you SAY it exists!

The URL patterns in the DD don't map to anything except other <servlet-name> elements in the DD.

The <servlet-name> elements are the key to servlet mapping—they match a request <url-pattern> to an actual servlet class.

Key point: clients request servlets by <url-pattern>, NOT by <servlet-name> or <servlet-class>!

BE the Container

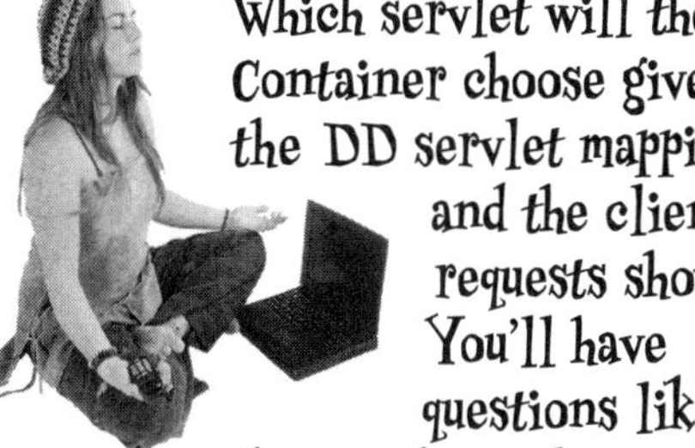

Which servlet will the Container choose given the DD servlet mappings and the client requests shown? You'll have questions like this on the real exam!

Key rules about servlet mappings

1) The Container looks for matches in the order shown on the opposite page. In other words, it looks first for an exact match. If it can't find an *exact* match, it looks for a directory match. If it can't find a *directory* match, it looks for an *extension* match.

2) If a request matches more than one directory <url-pattern>, the Container chooses the longest mapping. In other words, a request for /foo/bar/myStuff.do will map to the <url-pattern> /foo/bar/* even though it also matches the <url-pattern> /foo/*. The most *specific* match always wins.

Mappings:

```
<servlet>
  <servlet-name>One</servlet-name>
  <servlet-class>foo.DeployTestOne</servlet-class>
</servlet>

<servlet-mapping>
  <servlet-name>One</servlet-name>
  <url-pattern>*.do</url-pattern>
</servlet-mapping>


<servlet>
  <servlet-name>Two</servlet-name>
  <servlet-class>foo.DeployTestTwo</servlet-class>
</servlet>

<servlet-mapping>
  <servlet-name>Two</servlet-name>
  <url-pattern>/fooStuff/bar</url-pattern>
</servlet-mapping>


<servlet>
  <servlet-name>Three</servlet-name>
  <servlet-class>foo.DeployTestThree</servlet-class>
</servlet>

<servlet-mapping>
  <servlet-name>Three</servlet-name>
  <url-pattern>/fooStuff/*</url-pattern>
</servlet-mapping>
```

Requests:

http://localhost:8080/MapTest/blue.do
Container choice:

http://localhost:8080/MapTest/fooStuff/bar
Container choice:

http://localhost:8080/MapTest/fooStuff/bar/blue.do
Container choice:

http://localhost:8080/MapTest/fooStuff/blue.do
Container choice:

http://localhost:8080/MapTest/fred/blue.do
Container choice:

http://localhost:8080/MapTest/fooStuff
Container choice:

http://localhost:8080/MapTest/fooStuff/bar/foo.fo
Container choice:

http://localhost:8080/MapTest/fred/blue.fo
Container choice:

BE the Container

Answers

Mappings:

```
<servlet>
  <servlet-name>One</servlet-name>
  <servlet-class>foo.DeployTestOne</servlet-class>
</servlet>

<servlet-mapping>
  <servlet-name>One</servlet-name>
  <url-pattern>*.do</url-pattern>
</servlet-mapping>


<servlet>
  <servlet-name>Two</servlet-name>
  <servlet-class>foo.DeployTestTwo</servlet-class>
</servlet>

<servlet-mapping>
  <servlet-name>Two</servlet-name>
  <url-pattern>/fooStuff/bar</url-pattern>
</servlet-mapping>


<servlet>
  <servlet-name>Three</servlet-name>
  <servlet-class>foo.DeployTestThree</servlet-class>
</servlet>

<servlet-mapping>
  <servlet-name>Three</servlet-name>
  <url-pattern>/fooStuff/*</url-pattern>
</servlet-mapping>
```

Requests:

http://localhost:8080/MapTest/blue.do
Container choice: DeployTestOne
(matched the *.do *extension* pattern)

http://localhost:8080/MapTest/fooStuff/bar
Container choice: DeployTestTwo
(*exact* match with /fooStuff/bar pattern)

http://localhost:8080/MapTest/fooStuff/bar/blue.do
Container choice: DeployTestThree
(matched the /fooStuff/* *directory* pattern)

http://localhost:8080/MapTest/fooStuff/blue.do
Container choice: DeployTestThree
(matched /fooStuff/* *directory* pattern)

http://localhost:8080/MapTest/fred/blue.do
Container choice: DeployTestOne
(matched the *.do *extension* pattern)

http://localhost:8080/MapTest/fooStuff
Container choice: DeployTestThree
(matched the /fooStuff/* *directory* pattern)

http://localhost:8080/MapTest/fooStuff/bar/foo.fo
Container choice: DeployTestThree
(matched the /fooStuff/* *directory* pattern)

http://localhost:8080/MapTest/fred/blue.fo
Container choice: 404 NOT FOUND
(doesn't match ANYTHING)

Answers to the exercise on the opposite page:

1) DeployTestFour 2) DeployTestTwo

Subtle issues...

Just to make sure you understand servlet mappings, here's one more little example. Don't skim—look closely at both the mapping and the requests. (In this mini "Be the Container", the answers are at the bottom of the opposite page, so don't peek.)

BE the Container

Which servlet will the Container choose?

Mappings in the DD

```
<servlet>
    <servlet-name>Two</servlet-name>
    <servlet-class>foo.DeployTestTwo</servlet-class>
</servlet>
<servlet-mapping>
    <servlet-name>Two</servlet-name>
    <url-pattern>/fooStuff/bar</url-pattern>
</servlet-mapping>

<servlet>
    <servlet-name>Four</servlet-name>
    <servlet-class>foo.DeployTestFour</servlet-class>
</servlet>
<servlet-mapping>
    <servlet-name>Four</servlet-name>
    <url-pattern>/fooStuff/bar/*</url-pattern>
</servlet-mapping>
```

Requests:

1. http://localhost:8080/test/fooStuff/bar/
   Container choice:

2. http://localhost:8080/test/fooStuff/bar
   Container choice:

Configuring welcome files in the DD

You already know that if you type in the name of a web site and you don't specify a specific file, you (usually) still get something back. Entering *http://www.oreilly.com* into your browser takes you to the O'Reilly web site, and even though you didn't name a specific resource (like "home.html", for example), you still get a *default* page.

You can configure your server to define a default page for the entire *site*, but we're concerned here with default (also known as "welcome") pages for individual *web apps*. You configure welcome pages in the DD, and that DD determines what the Container chooses when the client enters a *partial* URL—a URL that includes a directory, for example, but not a specific resource in the directory.

In other words, what happens if the client request comes in for:

http://www.wickedlysmart.com/foo/bar ← "bar" is just a directory

and "bar" is simply a directory, and you don't have a specific servlet mapped to this URL pattern. What will the client see?

In the DD:

```
<web-app ...>
   <welcome-file-list>
       <welcome-file>index.html</welcome-file>
       <welcome-file>default.jsp</welcome-file>
   </welcome-file-list>
</web-app>
```

They must NOT start or end with a slash!

Imagine you have a web app where several different directories have their own default HTML page, named "index.html". But *some* directories use a "default.jsp" instead. It would be a huge pain if you had to specify a specific default page or JSP for each directory that needs one. Instead, you specify a list, in order, of the pages you want the Container to look for in whatever directory the partial request is for. In other words, no matter which directory is requested, the Container always looks through the same list—the one and only <welcome-file-list>.

The Container will pick the *first* match it finds, starting with the first welcome file listed in the <welcome-file-list>.

Multiple welcome files go in a single DD element.

*No matter how many welcome files you might list, you put them ALL into a single entry in the DD: <welcome-file-**list**>. It's tempting to think that each file might go in a separate <welcome-file-list> element, but that's not how it works! Each file has its own <welcome-file> element, but you put ALL of them within a single <welcome-file-**list**>.*

The files in the <welcome-file> element do NOT start with a slash!

Don't be confused. The way in which the Container matches and chooses welcome files is not the same as the way in which it matches URL patterns. If you put the slash in front of the file name, you'll be violating the spec, and bad things will happen.

BE the Container

Which welcome files will the Container choose given the DD and the client requests shown? You can expect something like this on the exam.

The DD:

```
<welcome-file-list>
   <welcome-file>index.html</welcome-file>
   <welcome-file>default.jsp</welcome-file>
</welcome-file-list>
```

Directory structure:

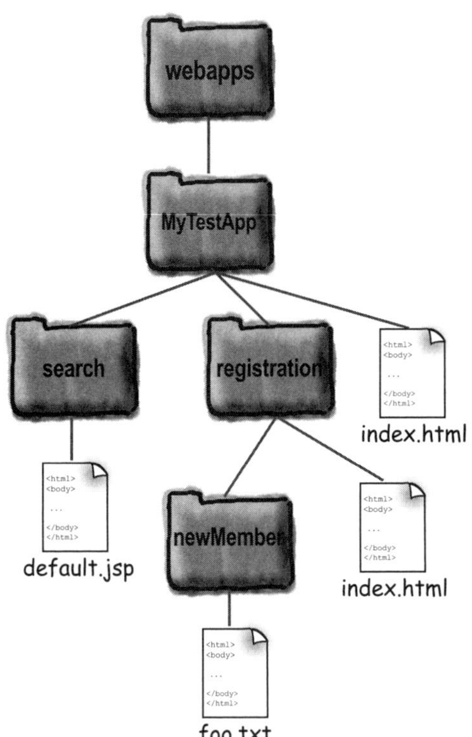

Requests:

http://localhost:8080/MyTestApp/

Container choice:

---

http://localhost:8080/MyTestApp/registration/

Container choice:

---

http://localhost:8080/MyTestApp/search

Container choice:

---

http://localhost:8080/MyTestApp/registration/newMember/

Container choice:

BE the Container

Answers

The DD:

```
<welcome-file-list>
   <welcome-file>index.html</welcome-file>
   <welcome-file>default.jsp</welcome-file>
</welcome-file-list>
```

Directory structure:

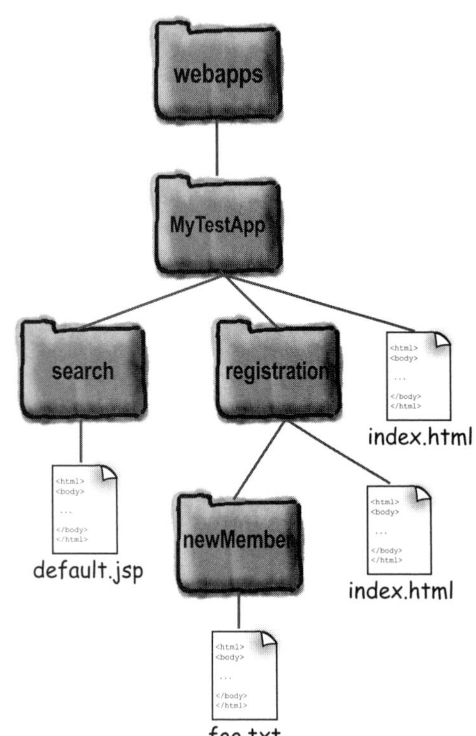

Requests:

http://localhost:8080/MyTestApp/

Container choice:
MyTestApp/index.html

---

http://localhost:8080/MyTestApp/registration/

Container choice:
MyTestApp/registration/index.html

---

http://localhost:8080/MyTestApp/search

Container choice:
MyTestApp/search/default.jsp
(If there HAD been both a default.jsp and an index.html in the "search" directory, the Container would have chosen the "index.html" file, since it is listed first in the DD.)

---

http://localhost:8080/MyTestApp/registration/newMember/

Container choice:
When no files from the <welcome-file-list> are found, the behavior is vendor-specific. *Tomcat* shows a directory listing for the newMember directory (which shows "foo.txt"). Another Container might show a 404 Not Found error.

How the Container chooses a welcome file

1

Client requests: http://www.wickedlysmart.com/MyTestApp/search

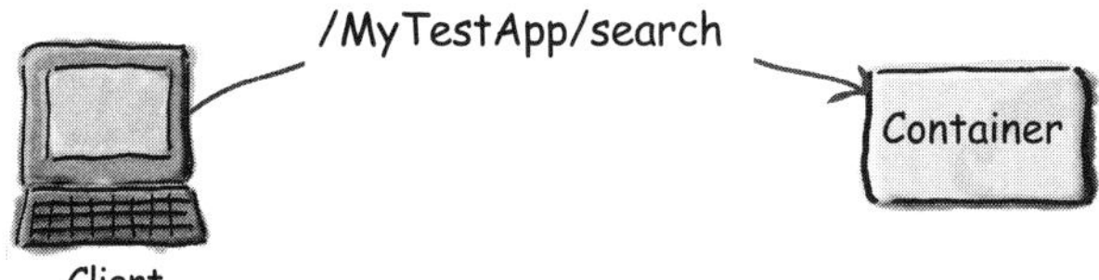

Container looks in the DD for a servlet mapping, and doesn't find a match. Next, the Container looks in the <welcome-file-list> and sees "index.html" at the top.

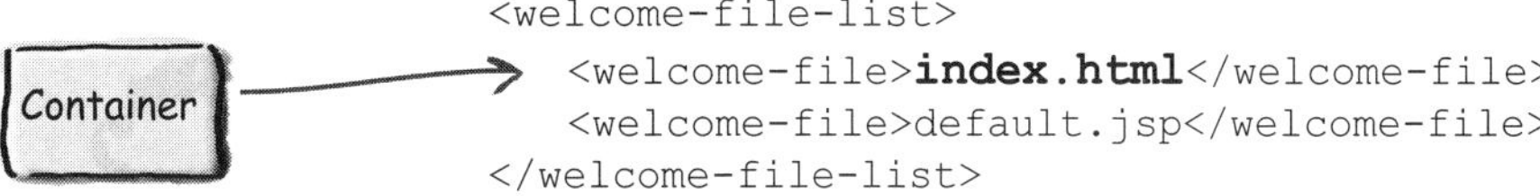

3

Container looks in the /MyTestApp/search directory for an "index.html" file, but does not find one.

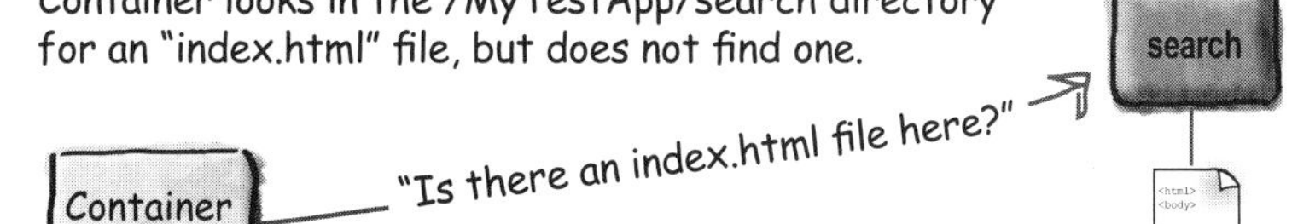

4

Container looks at the next <welcome-file> in the <welcome-file-list> in the DD, and sees "default.jsp".

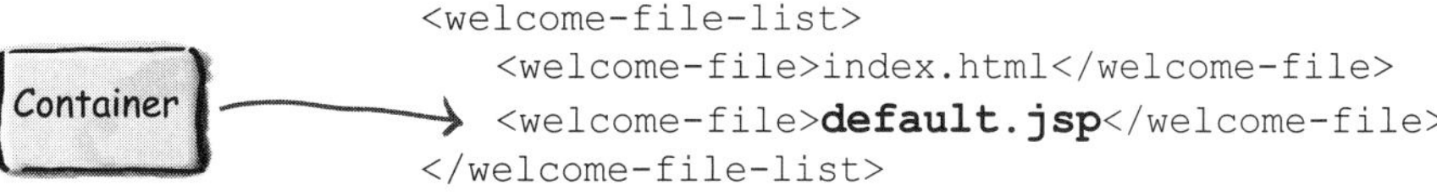

5

Container looks in the /MyTestApp/search directory for a "default.jsp" file, finds one, and serves its response to the client.

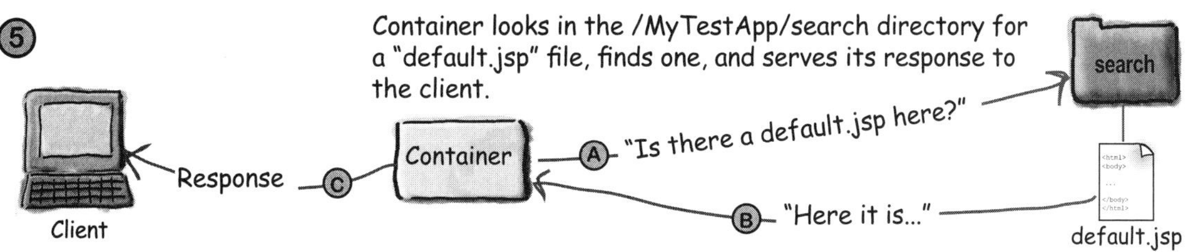

Configuring error pages in the DD

Sure, you want to be friendly when the user doesn't know the exact resource to ask for when they get to your site or web app, so you specify default/welcome files. But you also want to be friendly when *things go wrong*. We already looked at this in the chapter on Using Custom Tags, so this is just a review.

Declaring a catch-all error page

This applies to everything in your web app—not just JSPs.

```
<error-page>
  <exception-type>java.lang.Throwable</exception-type>
  <location>/errorPage.jsp</location>
</error-page>
```

(FYI: you can override this in individual JSPs by adding a page directive with an *errorPage* attribute.)

Declaring an error page for a more explicit exception

This configures an error page that's called only when there's an ArithmeticException. If you have both this declaration and the catch-all above, then any exception other than ArithmeticException will still end up at the "errorPage.jsp".

```
<error-page>
  <exception-type>java.lang.ArithmeticException</exception-type>
  <location>/arithmeticError.jsp</location>
</error-page>
```

Declaring an error page based on an HTTP status code

This configures an error page that's called only when the status code for the response is "404" (file not found).

```
<error-page>
  <error-code>404</error-code>
  <location>/notFoundError.jsp</location>
</error-page>
```

You can't use <error-code> and <exception-type> together!

You can configure an error page based on the HTTP status code OR based on the exception type thrown, but you CANNOT have both in the same <error-page> tag.

there are no Dumb Questions

Q: What are you allowed to declare as an exception type in <exception-type>?

A: Anything that's a Throwable, so that includes java.lang.Error, runtime exceptions, and any checked exception (as long as the checked exception class is on the Container's classpath, of course).

Q: Speaking of error handling, can you programmatically generate error codes yourself?

A: Yes, you can. You can invoke the sendError() method on the HttpServletResponse, and it'll tell the Container to generate that error just as if the Container generated the error on its own. And if you've configured an error page to be sent to the client based on that error code, that's what the client will get. And by the way, "error" codes are also known as "status" codes, so if you see either one, they mean the same thing—HTTP codes for errors.

Q: How about an example of generating your own error code?

A: OK, here's an example:

```
response.sendError(HttpServletResponse.SC_FORBIDDEN);
```

which is the same as:

```
response.sendError(403);
```

If you look in the HttpServletResponse interface, you'll see a bunch of constants defined for the common HTTP error/status codes. Keep in mind that for the exam, you don't need to memorize the status codes! It's enough to simply know that you *can* generate error codes, that the method is **response.sendError()**, and that in terms of the error pages you've defined in the DD, or any other error-handling you do in your JSPs, there's no difference between Container-generated and programmer-generated HTTP errors. A 403 is a 403 regardless of WHO sends the error. Oh yeah, there's also an overloaded two-argument version of sendError() that takes an int and a String message.

You must use the fully-qualified class name in <exception-type>!

Don't be fooled by something like this:

```
<exception-type>
      IOException
</exception-type>
```

You MUST use the fully-qualified class name, and any Throwable is allowed.

Configuring servlet initialization in the DD

You already know that servlets, by default, are initialized at first request. That means the first client suffers the pain of class loading, instantiation, and initialization (setting a ServletContext, invoking listeners, etc.), before the Container can do what it normally does—allocate a thread and invoke the servlet's service() method.

If you want servlets to be loaded at deploy time (or at server restart time) rather than on first request, use the <load-on-startup> element in the DD. Any non-negative value for <load-on-startup> tells the Container to initialize the servlet when the app is deployed (or any time the server restarts).

If you have multiple servlets that you want preloaded, and you want to control the order in which they're initialized, the value of <load-on-startup> determines the order! In other words, any non-negative value means load early, but the order in which servlets are loaded is based on the value of the different <load-on-startup> elements.

Being the ***first*** client to request a servlet SUCKS unless the developer uses <load-on-startup>.

In the DD

```
<servlet>
    <servlet-name>KathyOne</servlet-name>
    <servlet-class>foo.DeployTestOne</servlet-class>
    <load-on-startup>1</load-on-startup>
</servlet>
```

Any number greater than zero means "initialize this servlet at deployment or server startup time, rather than waiting for the first request."

Values greater than one do not affect the number of servlet instances!

The value you use:
*<load-on-startup>**4**</load-on-startup> does NOT mean "load four instances of the servlet". It means that this servlet should be loaded only AFTER servlets with a <load-on-startup> number less than four are loaded. And what if there's more than one servlet with a <load-on-startup> of **4**? The Container loads servlets with the same value in the order in which the servlets are declared in the DD.*

Q: Wouldn't you ALWAYS want to do this? Shouldn't everyone just use <load-on-startup>1</load-on-startup> by default?

A: To answer that question, you ask yourself, "How many servlets do I have in my app, and how likely is it that they'll all be used?" And you'll also need to ask, "How long does it take each servlet to load?" Some servlets are rarely used, so you might want to conserve resources by not loading the rarely-used servlets in advance. But some servlets take so painfully long to initialize (like the Struts *ActionServlet*), that you don't want even a single client to experience that much latency. So, only you can decide, and you'll probably decide on a servlet-by-servlet basis, evaluating both the pain level and likelihood of use for each servlet.

Making an XML-compliant JSP: a JSP Document

This topic didn't fit well anywhere else, so we decided to stick it in this chapter since we're talking about XML so much. The exam doesn't require you to be an XML expert, but you do have to know two things: the syntax for the key DD elements, and the basics of making what's known as a *JSP Document.* ("As opposed to *what*? If a normal JSP isn't a document, what is it?" That's what you're asking, right? Think of it this way—a normal JSP is a *page*, unless it's written with the XML alternatives to normal JSP syntax, in which case it becomes a *document.*)

All it means is that there are really *two* types of syntax you can use to make a JSP. The text in grey is the same across both types of syntax.

	Normal JSP *page* syntax	**JSP *document* syntax**
Directives (except taglib)	`<%@ page import="java.util.*" %>`	`<jsp:directive.page import="java.util.*"/>`

Declaration	`<%! int y = 3; %>`	`<jsp:declaration>`
		`int y = 3;`
		`</jsp:declaration>`

Scriptlet	`<% list.add("Fred"); %>`	`<jsp:scriptlet>`
		`list.add("Fred");`
		`</jsp:scriptlet>`

Text	`There is no spoon.`	`<jsp:text>`
		`There is no spoon.`
		`</jsp:text>`

Scripting Expression	`<%= it.next() %>`	`<jsp:expression>`
		`it.next()`
		`</jsp:expression>`

Relax ***This is all the exam covers on JSP Documents.***

We aren't going to say any more about it because writing XML-compliant JSP documents is probably not something you'll do. The XML syntax is used mainly by tools, and the table above just shows you how the tool would transform your normal JSP syntax into an XML document. There IS more you have to know if you write this by hand—the whole document, for example, must be enclosed in a <jsp:root> tag (which includes some other stuff), and the taglib directives go inside the <jsp:root> opening tag, rather than as a <jsp:directive>. But everything that might be on the exam is in the table above. So relax.

Memorizing the EJB-related DD tags

This exam is about web components, not business components (although in the Patterns chapter, you'll see a few things about business components). But if you're deploying a J2EE app, complete with Enterprise JavaBeans (EJBs) in the business tier, some of your web components will probably need to lookup and access the enterprise beans. If you're deploying an app in a full J2EE-compliant Container (one that has an EJB Container as well), you can define references to EJBs in the DD. You don't have to know *anything* about EJBs for this exam, other than what you declare in the DD, so we won't waste your time explaining it here.*

Reference to a local bean

The JNDI lookup name you'll use in code.

```
<ejb-local-ref>
   <ejb-ref-name>ejb/Customer</ejb-ref-name>
   <ejb-ref-type>Entity</ejb-ref-type>
   <local-home>com.wickedlysmart.CustomerHome</local-home>
   <local>com.wickedlysmart.Customer</local>
</ejb-local-ref>
```

These must be fully-qualified names of the bean's exposed interfaces.

A **LOCAL** bean means the client (in this case, a servlet) and the bean *must* be running in the same JVM.

Reference to a remote bean

```
<ejb-ref>
   <ejb-ref-name>ejb/LocalCustomer</ejb-ref-name>
   <ejb-ref-type>Entity</ejb-ref-type>
   <home>com.wickedlysmart.CustomerHome</home>
   <remote>com.wickedlysmart.Customer</remote>
</ejb-ref>
```

(Optional sub-elements for both tags include <description> and <ejb-link>, but you don't need to know that for the exam.)

A **REMOTE** bean means the client (in this case, a servlet) and the bean can be running in different JVMs (possibly on different physical machines as well).

* But if you're interested in EJB, there's this really good book...

The LOCAL and REMOTE tags are inconsistent!

Both the local and remote bean DD tags have two elements that are the same:

The <ejb-ref-name> that lists the logical lookup name you'll use in code to perform a JNDI lookup on an enterprise bean's home interface. (Don't worry if you haven't used EJBs before and don't know what that last sentence means—you don't need EJB knowledge for this exam.)

The <ejb-ref-type> describes whether this is an Entity or Session bean. Those two elements, the lookup name and the bean type, don't depend on whether the bean is local (running in the same JVM as the web component), or remote (potentially running in a different JVM).

But... look at the other elements starting with the outer tags: <ejb-local-ref> and <ejb-ref>. You might be tempted to think that it's:

<ejb-**local**-ref> ← Yes

<ejb-**remote**-ref> ← Wrong!!

But NO! For remote beans, it's just:

<ejb-ref> ← Right! There's no "remote" in the tag.

In other words, the local reference says it's local, but the remote reference does NOT include the word "remote" in its tag element name. Why? Because at the time <ejb-ref> was first defined, there was no such thing as "local" EJBs. Since ALL enterprise beans were "remote", there was no need to differentiate between local and remote, so no need to put "remote" in the name of the tag.

This also explains the OTHER tag naming inconsistency—the name of the tag for the bean's home interface. A local bean uses:

<**local**-home> ← Yes

but a remote bean does NOT use:

<**remote**-home> ← Wrong!!

For remote beans, it's just:

<home>

Memorizing the JNDI <env-entry> DD tag

If you're familiar with EJB and/or JNDI, this will make sense. If you're not, it doesn't really matter for the exam as long as you memorize the tag. (The details surrounding JNDI environment entries are covered in EJB/J2EE books like the lovely *Head First EJB.*)

Think of an environment entry as being something like a deploy-time constant that your app can use, much like servlet and context init parameters. In other words, a way for the deployer to pass values into the servlet (or in this case, an EJB as well if this is deployed as part of an enterprise application in a fully J2EE-compliant server).

At deploy time, the Container reads the DD and makes a JNDI entry (again, assuming this is a fully J2EE-compliant app, and not just a server with only a *web* Container), using the name and value you supply in this DD tag. At runtime, a component in the application can look up the value in JNDI, using the name listed in the DD. You probably won't care about <env-entry> unless you're also developing with EJBs, so the only reason you need to memorize this is for the exam.

Declaring an app's JNDI environment entry

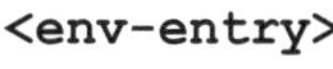

```
<env-entry>
    <env-entry-name>rates/discountRate</env-entry-name>
    <env-entry-type>java.lang.Integer</env-entry-type>
    <env-entry-value>10</env-entry-value>
</env-entry>
```

The lookup name you'll use in code.

This can be any type that takes a single String as a constructor parameter (or a single Character if it's java.lang.Character).

This will be passed in as a String (or a single Character if the <env-entry-type> is java.lang.Character).

The <env-entry-type> must NOT be a primitive!

When you see an <env-entry-value> that's an integer value (like the example above), you might think that the <env-entry-type> can be a primitive. But that would be... wrong.
You also might be tempted to think that you can have only Strings and wrappers, but that's wrong too—you can use any type that takes a single String in its constructor (or a single Character for a Character type).

Note: you can also include an optional <description>, which is a REALLY REALLY good idea.

Memorizing the <mime-mapping> DD tag

You can configure a mapping between an extension and a mime type in the DD. This will probably be the easiest tag to remember, because it just makes sense—you map between an *extension* and a *mime-type*, and guess what? In a rare moment of simplicity and clarity, they named the tag sub-elements "extension" and "mime-type". That means you have to remember only one thing—*that the tag elements are named for exactly what they are!*

Unless you start thinking of it as "file-type" and "content-type". But no, you won't do that. You'll memorize it just like this.

Declaring a <mime-mapping>

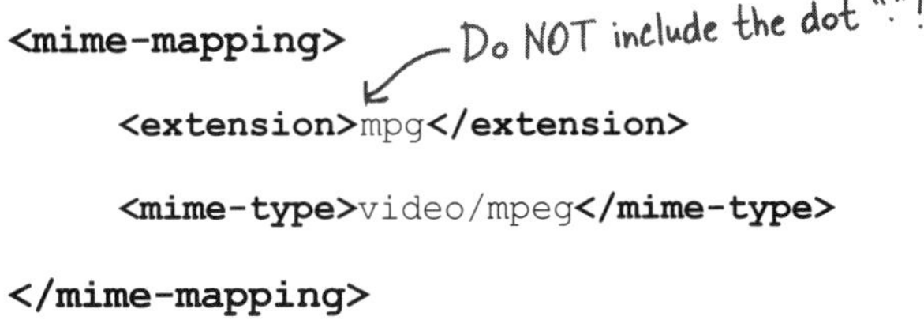


```
<mime-mapping>
    <extension>mpg</extension>
    <mime-type>video/mpeg</mime-type>
</mime-mapping>
```

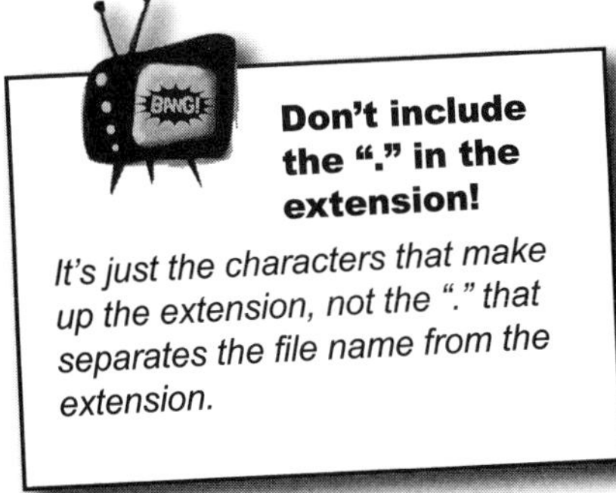

BANG!
Don't include the "." in the extension!
It's just the characters that make up the extension, not the "." that separates the file name from the extension.

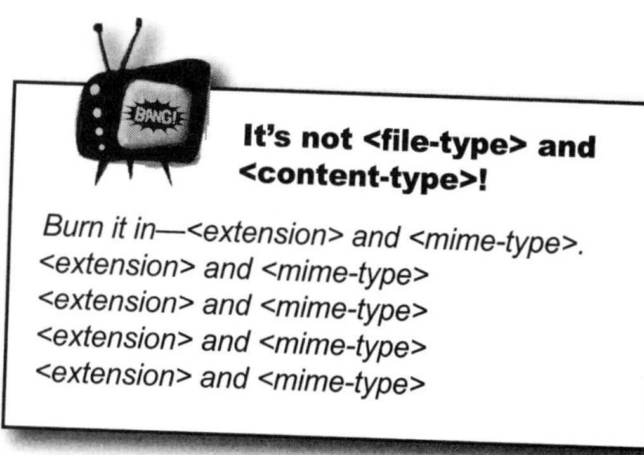

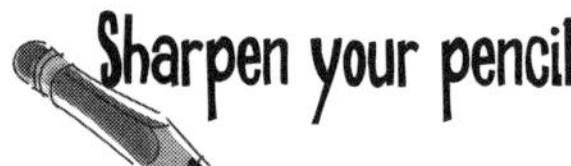

Where things go

Fill in this table with explicit notes on where in the web app the given resource must be placed. We did the first one for you. Turn the page for the answers.

Resource type	Deployment location
Deployment Descriptor (web.xml)	Directly inside WEB-INF (which is directly inside the root of the web app).
Tag Files (.tag or .tagx)	
HTML and JSPs (That you want to be directly accessible.)	
HTML and JSPs (That you want to "hide" from direct client access.)	
TLDs (.tld)	
Servlet classes	
Tag Handler classes	
JAR files	

Memorizing DD tags

If you're NOT planning on taking the exam, don't worry about getting all of these right (although the bottom two elements are important to almost everyone).

If you ARE going to take the exam, you should spend some time memorizing these.

```
<______________>

   <______________>ejb/Customer<______________>
   <ejb-ref-type>Entity</ejb-ref-type>

   <____________>com.wickedlysmart.CustomerHome<_____________>
   <local>com.wickedlysmart.Customer</local>

<______________>
```

```
<ejb-ref>

   <______________>ejb/LocalCustomer<______________>
   <ejb-ref-type>Entity</ejb-ref-type>

   <________>com.wickedlysmart.CustomerHome<_________>

   <________>com.wickedlysmart.Customer<_________>
</ejb-ref>
```

```
<env-entry>

   <________________>rates/discountRate<________________>

   <________________>java.lang.Integer<________________>

   <env-entry-value>10</env-entry-value>

</env-entry>
```

```
<error-page>
   <________________>java.io.IOException<________________>

   <________>/myerror.jsp<         >________
</error-page>
```

```
<________________>
   <welcome-file>index.html</welcome-file>

<________________>
```

Where things go

Fill in this table with explicit notes on where in the web app the resource must be placed. We did the first one for you.

Resource type	Deployment location
Deployment Descriptor (web.xml)	Directly inside WEB-INF (which is directly inside the root of the web app).
Tag Files (.tag or .tagx)	If NOT deployed inside a JAR, Tag Files must be inside WEB-INF/tags, or a subdirectory of WEB-INF/tags. If deployed in a JAR, Tag Files must be in META-INF/tags, or a subdirectory of META-INF/tags. Note: Tag Files deployed in a JAR must have a TLD in the JAR.
HTML and JSPs (That you want to be directly accessible.)	Client-accessible HTML and JSPs can be anywhere under the root of the web app or any of its subdirectories, EXCEPT they cannot be under WEB-INF (including subdirectories). In a WAR file, they can't be under META-INF (including subdirectories).
HTML and JSPs (That you want to "hide" from direct client access.)	Pages under WEB-INF (or META-INF in a WAR file) cannot be directly accessed by clients.
TLDs (.tld)	If NOT inside a JAR, TLD files must be somewhere under WEB-INF or a subdirectory of WEB-INF. If deployed in a JAR, TLD files must be somewhere under META-INF, or a subdirectory of META-INF.
Servlet classes	Servlet classes must be in a directory structure matching the package structure, placed directory under WEB-INF/classes (for example, class com.example.Ring would be inside WEB-INF/classes/com/example), or in the appropriate package directories within a JAR inside WEB-INF/lib).
Tag Handler classes	Actually ALL classes used by the web-app (unless they're part of the class libraries on the classpath) must follow the same rules as servlet classes—inside WEB-INF/classes, in a directory structure matching the package (or in the appropriate package directories within a JAR inside WEB-INF/lib).
JAR files	JAR files must be inside the WEB-INF/lib directory.

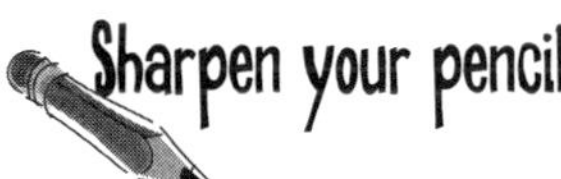

Memorizing DD tags

ANSWERS

If you are going to take the exam, you should spend some time memorizing ALL of these (plus any of the others from from this chapter and the security-related tags you'll see in the next chapter).

A reference to a bean that has a "local" interface.

```
< ejb-local-ref >
   < ejb-ref-name >ejb/Customer< /ejb-ref-name >
   <ejb-ref-type>Entity</ejb-ref-type>
   < local-home >com.wickedlysmart.CustomerHome< /local-home >
   <local>com.wickedlysmart.Customer</local>
< /ejb-local-ref >
```

A reference to a bean that has a "remote" interface.

```
<ejb-ref>
   < ejb-ref-name >ejb/LocalCustomer< /ejb-ref-name >
   <ejb-ref-type>Entity</ejb-ref-type>
   < home >com.wickedlysmart.CustomerHome< /home >
   < remote >com.wickedlysmart.Customer< /remote >
</ejb-ref>
```

An environment entry is a way to get deploy-time constants into a J2EE application.

```
<env-entry>
   < env-entry-name >rates/discountRate< /env-entry-name >
   < env-entry-type >java.lang.Integer< /env-entry-type >
   <env-entry-value>10</env-entry-value>
</env-entry>
```

Tells the Container which page to show when the specified <exception-type> occurs.

```
<error-page>
   < exception-type >java.io.IOException< /exception-type >
   < location >/myerror.jsp< /location >
</error-page>
```

Tells the Container which page to look for when a request comes in that doesn't match a specific resource. There can be more than one <welcome-file> specified in the <welcome-file-list>.

```
< welcome-file-list >
   <welcome-file>index.html</welcome-file>
< /welcome-file-list >
```

Mock Exam Chapter 11

1 Where can **<init-param>** elements appear in the DD? (Choose all that apply.)

- ❏ A. As child elements of **<servlet>**.
- ❏ B. As direct descendants of **<web-application>** elements.
- ❏ C. Just after the Document Type Declaration.
- ❏ D. Inside of **<context-param>** elements when you want to declare a context initialization parameter.

2 Where do you store Tag Library Descriptors (TLDs), in a web application? (Choose all that apply.)

- ❏ A. Only in **/WEB-INF/lib**.
- ❏ B. Only in **/WEB-INF/classes**.
- ❏ C. In the **/META-INF** directory of a JAR file inside **/WEB-INF/lib**
- ❏ D. At the application's top-level directory.
- ❏ E. In **/WEB-INF** or a sub-directory thereof.

3 Which statements about WAR files are true? (Choose all that apply.)

- ❏ A. WAR stands for Web Application Resources file.
- ❏ B. A valid WAR file must contain a deployment descriptor.
- ❏ C. Several WAR files can compose a web application.
- ❏ D. A WAR file cannot contain embedded JAR files.

4 The following servlet is declared in the DD:

```
<servlet>
  <servlet-name>MyServlet</servlet-name>
  <servlet-class>com.myorg.ServletClass</servlet-class>
</servlet>
```

Where can you store the servlet class in the web application? (Choose all that apply.)

- ❑ A. In **/META-INF** of a JAR file.
- ❑ B. In the package-related directory tree begining at the top level of the application directory.
- ❑ C. In **/WEB-INF/classes** or in a JAR file in **/WEB-INF/lib**.
- ❑ D. In **/WEB-INF/lib** outside of a JAR file.

---

5 What is the purpose of the deployment descriptor (DD)? (Choose all that apply.)

- ❑ A. To allow code-generation tools to dynamically create servlets from an XML file.
- ❑ B. To convey the web-application configuration information from developers to application assemblers and deployers.
- ❑ C. To configure vendor-specific aspects of the application.
- ❑ D. To configure only database and Enterprise JavaBean access from the web application.

---

6 Where should **web.xml** be stored in a WAR file? (Choose all that apply.)

- ❑ A. In **/WEB-INF/classes**.
- ❑ B. In **/WEB-INF/lib**.
- ❑ C. In **/WEB-INF**.
- ❑ D. In **/META-INF**.

---

7 Given:

```
10. <%@ page import="java.util.*" %>
11. <jsp:import import="java.util.*" />
12. <jsp:directive.page import="java.util.*" />
13. <jsp:page import="java.util.*" />
```

Assume the prefix "jsp" has been mapped to the namespace **`http://java.sun.com/JSP/Page`**.

Which are true? (Choose all that apply.)

❑ A. Lines 10 and 12 are equivalent in any type of JSP page.

❑ B. Line 10 is not valid in a JSP document (XML-based document).

❑ C. Line 11 will properly import the **`java.util`** package.

❑ D. Line 12 will properly import the **`java.util`** package.

❑ E. Line 13 will properly import the **`java.util`** package.

---

8 Which statements about **`<init-param>`** DD elements are true? (Choose all that apply.)

❑ A. They are used to declare initialization parameters for a specific servlet.

❑ B. They are used to declare initialization parameters for an entire web app.

❑ C. The method that retrieves these parameters returns an **`Object`**.

❑ D. The method that retrieves these parameters takes a String.

---

9 Which are DD elements that provide JNDI access to J2EE components? (Choose all that apply.)

❑ A. **`<ejb-ref>`**

❑ B. **`<entity-ref>`**

❑ C. **`<resource-ref>`**

❑ D. **`<session-ref>`**

❑ E. **`<message-ref>`**

10 The following servlet is registered in the DD:

```
<servlet>
  <servlet-name>action</servlet-name>
  <servlet-class>com.myorg.ActionClass</servlet-class>
</servlet>
```

Choose the correct mappings for this servlet. (Choose all that apply.)

❑ A.
```
<servlet-mapping>
    <servlet-name>action</servlet-name>
    <url-pattern>*.do</url-pattern>
</servlet-mapping>
```

❑ B.
```
<servlet-mapping>
    <servlet-name>com.myorg.ActionClass</servlet-name>
    <url-pattern>*.do</url-pattern>
</servlet-mapping>
```

❑ C.
```
<servlet-mapping>
    <servlet-name>action</servlet-name>
    <url-pattern>/controller</url-pattern>
</servlet-mapping>
```

❑ D.
```
<servlet-mapping>
    <url-pattern>*.do</url-pattern>
</servlet-mapping>
```

❑ E.
```
<servlet-mapping>
    <servlet-name>action</servlet-name>
</servlet-mapping>
```

11 For which type of web app components can dependencies be defined? (Choose all that apply.)

❑ A. JSP files

❑ B. WAR files

❑ C. classes

❑ D. libraries

❑ E. manifest files

12 Which are valid declarations in a JSP Document (XML-based document)? (Choose all that apply.)

- ❏ A.
```
<jsp:declaration
      xmlns:jsp="http://java.sun.com/JSP/Page">
  int x = 0;
  </jsp:declaration>
```
- ❏ B.
```
<jsp:declaration
       xmlns:jsp="http://java.sun.com/JSP/Page">
  int x;
  </jsp:declaration>
```
- ❏ C. `<%! int x = 0; %>`
- ❏ D. `<%! int x; %>`

13 Which 2.4 deployment descriptor elements may appear before the **<web-app>** element? (Choose all that apply.)

- ❏ A. **<listener>**
- ❏ B. **<context-param>**
- ❏ C. **<servlet>**
- ❏ D. No XML elements may appear before the **<web-app>** element.

14 Which statements concerning the container class loader are true? (Choose all that apply.)

- ❏ A. Web applications should NOT attempt to override container implementation classes.
- ❏ B. A web application must not attempt to load resources from within the WAR file using the J2SE semantics of getResource.
- ❏ C. A web application may override any J2EE classes in the javax.* namespace.
- ❏ D. A web developer may override J2EE platform classes provided they are contained in a library JAR within a WAR.

Chapter 11 Answers

1 Where can **<init-param>** elements appear in the DD? (Choose all that apply.)

(Servlet spec pg 107)

- [x] A. As child elements of **<servlet>**.
- [ ] B. As direct descendants of **<web-application>** elements.
- [ ] C. Just after the Document Type Declaration.
- [ ] D. Inside of **<context-param>** elements when you want to declare a context initialization parameter.

-Option B is incorrect because web.xml does not contain an element named <web-application>.

- Option D is incorrect because <context-param> elements do not contain <init-param>.

2 Where do you store Tag Library Descriptors (TLDs), in a web application? (Choose all that apply.)

(JSP spec pg 196)

- [ ] A. Only in **/WEB-INF/lib**.
- [ ] B. Only in **/WEB-INF/classes**.
- [x] C. In the **/META-INF** directory of a JAR file inside **/WEB-INF/lib**
- [ ] D. At the application's top-level directory.
- [x] E. In **/WEB-INF** or a sub-directory thereof.

-The container will not automatically discover TLDs if they are in /WEB-INF/classes or /WEB-INF/lib.

3 Which statements about WAR files are true? (Choose all that apply.)

(servlet spec 9.5 & 9.6)

- [ ] A. WAR stands for Web Application Resources file.
- [x] B. A valid WAR file must contain a deployment descriptor.
- [ ] C. Several WAR files can compose a web application.
- [ ] D. A WAR file cannot contain embedded JAR files.

-WAR stands for Web ARchive, and portions of a web application cannot be contained in a WAR file; only an entire application can reside within a WAR file.

4 The following servlet is declared in the DD: (Servlet spec p 70)

```
<servlet>
  <servlet-name>MyServlet</servlet-name>
  <servlet-class>com.myorg.ServletClass</servlet-class>
</servlet>
```

Where can you store the servlet class in the web application? (Choose all that apply.)

- [ ] A. In **/META-INF** of a JAR file.
- [ ] B. In the package-related directory tree begining at the top level of the application directory.
- [x] C. In **/WEB-INF/classes** or in a JAR file in **/WEB-INF/lib**.
- [ ] D. In **/WEB-INF/lib** outside of a JAR file.

–Option D is not correct because /WEB-INF/lib is designed as the container for JAR files.

5 What is the purpose of the deployment descriptor (DD)? (Choose all that apply.) (Servlet spec p 103)

- [ ] A. To allow code-generation tools to dynamically create servlets from an XML file.
- [x] B. To convey the web-application configuration information from developers to application assemblers and deployers.
- [ ] C. To configure vendor-specific aspects of the application.
- [ ] D. To configure only database and Enterprise JavaBean access from the web application.

–Option D is inaccurate because these concerns are just a subset of the DD's purpose.

6 Where should **web.xml** be stored in a WAR file? (Choose all that apply.) (Servlet spec p 70)

- [ ] A. In **/WEB-INF/classes**.
- [ ] B. In **/WEB-INF/lib**.
- [x] C. In **/WEB-INF**.
- [ ] D. In **/META-INF**.

–web.xml should be stored in /WEB-INF regardless of whether the deployment involves a WAR or an exploded directory structure.

7 Given:

(JSP v2.0 pg. 1-139)

```
10. <%@ page import="java.util.*" %>
11. <jsp:import import="java.util.*" />
12. <jsp:directive.page import="java.util.*" />
13. <jsp:page import="java.util.*" />
```

Assume the prefix "jsp" has been mapped to the namespace **http://java.sun.com/JSP/Page**.

Which are true? (Choose all that apply.)

- ☐ A. Lines 10 and 12 are equivalent in any type of JSP page.
- ☑ B. Line 10 is not valid in a JSP document (XML-based document).
- ☐ C. Line 11 will properly import the **java.util** package.
- ☑ D. Line 12 will properly import the **java.util** package.
- ☐ E. Line 13 will properly import the **java.util** package.

–Option A is incorrect because line 10 would be invalid in a JSP Document (XML–based document).

–Options C and E are invalid as they are not valid elements in the http://java.sun.com/JSP/Page namespace.

---

8 Which statements about **<init-param>** DD elements are true? (Choose all that apply.)

(servlet spec SRV.B & API)

- ☑ A. They are used to declare initialization parameters for a specific servlet.
- ☐ B. They are used to declare initialization parameters for an entire web app.
- ☐ C. The method that retrieves these parameters returns an **Object**.
- ☑ D. The method that retrieves these parameters takes a String.

–Initialization parameters can have web app scope or servlet scope. Those with servlet scope are named <init-param> in the DD, and take and return a String. Those with web app scope are named <context-param> in the DD and also take and return a String.

---

9 Which are DD elements that provide JNDI access to J2EE components? (Choose all that apply.)

(servlet spec 9.11)

- ☑ A. **<ejb-ref>**
- ☐ B. **<entity-ref>**
- ☑ C. **<resource-ref>**
- ☐ D. **<session-ref>**
- ☐ E. **<message-ref>**

–In addition, <ejb-local-ref> also provides the web app creator with a JNDI reference to J2EE components.

10 The following servlet is registered in the DD: (servlet spec pg 86)

```
<servlet>
  <servlet-name>action</servlet-name>
  <servlet-class>com.myorg.ActionClass</servlet-class>
</servlet>
```

Choose the correct mappings for this servlet. (Choose all that apply.)

☑ A.
```
<servlet-mapping>
    <servlet-name>action</servlet-name>
    <url-pattern>*.do</url-pattern>
  </servlet-mapping>
```

❑ B.
```
<servlet-mapping>
    <servlet-name>com.myorg.ActionClass</servlet-name>
    <url-pattern>*.do</url-pattern>
  </servlet-mapping>
```

–Option B is incorrect because it confuses the servlet name with the servlet class.

☑ C.
```
<servlet-mapping>
    <servlet-name>action</servlet-name>
    <url-pattern>/controller</url-pattern>
  </servlet-mapping>
```

❑ D.
```
<servlet-mapping>
    <url-pattern>*.do</url-pattern>
  </servlet-mapping>
```

–Option D is incorrect because it omits the <servlet-name> child element of <servlet-mapping>.

❑ E.
```
<servlet-mapping>
    <servlet-name>action</servlet-name>
  </servlet-mapping>
```

11 For which type of web app components can dependencies be defined? (Choose all that apply.) (servlet spec 9.7.1)

❑ A. JSP files

❑ B. WAR files

☑ C. classes

☑ D. libraries

❑ E. manifest files

– Libraries dependencies can be defined in the /META-INF/MANIFEST.MF file.

12 Which are valid declarations in a JSP Document (XML-based document)? (Choose all that apply.)

(JSP v2.0 pg. 1-139)

- [x] A.
```
<jsp:declaration
    xmlns:jsp="http://java.sun.com/JSP/Page">
int x = 0;
</jsp:declaration>
```

- [x] B.
```
<jsp:declaration
     xmlns:jsp="http://java.sun.com/JSP/Page">
int x;
</jsp:declaration>
```

- [ ] C. `<%! int x = 0; %>`

- [ ] D. `<%! int x; %>`

–Options C and D are incorrect because only the <jsp:declaration> syntax is valid in JSP Documents.

13 Which 2.4 deployment descriptor elements may appear before the **<web-app>** element? (Choose all that apply.)

(Servlet spec, p 107)

- [ ] A. **<listener>**
- [ ] B. **<context-param>**
- [ ] C. **<servlet>**
- [x] D. No XML elements may appear before the **<web-app>** element.

–The <web-app> element is the root element of the web application deployment descriptor.

14 Which statements concerning the container class loader are true? (Choose all that apply.)

(Servlet spec, 9.7.2)

- [x] A. Web applications should NOT attempt to override container implementation classes.
- [ ] B. A web application must not attempt to load resources from within the WAR file using the J2SE semantics of getResource.
- [ ] C. A web application may override any J2EE classes in the javax.* namespace.
- [ ] D. A web developer may override J2EE platform classes provided they are contained in a library JAR within a WAR.

–Option B is incorrect because the webapp may use the getResource method from the webapp's class loader to access any WAR file.

–Options C & D are incorrect because the webapp must NOT override any class in the java.* or javax.* namespaces.

12 web app security

Keep it secret, keep it safe

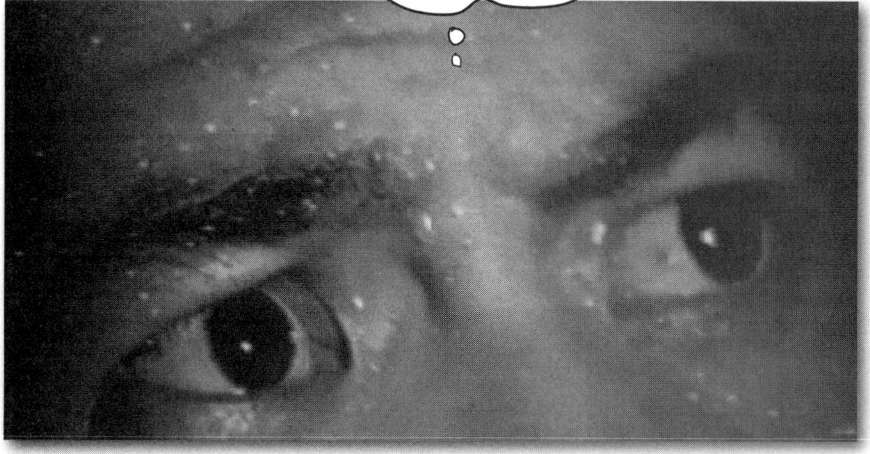

They're out there... The Bad Guys...they're everywhere! I *must* learn about Authentication, and Authorization... I *must* learn to transmit the data securely...I... I...
DID YOU HEAR THAT?

Your web app is in *danger*. Trouble lurks in every corner of the network, as crackers, scammers, and criminals try to break into your system to steal, take advantage, or just have a little fun with your site. You don't want the Bad Guys listening in to your online store transactions, picking off credit card numbers. You don't want the Bad Guys convincing your server that they're actually the Special Customers Who Get Big Discounts. And you don't want *anyone* (good OR bad) looking at sensitive employee data. Does Jim in marketing really need to know that Lisa in engineering makes three times as much as he does? And do you really want Jim to take matters into his own hands and login (unauthorized) to the UpdatePayroll servlet?

Servlets & JSP overview

5.1 Based on the servlet specification, compare and contrast the following security issues: (a) authentication, (b) authorization, (c) data integrity, and (d) confidentiality.

5.2 In the deployment descriptor, declare the following: a security constraint, a Web resource, the transport guarantee, the login configuration, and a security role.

5.3 Given an authentication type (BASIC, DIGEST, FORM, and CLIENT-CERT), describe its mechanism.

Coverage Notes:

All of the objectives in this section are covered completely in this chapter, including security-related DD elements that were NOT covered in the deployment chapter.

We can't make you a complete security being, but the content in this chapter is a start, and it's everything you need for the exam.

The Bad Guys are everywhere

As a web application developer you need to protect your web site. There are three main kinds of *bad guys* you need to watch out for: **Impersonators**, **Upgraders**, and **Eavesdroppers**.

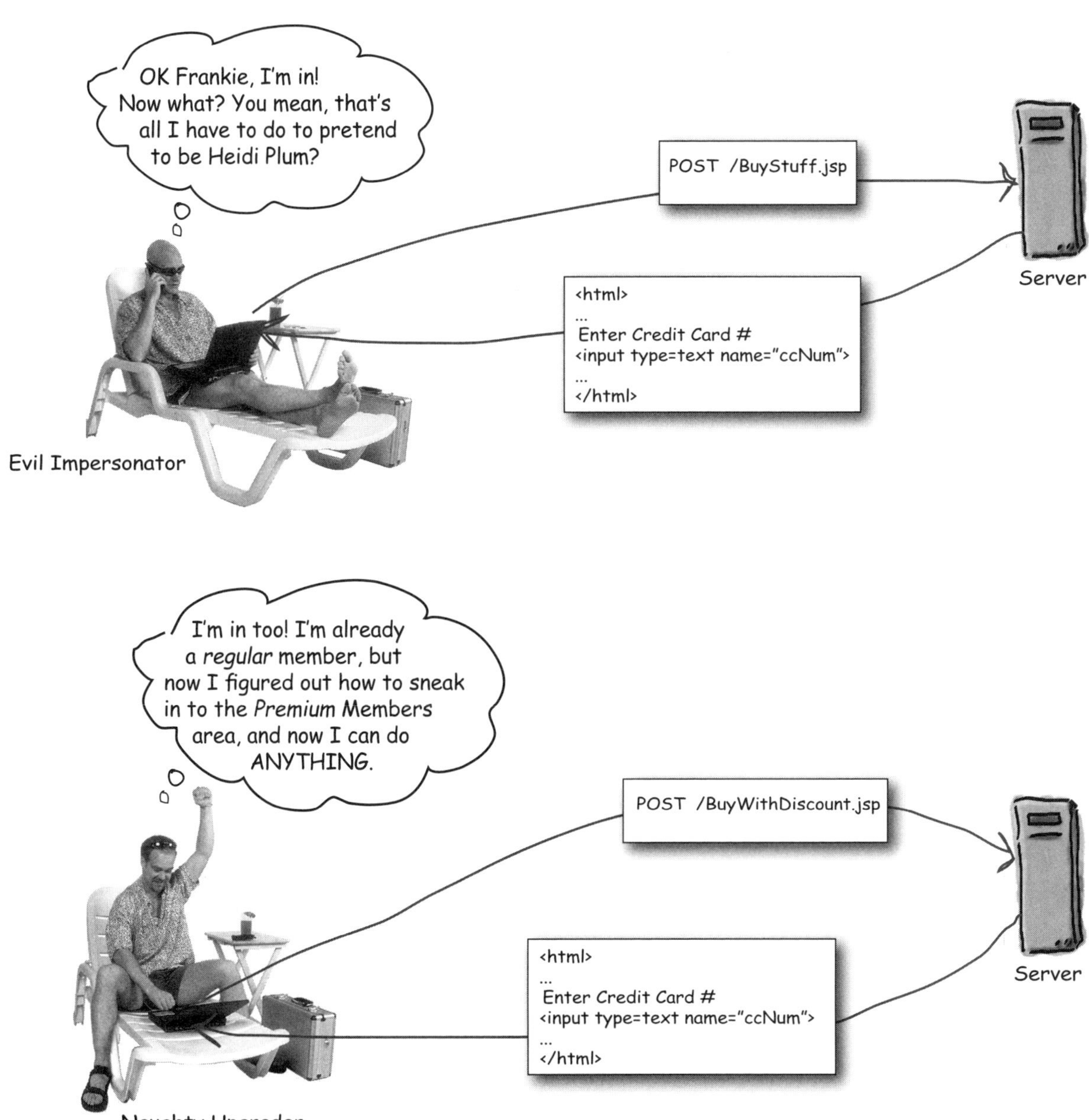

And it's not just the SERVER that gets hurt...

Eavesdroppers can be the worst. Not only are they trying to scam your *web app*, but they can burn some of your good *clients* too. A double hit. If an eavesdropper is successful, he'll swipe your client's credit card information and charge up a storm.

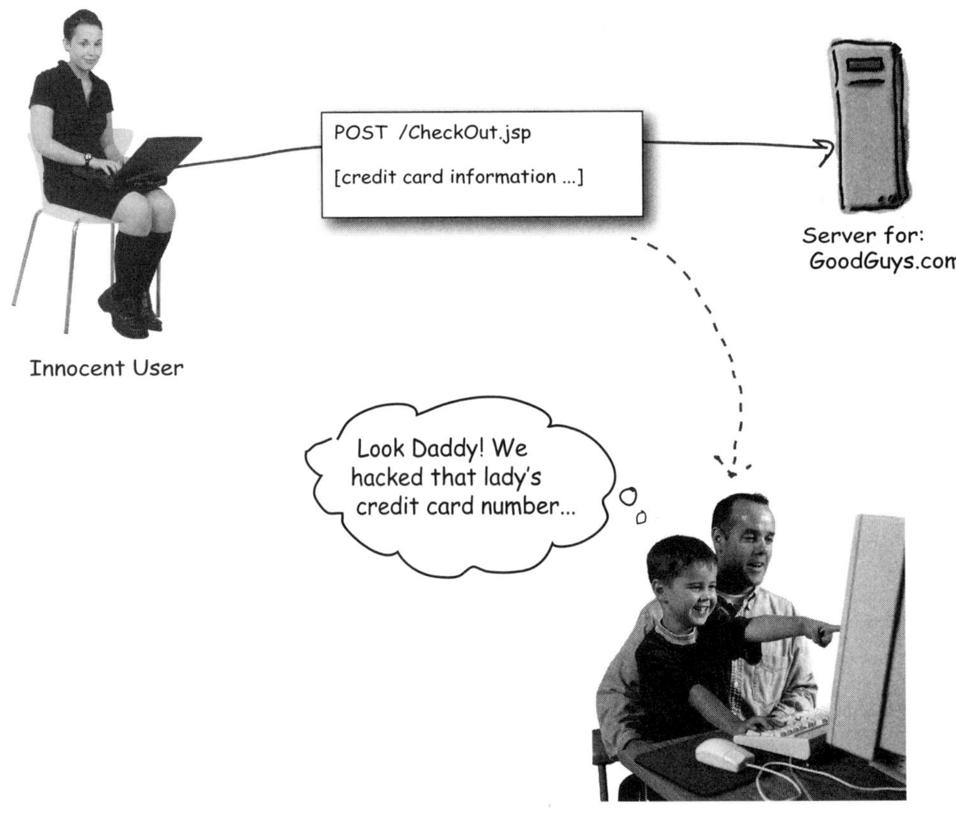

The Big 4 in servlet security

Servlet security helps you—the web app developer—foil Impersonators, Upgraders, and Eavesdroppers. As far as the servlet specification is concerned (and hence, the exam), servlet security boils down to four main concepts: **authentication**, **authorization**, **confidentiality**, and **data integrity.**

Busted...

Ok buddy, I got your request, but how do I know **you are who you say you are**?

HTTP request

POST

Server

① Authentication

(to foil Impersonators)

Busted...

Look Delbert, before I can send you this special *Premium* web page I have to make sure **you're allowed** to see it...

HTTP request

POST

Server

② Authorization

(to foil Upgraders)

Busted...

Shhh... Ok, we've got to make sure that no one can **look at** or **mess with** what I'm about to send out...

Encrypted response

e7x33f-
g7gwX11
sdf@11
f666d41dd
ddXXdes
R$3^ddEd

Server

③ Confidentiality ④ Data Integrity

(to foil Eavesdroppers)

A little security story

One day Bob's boss called Bob into his office. "I've got an exciting new project for you!" his boss said. Bob groaned. "I know I've handed you some bad jobs in the past, but this one should be really fun... I'd like you to design the security for our company's new eCommerce web site." "Security" Bob said, "is hard and boring." "No you're wrong..." the boss said. "In J2EE 1.4, servlet security is supposed to be pretty cool."

The boss continued, "Let me give you the elevator pitch to get you going, then we'll go into details once you've had a chance to think this through." "Ok," Bob sighed. "Lay it on me."

"As you know, this beer website is really hot right now. We've added several new features, and we're getting a great response. Some of our users are happy with just the *free* recipes we offer, but a lot more people than we thought are willing to *pay* for our rare hops and other premium ingredients. Oh, and our ***Frequent Brewer*** program is a huge hit. If a user decides he'll be a repeat ingredient buyer, he can pay a one time fee and upgrade to ***Brew Master*** status. A ***Brew Master*** get special discounts, and earns *Frequent Brewer* points which he can redeem for cool brew rewards."

Bob continued to listen, mentally calculating the code he'll have to write to implement all this, and kissing that tropical vacation goodbye. Meanwhile, the boss continued...

"But now we have to make sure that when one of our users makes a purchase, no one can swipe his credit card information. Oh, another thing, we'd better make sure that when a *member* logs in, it's not actually one of his *friends* trying to sneak in. I think we need to require that members have *passwords* from now on."

"It's all making sense so far." said Bob. "When users place an order with us, do we want to give them some sort of confirmation code?" "Great idea," said the boss. "Oh, and one more thing I forgot—you better make sure that only our ***Frequent Brewers*** get the special discounts."

"I think this is enough," said the boss. "But you know... the way things are going, it probably won't be too long before we offer some sort of *platinum* membership level..."

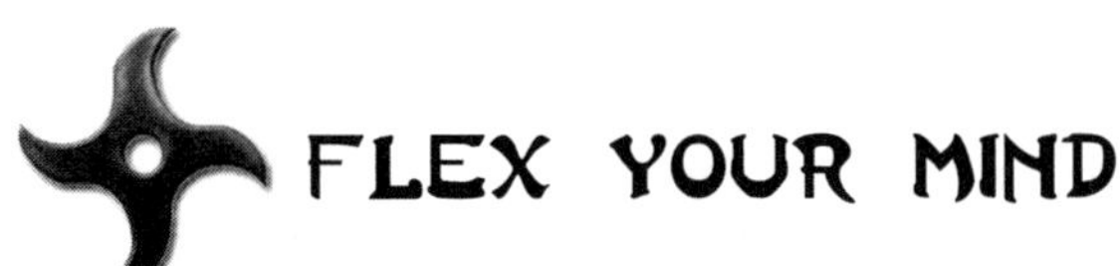

Which security concepts are mentioned in the story?

Reread the story and annotate the places where the boss's requirements call for:

- authentication
- authorization
- confidentiality
- data integrity

(Yeah, yeah, we know this is obvious, but we're just warming up the topic before it gets down and dirty.)

A little security story

One day Bob's boss called Bob into his office. "I've got an exciting new project for you!" his boss said. Bob groaned. "I know I've handed you some bad jobs in the past, but this one should be really fun... I'd like you to design the security for our company's new eCommerce web site."

"Security" Bob said, "is hard and boring." "No you're wrong..." the boss said. "In J2EE 1.4, servlet security is supposed to be pretty cool".

The boss continued, "Let me give you the elevator pitch to get you going, then we'll go into details once you've had a chance to think this through."

"OK." Bob sighed. "Lay it on me."

"As you know, this beer website is really hot right now! We've added several new features, and we're getting a great response. Some of our users are happy with just the *free* recipes we offer, but a lot more people than we thought are willing to *pay* for our rare hops and other premium ingredients. Oh, and our ***Frequent Brewer*** program is a *huge* hit. If a user decides he'll be a repeat ingredient buyer, he can pay a one time fee and upgrade to ***Brew Master*** status. A ***Brew Master*** get special discounts, and earns *Frequent Brewer* points which he can redeem for cool brew rewards."

Bob continued to listen, mentally calculating the code he'll have to write to implement all this, and kissing that tropical vacation goodbye. Meanwhile, the boss continued...

"But now we have to make sure that when one of our users makes a purchase, no one can swipe his credit card information. Oh, another thing, we'd better make sure that when a *member* logs in, it's not actually one of his *friends* trying to sneak in. I think we need to require that members have *passwords* from now on."

"It's all making sense so far." said Bob. "When a user places an order with us, do we want to give them some sort of confirmation code?" "Great idea", said the boss. "Oh, and one more thing I forgot—you better make sure that only our ***Frequent Brewers*** get the special discounts."

"I think this is enough," said the boss. "But you know... the way things are going, it probably won't be too long before we offer some sort of *platinum* membership level..."

CONFIDENTIALITY & DATA INTEGRITY- At this point the server is returning important and private information. It would be bad if the information was seen or altered by an eavesdropper.

AUTHORIZATION - Once we have established who we're talking to, we want to make sure that they're allowed to do what they want to do.

CONFIDENTIALITY - It would be a terrible security breach if a user's credit card number fell into the wrong hands!

AUTHENTICATION - Whenever someone mentions passwords, they're probably talking about authentication... is this guy who he says he is? If so, he should know his password!.

How to Authenticate in HTTP World: the beginning of a secure transaction

Let's start with a look at the communications that occur between a browser and a web container when the client asks for a secure resource on the web site. It's BASIC, really.

The HTTP perspective...

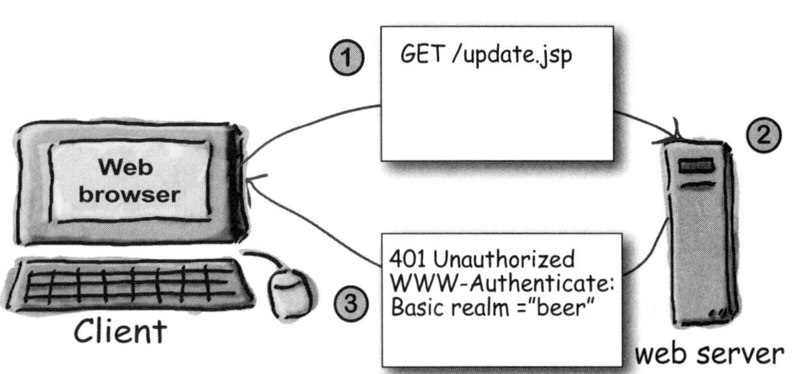

1 The browser makes a request for a web resource, "update.jsp".

2 The server determines that "update.jsp" is a constrained resource.

3 The container sends back an HTTP 401 ("Unauthorized"), with a www-authenticate header and realm information.

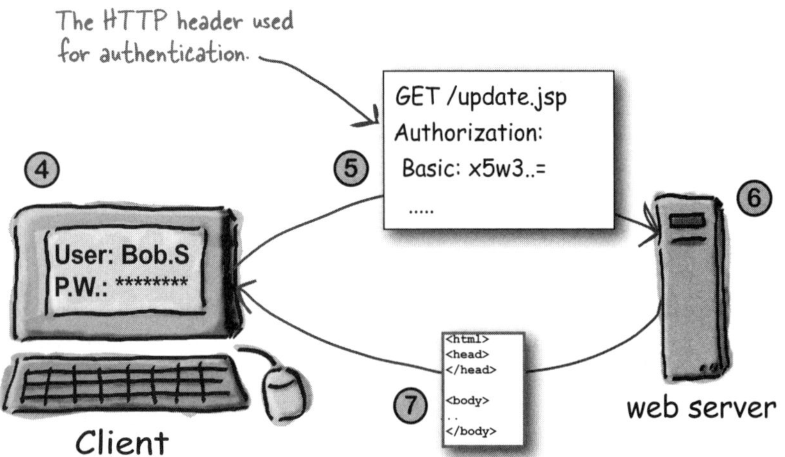

4 The browser gets the 401, and, based on the Realm info, asks the user for his username and password.

5 The browser asks for "update.jsp" again (stateless, remember), but this time the request includes a security HTTP header, and a username and password.

6 The Container verifies that the username and password match, and if they do, performs authorization.

7 If all the security stuff is good, the Container returns the HTML, if not it returns another HTTP 401...

A slightly closer look at how the Container does Authentication and Authorization

On the last page we skimmed over what the Container was doing. Throughout this chapter we'll hit different levels of detail, and here we zoom in just a little...

The Container perspective...

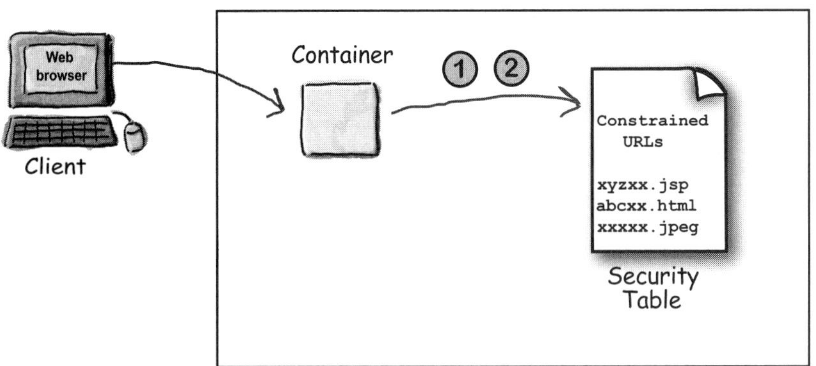

The initial request, NO password

1 Having received the request, the container finds the URL in the "security table" (stored in whatever the Container is using to keep security info).

2 If the Container finds the URL in the security table, it checks to see whether the requested resource is constrained. If it is, it returns 401...

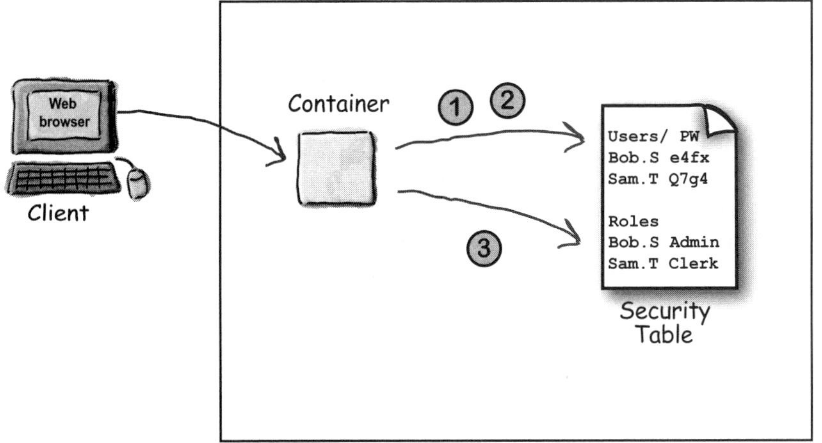

The second request, WITH password

1 When the Container receives a request with a username and password, it checks the URL in the security table.

2 If it finds the URL in the security table (and sees that it's constrained), it checks the username and password information to make sure they match.

3 If the username and password are OK, the Container checks to see if the user has been assigned the correct 'role' to access this resource (i.e. authorization). If so, the resource is returned to the client.

How did the Container do that?

You just got an overview of how the Container handles authentication and authorization. But what was going on inside the Container that made all that happen? Let's speculate a little on what was going on behind the scenes, deep down in the heart of the Container...

I put a LOT of cycles into security! *Anything* you can do to make security efficient will be a big help for performance.

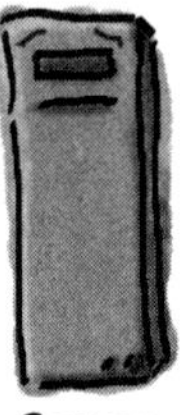

Things the Container did:

① Performed a ***lookup*** on the resource being requested

We already know that the Container is really good at finding resources. But now, once it finds the resource, it has to determine whether it's a resource that *anyone* can view, or whether the resource has *security constraints*. Does the servlet itself have some sort of security flag? Is there a table somewhere?

② Performed some ***authentication***

Once the Container determines that it's dealing with a secured resource, it has to *authenticate* the client. In other words, to find out if "Bob" really *is* Bob. (The most common way is to see if Bob knows his own password.)

③ Performed some ***authorization***

Once the Container determines that it *is* the real Bob asking for this resource, the Container has to see whether Bob is ***allowed*** access to that resource. Let's see, if we have 2,000,000 users, and 100 servlets in our webapp, we could throw together a little table with 200,000,000 cells...

Whoa! This could get out of hand in a hurry if we're not careful.

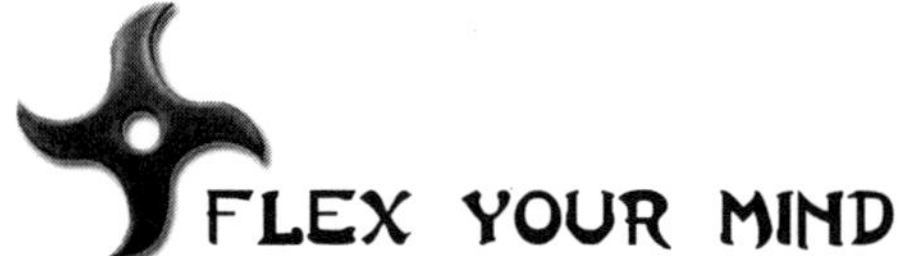

Which bits of security logic and information should be hardcoded in the servlet?

names and passwords?

users roles?

access rules for each servlet?

Keep security out of the code!

For most web apps, most of the time, the web app's security constraints should be handled *declaratively*, in the deployment descriptor. Why?

Top Ten Reasons to do your security declaratively

10. *Who doesn't need more XML practice?*
9. Often maps naturally to the existing job roles in a company's IT department.
8. Looks great on your resume.
7. Allows you to use servlets you've already written in more flexible ways.
6. It's on the exam.
5. Allows application developers to reuse servlets without access to the source code.
4. It's just cool.
3. Reduces ongoing maintenance when your application grows.
2. Finally, a way to justify the cost of that Container...
1. Supports the idea of component-based development.

Who implements security in a web app?

My job is easy. Most of the time, I don't even have to *think* about security when I'm writing a servlet. And that's good, because my philosophy is "Security is hard... don't do it."
Kim the servlet provider

My job is more involved. I decide which roles make sense in the application. For Kim's beer application Guest, Member, and Admin are key roles. Then I add these roles to the users in our Container's users file. Since we use tomcat, our file is called tomcat-users.xml.
Annie the application administrator

My job is huge! Once I have a list of Annie's roles, and a description of what Kim's servlets do, I can decide which roles should have access to which servlets. The deployment descriptor provides me with an easy, if somewhat verbose, way to tell the Container who has access to which servlets. And let me tell you, they don't pay me enough...
Dick the deployer

there are no Dumb Questions

Q: I'm confused—if I'm *creating* servlets, shouldn't I be thinking about security considerations?

A: Yes, you should; Kim the servlet provider was being a little sarcastic. A key point when designing servlets is their modularity. For instance, it makes sense to separate browsing capabilities from updating capabilities. If these two use cases are implemented in separate servlets then it will be easy for the deployer to assign *different* security constraints to them.

Q: I don't know where YOU work, but in my situation I have to wear all three hats: developer, admin, and deployer.

A: That's actually a very common situation. We still recommend that when you're implementing security you do it in *stages* and "imagine" that you're wearing one hat at a time.

Q: How does programmatic security fit into the picture?

A: We'll get to programmatic security later in the chapter. For now, what's important to know is that you'll probably find that 95% of the security work you'll do in servlets will be *declarative*. Programmatic security just isn't used very much. (See "Top Ten Reasons...")

Q: So far everything you've talked about is related to authentication and authorization, how about the other two in the "big 4"?

A: We'll talk about *confidentiality* and *data integrity* later in this chapter. The servlet specification makes implementing these concepts very easy, so we're focusing on authentication and authorization because they're the most complicated to understand and implement, and, hint hint, more likely to show up on the exam.

Q: It seems like when people talk about servlet security the term "role" is overloaded...

A: Good point! When Sun designs J2EE specs (EJBs, servlets, JSPs), they often think in terms of the *kinds* of people who might *create* and *administer* these components. In other words, IT-related ***job roles***. When developers tackle security for web apps, they think about the ***types of users*** that might exist. For instance a "guest" might have very few privileges within a web app, and a "member" might have more privileges. These "user roles" are defined, mapped, and fretted over in the Deployment Descriptor.

Q: I've heard about something called "cross-site'" hacking. What is that?

A: Cross-site hacking can happen when a website displays free form text entered by other users (for instance, a user book review). If a malicious user keys some HTML with, say, Javascript into a text area, and the server doesn't catch it, then unsuspecting browsers will render the potentially *dangerous* hidden code along with the *good* HTML when the page is served. In other words, the server sends to users something *another* user typed in, without checking or processing it for malicious scripting code.

Q: So we've got to deal with 'The Big Four'. How hard is it to set these babies up and maintain them, I mean is this going to be *painful*?

A: Yes, we're afraid it might hurt a *little*. Actually, *some* aspects of security are really low overhead, while others DO require a fair amount of work. But none of it is very complicated, just potentially tedious.

The Big Jobs in servlet security

The table below will give you a feel for the key items in servlet security. ***Authorization*** is the most time-consuming to implement and ***Authentication*** is next. From the servlet perspective, Confidentiality and Data Integrity are pretty easy to set up.*

Security concept	Who's responsible?	Complexity level	Effort level	Exam importance
Authentication	Admin	medium	high	medium
Authorization	Deployer (mostly)	high	high	high
Confidentiality	Deployer	low	low	low
Data Integrity	Deployer	low	low	low

We're going to emphasize Authorization in this chapter because it's the most important and complex of the vendor-neutral security concepts.

*Actually, getting the SSL certification is not trivial, so by "easy" we mean "you don't really do anything in your servlet code."

Just enough Authentication to discuss Authorization

Later in the chapter we'll go deeper into authentication, but for now we'll look at getting just enough *authentication* data into the system so that we can focus on *authorization.* A user can't be *authorized* until he's been *authenticated.*

The servlet specification doesn't talk about *how* a Container should implement support for authentication data, including usernames and passwords. But the general idea is that the Container will supply a vendor-specific table containing usernames and their associated passwords and roles. But virtually all vendors go beyond that and provide a way to hook into your company-specific authentication data, often stored in a relational database or LDAP system (which is beyond the scope of this book). Typically, this data is maintained by the administrator.

The security "realm"

Unfortunately, ***realm*** is yet another overloaded term in the security world. As far as the servlet spec is concerned, a ***realm*** is a place where ***authentication*** information is stored. When you're testing your application in Tomcat, you can use a file called "tomcat-users.xml" (located in tomcat's conf/directory, NOT within webapps). That one "tomcat-users.xml" file applies to ALL applications deployed under web-apps. It's commonly known as the ***memory realm*** because Tomcat reads this file into memory at startup time. While it's great for testing, it's not recommended for production. For one thing you can't modify its contents without restarting Tomcat.

The tomcat-users.xml file

Your app server will use something different... but SOMEHOW it will let you map users to passwords and roles.

```
<tomcat-users>
  <role rolename="Guest"/>
  <role rolename="Member"/>
  <user name="Bill" password="coder" roles="Member, Guest" />
  ...
</tomcat-users>
```

Remember! This is NOT part of the DD; it's vendor-specific.

The control for authentication is located in some sort of data structure like this. In Tomcat, you can use an XML file called "tomcat-users.xml" that holds name-password-role sets that the Container uses at authentication time.

Enabling authentication

To get authentication working (in other words, to get the Container to ask for a username and password), you need to stick something in the DD. Don't worry about what this means for now, but if you want to start playing around with authentication, use this:

```
<login-config>
  <auth-method>BASIC</auth-method>
</login-config>
```

We'll talk about this later in the chapter, but for now, you need this in your DD to get authentication.

Authorization Step 1: defining roles

The most common form of authorization in servlets is for the container to determine whether a specific servlet—and the invoking HTTP request method—can be called by a user who has been assigned a certain security "role". So the first step is to map the *roles* in the vendor-specific *"users" file* to *roles* established in the *Deployment Descriptor.*

Annie is an "Admin", a "Member" and a "Guest".

Diane is both a "Member" and a "Guest".

Ted is a "Guest".

VENDOR-SPECIFIC:

The <role> element in tomcat-users.xml

Vendor-specific users and roles data structure.

```
<tomcat-users>
  <role rolename="Admin"/>
  <role rolename="Member"/>
  <role rolename="Guest"/>
  <user username="Annie" password="admin" roles="Admin, Member, Guest" />
  <user username="Diane" password="coder" roles="Member, Guest" />
  <user username="Ted" password="newbie" roles="Guest" />
</tomcat-users>
```

In Tomcat, the tomcat-users.xml should look a lot like this. Notice that a single user can have multiple roles.

SERVLET-SPECIFICATION:

The DD <security-role> element in web.xml

When it's time for authorization, the container will map its vendor-specific "role" information to whatever <role-name>'s it finds in your DD's <security-role> elements.

```
<security-role>
  <role-name>Admin</role-name>
  <role-name>Member</role-name>
  <role-name>Guest</role-name>
</security-role>

<login-config>
  <auth-method>BASIC</auth-method>
</login-config>
```

Don't forget that you always need the <login-config> element if you want to enable authentication.

The deployer creates <role-name> elements in the DD, so that the Container can map roles to users.

Authorization Step 2: defining resource/method constraints

Finally, the cool part. This is where we get to specify, *declaratively*, that a given resource/method combination is accessible only by users in certain *roles*. Most of the security work you'll do is probably with <security-constraint> elements in your DD. (Lots of picky rules later.)

<security-constraint> element in the DD:

```
<web-app...>
  ...
  <security-constraint>

    <web-resource-collection>

      <web-resource-name>UpdateRecipes</web-resource-name>

      <url-pattern>/Beer/AddRecipe/*</url-pattern>
      <url-pattern>/Beer/ReviewRecipe/*</url-pattern>

      <http-method>GET</http-method>
      <http-method>POST</http-method>

    </web-resource-collection>

    <auth-constraint>
      <role-name>Admin</role-name>
      <role-name>Member</role-name>
    </auth-constraint>

  </security-constraint>
</web-app>
```

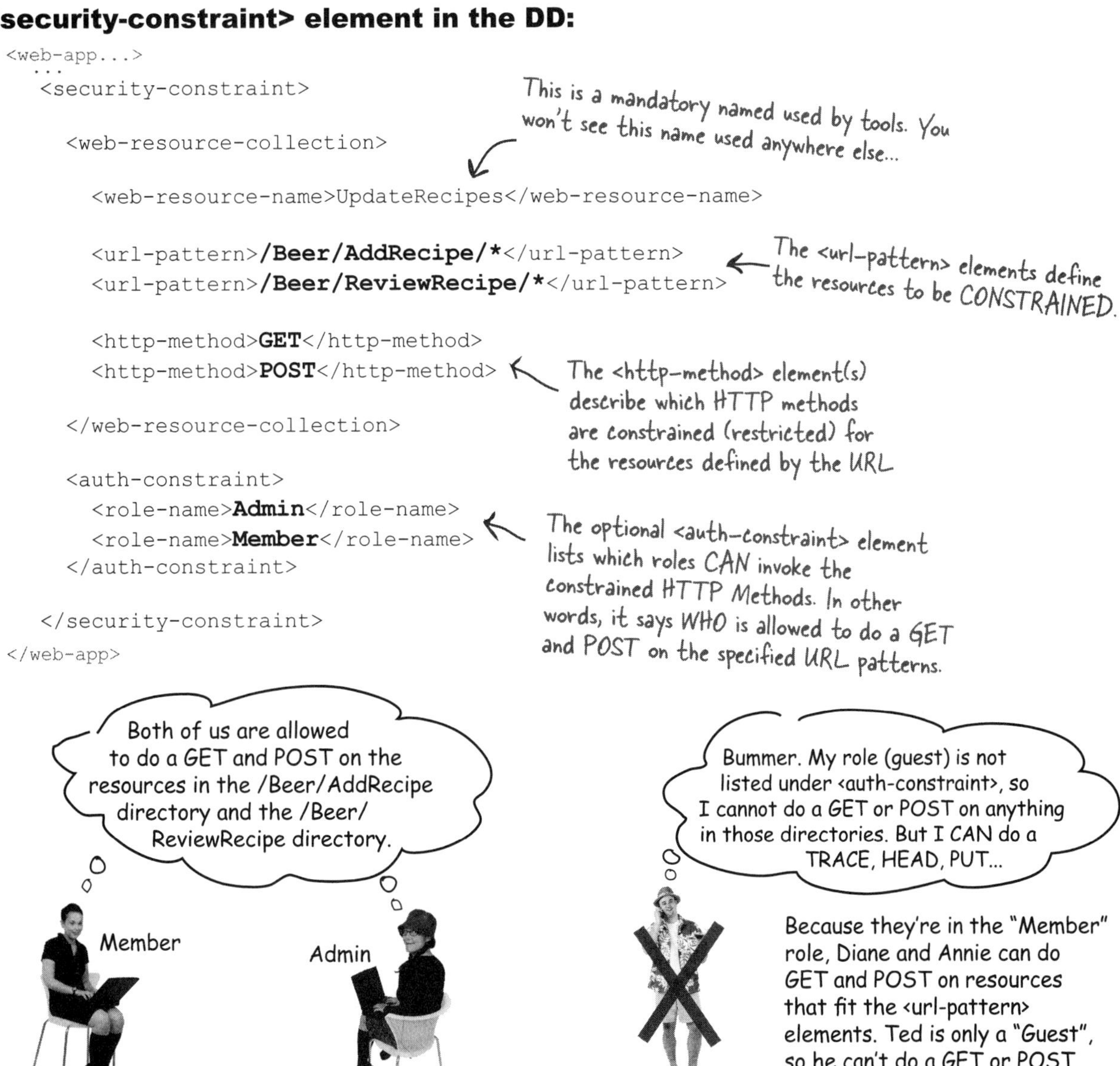

This is a mandatory named used by tools. You won't see this name used anywhere else...
The <url-pattern> elements define the resources to be CONSTRAINED.
The <http-method> element(s) describe which HTTP methods are constrained (restricted) for the resources defined by the URL
The optional <auth-constraint> element lists which roles CAN invoke the constrained HTTP Methods. In other words, it says WHO is allowed to do a GET and POST on the specified URL patterns.
Both of us are allowed to do a GET and POST on the resources in the /Beer/AddRecipe directory and the /Beer/ ReviewRecipe directory.
Member
Admin
Bummer. My role (guest) is not listed under <auth-constraint>, so I cannot do a GET or POST on anything in those directories. But I CAN do a TRACE, HEAD, PUT...
Guest
Because they're in the "Member" role, Diane and Annie can do GET and POST on resources that fit the <url-pattern> elements. Ted is only a "Guest", so he can't do a GET or POST.

The <security-constraint> rules for <web-resource-collection> elements

Remember; the purpose of the <web-resource-collection> sub-element is to tell the container which resources and HTTP Method combinations should be *constrained* in such a way that they can be accessed only by the roles in the corresponding <auth-constraint> tag. We wish we could tell you to relax here, but you really do need to know the details of these elements. If you make one little mistake in the security part of your DD, you could leave the most sensitive parts of your app open to... *everyone.*

The <web-resource-collection> sub-element of <security-constraint>

```
<web-app...>
  ...
  <security-constraint>

    <web-resource-collection>

      <web-resource-name>
          UpdateRecipes
      </web-resource-name>

      <url-pattern>/Beer/AddRecipe/*</url-pattern>
      <url-pattern>/Beer/ReviewRecipe/*</url-pattern>

      <http-method>GET</http-method>

    </web-resource-collection>

    <auth-constraint>
      ....
    </auth-constraint>

  </security-constraint>

</web-app>
```

These are the directories with constraints.
This says that the GET method can be accessed ONLY by the roles defined in the <auth-constraint>.
But the OTHER methods have no constraint, so they can be accessed by anyone.

Key points about <web-resource-collection>

- The <web-resource-collection> element has two primary sub-elements: <url-pattern> (one or more) <http-method> (optional, zero or more).
- The URL patterns and HTTP Methods together define resource requests that are ***constrained*** to be accessible by only those roles defined in <auth-constraint>.
- A <web-resource-name> element is MANDATORY (even though you probably won't use it for anything yourself). (Assume it's for IDE or future use.)
- A <description> element is OPTIONAL.
- The <url-pattern> element uses servlet standard naming and mapping rules (refer back to the deployment chapter for details on URL patterns).
- You **must specify at least *one* <url-pattern>**, but you *can* have many.
- Valid Methods for the <http-method> element are: GET, POST, PUT, TRACE, DELETE, HEAD, and OPTIONS.
- If *no* HTTP Methods are specified then ***ALL*** Methods will be constrained (which means they can be accessed only by the roles in <auth-constraint>)!!
- If you DO specify an <http-method>, then only those methods specified will be constrained. In other words, once you specify even a single <http-method>, you automatically enable any HTTP Methods which you have *not* specified.
- You can have more than one <web-resource-collection> element in the same <security-constraint>.
- The <auth-constraint> element applies to ALL <web-resource-collection> elements in the <security-constraint>.

Constraints are not at the RESOURCE level. Constraints are at the HTTP REQUEST level.

It's tempting to think that resources themselves are constrained. But it's really the combination of resource + HTTP Method. When you say, "This is a constrained resource", what you're really saying is, "This is a constrained resource with respect to HTTP GET." A resource is always constrained on an HTTP method by HTTP Method basis, although you CAN configure the <web-resource-collection> in such a way that ALL Methods are constrained, simply by not putting in ANY <http-method> elements.

The <auth-constraint> element does NOT define which roles are allowed to access the resources from the <web-resource-collection>. Instead, it defines which roles are allowed to make the ***constrained request****. Don't think of it as "Bob is a Member, so Bob can access the AddRecipe servlet". Instead, say "Bob is a Member, so Bob can make a GET or POST request on the AddRecipe servlet."*

If you specify an <http-method> element, all the HTTP methods you do NOT specify are UNconstrained!

The web server's job is to SERVE, so the default assumption is that you want the HTTP Methods to be UNconstrained unless you explicitly say (using <http-method>) that you want a method to be constrained (for the resources that match the <url-pattern>). If you put in ONLY an <http-method>GET</http-method> in the security constraint, then POST, TRACE, PUT, etc. are not constrained! That means anybody, regardless of security role (or even regardless of whether the client is authenticated), can invoke those HTTP Methods.

BUT... this is true ONLY if you have specified at least one <http-method> element. If you do NOT specify any <http-method>, then you're constraining ALL HTTP Methods. (You'll probably never do that, because the whole point of a security constraint is to constrain specific HTTP requests on a particular set of resources.)

Of course, HTTP Methods won't work in a servlet unless you've overridden the doXXX() method, so if you have only a doGet() in your servlet, and you specify an <http-method> element for only GET, nobody can do a POST anyway, because the server knows you don't support POST.

So we can modify the rule a little to say: any HTTP Methods supported by your servlet (because you overrode the matching service method) will be allowed UNLESS you do one of two things:

1) Do not specify ANY <http-method> elements in the <security-constraint>, which means that ALL Methods are constrained to the roles in <auth-constraint>.

2) Explicitly list the Method using the <http-method> element.

Picky <security-constraint> rules for <auth-constraint> sub-elements

Even though it's got *constraint* in its name, this is the sub-element that specifies which roles are ALLOWED to access the web resources specified by the **<web-resource-collection>** sub-element(s).

The <auth-constraint> sub-element of <security-constraint>

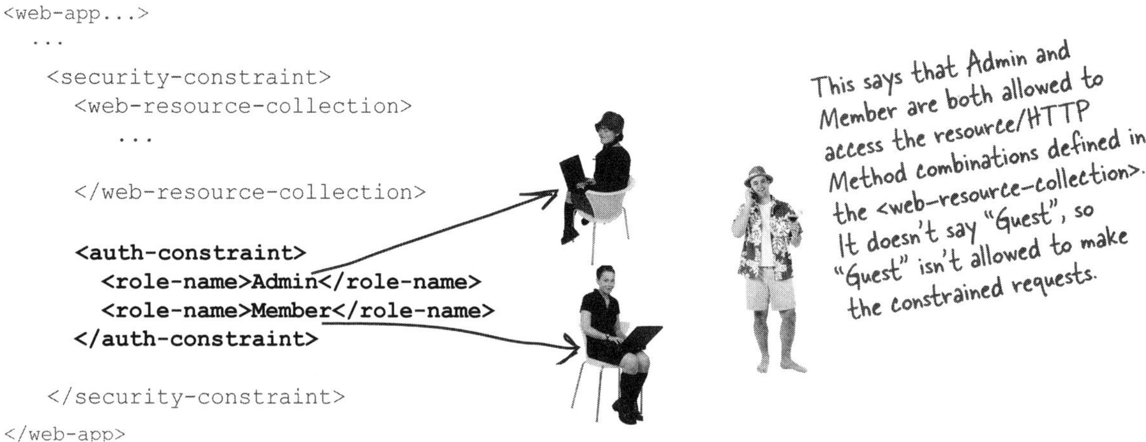

```
<web-app...>
  ...
    <security-constraint>
      <web-resource-collection>
         ...

      </web-resource-collection>

      <auth-constraint>
        <role-name>Admin</role-name>
        <role-name>Member</role-name>
      </auth-constraint>

    </security-constraint>
</web-app>
```

This says that Admin and Member are both allowed to access the resource/HTTP Method combinations defined in the <web-resource-collection>. It doesn't say "Guest", so "Guest" isn't allowed to make the constrained requests.

<role-name> rules

- Within an <auth-constraint> element, the <role-name> element is OPTIONAL.
- If <role-name> elements exist, they tell the Container which roles are ALLOWED.
- If an <auth-constraint> element exists with NO <role-name> element, then NO USERS ARE ALLOWED.
- If <role-name>*</role-name> then ALL users are ALLOWED.
- Role names are ***case-sensitive***.

<auth-constraint> rules

- Within a <security-constraint> element, the <auth-constraint> element is OPTIONAL.
- If an <auth-constraint> exists, the Container MUST perform authentication for the associated URLs.
- If an <auth-constraint> does NOT exist, the Container MUST allow unauthenticated access for these URLs.
- For readability, you can add a <description> inside <auth-constraint>.

The way <auth-constraint> works

Contents of <auth-constraint>	Which roles have access			
`<security-constraint> <auth-constraint> <role-name>Admin</role-name> <role-name>Member</role-name> </auth-constraint> </security-constraint>`	**Admin** **Member**			
`<security-constraint> <auth-constraint> <role-name>Guest</role-name> </auth-constraint> </security-constraint>`	**Guest**			
`<security-constraint> <auth-constraint> <role-name>*</role-name> </auth-constraint> </security-constraint>`	**Everybody**			
If there is NO <auth-constraint>	**Everybody**			
`<security-constraint> <auth-constraint/> </security-constraint>`	**Nobody**			

These two have the SAME effect.

Yikes! If you put in an empty tag, then NO roles have access.

NO <auth-constraint> is the opposite of an EMPTY <auth-constraint/>!

*Remember this: if you don't say **which** roles are constrained, then **NO** roles are constrained. But once you DO put in an <auth-constraint>, then ONLY the roles explicitly stated are allowed access (unless you use the wildcard "*" for the <role-name>). If you don't want ANY role to have access, you MUST put in the <auth-constraint/>, but just leave it empty. This tells the Container, "I am explicitly stating the roles allowed and, by the way, there aren't any!"*

How multiple <security-constraint> elements interact

Just when you thought you had <security-constraint> figured out, you realize that *multiple* <security-constraint> elements might conflict. Look at the DD fragments below, and imagine the different combinations of <auth-constraint> configurations that might be used. What happens, for example, if *one* <security-constraint> *denies* access while *another* <security-constraint> explicitly *grants* access... to the same constrained resource, for the same role? Which <security-constraint> wins? The table on the opposite page has all the answers.

Multiple <security-constraint> elements with the same (or partly-matching) URL patterns and <http-method> elements:

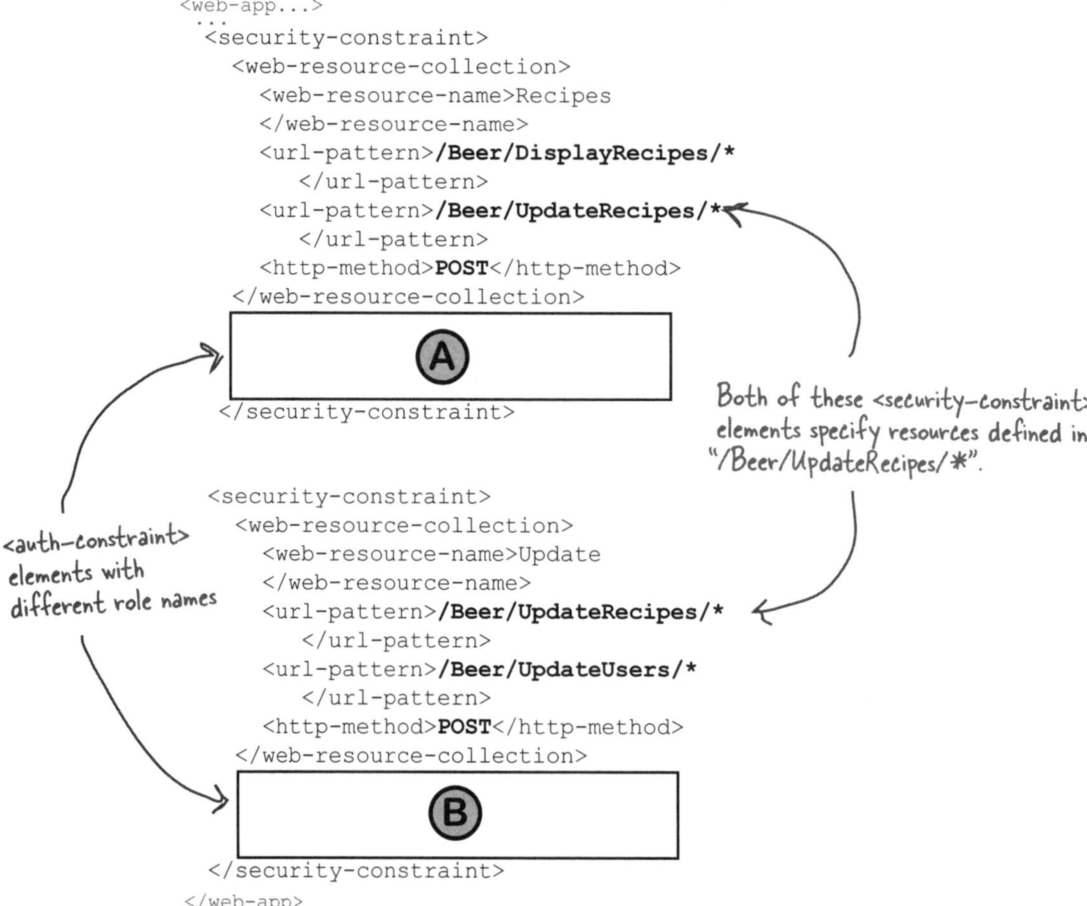


```
<web-app...>
...
  <security-constraint>
    <web-resource-collection>
      <web-resource-name>Recipes
      </web-resource-name>
      <url-pattern>/Beer/DisplayRecipes/*
         </url-pattern>
      <url-pattern>/Beer/UpdateRecipes/*
         </url-pattern>
      <http-method>POST</http-method>
    </web-resource-collection>
        [ A ]
  </security-constraint>

  <security-constraint>
    <web-resource-collection>
      <web-resource-name>Update
      </web-resource-name>
      <url-pattern>/Beer/UpdateRecipes/*
         </url-pattern>
      <url-pattern>/Beer/UpdateUsers/*
         </url-pattern>
      <http-method>POST</http-method>
    </web-resource-collection>
        [ B ]
  </security-constraint>
</web-app>
```

How should the container handle authorization when the same resource is used by more than one <security-constraint>?

Dueling <auth-constraint> elements

If two or more <security-constraint> elements have partially or fully overlapping <web-resource-collection> elements, here's how the container resolves access to the overlapping resources. A and B refer to the DD on the previous page.

	Contents of 	Contents of 	Who has Access to 'UpdateRecipes'
1	<auth-constraint> <role-name>**Guest**</role-name> </auth-constraint>	<auth-constraint> <role-name>**Admin**</role-name> </auth-constraint>	**Guests and Admins**   
2	<auth-constraint> <role-name>**Guest**</role-name> </auth-constraint>	<auth-constraint> <role-name>*****</role-name> </auth-constraint>	**Everybody**   
3	<auth-constraint/> empty tag	<auth-constraint> <role-name>**Admin**</role-name> </auth-constraint>	**Nobody**  
4	***NO <auth-constraint> element***	<auth-constraint> <role-name>**Admin**</role-name> </auth-constraint>	**Everybody**   

Rules for interpreting this table:

1 When combining individual role names, *all* of the role names listed will be allowed.

2 A role name of " * " combines with anything else to allow access to *everybody*.

3 An empty <auth-constraint> tag combines with *anything* else to allow access to nobody! In other words, an empty <auth-constraint> is always the final word!

4 If one of the <security-constraint> elements has *no* <auth-constraint> element, it combines with anything else to allow access to *everybody*.

When two different non-empty <auth-constraint> elements apply to the same constrained resource, access is granted to the union of all roles from both of the <auth-constraint> elements.

there are no Dumb Questions

Q: I understand that putting in an empty <auth-constraint/> element tells the Container that NOBODY from any role can access the constrained resource. But I don't understand WHY you would ever do that. What good is a resource that nobody can access?

A: When we said, "NOBODY", we meant, "Nobody from OUTSIDE the web app". In other words, a *client* can't access the constrained resource, but another part of the web app *can*. You might want to use a request dispatcher to forward to another part of the web app, but you don't ever want clients to request that resource directly. Think of 100% constrained resources as sort of like private methods in a Java class—for internal use only.

Q: Why does the <auth-constraint> element go inside <security-constraint> but NOT inside the <web-resource-collection> element?

A: This way, you can specify a single <auth-constraint> element (which could include multiple roles), and then specify multiple resource collections for which the <auth-constraint> role list applies. For example, you might define an <auth-constraint> for a Frequent Buyer role, and then put <web-resource-collection> elements in for the all the different parts of the web app where a Frequent Buyer gets special access.

Q: Do I actually have to sit there and type in every one of my users with their passwords and roles?

A: If you're using the test memory realm from Tomcat, yes. But chances are, in the real world you're using a production server that gives you a hook into the LDAP or database where your real user security info is stored.

Alice's recipe servlet, a story about programmatic security...

Alice knows that most of the time declarative security is the way to go. It's flexible, powerful, portable, and robust. As web application architectures have evolved, individual servlets have become more and more specialized. In the old days, a *single* servlet would be used to provide business logic to support employees and managers. Today, these functions would probably be split into at least two distinct servlets.

But, lucky Alice has just inherited someone else's "RecipeServlet". Alice has heard a rumour that RecipeServlet uses programmatic security, so she starts looking through the source code and finds this snippet...

```
if( request.isUserInRole("Manager")) {
    // do the UpdateRecipe page
    ...

} else {
    // do the ViewRecipe page
    ...

}
```

Who came up with "Manager" as a role name? What if the guy who wrote this servlet didn't know about your company's roles?

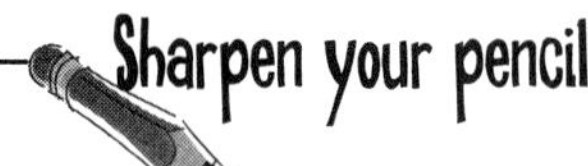

What are the implications?

Think about what you've learned so far in this chapter, look at the small code snippet above, and try to answer the questions.

What security step must have happened *before* this snippet runs?

What security step is implied by *this* snippet?

What part, if any, does the DD play in this snippet?

How do you think this code works?

What if the role of "Manager" doesn't exist in your container?

Customizing methods: isUserInRole()

In **HttpServletRequest,** three methods are associated with programmatic security:

getUserPrincipal(), which is mainly used with EJBs. We won't cover it in this book.*

getRemoteUser(), which can be used to check authentication status. It's not commonly used, so we don't cover it in this book (and there's nothing else you need to know about it for the exam).

isUserInRole(), which we'll look at *now.* Instead of authorizing at the HTTP method level (GET, POST, etc.), you can authorize access to *portions* of a method. This gives you a way to *customize* how a service method behaves based on the user's role. If you're in this service method (doGet(), doPost(), etc.), then the user made it through the declarative authorization, but now you want to do something in the method conditionally, based on whether the user is in a particular role.

I just got this servlet from Stan in accounting and he's hard-coded roles that we don't even *have.* (What the %$&# is a *superCustomer*?) No way am I gonna redefine all the roles in my container just so I can use Stan's stupid servlet...

How do you match up roles in the DD with roles in a servlet?

How it works:

1. Before isUserInRole() is called, the user needs to be **authenticated**. If the method is called on a user that has *not* been authenticated, the Container will always return false.

2. The Container takes the isUserInRole() argument, in this example "Manager", and compares it to the roles defined for the user in this request.

3. If the user *is* mapped to this role, the Container returns true.

* We do, however, know of this really nice EJB book...

The declarative side of programmatic security

There's a good chance that when a programmer hard-codes security role names in a servlet (to use as the argument to isUserInRole()), the programmer was just *making up a fake name*. He either didn't *know* the real role names, or he's writing a reusable component that'll be used by more than one company, and those companies aren't likely to have the exact role names the programmer used. (Of course, if the programmer really wants to build *reusable* components, hard-coding a role name is a Terrible Idea, but we'll suspend disbelief for now.)

It turns out that the Deployment Descriptor has a mechanism for mapping hard-coded (which means *made-up*) role names in a *servlet* to the "official" <security-role> declarations in your *Container*. Imagine, for example, that the programmer used "Manager" as the isUserInRole() argument, but your company uses "Admin" as the <security-role>, and you don't even have a "Manager" security role. So even if you can't stop a programmer from hard-coding a role name, you at least have a work-around when the hard-coded roles don't match your *real* role names. Because even if you *do* have the servlet source code, do you really want to change, recompile, and retest your code just to change every instance of "Manager" to "Admin"?

In the servlet

```
if( request.isUserInRole("Manager")) {
    // do the UpdateRecipe page
    ...

} else {
    // do the ViewRecipe page
    ...

}
```

In this case if the <security-role-ref> didn't exist, this would fail because there is no <security-role> named "Manager".

In the DD

```
<web-app...>
  <servlet>
    <security-role-ref>
      <role-name>Manager</role-name>
      <role-link>Admin</role-link>
    </security-role-ref>
   ...
  </servlet>
  ...
</web-app>
<web-app...>
  <security-role>
    <role-name>Admin</role-name>
    <role-name>Member</role-name>
    <role-name>Guest</role-name>
  </security-role>
  ...
</web-app>
```

The <security-role-ref> element maps programmatic (hard-coded) role names to declarative <security-role> elements.

The Container will use a <security-role-ref> mapping even IF the programmatic name matches a "real" <security-role> name.

When the Container hits an argument to "isUserInRole()", it looks FIRST for a matching <security-role-ref>. If it finds one, that's what it uses, even when the hard-coded name really DOES match a <security-role> name. Think about it—you might really HAVE a "Manager" security role in your company, but it might mean something completely different than what the programmer intended. So you could, for example, map hard-coded "Manager" to "Admin", and then map a hard-coded "Director" to "Manager". So, the <security-role-ref> always wins when both include the same <role-name>.

Sharpen your pencil

Assume all security constraints below have the same <url-pattern> and <http-method> elements. Based on the combinations shown, decide who can directly access the constrained resource.

		Nobody	Guest	Member	Admin	Everyone
1	<security-constraint> ... <auth-constraint> <role-name>Guest</role-name> </auth-constraint> </security-constraint>					
2	<security-constraint> ... <auth-constraint/> </security-constraint>					
3	<security-constraint> ... <auth-constraint> <role-name>Admin</role-name> </auth-constraint> </security-constraint> <security-constraint> ... <auth-constraint> <role-name>Guest</role-name> </auth-constraint> </security-constraint>					
4	<security-constraint> ... <auth-constraint> <role-name>Guest</role-name> </auth-constraint> </security-constraint> <security-constraint> ... <auth-constraint> <role-name>*</role-name> </auth-constraint> </security-constraint>					
5	<security-constraint> ... <auth-constraint> <role-name>Member</role-name> </auth-constraint> </security-constraint> <security-constraint> ← Assume that NO <auth-constraint> is defined ... </security-constraint>					
6	<security-constraint> ... <auth-constraint> <role-name>Member</role-name> </auth-constraint> </security-constraint> <security-constraint> ... <auth-constraint/> </security-constraint>					

OK, so I know all about authorization, but I still don't know how authentication happens, or exactly what I have to do to make the Container ask for a name and password...

Authentication revisited

For a J2EE Container, authentication comes down to this: ask for a user *name* and *password*, then verify that they *match*.

The first time an un-authenticated user asks for a constrained resource, the Container will automatically start the authentication process. There are four types of authentication the Container can provide, and the *main* difference between them is, "How securely is the name and password info transmitted?"

The FOUR authentication types

BASIC authentication transmits the login information in an encoded *(not encrypted)* form. That might *sound* secure, but you probably already know that since the encoding scheme (**base64**) is really well known, BASIC provides very weak security.

DIGEST authentication transmits the login information in a more secure way, but because the encryption mechanism isn't widely used, J2EE containers aren't required to support it. For more info on DIGEST authentication, check out the IETF RFC 2617 (www.ietf.org/rfc/rfc2617.txt).

CLIENT-CERT authentication transmits the login information in an extremely secure form, using Public Key Certificates (PKC). The downside to this mechanism is that your clients need to have a certificate before they can login to your system. It's fairly rare for consumers to have a certificate, so CLIENT-CERT authentication is used mainly in business to business scenarios.

The three types above—BASIC, DIGEST, and CLIENT-CERT—all use the browser's standard pop-up form for inputting the name and password. But the fourth type, FORM, is different.

FORM authentication lets you create your own custom login form out of anything that's legal HTML. But... of all four types, the form-based info is transmitted in the least secure way. The username and password are sent back in the HTTP request, with *no* encryption.

Implementing Authentication

This is the simple part—simply declare the authentication scheme in the DD. The main DD element for authentication is **<login-config>**.

Four <login-config> examples:

```
<web-app...>
 ...
  <login-config>
    <auth-method>BASIC</auth-method>
  </login-config>
</web-app>
```

BASIC is basic. Once you've declared this element in your DD, the container will do the rest, automatically requesting a username and password when a constrained resource is requested.

— or —

```
<web-app...>
 ...
  <login-config>
    <auth-method>DIGEST</auth-method>
  </login-config>
</web-app>
```

If your container supports DIGEST, it will handle ALL the details.

— or —

```
<web-app...>
 ...
  <login-config>
    <auth-method>CLIENT-CERT</auth-method>
  </login-config>
</web-app>
```

CLIENT is easy to configure, but your clients must have certificates. It does give you EXTRA-STRENGTH protection!

— or —

```
<web-app...>
 ...
  <login-config>
    <auth-method>FORM</auth-method>
    <form-login-config>
      <form-login-page>/loginPage.html</form-login-page>
      <form-error-page>/loginError.html</form-error-page>
    </form-login-config>
  </login-config>
</web-app>
```

FORM is the most complicated to implement; we'll look at it in detail on the next page.

Except for FORM, once you've declared the <login-config> element in the DD, implementing Authentication is done!
(Assuming you've already configured username/password/role info into your server.)

Form-Based Authentication

Although there's more to implementing it than with the *other* forms of authentication, FORM-based isn't that bad. First, you create your own custom HTML form for the user login (although this can certainly be generated by a JSP). Then you create a custom HTML error page for the Container to use when the user makes a login error. Finally, you tie the two forms together in the DD, using the <login-config> element. Note: if you're using Form-based authentication, be sure to turn on SSL or session tracking, or your Container might not recognize the login form when it's returned!

What YOU do:

1. **Declare <login-config> in the DD**
2. **Create an HTML login form**
3. **Create an HTML error form**

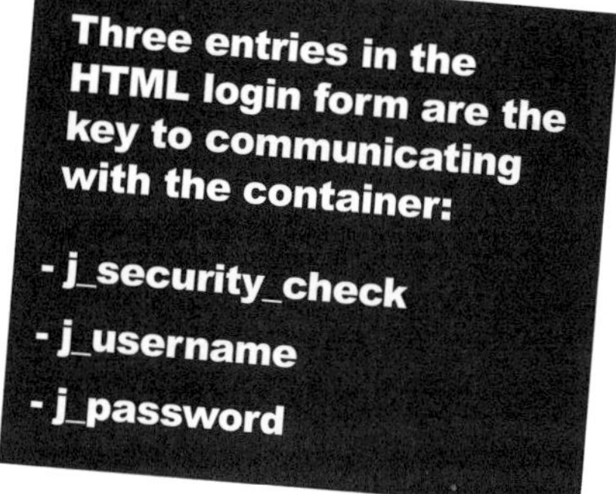

Three entries in the HTML login form are the key to communicating with the container:
- j_security_check
- j_username
- j_password

1 In the DD...

```
<login-config>
  <auth-method>FORM</auth-method>
  <form-login-config>
    <form-login-page>/loginPage.html</form-login-page>
    <form-error-page>/loginError.html</form-error-page>
  </form-login-config>
</login-config>
```

2 Inside the loginPage.html...

```
Please login daddy-o
<form method="POST" action="j_security_check">
  <input type="text" name="j_username">
  <input type="password" name="j_password">
  <input type="submit" value="Enter">
</form>
```

For the container to work, the action of the HTML login form MUST be: j_security_check

The Container requires that the HTTP request will store the user name in: j_username

The container requires that the HTTP request will store the password in: j_password

3 Inside the loginError.html...

```
<html><body>
  Sorry dude, wrong password
</body></html>
```

Don't relax! ***You need to know everything on this page for the exam!***

Summary of Authentication types

This table summarizes key attributes of the four authentication types. "Spec" refers to whether this type of authentication mechanism is defined in the HTTP spec or the J2EE spec. (Hint: you'll need to remember this table when you take the exam.)

Type	Spec	Data Integrity	Comments
BASIC	HTTP	Base64 - weak	HTTP standard, all browsers support it
DIGEST	HTTP	Stronger - but not SSL	Optional for HTTP and J2EE containers
FORM	J2EE	Very weak, no encryption	Allows a custom login screen
CLIENT-CERT	J2EE	Strong - public key, (PKC)	Strong, but users must have certificates

there are no Dumb Questions

Q: What does data integrity have to do with Authentication?

A: When you're authenticating a user, she's sending you her username and password. **Data integrity** and **confidentiality** refers to the degree to which an eavesdropper can steal or tamper with this information. In a moment, we'll talk about how to implement data integrity and confidentiality during login.

Data *integrity* means that the data that arrives is the same as the data that was sent. In other words, nobody tampered with it along the way. Data *confidentiality* means that nobody else can see the data along the way. Most of the time, though, we treat data integrity *and* confidentiality as a single goal—things you do to *protect data during transmission*.

Sharpen your pencil

Fill-in the missing pieces for this FORM-based authentication app. This is just to help you *memorize* the authentication-related pieces of the DD and the HTML form. (The answers are on the previous page.)

DD

```
<login-config>
   <auth-method>[          ]</auth-method>
   <form-login-config>
      <[          ]>/loginPage.html<[          ]/>
      <form-error-page>/loginError.html</form-error-page>
   </form-login-config>
</login-config>
```

HTML

```
Please login daddy-o
<form method="POST" action=[          ]>
   <input type="text" name=[          ]>
   <input type="password" name="j_password">
   <input type="submit" value="Enter">
</form>
```

Form-based authentication doesn't have any protection for the data. But I don't want to use the ugly browser login window that the other three authentication types use. Oh if only there were a way to use my own custom login form, but still protect the username and password when they're sent back...

She doesn't know about J2EE's "protected transport layer connection"

Don't Panic. You can have your custom login cake and secure it too. Login data is still ***data***, so you can secure it in the same way you'd want to protect an online shopper's credit card number—using your J2EE-compliant Container's data integrity and confidentiality features.

Securing data in transit: HTTPS to the rescue

When you tell a J2EE Container that you want to implement data confidentiality and/or integrity, the J2EE spec guarantees that the data to be transmitted will travel over a "**protected transport layer connection**". In other words, Containers are not *required* to use any specific protocol to handle secure transmissions, but in practice they nearly all use HTTPS over SSL.

HTTP request—*not secured*

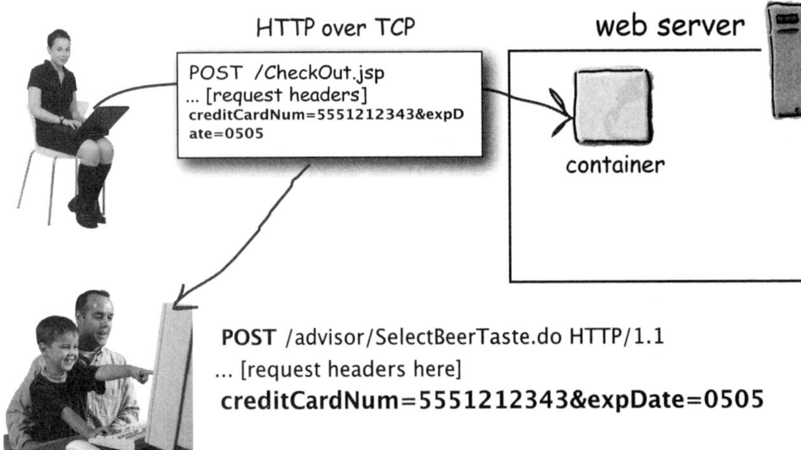

The Bad Eavesdropper gets a copy of the HTTP request that contains the client's credit card info. The data isn't protected, so it comes over in the body of the POST in a nice readable form. *The Eavesdropper is happy.*

A *secured* HTTPS over SSL request

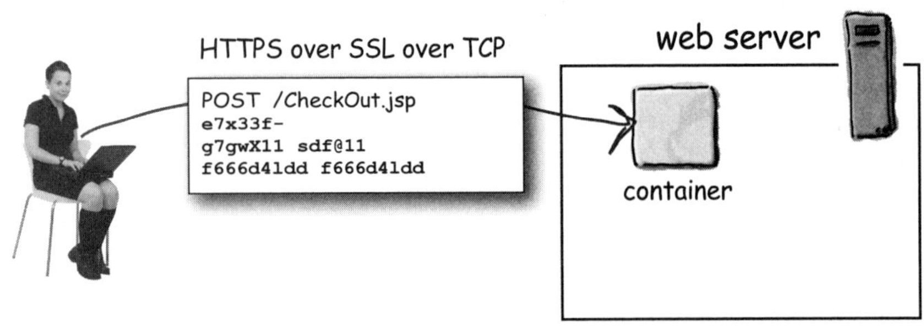

The Bad Eavesdropper gets a copy of the HTTP request that contains the client's credit card info.

But because it was sent with extra-strength HTTPS over SSL, he CANNOT read the information !!

Do NOT tell me that if I choose to use data protection it encrypts EVERY request and response in my app...

Sharpen your pencil

Think about what's been covered in this chapter. If your web application is going to be fast, efficient and secure, you've got some questions to answer... (there are no answers for this one; it's for you to figure out).

Do you need for every request and response to be secure? If not, which parts of your app need protected transmissions? __________________________________

What do you think data confidentiality means? __________________________________

What do you think data integrity means? __________________________________

If you could apply transmission security measures to only some requests and responses, how would you want to tell the Container *which* requests and responses? __________________________________

____

Can you think of any other DD elements that work on the same level of granularity that you want for declaring protected transmissions? __________________________________

How to implement data confidentiality and integrity sparingly and declaratively

Once again, we turn to the DD. In fact, we'll use our old friend **<security-constraint>** for both confidentiality and integrity by adding an element called **<user-data-constraint>**. And when you think about it, it makes sense—if you're thinking about authorization for a resource, you're probably going to consider whether you want the data transmitted securely.

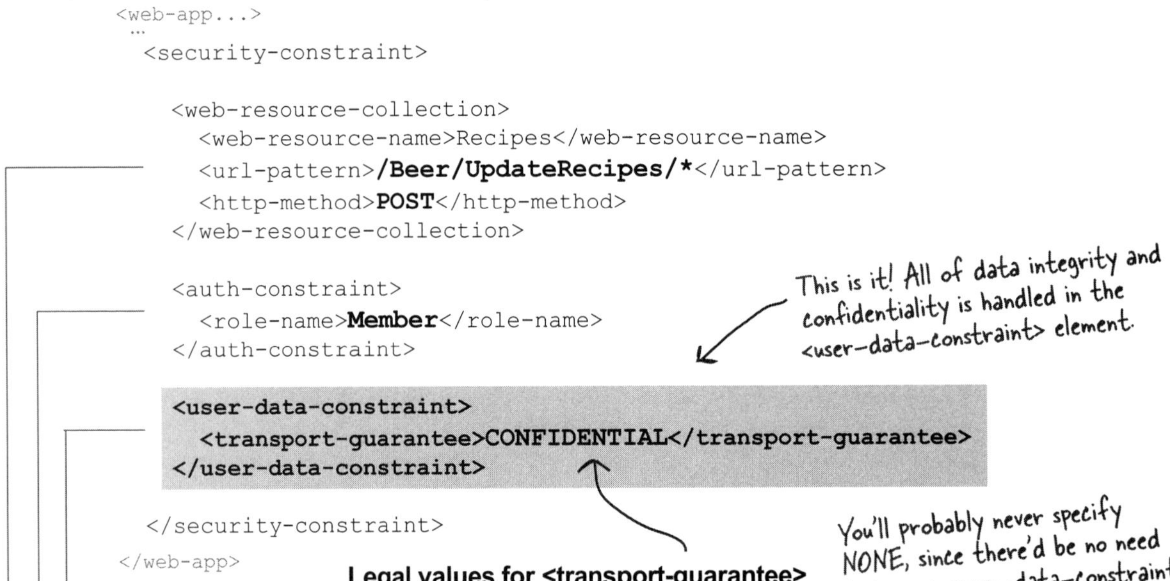

This is it! All of data integrity and confidentiality is handled in the <user-data-constraint> element.
You'll probably never specify NONE, since there'd be no need to have a <user-data-constraint> if you're not planning to protect the data!


```
<web-app...>
...
  <security-constraint>

    <web-resource-collection>
      <web-resource-name>Recipes</web-resource-name>
      <url-pattern>/Beer/UpdateRecipes/*</url-pattern>
      <http-method>POST</http-method>
    </web-resource-collection>

    <auth-constraint>
      <role-name>Member</role-name>
    </auth-constraint>

    <user-data-constraint>
      <transport-guarantee>CONFIDENTIAL</transport-guarantee>
    </user-data-constraint>

  </security-constraint>
</web-app>
```

Put these three sub-elements together to read:

Only ***Members*** can make POST requests to resources found in the ***UpdateRecipes*** directory, and make sure the transmission is secure.

Legal values for <transport-guarantee>

NONE

This is the default, and it means there's no data protection.

INTEGRAL

The data must not be changed along the way.

CONFIDENTIAL

The data must not be seen by anybody along the way.

NOTE: although not guaranteed by the spec, in practice virtually every Container uses SSL for guaranteed transport, which means that both INTEGRAL and CONFIDENTIAL do the same thing—either one gives you both confidentiality and integrity. Since you can have only one <user-data-constraint> per <security-constraint>, some people recommend you use CONFIDENTIAL, but again, it will probably never matter in practice, unless you move to a new (and unusual) Container that doesn't use SSL.

Wait... how do you guarantee that the *request* data is confidential? The Container doesn't even know it's supposed to protect the transmission until AFTER the client makes the request...

Protecting the request data

Remember that in the DD, the <security-constraint> is about what happens *after* the request. In other words, the client has already made the request when the Container starts looking at the <security-constraint> elements to decide how to respond. *The request data has already been sent over the wire.* How can you possibly remind the browser that, "Oh, by the way... if the user happens to request *this* resource, switch to secure sockets (SSL) *before* sending the request."

What can you do?

You already know how to force the client to get a login screen—by defining a constrained resource in the DD, the Container will automatically trigger the authentication process when an unauthenticated user makes the request.

So now we have to figure out how to protect the data coming in from a request... even (and sometimes *especially*) when the client has not yet logged in.

We might want to protect their login data!

Turn the page to see how it all works...

Unauthorized client requests a constrained resource that has NO transport guarantee

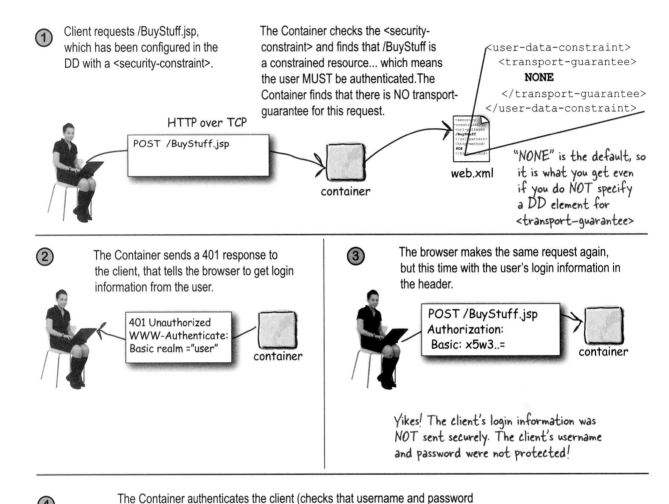

1 Client requests /BuyStuff.jsp, which has been configured in the DD with a <security-constraint>.

The Container checks the <security-constraint> and finds that /BuyStuff is a constrained resource... which means the user MUST be authenticated.The Container finds that there is NO transport-guarantee for this request.

HTTP over TCP

POST /BuyStuff.jsp

container

web.xml

```
<user-data-constraint>
  <transport-guarantee>
     NONE
  </transport-guarantee>
</user-data-constraint>
```

"NONE" is the default, so it is what you get even if you do NOT specify a DD element for <transport-guarantee>

2 The Container sends a 401 response to the client, that tells the browser to get login information from the user.

401 Unauthorized
WWW-Authenticate:
Basic realm ="user"

container

3 The browser makes the same request again, but this time with the user's login information in the header.

POST /BuyStuff.jsp
Authorization:
Basic: x5w3..=

container

Yikes! The client's login information was NOT sent securely. The client's username and password were not protected!

4 The Container authenticates the client (checks that username and password match the user data configured in the server). Then the Container authorizes the request to make sure that this user is in a role that's allowed to get the constrained resource. Everything checks out, so the response is sent.

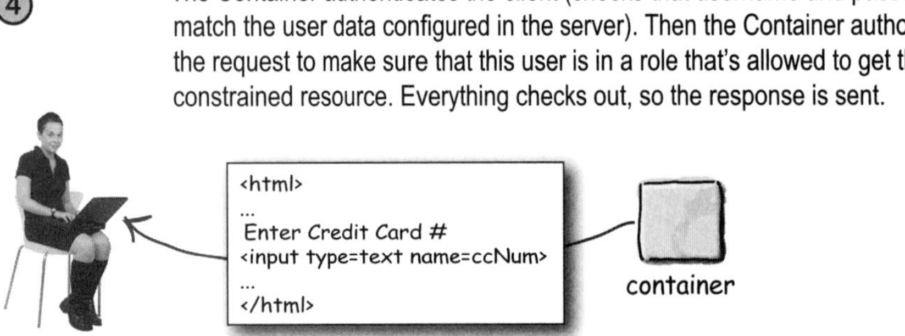

Unauthorized client requests a constrained resource that has a CONFIDENTIALITY transport guarantee

1 Client requests /BuyStuff.jsp, a constrained resource that also has a transport guarantee.

The Container sees that this constrained resource has a transport guarantee. The Container sees that the request did NOT come in securely...

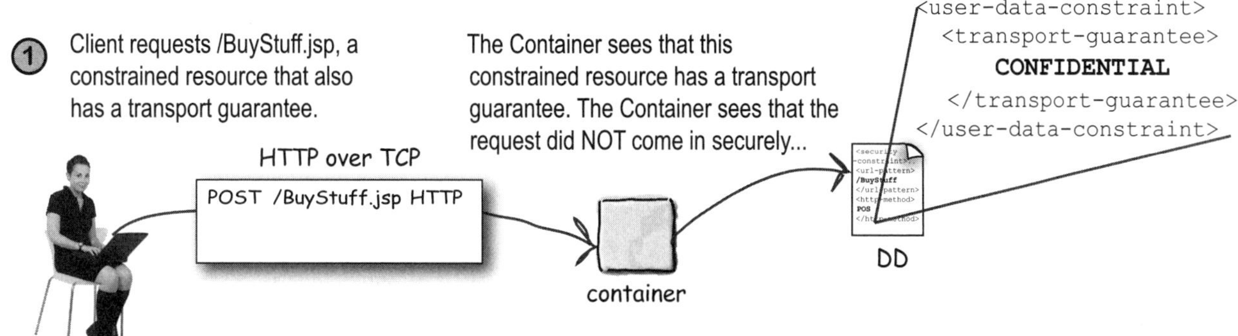

2 The Container sends a 301 response to the client, that tells the browser to redirect the request using a secure transport.

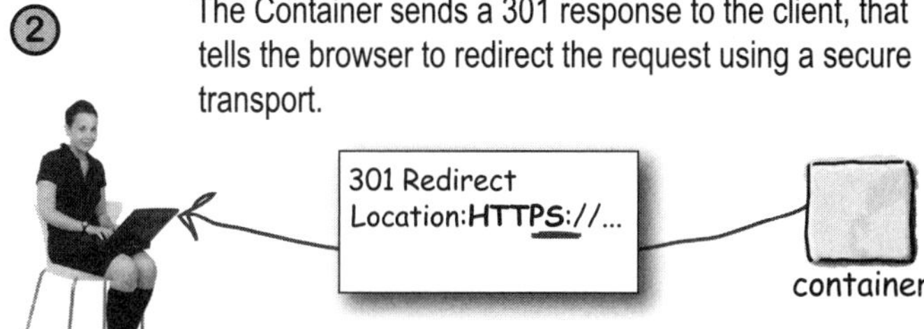

Yes, the "301" is used for normal redirects, but it's ALSO the way the Container tells the browser, "Hey, come back over a secure connection next time and THEN I'll see if we can talk..."

3 The browser makes the same resource request again, but this time, over a secure connection. In other words, the resource stays the same, but the protocol is now HTTPS.

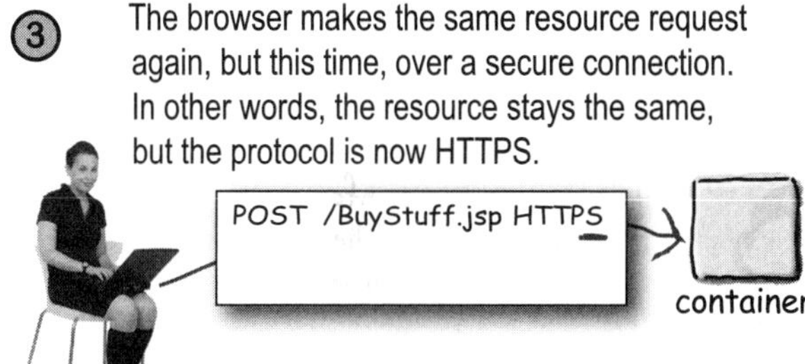

4 *Now* the Container sees that the resource is constrained, and that this user has not authenticated. So *now* the Container starts the authentication process by sending a "401" to the browser...

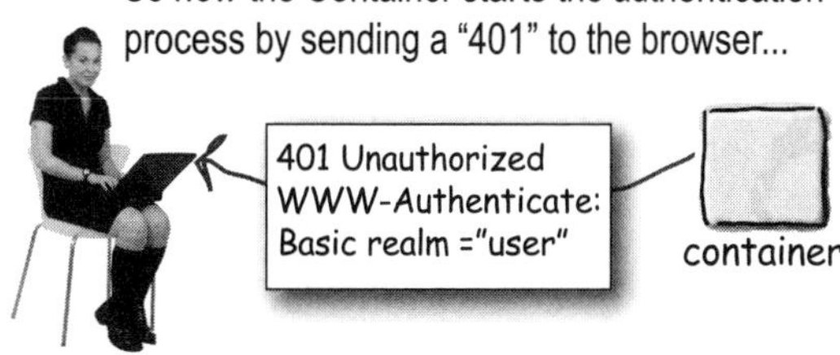

5 The browser makes the same request ***again***, (yes, for the THIRD time) but *this* time the request has the user's login data in the header AND the request comes over using a secure connection. So *this* time the client's login data is transmitted securely!

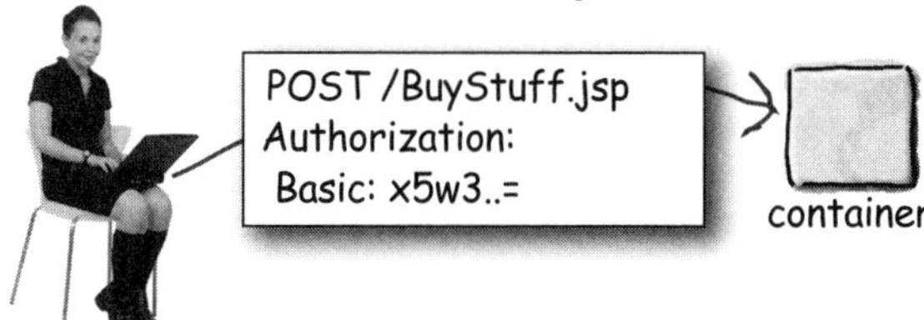

Bottom line: when a request comes in, the Container looks FIRST at the <transport-guarantee>, and if there IS one, the Container tries to deal with that issue first by asking, "Is this request over a secure connection?" If not, the Container doesn't even bother to look at authentication/authorization info. It just tells the client "Come back when you're secure, then we'll talk..."

To make sure the user's login info is submitted to the server securely, put a transport guarantee on EVERY constrained resource that could trigger the login process!

Remember, when you're using declarative authentication, the client never makes a direct request for the login. The client triggers the login/authentication process by requesting a constrained resource. So, if you want to make sure that your client's login data comes back to the server over a secure connection, you need to put a <transport-guarantee> on EVERY constrained resource that could trigger the login form on the client!

That way, the Container will get the request for the constrained resource, but BEFORE telling the browser to get the client's login data, the Container tells the browser, "You're not supposed to even MAKE this request until you're using a secure connection." Then when the client comes back the second time, the Container THEN says, "Oh, I see you're on a secure connection, but I still need authentication data from the user." The browser puts up the login form for the user, gets the user's info, and sends back this THIRD request over a secure connection.

there are no Dumb Questions

Q: I don't understand why the Container sends back a REDIRECT (301) to the client when the request comes in without a secure connection. Doesn't it just redirect back to the same original request?

A: Normally you think of a redirect as meaning "Hey browser, go to a *different* URL instead." The redirect is invisible to the client, remember; the client's browser automatically makes the new request on the URL specified in the redirect (301) header that comes from the server.

But with transport security, it's a little different. Instead of telling the client browser, "Redirect to a *different* resource", the Container says, "Re-direct to the *same* resource, but with a *different* protocol—use HTTP**S** instead of HTTP."

Q: So, is HTTPS over SSL just built-in to the Container somehow?

A: It's not guaranteed by the spec, but it's extremely likely that your Container is using HTTPS over SSL (secure sockets). ***But it won't necessarily be automatic!*** You probably have to configure SSL in your Container, and more importantly—you need a certificate!

You'll have to check your Container's documentation, but chances are, your Container can generate a certificate that you can use for testing, but for production, you'll need to get a Public Key certification from an "official" source such as VeriSign.

(Certificates and security protocols like HTTPS and SSL are way outside the scope of the exam, by the way. You're expected to know only what you have to do in the DD, and why. You're not expected to be the sys-admin and network security master.)

Sharpen your pencil

Configure the security aspects of a web application by filling in the three blocks in the DD. The web application must have the following behavior:

You want anyone to be able to do a GET on the resources within the Beer/UpdateRecipes directory (including any subdirectories), but you want ONLY those with the security role of "Admin" to be able to do a POST on resources within that directory. Also, you want the data to be protected so that nobody can eavesdrop.

```
<web-app...>

  <security-constraint>

  </security-constraint>

...
</web-app>
```

Fill out the following table by writing in the relevant DD elements. You'll see the answers when you turn the page (and don't even *LOOK* at the opposite page!).

Security goal	**What you'd put in the DD**
You want the Container to do BASIC authentication automatically.	
You want to use your own custom form page, named "loginPage.html" (and deployed directly at the root of the web app), and you want "loginError.html" to be displayed if the client cannot be authenticated.	
You want to constrain everything with a ".do" extension so that all clients can do a GET, but only Members can do a POST. (You do NOT need to include the DD elements needed to configure login information.)	
You want to constrain everything within the *foo/bar* directory so that only those with a security role of Admin can invoke ANY HTTP methods on those resources. (You do NOT need to include the DD elements needed to configure login information.)	

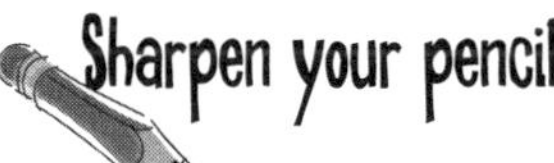

ANSWERS

You want everyone to be able to do a GET on the resources within the Beer/UpdateRecipes directory (including any subdirectories), but you want ONLY those with the security role of "Admin" to be able to do a POST on resources within that directory. Also, you want the data to be protected so that nobody can eavesdrop.

```
<web-app...>

  <security-constraint>

    <web-resource-collection>

      <web-resource-name>Recipes</web-resource-name>

      <url-pattern>/Beer/UpdateRecipes/*</url-pattern>

      <http-method>POST</http-method>

    </web-resource-collection>

    <auth-constraint>

      <role-name>Admin</role-name>

    </auth-constraint>

    <user-data-constraint>

      <transport-guarantee>CONFIDENTIAL</transport-guarantee>

    </user-data-constraint>

  </security-constraint>

...
</web-app>
```

Remember, the URL pattern for protected directories needs to end with a "/*".

If you didn't specify ANY <auth-constraint>, EVERYONE would be able to do a POST. Putting in Admin means that only Admin can access the combination of the URL pattern and the HTTP Method.

You could have said INTEGRAL here and for virtually all Containers, you'd still get confidentiality, because Containers use SSL for their transport guarantee (although that's not guaranteed by the spec).

ANSWERS

Security goal — **What you'd put in the DD**

You want the Container to do BASIC authentication automatically.

```
<web-app...>
  ...
  <login-config>
     <auth-method>BASIC</auth-method>
  </login-config>
</web-app>
```

You want to use your own custom form page, named "loginPage.html" (and deployed directly at the root of the web app), and you want "loginError.html" to be displayed if the client cannot be authenticated.

```
<web-app...>
  ...
  <login-config>
     <auth-method>FORM</auth-method>
     <form-login-config>
       <form-login-page>/loginPage.html</form-login-page>
       <form-error-page>/loginError.html</form-error-page>
     </form-login-config>
  </login-config>
</web-app>
```

You want to constrain everything with a ".do" extension so that all clients can do a GET, but only Members can do a POST.

You configure two things: a constrained resource (i.e. URL pattern plus HTTP Method), and the <auth-constraint> that defines the security role that can access the specified <http-method> on the specified <url-pattern>.

```
<web-app...>
  ...
  <security-constraint>
     <web-resource-collection>
        <web-resource-name>CoolThings</web-resource-name>
        <url-pattern>*.do</url-pattern>
        <http-method>POST</http-method>
     </web-resource-collection>

     <auth-constraint>
       <role-name>Member</role-name>
     </auth-constraint>

  </security-constraint>
</web-app>
```

We used the extension URL pattern that always starts with an asterisk (*).

You want to constrain everything within the foo/bar directory so that only those with a security role of Admin can invoke *any* HTTP methods on those resources.

```
<web-app...>
  ...
  <security-constraint>
     <web-resource-collection>
        <web-resource-name>Stuff</web-resource-name>
        <url-pattern>/foo/bar/*</url-pattern>
     </web-resource-collection>

     <auth-constraint>
        <role-name>Admin</role-name>
     </auth-constraint>
  </security-constraint>
</web-app>
```

We left off <http-method> so that ALL HTTP Methods are constrained to be accessible only to those in the Admin role.

Sharpen your pencil ANSWERS

		Nobody	Guest	Member	Admin	Everyone
1	<security-constraint> ... <auth-constraint> <role-name>Guest</role-name> </auth-constraint> </security-constraint>		X			
2	<security-constraint> ... <auth-constraint/> </security-constraint>	X				
3	<security-constraint> ... <auth-constraint> <role-name>Admin</role-name> </auth-constraint> </security-constraint> <security-constraint> ... <auth-constraint> <role-name>Guest</role-name> </auth-constraint> </security-constraint>		X		X	
4	<security-constraint> ... <auth-constraint> <role-name>Guest</role-name> </auth-constriant> </security-constraint> <security-constraint> ... <auth-constraint> <role-name>*</role-name> </auth-constraint> </security-constraint>					X
5	<security-constraint> ... <auth-constraint> <role-name>Member</role-name> </auth-constraint> </security-constraint> <security-constraint> ... </security-constraint> ← Assume that NO <auth-constraint> is defined.					X
6	<security-constraint> ... <auth-constraint> <role-name>Member</role-name> </auth-constraint> </security-constraint> <security-constraint> ... <auth-constraint/> </security-constraint>	X				

Mock Exam Chapter 12

---

1 Which security mechanisms always operate independently of the transport layer? (Choose all that apply.)

- ❑ A. authorization
- ❑ B. data integrity
- ❑ C. authentication
- ❑ D. confidentiality

---

2 Given a deployment descriptor with three valid `<security-constraint>` elements, all constraining web resource A, whose respective `<auth-constraint>` sub-elements are:

```
<auth-constraint>
    <role-name>Bob</role-name>
</auth-constraint>
<auth-constraint/>
<auth-constraint>
    <role-name>Alice</role-name>
</auth-constraint>
```

Who can access resource A?

- ❑ A. no one
- ❑ B. anyone
- ❑ C. only Bob
- ❑ D. only Alice

3 Which activities would be addressed via a J2EE 1.4 container's data integrity mechanism? (Choose all that apply.)

- ❑ A. Verifying that a specific user is allowed access to a specific HTML page.
- ❑ B. Ensuring that an eavesdropper can't read an HTTP message being sent from the client to the container.
- ❑ C. Verifying that a client making a request for a constrained JSP has the proper role credentials to access the JSP.
- ❑ D. Ensuring that a hacker can't alter the contents of an HTTP message while it is in transit from the container to a client.

---

4 Which are required fields in the login form when using Form Based Authentication? (Choose all that apply.)

- ❑ A. `pw`
- ❑ B. `id`
- ❑ C. `j_pw`
- ❑ D. `j_id`
- ❑ E. `password`
- ❑ F. `j_password`

---

5 Which authentication types require a specific type of HTML action? (Choose all that apply.)

- ❑ A. HTTP Basic Authentication
- ❑ B. Form Based Authentication
- ❑ C. HTTP Digest Authentication
- ❑ D. HTTPS Client Authentication

---

6 Which security mechanisms can be implemented by using a method in the `HttpServletRequest` interface? (Choose all that apply.)

- ❑ A. authorization
- ❑ B. data integrity
- ❑ C. authentication
- ❑ D. confidentiality

---

7 Which `HttpServletRequest` method is most closely associated with the use of the `<security-role-ref>` element?

- ❑ A. `getHeader`
- ❑ B. `getCookies`
- ❑ C. `isUserInRole`
- ❑ D. `getUserPrincipal`
- ❑ E. `isRequestedSessionIDValid`

---

8 Which deployment descriptor elements can contain a `<transport-guarantee>` sub-element? (Choose all that apply.)

- ❑ A. `<auth-constraint>`
- ❑ B. `<security-role-ref>`
- ❑ C. `<form-login-config>`
- ❑ D. `<user-data-constraint>`

---

9 Which authentication mechanism is recommended to be used only if cookies or SSL session tracking is in place?

- ❑ A. HTTP Basic Authentication
- ❑ B. Form Based Authentication
- ❑ C. HTTP Digest Authentication
- ❑ D. HTTPS Client Authentication

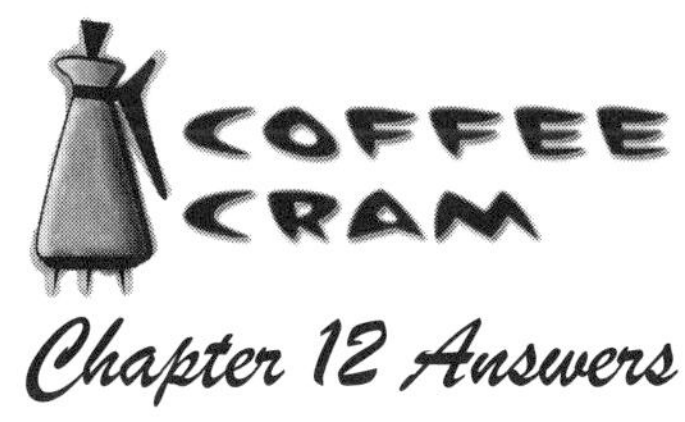

Chapter 12 Answers

1 Which security mechanisms always operate independently of the transport layer? (Choose all that apply.) (servlet spec: chap 12)

- [x] A. authorization
- [ ] B. data integrity
- [ ] C. authentication
- [ ] D. confidentiality

–Option A is correct. Authorization operates completely within the container once authentication has occurred. Authentication can affect the transport layer based on how the <auth-method> element is set.

---

2 Given a deployment descriptor with three valid **<security-constraint>** elements, all constraining web resource A, whose respective **<auth-constraint>** sub-elements are: (servlet spec: 12.8.1)

```
<auth-constraint>
    <role-name>Bob</role-name>
</auth-constraint>
<auth-constraint/>
<auth-constraint>
    <role-name>Alice</role-name>
</auth-constraint>
```

Who can access resource A?

- [x] A. no one
- [ ] B. anyone
- [ ] C. only Bob
- [ ] D. only Alice

–Option A is correct. The existence of an empty <auth-constraint> element overrides all other <auth-constraint> elements that refer to that resource, precluding access.

3 Which activities would be addressed via a J2EE 1.4 container's data integrity mechanism? (Choose all that apply.) (Servlet spec., 12.1)

- [ ] A. Verifying that a specific user is allowed access to a specific HTML page.
- [ ] B. Ensuring that an eavesdropper can't read an HTTP message being sent from the client to the container.
- [ ] C. Verifying that a client making a request for a constrained JSP has the proper role credentials to access the JSP.
- [x] D. Ensuring that a hacker can't alter the contents of an HTTP message while it is in transit from the container to a client.

–Option B describes confidentiality.

–Option D is correct. This would typically be accomplished through the use of HTTPS.

4 Which are required fields in the login form when using Form Based Authentication? (Choose all that apply.) (Servlet spec., 12.5.3:)

- [ ] A. **`pw`**
- [ ] B. **`id`**
- [ ] C. **`j_pw`**
- [ ] D. **`j_id`**
- [ ] E. **`password`**
- [x] F. **`j_password`**

–Option F is correct, the user's password must be stored in a field called j_password. In addition, the user's name must be stored in j_username.

5 Which authentication types require a specific type of HTML action? (Choose all that apply.) (Servlet spec., 12.5.3.1)

- [ ] A. HTTP Basic Authentication
- [x] B. Form Based Authentication
- [ ] C. HTTP Digest Authentication
- [ ] D. HTTPS Client Authentication

–Option B is correct. For form based authentication to work, the action of the login form must be j_security_check.

6 Which security mechanisms can be implemented by using a method in the **HttpServletRequest** interface? (Choose all that apply.) (Servlet spec., 12.3)

- [x] A. authorization
- [ ] B. data integrity
- [x] C. authentication
- [ ] D. confidentiality

-Option A is correct. The isUserInRole method can be used programatically, to help determine whether a client's role is authorized to access a given resource.

-Option C is correct. The getRemoteUser method can be used programatically, to help determine whether a client has been authenticated.

7 Which **HttpServletRequest** method is most closely associated with the use of the **<security-role-ref>** element? (Servlet spec., 12.3)

- [ ] A. **getHeader**
- [ ] B. **getCookies**
- [x] C. **isUserInRole**
- [ ] D. **getUserPrincipal**
- [ ] E. **isRequestedSessionIDValid**

-Option C is correct. The <security-role-ref> element is used to map roles hardcoded in a servlet element to roles declared in the deployment descriptor. The isUserInRole method is used in a servlet to test the contents of <security-role-ref> elements..

8 Which deployment descriptor elements can contain a **<transport-guarantee>** sub-element? (Choose all that apply.) (Servlet spec., 13.4)

- [ ] A. **<auth-constraint>**
- [ ] B. **<security-role-ref>**
- [ ] C. **<form-login-config>**
- [x] D. **<user-data-constraint>**

-Option D is correct. A <transport-guarantee> element is used within a <user-data-constraint> element to specify whether a web resource collection should be transmitted using a mechanism such as SSL.

9 Which authentication mechanism is recommended to be used only if cookies or SSL session tracking is in place? (Servlet spec., 12.5.3.1)

- [ ] A. HTTP Basic Authentication
- [x] B. Form Based Authentication
- [ ] C. HTTP Digest Authentication
- [ ] D. HTTPS Client Authentication

-Option B is correct. Form based login session tracking can be difficult to implement, therefore a separate session tracking mechanism is recommended.

The Power of Filters

Do not even THINK about trying to talk to the master without going through me first. I control what goes to the master, and I control what comes from the master...
They say that he was inspired by the Intercepting Filter pattern.

Filters let you intercept the request. And if you can intercept the *request*, you can also control the *response*. And best of all, **the servlet remains clueless**. It never knows that someone stepped in between the client request and the Container's invocation of the servlet's service() method. What does that mean to you? More vacations. Because the time you would have spent rewriting just *one* of your servlets can be spent instead writing and configuring a filter that has the ability to affect *all* of your servlets. Want to add user request tracking to *every* servlet in your app? No problem. Want to manipulate the output from every *servlet* in your app? No problem. And you don't even have to *touch* the servlet code. Filters may be the most powerful web app development tool you have.

Filters

Coverage Notes:

3.3 Describe the Web Container request processing model; write and configure a filter; create a request or response wrapper; and given a design problem, describe how to apply a filter or wrapper.

This objective is covered completely in this chapter.

11.1 *Given a scenario description with a list of issues, select a pattern that would solve the issues. The list of patterns you must know are:* **Intercepting Filter***, Model-View-Controller, Front Controller, Service Locator, Business Delegate, and Transfer Object.*

11.2 *Match design patterns with statements describing potential benefits that accrue from the use of the pattern, for any of the following patterns:* **Intercepting Filter***, Model-View-Controller, Service Locator, Business Delegate, and Transfer Object.*

Filters, which are covered in this chapter, are an example of (imagine this) the Intercepting Filter pattern. We don't cover pattern-specific info until the Patterns chapter, but it's in THIS chapter where you actually see a design that demonstrates the Intercepting Filter pattern.

Enhancing the entire web application

Sometimes you need to enhance your system in ways that span many different use cases or requests. For example, you might want to keep track of your system's response times, across all of its different user interactions.

I got good news and bad news today. The good news is that the new "Add your favorite recipe" feature on the Beer site is very popular! The bad news is that the boss wants us to keep track of all the users who access these servlets...

I sure don't want to go modify a bunch of working servlets, *especially* when I know that as soon as I *add* user tracking, the boss will tell me to take it out again...

How about some kind of "filter"?

Filters are Java components—very similar to servlets—that you can use to intercept and process requests *before* they are sent to the servlet, or to process responses *after* the servlet has completed, but *before* the response goes back to the client.

The Container decides when to invoke your filters based on declarations in the DD. In the DD, the deployer maps which filters will be called for which request URL patterns. So it's the deployer, not the programmer, who decides which subset of requests or responses should be processed by which filters.

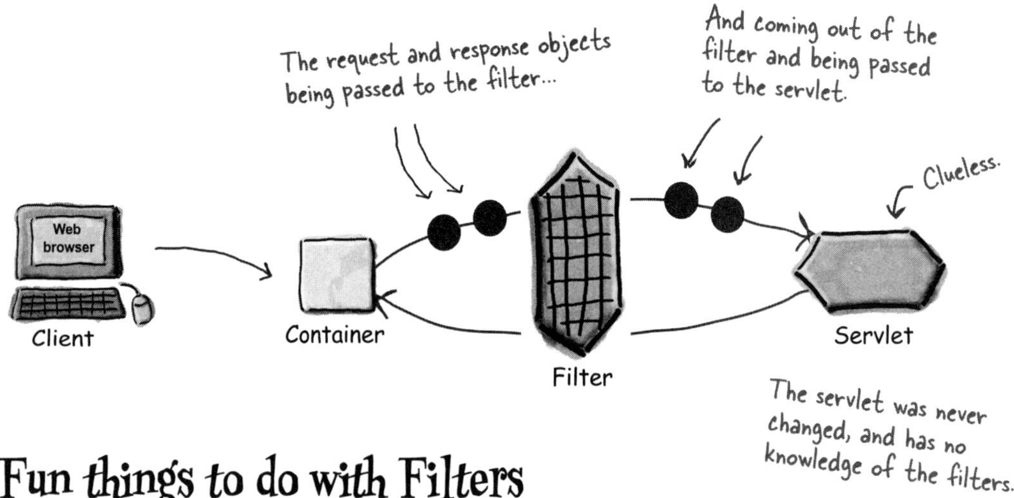
The request and response objects being passed to the filter...
And coming out of the filter and being passed to the servlet.
Clueless.
Web browser
Client
Container
Filter
Servlet
The servlet was never changed, and has no knowledge of the filters.

Fun things to do with Filters

Request filters can:

- perform security checks
- reformat request headers or bodies
- audit or log requests

Response filters can:

- compress the response stream
- append or alter the response stream
- create a different response altogether

BANG!

There is only ONE filter interface, Filter.

There's no such thing as a RequestFilter or ResponseFilter interface—it's just Filter. When we talk about a request filter vs. a response filter, we're talking only about how you USE the filter, not the actual filter interface. As far as the Container is concerned, there is only one kind of filter—anything that implements the Filter interface.

Filters are modular, and configurable in the DD

Filters can be chained together, to run one after the other. Filters are designed to be totally self-contained. A filter doesn't care which (if any) filters ran before *it* did, and it doesn't care which one will run next.*

The DD controls the order in which filters run; we'll talk about filter DD configuration a little later in the chapter.

DD configuration 1:

Using the DD, you can link them together by telling the Container: "For these URLs, run filter 1, then filter 7, then filter 3, then run the target servlet."

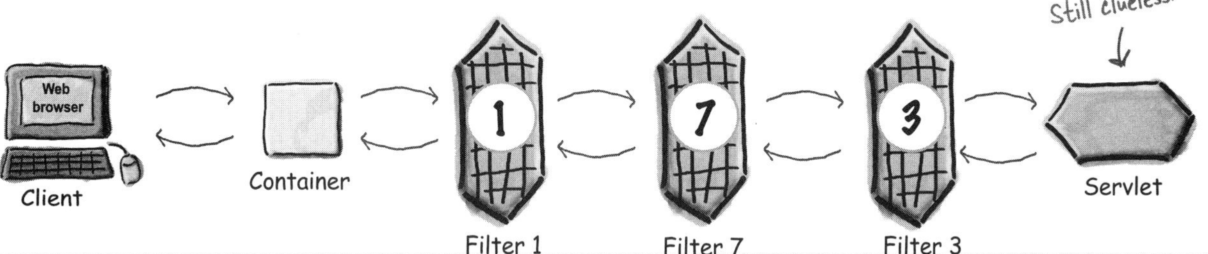

DD configuration 2:

Then, with a quick change to the DD, you can delete and swap them with: "For these URLs, run filter 3, then filter 7, and then the target servlet."

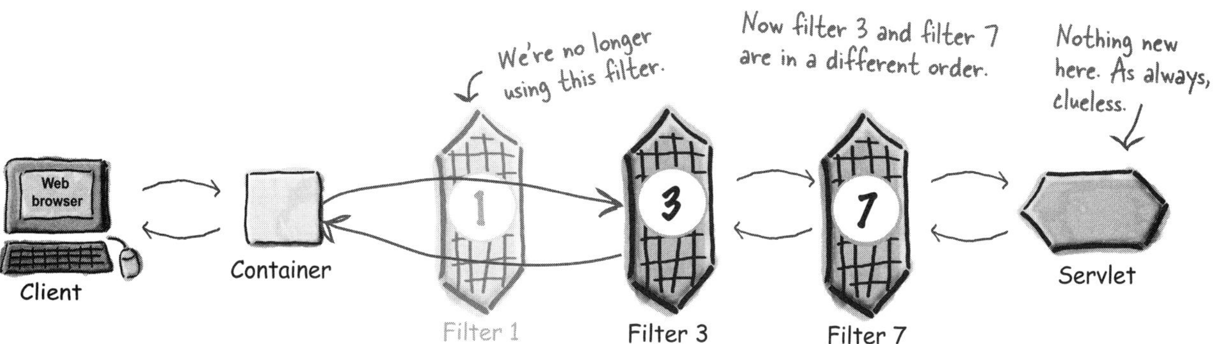

* We're fudging a little. The deployer often *does* need to configure the order based on the consequences of the transformations performed by the filters. You wouldn't, for example, add a watermark to an image after you applied a compression filter. In that example, the watermark filter would have to do its thing before the data hits the compression filter. The point is, you as the *programmer* will not build dependencies into your code.

If filters are like servlets, then I'm guessing they must be invoked by the Container, just like servlets. They probably have their own lifecycle...

Three ways filters are like servlets

Kim's right, filters live in the Container. In many ways they're similar to their co-residents, servlets. Here are a few ways in which filters are like servlets:

The Container knows their API

Filters have their own API. When a Java class implements the **Filter interface**, it's striking a deal with the Container, and it goes from being a plain old class to being an official J2EE Filter. Other members of the filter API allow filters to get access to the ServletContext, and to be linked to other filters.

The Container manages their lifecycle

Just like servlets, filters have a lifecycle. Like servlets, they have **init()** and **destroy()** methods. Similar to a servlet's **doGet()/doPost()** method, filters have a **doFilter()** method.

They're declared in the DD

A web app can have **lots of filters**, and a given request can cause more than one filter to execute. The DD is the place where you declare which filters will run in response to which requests, and in which *order*.

Building the request tracking filter

Our task is to enhance the Beer application so that whenever someone requests any of the resources associated with updating recipes, we'll be able to keep track of who made the request. Here's one version of what such a filter might look like.

Filters have no idea who's going to call them or who's next in line!

```
package com.example.web;

import java.io.*;
import javax.servlet.*;
import javax.servlet.http.HttpServletRequest;

public class BeerRequestFilter implements Filter {

   private FilterConfig fc;


   public void init(FilterConfig config) throws ServletException {
      this.fc = config;
   }

   public void doFilter(ServletRequest req,
                        ServletResponse resp,
                        FilterChain chain)
           throws ServletException, IOException {

      HttpServletRequest httpReq = (HttpServletRequest) req;

      String name = httpReq.getRemoteUser();

      if (name != null) {

        fc.getServletContext().log("User " + name + " is updating");
      }

      chain.doFilter(req, resp);
   }

   public void destroy() {
      // do cleanup stuff
   }
}
```

Filter and FilterChain are in javax.servlet

Every filter MUST implement the Filter interface.

You must implement init(), usually you just save the config object.

doFilter() is where you do the real work.. Notice that the method doesn't take HTTP request and response objects... just regular ServletRequest and ServletResponse objects.

But we're pretty sure that we can cast the request and response to their HTTP subtypes.

This is how the next filter or servlet in line gets called – lots more on this in the next couple of pages.

You must implement destroy() but usually it's empty.

A filter's life cycle

Every filter must implement the three methods in the Filter interface: **init()**, **doFilter()**, and **destroy()**.

First there's init()

When the Container decides to instantiate a filter, the **init()** method is your chance to do any set-up tasks before the filter is called. The most common implementation was shown on the previous page; saving a reference to the **FilterConfig** object for later use in the filter.

doFilter() does the heavy lifting

The **doFilter()** method is called every time the Container determines that the filter should be applied to the current request. The doFilter() method takes three arguments:

- A **ServletRequest** (**not** an **HttpServletRequest**)!
- A **ServletResponse** (**not** an **HttpServletResponse**)!
- A **FilterChain**

The doFilter() method is your chance to implement your filter's function. If your filter is supposed to log user names to a file, do it in doFilter(). Want to compress the response output? Do it in doFilter().

In the end there's destroy()

When the Container decides to remove a filter instance, it calls the **destroy()** method, giving you a chance to do any cleanup you need to do before the instance is destroyed.

there are no Dumb Questions

Q: What is a *FilterChain?*

A: A FilterChain is the coolest thing in all of Filter-dom. Filters are designed to be modular building blocks you can mix together in a variety of ways to make a combination of things happen, and the FilterChain is a big part of what makes this possible. *It's the thing that knows what comes next.* We already mentioned that the filters (not to mention the servlet) shouldn't know anything about the other filters involved in the request... but someone needs to know the order, and that someone is the FilterChain, driven by the filter elements you specify in the DD.

By the way, FilterChain is in the same package as Filter, *javax.servlet*.

Q: I noticed that in your doFilter() method you made this call: *chain.doFilter()*... What's a doFilter() doing inside a doFilter()? You're not gonna get all recursive on us, are you?

A: The ***FilterChain*** interface's doFilter() is a little bit different than the **Filter** interface's doFilter(). Here's the main difference:

The doFilter() method of the ***FilterChain*** takes care of figuring out whose doFilter() method to invoke next (or, if it's the end of the chain, which servlet's service() method). but the doFilter() method in a ***Filter*** actually *does* the filtering—the thing the filter was created to do.

This means a FilterChain can invoke EITHER a filter or a servlet, depending on whether it's the end of the chain. The end of the chain is *always* either a servlet or a JSP (which means a JSP's generated servlet, of course), assuming the Container is able to map the request URL to a servlet or JSP. (If the Container can't locate the right resource for the request, the filter is never invoked.)

Think of filters as being "stackable"

The servlet spec doesn't dictate how the **chain.doFilter(req, resp)** method is handled inside the container. In practice, though, you can think of the process of filters chaining to each other as if they were simply method calls on a single **stack**. We know there's more going on behind the scenes in the Container, but we don't care, as long as we can predict how our filters will run, and a *conceptual* (if not physical) stack lets us do that.

This "conceptual stack" is just a way to think about filter chain invocations. We don't know (or care) how the Container actually implements this—but thinking of it this way lets you predict how your filter chain will behave.

A conceptual call stack example

In this example, a request for ServletA will be filtered by two filters, Filter3, then Filter7.

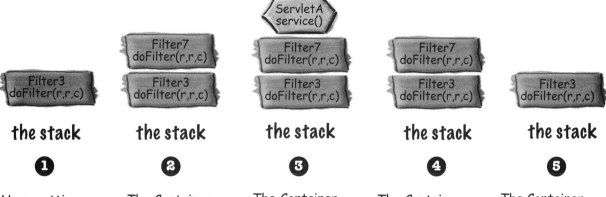

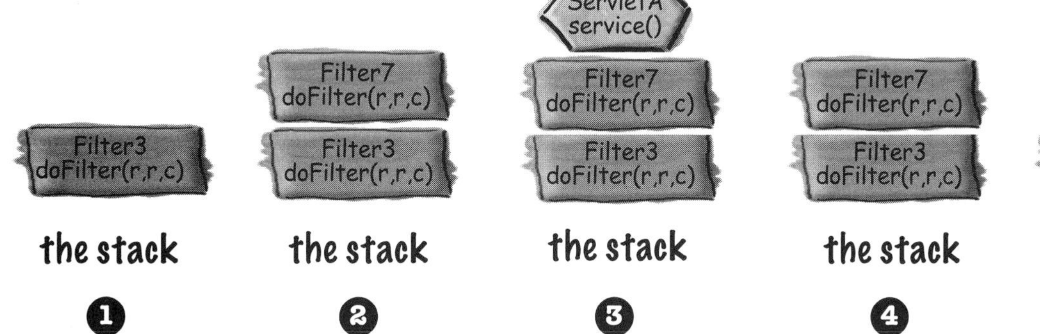

1. Upon getting the request, the Container calls Filter3's doFilter() method, which runs until it encounters its chain.doFilter() call.

2. The Container pushes Filter7's doFilter() method on the top of the stack - where it executes until it reaches its chain. doFilter ()call.

3. The Container pushes ServletA's service() method on the top of the stack where it executes to completion, and is then popped off the stack.

4. The Container returns control to Filter7, where its doFilter() method completes and is then popped off.

5. The Container returns control to Filter3, where its doFilter() method completes, and is popped off. Then the Container completes the response.

Declaring and ordering filters

When you configure filters in the DD, you'll usually do three things:

- Declare your filter
- Map your filter to the web resources you want to filter
- Arrange these mappings to create filter invocation sequences

Declaring a filter

```
<filter>
  <filter-name>BeerRequest</filter-name>
  <filter-class>com.example.web.BeerRequestFilter
        </filter-class>
  <init-param>
    <param-name>LogFileName</param-name>
    <param-value>UserLog.txt</param-value>
  </init-param>
</filter>
```

Rules for <filter>

- The <filter-name> is mandatory.
- The <filter-class> is mandatory.
- The <init-param> is optional, and you can have many.

Declaring a filter mapping to a URL pattern

```
<filter-mapping>
  <filter-name>BeerRequest</filter-name>
  <url-pattern>*.do</url-pattern>
</filter-mapping>
```

Rules for <filter-mapping>

- The <filter-name> is mandatory and it is used to link to the correct <filter> element.
- Either the <url-pattern> or the the <servlet-name> element is mandatory.
- The <url-pattern> element defines which web app resources will use this filter.

Declaring a filter mapping to a servlet name

```
<filter-mapping>
  <filter-name>BeerRequest</filter-name>
  <servlet-name>AdviceServlet</servlet-name>
</filter-mapping>
```

- The <servlet-name> element defines which single web app resource will use this filter.

IMPORTANT: The Container's rules for ordering filters:

When more than one filter is mapped to a given resource, the Container uses the following rules:

1) ALL filters with matching URL patterns are located first. This is NOT the same as the URL mapping rules the Container uses to choose the "winner" when a client makes a request for a resource, because ALL filters that match will be placed in the chain!! Filters with matching URL patterns are placed in the chain in the order in which they are declared in the DD.

2) Once all filters with matching URLs are placed in the chain, the Container does the same thing with filters that have a matching <servlet-name> in the DD.

Isn't THAT typical... they give us a way to filter requests coming from a *client*, and they just forget all about requests that WE generate through *forwards* and *request dispatches.* Geez... they treat request dispatching like it's a second-class invocation technique?!

News Flash: As of version 2.4, filters can be applied to request dispatchers

Think about it. It's great that filters can be applied to requests that come directly from the *client.* But what about resources requested from a **forward** or **include**, **request dispatch**, and/or the **error** handler? Servlet spec 2.4 to the rescue.

Declaring a filter mapping for request-dispatched web resources

```
<filter-mapping>
  <filter-name>MonitorFilter</filter-name>
  <url-pattern>*.do</url-pattern>
  <dispatcher>REQUEST</dispatcher>

        - and / or -

  <dispatcher>INCLUDE</dispatcher>

        - and / or -

  <dispatcher>FORWARD</dispatcher>

        - and / or -

  <dispatcher>ERROR</dispatcher>
</filter-mapping>
```

Declaration Rules

- The <filter-name> is mandatory.
- Either the <url-pattern> or <servlet-name> element is mandatory.
- You can have from 0 to 4 <dispatcher> elements.
- A REQUEST value activates the filter for client requests. If no <dispatcher> element is present, REQUEST is the default.
- An INCLUDE value activates the filter for request dispatching from an include() call.
- A FORWARD value activates the filter for request dispatching from a forward() call.
- An ERROR value activates the filter for resources called by the error handler.

Based on the following DD fragment, write down the sequence in which the filters will be executed for each request path. Assume Filter1 through Filter5 have been properly declared, and that the servlet names are the same as their mappings. (Answers are at the end of this chapter.)

```
<filter-mapping>
  <filter-name>Filter1</filter-name>
  <url-pattern>/Recipes/*</url-pattern>
</filter-mapping>

<filter-mapping>
  <filter-name>Filter2</filter-name>
  <servlet-name>/Recipes/HopsList.do</servlet-name>
</filter-mapping>

<filter-mapping>
  <filter-name>Filter3</filter-name>
  <url-pattern>/Recipes/Add/*</url-pattern>
</filter-mapping>

<filter-mapping>
  <filter-name>Filter4</filter-name>
  <servlet-name>/Recipes/Modify/ModRecipes.do</servlet-name>
</filter-mapping>

<filter-mapping>
  <filter-name>Filter5</filter-name>
  <url-pattern>/*</url-pattern>
</filter-mapping>
```

Request path	**Filter Sequence**
/Recipes/HopsReport.do	Filters:
/Recipes/HopsList.do	Filters:
/Recipes/Modify/ModRecipes.do	Filters:
/HopsList.do	Filters:
/Recipes/Add/AddRecipes.do	Filters:

Compressing output with a response-side filter

Earlier we showed a very simple *request* filter. But now we'll look at a *response* filter. Response filters are a bit trickier, but they can be incredibly useful. They let us do something to the response output after the servlet does its thing, but before the response is sent to the client. So instead of stepping in at the beginning—*before* the servlet gets the request—we step in at the end—*after* the servlet gets the request and generates a response.

Well, *sort of*... think about it. Filters are *always* invoked in the chain *before* the servlet. There's no such thing as a filter that is invoked only after the servlet. But... remember that stack picture. **The filter gets another shot at this *after* the servlet completes its work and is popped off the (virtual) stack!**

My boss liked my first filter so much he wants me to write another one. The company's pipe to the Internet is getting really busy, so now he wants us to compress all of our response streams...

Seems like a filter would be the way to go... But since we're dealing with responses, I'll have to put the compression code AFTER the chain.doFilter() call...

Architecture of a response filter

Rachel is talking about the basic structure of what you put in a doFilter() method—first you do work related to the request, then you call chain.doFilter(), then finally, when the servlet (and any other filter in the chain after your filter) completes and control is returned to your original doFilter()method, you can do something to the response.

Rachel's pseudo-code for the compression filter

```
class MyCompressionFilter implements Filter {

  init();

  public void doFilter(request, response, chain) {

    // this is where request handling would go

    chain.doFilter(request, response);

    // do compression logic here
  }

  destroy();
}
```

The servlet does its work at this point. (annotation on `chain.doFilter(request, response);`)

Now that the servlet is done, we can get to work on compressing the response the servlet generated... (annotation on `// do compression logic here`)

The conceptual call stack

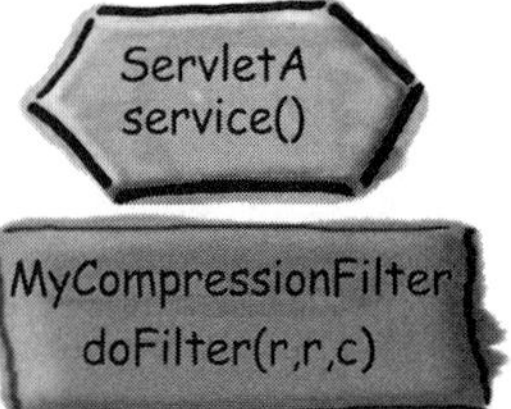

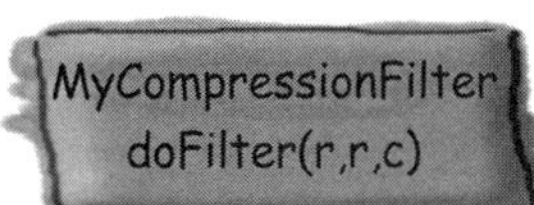

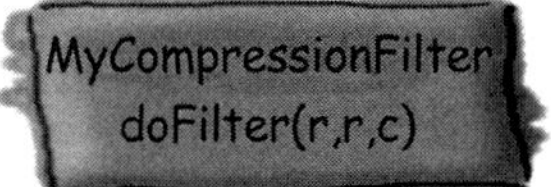

MyCompressionFilter doFilter(r,r,c)

The Compression filter's doFilter() method runs, and invokes chain.doFilter(). It's too early to do any compression—the goal is to compress the response output from the servlet.

The Servlet's service() method goes on the top of the stack, does some work, generates a response output, and completes.

Now that the Servlet's service() method has popped off the stack, the rest of the compression filter's doFilter() method can run, and (it hopes) do the compression on whatever the servlet wrote to the response output!

But is it really that simple?

Does compressing the response really involve nothing more than waiting for the servlet to finish, then compressing the servlet's response output? After all, the filter's doFilter() method has a reference to the same response object that went to the servlet, so in theory, the filter should have access to the response output...

```
public void doFilter(request, response, chain) {
   // this is where request handling would go
   chain.doFilter(request, response); (1) (2)
   // do compression logic here (3)
}
```

1 The filter passes the request and response to the servlet, and waits patiently for its chance to compress stuff.

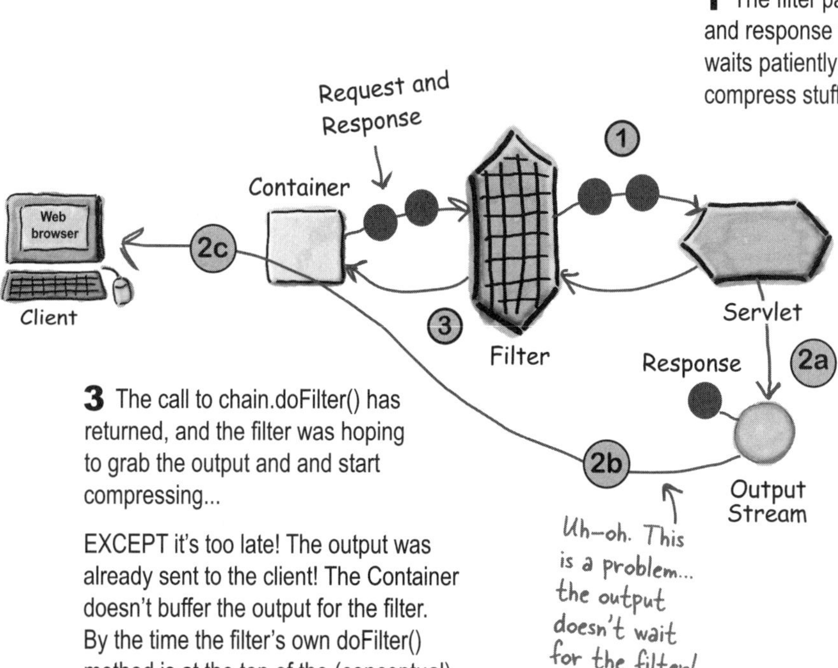

2a The servlet does its thing, creating output, blissfully unaware that this very same output was supposed to be compressed.

2b The output goes back through the Container and...

2c It's sent back to the client! Hmmm... this could be a problem. The filter was hoping to have a chance to do something to the output (compress it) before the output went to the client.

3 The call to chain.doFilter() has returned, and the filter was hoping to grab the output and and start compressing...

EXCEPT it's too late! The output was already sent to the client! The Container doesn't buffer the output for the filter. By the time the filter's own doFilter() method is at the top of the (conceptual) stack, it's ***too late for the filter to affect the output.***

The output has left the building

This won't work! I can't compress something on the way ***out*** of the servlet, because it's too late. The output goes straight from the servlet back to the client. But the whole point is to compress the output, so how can I get control of the output BEFORE it goes to the client?

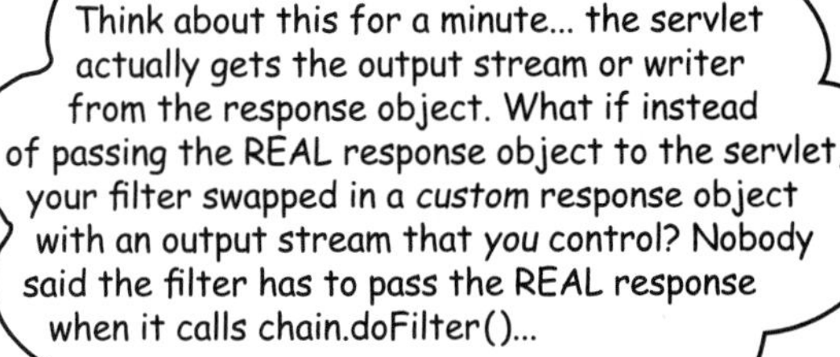

Think about this for a minute... the servlet actually gets the output stream or writer from the response object. What if instead of passing the REAL response object to the servlet, your filter swapped in a *custom* response object with an output stream that *you* control? Nobody said the filter has to pass the REAL response when it calls chain.doFilter()...

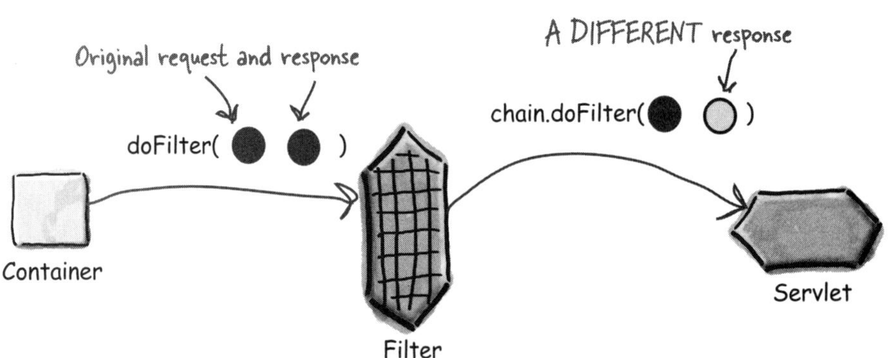

We can implement our OWN response

The Container already implements the HttpServletResponse interface; that's what you get in the doFilter() and service() methods. But to get this compression filter working, we have to make our *own* custom implementation of the HttpServletResponse interface and pass *that* to the servlet via the chain.doFilter() call. And that custom implementation has to also include a *custom output stream* as well, since that's the goal—to capture the output *after* the servlet writes to it but *before* it goes back to the client.

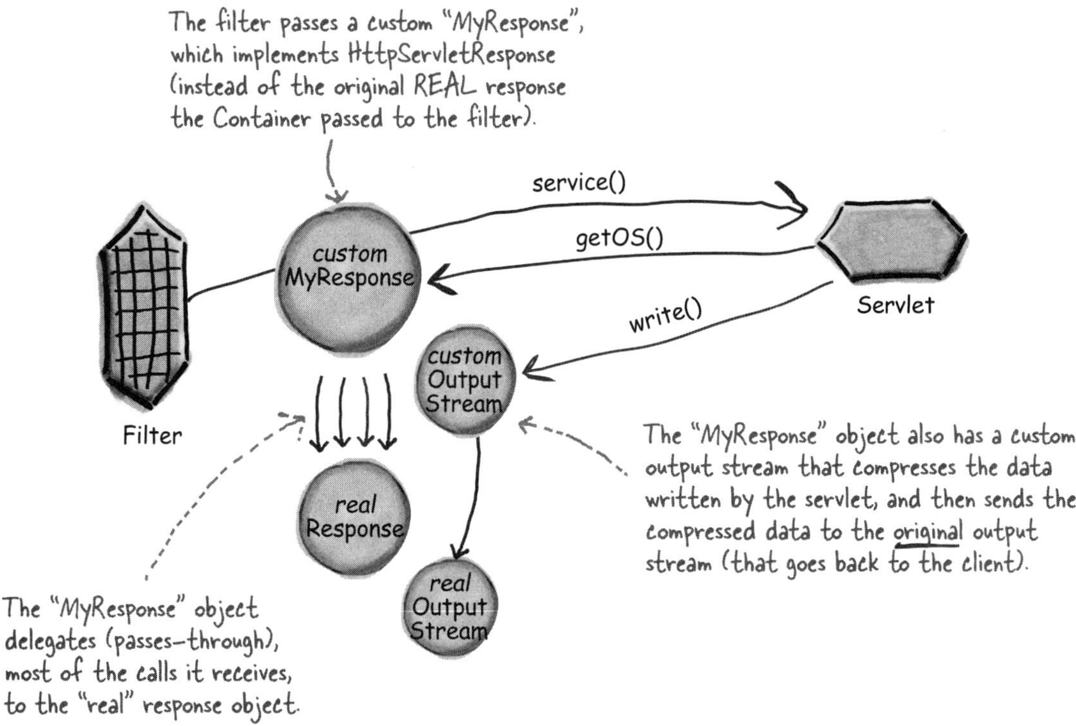
The filter passes a custom "MyResponse", which implements HttpServletResponse (instead of the original REAL response the Container passed to the filter).
service()
getOS()
write()
custom MyResponse
Servlet
Filter
custom Output Stream
real Response
real Output Stream
The "MyResponse" object also has a custom output stream that compresses the data written by the servlet, and then sends the compressed data to the original output stream (that goes back to the client).
The "MyResponse" object delegates (passes-through), most of the calls it receives, to the "real" response object.

Q: Filters pass ServletRequest and ServletResponse objects to the next thing in the chain, NOT HttpServlet Response! So why are you talking about implementing HttpServletResponse?

A: Filters were designed to be generic, and so officially, you're right. If we thought one of our filters might be used in a *non*-web app, we'd be implementing the *non*-HTTP interface (ServletResponse), but today, the chances of someone developing non-HTTP servlets is close to zero, so we're not worried. And since ServletResponse is the supertype of HttpServletResponse, there's no problem passing an HttpServletResponse where a ServletResponse is expected.

HttpServletResponse is such a complicated interface... if only there were a way to avoid implementing all those methods and delegating calls to the real response...

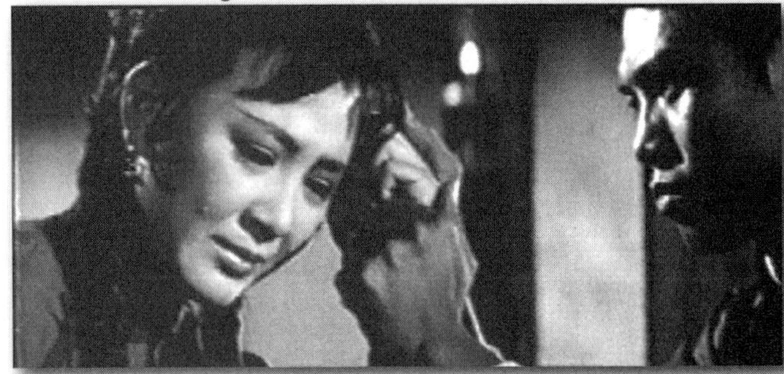

She doesn't know about the servlet Wrapper classes

Creating your own custom HttpServletResponse implementation *would* be a pain. Especially when all you want to implement are just a *few* of the methods. And since HttpServletResponse is an interface that extends another interface, to implement your own custom response, you'd have to implement *everything* in both HttpServletResponse *and* its superinterface, ServletResponse.

But fortunately, someone at Sun did that for you, by creating a support convenience class that implements the HttpServletResponse interface. All of the methods in that class delegate the calls to the underlying real response created by the Container.

ServletResponse interface
(javax.servlet.ServletResponse)

<<interface>>
ServletResponse

getBufferSize()
setContentType()
getOutputStream()
getWriter()
// MANY more methods...

HttpServletResponse interface
(javax.servlet.http.HttpServletResponse)

<<interface>>
HttpServletResponse

addCookie()
addDateHeader()
addHeader()
encodeRedirectURL()
encodeURL()
sendError()
sendRedirect()
setDateHeader()
setHeader()
setStatus()
// more methods

Remember, to implement HttpServletResponse you have to implement EVERYTHING from both it and its superinterface ServletResponse.

Wrappers rock

The wrapper classes in the servlet API are awesome—they implement all the methods needed for the thing you're trying to wrap, delegating all calls to the underlying request or response object. All you need to do is extend one of the wrappers, and override just the methods you need to do your custom work.

You've seen support classes in the J2SE API, of course, with things like the Listener adapter classes for GUIs. And you've seen them in the JSP API with the custom tag support classes. But while those support classes and these request and response wrappers are all convenience classes, the wrappers are a little different because they, well, *wrap* an object of the type they implement. In other words, they don't just provide an *interface implementation*, they actually hold a reference to an object of the same interface type to which they delegate method calls. (By the way, this has nothing whatsoever to do with the J2SE "primitive wrapper" classes like Integer, Boolean, Double, etc.)

Creating a specialized version of a request or response is such a common approach when creating filters, that Sun has created four "convenience" classes to make the job easier:

- `ServletRequestWrapper`
- `HttpServletRequestWrapper`
- `ServletResponseWrapper`
- `HttpServletResponseWrapper`

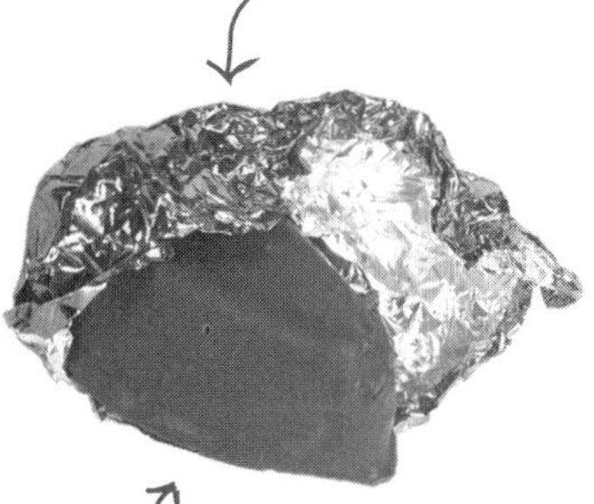

Whenever you want to create a custom request or response object, just subclass one of the convenience request or response "wrapper" classes.

A wrapper wraps the REAL request or response object, and delegates (passes through) calls to the real thing, while still letting you do the extra things you need for your custom request or response.

Although not explicitly listed in the official objectives, you MIGHT see "Decorator" on the exam.

If you're familiar with regular old (non-J2EE) design patterns, then you probably recognize this wrapper classes as an example of using a Decorator pattern (although it is also sometimes called Wrapper) pattern. The Decorator/Wrapper decorates/wraps one kind of an object with an "enhanced" implementation. And by "enhanced", we mean "adds new capabilities" while still doing everything the original wrapped thing did. It's like saying, "I'm just a BETTER version of the thing I'm wrapping—I do everything it does, and more." One characteristic of a Decorator/Wrapper is that it delegates method invocations to the thing it wraps, rather than being a complete replacement.

Adding a simple Wrapper to the design

Let's enhance Rachel's first pseudo-code by adding a wrapper.

Let's subclass this wrapper class for our own evil purposes...

Compression filter design, version 2 (pseudocode)

```
class CompressionResponseWrapper extends HttpServletResponseWrapper {

  // override any methods you want to customize
}
```

We'll be doing some real overriding in a few pages!

```
class MyCompressionFilter implements Filter {

   public void init(FilterConfig cfg) { }

   public void doFilter( request, response, chain) {

     CompressionResponseWrapper wrappedResp
       = new CompressionResponseWrapper(response);

     chain.doFilter(request, wrappedResp);

     // do compression logic here
   }
   public void destroy() { }
 }
}
```

The act of "wrapping" the response with our custom Wrapper class.

Now we send this along down the filter chain. None of the components down the chain will ever know that the response object they got was a custom job.

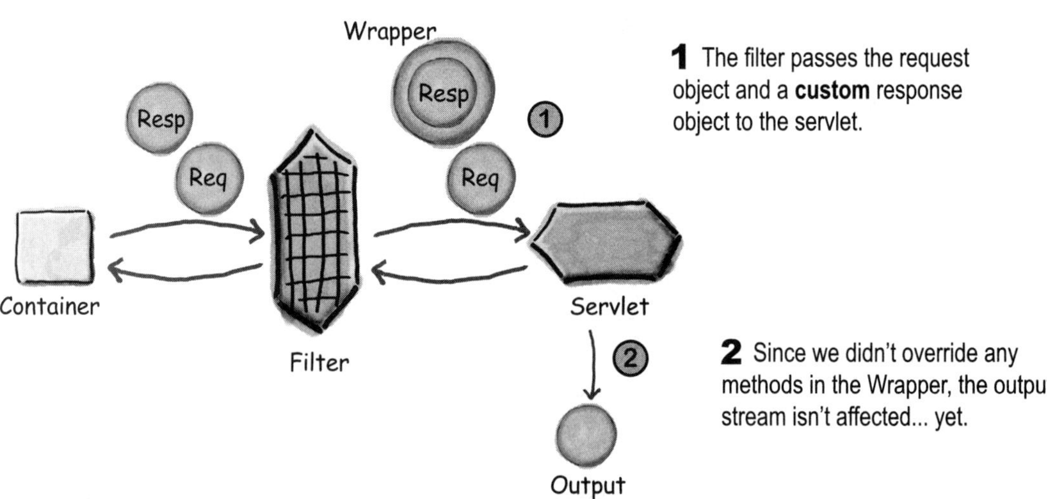

1 The filter passes the request object and a **custom** response object to the servlet.

2 Since we didn't override any methods in the Wrapper, the output stream isn't affected... yet.

Add an output stream Wrapper

Let's add a second Wrapper...

Compression filter design, version 3 (pseudocode)

```
class CompressionResponseWrapper extends HttpServletResponseWrapper {

   public ServletOutputStream getOutputStream() throws... {
     ...
     servletGzipOS = new GzipSOS(resp.getOutputStream());
     return servletGzipOS;
   }

  // maybe override other methods
}
```

Override this method to return a custom output stream.

"Wrapping" the ServletOutputStream with our custom ServletOutputStream Wrapper class. For now let's assume GzipServletOutputStream extends ServletOutputStream.

Return a "special" ServletOutputStream to whoever asks for one.

```
class MyCompressionFilter implements Filter {

  public void init(FilterConfig cfg) { }

  public void doFilter( request, response, chain) {

    CompressionResponseWrapper wrappedResp
       = new CompressionResponseWrapper(response);

    chain.doFilter(request, wrappedResp);

    // do compression logic here
  }
  public void destroy() { }

}
```

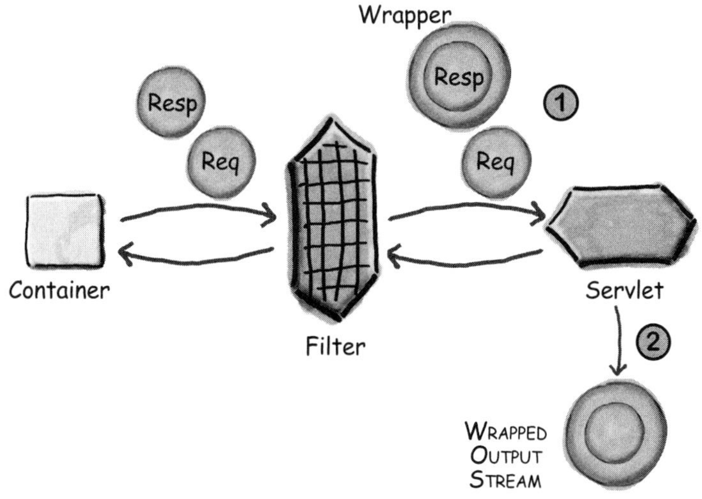

1 The filter passes the request object and a ***custom*** response object to the servlet. The custom response has a special **getOutputStream** method.

2 When the servlet asks for an output stream, it doesn't KNOW that it will get a "special" output stream.

The real compression filter code

Time to code. We end this chapter by looking at the code for both the compression filter and the wrapper it uses. We're expanding from the previous discussion, and while there is some new stuff here, it's mostly just plain Java code.

This filter provides a mechanism to compress the response body content. This type of filter would commonly be applied to any text content such as HTML, but not to most media formats such as PNG or MPEG, because they are already compressed.

Relax **You don't need to study this code for the exam.**

The rest of this example is a demonstration of a response filter in action, just so that you can see something a little more real-world. You don't need to learn or understand this particular example for the exam, so consider the rest of this chapter completely optional.

```
package com.example.web:

import javax.servlet.*;
import javax.servlet.http.*;
import java.io.*;
import java.util.zip.GZIPOutputStream;

public class CompressionFilter implements Filter {

  private ServletContext ctx;
  private FilterConfig cfg;

  public void init(FilterConfig cfg)
       throws ServletException {
    this.cfg = cfg;
    ctx = cfg.getServletContext();
    ctx.log(cfg.getFilterName() + " initialized.");
  }

  public void doFilter(ServletRequest req,
                       ServletResponse resp,
                       FilterChain fc)
       throws IOException, ServletException {
    HttpServletRequest request = (HttpServletRequest) req;
    HttpServletResponse response = (HttpServletResponse) resp;

    String valid_encodings = request.getHeader("Accept-Encoding");
    if ( valid_encodings.indexOf("gzip") > -1 ) {

      CompressionResponseWrapper wrappedResp
       = new CompressionResponseWrapper(response);
```

The init method saves the config object and a quick reference to the servlet context object (for logging purposes).

The heart of this filter wraps the response object with a Decorator that wraps the output stream with a compression I/O stream.

Compression of the output stream is performed if and only if the client includes an Accept-Encoding header (specifically, for gzip).

Does the client accept GZIP compression?

If so, wrap the response object with a compression wrapper.

Compression filter code, cont.

Debugging Tip!

To test this filter, comment out this line of code. You should see illegible, compressed data in your browser.

```
      wrappedResp.setHeader("Content-Encoding", "gzip");

      fc.doFilter(request, wrappedResp);


      GZIPOutputStream gzos = wrappedResp.getGZIPOutputStream();
      gzos.finish();

      ctx.log(cfg.getFilterName() + ": finished the request.");

    } else {
      ctx.log(cfg.getFilterName() + ": no encoding performed.");
      fc.doFilter(request, response);
    }
  }

  public void destroy() {
      // nulling out my instance variables
      cfg = null;
      ctx = null;
  }
}
```

Declare that the response content is being GZIP encoded.

Chain to the next component.

A GZIP compression stream must be "finished", which also flushes the GZIP stream buffer, and sends all of its data to the original response stream.

The container handles the rest of the work.

"Off the path"

Compression meets HTTP

How does the server know it can send compressed data? How does the browser know when it's getting compressed data? It turns out that HTTP is "compression-aware"; here's how it works:

- One of the headers that the browser sends ("Accept-Encoding: gzip"), tells the server about the browser's capabilities for dealing with different types of content.
- If the server sees that the browser can deal with compressed data, it will perform the compression, and add a header ("Content-Encoding: gzip"), to the response.
- When the browser receives the response, the "Content-Encoding: gzip" header tells the browser to de-compress the data before it is displayed.

So far so good. How hard can a little thing like a wrapper be?

(Famous last words...)

Compression wrapper code

We looked at the Compression filter; now let's take a look at the wrapper it uses. This is one of the most complicated topics in all of servlet-dom, so don't panic if you don't grok it the first time.

This response wrapper decorates the original response object by adding a compression decorator on the original servlet output stream.

```
package com.example.web;

// Servlet imports
import javax.servlet.http.*;
import javax.servlet.*;
// I/O imports
import java.io.*;
import java.util.zip.GZIPOutputStream;

class CompressionResponseWrapper extends HttpServletResponseWrapper {

  private GZIPServletOutputStream servletGzipOS = null;

  private PrintWriter pw = null;

  CompressionResponseWrapper(HttpServletResponse resp) {
    super(resp);
  }

  public void setContentLength(int len) { }

  public GZIPOutputStream getGZIPOutputStream() {
    return this.servletGzipOS.internalGzipOS;
  }
```

The compressed output stream for the servlet response.

The PrintWriter object to the compressed output stream.

The super constructor performs the Decorator responsibility of storing a reference to the object being decorated, in this case the HTTP response object.

Ignore this method—the output will be compressed.

This decorator method, used by the filter, gives the compression filter a handle on the GZIP output stream so that the filter can "finish" and flush the GZIP stream.

Compression wrapper code, cont.

```
  private Object streamUsed = null;

  public ServletOutputStream getOutputStream() throws IOException {

    if ((streamUsed != null) && (streamUsed != pw)) {
      throw new IllegalStateException();
    }

    if ( servletGzipOS == null ) {
      servletGzipOS
         = new GZIPServletOutputStream(getResponse()
                                   .getOutputStream());
      streamUsed = servletGzipOS;
    }
    return servletGzipOS;
  }

  public PrintWriter getWriter() throws IOException {

    if ( (streamUsed != null) && (streamUsed != servletGzipOS)) {
      throw new IllegalStateException();
    }

    if ( pw == null ) {

      servletGzipOS
          = new GZIPServletOutputStream(getResponse()
                                   .getOutputStream());
      OutputStreamWriter osw
          = new OutputStreamWriter(servletGzipOS,
                 getResponse().getCharacterEncoding());

      pw = new PrintWriter(osw);
      streamUsed = pw;
    }
    return pw;
  }
}
```

Provide access to a decorated servlet output stream.

Allow the servlet to access a servlet output stream, only if the servlet has not already accessed the print writer.

Wrap the original servlet output stream with our compression servlet output stream.

Provide access to a decorated print writer.

Allow the servlet to access a print writer, only if the servlet has not already accessed the servlet output stream.

To make a print writer, we have to first wrap the servlet output stream and then wrap the compression servlet output stream in two additional output stream decorators: OutputStreamWriter which converts characters into bytes, and then a PrintWriter on top of the OutputStreamWriter object.

Compression wrapper, helper class code

This helper class is a Decorator on the ServletOutputStream abstract class which delegates the real work of compressing the generated content using a standard GZIP output stream.

There is only one abstract method in the ServletOutputStream that this Decorator must implement: write(int). This is where all of the delegation magic occurs!

```
class GZIPServletOutputStream extends ServletOutputStream {

  GZIPOutputStream internalGzipOS;

  /** Decorator constructor */
  GZIPServletOutputStream(ServletOutputStream sos) throws IOException {
    this.internalGzipOS = new GZIPOutputStream(sos);
  }

  public void write(int param) throws java.io.IOException {
    internalGzipOS.write(param);
  }
}
```

Keep a reference to the raw GZIP stream. This instance variable is package-private to allow the compression response wrapper access to this variable..

This method implements the compression decoration by delegating the write() call to the GZIP compression stream, which is wrapping the original ServletOutputStream, (which in turn is ultimately wrapping the TCP network output stream to the client).

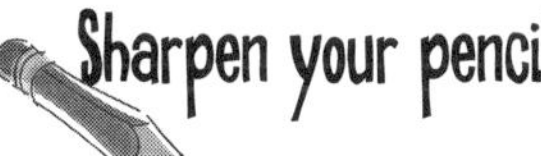

ANSWERS

Write down the sequence in which the filters will be executed for each request path. Assume Filter1 - Filter5 have been properly declared.

```
<filter-mapping>
  <filter-name>Filter1</filter-name>
  <url-pattern>/Recipes/*</url-pattern>
</filter-mapping>

<filter-mapping>
  <filter-name>Filter2</filter-name>
  <servlet-name>/Recipes/HopsList.do</servlet-name>
</filter-mapping>

<filter-mapping>
  <filter-name>Filter3</filter-name>
  <url-pattern>/Recipes/Add/*</url-pattern>
</filter-mapping>

<filter-mapping>
  <filter-name>Filter4</filter-name>
  <servlet-name>/Recipes/Modify/ModRecipes.do</servlet-name>
</filter-mapping>

<filter-mapping>
  <filter-name>Filter5</filter-name>
  <url-pattern>/*</url-pattern>
</filter-mapping>
```

Request path	Filter Sequence
/Recipes/HopsReport.do	Filters: **1, 5**
/Recipes/HopsList.do	Filters: **1, 5, 2**
/Recipes/Modify/ModRecipes.do	Filters: **1, 5, 4**
/HopsList.do	Filters: **5**
/Recipes/Add/AddRecipes.do	Filters: **1, 3, 5**

---

1 Which are true about filters? (Choose all that apply.)

- ❏ A. A filter can act on only the request or response object, not both.
- ❏ B. The **`destroy`** method is always a container callback method.
- ❏ C. The **`doFilter`** method is always a container callback method.
- ❏ D. The only way a filter can be invoked is through a declaration in the DD.
- ❏ E. The next filter in a filter chain can be specified either by the previous filter or in the DD.

---

2 Which are true about declaring filters in the DD? (Choose all that apply.)

- ❏ A. Unlike servlets, filters CANNOT declare initialization parameters.
- ❏ B. Filter chain order is always determined by the order the elements appear in the DD.
- ❏ C. A class that extends an API request or response wrapper class must be declared in the DD.
- ❏ D. A class that extends an API request or response wrapper class is using the Intercepting Filter pattern.
- ❏ E. Filter chain order is affected by whether filter mappings are declared via **`<url-pattern>`** or via **`<servlet-name>`**.

3 Given the class UserRequest is an implementation of HttpServletRequest, and given that this method in an otherwise properly defined **`Filter`** implementation:

```
20. public void doFilter(ServletRequest req,
21.                      ServletResponse response,
22.                      FilterChain chain)
22.        throws IOException, ServletException {
23.   HttpServletRequest request = (HttpServletRequest) req;
23.   HttpSession session = request.getSession();
25.   Object user = session.getAttribute("user");
26.   if (user != null) {
27.     UserRequest ureq = new UserRequest(request, user);
28.     chain.doFilter(ureq, response);
29.   } else {
30.     RequestDispatcher rd = request.getRequestDispatcher("/login.jsp");
31.     rd.forward(request, response);
32.   }
33. }
```

Which is true?

- ❑ A. An exception will always be thrown if line 31 executes.
- ❑ B. Line 28 is invalid because **`request`** must be passed as the first argument.
- ❑ C. This line: **`chain.doFilter(request, response)`** must be inserted somewhere in the **`else`** block.
- ❑ D. This method does not properly implement **`Filter.doFilter()`** because the method signature is incorrect.

4 Given a partial deployment descriptor:

```
<filter>
  <filter-name>My Filter</filter-name>
  <filter-class>com.example.MyFilter</filter-class>
</filter>
<filter-mapping>
   <filter-name>My Filter</filter-name>
   <url-pattern>/my</url-pattern>
</filter-mapping>
<servlet>
  <servlet-name>My Servlet</servlet-name>
  <servlet-class>com.example.MyServlet</servlet-class>
</servlet>
<servlet-mapping>
  <servlet-name>My Servlet</servlet-name>
  <url-pattern>/my</url-pattern>
</servlet-mapping>
```

Which is true? (Choose all that apply.)

❑ A. The file is invalid because the URL pattern **/my** is mapped to both a servlet and a filter.

❑ B. The file is invalid because neither the servlet name nor the filter name is allowed to contain spaces.

❑ C. The filter **MyFilter** will be invoked after the **MyServlet** servlet for each request that matches the pattern **/my**.

❑ D. The filter **MyFilter** will be invoked before the **MyServlet** servlet for each request that matches the pattern **/my**.

❑ E. The file is invalid because the **<filter>** element must contain a **<servlet-name>** element that defines which servlet the filter should be applied to.

5 Which about filters are true? (Choose all that apply.)

- ❑ A. Filters may be used to create request or response wrappers.
- ❑ B. Wrappers may be used to create request or response filters.
- ❑ C. Unlike servlets, all filter initialization code should be placed in the constructor since there is no **`init()`** method.
- ❑ D. Filters support an initialization mechanism that includes an **`init()`** method that is guaranteed to be called before the filter is used to handle requests.
- ❑ E. A filter's **`doFilter()`** method must call **`doFilter()`** on the input **`FilterChain`** object in order to ensure that all filters have a chance to execute.
- ❑ F. When calling **`doFilter()`** on the input **`FilterChain`**, a filter's **`doFilter()`** method must pass in the same **`ServletRequest`** and **`ServletResponse`** objects that were passed into it.
- ❑ G. A filter's **`doFilter()`** may block further request processing.

6 Which are true about the servlet Wrapper classes? (Choose all that apply.)

- ❑ A. They provide the only mechanism for wrapping **`ServletResponse`** objects.
- ❑ B. They can be used to decorate classes that implement **`Filter`**.
- ❑ C. They can be used even when the application does NOT support HTTP.
- ❑ D. The API provides wrappers for **`ServletRequest`**, **`ServletResponse`**, and **`FilterChain`** objects.
- ❑ E. They implement the Intercepting Filter pattern.
- ❑ F. When you subclass a wrapper class, you must override at least one of the wrapper class's methods.

Chapter 13 Answers

---

1 Which are true about filters? (Choose all that apply.)

(Servlet v2.4 section 6)

- [ ] A. A filter can act on only the request or response object, not both.
- [x] B. The **destroy** method is always a container callback method.
- [ ] C. The **doFilter** method is always a container callback method.

  -Option C is incorrect, doFilter is both a callback and an inline method.

- [x] D. The only way a filter can be invoked is through a declaration in the DD.
- [ ] E. The next filter in a filter chain can be specified either by the previous filter or in the DD.

  -Option E is incorrect, the order of filter execution is always determined in the DD.

---

2 Which are true about declaring filters in the DD? (Choose all that apply.)

(Servlet v2.4 section 6)

- [ ] A. Unlike servlets, filters CANNOT declare initialization parameters.
- [ ] B. Filter chain order is always determined by the order the elements appear in the DD.

  -Option B is incorrect, because <url-pattern> mappings will be chained before <servlet-name> mappings.

- [ ] C. A class that extends an API request or response wrapper class must be declared in the DD.
- [ ] D. A class that extends an API request or response wrapper class is using the Intercepting Filter pattern.

  -Option D is incorrect, wrappers are examples of the Decorator pattern.

- [x] E. Filter chain order is affected by whether filter mappings are declared via **<url-pattern>** or via **<servlet-name>**.

3 Given the class UserRequest is an implementation of HttpServletRequest, and given that this method in an otherwise properly defined **Filter** implementation:

(Servlet v2.4 pg. 49)

```
20. public void doFilter(ServletRequest req,
21.                      ServletResponse response,
22.                      FilterChain chain)
22.        throws IOException, ServletException {
23.   HttpServletRequest request = (HttpServletRequest) req;
23.   HttpSession session = request.getSession();
25.   Object user = session.getAttribute("user");
26.   if (user != null) {
27.     UserRequest ureq = new UserRequest(request, user);
28.     chain.doFilter(ureq, response);
29.   } else {
30.     RequestDispatcher rd = request.getRequestDispatcher("/login.jsp");
31.     rd.forward(request, response);
32.   }
33. }
```

Which is true?

- ☐ A. An exception will always be thrown if line 31 executes.

  –Option A is incorrect as it is valid for a filter to forward a request.

- ☐ B. Line 28 is invalid because **request** must be passed as the first argument.

  –Option B is incorrect because it is valid for a filter to wrap a request (note that UserRequest must implement ServletRequest).

- ☐ C. This line: **chain.doFilter(request, response)** must be inserted somewhere in the **else** block.

  –Option C is incorrect because the doFilter method is NOT required to call chain.doFilter().

- ☐ D. This method does not properly implement **Filter.doFilter()** because the method signature is incorrect.

  –Option D is incorrect because the method signature is correct.

- ☑ E. None of the above.

(Servlet v2.4 pg. 53)

4 Given a partial deployment descriptor:

```
<filter>
  <filter-name>My Filter</filter-name>
  <filter-class>com.example.MyFilter</filter-class>
</filter>
<filter-mapping>
   <filter-name>My Filter</filter-name>
   <url-pattern>/my</url-pattern>
</filter-mapping>
<servlet>
  <servlet-name>My Servlet</servlet-name>
  <servlet-class>com.example.MyServlet</servlet-class>
</servlet>
<servlet-mapping>
  <servlet-name>My Servlet</servlet-name>
  <url-pattern>/my</url-pattern>
</servlet-mapping>
```

Which is true? (Choose all that apply.)

- ☐ A. The file is invalid because the URL pattern **/my** is mapped to both a servlet and a filter.

  –Option A is incorrect because this is proper syntax used to map a filter to the same pattern as a servlet.

- ☐ B. The file is invalid because neither the servlet name nor the filter name is allowed to contain spaces.

  –Option B is incorrect because there is no such restriction.

- ☐ C. The filter **MyFilter** will be invoked after the **MyServlet** servlet for each request that matches the pattern **/my**.

  –Option C is incorrect because filters are executed before servlets, not after.

- ☑ D. The filter **MyFilter** will be invoked before the **MyServlet** servlet for each request that matches the pattern **/my**.

- ☐ E. The file is invalid because the **<filter>** element must contain a **<servlet-name>** element that defines which servlet the filter should be applied to.

  –Option E is incorrect because either a <servlet-name> element or a <url-pattern> may be used within a <filter-mapping> element.

5 Which about filters are true? (Choose all that apply.) (Servlet v2.4 pg. 51)

- [x] A. Filters may be used to create request or response wrappers.
- [ ] B. Wrappers may be used to create request or response filters.
  -Option B is incorrect because the terminology is reversed.
- [ ] C. Unlike servlets, all filter initialization code should be placed in the constructor since there is no **`init()`** method.
  -Option C is incorrect because there is an init() method that should be used for filter initialization.
- [x] D. Filters support an initialization mechanism that includes an **`init()`** method that is guaranteed to be called before the filter is used to handle requests.
- [ ] E. A filter's **`doFilter()`** method must call **`doFilter()`** on the input **`FilterChain`** object in order to ensure that all filters have a chance to execute.
  -Option E is incorrect because calling doFilter() is not necessary if a filter wishes to block further request processing.
- [ ] F. When calling **`doFilter()`** on the input **`FilterChain`**, a filter's **`doFilter()`** method must pass in the same **`ServletRequest`** and **`ServletResponse`** objects that were passed into it.
  -Option F is incorrect because the filter may choose to "wrap" the request or the response object and pass those instead.
- [x] G. A filter's **`doFilter()`** may block further request processing.

---

6 Which are true about the servlet Wrapper classes? (Choose all that apply.) (API)

- [ ] A. They provide the only mechanism for wrapping **`ServletResponse`** objects.
  -Option A is incorrect because you can create your own wrapper class.
- [ ] B. They can be used to decorate classes that implement **`Filter`**.
  -Option B is incorrect because these classes are used to wrap requests and responses.
- [x] C. They can be used even when the application does NOT support HTTP.
- [ ] D. The API provides wrappers for **`ServletRequest`**, **`ServletResponse`**, and **`FilterChain`** objects.
  -Option D is incorrect because the API does NOT provide a FilterChain wrapper.
- [ ] E. They implement the Intercepting Filter pattern.
  -Option E is incorrect because these wrappers implement the Decorator pattern..
- [ ] F. When you subclass a wrapper class, you must override at least one of the wrapper class's methods.

Enterprise Design Patterns

Someone has done this already. If you're just starting to develop web applications in Java, you're lucky. You get to exploit the collective wisdom of the tens of thousands of developers who've been down that road and got the t-shirt. Using both J2EE-specific and *other* design patterns, you can can simplify your code *and* your life. And the most significant design pattern for web apps, MVC, even has a wildly popular framework, Struts, that'll help you craft a flexible, maintainable servlet Front Controller. You owe it to yourself to take advantage of everyone *else's* work so that you can spend more time on the more important things in life (skiing, golf, salsa dancing, soccer, poker, playing the accordian...).

J2EE Patterns

11.1 Given a scenario description with a list of issues, select the one of the following patterns that would solve those issues: Intercepting Filter, Model-View-Controller, Front Controller, Service Locator, Business Delegate, and Transfer Object.

11.2 Match design patterns with statements describing potential benefits that accrue from the use of the pattern, for any of the following patterns: Intercepting Filter, Model-View-Controller, Front Controller, Service Locator, Business Delegate, and Transfer Object.

Coverage Notes:

The objectives in this section are covered completely in this chapter. No, make that MORE than completely. The exam questions on patterns are the least tricky of all the possible questions you'll see on the exam, so you can almost relax in this section.
If you're already familiar with the fundamental enterprise design patterns, you can probably answer the exam questions on patterns.

And although Struts is not on the exam, this chapter also includes an introduction to Struts, currently the most commonly-used framework for an MVC web application.

Web site hardware can get complicated

In the Real World, web apps can get complicated. A popular web site can get hundreds of thousands of hits per day. To handle this kind of volume, most big web sites create complex hardware architectures in which the software and data is distributed across many machines.

A common architecture you're probably quite familiar with is configuring the hardware in layers or "tiers" of functionality. Adding more computers to a tier is known as **horizontal scaling**, and is considered one of the best ways to increase throughput.

Most of the software for a big web application lives in either the "Web Tier" or the "Business Tier".

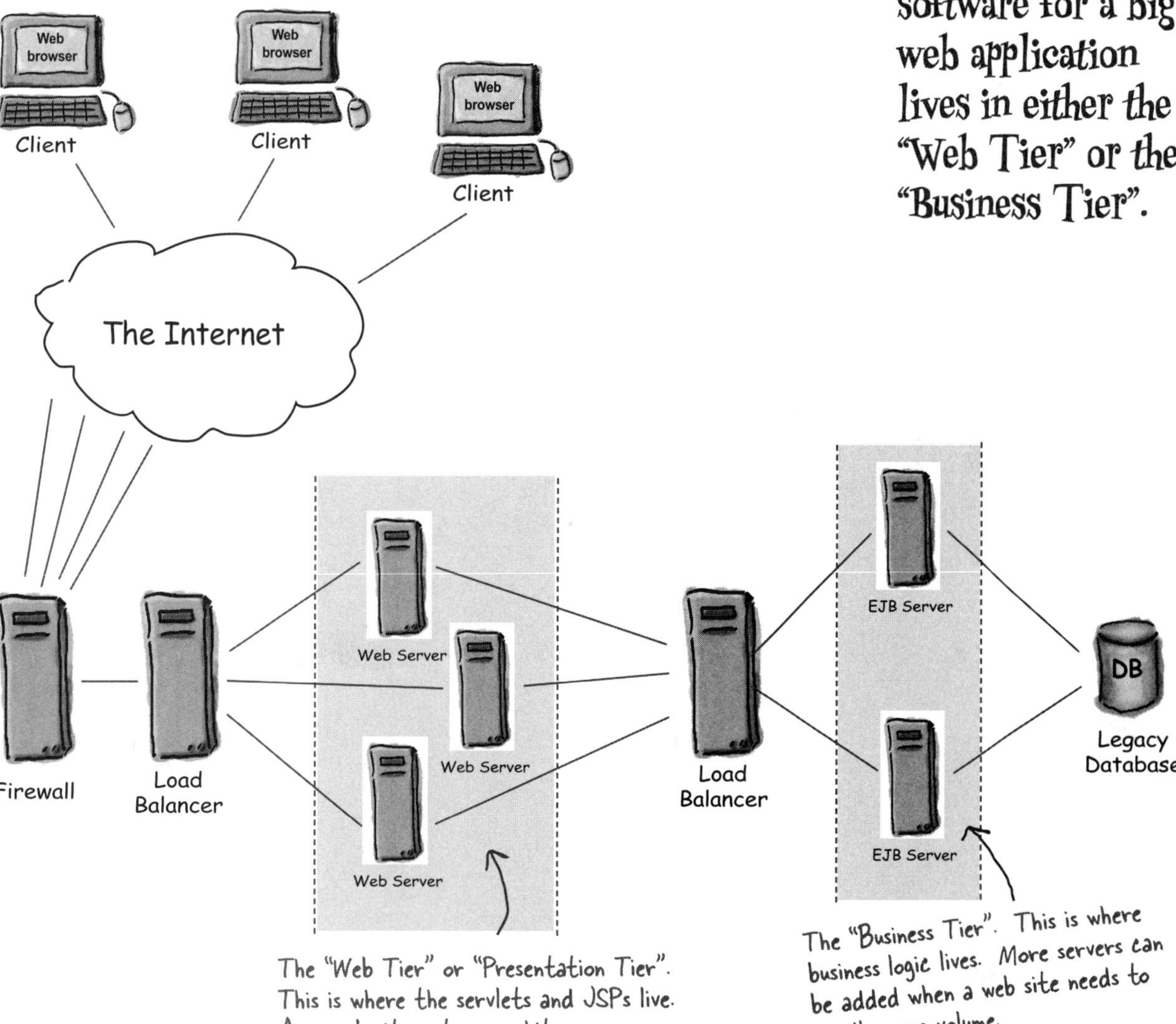
Web browser
Client
Web browser
Client
Web browser
Client
The Internet
Firewall
Load Balancer
Web Server
Web Server
Web Server
Load Balancer
EJB Server
EJB Server
DB
Legacy Database
The "Web Tier" or "Presentation Tier". This is where the servlets and JSPs live. As a web site gets more hits, more servers can be added to handle the load.
The "Business Tier". This is where business logic lives. More servers can be added when a web site needs to handle more volume.

Web application software can get complicated

As we've seen, it's very common for a web application to be made up of many different kinds of software components. The web tier frequently contains HTML pages, JSPs, servlets, controllers, model components, images, and so on. The business tier can contain EJBs, legacy applications, lookup registries, and in most cases database drivers, and databases.

drivers
filters
controllers
views
images
JSPs
servlets
models
JNDI
How am I going to keep all this stuff organized? What if the requirements change? How can I get this to run fast?
This is Internet time, baby. That code is *weeks* old... Time for some new features!

Lucky for us, we have J2EE patterns

The good news is that a *lot* of people have been using J2EE containers to solve the very same problems you're likely to encounter. They found reoccuring themes in the nature of the problems they were dealing with, and they came up with reusable solutions to these problems. These **design patterns** have been used, tested, and refined by other developers, so *you* don't have to reinvent the wheel.

A software design pattern is "a repeatable solution for a commonly-occuring software problem."

Common pressures

The most important job for a web app is to provide the end user with a reliable, useful, and correct experience. In other words, the program must satisfy the *functional requirements* such as "select a beer style" or "add malt to my shopping cart". Once you've made sure that the system supports the use cases, you'll most likely be faced with another set of requirements—requirements for what happens *behind* the scenes, i.e. the *non*-functional requirements.

What are the "ilities"?

What are some of the important non-functional requirements of a system you've worked on (or could imagine working on)? One clue is that most of the requirements words end with "ility" (for example, "maintainab*ility*").

Performance (and the "ilities")

Here are three of the most important non-functional requirements you're likely to face:

① Performance

If your website is too slow, you'll (obviously) lose users. In this chapter, we'll look at how patterns can help an individual user experience faster **response time**, and how patterns can help your system support a greater number of simultaneous users (**throughput**). (More on this when we discuss the ***Transfer Object***.)

If J2EE patterns can help me solve all of these issues, I'll be the hero around here. And that could lead to more stock options. And when we get another dot com bubble... those options could actually be *worth* something.

② Modularity

In order for different pieces of your application to run on different boxes at the same time, your software is going to have to be modular... and modular in *just the right ways.*

③ Flexibility, Maintainability, and Extensibility

Flexibility: You need to change your system without going through some big development cycle. You might need to swap in the "limited time, special offer" components for a big sale. You might find a bug in a new component and need to swap in the older component temporarily. You need your system to be flexible.

Maintainability: You might need to change database vendors, and update your system quickly. You might get obscure bugs and need to track them down ASAP. The admins might decide to restructure the company's naming service, and you'll have to adjust—**right now!** You need your system to be maintainable.

Extensibility: The guys over in marketing might need a new feature to land that big client. Your users might demand that you support a brand new feature that their browsers have. Your system had better be extensible!

Aligning our vernaculars...

All of the J2EE patterns rely heavily on common software design principles you're probably very familiar with. In the next few pages, we fling around several terms for these design principles. Different people and books might have different perspectives on the same terms, so we're giving you *our* definitions now, so that you'll know what *we* mean.

Code to interfaces

As you recall, an interface is a kind of a **contract between two objects.** When a class implements an interface, it's saying in effect: "My objects can speak your language." Another huge benefit of interfaces is **polymorphism**. Many classes can implement the same interface. The calling object doesn't care who it's talking to as long as the contract is upheld. For example, the web container can use any component that implements the Servlet interface.

Separation of Concerns & Cohesion

We all know that when we specialize the capabilities of our software components, they get easier to create, maintain, and reuse. A natural fallout of separating concerns is that **cohesion** tends to increase. Cohesion means the degree to which a class is designed for one, *cohesive,* task or purpose.

Hide Complexity

Hiding complexity often goes hand in hand with separating concerns. For instance if your system needs to communicate with a lookup service, it's best to hide the complexity of that operation in a single component, and allow all the other components that need access to the lookup service to use that specialized component. This approach simplifies all of the system components that are involved.

More design principles...

Loose Coupling

By their very nature, OO systems involve objects talking to each other. By coding to interfaces, you can reduce the number of things that one class needs to know about another class to communicate with it. The less two classes know about each other, the more **loosely coupled** they are to each other. A very common approach when class A wants to use methods in class B is to create an interface between the two. Once class B implements this interface, class A can use class B via the interface. This is useful, because later on you can use an updated class B or even an entirely different class, as long as it upholds the contract of the interface.

Remote Proxy

Today, when a web site grows, the answer is to lash together more servers, as opposed to upgrading a single, huge, monolithic server. The outcome is that Java objects on different machines, in their own separate heaps, have to communicate with each other.

Leveraging the power of interfaces, a remote proxy is an object local to the "client" object that *pretends* to be a remote object. (The proxy is remote in that it is remote from the object it is emulating.) The client object communicates with the proxy, and the proxy handles all the networking complexities of communicating with the actual "service" object. As far as the client object is concerned, it's talking to a local object.

Increase Declarative Control

Declarative control over applications is a powerful feature of J2EE Containers. Most commonly, this declarative control is implemented using the application's deployment descriptor (or DD). Modifying the DD gives us the power to change system behaviors without changing code. The DD is an XML file that can be maintained and updated by non-programmers. The more that we write our web applications to leverage the power of the DD, the more abstract and generic our code becomes.

Patterns to support remote model components

We've talked at a very theoretical level about how J2EE patterns can help simplify complex web applications. We've also talked about the software design principles that underlie J2EE patterns. With that foundation in place, let's get our feet wet by talking about a few of the simpler J2EE patterns. All three of the patterns we're about to discuss share the goal of making remote *model* components manageable.

A Fable: The Beer App Grows

Once upon a time there was a small dot com that had a website that offered home brewing recipes, advice, ingredients and supplies for beer aficionados. Being a small company (with big plans), they had only one production server to support the site, but they had created two separate software development teams to grow the application. The first team, known as the "Web Designers" focused their attentions on the *view* components of the system. The second team, known as the "Business Team" focused on the *controller* components (Rachel's focus), and the *model* components (Kim's area).

How the Business Team supports the web designers when the MVC components are running on one JVM

As long as the business guys keep the interfaces to their model components consistent, everyone will be happy. The two key interface points in their design are when the *controller* first interacts with a *model* component (steps 1 and 2 below), and then later, when a JSP *view* interacts with the bean it needs (steps 3 and 4 below).

Getting customer data for a client...

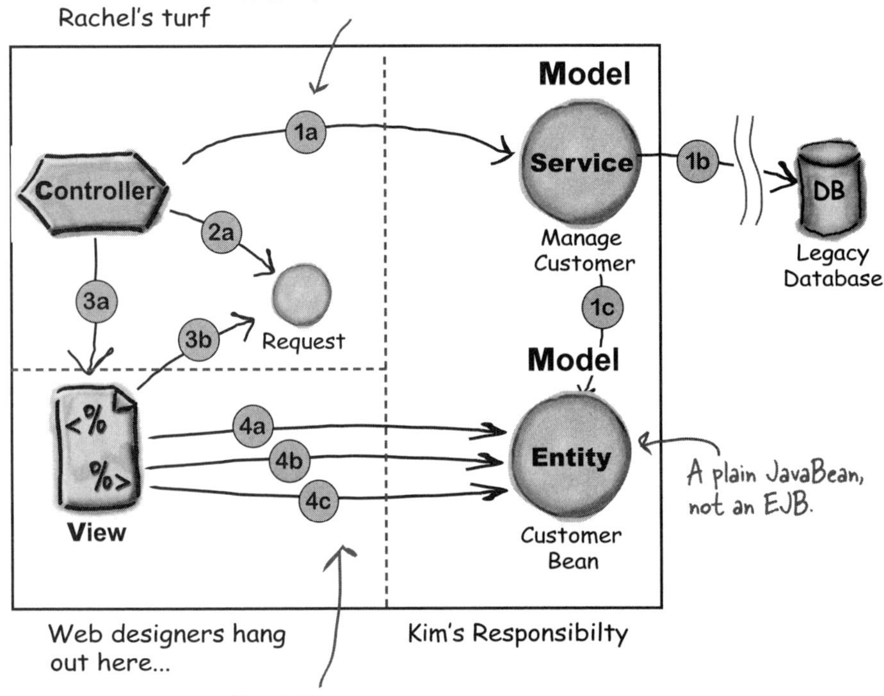
The client's "getCustomerData" request being sent to the model. Rachel's need is for this interface to be stable.
Rachel's turf
Model
1a
Controller
Service
1b
DB
2a
Manage Customer
Legacy Database
3a
1c
3b
Request
Model
<%
%>
4a
4b
4c
Entity
A plain JavaBean, not an EJB.
View
Customer Bean
Web designers hang out here...
Kim's Responsibilty
The JSP uses EL to access the Customer Bean properties. The web designer's need is for this interface to be stable.

1 Having received a request for customer information, the **Controller** calls the **ManageCustomer** service component (a **Model**). The service component does a JDBC call to the legacy database, then creates a **Customer** bean (this is NOT an EJB, just a plain old JavaBean), populated with customer data from the database.

2 The Controller adds the Customer bean reference to the request object, as an attribute.

3 The Controller forwards to the **View** JSP. The JSP gets the reference to the Customer bean from the request object.

4 The View JSP uses EL to get the Customer Bean properties it needs to satisfy the original request.

How will they handle remote objects?

Things are fairly simple when all the web app components (model, view, controller) are on the same server, running in the same JVM. It's just plain old Java—get a reference, call a method. But Kim and Rachel *now* have to figure out what to do when their model components are *remote* to the web app.

So, we have to move some of our model components off of the web server hardware and on to the business tier servers. You *know* this won't be the last time...

JNDI and RMI, a quick overview

Java and J2EE provide mechanisms that handle two of the most common difficulties that arise when objects need to communicate across a network—***locating*** remote objects, and handling all the low level network/IO ***communications*** between local and remote objects. (In other words, how to *find* remote objects, and how to *invoke* their methods.)

JNDI in a nutshell

JNDI stands for Java Naming and Directory Interface, and it's an API to access naming and directory services. JNDI gives a network a centralized location to find things. If you've got objects that you want other programs on your network to find and access, you register your objects with JNDI. When some other program wants to *use* your objects, that program uses JNDI to look them up.

JNDI makes relocating components on your network easier. Once you've relocated a component, all you need to do is tell *JNDI* the new location. That way, other client component only need to know how to find JNDI, without knowing where the objects *registered* with JNDI are actually located.

Exactly! Plus, you can bet that, in the end, we'll be affecting a lot of objects. Our design for network communications better be as simple as possible.

RMI in a nutshell

RMI stands for Remote Method Invocation, a mechanism that greatly simplifies the process of getting objects to communicate across a network. Turn the page and we'll do a quick refresh, in case you're a little rusty. Why think about RMI here? Because it will help make two of the J2EE design patterns easier to understand and appreciate.

RMI makes life easy

You want your objects to communicate across a network. In other words, you want an object in one JVM to cause a method invocation on a **remote** object (i.e. an object in a *different* JVM), but you want to *pretend* that you're invoking a method on a *local* object. That's what RMI gives you—the ability to pretend (almost) that you're making a regular old local method call.

What we want...

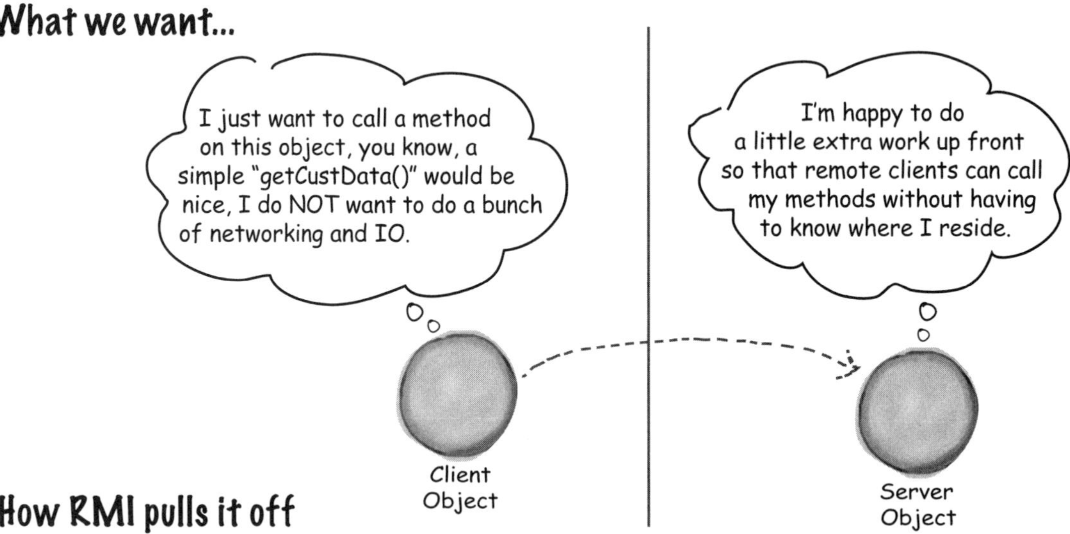

I just want to call a method on this object, you know, a simple "getCustData()" would be nice, I do NOT want to do a bunch of networking and IO.
I'm happy to do a little extra work up front so that remote clients can call my methods without having to know where I reside.
Client Object
Server Object

How RMI pulls it off

Let's say your "business guy" hat is on, and you want to make an object available to remote clients. Using RMI, you'll create a **proxy** and you'll **register** your object with some sort of registry. Any client who wants to call your methods will do a lookup on the registry and get a copy of the remote *proxy*. Then the client will make calls on the remote proxy, **pretending it's the real thing**. The remote proxy (called a **stub**), handles all the communications details like sockets, I/O streams, TCP/IP, serializing and deserializing method arguments and return values, handling exceptions, and so forth.

(Oh, by the way, there's usually a proxy on the server side (often called a "**skeleton**"), doing similar chores on the server side where the remote object lives.)

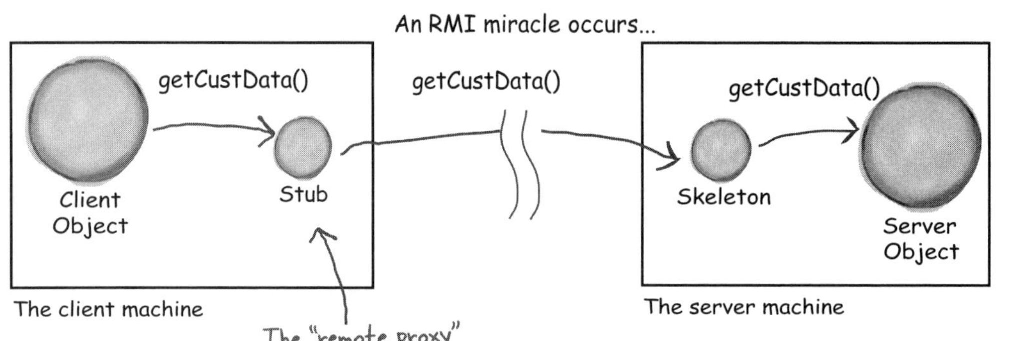

There are 3 versions of getCustData()!

The remote proxy's, the skeleton's and the server's, which is the real one.

Just a little more RMI review

Without doing an entire RMI tutorial,* we'll look at a few more high level RMI topics to make sure we're all talking the same talk. Specifically, we'll look at the server side and client side of using RMI.

RMI on the Server side in 4 steps

(An overview of the steps to make a remote model service that runs on the server.)

1. Create a **remote interface**. This is where the signature for methods like **getCustData()** will reside. Both the **stub** (proxy) and the actual model **service** (the remote object) will implement this interface.

2. Create the **remote implementation**, in other words, the actual model object that will reside on the model server. This includes code that registers the model with a well-known registry service such as JNDI or the RMI registry.

3. Generate the stub and (possibly) skeleton. RMI provides a compiler called **rmic** that will create the proxies for you.

4. Start/run the model service (which will register itself with the registry and wait for calls from far-away clients).

The client side, with and without RMI

Let's compare the pseudo-code of a client using RMI to the pseudo-code of a client NOT using RMI.

The client *without* RMI

```
public void goClient() {

  try {
     // get a new Socket

     // get an OutputStream
     // chain it to an ObjectOutputStream

     // send an opcode & op arguments
     // flush OS

     // get the InputStream
     // chain it to an ObjectInputStream

     // read the return value and/or
     // handle exceptions

     // close stuff

  } // catch and handle remote exceptions
}
```

The client *with* RMI

```
public void goClient() {

   try {

      // lookup the remote object (stub)

      // call the remote object's method

   } // catch and handle remote exceptions
}
```

*If you aren't really familiar with RMI, drive to your local bookstore, pick up (but don't *buy*) a copy of Head First Java, and just read the sections on RMI. Then put the book back on the shelf, face forward, in *front* of the competing book of your choice. Make sure that the cover is dusted and don't spill coffee on it.

Adding RMI and JNDI to the controller

Let's focus on what we need to do to keep Rachel's life as simple as possible. In other words, what impact does adding JNDI and RMI have on the controller?

3 steps to using a remote object

1. Kim, the model guy, *registers* his model component with the *JNDI* service.

2. When Rachel's controller gets a request, the controller code does a JNDI *lookup* to get the stub proxy for Kim's remote model service.

3. The controller makes business method calls against the stub, just as though the stub were the actual model object iself. *Almost...*

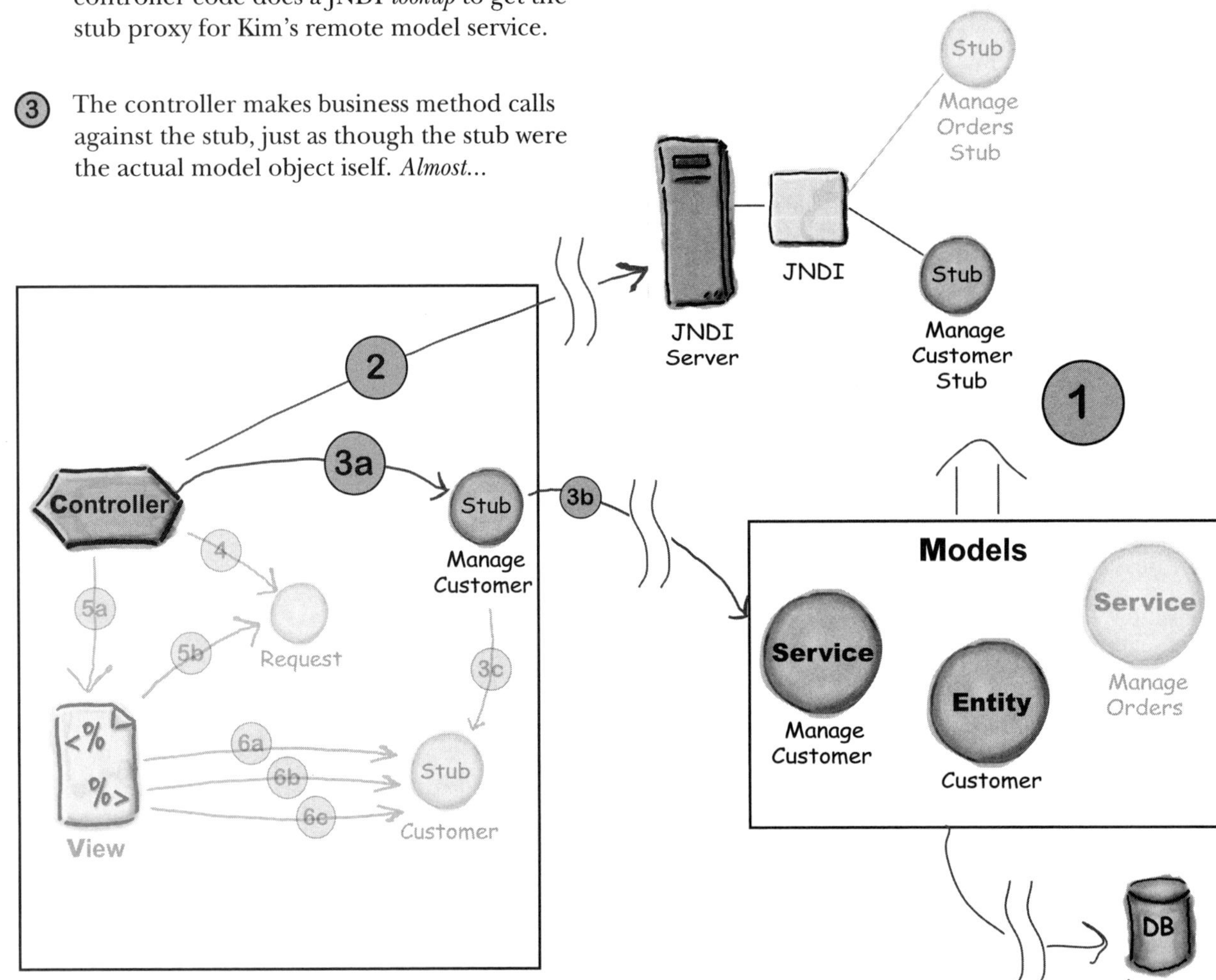

Sure, the method calls are pretty close to what I was doing before when the model was local, but I still have to change the Controller code to put in the whole JNDI lookup. I was hoping for something that would let me use the same Controller regardless of whether the model is local or remote.

Sharpen your pencil

How can this design be improved?

1 - What are the problems with this design (list at least two)?

2 - How might you change this design to handle those problems?

Problems:

Solution:

How about a "go-between" object?

A common solution to the design problems we left you with is to create a new object—a single, "go-between" object for the controller to talk to rather than having the controller deal directly with the *remoteness* of the remote model.

Problem 1: Hide the complex JNDI lookup

If Rachel's controller lets a "go-between" object handle the JNDI lookup, the controller code can stay simpler, free from having to know where (and how) to look up the model.

Problem 2: Hide "remote-ness complexity"

If the "go-between" object can handle talking to the stub, Rachels' controller can be shielded from all the remote issues including remote *exceptions.*

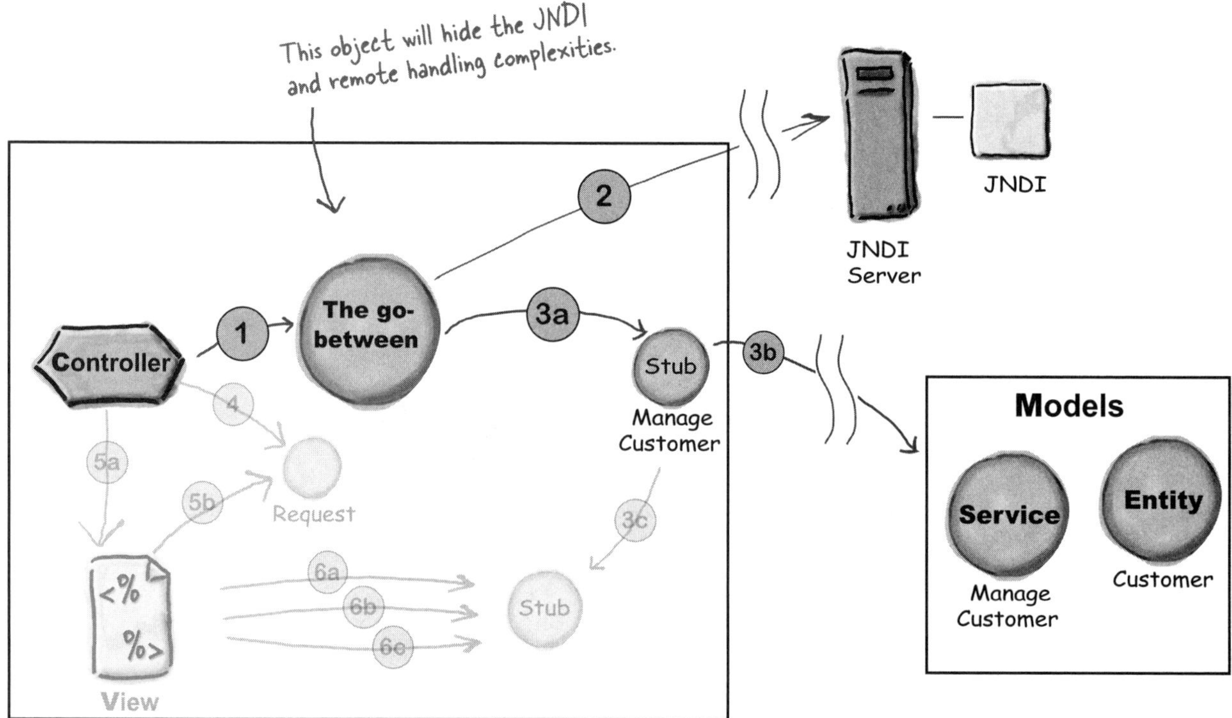

The "go-between" is a Business Delegate

Let's take a look at the pseudo-code for a typical Business Delegate, and at how Business Delegates tend to be deployed in the web container.

Notice that there will be LOTS of Business Delegates on the web tier.

A Business Delegate's pseudo-code

```
// get the request and do a JNDI lookup
// get back a stub

// call to the business method
// handle & abstract any remote exceptions
// send the return value to the controller
```

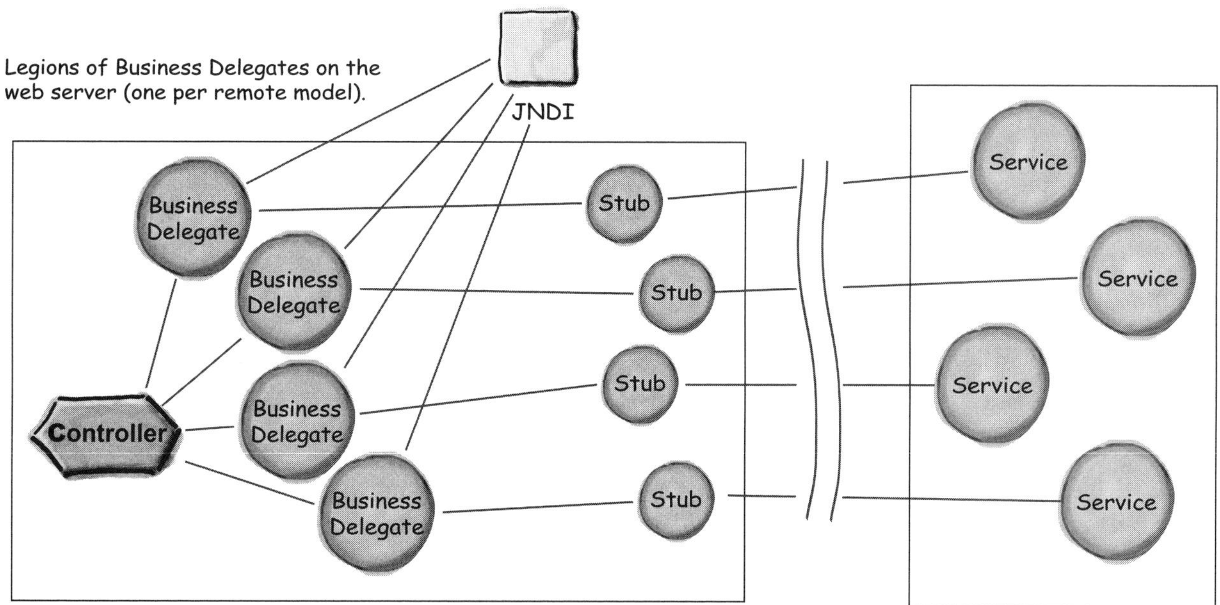

Sharpen your pencil

Uh-oh. ***Duplicate Code Alert.***

(Describe where the duplicate code exists and how you could solve that problem.)

Simplify your Business Delegates with the Service Locator

Unless your Business Delegates use a Service Locator, they will have duplicate code for dealing with the lookup service.

To implement a Service Locator, we'll take all of the logic for doing the JNDI lookup and move it *out* of the multiple Business Delegates and *into* a single Service Locator.

Typically in J2EE applications, there will be a number of components that all use the same JNDI service. While a complex application might use several different registries such as JNDI and UDDI (for web service endpoints), an individual *component* will typically need access to only *one* registry. In general, a single Service Locator will support a single, specific registry.

By making the ***Business*** Delegate an object that handles only the ***business*** methods rather than *also* handling the registry lookup code, you increase the cohesion for the Business Delegates.

A Service Locator's pseudo-code

```
// obtain an InitialContext object
// perform remote lookup
// handle remote issues
// optionally, cache references
```

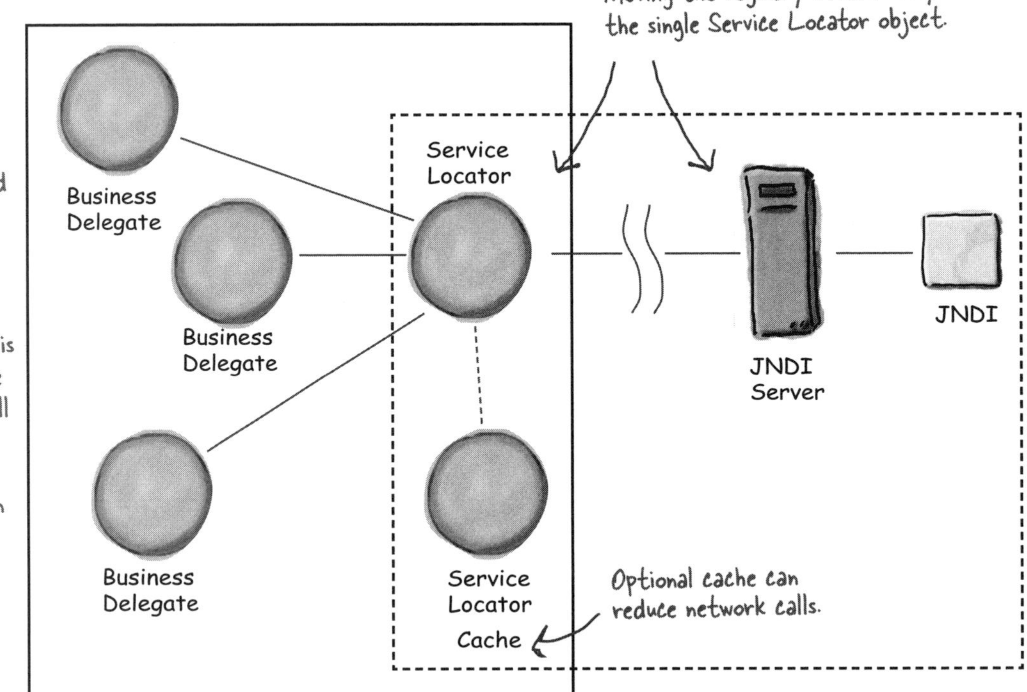
Moving the registry affects only the single Service Locator object.
Cohesion is increased for all of these Business Delegates.
Obtaining the stub is now handled by the Service Locator. All the Delegate has to do is deal with business methods on the stub.
Business Delegate
Business Delegate
Business Delegate
Service Locator
Service Locator
Cache
JNDI Server
JNDI
Optional cache can reduce network calls.
Web Server

there are no Dumb Questions

Q: This whole discussion has assumed RMI; what if our company is using CORBA?

A: All of the patterns we're discussing can be implemented more or less independently of J2EE technologies. Admittedly, they will be easiest to implement in J2EE, but they do apply to other situations.

Q: Is the same thing true for JNDI?

A: Well, there *are* other Java-related registries *besides* JNDI—RMI and Jini come to mind. Of those three, JNDI is probably the best choice for most web apps, it's easy and powerful. (Although the authors would *personally* love to see Jini take its rightful place in the distributed world.) You might also be dealing with non-Java registries like UDDI. In any case, the *patterns* will still work, even though the code changes, of course.

Q: It seems like these patterns are forever adding a new layer of objects to the architecture. Why is this approach so common?

A: You're right that this is a common part of a lot of patterns. Assuming that your design is good, think about the software design benefits inherent in this approach...

Q: OK, well, *cohesion* comes to mind...

A: Right! Both the Business Delegate and the Service Locator increase the **cohesiveness** of the objects they support. Another driving force is **network transparency**. Adding a layer often shields existing objects from being network aware. Then of course, closely related to **cohesion** is **separation of concerns**.

Q: Separation of concerns buys me...?

A: Let's take the Service Locator as an example. In the event that your registry gets a new network address and/or registry interface, it's far easier to modify a single Service Locator than change a whole flotilla of Business Delegates. In general, separation of concerns buys us a lot of flexibility and maintainability.

Q: In your examples so far, you've taken POJOs that were local, and made them remote. Isn't it more likely that I'll be faced with integrating existing EJBs into my web app?

A: By POJOs, we assume you mean "Plain Old Java Objects", of course. And yes, it is likely that you'll be integrating EJBs into your app. And in fact that's yet another reason to use these two patterns... your controller (and view) should never have to care whether the model is a local JavaBean, a remote POJO, or an *enterprise* JavaBean (EJB). Without using ServiceLocator and Business Delegate, that difference means a lot—enterprise beans and plain old remote objects don't use the same lookup code!

Using these patterns, you can encapsulate the issues related to how and where the model is discovered and used, and keep the controller happy and clueless, so that you won't have to change your controller code when the business guys change things and move things around on the business tier. You'll update only the Service Locator and (possibly) the Business Delegate.

Protecting the web designer's JSPs from remote model complexity

By using the Business Delegate and Service Locator patterns, we've got Rachel's controllers protected from the complexities of remote model components. Now let's see if we can do the same for the web designer's JSPs.

Quick review of the old *non-remote* way— the JSP uses EL to get info from the local model.

This diagram should look familiar from earlier in the chapter. The JSP gets the bean reference from the request object (step 3), then calls getters on the bean (step 4).

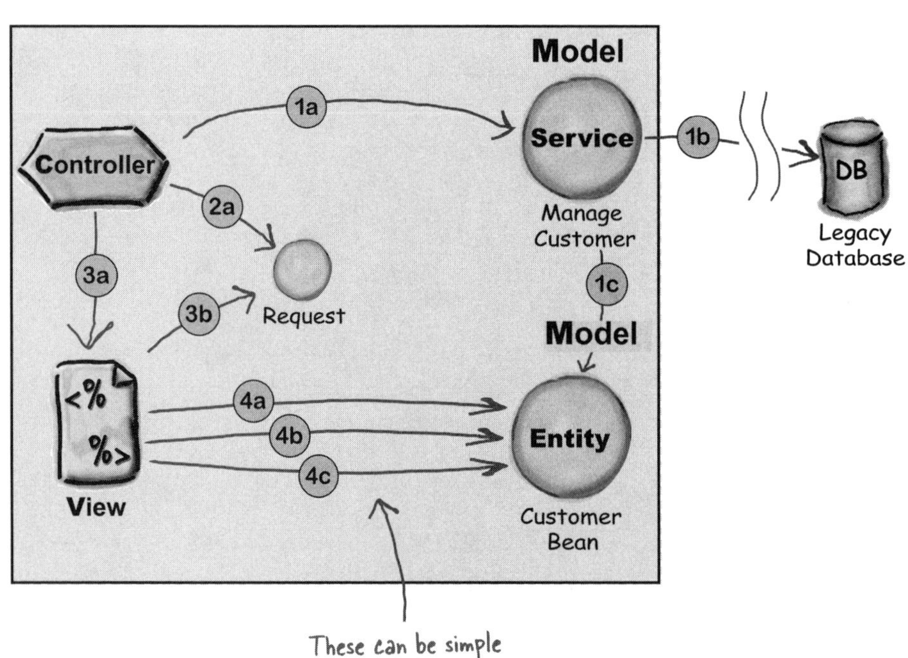

1 Having received a request for customer information, the **Controller** calls the **ManageCustomer** model component. The model component does a remote call to the legacy database, then creates a **Customer** bean, populated with customer data from the database.

2 The Controller adds the Customer reference to the request, as an attribute.

3 The controller forwards to the **View** JSP. The JSP gets a reference to the Customer bean from the request object.

4 The View JSP uses EL to get the Customer Bean properties it needs to satisfy the original request.

Compare the local model diagram to this remote model diagram

Don't Panic!

The shaded area in this diagram should look a LOT like the previous diagram, especially if you remember that the **Business Delegate** is pretending to be the **Manage Customer** model.

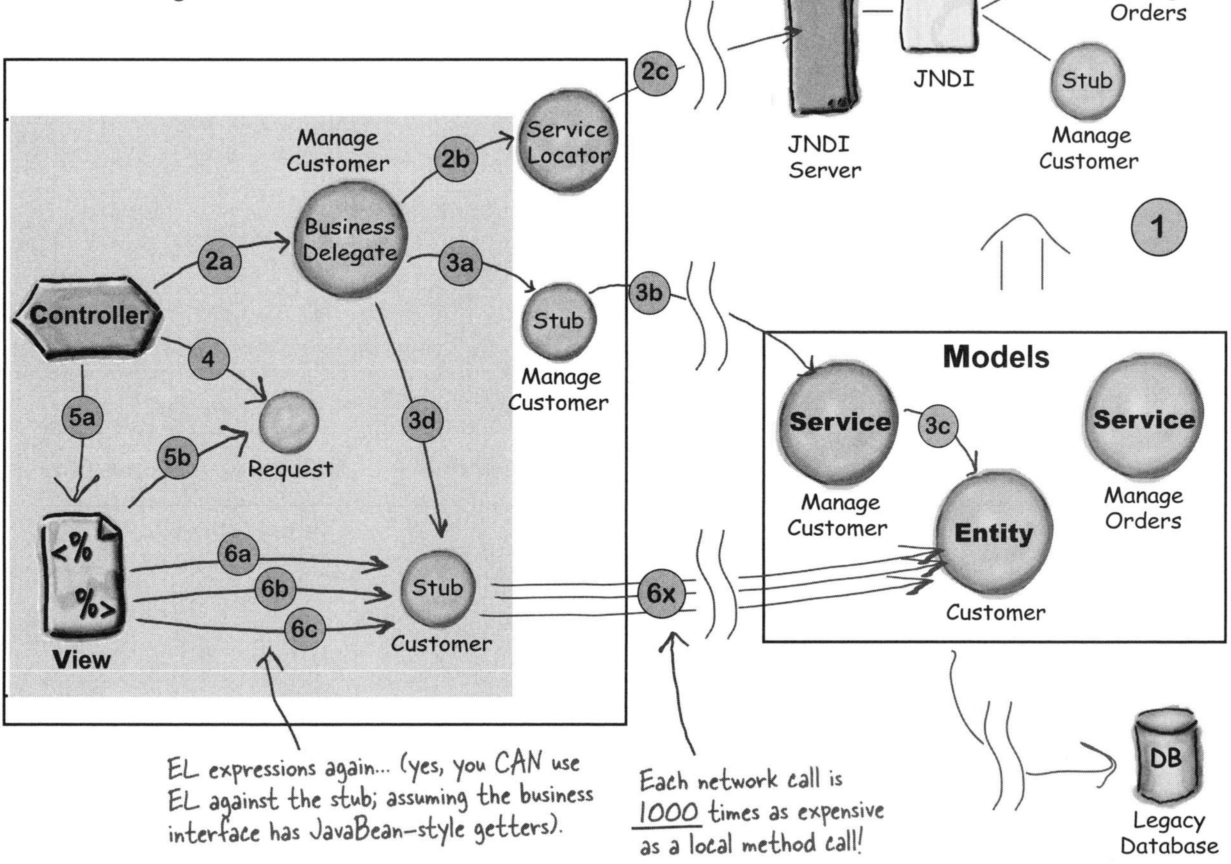

EL expressions again... (yes, you CAN use EL against the stub; assuming the business interface has JavaBean-style getters).

Each network call is 1000 times as expensive as a local method call!

A 6-step review:

1 Register your services with JNDI.

2 Use Busines Delegate and Service Locator to get the Manage Customer stub from JNDI.

3 Use the Business Delegate and the stub to get the "Customer Bean", which in this case is another stub. Return this stub's reference to the controller.

4 Add the Customer stub reference to the request.

5 The controller forwards to the **View** JSP. The JSP gets a reference to the Customer bean (stub) from the request object.

6 The View JSP uses EL to get the Customer Bean properties it needs to satisfy the original request.

BIG NOTE: Every time the JSP invokes a getter, the Customer stub makes a network call.

There's good news and bad news...

The previous architecture succeeds in hiding complexity from both the controllers and the JSPs. And it makes good use of the Business Delegate and Service Locator patterns.

The bad news:

When it's time for the JSP to get data, there are two problems, both related to the fact that the bean the JSP is dealing with is actually a *stub to a remote object.*

1 - ***All those fine-grained network calls are likely to be a big performance hit.*** Think about it. Each EL expression triggers a remote method invocation. Not only is this a bandwidth/latency issue, but all those calls cause the server some problems too. Each call might lead to a separate transaction and database load (and possibly store!) on the server.

2 - The JSP is ***NOT a good place to be handling exceptions*** that might occur if the remote server crashes.

Why not have the JSP talk to a plain old bean instead of a stub?

Q: If you want the JSP to talk to a JavaBean, where will this bean come from?

A: Well, it used to come from the local model/service object, so why not have it come from the *remote* model/service object?

Q: How do you get a bean across the network?

A: Hey, as long as it's serializable, RMI has no problem sending an object across the network.

Q: So what would this buy us again?

A: First of all, we'd have one big network call instead of a lot of little ones. Second, since the JSP would be talking to a local object, there'd be no remote exceptions to worry about!

Q: Wait a minute... I see a little problem here. Or maybe a big problem—if you're using a bean on the client side, doesn't that bean's data become stale the moment it's sent?

A: Yes, you're right, and this IS a trade-off: performance vs. how current the data is. You have to decide which makes sense based on your requirements. If the data used by your view component must absolutely, positively, represent the current state of the database at all times, then you need a remote reference. For example, if you make three calls, say, getName(), getAddress(), and getPhone() on customer, you'll probably decide that this information doesn't change rapidly enough to make it worth going *back* to the database (via the remote object) just in case the customer's phone number changed IN BETWEEN the call to getName() and getAddress().

On the other hand, you might decide that in a highly dynamic environment, where a customer is making transactions 24/7, you DO need to show the most up-to-date info. Sending a JavaBean back for the client means the View would have a snapshot of the database at the moment the bean was populated, but since the bean has no connection to the database, the data begins to go stale immediately.

Time for a Transfer Object?

If it's likely that a business service might be asked to send or receive all or most of its data in a big, coarse-grained message, it's common for that service to provide that feature in its API. Commonly, the business service creates a serializable Java object that contains lots of instance variables. Sun calls this object a **Transfer Object**. Outside of Sun there is a pattern called ***Data* Transfer Object**. Guess what? They're the same thing. (Yeah, we feel the same way about that.)

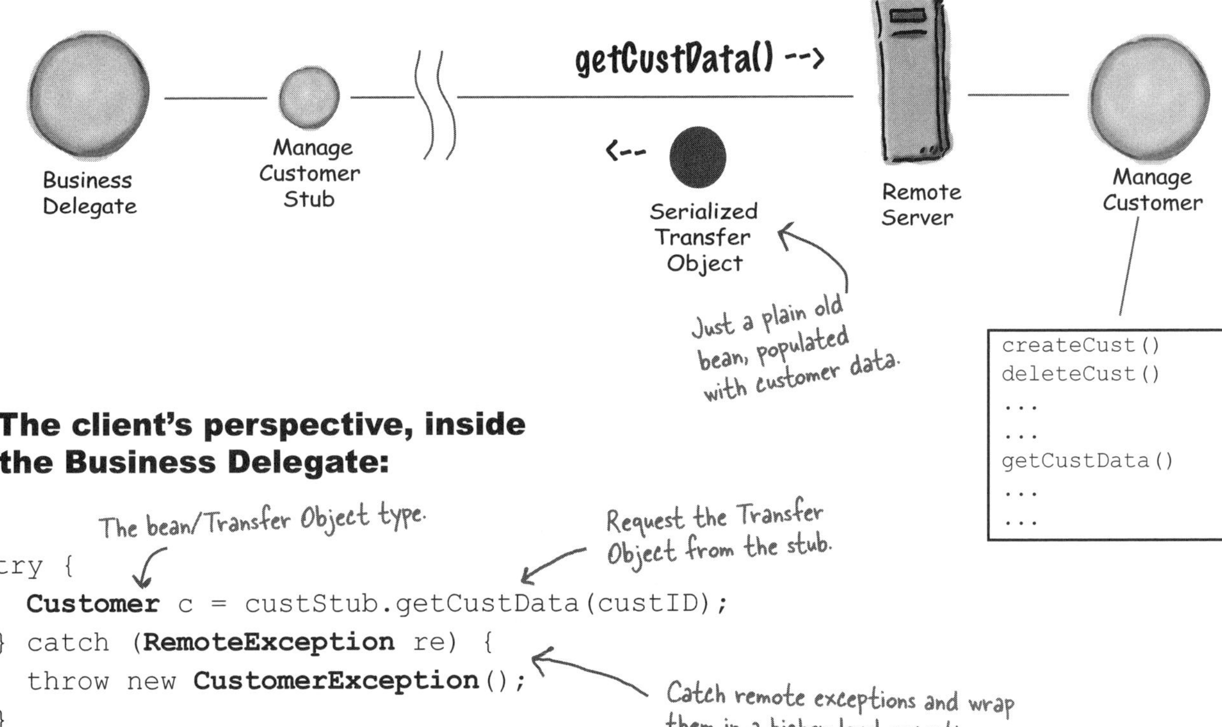

The client's perspective, inside the Business Delegate:

The bean/Transfer Object type.

Request the Transfer Object from the stub.

```
try {
  Customer c = custStub.getCustData(custID);
} catch (RemoteException re) {
  throw new CustomerException();
}
```

Catch remote exceptions and wrap them in a higher level exception.

That's it. Under the covers, the Transfer Object is serialized, shipped, and deserialized on to the client's local JVM heap. At that point, it is just like any other local bean.

The data in a Transfer Object grows stale!

Once it's shipped across the network, the Transfer Object is completely out of touch with its source, and begins to fall out of sync with the state of the data in the underlying database. You'll have to decide for each use case whether data integrity/ synchronization is worth the performance hits.

Service Locator and Business Delegate both simplify model components

Listen in as our two black-belts debate which pattern is better—Service Locator or Business Delegate.

Service Locator

Business Delegate

Service Locator: Service Locator is the superior pattern. First of all, unlike the Business Delegate, one Service Locator instance can support an entire application tier.

Business Delegate: That's true, but Service Locator needs to talk to only *one* remote entity. Business Delegate must handle *many* entity objects.

Service Locator: Service Locator is more efficient with network calls. It can cache references to stubs or service stubs once it has located them, reducing network traffic for subsequent calls.

Business Delegate: With much respect, you are forgetting that Service Locator has a much easier task. The Business Delegate must carry the heavy burden of communicating with a dynamic object, whose data might change at any moment.

Service Locator: Heavy burden? Your simple business data does not impress me.

Business Delegate: A Business Delegate gives web application programmers much more *benefit* than your Service Locator.

Service Locator: Ah, maybe programmers do benefit, but your simple pattern seems to forget that it often exists in a *network* environment. It will make many calls to business services with no restraint, no consideration for the *overhead* of remote calls.

Business Delegate: Ah ha! The Business Delegate is not ashamed to form an alliance with the Transfer Object! Working as a team, they help the programmer AND minimize remote calls.

Service Locator: Yes, yes, your weak pattern needs *assistance*, we all know that. But when you partner with a Transfer Object other demons can haunt you... you haven't forgotten your little problems with data staleness and concurrency, have you?

Business Delegate: No, I haven't forgotten. But when these issues come up they can be solved. You cannot expect to achieve great things without a little extra effort... nothing in J2EE is ever black and white.

Business tier patterns: quick review

To wrap up our discussion of business tier patterns, here's a diagram that shows a Business Delegate, a Service Locator, and a Transfer Object in action. At the end of the chapter you'll find a couple of summary pages for these patterns and the presentation tier patterns we'll discuss next.

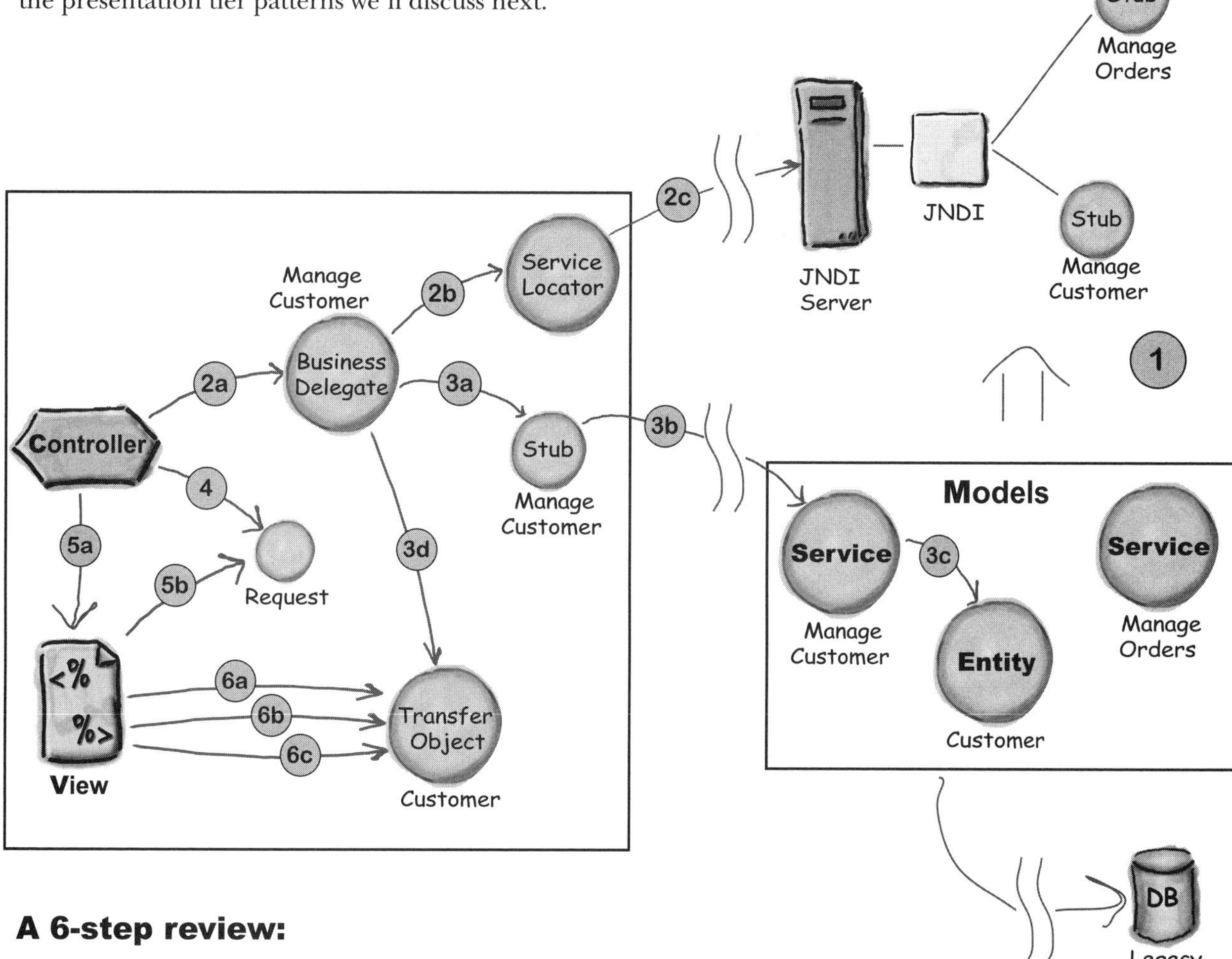

A 6-step review:

1 Register your services with JNDI.

2 Use Business Delegate and Service Locator to get the Manage Customer stub from JNDI.

3 Use the Business Delegate and the stub to get the "Customer Bean", which in this case is a Transfer Object. Return this Transfer Object's reference to the controller.

4 Add the bean's reference to the request.

5 The controller forwards to the **View** JSP. The JSP gets the reference to the Customer Transfer Object bean from the request object.

6 The View JSP uses EL to get the Customer Transfer Object Bean's properties it needs to satisfy the original request.

Our very first pattern revisited... MVC

As luck would have it, the very same pattern we've been using in the book is on the exam. The last two patterns we're covering are presentation tier patterns, as was the Intercepting Filter. First we'll pick up where we left off talking about MVC. That discussion will lead us into Struts and finally Front Controller.

Where we left off...

Let's do a quick review of where we left off in chapter 2.

MODEL

Holds the real business logic and the state. In other words, it knows the rules for getting and updating state.

A Shopping Cart's contents (and the rules for what to do with it) would be part of the Model in MVC.

It's the only part of the application that talks to the database.

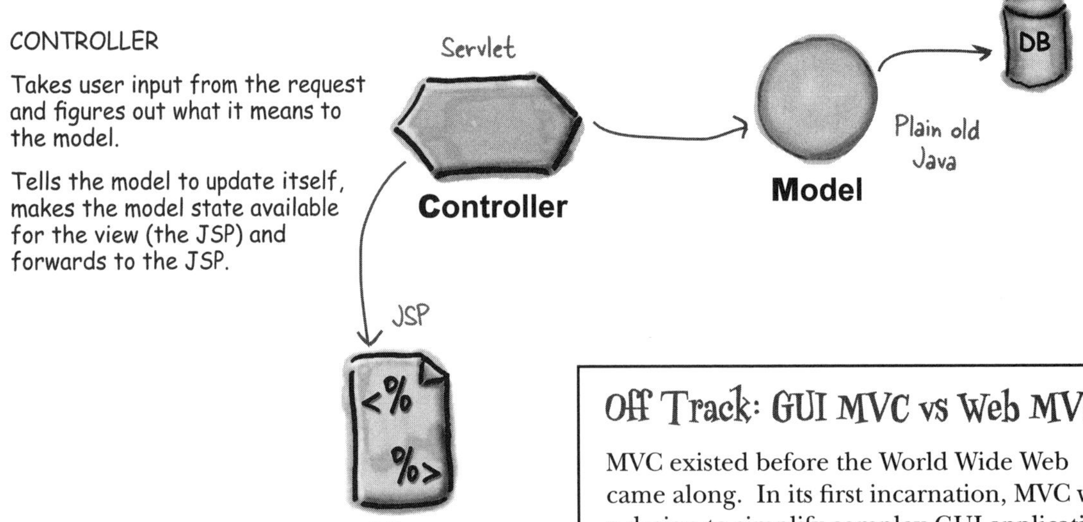

CONTROLLER
Takes user input from the request and figures out what it means to the model.
Tells the model to update itself, makes the model state available for the view (the JSP) and forwards to the JSP.
Servlet
Controller
Model
Plain old Java
DB
JSP
<% %>
View

VIEW

Responsible for the presentation. It gets the state of the model from the Controller (although not directly; the Controller puts the model data in a place where the View can find it).

Off Track: GUI MVC vs Web MVC

MVC existed before the World Wide Web came along. In its first incarnation, MVC was a design to simplify complex GUI applications. First created in Smalltalk, one of MVC's chief attributes was that the View would be notified automatically of changes to the Model.

More recently, MVC has been used on the web, even though the View is in the browser and cannot be automatically updated when the Model changes in the web tier. Our focus is entirely on the web version of MVC.

Finally, we're always talking about MVC, model 2, never the older Model 1 or 1.5 MVCs.

MVC in a real web app

Way back in chapter two, we left you with a "Flex your mind" exercise about potential problems with our Dating App MVC architecture. Let's review where we left off and get around to answering the question that's certainly been haunting you for all these chapters: what could possibly be better than MVC?

For each browser use case, there will be a corresponding set of Model, View, and Controller components, which might be mixed and matched and recombined in many different ways from use case to uses case.

The problem we had in the dating app was that we had many specialized controllers, which sounded good from an OO perspective, but left us with duplicate code across all the different controllers in our app, and didn't give us a nice happy feeling about maintainability and flexibility.

A single MVC app will have many models, views, and controllers.

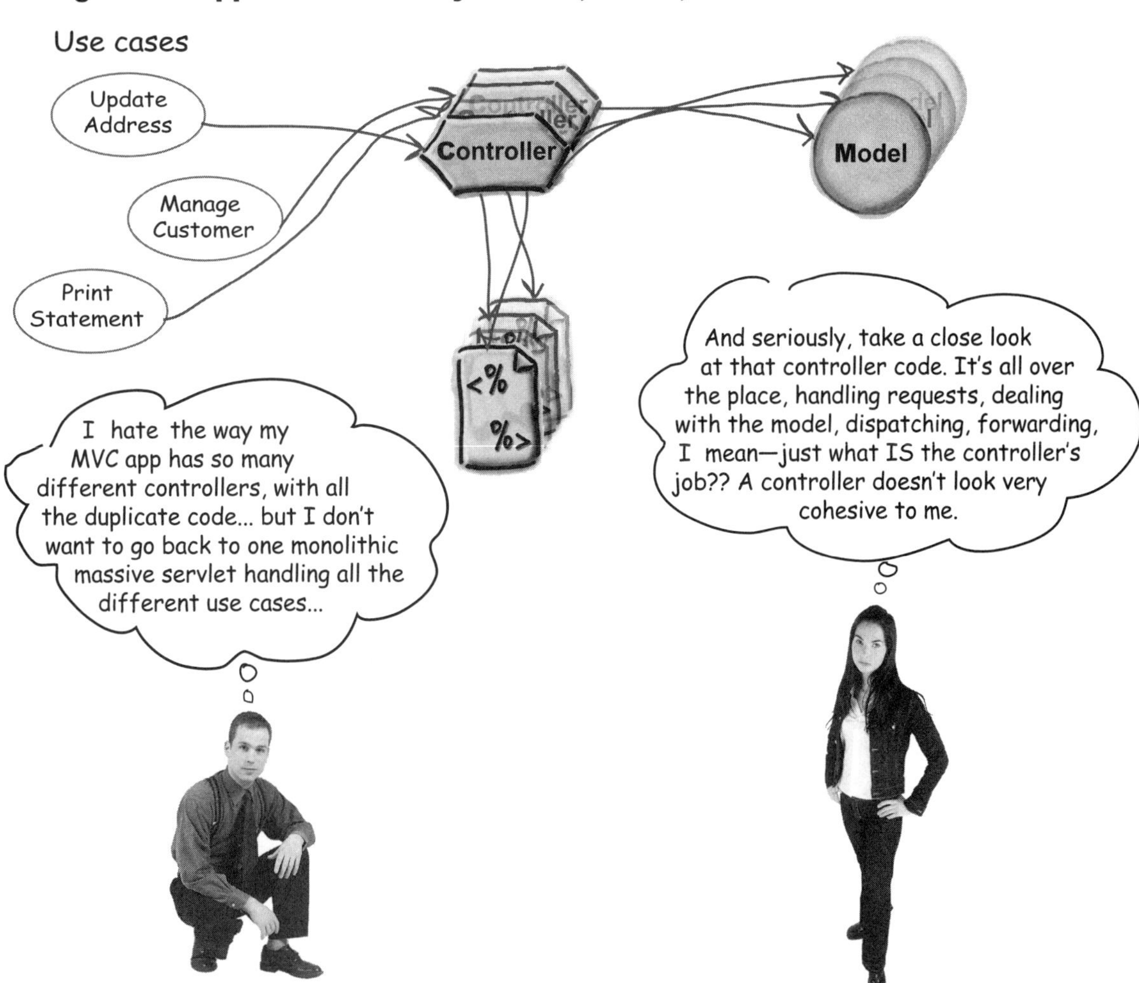

Looking at the MVC controller

Let's see if we agree with what's been said about controllers. First, a reminder about the controller servlet's job:

Pseudo-code for a generic MVC controller

```
public class ControllerServlet extends HttpServlet {

  public void doPost(request, response) {

(1)  String c = req.getParameter("startDate");

     // do a data conversation on the date parameter

     // validate that date is in range

     // if any errors happen in validation,
     // forward to hardcoded "retry" JSP
```

Deal with the **request parameters**

```
(2)  // invoke the hardcoded model component(s)

     // add model results to the request obj.
     // (maybe a reference to a bean)
```

Deal with the **model**

```
(3)  // dispatch to the view JSP
     // (of course it's hard coded)
  }
}
```

Deal with the **view**

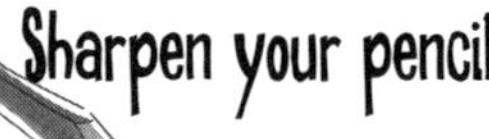

What principles does this component violate?

List three or more software design principles this pseudo-code violates.

Improving the MVC controllers

Besides a lack of cohesiveness, the controller is also tightly coupled to the model and the view components. And there's yet another Duplicate Code Alert here. How can we fix things?

	The controller's three main tasks	A better way to handle it?
1	Get and deal with the **request parameters**	Give this task to a separate form validation component that can get the form parameters, convert them, validate them, handle validation errors, and create an object to hold the parameter values.
2	Invoke the **model**	Hmmm... we don't like hard-coding the model into the controller, so maybe we could do it declaratively, listing a bunch of models in our own custom deployment descriptor that the controller could read and, based on the request, figure out which model(s) to use.
3	Dispatch to the **View**	Why not make this declarative as well? That way, based on the request URL, the controller can tell (from our custom deployment descriptor) which view to dispatch to.

New and (shorter) controller pseudo-code

```
public class ControllerServlet extends HttpServlet {

  public void doPost(request, response) {

    // call a validation component declaratively
    //  (have it handle validation errors too!)

    // declaratively invoke a request processing
    // component, to call a Model component

    // dispatch to the view JSP declaratively
  }
}
```

This looks great to me! I'll feel a lot less schizophrenic if I'm designed this way.

Controller

Designing our fantasy controller

Let's do another one of our now-infamous architectural diagrams to see what this controller and its support components might look like.

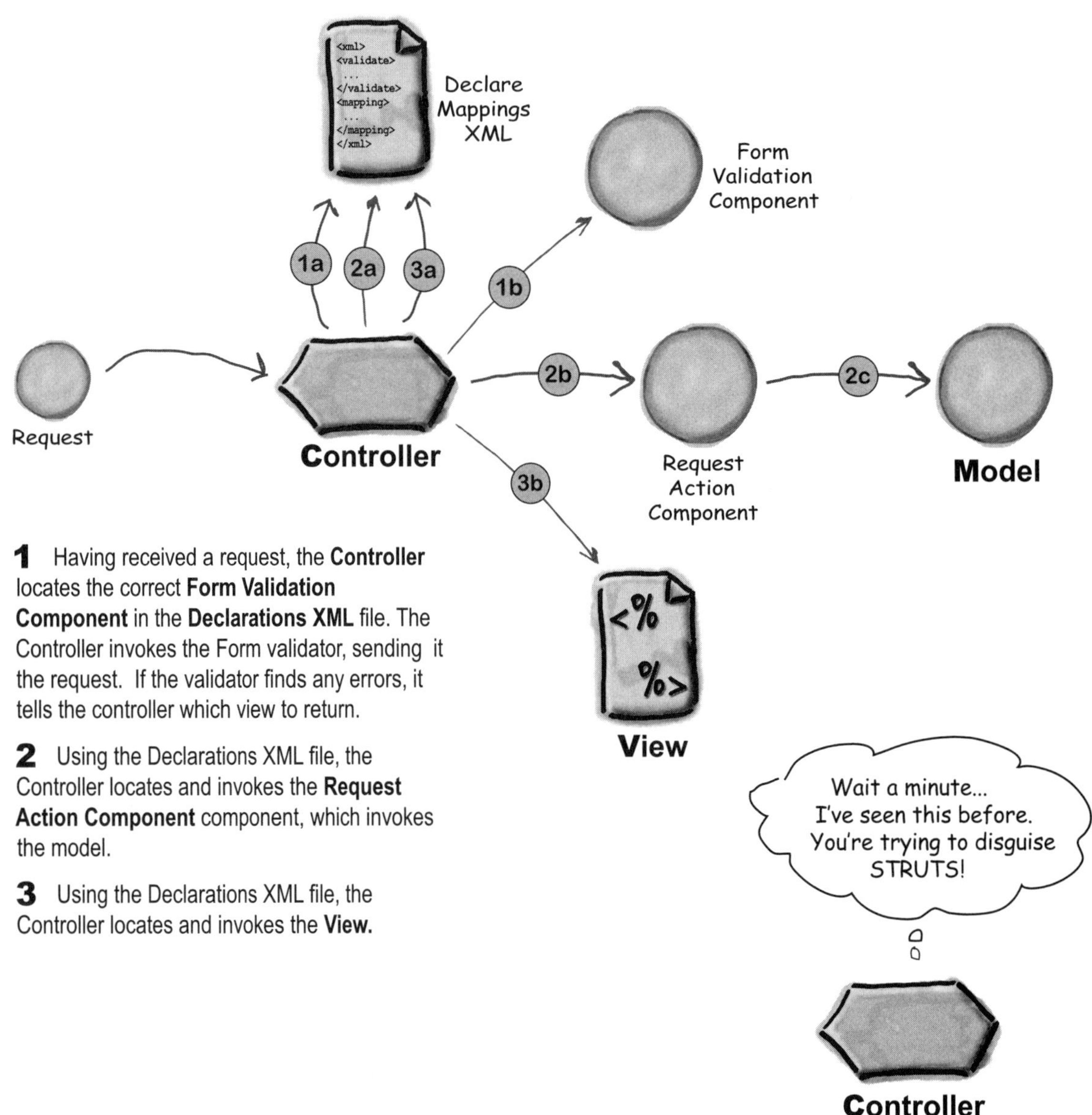

1 Having received a request, the **Controller** locates the correct **Form Validation Component** in the **Declarations XML** file. The Controller invokes the Form validator, sending it the request. If the validator finds any errors, it tells the controller which view to return.

2 Using the Declarations XML file, the Controller locates and invokes the **Request Action Component** component, which invokes the model.

3 Using the Declarations XML file, the Controller locates and invokes the **View.**

Yes! It's Struts in a nutshell

Obviously this is an overview, and we've left out pretty much all of the details, but this is the basic idea behind the Struts framework. Let's look at a few more details, starting with the fact that we've changed all the names...

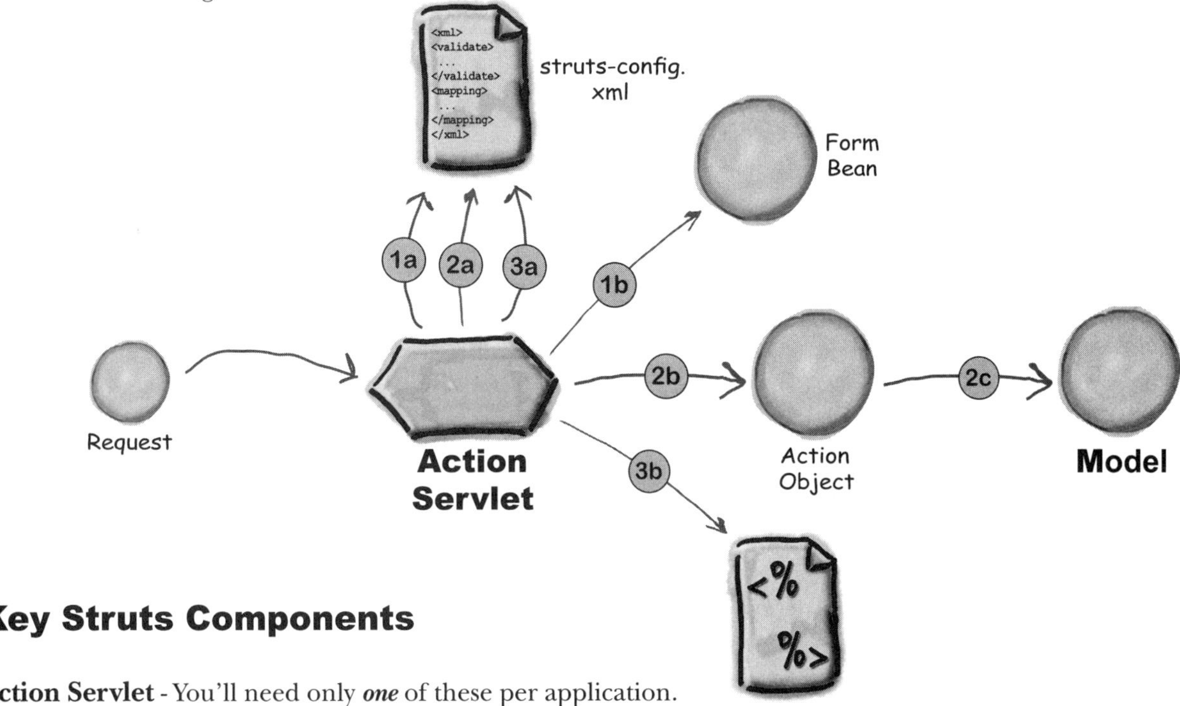

Key Struts Components

Action Servlet - You'll need only ***one*** of these per application. Best of all, *you* don't even have to write it, **Struts provides it**.

Form Beans - You'll write one of these for each HTML form your app needs to process. They are Java beans, and once the Struts Action Servlet has called the setters on the form bean (to populate the bean with form parameters), it will call the bean's validate() method. This is a great place to put data conversion and error handling logic.

Action Objects - Generally, an action maps to a single activity in a use-case. It has a call-back-like method called **execute()**, which is a great place to *get* the validated form params, and call model components. Think of the Action object as kind of a "servlet lite".

struts-config.xml - This is the Struts-specific deployment descriptor. In it you'll map: **request URLs to Actions**, **Actions to Form beans**, and **Actions to views**.

Is Struts a container?

Officially, Struts is considered a framework.

Frameworks are collections of interfaces and classes that are designed to work together to handle a particular type of problem. In the case of Struts, the problem space is web applications. The goal of a framework is to "aid programmers in the development and maintenance of complex applications".

So, Struts isn't a container, but in some ways it acts like one.

I feel an analogy coming on... you've said Struts has "call-back" methods and a deployment descriptor. So is Struts like a mini-container?

Top five ways Struts is like a servlets container

1 Declarative: They both use an XML file to configure the application declaratively.

2 Lifecycle: They both provide lifecycles for predetermined types of objects.

3 Callbacks: They both perform automatic callbacks of key lifecycle methods.

4 APIs: They both provide APIs for key types of objects that are supported.

5 Application Control: They both provide a controlled environment in which your application runs. They are your application's window to the outside world.

In Struts, I've been promoted to "Action Servlet". Sometimes I'm also referred to as a Front Controller. (That's on the exam, by the way.)

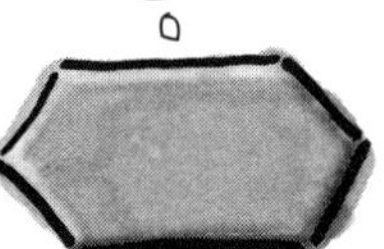

Action Servlet

Relax

There is nothing about Struts on the exam!

You ARE expected to know the purpose and function of a Front Controller (and Struts is just a tricked-out Front Controller), but you will not have any questions about the Struts framework. So, you can relax and follow along without having to memorize every picky detail.

How does Front Controller fit in?

Oh yeah. Front Controller is another J2EE pattern, and it just happens to be on the exam. Actually, ***Struts is a really fancy example of using a Front Controller pattern.*** The basic idea of the Front Controller pattern is that a single component, usually a servlet but possibly a JSP, acts as the single control point for the presentation tier of a web application. With the Front Controller pattern, all of the app's requests go through a single controller, which handles dispatching the request to the appropriate places.

In the real world, it's rare to implement a Front Controller all by itself. Even a really simple implementation usually includes another J2EE pattern called an **Application Controller**. Struts includes a class called the RequestProcessor, which is ultimately responsible for the handling of HTTP requests.

Although the exam might contain questions about the Front Controller pattern, you'll be fine if you remember the benefits of Struts, and the fact that Struts is simply a Front Controller with all the bells and whistles.

Eight features that Struts adds to a Front Controller

1 Declarative Control: Struts allows you to create declarative maps between request URLs, validation objects, model-invoking objects, and views.

2 Automated Request Dispatching: The Action.execute() method returns a symbolic ActionForward which tells the ActionServlet which view to dispatch to. This provides another layer of abstraction (and loose coupling) between the controller and view components.

3 DataSources: Struts can provide DataSource management.

4 Custom Tags: Struts provides dozens of custom tags.

5 Internationalization Support: Error classes and custom tags have internationalization support.

6 Declarative Validation: Struts provides a validation framework that removes the need to code the validate method in your form beans. The rules for validating a form are configured in an XML file and can be changed without affecting your form bean code.

7 Global exception handling: Struts provides a declarative error handling mechanism similar to <error-page> in the DD. However, with Struts the exceptions can be specific to the application code in your Action object.

8 Plug-ins: Struts provides a PlugIn interface with two methods: init() and destroy(). You can create your own plug-ins to enhance your Struts application, and they will be managed for you. For example, the Validator framework is initialized using a plug-in.

Refactoring the Beer app for Struts

Enough theory, let's write a Struts app. First off, let's review our MVC Beer app from chapter 3. The only code that's going to change when we refactor to Struts is related to the MVC controller. (The model and view are not affected.)

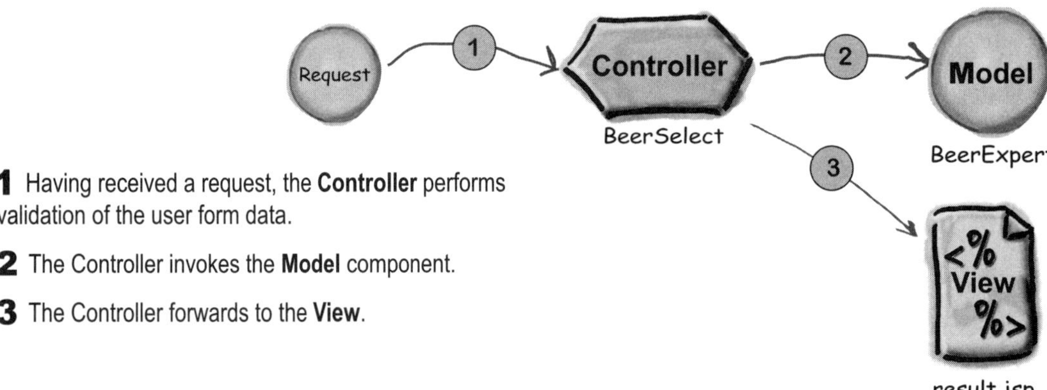

1 Having received a request, the **Controller** performs validation of the user form data.

2 The Controller invokes the **Model** component.

3 The Controller forwards to the **View**.

MVC controller code (from chapter 3)

```
package com.example.web;
import com.example.model.*;
import javax.servlet.*;
import javax.servlet.http.*;
import java.io.*;
import java.util.*;

public class BeerSelect extends HttpServlet {
  public void doPost(HttpServletRequest request,
                     HttpServletResponse response)
          throws IOException, ServletException {

  String c = request.getParameter("color");

  BeerExpert be = new BeerExpert();
  List result = be.getBrands(c);

  request.setAttribute("styles", result);
  RequestDispatcher disp =
     request.getRequestDispatcher("result.jsp");
  disp.forward(request, response);
  }
}
```

Not a lot of form validation going on here. :)

Invoke the model.

Forward to the hardcoded View.

The Struts Beer app architecture

Here's the Beer app architecture, all done up in Struts...

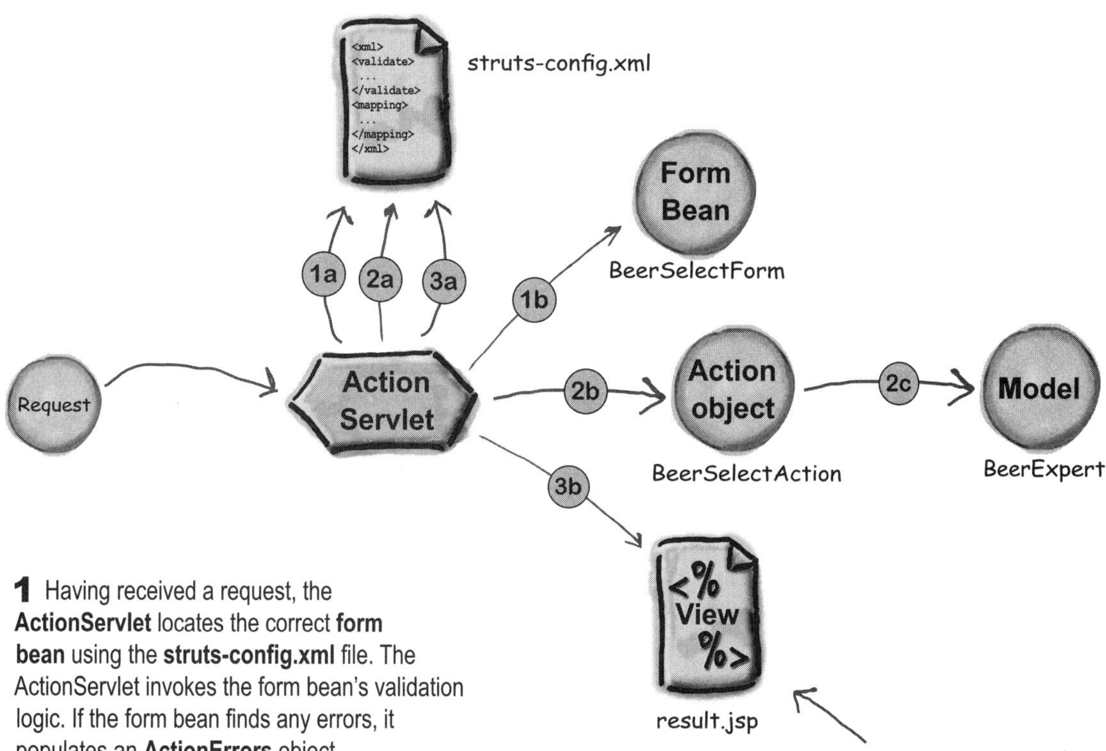

1 Having received a request, the **ActionServlet** locates the correct **form bean** using the **struts-config.xml** file. The ActionServlet invokes the form bean's validation logic. If the form bean finds any errors, it populates an **ActionErrors** object.

2 Using the struts-config.xml file, the ActionServlet locates and invokes the **Action** object, which invokes the model and returns an **ActionForward** object to the ActionServlet.

3 Having previously extracted the necessary mappings from struts-config.xml, the ActionServlet uses the ActionForward object to dispatch to the correct view component.

Well, OK, the view *will* change in a Struts web app. For one thing, Struts provides a tag library that provides a tag, <html:errors/>, that displays the form bean validation errors. Also, the HTML tag library provides tags that repopulate the form on an error.

A form bean exposed

Remember, the form bean's job is to validate the user's form params. A nice benefit of Struts is that a validation step is built right into the architecture.

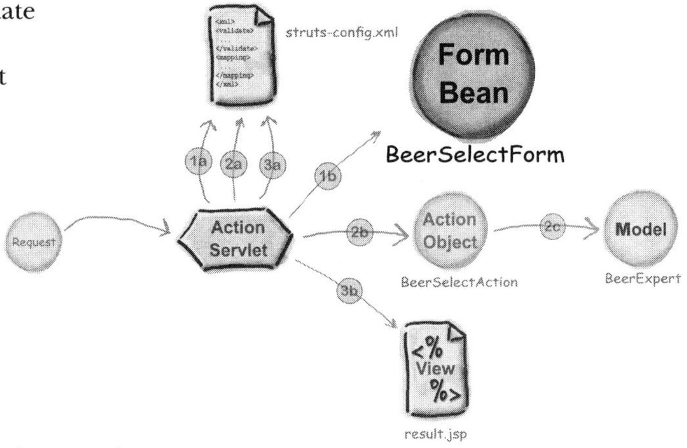

struts-config.xml

Form Bean

BeerSelectForm

Request

Action Servlet

Action Object

Model

BeerSelectAction

BeerExpert

View

result.jsp

```
package com.example.web;

// Struts imports
import org.apache.struts.action.ActionMapping;
import org.apache.struts.action.ActionForm;
import org.apache.struts.action.ActionError;
import org.apache.struts.action.ActionErrors;

import javax.servlet.http.HttpServletRequest;

public class BeerSelectForm extends ActionForm {

  private String color;
  public void setColor(String color) {
    this.color = color;
  }
  public String getColor() {
    return color;
  }
  private static final String VALID_COLORS = "amber,dark,light,brown";

  public ActionErrors validate(ActionMapping mapping,
                               HttpServletRequest request) {
    ActionErrors errors = new ActionErrors();

    if ( VALID_COLORS.indexOf(color) == -1 ) {
      errors.add("color", new ActionError("error.colorField.notValid"));
    }
    return errors;
  }
}
```

Form beans must extend ActionForm.

Usually, you'll want your Form beans to have getters and setters for all of the form params.

The ActionServlet calls validate().

Struts provides ActionErrors to manage validation errors.

The ActionError constructor takes a String that is a symbolic key into a resource bundle. This is done to facilitate internationalization.

How an Action object ticks

The Action object is mainly a dispatcher. It is invoked by the ActionServlet, which calls the Action object's execute() method.

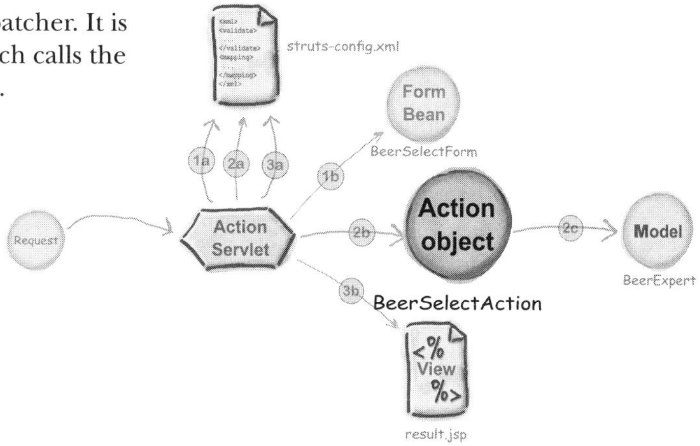

```
package com.example.web;

// Model imports
import com.example.model.*;
import java.util.*;

// Struts imports
import org.apache.struts.action.Action;
import org.apache.struts.action.ActionMapping;
import org.apache.struts.action.ActionForm;
import org.apache.struts.action.ActionForward;

// Servlet imports
import javax.servlet.http.HttpServletRequest;
import javax.servlet.http.HttpServletResponse;

public class BeerSelectAction extends Action {

  public ActionForward execute(ActionMapping mapping, ActionForm form,
                               HttpServletRequest request,
                               HttpServletResponse response) {

      // Cast the form to the application-specific form
      BeerSelectForm myForm = (BeerSelectForm) form;

      // Process the business logic
      BeerExpert be = new BeerExpert();
      ArrayList result = be.getBrands(myForm.getColor());

      // Forward to the Results view
      // (and store the data in the request-scope)
      request.setAttribute("styles", result);
      return mapping.findForward("show_results");
    }
}
```

Your controllers MUST extend the Action class.

Sent from the ActionServlet, so we can return the right view.

Provides access to the validated user form params.

Sending a user form param to the model component.

The execute method returns an ActionForward to the ActionServlet that directs Struts to dispatch to the next appropriate view. These symbolic "forwards" are declared in the struts-config.xml file.

struts-config.xml: tying it all together

The struts-config.xml file is analogous to the DD. You can actually call it whatever you want, although struts-config.xml is its conventional name. Similar to the DD, this file is where you'll declare and map Struts components in your web app. This mechanism helps your application become more loosely coupled.

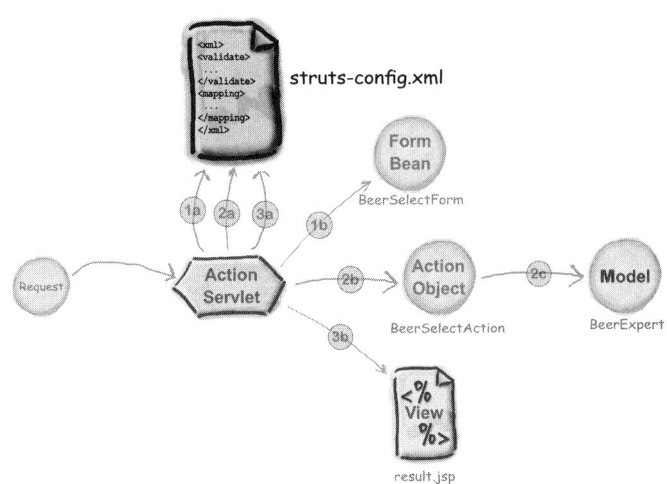


```
<?xml version="1.0" encoding="ISO-8859-1" ?>
<!DOCTYPE struts-config PUBLIC
      "-//Apache Software Foundation//DTD Struts Configuration 1.0//EN"
      "http://jakarta.apache.org/struts/dtds/struts-config_1_0.dtd">

<struts-config>

  <form-beans>
    <form-bean name="selectBeerForm"
               type="com.example.web.BeerSelectForm" />
  </form-beans>


  <action-mappings>
    <action path="/SelectBeer"
           type="com.example.web.BeerSelectAction"
           name="selectBeerForm" scope="request"
           validate="true" input="/form.jsp">


        <forward name="show_results"
               path="/result.jsp" />
    </action>
  </action-mappings>


  <message-resources parameter="ApplicationResources" null="false" />
</struts-config>
```

The <form-bean> element declares the symbolic name and class of a form bean object.

An <action> element maps the URL path to the controller class; notice that the .do extension for the path is NOT included in the Struts configuration.

The <action> also associates a form bean with the action. This is specified by the symbolic form bean name. Struts will create this bean and store it in the specified scope. If validation occurs and errors are returned from the validate method, then the input attribute declares the View responsible for displaying the error message; this is usually the form that submitted this action.

The <forward> element creates a mapping between the symbolic view name, used by the Action object, and the physical path to the view component.

Specifying Struts in the web.xml DD

As far as the Container is concerned, the ActionServlet is just another servlet. So, you have to declare it and make sure all of the web app's requests are mapped to it.

```
<web-app xmlns="http://java.sun.com/xml/ns/j2ee"
    xmlns:xsi="http://www.w3.org/2001/XMLSchema-instance"
    xsi:schemaLocation="http://java.sun.com/xml/ns/j2ee/web-app_2_4.xsd"
    version="2.4">

  <!-- Define the controller servlet -->
  <servlet>
    <servlet-name>FrontController</servlet-name>
    <servlet-class>org.apache.struts.action.ActionServlet</servlet-class>

    <!-- Name the struts configuration file -->
    <init-param>
      <param-name>config</param-name>
      <param-value>/WEB-INF/struts-config.xml</param-value>
    </init-param>

    <!-- Guarantee that this servlet is loaded on startup. -->
    <load-on-startup>1</load-on-startup>
  </servlet>

  <!-- The Struts controller mapping -->
  <servlet-mapping>
    <servlet-name>FrontController</servlet-name>
    <url-pattern>*.do</url-pattern>
  </servlet-mapping>
  <!-- END: The Struts controller mapping -->

</web-app>
```

Naming the ActionServlet "FrontController" isn't required, but it'll help remind you of its purpose in the app.

The "config" init param tells the ActionServlet where to find the Struts config file.

The ActionServlet has a complex init method; you better load this servlet at startup.

Wow! This one servlet is going to handle ALL of this app's requests (assuming you name the request URLs with a ".do" extension).

BANG!

You should name the Struts DD "struts-config.xml"

And if you do NOT, then in your web.xml DD, you MUST declare an init-param "config", to define the name of the Struts DD. If you DO use the name "struts-config.xml", then Struts will find it automatically, without an init-parameter, but it's still considered "good practice" to declare it in the DD.

Install Struts, and Just Run It!

Installing Struts is simple.

The links and versions mentioned on this page were current at the time of this writing. Which is no help at all for you, but means simply: *we have no idea what things will be like by the time you read this, but we gave it our best shot anyway.*

Six easy steps to installing Struts

1. Crank up your browser and navigate to:

   `http://jakarta.apache.org/site/binindex.cgi`

2. Scroll down to the Struts section and select the link to:

   `1.1 zip`

3. Download the zip file to a temporary directory.

4. Unzip the file which unpacks to:

```
jakarta-struts-1.1/
   README
   lib/
      struts.jar
      commons-beanutils.jar
      commons-digester.jar
   webapps/
   .....
```

5. Copy the following files to your webapp's **WEB-INF/lib/** directory:

```
struts.jar
commons-beanutils.jar
commons-digester.jar
```

6. FYI: make sure that there is a copy of **struts.jar** in your classpath when you compile your form beans and action objects. (Remember, the ActionServlet front controller is created for you automatically.)

Creating the deployment environment

This is the directory structure you will create to run the Struts version of the Beer app.

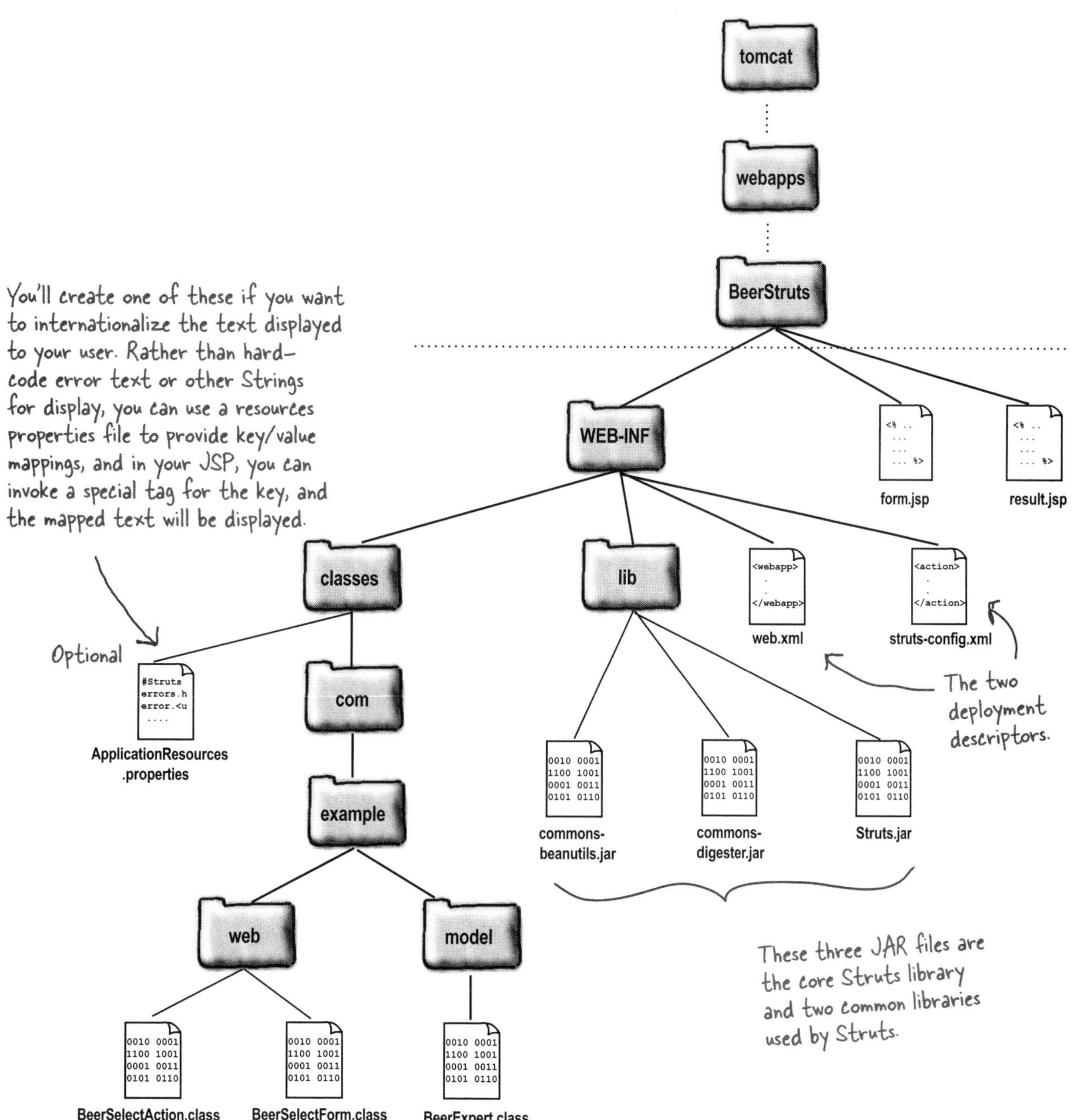

tomcat
webapps
BeerStruts
WEB-INF
form.jsp
result.jsp
classes
lib
web.xml
struts-config.xml
<webapp>
</webapp>
<action>
</action>
You'll create one of these if you want to internationalize the text displayed to your user. Rather than hard-code error text or other Strings for display, you can use a resources properties file to provide key/value mappings, and in your JSP, you can invoke a special tag for the key, and the mapped text will be displayed.
Optional
ApplicationResources .properties
com
example
web
model
commons-beanutils.jar
commons-digester.jar
Struts.jar
The two deployment descriptors.
These three JAR files are the core Struts library and two common libraries used by Struts.
BeerSelectAction.class
BeerSelectForm.class
BeerExpert.class

Patterns review for the SCWCD

We've covered a lot of patterns in the last two chapters. The next few pages pull together a lot of the details you'll want to study for the SCWCD exam.

Business Delegate

Use the Business Delegate pattern to shield your web tier controllers from the fact that some of your app's model components are remote.

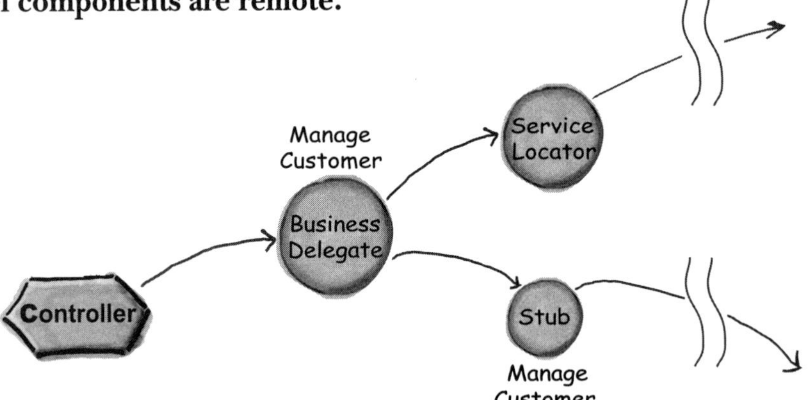

Business Delegate features

- Acts as a proxy, implementing the remote service's interface.
- Initiates communications with a remote service.
- Handles communication details and exceptions.
- Receives requests from a controller component.
- Translates the request and forwards it to the business service (via the stub).
- Translates the response and returns it to the controller component.
- By handling the details of remote component lookup and communications, allows controllers to be more cohesive.

Business Delegate principles

- The Business delegate is based on:
  - hiding complexity
  - coding to interfaces
  - loose coupling
  - separation of concerns
- Minimizes the impact on the web tier when changes occur on the business tier.
- Reduces coupling between tiers.
- Adds a layer to the app, which increases complexity.
- Method calls to the Business Delegate should be coarse-grained to reduce network traffic.

Service Locator

Use the Service Locator pattern to perform registry lookups so you can simplify all of the other components (such as Business Delegates) that have to do JNDI (or other registry types) lookups.

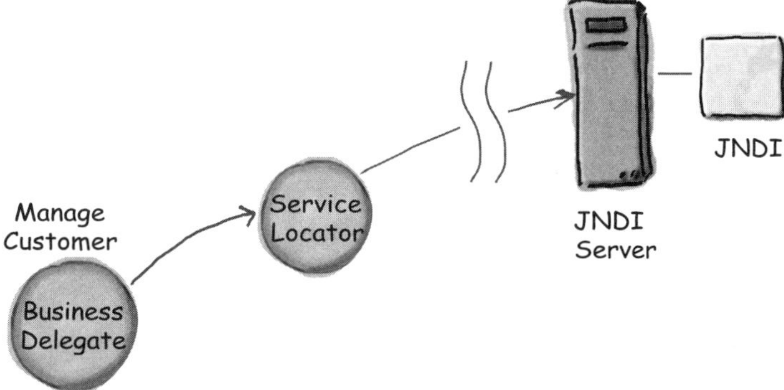

Service Locator features

- Obtains InitialContext objects.
- Performs registry lookups.
- Handles communication details and exceptions.
- Can improve performance by caching previously obtained references.
- Works with a variety of registries such as: JNDI, RMI, UDDI, and COS naming.

Service Locator principles

- The Service Locator is based on:
  - hiding complexity
  - separation of concerns
- Minimizes the impact on the web tier when remote components change locations or containers.
- Reduces coupling between tiers.

Transfer Object

Use the Transfer Object pattern to minimize network traffic by providing a local representation of a fine-grained remote component (usually an entity).

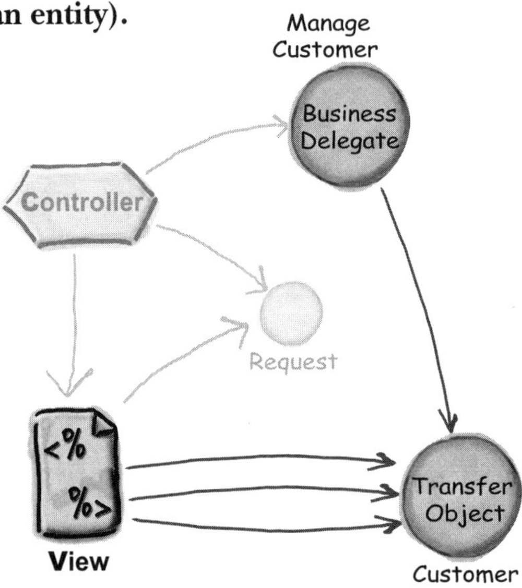

Transfer Object functions

- Provides a local representation of a remote entity (i.e., an object that maintains some data state).
- Minimizes network traffic.
- Can follow Java bean conventions so that it can be easily accessed by other objects.
- Implemented as a serializable object so that it can move across the network.
- Typically easily accessible by view components.

Transfer Object principles

- The Transfer Object is based on:
    - reducing network traffic
- Minimizes the performance impact on the web tier when remote components' data is accessed with fine-grained calls.
- Reduces coupling between tiers.
- A drawback is that components accessing the Transfer Object can receive out-of-date data, because the Transfer Object's data is really representing state that's stored somewhere else.
- Making updatable Transfer Objects concurrency-safe is typically complex.

Intercepting Filter

Use the Intercepting Filter pattern to modify requests being sent to servlets, or to modify responses being sent to users.

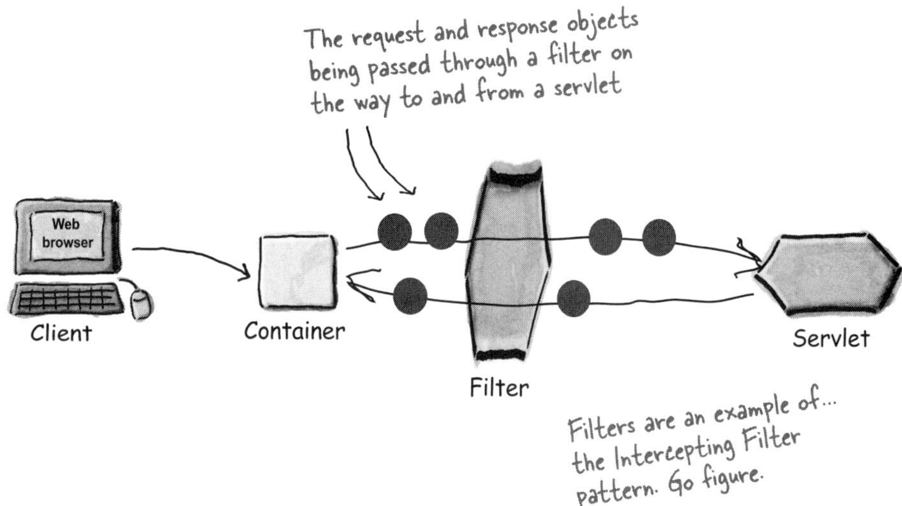
The request and response objects being passed through a filter on the way to and from a servlet
Web browser
Client
Container
Filter
Servlet
Filters are an example of... the Intercepting Filter pattern. Go figure.

Intercepting Filter functions

- Can intercept and/or modify requests before they reach the servlet.
- Can intercept and/or modify responses before they are returned to the client.
- Filters are deployed declaratively using the DD.
- Filters are modular so that they can be executed in chains.
- Filters have lifecycles managed by the Container.
- Filters must implement Container callback methods.

Intercepting Filter principles

- The Intercepting Filter is based on:
  - cohesion
  - loose coupling
  - increasing declarative control
- Declarative control allows Filters to be easily implemented on either a temporary or permanent basis.
- Declarative control allows the sequence of invocation to be easily updated.

Model, View, Controller (MVC)

Use the MVC pattern to create a logical structure that separates the code into three basic types of components (Model, View, Controller) in your application. This increases the cohesiveness of each component and allows for greater reusability, especially with model components.

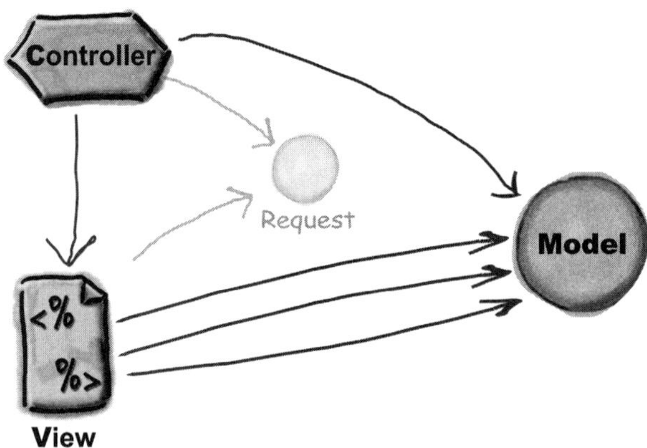

Model, View, Controller features

- Views can change independently from controllers and models.
- Model components hide internal details (data structures), from the view and controller components.
- If the model adheres to a strict contract (interface), then these components can be reused in other application areas such as GUIs or J2ME.
- Separation of model code from controller code allows for easier migration to using remote business components.

Model, View, Controller principles

- Model, View, Controller is based on:
  - separation of concerns
  - loose couplings
- Increases cohesion in individual components.
- Increases the overall complexity of the application. (This is true because even though individual components become more cohesive, MVC adds many new components to the application.)
- Minimizes the impact of changes in other tiers of the application.

Front Controller

Use the Front Controller pattern to gather common, often redundant, request processing code into a single component. This allows the application controller to be more cohesive and less complex.

```
<xml>
<validate>
...
</validate>
<mapping>
...
</mapping>
</xml>
```

struts-config.xml

Form Bean

Request

Action Servlet

Action object

Model

<% %>

View

A Struts implementation of the Front Controller pattern.

Front Controller features

- Centralizes a web app's initial request handling tasks in a single component.
- Using the Front Controller with other patterns can provide loose coupling by making presentation tier dispatching declarative.
- A drawback of Front Controller (on its own, without Struts) is that it's very barebones compared to Struts. To create a reasonable application from scratch using the Front Controller pattern, you would end up rewriting many of the features already found in Struts.

Front Controller principles

- The Front Controller is based on:
  - hiding complexity
  - separation of concerns
  - loose coupling
- Increases cohesion in application controller components.
- Decreases the overall complexity of the application.
- Increases the maintainability of the infrastructure code.

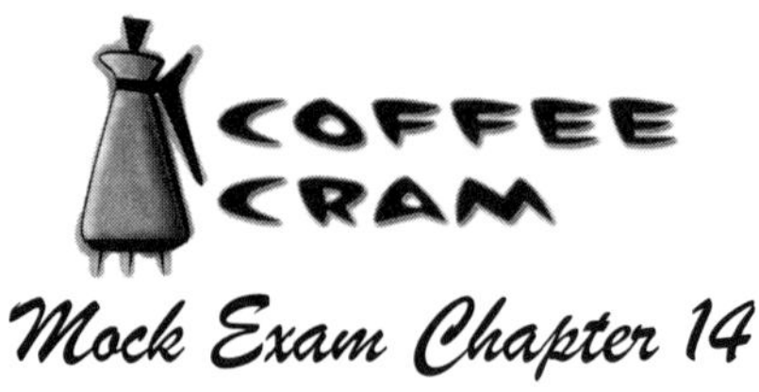

Mock Exam Chapter 14

1 Given this list of attributes:

- related to Intercepting Filter
- supports role separation between developers
- adds reusability

Which design pattern is being described?

- ❏ A. Transfer Object
- ❏ B. Service Locator
- ❏ C. Front Controller
- ❏ D. Business Delegate

2 The design of your web application calls for certain security measures to be taken for every request received. Some of these security checks will be applied, regardless of the type of request.

Which design pattern can be used to achieve this design requirement?

- ❏ A. Transfer Object
- ❏ B. Service Locator
- ❏ C. Composite Entity
- ❏ D. Business Delegate
- ❏ E. Intercepting Filter

3 Your company wants to leverage its distributed silos. Your job is to seamlessly integrate your application's web service endpoints with its DAOs. In addition, your coarse-grained Controller Locators must be enhanced to support J2ME, UDDI registries.

Which design pattern can be used to achieve these design requirements?

- ❏ A. Domain Activator
- ❏ B. Intercepting Observer
- ❏ C. Composite Delegate
- ❏ D. Transfer Facade

---

4 This statement describes the potential benefits of a design pattern:

The pattern reduces network roundtrips between a client and an Enterprise Bean, and gives the client a local copy of the data encapsulated by an Enterprise Bean after a single method call, instead of requiring several method calls. Which design pattern is being described?

- ❑ A. Transfer object
- ❑ B. Intercepting Filter
- ❑ C. Model-View-Controller
- ❑ D. Business Delegate

---

5 Your company, Models 'R Us, is creating an advanced inventory maximization component that can be used with all major J2EE container vendors. Your job is to design the piece of this component that will perform JNDI lookups with whatever vendor the client is using.

What design pattern can help you accomplish this task?

- ❑ A. Transfer object
- ❑ B. Intercepting Filter
- ❑ C. Model-View-Controller
- ❑ D. Business Delegate
- ❑ E. Service Locator

---

6 While fine tuning your multi-tiered J2EE business application, you've discovered that you'd get better performance if you reduced the number of remote requests your app makes, and increased the amount of data collected for each request you make.

What design pattern should you consider to implement this change in your application?

- ❑ A. Transfer object
- ❑ B. Service Locator
- ❑ C. Front Controller
- ❑ D. Intercepting Filter
- ❑ E. Model-View-Controller

7 Given this list of attributes:

- related to Service Locator
- reduces coupling
- can add a layer and some complexity

Which design pattern is being described?

- ❑ A.Transfer Object
- ❑ B. Front Controller
- ❑ C. Business Delegate
- ❑ D. Intercepting Filter
- ❑ E. Model-View-Controller

---

8 Your web application uses a SessionBean component in a distributed application to make a specialized calculation, such as validating credit-card numbers. However, you want to shield your web components from the code involved with looking up the SessionBean component and using its interface. You want to decouple local application classes from the looking up and use of the distributed component, whose interface could change. Which J2EE design pattern can you use in this case?

- ❑ A. Transfer object.
- ❑ B. Service Locator.
- ❑ C. Model-View-Controller.
- ❑ D. Business Delegate.

---

9 Given this list of attributes:

- related to Business Delegate
- improves network performance
- can improve client performance through caching

Which design pattern is being described?

- ❑ A.Transfer Object
- ❑ B. Service Locator
- ❑ C. Front Controller
- ❑ D. Intercepting Filter
- ❑ E. Model-View-Controller

Chapter 14 Answers

1 Given this list of attributes:

- related to Intercepting Filter
- supports role separation between developers
- adds reusability

(Core J2EE Patterns, pg. 180)

Which design pattern is being described?

- ❑ A. Transfer Object
- ❑ B. Service Locator
- ☑ C. Front Controller
- ❑ D. Business Delegate

–This pattern (among others), helps separate the tasks performed by application developers from the tasks performed by web designers.

2 The design of your web application calls for certain security measures to be taken for every request received. Some of these security checks will be applied, regardless of the type of request.

(Core J2EE Patterns, pg. 144)

Which design pattern can be used to achieve this design requirement?

- ❑ A. Transfer Object
- ❑ B. Service Locator
- ❑ C. Composite Entity
- ❑ D. Business Delegate
- ☑ E. Intercepting Filter

–The Intercepting Filter is a good choice when you want to intercept and manipulate requests before the normal request processing happens.

3 Your company wants to leverage its distributed silos. Your job is to seamlessly integrate your application's web service endpoints with its DAOs. In addition, your coarse-grained Controller Locators must be enhanced to support J2ME, UDDI registries.

(Dating Design Patterns ch. 7)

Which design pattern can be used to achieve these design requirements?

- ❑ A. Domain Activator
- ❑ B. Intercepting Observer
- ☑ C. Composite Delegate
- ❑ D. Transfer Facade

– Given the irregularities in the requirements, the Composite Delegate pattern will provide the greatest refactoring flexibility :)

4 This statement describes the potential benefits of a design pattern:

The pattern reduces network roundtrips between a client and an Enterprise Bean, and gives the client a local copy of the data encapsulated by an Enterprise Bean after a single method call, instead of requiring several method calls. Which design pattern is being described?

(Core J2EE Patterns, pg. 424)

- [x] A. Transfer object
- [ ] B. Intercepting Filter
- [ ] C. Model-View-Controller
- [ ] D. Business Delegate

–A key benefit of a Transfer Object is the reduction of network traffic.

5 Your company, Models 'R Us, is creating an advanced inventory maximization component that can be used with all major J2EE container vendors. Your job is to design the piece of this component that will perform JNDI lookups with whatever vendor the client is using.

(Core J2EE Patterns, pg. 316)

What design pattern can help you accomplish this task?

- [ ] A. Transfer object
- [ ] B. Intercepting Filter
- [ ] C. Model-View-Controller
- [ ] D. Business Delegate
- [x] E. Service Locator

–The Service Locator can be used when you want to encapsulate vendor dependencies concerning service lookups. Using this pattern will help isolate the code that will be unique from vendor to vendor.

6 While fine tuning your multi-tiered J2EE business application, you've discovered that you'd get better performance if you reduced the number of remote requests your app makes, and increased the amount of data collected for each request you make.

(Core J2EE Patterns, pg. 415-416)

What design pattern should you consider to implement this change in your application?

- [x] A. Transfer object
- [ ] B. Service Locator
- [ ] C. Front Controller
- [ ] D. Intercepting Filter
- [ ] E. Model-View-Controller

–The Transfer Object can be used to aggregate multiple, fine-grained remote calls into a single call. Often, the reduction in network traffic more than makes up for the overhead of populating a larger object, and an increase in performance can be achieved.

7 Given this list of attributes:

(Core J2EE Patterns, pg. 308-309)

- related to Service Locator
- reduces coupling
- can add a layer and some complexity

Which design pattern is being described?

- [ ] A.Transfer Object
- [ ] B. Front Controller
- [x] C. Business Delegate
- [ ] D. Intercepting Filter
- [ ] E. Model-View-Controller

-Although a layer is added, the benefits of this pattern (such as reduced coupling and a simpler business tier interface), make it worthwhile.

---

8 Your web application uses a SessionBean component in a distributed application to make a specialized calculation, such as validating credit-card numbers. However, you want to shield your web components from the code involved with looking up the SessionBean component and using its interface. You want to decouple local application classes from the looking up and use of the distributed component, whose interface could change. Which J2EE design pattern can you use in this case?

(Core J2EE Patterns, pg. 308)

- [ ] A. Transfer object.
- [ ] B. Service Locator.
- [ ] C. Model-View-Controller.
- [x] D. Business Delegate.

-A key benefit of the Business Delegate is reduced coupling between the presentation tier and the business tier.

---

9 Given this list of attributes:

(Core J2EE Patterns, pg. 329)

- related to Business Delegate
- improves network performance
- can improve client performance through caching

Which design pattern is being described?

- [ ] A.Transfer Object
- [x] B. Service Locator
- [ ] C. Front Controller
- [ ] D. Intercepting Filter
- [ ] E. Model-View-Controller

-By using this pattern you can combine the network calls necessary to lookup and create business objects.

Appendix A: Final Mock Exam

Do NOT try to take this exam until you believe you're ready for the real thing. If you take it too soon, then when you come back to it again you'll already have some memory of the questions, and it could give you an artificially high score. We really do want you to pass the *first* time. (Unless there were some way to convince you that you need to buy a fresh copy of this book each time you retake the exam...)

To help defeat the "I remember this question" problem, we've made this exam just a little *harder* than the real exam, by *not* telling you how many answers are correct for each of our questions. Our questions and answers are virtually identical to the tone, style, difficulty, and topics of the real exam, but by not telling you how many answers to choose, you can't automatically eliminate any of the answers. It's cruel of us, really, and we wish we could tell you that it hurts us more than it hurts you to have to take the exam this way. (But be grateful—until a few years ago, Sun's real Java exams *were* written this way, where most questions ended with "Choose all that apply.")

Most exam candidates have said that our mock exams *are* a little more difficult than the real SCWCD, but that their scores on our exam and on the real one were very close. This mock exam is a perfect way to see if you're ready, but only if you:

1) Give yourself no more than two hours and 15 minutes to complete it, just like the real exam.

2) Don't look anywhere else in the book while you're taking the exam!

3) Don't take it over and over again. By the fourth time, you might be getting 98% and yet still not be able to pass the real exam, simply because you were memorizing our exact questions and answers.

4) Wait until *after* you finish the exam to consume large quantities of alcohol or other mind-altering substances...

Final Mock Exam

---

1 This statement describes the potential benefits of a design pattern:

These components pre-process or post-process incoming requests and outgoing responses in a web application, and can be cleanly plugged into the application depending on whether the application requires the component's specialized task.

Which design pattern is being described?

- ❑ A. Transfer Object
- ❑ B. Intercepting Filter
- ❑ C. Model-View-Controller
- ❑ D. Business Delegate
- ❑ E. Front Controller

---

2 Which are true about the **`jsp:useBean`** standard action? (Choose all that apply.)

- ❑ A. The **`name`** attribute is mandatory.
- ❑ B. The **`scope`** attribute defaults to the page scope.
- ❑ C. The **`type`** and **`class`** attributes must NOT be used together.
- ❑ D. The **`type`** attribute is ONLY used when the bean already exists in one of the four JSP scopes.
- ❑ E. The **`jsp:useBean`** standard action may be used to declare a scripting variable that may be used in scriptlets, such as **`<% myBean.method(); %>`**

3 Given this partial deployment descriptor:

```
<context-param>
  <param-name>email</param-name>
  <param-value>foo@bar.com</param-value>
</context-param>
<servlet>
  <servlet-name>a</servlet-name>
  <servlet-class>com.bar.Foo</servlet-class>
  <init-param>
    <param-name>email</param-name>
    <param-value>baz@bar.com</param-value>
  </init-param>
</servlet>
```

And, assuming **scfg** is a **ServletConfig** object and **sctx** is a **ServletContext** object, which statement is true?

❑ A. `sctx.getInitParameter("email")`
will return **baz@bar.com**.

❑ B. `scfg.getInitParameter("email")`
will return **foo@bar.com**.

❑ C. An error will occur because the **email** parameter is defined twice.

❑ D. `scfg.getServletContext().getInitParameter("email")`
will return **baz@bar.com**.

❑ E. `scfg.getServletContext().getInitParameter("email")`
will return **foo@bar.com**.

❑ F. An error will occur because servlet context initialization parameters should be defined using **init-param**, NOT **context-param**.

4 Given:

```
public class DoubleTag extends SimpleTagSupport {
  private String data;
  public void setData(String d) { data = d; }
  public void doTag() throws JspException, IOException {
    getJspContext().getOut().print(data + data);
  }
}
```

Which is an equivalent tag file?

- ❑ A. `${param.data}${param.data}`
- ❑ B.
```
<%@ attribute name="data" %>
${data}${data}
```
- ❑ C.
```
<%@ variable name-given="data" %>
${data}${data}
```
- ❑ D.
```
<%@ attribute name="data" %>
<% pageContext.getOut().print(data + data); %>
```
- ❑ E.
```
<%@ variable name-given="data" %>
<% pageContext.getOut().print(data + data); %>
```

---

5 Given a session object **sess** with an attribute named **myAttr**, and an **Http-SessionBindingEvent** object **bind** bound to **sess**.

Which will retrieve **myAttr**? (Choose all that apply.)

- ❑ A. `long myAttr = sess.getAttribute("myAttr");`
- ❑ B. `Object o = sess.getAttribute("myAttr");`
- ❑ C. `String s = sess.getAttribute("myAttr");`
- ❑ D. `Object o = bind.getAttribute("myAttr");`
- ❑ E. `Object o = bind.getSession().getAttribute("myAttr");`

6 Which about JSP Documents (XML-based documents) are true? (Choose all that apply.)

- ❑ A. A JSP document must have a **`<jsp:root>`** as its top element.
- ❑ B. The following would be valid as the first line of a JSP document: **`<jsp:root xmlns:uri="http://java.sun.com/JSP/Page" version="2.0">`**.
- ❑ C. In a JSP document, page directives are defined using **`<jsp:directive.page>`** instead of **`<%@ %>`**.
- ❑ D. The **`<c:forEach>`** tag CANNOT be used unless the **`c`** prefix has been introduced through a namespace attribute.
- ❑ E. Both the standard **`<%! %>`** syntax as well as **`<jsp:declaration>`** may be used to declare variables in a JSP document.

7 Which statements about EL implicit objects are true? (Choose all that apply.)

- ❑ A. **`${param.name}`** produces the value of the parameter **`name`**.
- ❑ B. **`${init.foo}`** produces the value of the context initialization parameter named **`foo`**.
- ❑ C. The implicit object **`param`** is a **`Map`** that maps parameter names to single String parameter values.
- ❑ D. **`pageContext`**, **`param`**, **`header`**, and **`cookie`** are all implicit objects available to EL expressions in JSP pages.
- ❑ E. **`page`**, **`request`**, **`session`**, and **`application`** are implicit objects that map attribute names to values in the corresponding scopes.

8 Given this JSP snippet:

```
<!--X-->
<%=A.b()%>
<!--<%=A.b()%>-->
<%--Y--%>
```

Assume that a call to **A.b()** is valid and returns the text **test**. Ignoring whitespace in the generated response, which represents the HTML this JSP would produce?

- ❑ A. **<!--X-->test<!--<%=A.b()%>-->**
- ❑ B. **<!--X-->test<!--test-->**
- ❑ C. **test**
- ❑ D. **<!--X-->test<!--<%=A.b()%>-->**
  <%--Y--%>
- ❑ E. **test<%--Y--%>**
- ❑ F. The generated HTML will be blank.

9 Which are true about tag libraries in web applications? (Choose all that apply.)

- ❑ A. A TLD file must exist in the **WEB-INF/tlds/** directory.
- ❑ B. A TLD file may exist in any subdirectory of **WEB-INF**.
- ❑ C. A TLD file may exist in the **WEB-INF** directory in a JAR file.
- ❑ D. A TLD file may exist in the **META-INF** directory in a JAR file.
- ❑ E. A TLD file in a JAR file must be located at **META-INF/taglib.tld**.

10 You store the SQL source files for web-database work in a web application's top-level **sql** directory, but you do NOT want to make this directory accessible to HTTP requests.

How do you configure the web application to forbid requests to this directory? (Choose all that apply.)

- ☐ A. Protect the server with a firewall.
- ☐ B. Specify the directory with a **<security-role>** element in deployment descriptor.
- ☐ C. Move the directory beneath **WEB-INF**, the contents of which are NOT accessible to application users.
- ☐ D. Create a **<security-constraint>** element in the DD to prevent access to the **sql** directory.

---

11 Given:

```
11. <% java.util.Map map = new java.util.HashMap();
12.     map.put("a", "1");
13.     map.put("b", "2");
14.     map.put("c", "3");
15.     request.setAttribute("map", map);
16.     request.setAttribute("map-index", "b");
17. %>
18. <%-- insert code here --%>
```

Which , inserted at line 18, are valid and evaluate to **2**? (Choose all that apply.)

- ☐ A. `${map.b}`
- ☐ B. `${map[b]}`
- ☐ C. `${map.map-index}`
- ☐ D. `${map[map-index]}`
- ☐ E. `${map['map-index']}`
- ☐ F. `${map[requestScope['map-index']]}`

12 Given this tag handler class excerpt:

```
public class WorthlessTag extends TagSupport {
  private String x;
  public void setX(String x) { this.x = x; }
  public int doStartTag() throws JspException {
    try { pageContext.getOut().print(x); }
    catch (IOException e) { }
    if ("x".equals(x))
      return SKIP_BODY;
    else
      return EVAL_BODY_INCLUDE;
  }
  public int doEndTag() throws JspException {
    try { pageContext.getOut().print("E"); }
    catch (IOException e) { }
    if ("y".equals(x))
      return SKIP_PAGE;
    else
      return EVAL_PAGE;
  }
}
```

and given this TLD excerpt:

```
<tag>
    <name>worthless</name>
    <tag-class>com.mycom.WorthlessTag</tag-class>
    <body-content>empty</body-content>
    <attribute>
        <name>x</name>
        <required>true</required>
        <rtexprvalue>true</rtexprvalue>
    </attribute>
</tag>
```

(continued on next page.)

12, cont.

and given this complete JSP page:

```
<%@ taglib uri="somevaliduri" prefix="w" %>
<w:worthless x="x" />
<w:worthless x="<%=Boolean.TRUE.toString()%>" />
<w:worthless x="y" />
<w:worthless x="z" />
```

What output does the JSP generate?

❑ A. `xE`

❑ B. `x trueE yE`

❑ C. `xE trueE yE`

❑ D. `xE trueE yE zE`

❑ E. `x <%=Boolean.TRUE.toString()%>E yE`

❑ F. `xE <%=Boolean.TRUE.toString()%>E yE`

❑ G. `xE <%=Boolean.TRUE.toString()%>E yE zE`

13 A user submits a form using an HTML page containing :

```
<form action="/handler">
  <!-- form tags here -->
</form>
```

The URL pattern **/handler** is mapped to an HTTP servlet.

Which **HttpServlet** service method will the web container call in response to this form submit?

- [ ] A. **doHead**
- [ ] B. **doPost**
- [ ] C. **Get**
- [ ] D. **doGet**

14 Which statements concerning welcome files are true? (Choose all that apply.)

- [ ] A. They can be declared in the DD.
- [ ] B. They can be used to respond to 'partial requests'.
- [ ] C. If multiple welcome files are declared for a web app, their ordering in the DD is NOT meaningful.
- [ ] D. J2EE 1.4 compliant containers are required to match partial requests to URLs in the welcome file list using a specified algorithm.
- [ ] E. If a J2EE 1.4 compliant container receives a partial request for which it CANNOT find a match, it must return an HTTP 404 error code.

15 Once a session has been invalidated, which **HttpSession** methods can be called on that session without throwing an **IllegalStateException**? (Choose all that apply.)

- [ ] A. **invalidate**
- [ ] B. **getAttribute**
- [ ] C. **setAttribute**
- [ ] D. **getServletContext**
- [ ] E. **getAttributeNames**

16 Which statements about the **taglib** directive are true? (Choose all that apply.)

❑ A. A **taglib** directive always identifies a tag prefix that will distinguish usage of actions in the library.

❑ B. `<%@ taglib uri="http://www.mytags.com/mytags" prefix="mytags" %>` is an example of a valid taglib directive.

❑ C. Every **taglib** directive must specify a value for the **uri** attribute.

❑ D. Every **taglib** directive must specify a non-empty value for the **prefix** attribute.

❑ E. There are three attributes defined for the **taglib** directive: **uri**, **tagdir**, and **prefix**.

---

17 Which statements about making a servlet's **doGet()** method **synchronized** are true? (Choose all that apply.)

❑ A. It will make access to **ServletRequest** attributes thread-safe.

❑ B. It will NOT make access to **HttpSession** attributes thread-safe.

❑ C. It may have a negative performance impact because the servlet will only be able to process one request at a time.

❑ D. It is necessary if the method will be using **HttpSession.getAttribute()** or **HttpSession.setAttribute()**.

❑ E. It is necessary if the method will be using **ServletContext.getAttribute()** or **ServletContext.setAttribute()**.

---

18 Which are valid EL implicit variables? (Choose all that apply.)

❑ A. **out**

❑ B. **request**

❑ C. **response**

❑ D. **pageContext**

❑ E. **contextParam**

19 Given the following URL:

http://www.example.com/userConfig/searchByName.do ?first=Bruce&middle=W&last=Perry

Which servlet code fragment from a service method, for example **doPost()**, will retrieve the values of all of the query string parameters?

❑ A.
```
String value
    = request.getParameter("Bruce");
```

❑ B.
```
String value
    = getServletContext().getInitParameter("first");
```

❑ C.
```
String value
    = getServletConfig().getInitParameter("first")
```

❑ D.
```
java.util.Enumeration enum
    = request.getParameterNames();
  while (enum.hasMoreElements()) {
    String name = (String) enum.nextElement();
    String value = request.getParameter(name);
  }
```

❑ E.
```
java.util.Enumeration enum
    = request.getParameterNames();
  while (enum.hasMoreElements()) {
    String value = (String) enum.nextElement();
  }
```

---

20 Which are true about EL operators? (Choose all that apply.)

❑ A. The logical operators treat a **null** value as **false**.

❑ B. The arithmetic operators treat a **null** value as **Double.NaN** (not a number).

❑ C. Divide by zero, **${x div 0}**, throws a runtime exception.

❑ D. Strings in EL expressions are automatically converted into the appropriate numeric or boolean values.

❑ E. A **NullPointerException** is thrown when a **null** is encountered in an arithmetic EL expression.

21 Given the partial TLD:

```
<tag>
  <name>getTitle</name>
  <tag-class>com.example.taglib.GetTitleTagHandler</tag-class>
  <body-content>empty</body-content>
  <attribute>
    <name>story</name>
    <required>false</required>
  </attribute>
</tag>
<tag>
  <name>printMessage</name>
  <tag-class>com.example.taglib.PrintMessageTagHandler</tag-class>
  <body-content>JSP</body-content>
  <attribute>
    <name>section</name>
    <required>true</required>
  </attribute>
</tag>
```

Which are valid invocations of these tags within a JSP? (Choose all that apply)

❑ A.
```
<my:getTitle>
  <my:printMessage />
</my:getTitle>
```

❑ B.
```
<my:printMessage section="47">
  <my:getTitle />
</my:printMessage>
```

❑ C.
```
<my:getTitle story="">
  <my:printMessage section="47" />
</my:getTitle>
```

❑ D.
```
<my:printMessage section="47">
  <my:getTitle story="Shakespear_RJ"></my:getTitle>
</my:printMessage>
```

22 Which JSP code would you use to include static content in a JSP? (Choose all that apply.)

❑ A. `<%@ include file="/segments/footer.html" %>`

❑ B. `<jsp:forward page="/segments/footer.html" />`

❑ C. `<jsp:include page="/segments/footer.html" />`

❑ D.
```
RequestDispatcher dispatcher
    = request.getRequestDispatcher("/segments/footer.html");
dispatcher.include(request,response);
```

23 Which statements about the deployment descriptor (DD) are true? (Choose all that apply.)

❑ A. The DD must contain at least one **<context-param>** element.

❑ B. The DD must be a well-formed XML file.

❑ C. The DD can be a text-based properties file or an XML file.

❑ D. You can leave out the XML form of the DD and provide a DD as a Java object.

❑ E. The **<web-app>** element must be the parent element of all of the other DD elements.

24 Which steps occur before **jspInit()** is called? (Choose all that apply.)

❑ A. A class instantiation occurs.

❑ B. A Java source file is compiled.

❑ C. The **_jspService()** method is called.

❑ D. The JSP page is translated to source.

❑ E. The **jspCreate()** method is called.

❑ F. The container supplies a **ServletConfig** reference.

25 Given a Simple tag handler class:

```
11. public class MyTagHandler
        extends SimpleTagSupport {
12.   public void doTag() throws JspException {
13.     try {
14.       // insert code 1
15.       // insert code 2
16.       // insert code 3
17.       JspWriter out = tagContext.getOut();
18.       out.print(requestURI);
19.     } catch (IOException ioe) {
20.       throw new JspException(ioe);
21.     }
22.   }
23. }
```

Which, inserted at lines 14, 15, and 16, will print the request-URI to the response stream?

❑ A.
```
14. JspContext tagContext = pageContext;
15. ServletRequest request
        = (ServletRequest) tagContext.getRequest();
16. String requestURI = request.getRequestURI();
```

❑ B.
```
14. PageContext tagContext = (PageContext) jspContext;
15. ServletRequest request
        = (ServletRequest) tagContext.getRequest();
16. String requestURI = request.getRequestURI();
```

❑ C.
```
14. JspContext tagContext = getJspContext();
15. HttpServletRequest request
        = (HttpServletRequest) tagContext.getRequest();
16. String requestURI = request.getRequestURI();
```

❑ D.
```
14. PageContext tagContext = (PageContext) getJspContext();
15. HttpServletRequest request
        = (HttpServletRequest) tagContext.getRequest();
16. String requestURI = request.getRequestURI();
```

26

Given the following scriptlet code:

```
<% String cityParam = request.getParameter("city");
   if ( cityParam != null ) { %>
     City: <input type='text' name='city' value='<%= cityParam %>' />
<% } else { %>
     City: <input type='text' name='city' value='Paris' />
<% } %>
```

Which JSTL code snippet produces the same result?

❑ A.

```
<c:if test='${not empty param.city}'>
    City: <input type='text' name='city' value='${param.city}' />
  <c:else/>
    City: <input type='text' name='city' value='Paris' />
  </c:if>
```

❑ B.

```
<c:if test='${not empty param.city'>
      <c:then>
        City: <input type='text' name='city' value='${param.city}' />
      </c:then>
      <c:else>
        City: <input type='text' name='city' value='Paris' />
      </c:else>
  </c:if>
```

❑ C.

```
<c:choose test='${not empty param.city}'>
    City: <input type='text' name='city' value='${param.city}' />
  <c:otherwise/>
    City: <input type='text' name='city' value='Paris' />
  </c:choose>
```

❑ D.

```
<c:choose>
      <c:when test='${not empty param.city}'>
        City: <input type='text' name='city' value='${param.city}' />
      </c:when>
      <c:otherwise>
        City: <input type='text' name='city' value='Paris' />
      </c:otherwise>
  </c:choose>
```

---

27 How would you redirect an HTTP request to another URL? (Choose all that apply)

❑ A. `response.sendRedirect("/anotherUrl");`

❑ B. `response.encodeRedirectURL("/anotherUrl");`

❑ C.
```
response.sendRedirect(
    response.encodeRedirectURL("/anotherUrl"));
```

❑ D.
```
RequestDispatcher dispatcher
    = request.getRequestDispatcher("/anotherUrl");
  dispatcher.forward(request,response);
```

❑ E.
```
RequestDispatcher dispatcher
    = request.getRequestDispatcher("/anotherUrl");
  dispatcher.redirect(request,response);
```

---

28 Given:

```
<%@ page isELIgnored="true" %>
```

Which statements are true? (Choose all that apply.)

❑ A. This is an example of a directive.

❑ B. This is NOT an example of a directive.

❑ C. It will cause **${a.b}** to be ignored by the container.

❑ D. It will NOT cause **${a.b}** to be ignored by the container.

❑ E. It will cause the EL expression in **<c:out value="${a.b}"/>** to be ignored by the container.

❑ F. It will NOT cause the EL expression in **<c:out value="${a.b}"/>** to be ignored by the container.

---

29 Given a deployment descriptor with three valid **<security-constraint>** elements, all constraining web resource A. And, given that two of the **<security-constraint>** elements respective **<auth-constraint>** sub–elements are:

```
<auth-constraint>Bob</auth-constraint>
```

and

```
<auth-constraint>Alice</auth-constraint>
```

And that the third **<security-constraint>** element has no **<auth-constraint>** sub-element.

Who can access resource A?

- ❑ A. no one
- ❑ B. anyone
- ❑ C. only Bob
- ❑ D. only Alice
- ❑ E. only Bob and Alice
- ❑ F. anyone but Bob or Alice

---

30 Given:

```
<function>
   <name>myfun</name>
   <function-class>com.example.MyFunctions</function-class>
   <function-signature>
     java.util.List getList(java.lang.String name)
   </function-signature>
</function>
```

Which is true about an invocation of this EL function mapping?

Assume that **pre** is correctly declared by a **taglib** directive.

- ❑ A. EL functions are NOT allowed to return collections.
- ❑ B. `${pre:getList("visitors")[0]}` is a valid invocation.
- ❑ C. `${pre:myfun("visitors")[0]}` is a valid invocation.
- ❑ D. The function signature is invalid because you do NOT need to specify the package information **java.lang** on the method parameter.

31 In an HTML page with a rich, graphical layout, how would you write the JSP standard action code to import a JSP segment that generates a menu that is parameterized by the user's role?

- [ ] A.
```
<jsp:include page="user-menu.jsp">
    <jsp:param name="userRole"
               value="${user.role}" />
</jsp:include>
```
- [ ] B.
```
<jsp:import page="user-menu.jsp">
    <jsp:param name="userRole"
               value="${user.role}" />
</jsp:import>
```
- [ ] C.
```
<jsp:include page="user-menu.jsp">
    <jsp:parameter name="userRole"
                   value="${user.role}" />
</jsp:include>
```
- [ ] D.
```
<jsp:import page="user-menu.jsp">
    <jsp:parameter name="userRole"
                   value="${user.role}" />
</jsp:import>
```
- [ ] E. This CANNOT be done using a JSP standard action.

---

32 Given that **resp** is an **HttpServletResponse**, and no custom headers exist in this response before this snippet executes:

```
resp.addHeader("myHeader", "foo");
resp.addHeader("myHeader", "bar");
resp.setHeader("myHeader", "baz");
String [] s = resp.getHeaders("myHeader");
```

What is the value of **s[0]**?

- [ ] A. **foo**
- [ ] B. **bar**
- [ ] C. **baz**
- [ ] D. Compilation fails
- [ ] E. An exception is thrown at runtime

33 Given a servlet that stores a customer bean in the session scope with the following code snippet:

```
public void doPost(HttpServletRequest req,
                          HttpServletResponse resp) {
  HttpSession session = req.getSession();
  com.example.Customer cust
    = new com.example.Customer();
  cust.setName(req.getParameter("full_name"));
  session.setAttribute("customer", cust);
  RequestDispatcher page
    = req.getRequestDispatcher("page.jsp");
  page.forward(req, resp);
}
```

Which of these complete JSPs will print the customer's name?
(Choose all that apply..)

❑ A.

```
<%= customer.getName() %>
```

❑ B.

```
<jsp:useBean id="customer"
             type="com.example.Customer"
             scope="session" />
<%= customer.getName() %>
```

❑ C.

```
<jsp:useBean id="customer"
             type="com.example.Customer"
             scope="session">
  <%= customer.getName() %>
</jsp:useBean>
```

❑ D.

```
<jsp:useBean id="customer"
             type="com.example.Customer"
             scope="session" />
<jsp:getProperty name="customer"
                 property="name" />
```

❑ E.

```
<jsp:useBean id="customer"
             type="com.example.Customer"
             scope="session">
  <jsp:getProperty name="customer"
                   property="name" />
</jsp:useBean>
```

34 Which are valid elements in a DD? (Choose all that apply.)

- [ ] A.
```
<filter>
  ...
  <dispatcher>ERROR</dispatcher>
</filter>
```
- [ ] B.
```
<filter>
  ...
  <dispatcher>CHAIN</dispatcher>
</filter>
```
- [ ] C.
```
<filter>
  ...
  <dispatcher>FORWARD</dispatcher>
</filter>
```
- [ ] D.
```
<filter-mapping>
  ...
  <dispatcher>INCLUDE</dispatcher>
</filter-mapping>
```
- [ ] E.
```
<filter-mapping>
  ...
  <dispatcher>REQUEST</dispatcher>
</filter-mapping>
```
- [ ] F.
```
<filter-mapping>
  ...
  <dispatcher>RESPONSE</dispatcher>
</filter-mapping>
```

---

35 Given that **req** is an **HttpServletRequest**, which returns the names of all the parameters in the request? (Choose all that apply.)

- [ ] A. `Map names = req.getParameterNames();`
- [ ] B. `String [] names = req.getParameters();`
- [ ] C. `Enumeration names = req.getParameters();`
- [ ] D. `String [] names = req.getParameterNames();`
- [ ] E. `Enumeration names = req.getParameterNames();`

36 Which of the following are legal <error-page> elements? (Choose all that apply.)

❑ A.
```
<error-page>
    <exception-type>java.lang.Throwable</exception-type>
    <location>/error/generic-error.jsp</location>
</error-page>
```

❑ B.
```
<error-page>
    <error-code>404</error-code>
    <location>/error/file-not-found.jsp</location>
</error-page>
```

❑ C.
```
<error-page>
    <error-code>404</error-code>
    <error-code>403</error-code>
    <location>/error/generic-error.jsp</location>
</error-page>
```

❑ D.
```
<error-page>
    <error-code>404</error-code>
    <location>/error/file-not-found.jsp</location>
    <location>/error/generic-error.jsp</location>
</error-page>
```

❑ E.
```
<error-page>
    <error-code>404</error-code>
    <exception-type>java.lang.Throwable</exception-type>
    <location>/error/generic-error.jsp</location>
</error-page>
```

37 Given that there exists a **HashMap** attribute called **preferences** in the session-scope.

Which JSTL code structure will put an entry, **color**, into the map with the value of the color request parameter?

❑ A.
```
<c:set target="${sessionScope.preferences}"
    property="color" value="${param.color}" />
```

❑ B.
```
<c:put map="${sessionScope.preferences}"
    property="color" value="${param.color}" />
```

❑ C.
```
<c:set scope="session" var="preferences"
    property="color" value="${param.color}" />
```

❑ D.
```
<c:put scope="session" map="preferences"
    property="color" value="${param.color}" />
```

Note: This is a simulated 'Drag and Drop' question, something like what you'll see on the exam:

38 Given the Implicit Objects listed on the left, and actual Java types listed on the right, match the Implicit Objects to their correct Java type:

Implicit Objects	Java types
`out`	`Object`
`application`	`JspWriter`
`config`	`PageAttributes`
`page`	`Writer`
	`JspContext`
	`JspConfig`
	`System`
	`ServletConfig`
	`ServletContext`

39 Which Simple tag handler will iterate over the body content five times?

❑ A.
```
public class MySimpleTag extends SimpleTagSupport {
    public void doTag() throws IOException, JspException {
      for ( int i=0; i<5; i++ ) {
        getJspBody().invoke(null);
      }
    }
)
```

❑ B.
```
public class MySimpleTag extends SimpleTagSupport {
    int count=0;
    public int doTag() throws IOException, JspException {
      getJspBody().invoke(null);
      count++;
      return ( (count<5) ? EVAL_BODY_AGAIN : SKIP_BODY );
    }
}
```

❑ C.
```
public class MySimpleTag extends SimpleTagSupport {
    int count=0;
    public int doStartTag() {
      return EVAL_BODY_INCLUDE;
    }
    public int doEndTag() {
      count++;
      return ( (count<5) ? EVAL_BODY_AGAIN : SKIP_BODY );
    }
}
```

❑ D.
```
public class MySimpleTag extends SimpleTagSupport {
    int count=0;
    public int doStartTag() {
      return EVAL_BODY_INCLUDE;
    }
    public int doAfterBody() {
      count++;
      return ( (count<5) ? EVAL_BODY_AGAIN : SKIP_BODY );
    }
}
```

40 Which of the following statements about the servlet lifecycle are true? (Choose all that apply.)

❑ A. The web container calls the **`init()`** and **`service()`** methods in response to each servlet request.

❑ B. The web application developer uses an object that implements the **`java.servlet.Filter`** interface to instantiate one or more servlets.

❑ C. The web container calls the servlet's **`destroy()`** method when the servlet is destroyed or unloaded.

❑ D. The web container loads and instantiates a servlet class, then initializes the servlet by calling its **`init()`** method exactly once, passing into **`init()`** an object that implements the **`javax.servlet.ServletConfig`** interface that the container creates for the servlet.

41 Which about web attributes are true? (Choose all that apply.)

❑ A. No attributes are longer lived than session attributes.

❑ B. In all scopes, attributes can be retrieved using a **`getAttribute()`** method.

❑ C. Context attributes survive a session time-out.

❑ D. Only session and context attributes can be retrieved in an enumeration.

❑ E. Data stored in both request and session objects is thread safe.

42 Given a JSP page:

```
<my:tag1>
  <my:tag2>
    <%-- JSP content --%>
  </my:tag2>
</my:tag1>
```

The tag handler for **`my:tag1`** is **`Tag1Handler`** and extends TagSupport. The tag handler for **`my:tag2`** is **`Tag2Handler`** and extends SimpleTagSupport.

The tag handler for **`my:tag1`** must have access to the tag handler for **`my:tag2`**. What must you do to make this work?

❑ A. The instance of **`Tag1Handler`** must use the **`getChildren`** method in order to retrieve the collection of child tag instances. The instance of **`Tag1Handler`** will only be able to access the registered tags during the **`doAfterBody`** and **`doEndTag`** methods.

❑ B. The instance of **`Tag2Handler`** must use the **`getParent`** method in order to register itself with the instance of **`Tag1Handler`**. The instance of **`Tag1Handler`** will only be able to access the registered tags during the **`doAfterBody`** and **`doEndTag`** methods.

❑ C. The instance of **`Tag1Handler`** must use the **`getChildren`** method in order to retrieve the collection of child tag instances. The instance of **`Tag1Handler`** will be able to access the registered tags in any of the tag event methods, but NOT in the attribute setter methods.

❑ D. The instance of **`Tag2Handler`** must use the **`getParent`** method in order to register itself with the instance of **`Tag1Handler`**. The instance of **`Tag1Handler`** will be able to access the registered tags in any of the tag event methods, but NOT in the attribute setter methods.

43 Given that a deployment descriptor has only one security role, defined as:

```
<security-role>
   <role-name>Member</role-name>
</security-role>
```

Which are valid **<auth-constraint>** elements that will allow users to access resources constrained by the security role declared? (Choose all that apply.)

- ❏ A. **<auth-constraint/>**
- ❏ B. **<auth-constriant>*</auth-constraint>**
- ❏ C. **<auth-constraint>Member</auth-constraint>**
- ❏ D. **<auth-constraint>MEMBER</auth-constraint>**
- ❏ E. **<auth-constraint>"Member"</auth-constraint>**

44 Given this list of features:

- might create stale data
- can increase the complexity of code having to deal with concurrency issues

Which design pattern is being described?

- ❏ A. Transfer Object
- ❏ B. Service Locator
- ❏ C. Front Controller
- ❏ D. Business Delegate
- ❏ E. Intercepting Filter
- ❏ F. Model-View-Controller

45 Where are servlet classes located inside a Web Application Archive (WAR) file?

- ❏ A. Only in **/WEB-INF/classes**.
- ❏ B. Only in a JAR file in **/WEB-INF/lib**.
- ❏ C. Either in a JAR file in **/WEB-INF/lib** or under **/WEB-INF/classes**.
- ❏ D. At the top level of the directory tree inside the WAR so that the web container can easily find them upon deployment.

46 Which code snippets properly map the **com.example.web.BeerSelect** servlet to the **/SelectBeer.do** URL? (Choose all that apply.)

❑ A.
```
<servlet-map>
    <servlet-class>com.example.web.BeerSelect</servlet-class>
    <url-pattern>/SelectBeer.do</url-pattern>
<servlet-map>
```

❑ B.
```
<servlet>
    <servlet-mapping>
      <servlet-class>com.example.web.BeerSelect</servlet-class>
      <url-pattern>/SelectBeer.do</url-pattern>
    </servlet-mapping>
</servlet>
```

❑ C.
```
<servlet-mapping>
    <servlet-name>com.example.web.BeerSelect</servlet-name>
    <url-pattern>/SelectBeer.do</url-pattern>
</servlet-mapping>
```

❑ D.
```
<servlet>
    <servlet-name>BeerServlet</servlet-name>
    <servlet-class>com.example.web.BeerSelect</servlet-class>
</servlet>
<servlet-mapping>
    <servlet-name>BeerServlet</servlet-name>
    <url-pattern>/SelectBeer.do</url-pattern>
</servlet-mapping>
```

47 Which statements about **HttpSession** objects are true? (Choose all that apply.)

❑ A. A session may become invalid due to inactivity.

❑ B. A new session is created each time a user makes a request.

❑ C. A session may become invalid as a result of a specific call by a servlet.

❑ D. Multiple requests made from the same browser may have access to the same session object.

❑ E. A user who accesses the same web application from two browser windows is guaranteed to have two distinct session objects.

---

48 Given a partial deployment descriptor:

```
11.   <servlet>
12.     <servlet-name>ServletIWantToListenTo</servlet-name>
13.     <servlet-class>com.example.MyServlet</servlet-class>
14.   </servlet>
15.   <listener>
16.     <listener-class>com.example.ListenerA</listener-class>
17.   </listener>
18.   <listener>
19.     <listener-class>com.example.ListenerB</listener-class>
20.     <listener-type>Session</listener-type>
21.   </listener>
22.   <listener>
23.     <listener-class>com.example.ListenerC</listener-class>
24.     <description>A session listener.</description>
25.   </listener>
26.   <listener>
27.     <listener-class>com.example.ReqListener</listener-class>
28.     <servlet-name>ServletIWantToListenTo</servlet-name>
29.   </listener>
```

Which are valid **listener** elements (identify each listener by the line number it starts on)? (Choose one.)

- ❑ A. Only 15.
- ❑ B. Only 18.
- ❑ C. Only 26.
- ❑ D. Both 15 and 22.
- ❑ E. Both 18 and 26.
- ❑ F. 15, 22 and 26.
- ❑ G. All four are valid.

---

49 Which statements concerning **/META-INF** are true? (Choose all that apply.)

- ❑ A. This directory is optional when creating a WAR file.
- ❑ B. The contents of this directory can be served directly to clients only if HTTPS is activated.
- ❑ C. Servlets can access the contents of the **/META-INF** directory via methods in the **ServletContext** class.
- ❑ D. Servlets can access the contents of the **/META-INF** directory via methods in the **ServletConfig** class.

50 Which security mechanisms can be applied to specific resources by specifying URL patterns in the deployment descriptor? (Choose all that apply.)

- ❑ A. authorization
- ❑ B. data integrity
- ❑ C. authentication
- ❑ D. confidentiality
- ❑ E. form-based login

---

51 Your company is in the process of integrating several different back office applications and creating a single web UI to present the entire back office suite to your clients. The design of the front end will be finished long before the design of the back end. Although the details of the back end design are still very rough, you have enough information to create some temporary back end 'stubs' to use to test the UI.

Which design pattern can be used to minimize the overhead of modifying the UI once the back end is complete?

- ❑ A. Transfer Object
- ❑ B. Front Controller
- ❑ C. Business Delegate
- ❑ D. Intercepting Filter
- ❑ E. Model-View-Controller

---

52 Given:

`fc` is of type **`FilterChain`** and **`req`** and **`resp`** are request and response objects.

Which line of code in a class implementing **`Filter`** will invoke the target servlet if there is only one filter in the chain?

- ❑ A. `fc.chain(req, resp);`
- ❑ B. `fc.doFilter(req, resp);`
- ❑ C. `fc.doForward(req, resp);`
- ❑ D. `req.chain(req, resp, fc);`
- ❑ E. `req.doFilter(req, resp, fc);`
- ❑ F. `req.doForward(req, resp, fc);`

---

53 What type of listener could be used to log the user name of a user at the time that she logs into a system? (Choose all that apply.)

- ❑ A. `HttpSessionListener`
- ❑ B. `ServletContextListener`
- ❑ C. `HttpSessionAttributeListener`
- ❑ D. `ServletContextAttributeListener`

---

54 Given a tag library descriptor located at **`/mywebapp/WEB-INF/tlds/mytags.tld`**, which would be the correct **`taglib`** directive? Assume **`mywebapp`** is the web application root and that there are no **`<taglib>`** tags in the deployment descriptor.

❑ A.
```
<%@ taglib uri="/mytags.tld"
        prefix="my" %>
```

❑ B.
```
<%@ taglib uri="/tlds/mytags.tld"
        prefix="my" %>
```

❑ C.
```
<%@ taglib uri="/WEB-INF/tlds/mytags.tld"
        prefix="my" %>
```

❑ D.
```
<%@ taglib uri="/mywebapp/WEB-INF/tlds/mytags.tld"
        prefix="my" %>
```

❑ E. **`/mywebapp/WEB-INF/tlds/mytags.tld`** is NOT a valid location for a tag library descriptor, so none of these will work.

55 Given:

```
public class ServletX extends HttpServlet {
  public void doGet(HttpServletRequest req,
                    HttpServletResponse res)
         throws IOException, ServletException {
    req.getSession().setAttribute("key", new X());
    req.getSession().setAttribute("key", new X());
    req.getSession().setAttribute("key", "x");
    req.getSession().removeAttribute("key");
  }
}
```

and given a listener class:

```
public class X implements HttpSessionBindingListener {
  public void valueBound(HttpSessionBindingEvent event) {
    System.out.print("B");
  }
  public void valueUnbound(HttpSessionBindingEvent event) {
    System.out.print("UB");
  }
}
```

Which logging output would be generated by an invocation of the **doGet** method?

- ❑ A. **UBUBUB**
- ❑ B. **BBUBUB**
- ❑ C. **BBUBUBB**
- ❑ D. **BUBBUBB**
- ❑ E. **BBUBUBBUB**
- ❑ F. **BBUBBUBBUB**

---

56 Given:

```
public void doGet(HttpServletRequest req,
                  HttpServletResponse res)
      throws IOException, ServletException {
  RequestDispatcher rd1
    = getServletContext().getRequestDispatcher("/xyz");
  RequestDispatcher rd2
    = req.getRequestDispatcher("/xyz");
  RequestDispatcher rd3
    = getServletContext().getRequestDispatcher("xyz");
  RequestDispatcher rd4
    = req.getRequestDispatcher("xyz");
}
```

Which statements are true? (Choose all that apply.)

- ❑ A. **rd3** will never map to a servlet since the given path does NOT begin with **/**.
- ❑ B. **rd4** will never map to a servlet since the given path does NOT begin with **/**.
- ❑ C. **rd2.forward(req, res)** and **rd4.forward(req, res)** may forward to the same resource.
- ❑ D. **rd1.forward(req, res)** and **rd2.forward(req, res)** would always forward to the same resource.
- ❑ E. **rd3.forward(req, res)** and **rd4.forward(req, res)** would always forward to the same resource.

---

57 Which JSTL tag performs URL rewriting?

- ❑ A. **link**
- ❑ B. **aHref**
- ❑ C. **import**
- ❑ D. **url**

58 Given:

```
11. public void doGet(HttpServletRequest req,
12.                   HttpServletResponse res)
13.        throws IOException, ServletException {
14.     String url = res.encodeRedirectURL("/redirectme");
15.     boolean test = "/redirectme".equals(url);
16.     res.sendRedirect(url);
17. }
```

Which statements are true? (Choose all that apply.)

- ❑ A. After line 15, **test** will always be **true**.
- ❑ B. After line 15, **test** will always be **false**.
- ❑ C. Line 14 demonstrates a session management mechanism called URL rewriting.
- ❑ D. After line 15, **test** could be either **true** ot **false**.
- ❑ E. The **encodeURL** method should have been used instead of the **encodeRedirectURL** method in line 14.
- ❑ F. The **encodeRedirectURL** method shown in line 14 should only be used when clients have disabled cookies.

59 What happens when a container migrates a session from one VM to another?

- ❑ A. **sessionWillPassivate()** will be called on any objects that implement the **HttpSessionActivationListener** and are currently bound to the session.
- ❑ B. **sessionWillPassivate()** will be called on any objects that implement the **HttpSessionPassivationListener** and are currently bound to the session.
- ❑ C. **sessionWillPassivate()** will be called on any objects that implement the **HttpSessionListener** interface.
- ❑ D. **sessionWillPassivate()** will be called on any objects that implement the **HttpSessionBindingListener** and are currently bound to the session.

60 Given an existing class:

```
package com.example;
public class MyFunctions {
  private int x;
  public MyFunctions()
    { x = 0; }
  public int modX(int y)
    { return (y mod x); }
  public static int funct(int x, int y)
    { return (2*x + y - 5); }
}
```

Which are true about EL functions? (Choose all that apply.)

❑ A. The `MyFunctions` class may NOT be used by EL because it has NOT been declared `final`.

❑ B. The `funct` method may be used by EL because it has been declared static.

❑ C. The `funct` method may NOT be use by EL because the calling arguments and return value must be object references.

❑ D. The `modX` method may be used by EL because it is an instance method.

❑ E. The `MyFunctions` class may be used by EL even though it has a public constructor.

61 Which statements about ignoring EL in your JSPs are true? (Choose all that apply.)

❑ A. You can instruct the container to ignore EL in your JSPs by using the **<el-ignored>** tag in the DD.

❑ B. You can instruct the container to ignore EL in your JSPs by using the **<is-el-ignored>** tag in the DD.

❑ C. You can instruct the container to ignore EL in a JSP by using the `elIgnored` attribute of the `page` directive.

❑ D. When using the DD to instruct the container to ignore EL, you can specify which JSPs to constrain.

❑ E. You CANNOT constrain both scripting and EL in the same JSP.

62 You have purchased a purchase order web application that uses programmatic authorization that uses security roles that are not used in your organization.

Which deployment descriptor element must you use to make this webapp work in your organization?

- ❑ A. **<login-config>**
- ❑ B. **<security-role>**
- ❑ C. **<security-role-ref>**
- ❑ D. **<security-constraint>**

63 Given:

```
1. <%@ taglib uri="http://www.mycompany.com/mytags"
              prefix="mytags" %>
2. <mytags:foo bar="abc" />
3. <mytags:forEach><mytags:doSomething /></mytags:forEach>
4. <jsp:setProperty name="x" property="a" value="b" />
5. <c:out value="hello" />
```

Assuming this is a complete JSP, which is true?

(For options E and F, ignore the fact that an error in one line might keep a subsequent line from being reached)

- ❑ A. Only line 2 will definitely generate an error.
- ❑ B. Only line 3 will definitely generate an error.
- ❑ C. Only line 4 will definitely generate an error.
- ❑ D. Only line 5 will definitely generate an error.
- ❑ E. Lines 4 and 5 will both definitely generate errors.
- ❑ F. Lines 2, 3, 4 and 5 will all definitely generate errors.
- ❑ G. The entire JSP could execute without generating any errors.

64 Which authentication mechanism employs a base64 encoding scheme to protect user passwords?

- ❑ A. HTTP Basic Authentication
- ❑ B. Form Based Authentication
- ❑ C. HTTP Digest Authentication
- ❑ D. HTTPS Client Authentication

65 Which concepts are common to all four authentication mechanisms supported by J2EE 1.4 compliant web containers? (Choose all that apply.)

- ❑ A. passwords
- ❑ B. realm names
- ❑ C. generic error pages
- ❑ D. secured web resources
- ❑ E. automatic SSL support
- ❑ F. target server authentication

---

66 How are cookies used to support session management?

- ❑ A. A cookie is created for each attribute stored in the session.
- ❑ B. A single cookie is created to hold an ID that uniquely identifies a session.
- ❑ C. A single cookie is created to hold the serialized **`HttpSession`** object.
- ❑ D. The session ID is encoded as a path parameter in the URL string called **`jsessionid`**.
- ❑ E. Cookies CANNOT be used to support session management because it is possible for a user to disable cookies in their browser.

---

67 You are developing a web application for an organization that needs to display the results of database searches to several different types of clients, including browsers, PDAs, and kiosks. The application will have to examine the request to determine which type of client has initiated it, and then dispatch the request to the proper component.

Which J2EE design pattern is designed for this type of application?

- ❑ A. Transfer Object
- ❑ B. Service Locator
- ❑ C. Model-View-Controller
- ❑ D. Business Delegate
- ❑ E. Intercepting Filter

68 Which is true about the differences between the Classic and Simple tag models?

- ❑ A. A nested Classic tag is allowed to access its parent tag, but this is NOT supported in the Simple tag model.
- ❑ B. In the Classic model, you may gain access to the evaluated body content using the **`BodyTag`** interface. In the Simple model, you can invoke the body, but you CANNOT gain access to the content generated in the invocation.
- ❑ C. The Tag interface has two event methods (**`doStartTag`** and **`doEndTag`**), but the **`SimpleTag`** interface only has one event method (**`doTag`**).
- ❑ D. Both tag models support iteration. In the **`SimpleTag.doTag`** method, you can invoke the body within a Java-based iteration. In the Classic model, iteration may be supported by returning the **`EVAL_BODY_AGAIN`** constant from the **`Tag.doEndTag`** method.

69 Given this class:

```
package biz.mybiz;
public class BeanX {
   private String a,b,c;
   public BeanX() {a="A";b="B";c="C";}
   public void setA(String a) { this.a = a; }
   public void setB(String b) { this.b = b; }
   public void setC(String c) { this.c = c; }
   public String getAll() { return a+b+c; }
}
```

and the JSP:

```
<jsp:useBean id="x" class="biz.mybiz.BeanX" />
<jsp:setProperty name="x" property="*" />
<jsp:getProperty name="x" property="all" />
<jsp:setProperty name="x" property="a" param="b" />
<jsp:setProperty name="x" property="b" param="c" />
<jsp:setProperty name="x" property="c" param="a" />
<jsp:getProperty name="x" property="all" />
```

What will be generated by the JSP when invoked with the query string **a=X&b=Y&c=Z**?

- ❑ A. **ABC YZX**
- ❑ B. **XYZ XYZ**
- ❑ C. **ABC ABC**
- ❑ D. **YXZ YZX**
- ❑ E. **XYZ ZXY**
- ❑ F. **XYZ YZX**
- ❑ G. **nullnullnull YZX**

Final Exam Answers

---

1 This statement describes the potential benefits of a design pattern: (Core J2EE Patterns 2nd ed. pg. 145)

These components pre-process or post-process incoming requests and outgoing responses in a web application, and can be cleanly plugged into the application depending on whether the application requires the component's specialized task.

Which design pattern is being described?

- [ ] A. Transfer Object
- [x] B. Intercepting Filter
- [ ] C. Model-View-Controller
- [ ] D. Business Delegate
- [ ] E. Front Controller

-One of the most powerful features of Intercepting Filter is that filters can be chained together in different sequences and added and subtracted from an application declaratively.

---

2 Which are true about the **jsp:useBean** standard action? (Choose all that apply.) (JSP v2.0 section 5.1)

- [ ] A. The **name** attribute is mandatory.

-Option A is invalid because there is no name attribute in this standard action (pg 1-104).

- [x] B. The **scope** attribute defaults to the page scope.
- [ ] C. The **type** and **class** attributes must NOT be used together.

-Option C is invalid because type and class may be used together (pg 1-103).

- [ ] D. The **type** attribute is ONLY used when the bean already exists in one of the four JSP scopes.

-Option D is invalid because the type attribute may be used in conjunction with the class attribute when creating a new object.

- [x] E. The **jsp:useBean** standard action may be used to declare a scripting variable that may be used in scriptlets, such as `<% myBean.method(); %>`

-Option E is correct, because the bean name specified in the id attribute creates a local variable in the JSP's _jspService method.

3 Given this partial deployment descriptor:

(Servlet v2.4 pg. 135)

```
<context-param>
  <param-name>email</param-name>
  <param-value>foo@bar.com</param-value>
</context-param>
<servlet>
  <servlet-name>a</servlet-name>
  <servlet-class>com.bar.Foo</servlet-class>
  <init-param>
    <param-name>email</param-name>
    <param-value>baz@bar.com</param-value>
  </init-param>
</servlet>
```

And, assuming **`scfg`** is a **`ServletConfig`** object and **`sctx`** is a **`ServletContext`** object, which statement is true?

- ❑ A. **`sctx.getInitParameter("email")`** will return **`baz@bar.com`**.

  -Option A is invalid because this call would return the servlet context initialization parameter (foo@bar.com).

- ❑ B. **`scfg.getInitParameter("email")`** will return **`foo@bar.com`**.

  -Option B is invalid because this call would return the servlet-specific value baz@bar.com.

- ❑ C. An error will occur because the **`email`** parameter is defined twice.

  -Option C is invalid because there are no naming restrictions between servlet context parameter names and servlet parameter names.

- ❑ D. **`scfg.getServletContext().getInitParameter("email")`** will return **`baz@bar.com`**.

  -Option D is invalid because this call would return the servlet context initialization parameter (foo@bar.com).

- ☑ E. **`scfg.getServletContext().getInitParameter("email")`** will return **`foo@bar.com`**.

- ❑ F. An error will occur because servlet context initialization parameters should be defined using **`init-param`**, NOT **`context-param`**.

  -Option F is invalid because servlet context initialization parameters are defined using <context-param>.

4 Given: (JSP v2.0 pg. 1-182)

```
public class DoubleTag extends SimpleTagSupport {
  private String data;
  public void setData(String d) { data = d; }
  public void doTag() throws JspException, IOException {
    getJspContext().getOut().print(data + data);
  }
}
```

Which is an equivalent tag file?

- [ ] A. `${param.data}${param.data}`

  – Option A is invalid because it would print the parameter named data, not the tag attribute data.

- [x] B. `<%@ attribute name="data" %>`
  `${data}${data}`

- [ ] C. `<%@ variable name-given="data" %>`
  `${data}${data}`

  – Option C is invalid because the attribute directive should be used, not the variable directive.

- [ ] D. `<%@ attribute name="data" %>`
  `<% pageContext.getOut().print(data + data); %>`

  – Option D is invalid because the JSP variable pageContext is not available here. However, replacing pageContext with getJspContext() would work here instead.

- [ ] E. `<%@ variable name-given="data" %>`
  `<% pageContext.getOut().print(data + data); %>`

  – Option E is invalid for the reasons listed for Options C and D.

---

5 Given a session object **sess** with an attribute named **myAttr**, and an **HttpSessionBindingEvent** object **bind** bound to **sess**. (API)

Which will retrieve **myAttr**? (Choose all that apply.)

- [ ] A. `long myAttr = sess.getAttribute("myAttr");`
- [x] B. `Object o = sess.getAttribute("myAttr");`
- [ ] C. `String s = sess.getAttribute("myAttr");`
- [ ] D. `Object o = bind.getAttribute("myAttr");`
- [x] E. `Object o = bind.getSession().getAttribute("myAttr");`

–Options A and C are invalid because getAttribute returns an Object.

–Option D is invalid because the event class has no getAttribute method.

6 Which about JSP Documents (XML-based documents) are true? (Choose all that apply.)

(JSP v2.0 section 6)

- ❑ A. A JSP document must have a **<jsp:root>** as its top element.

-Option A is invalid because the <jsp:root> elements is optional in JSP v2.0 (section 6.2.2).

- ❑ B. The following would be valid as the first line of a JSP document: **<jsp:root xmlns:uri="http://java.sun.com/JSP/Page" version="2.0">**.

-Option B is invalid because it does not introduce the prefix jsp used in the <jsp:root> element (it introduces the prefix uri).

- ☑ C. In a JSP document, page directives are defined using **<jsp:directive.page>** instead of **<%@ %>**.
- ☑ D. The **<c:forEach>** tag CANNOT be used unless the **c** prefix has been introduced through a namespace attribute.
- ❑ E. Both the standard **<%! %>** syntax as well as **<jsp:declaration>** may be used to declare variables in a JSP document.

-Option E is invalid because only the <jsp:declaration> syntax is valid in a JSP document.

7 Which statements about EL implicit objects are true? (Choose all that apply.)

(JSP v2.0 section 2.2.3)

- ☑ A. **${param.name}** produces the value of the parameter **name**.
- ❑ B. **${init.foo}** produces the value of the context initialization parameter named **foo**.

-Option B is invalid because the implicit object used for initialization parameters is initParam not init.

- ☑ C. The implicit object **param** is a **Map** that maps parameter names to single String parameter values.
- ☑ D. **pageContext**, **param**, **header**, and **cookie** are all implicit objects available to EL expressions in JSP pages.
- ❑ E. **page**, **request**, **session**, and **application** are implicit objects that map attribute names to values in the corresponding scopes.

-Option E is invalid because each of the implicit object names need the word Scope appended to the (e.g. sessionScope).

8 Given this JSP snippet: (JSP v2.0 section 1.5)

```
<!--X-->
<%=A.b()%>
<!--<%=A.b()%>-->
<%--Y--%>
```

Assume that a call to **A.b()** is valid and returns the text **test**. Ignoring whitespace in the generated response, which represents the HTML this JSP would produce?

- ❏ A. **<!--X-->test<!--<%=A.b()%>-->**

  –Options A and D are invalid because the expression A.b() is evaluated, despite being part of a comment.

- ☑ B. **<!--X-->test<!--test-->**

- ❏ C. **test**

  –Option C is invalid because simple HTML comments are not removed.

- ❏ D. **<!--X-->test<!--<%=A.b()%>-->**
  <%--Y--%>

  –Option D is also invalid because the JSP comments are removed from the page.

- ❏ E. **test<%--Y--%>**

  –Option E is invalid for the reasons described for Options C and D.

- ❏ F. The generated HTML will be blank.

  –Option F is invalid for many of the reasons described above.

---

9 Which are true about tag libraries in web applications? (Choose all that apply.) (JSP v2.0 section 7.3.1)

- ❏ A. A TLD file must exist in the **WEB-INF/tlds/** directory.

  –Option A is invalid because the statement is too strong; TLDs can exist in other WEB-INF subdirectories.

- ☑ B. A TLD file may exist in any subdirectory of **WEB-INF**.

- ❏ C. A TLD file may exist in the **WEB-INF** directory in a JAR file.

  –Option C is invalid because a JAR file need not have a WEB-INF directory.

- ☑ D. A TLD file may exist in the **META-INF** directory in a JAR file.

- ❏ E. A TLD file in a JAR file must be located at **META-INF/taglib.tld**.

  –Option E is invalid because the statement is too strong; more than one TLD file can exist in a single JAR with different file names.

---

10 You store the SQL source files for web-database work in a web application's top-level **sql** directory, but you do NOT want to make this directory accessible to HTTP requests.

(Servlet v2.4 pg. 70)

How do you configure the web application to forbid requests to this directory? (Choose all that apply.)

❑ A. Protect the server with a firewall.

❑ B. Specify the directory with a **<security-role>** element in deployment descriptor.

☑ C. Move the directory beneath **WEB-INF**, the contents of which are NOT accessible to application users.

☑ D. Create a **<security-constraint>** element in the DD to prevent access to the **sql** directory.

–Option A is invalid because the firewall would not affect access to the /sql/ components in the webapp file structure.*

–Option D could be used to restrict directory access using the <security-constraint> element's child element <web-resource-collection>, for instance.

---

11 Given:

(JSP v2.0 section 2.3.4, 2.3.5, and 2.2.3)

```
11. <% java.util.Map map = new java.util.HashMap();
12.    map.put("a", "1");
13.    map.put("b", "2");
14.    map.put("c", "3");
15.    request.setAttribute("map", map);
16.    request.setAttribute("map-index", "b");
17. %>
18. <%-- insert code here --%>
```

Which , inserted at line 18, are valid and evaluate to **2**? (Choose all that apply.)

☑ A. `${map.b}`

–Option A is correct because map.b is equivalent to map['b'].

❑ B. `${map[b]}`

–Option B is invalid because 'b' is not a defined attribute.

❑ C. `${map.map-index}`

–Option C is invalid because this expression is really ${map.map – index} --a subtraction-- which is invalid no matter how you look at it.

❑ D. `${map[map-index]}`

–Option D is invalid because this expression is really ${map[map – index]} which is invalid for the same reasons as in Option C.

❑ E. `${map['map-index']}`

–Option E is invalid because there is no map key called 'map-index'.

☑ F. `${map[requestScope['map-index']]}`

12 Given this tag handler class excerpt:

(JSP v2.0 sections 7.3 and 13)

```
public class WorthlessTag extends TagSupport {
  private String x;
  public void setX(String x) { this.x = x; }
  public int doStartTag() throws JspException {
    try { pageContext.getOut().print(x); }
    catch (IOException e) { }
    if ("x".equals(x))
      return SKIP_BODY;
    else
      return EVAL_BODY_INCLUDE;
  }
  public int doEndTag() throws JspException {
    try { pageContext.getOut().print("E"); }
    catch (IOException e) { }
    if ("y".equals(x))
      return SKIP_PAGE;
    else
      return EVAL_PAGE;
  }
}
```

and given this TLD excerpt:

```
<tag>
    <name>worthless</name>
    <tag-class>com.mycom.WorthlessTag</tag-class>
    <body-content>empty</body-content>
    <attribute>
        <name>x</name>
        <required>true</required>
        <rtexprvalue>true</rtexprvalue>
    </attribute>
</tag>
```

(continued on next page.)

12, cont. and given this complete JSP page:

```
<%@ taglib uri="somevaliduri" prefix="w" %>
<w:worthless x="x" />
<w:worthless x="<%=Boolean.TRUE.toString()%>" />
<w:worthless x="y" />
<w:worthless x="z" />
```

What output does the JSP generate?

- ❑ A. **xE** — Option A is invalid because the SKIP_BODY return value does not keep the rest of the page from being evaluated.
- ❑ B. **x trueE yE** — Option B is invalid because the SKIP_BODY return value does not keep doEndTag() from being called.
- ❑ ✓ C. **xE trueE yE**
- ❑ D. **xE trueE yE zE** — Option D is invalid because the value SKIP_PAGE is returned from the third use of the tag, so the remainder of the page is ignored.
- ❑ E. **x <%=Boolean.TRUE.toString()%>E yE**
- ❑ F. **xE <%=Boolean.TRUE.toString()%>E yE** — Options E, F and G are invalid because the expression is properly evaluated before being passed to the setX() method.
- ❑ G. **xE <%=Boolean.TRUE.toString()%>E yE zE**

13 A user submits a form using an HTML page containing : (Servlet v2.4 pg. 23)

```
<form action="/handler">
  <!-- form tags here -->
</form>
```

The URL pattern **/handler** is mapped to an HTTP servlet.

Which **HttpServlet** service method will the web container call in response to this form submit?

- ☐ A. **doHead**
- ☐ B. **doPost**
- ☐ C. **Get**
- ☑ D. **doGet**

–The default HTTP method for the form tag, if not specified by the tag's method attibute, is GET. The correct answer is option D, the HttpServlet's doGet() method.

---

14 Which statements concerning welcome files are true? (Choose all that apply.) (Servlet v2.4 section 9.10)

- ☑ A. They can be declared in the DD.
- ☑ B. They can be used to respond to 'partial requests'.
- ☐ C. If multiple welcome files are declared for a web app, their ordering in the DD is NOT meaningful.
- ☑ D. J2EE 1.4 compliant containers are required to match partial requests to URLs in the welcome file list using a specified algorithm.
- ☐ E. If a J2EE 1.4 compliant container receives a partial request for which it CANNOT find a match, it must return an HTTP 404 error code.

–Option C is invalid because the list of welcome files is searched by the container in the order declared in the DD.

–Option E is invalid because while a given container might return a 404, it is not required to do so.

---

15 Once a session has been invalidated, which **HttpSession** methods can be called on that session without throwing an **IllegalStateException**? (Choose all that apply.) (API)

- ☐ A. **invalidate**
- ☐ B. **getAttribute**
- ☐ C. **setAttribute**
- ☑ D. **getServletContext**
- ☐ E. **getAttributeNames**

–Since the ServletContext survives, getServletContext can be called successfully on an invalid session.

16 Which statements about the **taglib** directive are true? (Choose all that apply.)

(JSP v2.0 section 1.10.2)

- [x] A. A **taglib** directive always identifies a tag prefix that will distinguish usage of actions in the library.
- [ ] B. `<% taglib uri="http://www.mytags.com/mytags" prefix="mytags" %>` is an example of a valid taglib directive.
- [ ] C. Every **taglib** directive must specify a value for the **uri** attribute.
- [x] D. Every **taglib** directive must specify a non-empty value for the **prefix** attribute.
- [x] E. There are three attributes defined for the **taglib** directive: **uri**, **tagdir**, and **prefix**.

-Option B is invalid because directives must begin with <%@.

-Option C is invalid because the uri attribute is not required as long as the tagdir attribute is included instead.

17 Which statements about making a servlet's **doGet()** method **synchronized** are true? (Choose all that apply.)

(Servlet v2.4 section 2.3.3.1)

- [ ] A. It will make access to **ServletRequest** attributes thread-safe.
- [x] B. It will NOT make access to **HttpSession** attributes thread-safe.
- [x] C. It may have a negative performance impact because the servlet will only be able to process one request at a time.
- [ ] D. It is necessary if the method will be using **HttpSession.getAttribute()** or **HttpSession.setAttribute()**.
- [ ] E. It is necessary if the method will be using **ServletContext.getAttribute()** or **ServletContext.setAttribute()**.

-Option A is invalid because it doesn't make request attributes any more thread-safe than they already are.

-Options D and E are invalid because it does nothing to help make these attribute scopes more thread-safe since other servlets could access them concurrently despite the synchronization.

18 Which are valid EL implicit variables? (Choose all that apply.)

(JSP v2.0 section 2.2.3)

- [ ] A. **out**
- [ ] B. **request**
- [ ] C. **response**
- [x] D. **pageContext**
- [ ] E. **contextParam**

-Options A, B, and C are JSP implicit variables, but not in EL.

-Option E is a tricky one because context params are available in EL, but the variable is called initParam.

19 Given the following URL: (API)

http://www.example.com/userConfig/searchByName.do ?first=Bruce&middle=W&last=Perry

Which servlet code fragment from a service method, for example **doPost()**, will retrieve the values of all of the query string parameters?

❑ A.
```
String value
     = request.getParameter("Bruce");
```

❑ B.
```
String value
     = getServletContext().getInitParameter("first");
```

❑ C.
```
String value
     = getServletConfig().getInitParameter("first")
```

☑ D.
```
java.util.Enumeration enum
     = request.getParameterNames();
   while (enum.hasMoreElements()) {
     String name = (String) enum.nextElement();
     String value = request.getParameter(name);
   }
```

-Option D stores all parameter names in a java.util.Enumeration, then gets each value by calling request.getParameter().

❑ E.
```
java.util.Enumeration enum
     = request.getParameterNames();
   while (enum.hasMoreElements()) {
     String value = (String) enum.nextElement();
   }
```

NOTE: You can also use the getParameterMap() method on the request to access all querystring values.

20 Which are true about EL operators? (Choose all that apply.) (JSP v2.0 section 2.8)

☑ A. The logical operators treat a **null** value as **false**. -Option A is correct (2.8.5).

❑ B. The arithmetic operators treat a **null** value as **Double.NaN** (not a number). -Option B is invalid because a null is coerced to a zero (2.8.3).

❑ C. Divide by zero, **${x div 0}**, throws a runtime exception. -Option C is invalid because division by zero returns infinity.

☑ D. Strings in EL expressions are automatically converted into the appropriate numeric or boolean values.

❑ E. A **NullPointerException** is thrown when a **null** is encountered in an arithmetic EL expression. -Option E is invalid because null is coerced to a zero (2.8.3).

21 Given the partial TLD:

(JSP v2.0 pgs 3-21 and 3-30)

```
<tag>
  <name>getTitle</name>
  <tag-class>com.example.taglib.GetTitleTagHandler</tag-class>
  <body-content>empty</body-content>
  <attribute>
    <name>story</name>
    <required>false</required>
  </attribute>
</tag>
<tag>
  <name>printMessage</name>
  <tag-class>com.example.taglib.PrintMessageTagHandler</tag-class>
  <body-content>JSP</body-content>
  <attribute>
    <name>section</name>
    <required>true</required>
  </attribute>
</tag>
```

Which are valid invocations of these tags within a JSP? (Choose all that apply)

❑ A.
```
<my:getTitle>
   <my:printMessage />
</my:getTitle>
```

☑ B.
```
<my:printMessage section="47">
   <my:getTitle />
</my:printMessage>
```

❑ C.
```
<my:getTitle story="">
   <my:printMessage section="47" />
</my:getTitle>
```

☑ D.
```
<my:printMessage section="47">
   <my:getTitle story="Shakespear_RJ"></my:getTitle>
</my:printMessage>
```

-The getTitle tag must have an empty body, which knocks out options A and C.

The printMessage tag is required to use the section attribute, which also knocks out option A.

That leaves options B and D as valid uses of these tags.

---

22 Which JSP code would you use to include static content in a JSP? (Choose all that apply.)

(JSP v2.0 sections 1.10.3 and 5.4)

- [x] A. `<%@ include file="/segments/footer.html" %>`
- [ ] B. `<jsp:forward page="/segments/footer.html" />`
- [x] C. `<jsp:include page="/segments/footer.html" />`
- [ ] D.
```
RequestDispatcher dispatcher
    = request.getRequestDispatcher("/segments/footer.html");
dispatcher.include(request,response);
```

–Option A is correct because it uses an include directive, which includes the bytes of the referenced resource prior to the JSP's translation into a servlet.

---

23 Which statements about the deployment descriptor (DD) are true? (Choose all that apply.)

(Servlet v2.4 section 13)

- [ ] A. The DD must contain at least one **<context-param>** element.
- [x] B. The DD must be a well-formed XML file.
- [ ] C. The DD can be a text-based properties file or an XML file.
- [ ] D. You can leave out the XML form of the DD and provide a DD as a Java object.
- [x] E. The **<web-app>** element must be the parent element of all of the other DD elements.

–The deployment descriptor has to be well-formed XML and <web-app> is the parent element.

---

24 Which steps occur before **jspInit()** is called? (Choose all that apply.)

(JSP v2.0 section 1.1)

- [x] A. A class instantiation occurs.
- [x] B. A Java source file is compiled.
- [ ] C. The **_jspService()** method is called.
- [x] D. The JSP page is translated to source.
- [ ] E. The **jspCreate()** method is called.
- [x] F. The container supplies a **ServletConfig** reference.

–There is no jspCreate() method, and the _jspService() method is called after jspInit is called.

25 Given a Simple tag handler class:

(JSP v2.0 SimpleTagSupport API pg 2-86, JSP v2.0 PageContext API pg 2-30, and Servlet v2.4 HttpServletRequest API pg 242)

```
11. public class MyTagHandler
           extends SimpleTagSupport {
12.   public void doTag() throws JspException {
13.     try {
14.       // insert code 1
15.       // insert code 2
16.       // insert code 3
17.       JspWriter out = tagContext.getOut();
18.       out.print(requestURI);
19.     } catch (IOException ioe) {
20.       throw new JspException(ioe);
21.     }
22.   }
23. }
```

This item is testing two APIs. First, that a Simple tag handler must use the getJspContext (and cast it) to retrieve the PageContext object. Second, that the request object can only be retrieved from a PageContext and not a JspContext. Option D is the only valid combination of code to make the question of this item true.

Which, inserted at lines 14, 15, and 16, will print the request-URI to the response stream?

- [ ] A.
```
14. JspContext tagContext = pageContext;
15. ServletRequest request
        = (ServletRequest) tagContext.getRequest();
16. String requestURI = request.getRequestURI();
```

-Option A is invalid because there is no protected pageContext variable as there is for Classic tags.

- [ ] B.
```
14. PageContext tagContext = (PageContext) jspContext;
15. ServletRequest request
        = (ServletRequest) tagContext.getRequest();
16. String requestURI = request.getRequestURI();
```

-Option B is invalid because there is no jspContext protected variable.

- [ ] C.
```
14. JspContext tagContext = getJspContext();
15. HttpServletRequest request
        = (HttpServletRequest) tagContext.getRequest();
16. String requestURI = request.getRequestURI();
```

-Option C is invalid because you cannot access the request object from the JspContext API.

- [x] D.
```
14. PageContext tagContext = (PageContext) getJspContext();
15. HttpServletRequest request
        = (HttpServletRequest) tagContext.getRequest();
16. String requestURI = request.getRequestURI();
```

26 Given the following scriptlet code: (JSTL v1.1 section 5.1)

```
<% String cityParam = request.getParameter("city");
   if ( cityParam != null ) { %>
     City: <input type='text' name='city' value='<%= cityParam %>' />
<% } else { %>
     City: <input type='text' name='city' value='Paris' />
<% } %>
```

Which JSTL code snippet produces the same result?

- [ ] A.
```
<c:if test='${not empty param.city}'>
    City: <input type='text' name='city' value='${param.city}' />
  <c:else/>
    City: <input type='text' name='city' value='Paris' />
  </c:if>
```

- [ ] B.
```
<c:if test='${not empty param.city'>
    <c:then>
      City: <input type='text' name='city' value='${param.city}' />
    </c:then>
    <c:else>
      City: <input type='text' name='city' value='Paris' />
    </c:else>
  </c:if>
```

- [ ] C.
```
<c:choose test='${not empty param.city}'>
    City: <input type='text' name='city' value='${param.city}' />
  <c:otherwise/>
    City: <input type='text' name='city' value='Paris' />
  </c:choose>
```

- [x] D.
```
<c:choose>
    <c:when test='${not empty param.city}'>
      City: <input type='text' name='city' value='${param.city}' />
    </c:when>
    <c:otherwise>
      City: <input type='text' name='city' value='Paris' />
    </c:otherwise>
  </c:choose>
```

–To mimic an if-then-else statement you need to use the choose/when/otherwise tags. Option D is the only valid usage pattern.

---

27 How would you redirect an HTTP request to another URL? (Choose all that apply)

(HttpServletResponse API)

☑ A. `response.sendRedirect("/anotherUrl");`

☐ B. `response.encodeRedirectURL("/anotherUrl");`

-Option B is invalid because the encodeRedirectURL method only performs the URL rewriting, and not the actual redirection.

☑ C.
```
response.sendRedirect(
    response.encodeRedirectURL("/anotherUrl"));
```

☐ D.
```
RequestDispatcher dispatcher
    = request.getRequestDispatcher("/anotherUrl");
dispatcher.forward(request,response);
```

-Option D is invalid because a forward is server-side only, but a redirect must tell the browser to change URLs.

☐ E.
```
RequestDispatcher dispatcher
    = request.getRequestDispatcher("/anotherUrl");
dispatcher.redirect(request,response);
```

-Option E is invalid because there is no such method on a RequestDispatcher.

---

28 Given:

(JSP v2.0 pg. 1-49)

```
<%@ page isELIgnored="true" %>
```

Which statements are true? (Choose all that apply.)

☑ A. This is an example of a directive.

☐ B. This is NOT an example of a directive.

☑ C. It will cause `${a.b}` to be ignored by the container.

☐ D. It will NOT cause `${a.b}` to be ignored by the container.

☑ E. It will cause the EL expression in `<c:out value="${a.b}"/>` to be ignored by the container.

☐ F. It will NOT cause the EL expression in `<c:out value="${a.b}"/>` to be ignored by the container.

-Options D and F are invalid because the isELIgnored directive, when set to true, indicates that the container should ignore all EL expressions in this JSP.

29 Given a deployment descriptor with three valid **<security-constraint>** elements, all constraining web resource A. And, given that two of the **<security-constraint>** elements respective **<auth-constraint>** sub–elements are: (Servlet v2.4 sec. 12.8.1)

<auth-constraint>Bob</auth-constraint>

and

<auth-constraint>Alice</auth-constraint>

And that the third **<security-constraint>** element has no **<auth-constraint>** sub-element.

Who can access resource A?

- ❑ A. no one
- ☑ B. anyone
- ❑ C. only Bob
- ❑ D. only Alice
- ❑ E. only Bob and Alice
- ❑ F. anyone but Bob or Alice

-Option B is correct. The existence of a <security-constraint> element with no <auth-constraint> element overrides all other <auth-constraint> elements that refer to that resource, granting access to everyone.

30 Given: (JSP v2.0 section 2.6)

```
<function>
  <name>myfun</name>
  <function-class>com.example.MyFunctions</function-class>
  <function-signature>
    java.util.List getList(java.lang.String name)
  </function-signature>
</function>
```

Which is true about an invocation of this EL function mapping?

Assume that **pre** is correctly declared by a **taglib** directive.

- ❑ A. EL functions are NOT allowed to return collections.
- ❑ B. **${pre:getList("visitors")[0]}** is a valid invocation.
- ☑ C. **${pre:myfun("visitors")[0]}** is a valid invocation.
- ❑ D. The function signature is invalid because you do NOT need to specify the package information **java.lang** on the method parameter.

-Option A is invalid because an EL function may return any object type.

-Option B is invalid because EL uses the <name> mapping, not the real method name.

-Option C is correct because it uses the <name> mapping.

-Option D is invalid because you DO need the package information on all reference types, including classes in the java.lang package.

31 In an HTML page with a rich, graphical layout, how would you write the JSP standard action code to import a JSP segment that generates a menu that is parameterized by the user's role?

(JSP v2.0 section 5.4 and 5.6)

☑ A.
```
<jsp:include page="user-menu.jsp">
    <jsp:param name="userRole"
               value="${user.role}" />
</jsp:include>
```

☐ B.
```
<jsp:import page="user-menu.jsp">
    <jsp:param name="userRole"
               value="${user.role}" />
</jsp:import>
```
–Option B is invalid because there is no import standard action.

☐ C.
```
<jsp:include page="user-menu.jsp">
    <jsp:parameter name="userRole"
                   value="${user.role}" />
</jsp:include>
```
–Option C is invalid because there is no parameter standard action.

☐ D.
```
<jsp:import page="user-menu.jsp">
    <jsp:parameter name="userRole"
                   value="${user.role}" />
</jsp:import>
```
–Option D is invalid because there are no import and parameter standard actions.

☐ E. This CANNOT be done using a JSP standard action.

–Option E is invalid because this CAN be done using the include/param actions.

---

32 Given that **resp** is an **HttpServletResponse**, and no custom headers exist in this response before this snippet executes:

(API)

```
30.  resp.addHeader("myHeader", "foo");
31.  resp.addHeader("myHeader", "bar");
32.  resp.setHeader("myHeader", "baz");
33.  String [] s = resp.getHeaders("myHeader");
```

What is the value of **s[0]**?

☐ A. **foo**

☐ B. **bar**

☐ C. **baz**

☑ D. Compilation fails

☐ E. An exception is thrown at runtime

–Option D is correct. Compilation fails because there is no getHeaders() method in HttpServletResponse. Note that line 31 would add "bar" as an additional value, and line 32 would reset the value of "myHeader" to "baz".

---

33 Given a servlet that stores a customer bean in the session scope with the following code snippet:

(JSP v2.0 sections 5.1 and 5.3)

```
public void doPost(HttpServletRequest req,
                         HttpServletResponse resp) {
  HttpSession session = req.getSession();
  com.example.Customer cust
    = new com.example.Customer();
  cust.setName(req.getParameter("full_name"));
  session.setAttribute("customer", cust);
  RequestDispatcher page
    = req.getRequestDispatcher("page.jsp");
  page.forward(req, resp);
}
```

Which of these complete JSPs will print the customer's name? (Choose all that apply..)

☐ A.

```
<%= customer.getName() %>
```

-Option A is invalid because the customer variable has not yet been initialized.

☑ B.

```
<jsp:useBean id="customer"
             type="com.example.Customer"
             scope="session" />
<%= customer.getName() %>
```

-Option B is correct because the useBean tag initializes the customer variable.

☐ C.

```
<jsp:useBean id="customer"
             type="com.example.Customer"
             scope="session">
  <%= customer.getName() %>
</jsp:useBean>
```

-Option C is invalid because the body of the useBean tag will not be invoked because the bean already exists in the session scope.

☑ D.

```
<jsp:useBean id="customer"
             type="com.example.Customer"
             scope="session" />
<jsp:getProperty name="customer"
                 property="name" />
```

-Option D is correct because the getProperty tag prints the property.

☐ E.

```
<jsp:useBean id="customer"
             type="com.example.Customer"
             scope="session">
  <jsp:getProperty name="customer"
                   property="name" />
</jsp:useBean>
```

-Option E is invalid because the body of the useBean tag will not be invoked because the bean already exists in the session scope.

34 Which are valid elements in a DD? (Choose all that apply.)

(Servlet v2.4 section 6.2.5)

☐ A.
```
<filter>
  ...
  <dispatcher>ERROR</dispatcher>
</filter>
```

☐ B.
```
<filter>
  ...
  <dispatcher>CHAIN</dispatcher>
</filter>
```

☐ C.
```
<filter>
  ...
  <dispatcher>FORWARD</dispatcher>
</filter>
```

☑ D.
```
<filter-mapping>
  ...
  <dispatcher>INCLUDE</dispatcher>
</filter-mapping>
```

☑ E.
```
<filter-mapping>
  ...
  <dispatcher>REQUEST</dispatcher>
</filter-mapping>
```

☐ F.
```
<filter-mapping>
  ...
  <dispatcher>RESPONSE</dispatcher>
</filter-mapping>
```

-Options A, B and C are invalid because the <dispatcher> element is a sub-element of <filter-mapping>, although ERROR is a valid value for the <dispatcher> element.

-Option F is invalid because the <dispatcher> is only applied to requests.

35 Given that **req** is an **HttpServletRequest**, which returns the names of all the parameters in the request? (Choose all that apply.)

(API)

☐ A. `Map names = req.getParameterNames();`

☐ B. `String [] names = req.getParameters();`

☐ C. `Enumeration names = req.getParameters();`

☐ D. `String [] names = req.getParameterNames();`

☑ E. `Enumeration names = req.getParameterNames();`

-Option E specifies the correct method name and the correct return type.

36 Which of the following are legal **<error-page>** elements? (Choose all that apply.)

(Servet v2.4 pgs. 142 & 306)

☑ A.
```
<error-page>
    <exception-type>java.lang.Throwable</exception-type>
    <location>/error/generic-error.jsp</location>
</error-page>
```

☑ B.
```
<error-page>
    <error-code>404</error-code>
    <location>/error/file-not-found.jsp</location>
</error-page>
```

☐ C.
```
<error-page>
    <error-code>404</error-code>
    <error-code>403</error-code>
    <location>/error/generic-error.jsp</location>
</error-page>
```

☐ D.
```
<error-page>
    <error-code>404</error-code>
    <location>/error/file-not-found.jsp</location>
    <location>/error/generic-error.jsp</location>
</error-page>
```

☐ E.
```
<error-page>
    <error-code>404</error-code>
    <exception-type>java.lang.Throwable</exception-type>
    <location>/error/generic-error.jsp</location>
</error-page>
```

-An <error-page> element can have either a single <error-code> element OR a single <exception-type> element, but not both. In addition, an <error-page> element must have a single <location> subelement.

37 Given that there exists a **HashMap** attribute called **preferences** in the session-scope.

(JSTL v1.1 section 4.3)

Which JSTL code structure will put an entry, **color**, into the map with the value of the color request parameter?

☑ A.
```
<c:set target="${sessionScope.preferences}"
    property="color" value="${param.color}" />
```

☐ B.
```
<c:put map="${sessionScope.preferences}"
    property="color" value="${param.color}" />
```

☐ C.
```
<c:set scope="session" var="preferences"
    property="color" value="${param.color}" />
```

☐ D.
```
<c:put scope="session" map="preferences"
    property="color" value="${param.color}" />
```

-Option B is invalid because there is no put tag.

-Option C is invalid because the var and property attributes of the set tag are not a valid combination.

-Option D is invalid because there is no put tag and no map attribute.

Note: This is a simulated 'Drag and Drop' question, something like what you'll see on the exam:

(JSP v2.0 section 1.8.3)

38 Given the Implicit Objects listed on the left, and actual Java types listed on the right, match the Implicit Objects to their correct Java type:

```
out                          Object
application        JspWriter
config             PageAttributes
page                         Writer
                             JspContext
                             JspConfig
                             System
                             ServletConfig
                             ServletContext
```

Answer:

```
out ----------> JspWriter
application --> ServletContext
config --------> ServletConfig
page ---------> Object
```

–These are the correct mappings from implicit object type to Java type.

39 Which Simple tag handler will iterate over the body content five times? (JSP v2.0 section 13.6)

☑ A.
```
public class MySimpleTag extends SimpleTagSupport {
    public void doTag() throws IOException, JspException {
      for ( int i=0; i<5; i++ ) {
        getJspBody().invoke(null);
      }
    }
)
```

– Option A is correct; iteration can be performed right in the doTag method.

☐ B.
```
public class MySimpleTag extends SimpleTagSupport {
    int count=0;
    public int doTag() throws IOException, JspException {
      getJspBody().invoke(null);
      count++;
      return ( (count<5) ? EVAL_BODY_AGAIN : SKIP_BODY );
    }
}
```

– Option B is invalid because the doTag method does not return an int flag as is done in the Classic tag model.

☐ C.
```
public class MySimpleTag extends SimpleTagSupport {
    int count=0;
    public int doStartTag() {
      return EVAL_BODY_INCLUDE;
    }
    public int doEndTag() {
      count++;
      return ( (count<5) ? EVAL_BODY_AGAIN : SKIP_BODY );
    }
}
```

– Options C and D are invalid because a Simple tag does not have the doStartTag, doAfterBody, or doEndTag methods, which are part of the Classic model.

☐ D.
```
public class MySimpleTag extends SimpleTagSupport {
    int count=0;
    public int doStartTag() {
      return EVAL_BODY_INCLUDE;
    }
    public int doAfterBody() {
      count++;
      return ( (count<5) ? EVAL_BODY_AGAIN : SKIP_BODY );
    }
}
```

BTW, Option D is a valid implementation of this tag behavior using the Classic model; except that MySimpleTag must extend TagSupport.

40 Which of the following statements about the servlet lifecycle are true? (Choose all that apply.)

(Servlet v2.4 section 2.3)

- [ ] A. The web container calls the **`init()`** and **`service()`** methods in response to each servlet request.

-Option A is invalid because the init() method is only called once after the servlet has been initialized.

- [ ] B. The web application developer uses an object that implements the **`java.servlet.Filter`** interface to instantiate one or more servlets.

-Option B is completely bogus because filters are not used this way.

- [x] C. The web container calls the servlet's **`destroy()`** method when the servlet is destroyed or unloaded.

- [x] D. The web container loads and instantiates a servlet class, then initializes the servlet by calling its **`init()`** method exactly once, passing into **`init()`** an object that implements the **`javax.servlet.ServletConfig`** interface that the container creates for the servlet.

-Option D shows the process by which a web container loads and initializes a servlet.

41 Which about web attributes are true? (Choose all that apply.)

(Servlet v2.4 general knowledge)

- [ ] A. No attributes are longer lived than session attributes.

-Option A is wrong because context attributes tend to be longer lived.

- [x] B. In all scopes, attributes can be retrieved using a **`getAttribute()`** method.

- [x] C. Context attributes survive a session time-out.

- [ ] D. Only session and context attributes can be retrieved in an enumeration.

-Option D is wrong because request attributes can also be retrieved in an enumeration.

- [ ] E. Data stored in both request and session objects is thread safe.

-Option E is wrong because, in the 'two-browser windows' scenario, session objects may not be thread safe.

42 Given a JSP page:

```
<my:tag1>
  <my:tag2>
    <%-- JSP content --%>
  </my:tag2>
</my:tag1>
```

(JSP v2.0 SimpleTagSupport API, JSP v2.0 TagSupport API, and JSP v2.0 Classic tag lifecycle pg 2-59)

The tag handler for **`my:tag1`** is **`Tag1Handler`** and extends TagSupport. The tag handler for **`my:tag2`** is **`Tag2Handler`** and extends SimpleTagSupport.

The tag handler for **`my:tag1`** must have access to the tag handler for **`my:tag2`**. What must you do to make this work?

- [ ] A. The instance of **`Tag1Handler`** must use the **`getChildren`** method in order to retrieve the collection of child tag instances. The instance of **`Tag1Handler`** will only be able to access the registered tags during the **`doAfterBody`** and **`doEndTag`** methods.
- [x] B. The instance of **`Tag2Handler`** must use the **`getParent`** method in order to register itself with the instance of **`Tag1Handler`**. The instance of **`Tag1Handler`** will only be able to access the registered tags during the **`doAfterBody`** and **`doEndTag`** methods.
- [ ] C. The instance of **`Tag1Handler`** must use the **`getChildren`** method in order to retrieve the collection of child tag instances. The instance of **`Tag1Handler`** will be able to access the registered tags in any of the tag event methods, but NOT in the attribute setter methods.
- [ ] D. The instance of **`Tag2Handler`** must use the **`getParent`** method in order to register itself with the instance of **`Tag1Handler`**. The instance of **`Tag1Handler`** will be able to access the registered tags in any of the tag event methods, but NOT in the attribute setter methods.

-TagSupport and SimpleTagSupport both have a getParent method, but there is no such method as getChildren. This fact eliminates Options A and C.

-The child tags must be activated (via the attribute setters or tag event methods) in order to register with the parent. Therefore, the parent tag must have invoked the tag body at least once. Thus, only the doAfterBody and doEndTag methods will have access to the registered inner tags. This fact eliminates Option D.

43 Given that a deployment descriptor has only one security role, defined as: (Servlet v2.4 section 12.8)

```
<security-role>
  <role-name>Member</role-name>
</security-role>
```

Which are valid **<auth-constraint>** elements that will allow users to access resources constrained by the security role declared? (Choose all that apply.)

- [ ] A. **<auth-constraint/>**
- [x] B. **<auth-constriant>*</auth-constraint>**
- [x] C. **<auth-constraint>Member</auth-constraint>**
- [ ] D. **<auth-constraint>MEMBER</auth-constraint>**
- [ ] E. **<auth-constraint>"Member"</auth-constraint>**

-Options B and C are correct. Role names are case sensitive in the deployment descriptor, and an empty <auth-constraint> element signifies that no users can access the resource being requested.

44 Given this list of features: (Core J2EE Patterns 2nd ed., pg. 424)

- might create stale data
- can increase the complexity of code having to deal with concurrency issues

Which design pattern is being described?

- [x] A. Transfer Object
- [ ] B. Service Locator
- [ ] C. Front Controller
- [ ] D. Business Delegate
- [ ] E. Intercepting Filter
- [ ] F. Model-View-Controller

-The creation of stale data is a common side effect whenever you decouple data from its remote source. Remote sources do not typically broadcast updates to 'subscribers' to their data.

45 Where are servlet classes located inside a Web Application Archive (WAR) file? (Servlet v2.4 section 9.5)

- [ ] A. Only in **/WEB-INF/classes**.
- [ ] B. Only in a JAR file in **/WEB-INF/lib**.
- [x] C. Either in a JAR file in **/WEB-INF/lib** or under **/WEB-INF/classes**.
- [ ] D. At the top level of the directory tree inside the WAR so that the web container can easily find them upon deployment.

-Option C shows the correct options for storing servlet classes in a WAR.

46 Which code snippets properly map the **com.example.web.BeerSelect** servlet to the **/SelectBeer.do** URL? (Choose all that apply.)

(Servlet v2.4 section 13.5.1)

❑ A.
```
<servlet-map>
    <servlet-class>com.example.web.BeerSelect</servlet-class>
    <url-pattern>/SelectBeer.do</url-pattern>
<servlet-map>
```

❑ B.
```
<servlet>
    <servlet-mapping>
      <servlet-class>com.example.web.BeerSelect</servlet-class>
      <url-pattern>/SelectBeer.do</url-pattern>
    </servlet-mapping>
</servlet>
```

❑ C.
```
<servlet-mapping>
    <servlet-name>com.example.web.BeerSelect</servlet-name>
    <url-pattern>/SelectBeer.do</url-pattern>
</servlet-mapping>
```

☑ D.
```
<servlet>
    <servlet-name>BeerServlet</servlet-name>
    <servlet-class>com.example.web.BeerSelect</servlet-class>
</servlet>
<servlet-mapping>
    <servlet-name>BeerServlet</servlet-name>
    <url-pattern>/SelectBeer.do</url-pattern>
</servlet-mapping>
```

–Option D is correct. The <servlet-name> element is used internally within the DD to tie the <servlet> and <servlet-mapping> elements to each other.

47 Which statements about **HttpSession** objects are true? (Choose all that apply.)

(Servlet v2.4 section 7)

☑ A. A session may become invalid due to inactivity.

❑ B. A new session is created each time a user makes a request.

☑ C. A session may become invalid as a result of a specific call by a servlet.

☑ D. Multiple requests made from the same browser may have access to the same session object.

❑ E. A user who accesses the same web application from two browser windows is guaranteed to have two distinct session objects.

–Option B is invalid because the purpose of a session is to span multiple requests.

–Option E is invalid because multiple browser windows will typically share a session.

48 Given a partial deployment descriptor:

(Servlet v2.4 pg. 139)

```
11.   <servlet>
12.     <servlet-name>ServletIWantToListenTo</servlet-name>
13.     <servlet-class>com.example.MyServlet</servlet-class>
14.   </servlet>
15.   <listener>
16.     <listener-class>com.example.ListenerA</listener-class>
17.   </listener>
18.   <listener>
19.     <listener-class>com.example.ListenerB</listener-class>
20.     <listener-type>Session</listener-type>
21.   </listener>
22.   <listener>
23.     <listener-class>com.example.ListenerC</listener-class>
24.     <description>A session listener.</description>
25.   </listener>
26.   <listener>
27.     <listener-class>com.example.ReqListener</listener-class>
28.     <servlet-name>ServletIWantToListenTo</servlet-name>
29.   </listener>
```

Which are valid **listener** elements (identify each listener by the line number it starts on)? (Choose one.)

- [ ] A. Only 15.
- [ ] B. Only 18.
- [ ] C. Only 26.
- [x] D. Both 15 and 22.
- [ ] E. Both 18 and 26.
- [ ] F. 15, 22 and 26.
- [ ] G. All four are valid.

-Option A is invalid because servlets do not act as listeners.

-Options B, E and G are incorrect because there is no <listener-type> element.

-Options C, E, F and G are invalid because the <servlet-name> element is not applicable to the <listener> element.

49 Which statements concerning **/META-INF** are true? (Choose all that apply.)

(Servlet v2.4 section 9.6)

- [ ] A. This directory is optional when creating a WAR file.
- [ ] B. The contents of this directory can be served directly to clients only if HTTPS is activated.
- [x] C. Servlets can access the contents of the **/META-INF** directory via methods in the **ServletContext** class.
- [ ] D. Servlets can access the contents of the **/META-INF** directory via methods in the **ServletConfig** class.

---

50 Which security mechanisms can be applied to specific resources by specifying URL patterns in the deployment descriptor? (Choose all that apply.)

(Servlet v2.4 section 12)

- [x] A. authorization
- [x] B. data integrity
- [ ] C. authentication
- [x] D. confidentiality
- [ ] E. form-based login

-Options A, B, and D are correct. The <security-constraint> element allows security to be mapped to specific URLs and within that element, the <user-data-constraint> element allows the deployer to declare a transport guarantee to provide data integrity and confidentiality.

---

51 Your company is in the process of integrating several different back office applications and creating a single web UI to present the entire back office suite to your clients. The design of the front end will be finished long before the design of the back end. Although the details of the back end design are still very rough, you have enough information to create some temporary back end 'stubs' to use to test the UI.

(Core J2EE Patterns 2nd ed., pg. 302)

Which design pattern can be used to minimize the overhead of modifying the UI once the back end is complete?

- [ ] A. Transfer Object
- [ ] B. Front Controller
- [x] C. Business Delegate
- [ ] D. Intercepting Filter
- [ ] E. Model-View-Controller

-The Business Delegate can be used when you want to minimize coupling between clients and business services. It is also appropriate when you need to hide implementation details or, in this case, partition them since they are temporary.

---

52 Given:

(Filter API)

`fc` is of type **`FilterChain`** and
`req` and **`resp`** are request and response objects.

Which line of code in a class implementing **`Filter`** will invoke the target servlet if there is only one filter in the chain?

- [ ] A. `fc.chain(req, resp);`
- [x] B. `fc.doFilter(req, resp);`
- [ ] C. `fc.doForward(req, resp);`
- [ ] D. `req.chain(req, resp, fc);`
- [ ] E. `req.doFilter(req, resp, fc);`
- [ ] F. `req.doForward(req, resp, fc);`

-Option B is the correct method call regardless of whether the target servlet is next in the chain.

53 What type of listener could be used to log the user name of a user at the time that she logs into a system? (Choose all that apply.) (API)

- ❑ A. **HttpSessionListener**
- ❑ B. **ServletContextListener**
- ☑ C. **HttpSessionAttributeListener**
- ❑ D. **ServletContextAttributeListener**

–Option A is incorrect because the user name would not be known when the session is initially created. Since logging is desired at the time of the login, the listener's invalidation and timeout methods would not be helpful.

–Options B and D are incorrect because these listeners are used for servlet-context notifications.

54 Given a tag library descriptor located at **/mywebapp/WEB-INF/tlds/mytags.tld**, which would be the correct **taglib** directive? Assume **mywebapp** is the web application root and that there are no **<taglib>** tags in the deployment descriptor. (JSP v2.0 section 7.3.6.3)

- ❑ A. `<%@ taglib uri="/mytags.tld" prefix="my" %>`
- ❑ B. `<%@ taglib uri="/tlds/mytags.tld" prefix="my" %>`
- ☑ C. `<%@ taglib uri="/WEB-INF/tlds/mytags.tld" prefix="my" %>`
- ❑ D. `<%@ taglib uri="/mywebapp/WEB-INF/tlds/mytags.tld" prefix="my" %>`
- ❑ E. **/mywebapp/WEB-INF/tlds/mytags.tld** is NOT a valid location for a tag library descriptor, so none of these will work.

–Option C is correct because, in the absence of a <taglib> element in the DD, the URI must be a full path relative to the application root.

55 Given:

(Servlet v2.4 sections 7.4 and 15.1.11)

```
public class ServletX extends HttpServlet {
  public void doGet(HttpServletRequest req,
                    HttpServletResponse res)
        throws IOException, ServletException {
    req.getSession().setAttribute("key", new X());
    req.getSession().setAttribute("key", new X());
    req.getSession().setAttribute("key", "x");
    req.getSession().removeAttribute("key");
  }
}
```

and given a listener class:

```
public class X implements HttpSessionBindingListener {
  public void valueBound(HttpSessionBindingEvent event) {
    System.out.print("B");
  }
  public void valueUnbound(HttpSessionBindingEvent event) {
    System.out.print("UB");
  }
}
```

Which logging output would be generated by an invocation of the **doGet** method?

- ☐ A. **UBUBUB**

  –Option A is incorrect because it implies that the valueBound method is never called.

- ☑ B. **BBUBUB**

- ☐ C. **BBUBUBB**

- ☐ D. **BUBBUBB**

  –Options C and D are incorrect because they imply an extra call to the valueBound method when a String value is added to the session.

- ☐ E. **BBUBUBBUB**

- ☐ F. **BBUBBUBBUB**

  –Options E and F are incorrect because they include calls to the valueBound and the valueUnbound methods when a String value is added to the session.

56 Given:

(Servlet v2.4 section 8)

```
public void doGet(HttpServletRequest req,
                   HttpServletResponse res)
        throws IOException, ServletException {
   RequestDispatcher rd1
     = getServletContext().getRequestDispatcher("/xyz");
   RequestDispatcher rd2
     = req.getRequestDispatcher("/xyz");
   RequestDispatcher rd3
     = getServletContext().getRequestDispatcher("xyz");
   RequestDispatcher rd4
     = req.getRequestDispatcher("xyz");
}
```

Which statements are true? (Choose all that apply.)

- [x] A. **rd3** will never map to a servlet since the given path does NOT begin with /.

  –Option A is correct because the path in this call must begin with "/".

- [ ] B. **rd4** will never map to a servlet since the given path does NOT begin with /.

  –Option B is incorrect because a relative path is valid here.

- [x] C. **rd2.forward(req, res)** and **rd4.forward(req, res)** may forward to the same resource.

  –Option C is correct because these calls would refer to the same resource if the original request was for a resource at the top level (e.g. "/foo").

- [x] D. **rd1.forward(req, res)** and **rd2.forward(req, res)** would always forward to the same resource.

  –Option D is correct because both calls are using an absolute path relative to the servlet context root.

- [ ] E. **rd3.forward(req, res)** and **rd4.forward(req, res)** would always forward to the same resource.

  –Option E is incorrect because rd3 is null.

57 Which JSTL tag performs URL rewriting?

(JSTL v1.1 section 7.6)

- [ ] A. **link**
- [ ] B. **aHref**
- [ ] C. **import**
- [x] D. **url**

–Options A and B are not JSTL tags.

–Option C is invalid because the import tag does not perform URL rewriting.

58 Given:

(Servlet v2.4 pg. 258)

```
11. public void doGet(HttpServletRequest req,
12.                   HttpServletResponse res)
13.       throws IOException, ServletException {
14.    String url = res.encodeRedirectURL("/redirectme");
15.    boolean test = "/redirectme".equals(url);
16.    res.sendRedirect(url);
17. }
```

Which statements are true? (Choose all that apply.)

☐ A. After line 15, **test** will always be **true**.

☐ B. After line 15, **test** will always be **false**.

-Options A and B are incorrect because the URL will be modified by line 14 only if necessary.

☑ C. Line 14 demonstrates a session management mechanism called URL rewriting.

☑ D. After line 15, **test** could be either **true** ot **false**.

☐ E. The **encodeURL** method should have been used instead of the **encodeRedirectURL** method in line 14.

-Option E is incorrect because this is the correct method to be used with URLs that are to be passed to the sendRedirect method.

☐ F. The **encodeRedirectURL** method shown in line 14 should only be used when clients have disabled cookies.

-Option F is incorrect because the encodeRedirectURL method should be used for all URLs sent through the sendRedirect method in order to support session management with browsers that do not support cookies.

59 What happens when a container migrates a session from one VM to another?

(Servlet v2.4 pg. 80)

☑ A. **sessionWillPassivate()** will be called on any objects that implement the **HttpSessionActivationListener** and are currently bound to the session.

☐ B. **sessionWillPassivate()** will be called on any objects that implement the **HttpSessionPassivationListener** and are currently bound to the session.

☐ C. **sessionWillPassivate()** will be called on any objects that implement the **HttpSessionListener** interface.

☐ D. **sessionWillPassivate()** will be called on any objects that implement the **HttpSessionBindingListener** and are currently bound to the session.

-Option A is the only one that refers to a valid interface/method combination.

60 Given an existing class:

(JSP v2.0 section 2.6)

```
package com.example;
public class MyFunctions {
  private int x;
  public MyFunctions()
    { x = 0; }
  public int modX(int y)
    { return (y mod x); }
  public static int funct(int x, int y)
    { return (2*x + y - 5); }
}
```

Which are true about EL functions? (Choose all that apply.)

☐ A. The **MyFunctions** class may NOT be used by EL because it has NOT been declared **final**.

-Option A is invalid because a class of functions need not be final.

☑ B. The **funct** method may be used by EL because it has been declared static.

-Option B is correct because only static methods may be used by EL.

☐ C. The **funct** method may NOT be use by EL because the calling arguments and return value must be object references.

-Option C is invalid because EL handles primitive values as well as objects.

☐ D. The **modX** method may be used by EL because it is an instance method.

-Option D is invalid because only static methods may be used by EL.

☑ E. The **MyFunctions** class may be used by EL even though it has a public constructor.

-Option E is correct because EL ignores all instance methods. EL doesn't care that it's dealing with a concrete class.

---

61 Which statements about ignoring EL in your JSPs are true? (Choose all that apply.)

(JSP v2.0 section 3.3.3)

☑ A. You can instruct the container to ignore EL in your JSPs by using the **<el-ignored>** tag in the DD.

☐ B. You can instruct the container to ignore EL in your JSPs by using the **<is-el-ignored>** tag in the DD.

☐ C. You can instruct the container to ignore EL in a JSP by using the **elIgnored** attribute of the **page** directive.

-Option C is invalid because the correct page directive attribute is isELIgnored.

☑ D. When using the DD to instruct the container to ignore EL, you can specify which JSPs to constrain.

☐ E. You CANNOT constrain both scripting and EL in the same JSP.

-Option E is invalid because it's OK to constrain a given JSP from using both scripting and EL.

62 You have purchased a purchase order web application that uses programmatic authorization that uses security roles that are not used in your organization.

(Servlet v2.4 section 12.3)

Which deployment descriptor element must you use to make this webapp work in your organization?

- ❑ A. **<login-config>**
- ❑ B. **<security-role>**
- ☑ C. **<security-role-ref>**
- ❑ D. **<security-constraint>**

–Option C is correct. The <security-role-ref> element is used to map roles hardcoded in a servlet to roles declared in the deployment descriptor. The other elements are used for declarative security.

---

63 Given:

(JSP v2.0 section 7)

```
1. <%@ taglib uri="http://www.mycompany.com/mytags"
              prefix="mytags" %>
2. <mytags:foo bar="abc" />
3. <mytags:forEach><mytags:doSomething /></mytags:forEach>
4. <jsp:setProperty name="x" property="a" value="b" />
5. <c:out value="hello" />
```

Assuming this is a complete JSP, which is true?

(For options E and F, ignore the fact that an error in one line might keep a subsequent line from being reached)

- ❑ A. Only line 2 will definitely generate an error.
- ❑ B. Only line 3 will definitely generate an error.
- ❑ C. Only line 4 will definitely generate an error.
- ☑ D. Only line 5 will definitely generate an error.
- ❑ E. Lines 4 and 5 will both definitely generate errors.
- ❑ F. Lines 2, 3, 4 and 5 will all definitely generate errors.
- ❑ G. The entire JSP could execute without generating any errors.

–Options A and B are incorrect because, assuming the tags used are appropriately defined in the mytags tag library, there is nothing wrong with them.

–Option C is incorrect because this is a valid JSP standard action. The jsp prefix does not need to be referenced in a taglib directive.

–Option D is correct because there is no taglib directive shown for the prefix c.

---

64 Which authentication mechanism employs a base64 encoding scheme to protect user passwords?

(Servlet v2.4 section 12.5.1)

- ☑ A. HTTP Basic Authentication
- ❑ B. Form Based Authentication
- ❑ C. HTTP Digest Authentication
- ❑ D. HTTPS Client Authentication

–Option A is correct. BTW, the base64 encoding scheme is considered to be a very weak protection scheme.

---

65 Which concepts are common to all four authentication mechanisms supported by J2EE 1.4 compliant web containers? (Choose all that apply.)

(Servlet v2.4 section 12.5)

- [x] A. passwords
- [ ] B. realm names
- [ ] C. generic error pages
- [x] D. secured web resources
- [ ] E. automatic SSL support
- [ ] F. target server authentication

–Options A and D are correct. All authentication schemes rely on passwords, and in J2EE 1.4, authentication is initiated only when a secured web resource is requested.

---

66 How are cookies used to support session management?

(Servlet v2.4 section 7.1.1)

- [ ] A. A cookie is created for each attribute stored in the session.
- [x] B. A single cookie is created to hold an ID that uniquely identifies a session.
- [ ] C. A single cookie is created to hold the serialized `HttpSession` object.
- [ ] D. The session ID is encoded as a path parameter in the URL string called `jsessionid`.
- [ ] E. Cookies CANNOT be used to support session management because it is possible for a user to disable cookies in their browser.

–Option A is incorrect because session data is not stored in cookies, just a session ID.

–Option C is incorrect because the session itself is not stored in the cookie, just a session ID.

–Option D is incorrect because it describes URL rewriting, not cookies.

–Option E is incorrect because cookies are the most commonly used session tracking mechanism (despite the possibility described here).

---

67 You are developing a web application for an organization that needs to display the results of database searches to several different types of clients, including browsers, PDAs, and kiosks. The application will have to examine the request to determine which type of client has initiated it, and then dispatch the request to the proper component.

(HFS – chap 14)

Which J2EE design pattern is designed for this type of application?

- [ ] A. Transfer Object
- [ ] B. Service Locator
- [x] C. Model-View-Controller
- [ ] D. Business Delegate
- [ ] E. Intercepting Filter

–One clue that MVC might be a good choice is when your application has to represent the same business data in several different views.

---

68 Which is true about the differences between the Classic and Simple tag models?

(JSP v2.0 section 13)

- ❑ A. A nested Classic tag is allowed to access its parent tag, but this is NOT supported in the Simple tag model.
- ❑ B. In the Classic model, you may gain access to the evaluated body content using the **`BodyTag`** interface. In the Simple model, you can invoke the body, but you CANNOT gain access to the content generated in the invocation.
- ☑ C. The Tag interface has two event methods (**`doStartTag`** and **`doEndTag`**), but the **`SimpleTag`** interface only has one event method (**`doTag`**).
- ❑ D. Both tag models support iteration. In the **`SimpleTag.doTag`** method, you can invoke the body within a Java-based iteration. In the Classic model, iteration may be supported by returning the **`EVAL_BODY_AGAIN`** constant from the **`Tag.doEndTag`** method.

-Option A is invalid because a Simple tag is allowed to access its parent.

-Option B is invalid because a Simple tag can pass in a Writer object to the JspFragment.invoke method that captures the output.

-Option D is invalid because it is not the doEndTag method that is used to perform iteration (it is the doAfterBody method).

69 Given this class:

(JSP v2.0 section 5.2)

```
package biz.mybiz;
public class BeanX {
   private String a,b,c;
   public BeanX() {a="A";b="B";c="C";}
   public void setA(String a) { this.a = a; }
   public void setB(String b) { this.b = b; }
   public void setC(String c) { this.c = c; }
   public String getAll() { return a+b+c; }
}
```

and the JSP:

```
<jsp:useBean id="x" class="biz.mybiz.BeanX" />
<jsp:setProperty name="x" property="*" />
<jsp:getProperty name="x" property="all" />
<jsp:setProperty name="x" property="a" param="b" />
<jsp:setProperty name="x" property="b" param="c" />
<jsp:setProperty name="x" property="c" param="a" />
<jsp:getProperty name="x" property="all" />
```

What will be generated by the JSP when invoked with the query string **a=X&b=Y&c=Z**?

- ❑ A. **ABC YZX**
- ❑ B. **XYZ XYZ**
- ❑ C. **ABC ABC**
- ❑ D. **YXZ YZX**
- ❑ E. **XYZ ZXY**
- ☑ F. **XYZ YZX**
- ❑ G. **nullnullnull YZX**

–Option F is correct because the first jsp:setProperty call sets all three properties based on the parameters in the query string and then the subsequent jsp:setProperty calls change their values.

Index

Symbols & Tags

A

B

C

D

E

F

G

H

L

M

N

O

P

R

S

T

U

V

JavaCross 2.4

Let's give your right brain something to do.

It's a standard crossword, but almost all of the solution words are from chapters 13 and 14.

If you aren't a veteran puzzler, we've provided less "ornery" clues at the bottom of the page.

Across

3. Performance pattern
5. Architecture layer
7. Don't invoke me
9. Trickier filters
10. HTTP's stomping ground
11. One per Struts app.
12. Socket shielder
13. Could be moldy (abbr.)
14. Browser jockey
15. A Struts callback
18. Web developer's tool
19. Smalltalk pattern
21. Some kind of event
23. XML hotbed
24. Could be a browser
25. Crupi's bailiwick
27. JavaScript inspired
28. Fancy models
30. Inter-server ether
31. 1st step towards looseness
32. Hand off

Down

1. Data communicator
2. Convenient class
3. JSP super-chargers
4. Stackable component
6. DD brick
8. Single minded
11. Declarative reducer
16. The blueprints
17. State component
18. The yellow pages
19. Blind to the GUI
20. SL's shortcut
22. Filter's fate
26. Validate's home
29. Controller protecto (abbr.)

Extra Hints:

. Container invokes me
2. Local call, not!
3. Could be stale
3. The big mapper

25. MVC is one
28. SCBCD stars
31. Announce

1. All scopes have'em
2. Decorate me
6. XML chunk

11. Less hard-coding
26. Getters and setters

This isn't goodbye

Bring your brain over to wickedlysmart.com

And don't forget to write and tell us when you pass the exam!

Ikickedbutt@wickedlysmart.com
So we can have a drink in your honor.

Don't you know there's more on the wickedlysmart.com website? And if you're going to take the exam be sure to drop by javaranch.com and spend some time in the SCWCD study forum. Folks there are just so damn friendly it'll make you want to throw up.

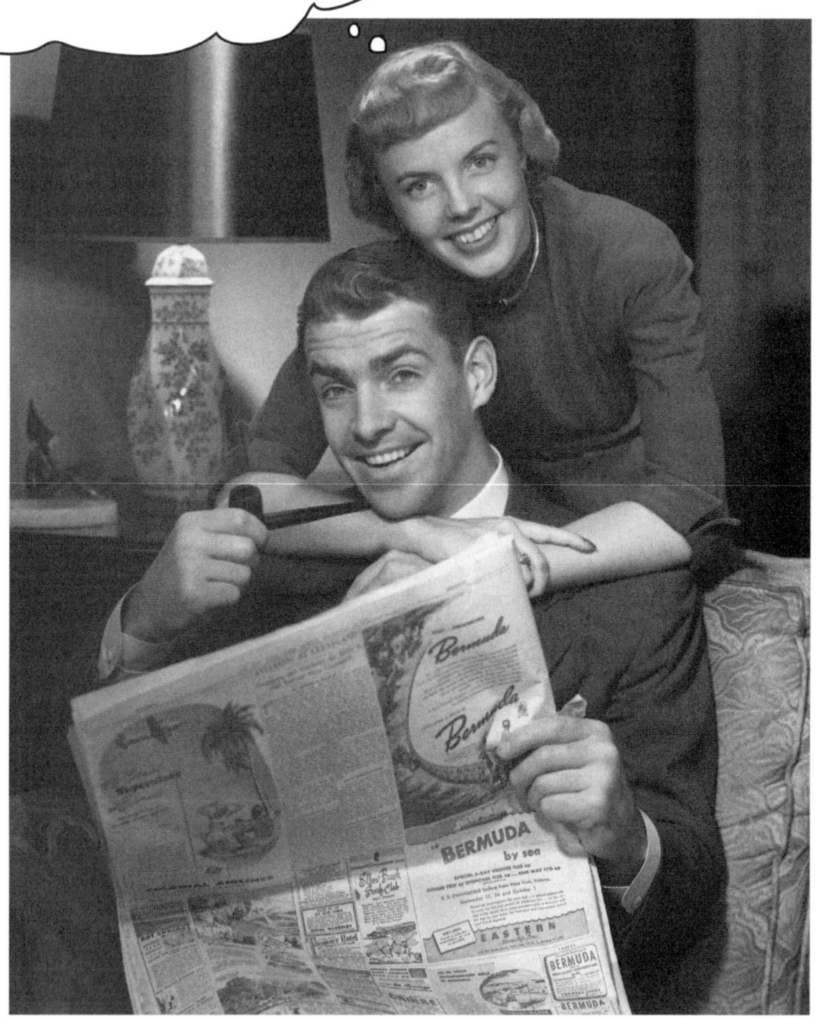

Cover Rough Drafts for the Head First series

**It was a tough decision.
Before we finally settled on:**

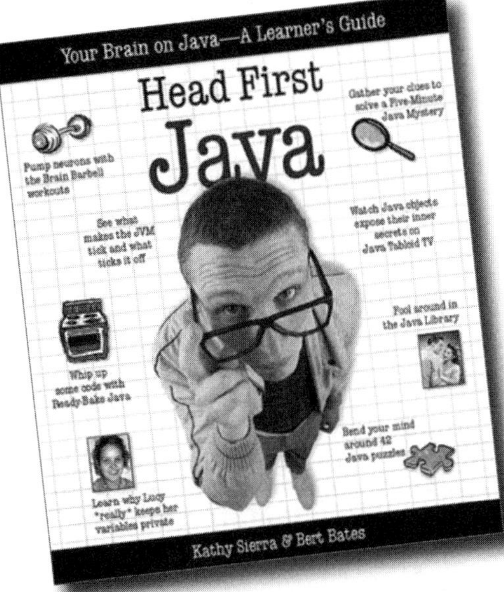

...we kicked around a lot of promising candidates...

1 We were thinking this might play up the whole hands-on approach... what do you think? -K & B

well since it's brain-based, why don't we emphasize the HEAD and call it Head First?
-marketing

2 Hey, is this what you had in mind by "emphasize the Head?" - K & B

[um, no. -marketing]

3 Wasn't this the one we agreed on last week? - K & B

4 Yes we know this one is more festive, but what the #%^@! does it mean? PLEASE leave it to the professionals.
-marketing

Behind the scenes...

Dude..what's with that obnoxious brat girl who whines about frickin' everything? Can't you get her to lighten up a little?

Actually... she's my girlfriend. And she's really not like that once you get to know her...

They always cast me as the "thoughtful professional". I have to wear this horrid suit. How come *I* never get to play the bad girl or the "party dude"? And they make me *look* like I'm always *wondering*... trying to figure it all out... when I've probably *refactored* more code than the rest of them combined have *written*.

Am I the ONLY ONE here who appreciates that this is a serious topic? I could lose my job if I use scriptlets in a JSP and EVERYONE IS OK WITH THAT?? And for the record, Kim and I dated, like, *twice*. So, yeah, I'm his girlfriend all right... in his *dreams!*

Answers!

JavaCross 2.4

Let's give your right brain something to do.

It's your standard crossword, but almost all of the solution words are from chapters 13 and 14.

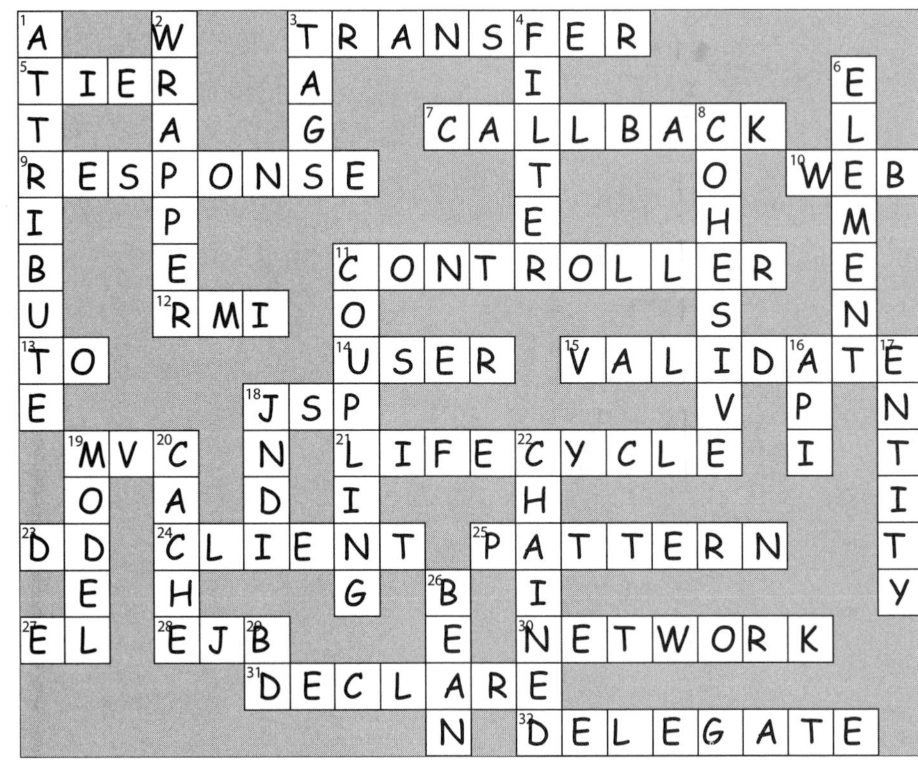

Across

3. Performance pattern
5. Architecture layer
7. Don't invoke me
9. Trickier filters
10. HTTP's stomping ground
11. One per Struts app.
12. Socket shielder
13. Could be moldy (abbr.)
14. Browser jockey
15. A Struts callback
18. Web designer's tool
19. Smalltalk pattern
21. Some kind of event
23. XML hotbed
24. Could be a browser
25. Crupi's bailiwick
27. JavaScript inspired
28. Fancy models
30. Inter-server ether
31. 1st step towards looseness
32. Really fancy proxy

Down

1. Communicator
2. Convenient class
3. JSP super-chargers
4. Stackable component
6. DD brick
8. Single minded
11. Declarative reducer
16. The blueprints
17. State component
18. The yellow pages
19. Blind to the GUI
20. SL's shortcut
22. Filter's fate
26. Validate's home

Related Titles Available from O'Reilly

Java

Ant: The Definitive Guide
Eclipse: A Java Developer's Guide
Enterprise JavaBeans, *3rd Edition*
Hardcore Java
Head First Java
Head First Servlets & JSP
Head First EJB
J2EE Design Patterns
Java and SOAP
Java & XML Data Binding
Java & XML
Java Cookbook
Java Data Objects
Java Database Best Practices
Java Enterprise Best Practices
Java Enterprise in a Nutshell, *2nd Edition*
Java Examples in a Nutshell, *3rd Edition*
Java Extreme Programming Cookbook
Java in a Nutshell, *4th Edition*
Java Management Extensions
Java Message Service
Java Network Programming, *2nd Edition*
Java NIO
Java Performance Tuning, *2nd Edition*
Java RMI
Java Security, *2nd Edition*
Java ServerPages, *2nd Edition*
Java Serlet & JSP Cookbook
Java Servlet Programming, *2nd Edition*
Java Swing, *2nd Edition*
Java Web Services in a Nutshell
Learning Java, *2nd Edition*
Mac OS X for Java Geeks
NetBeans: The Definitive Guide
Programming Jakarta Struts
Tomcat: The Definitive Guide
WebLogic: The Definitive Guide

O'REILLY®

Our books are available at most retail and online bookstores.
To order direct: 1-800-998-9938 • *order@oreilly.com* • *www.oreilly.com*
Online editions of most O'Reilly titles are available by subscription at *safari.oreilly.com*

Keep in touch with O'Reilly

1. Download examples from our books

To find example files for a book, go to:

www.oreilly.com/catalog

select the book, and follow the "Examples" link.

2. Register your O'Reilly books

Register your book at *register.oreilly.com*

Why register your books?
Once you've registered your O'Reilly books you can:

- Win O'Reilly books, T-shirts or discount coupons in our monthly drawing.
- Get special offers available only to registered O'Reilly customers.
- Get catalogs announcing new books (US and UK only).
- Get email notification of new editions of the O'Reilly books you own.

3. Join our email lists

Sign up to get topic-specific email announcements of new books and conferences, special offers, and O'Reilly Network technology newsletters at:

elists.oreilly.com

It's easy to customize your free elists subscription so you'll get exactly the O'Reilly news you want.

4. Get the latest news, tips, and tools

www.oreilly.com

- "Top 100 Sites on the Web"—PC Magazine
- CIO Magazine's Web Business 50 Awards

Our web site contains a library of comprehensive product information (including book excerpts and tables of contents), downloadable software, background articles, interviews with technology leaders, links to relevant sites, book cover art, and more.

5. Work for O'Reilly

Check out our web site for current employment opportunities:

jobs.oreilly.com

6. Contact us

O'Reilly & Associates
1005 Gravenstein Hwy North
Sebastopol, CA 95472 USA

TEL: 707-827-7000 or 800-998-9938
(6am to 5pm PST)

FAX: 707-829-0104

order@oreilly.com
For answers to problems regarding your order or our products. To place a book order online, visit:

www.oreilly.com/order_new

catalog@oreilly.com
To request a copy of our latest catalog.

booktech@oreilly.com
For book content technical questions or corrections.

corporate@oreilly.com
For educational, library, government, and corporate sales.

proposals@oreilly.com
To submit new book proposals to our editors and product managers.

international@oreilly.com
For information about our international distributors or translation queries. For a list of our distributors outside of North America check out:

international.oreilly.com/distributors.html

adoption@oreilly.com
For information about academic use of O'Reilly books, visit:

academic.oreilly.com

O'REILLY®

Our books are available at most retail and online bookstores.
To order direct: 1-800-998-9938 • *order@oreilly.com* • *www.oreilly.com*
Online editions of most O'Reilly titles are available by subscription at *safari.oreilly.com*